A Counselor's Guide to Career Assessment Instruments

Sixth Edition

Chris Wood
Danica G. Hays
Editors

National Career Development Association
In Cooperation with the Association for Assessment
and Research in Counseling

National Career Development Association
In Cooperation with the
Association for Assessment and Research in Counseling

Copyright 2013 by the National Career Development Association
305 North Beech Circle
Broken Arrow, OK 74012

No part of this book may be reproduced, stored in a retrieval system, or transmitted in any form or by any means, electronic, mechanical, photocopying, recording, or otherwise without prior permission of the National Career Development Association.

Printed in the United States of America

Library of Congress Cataloging-in-Publication Data

Wood, Chris (Christopher Todd)
A counselor's guide to career assessment instruments / Dr. Chris Wood and
Dr. Danica Hays. -- 6th ed.
    pages cm
Includes bibliographical references and index.
ISBN 978-1-885333-38-4
1. Occupational aptitude tests--Evaluation.   2. Vocational
interest--Testing--Evaluation   I. Hays, Danica G. II. Title
HF5381.7.C68 2013
153.9'4--dc23
                              2013008616

NCDA opposes discrimination against any individual based on age, culture, disability, ethnicity, race, religion/spirituality, creed, gender, gender identity and expression, sexual orientation, marital/partnership status, language preference, socioeconomic status, or any other personal characteristic not specifically relevant to job performance. (Approved by the NCDA Board – October 2012)

For Charlotte — Our miracle beyond measure

ACKNOWLEDGEMENTS

We thank Mary Ann Powell, NCDA Special Projects Director, for her support and responsiveness throughout the writing and production process. We are also grateful for the support of Deneen Pennington, NCDA Executive Director, and others who made this edition possible – particularly Melanie Reinersman and Michael Blechner, copy editors, and Katherine Kinnamon, as well as members of the Publications Development Council – Robert Reardon, Jane Goodman, Don Schutt, Julia Panke Makela, and Tracy Lara.

We appreciate the previous editors of *A Counselor's Guide to Career Assessment Instruments:* Jerome T. Kapes, Edwin A. Whitfield, Marjorie M. Mastie, and Rich W. Feller. We hope the current edition honors your legacy.

FOREWORD

During the decade prior to the 1982 publication of the first edition of *A Counselor's Guide to Vocational Guidance Instruments,* considerable attention and discussion were given to the value and appropriateness of standardized assessment instruments to measure and evaluate the progress of counselees/clients. Near the close of that decade, the Association for Measurement and Evaluation in Guidance (AMEG), (now the Association of Assessment and Research in Counseling, AARC) and the National Vocational Guidance Association (NVGA, now The National Career Development Association; NCDA) — two divisions of the American Personnel and Guidance Association (APGA, now the American Counseling Association, ACA) — devoted time and resources to develop publications addressing the use and value of measurement, assessment and evaluation in counseling and guidance practice and in assisting counselees' in their career planning needs and development.

AMEG through a special issue of its *Measurement and Evaluation in Guidance Journal* (Volume 15, No. 1) edited by Nicholas Vacc and Jack Bardon published 16 articles related to assessment and counseling. Specifically, the editors' stated purpose was to examine "issues and practices concerning assessment and appraisal as they relate to counselors for the purpose of offering a wide range of information to let readers make up their own minds." Donald Zytowski's article in that issue traced "the historical relationship between testing and counseling, which culminated in the apparent mutual mistrust of the 1970s" and to the intervening developments that brought the two closer near the end of the decade. In that same issue, Leo Goldman stated that "tests seem to have made little difference in the decision making, problem solving, and planning activities of pupils and clients." In this special issue, the National Education Association (NEA) called for a moratorium on the use of standardized tests.

In 1979, just prior to work beginning on the special issue and parallel to but separate from its development and publication, Edwin Herr, President of the NVGA charged the NVGA Commission of Assessment and Testing "to develop a publication which would comprehensively, but succinctly, portray the major instruments appropriate to various vocational purposes." Dale Prediger was appointed Chairperson of the Commission with Nancy Garfield, David Jepsen, Alan Robertson, Dale Woolly, Marjorie Mastie, and Jerome Kapes as members. During the fall of 1979, the commission identified the tasks needed to be accomplished, and Kapes and Mastie agreed to serve as co-leaders for the project that would become *A Counselor's Guide to Career Assessment Instruments* ("A Counselor's Guide").

A national advisory group was assembled consisting of Jepsen, Prediger, Christopher Borman, Joseph Kandor (Chairperson of the AMEG Committee to Screen Career Guidance Instruments), and Bert Westerbrook (test review editor for the AMEG journal). As the NVGA Publication Chairperson, I attended the advisory committee meetings when possible, worked with Kapes and Mastie, provided final editing, designed page layout for the final product, and worked with APGA Press to bring the work of the committee to fruition. Many of the advisory group were members of and involved in the work of both NVGA and AMEG. Later, for example, Prediger, Kapes, Mastie, and Kandor each would be elected president of AACE. The advisory group determined the content of the publication and the selection of instruments and reviewers. Upon publication of *A Counselor's Guide,* Herr noted "that without the considerable unselfish support of AMEG in this effort, the outcome would undoubtedly be less than achieved."

Once instruments to be reviewed were chosen, the advisory committee sought the cooperation and permission of the Buros Center for Testing, the AMEG journal, and ProEd (publisher of *Test Critiques*) to contact their test reviewers of the selected instruments and permit them to update and abridge their published reviews to conform to *A Counselor's Guide* format that included a section addressing the use of the instrument in counseling.

The success of the first edition (6,000 copies sold) resulted in the NCDA Board of Directors requesting the co-editors to develop a second edition of *A Counselor's Guide,* and in 1985 work began on it. Kapes and Mastie continued as co-editors and at their invitation, I continued as production editor. Later, at their request I would join them as co-editor for the third edition and continue in that role for the fourth and fifth editions. To reflect the name change of NVGA to NCDA the title of the second and all later editions changed to *A Counselor's*

Guide to Career Assessment Instruments. The second edition contained 21 instruments not reviewed in the first edition and 22 repeats (with different reviewers). All subsequent editions would follow this practice.

The advisory committee decided to not review computerized instruments in the second edition. It was thought that the number of such instruments would make it difficult to do justice to them while covering the traditional instruments. Research on these computerized instruments was scarce and at that time the Test Corporation of America and the AACD (formerly APGA) Media Committee had publications in the pipeline addressing these products in more detail than possible in the page limitations of *A Counselor's Guide.*

Originally, it was hoped that each edition would not repeat an instrument review unless major changes had occurred in it. The fact that previous editions would not be reprinted nor be available, led to the practice of repeating reviews of popular instruments (with new reviewers). Also, the less than sturdy binding of the first three editions made any lengthy shelf life doubtful at best. In addition, the lack of electronic processing in the development of the early editions did not allow for electronic retrieval. Actually, the fifth edition of *A Counselor's Guide* was the first produced electronically.

In the earlier editions, contact with publishers was through personal contact. A packet containing review samples, and information concerning our procedures was mailed directly to the president of the test company, followed by a personal phone call to answer any questions and ask whom to contact for the information we needed. In the fourth and fifth editions there was little or no personal communication with the company president, when such packets were transmitted solely electronically, they were then forwarded to appropriate staff less familiar with our work and our product, and the urgency given to our needs and timelines diminished, and our workload increased. It should be noted, however, that without the willingness of the test publishers to entrust their products to the professional judgment of our reviewers and to assist them by providing supportive, statistical and descriptive information, our final product would have been diminished.

Subsequent editions mainly followed the usual procedures and similar content of previous editions. The third edition was the first to include the formal involvement of the AARC, formerly Association for Assessment in Counseling and Education (AACE), Association for Assessment in Counseling (AAC), and AMEG. Presidents of both AAC and NVGA jointly endorsed our work in the Preface to that edition and to all future editions. Chapters addressing computer-based guidance systems, card sorts, and portfolio assessments were included in the third edition.

The fourth edition, similar to previous editions contained some chapter additions such as addressing personal and program advocacy and a thorough presentation addressing computer-assisted assessments. The number of reviews had grown to 85, more than double the number of reviews in the first edition. Due to other priorities that required her full attention, Mastie did not continue as a co-editor on the fourth edition.

The fifth edition was the first without the leadership and commitment of Kapes. Kapes passed away prior to the initiation of the fifth edition. Rich Feller and Chris Wood joined me in co-editing the fifth edition of *A Counselor's Guide,* which would be my last. As before, the fifth edition had few changes in content. A chapter was added to address assessment strategies in career planning that can reduce or eliminate barriers to successful outcomes for persons with disabilities. The absence of Kapes also resulted in the loss of the extraordinary support for our publication from Texas A&M University where he was a faculty member. Texas A&M provided both faculty and financial support from the very initiation of the first edition through the fourth edition. Sharing the cost of a graduate assistant position devoted to the project, day to day clerical support, and faculty involvement through serving as reviewers and professional consultation.

Time and space do not allow the identification of all the contributors to this work. Through five editions of *A Counselor's Guide,* over a span of 30 years, 279 reviewers from various divisions in the American Counseling Association as well as the American Psychological Association and other professional groups reviewed 285 instruments. Many participated in multiple editions of the project. In addition, 34 professionals authored content chapters and other chapters dealing with additional instruments and other assessment topics. *A Counselor's Guide* truly has been a collaboration and collegial undertaking to address a problem of the 1970s, and it continues to provide a platform and process to continue to address the use of assessment in career counseling and to help readers make up their own minds concerning assessment instruments and their use.

The sixth edition is in the capable hands of Chris Wood and Danica G. Hays, two professionals who reflect the origin and collaboration that resulted in the success of the first five editions. Once again, as in the 1970s, there is consternation and discussion in the education world on the value and use of standardized tests. And, as in 1982, the co-editors of *A Counselor's Guide* represent various divisions of the American Counseling Association. Chris Wood, co-editor of the fifth edition, is active in both NCDA and the American School Counselor Association (ASCA). Danica Hays is involved in the activities of the AARC and is past-president of that division. Both bring the strengths of these divisions to a publication created to promote and explain the use and value of assessment in counseling.

Edwin A. Whitfield
Former Co-Editor, *A Counselor's Guide to Career Assessment Instruments*
NCDA Past-President
Former Editor, *The Vocational Guidance Quarterly* (now *The Career Development Quarterly*)

PREFACE

Danica G. Hays
President, Association for Assessment and Research in Counseling (2011-2012)

Debra S. Osborn
President, National Career Development Association (2011-2012)

Careers are an integral part of an individual's experiences across the life span. As such, it is imperative that counselors and other career practitioners engage in the intentional practice of the comprehensive evaluation of skills, interests, values, degree of readiness, and other variables as they facilitate career development. Career assessments enhance a client or student's career development in various counseling settings: a client seeing a mental health counselor for depression related to underemployment; a student talking with a student counselor about post high school plans; an individual with an acquired disability exploring new career avenues with a vocational rehabilitation counselor; or a client seeking to expand career options with a career counselor. Counselors, researchers, and educators who value assessments for practice and research will find this text a vital go-to manual for key information about the most commonly used career assessments.

The sixth edition of *A Counselor's Guide to Career Assessment Instruments,* while providing a plethora of career instruments from which to choose, also provides advice on choosing appropriate assessment strategies and using the assessment results to best serve the client or student. The text offers information on popular career assessment instruments — both quantitative and qualitative — for the following assessment categories: aptitude and achievement, comprehensive or combined, interest and values, career development/career maturity, personality, special populations, and qualitative and alternative approaches.

The first nine chapters include foundational material for the career practitioner or trainee to gain knowledge of several career assessment considerations. In the sixth edition, chapters have been updated to include concrete assessment strategies for counselors, provide case examples as applicable, and offer chapter review questions. Further, the editors include two new chapters: one to highlight the importance of multicultural considerations in the career assessment process (Chapter 5), and another to extend the discussion of the career assessment process beyond test selection. In addition, instructors can find supplemental materials at the NCDA website (http://www.ncda.org), which include PowerPoint presentations and multiple choice items.

Wood and Hays (Chapter 1, *Uses of Career Assessment*) provide a comprehensive definition of career assessment and cite several uses of these tools in a variety of settings; articulate a brief history on career assessment use; outline legal, ethical and social considerations; and discuss the selection process and inclusion and exclusion criteria for career assessment instruments in this edition. Herr and Niles (Chapter 2, *Trends in Career Assessment*) provide the reader information about the changing context of assessment and the world of work; offer perspectives on the nature of career assessment; and articulate trends that include the integration of technology, instrument adaptation, and globalization. In Chapter 3 *(Career Assessment Standards and Competencies for Practitioners),* Wall includes a comprehensive summary of professional guidelines for the assessment community in general, professional counselors, career counselors and practitioners, specialty standards for counseling sub-disciplines and test users, and those related to specific uses for various sub-populations. Sampson, McClain, Dozier, Carr, Lumsden, and Osborn (Chapter 4, *Computer-Assisted Career Assessment*) explore the benefits, limitations, and potential of computer applications in career assessment. Their discussion of necessary competence and experience for persons who use computer-assisted assessment focuses on the various roles of the computer, counselor, and client in career assessment.

Chapter 5 *(Multicultural Considerations in Career Assessment)* is a new chapter in the sixth edition. Evans advocates for infusing multicultural factors into the career assessment process. After providing a rationale for the need for multicultural assessment, Evans highlights culturally-related issues across the assessment categories presented in this text. Podmostko, Timmons, and Bremer in Chapter 6 *(Assessing Youth and Adolescents with Educational and Career Development Challenges)* address the four domains of assessment strategies (educational, vocational, psychological, and medical) in career planning and development that can reduce or eliminate barriers created by disability. This chapter focuses primarily on supporting clients in the vocational domain. In Chapter 7 *(Using Assessment for Personal, Program, and Policy Advocacy)*, Gysbers, Lapan, and Cato look at societal changes, the challenges they represent for assessment, as well as the potential for career assessments to help shape sound policy and guide program implementation and evaluation. They envision three roles of assessment: personal advocacy, program evaluation, and formulation of public policy. New to this edition is the increased discussion of social advocacy in the career assessment process. Chapters 8 and 9 offer expanded information for a previously published chapter on instrument selection. In Chapter 8 *(Selecting Career Assessment Instruments)*, Wilson, Tang, and Wilson present client, counselor, and testing factors to consider when selecting a career assessment instrument, sources of information in test selection, as well as technical material on reliability, validity, and norms. The chapter concludes with a brief overview of the test review structure used in the second half of the text. Finally in another new chapter for this edition, Whiston and Rose in Chapter 9 *(Test Administration, Interpretation, and Communication)* articulate administration, scoring, interpretation and communication factors in career assessment while including the latest research on these components of the assessment process and addressing some multicultural considerations.

Chapters 10 through 16 present select career assessment instruments based on inclusion criteria outlined in Chapter 1. Specifically, the following chapters, which include predominant career assessment tools, may be found in the sixth edition: Chapter 10: *Aptitude and Achievement Measures,* Chapter 11: *Comprehensive or Combined Measures,* Chapter 12: *Interest and Values Inventories,* Chapter 13: *Career Development/Career Maturity Measures,* Chapter 14: *Personality Measures,* Chapter 15: *Instruments for Special Populations,* and Chapter 16: *Qualitative and Alternative Approaches to Standardized Assessments.* Chapter 16 is a new addition in the text to highlight available tools that can stand alone or supplement quantitative assessments.

In the final chapter (Chapter 17: *Additional Career Assessment Instruments*), Wood and Hays provide an overview of additional career assessment instruments that are available to the career practitioner. When such are available, readers are referred to more complete reviews. The sixth edition concludes with two appendices. Appendix A, *A Counselor's Guide User's Matrix,* lists all instruments included in the guide and should help the reader to find instruments appropriate for selected purposes. Appendix B, *Supplemental Online Resources,* provides a list of specific items to enhance the book (e.g., instructor materials, publisher contact information, and links to assessment- and career-related organizations, websites, and publications).

Once the reader has an overall picture of what is available here, thoughtful consideration should be given to perspective. Fairness and balance in the treatment of reviewed instruments drove all deliberations by the editors, reviewers, and authors. We believe the reader will find this text to be as accurate as possible. Nevertheless, limitations of length, technical documentation, and the occasional divided professional opinion suggest that serious readers will need to undertake additional investigation using the technical manuals and sources referenced. Further, given continual changes in test pricing, purpose, and technical data available, readers are encouraged to review additional materials as they select career assessment instruments. We believe — given the intent, benefits, and potential limitations of the text — that the sixth edition will be an invaluable tool to counselors and other career practitioners to assist in clarifying and managing the complex body of knowledge about career assessment.

TABLE OF CONTENTS

Dedication iii

Acknowledgements iv

Foreword v
    Edwin A. Whitfield

Preface viii
    Danica G. Hays and Debra S. Osborn

Part I: Introduction to Career Assessment 1

Chapter 1: Uses of Career Assessment 3
    Chris Wood and Danica G. Hays

Chapter 2: Trends and Issues in Career Assessment 11
    Edwin L. Herr and Spencer G. Niles

Chapter 3: Career Assessment Standards and Competencies for Practitioners 23
    Janet E. Wall

Chapter 4: Computer-Assisted Career Assessment 33
    James P. Sampson, Jr., Mary-Catherine McClain, Casey Dozier, Darrin L. Carr,
    Jill A. Lumsden, and Debra S. Osborn

Chapter 5: Multicultural Considerations in Career Assessment 49
    Kathy M. Evans

Chapter 6: Assessing Youth and Adolescents with Educational and Career Development Challenges 63
    Mary Podmostko, Joe Timmons, Christine Bremer, and Chris Opsal

Chapter 7: Using Assessment for Personal, Program, and Policy Advocacy 75
    Norman C. Gysbers, Richard T. Lapan, and Sibyl Cato

Chapter 8: Selecting Career Assessment Instruments 85
    F. Robert Wilson, Mei Tang, and Cornelia R. Wilson

Chapter 9: Test Administration, Interpretation, and Communication 101
    Susan C. Whiston and Ciemone S. Rose

Part II: Career Assessment Instruments 113

Chapter 10: Aptitude and Achievement Measures 115

    Ability Explorer, Third Edition 116
        Wei-Cheng J. Mau, Reviewer

    Adult Basic Learning Examination, Second Edition 121
        Kurt F. Geisinger, Reviewer

    Armed Services Vocational Aptitude Battery – Career Exploration Program 125
        John Patrick, Jeff Samide, Nikki S. Comito, Deidre L. Muth, and Christi L. Gross, Reviewers

The Highlands Ability Battery 135
  Manivong J. Ratts and Julian R. McCullough, Reviewers

O*NET Ability Profiler 141
  Richard T. Kinnier and Joanna Gorin, Reviewers

Tests of Adult Basic Education..147
  Andrew M. Burck, Reviewer

Wonderlic Basic Skills Test 153
  Sally J. Power, Reviewer

WorkKeys Assessments..157
  Debra S. Osborn, Reviewer

Workplace Skills Survey 163
  Erika Raissa Nash Cameron, Reviewer

Chapter 11: Comprehensive or Combined Measures 167

Career Interests, Preferences, and Strengths Inventory 168
  Maria I. Kuznetsova and Shawn Powell, Reviewers

CareerScope: Career Assessment and Reporting System, Version 10 171
  Gabriel I. Lomas, Reviewer

COPSystem Career Guidance Program 177
  Emily E. Bullock-Yowell and Lauren K. Osborne, Reviewers

Differential Aptitude Tests for Personnel and Career Assessment and the 183
Career Interest Inventory, Fifth Edition
  Karl N. Kelley, Reviewer

Employability Competency System Appraisal Test...189
  Marie F. Shoffner, Reviewer

EXPLORE and PLAN...195
  Linda H. Foster, Reviewer

Kuder Career Planning System 203
  Melinda M. Gibbons, Reviewer

Occupational Aptitude Survey and Interest Schedule, Third Edition..211
  A. Stephen Lenz, Reviewer

World of Work Inventory..219
  Eugene P. Sheehan, Reviewer

Chapter 12: Interest and Values Inventories 225

Campbell Interest and Skill Survey 226
  Lisa E. Severy, Reviewer

Career Directions Inventory, Second Edition 233
  Aaron H. Carlstrom and Kenneth F. Hughey, Reviewers

Career and Life Explorer, Third Edition 239
  Tara Hill, Reviewer

Expanded Skills Confidence Inventory...243
  Jacqueline M. Swank, Reviewer

Hall Occupational Orientation Inventory, Fourth Edition....................................247
  Bryan J. Dik, Reviewer

Harrington-O'Shea Career Decision Making System – Revised 251
  Vicki L. Campbell and QuaVaundra A. Perry, Reviewers

Jackson Vocational Interest Survey, Second Edition 255
  Eleanor E. Sanford-Moore, Reviewer

O*NET Interest Profiler and Computerized O*NET Interest Profiler....................261
  Stephanie A. Crockett, Reviewer

O*NET Work Importance Profiler and Work Importance Locator 269
  Jennifer J. Del Corso, Reviewer

Self-Directed Search, Fourth Edition, and Career Explorer...............................275
  Caroline A. Baker, Reviewer

Strong Interest Inventory and Skills Confidence Inventory.................................279
  Jeffrey A. Jenkins, Reviewer

Study of Values, Fourth Edition 285
  W. Matthew Shurts, Reviewer

Values Preference Indicator..291
  Donna S. Sheperis, Reviewer

Wide Range Interest and Occupation Test, Second Edition.................................295
  Albert M. Bugaj, Reviewer

Chapter 13: Career Development/Career Maturity Measures.................................301

Adult Career Concerns Inventory..302
  Spencer R. Baker, Reviewer

Barriers to Employment Success Inventory, Fourth Edition.................................307
  Kathy E. Green, Reviewer

Career Commitment Measure 311
  Carrie Wachter Morris, Reviewer

Career Decision Self-Efficacy Scale and Career Decision Self-Efficacy Scale – Short Form 315
  Joshua C. Watson, Reviewer

Career Development Inventory 319
  Dale Pietrzak, Reviewer

Career Factors Inventory..325
  Ayres D'Costa, Reviewer

Career Search Efficacy Scale...329
  Pamela Doubrava-Smith and Richard S. Balkin, Reviewers

Career Thoughts Inventory...333
  Jacqueline J. Peila-Shuster and Rich Feller, Reviewers

Career Transitions Inventory 339
    Jean Powell Kirnan and David J. Rothman, Reviewers

Childhood Career Development Scale 343
    Cass Dykeman, Reviewer

Job Search Attitude Inventory, Fourth Edition 347
    John W. Fleenor, Reviewer

Job Search Knowledge Scale 351
    Dixie Meyer, Reviewer

Job Survival and Success Scale, Second Edition 355
    William I. Sauser, Jr., Reviewer

Quality of Life Inventory 359
    Laurie A. Carlson, Reviewer

WorkLife Indicator 363
    Rebecca A. Newgent, Reviewer

Chapter 14: Personality Measures 367

California Psychological Inventory, Third Edition 368
    Robert C. Chope, Reviewer

Career Key 373
    Margaret M. Nauta, Reviewer

Clifton StrengthsFinder or StrengthsFinder 2.0 377
    Mike Hauser and Katie Hillis, Reviewers

Jackson Personality Inventory – Revised 381
    Peter Zachar, Reviewer

Myers-Briggs Type Indicator 385
    Amanda C. La Guardia, Reviewer

NEO Personality Inventory-3 391
    Michael J. Stebleton, Reviewer

Personal Style Indicator 397
    Paul R. Peluso, Reviewer

Sixteen Personality Factor Questionnaire and Career Development Report 401
    Michelle Perepiczka, Reviewer

Student Styles Questionnaire 409
    Michelle L. Bruno, Reviewer

Chapter 15: Instruments for Special Populations 415

Ashland Interest Assessment 416
    Lori Ellison, Reviewer

Becker Work Adjustment Profile, Second Edition 421
    James T. Austin, Reviewer

BRIGANCE Transition Skills Inventory 427
    Jonna L. Bobzien, Reviewer

Geist Picture Interest Inventory, Revised Eighth Printing 433
   Tammi Vacha-Haase and Serena Enke, Reviewers

Life Centered Career Education Competency Assessment: Knowledge and Performance Batteries 437
   Steven R. Sligar and Matthew Putts, Reviewers

Picture Interest Career Survey, Second Edition 443
   Julia Y. Porter, Reviewer

Reading-Free Vocational Interest Inventory, Second Edition 447
   Zandra S. Gratz, Reviewer

Workplace Sexual Identity Management Measure 451
   Cirleen DeBlaere and Bethany L. Perkins, Reviewers

Chapter 16: Qualitative and Alternative Approaches to Standardized Assessments 457

Career Genogram 459
   Elizabeth A. Prosek, Reviewer

Career Style Interview 465
   Mark C. Rehfuss, Reviewer

Future Career Autobiography 471
   Kaprea F. Johnson, Reviewer

Intelligent Career Card Sort 475
   Ana C. Berríos-Allison, Reviewer

Knowdell Card Sorts 481
   Justin R. Fields, Reviewer

Life Role Analysis 487
   Sonya Lorelle, Reviewer

My Career Chapter 493
   Hannah B. Bayne, Reviewer

My System of Career Influences 499
   Malik S. Henfield, Reviewer

Possible Selves Mapping 503
   Rebecca E. Michel, Reviewer

Chapter 17: Additional Career Assessment Instruments 509
   Chris Wood and Danica G. Hays

About the Authors 531

Appendix A: A Counselor's Guide User's Matrix 545

Appendix B: Supplemental Online Resources 553

Index 557

PART I

INTRODUCTION TO CAREER ASSESSMENT

CHAPTER 1

USES OF CAREER ASSESSMENT

Chris Wood

Danica G. Hays

Department of Counseling and Human Services
Old Dominion University

Introduction

Assessment is an integral component of practice for counselors working with clients or students on career-related issues. Career assessment may occur in a variety of settings, including career centers, mental health agencies, schools, colleges/universities, residential facilities, emergency shelters, and hospitals, to name a few. Further, counselors — whether they identify primarily as career counselors or not — will encounter clients or students with career-related concerns that often interface with other presenting issues such as interpersonal difficulties, mental health symptoms such as depression or anxiety, or other personal adjustment considerations. Thus, it is imperative, no matter the setting, focus, population, or clinical interest, that counselors be familiar with career assessment and the uses for career assessment instruments.

The information age and the explosion of the Internet have made what some may call "career assessments" more widely available. This increased accessibility comes without quality control or consumer protections as to what meets the definition of *career assessment instrument,* much less any filter as to what instruments are most appropriate for what purpose with what population. While the World Wide Web has created increased access to career information and what may be proselytized as career guidance, there is still more federal oversight on the definitions and claims made by cosmetics manufacturers than by creators of career assessment instruments.

Moreover, access to career development assistance that includes the use of career assessment instruments continues to be a social justice issue. Although legislation has been targeted toward increasing career opportunities for some traditionally marginalized groups of Americans, there is still inequity regarding who receives good career/college planning assistance, including the use of quality career assessment instruments in such endeavors.

Most certainly to define career assessment instrument, it is important to define assessment. *The Standards for Educational and Psychological Testing* (American Educational Research Association [AERA], American Psychological Association [APA], & National Council on Measurement in Education [NCME], 1999) defines assessment as "any systematic method of obtaining information from tests and other sources, used to draw inferences about characteristics of people, objects, or programs" (p. 172). This definition indicates that assessment is a comprehensive process to increase client or student understanding that involves a broad array of methods that include standardized assessments, rating scales, observations and interviews, card sorts, projective techniques, archived records, and so on. Tests, what many counselors consider synonymous with assessment, is only one aspect of assessment. The assessment process can and should involve both quantitative and qualitative evaluation methods to present a client a holistic picture of interests, abilities, and values.

It is also important to note certain principles that apply to all assessment:

- Assessment is something that is done with and by clients, not something that is done to them. Assessment is a process, a part of instruction, not an event. It is a process for gathering information and using results to inform decisions.
- All assessments must complement and supplement each other. Assessment of achievement, aptitudes, interests, values, career development, and personality traits are a part of learning and development.
- All assessments should promote self-awareness, the involvement of the client, and his or her ownership of the process and the results.

- Two major purposes of assessment are to improve and to prove: to improve clients' learning and development and the programs provided for them and to prove the effectiveness of such programs.

- Assessment is inseparable from instruction, learning, and development.

Career assessment is a measure of a client or student's career development process as well as the content domains of that process. In essence, it is the evaluation of the process and content of career decision making using a variety of assessment tools. Process variables related to career assessment include career readiness, maturity, concerns, and planning. Content variables involve values and interests (Hays, 2013). Although process and content evaluation are not necessarily independent constructs, career assessments can hone in on specific aspects of career development to aid counselors in working with clients on specific concerns. Career assessments, whether they measure process and/or content considerations, can include individual tools or more comprehensive assessment tools. In this text you will find that both types of tools — in quantitative and qualitative formats — are presented.

Although all assessments of clients contribute to their overall growth and development, career assessment provides additional information for the enhancement of career development and career success. When combined with other assessment modes, experiences, professional assistance, and other influences, these assessments assist clients in forming and seeking answers to questions such as *What can I do? What can I be? What do I want to be? How can I be what I want to be?*

To choose wisely from the array of assessment instruments in this sixth edition, it is helpful to reflect on the purpose of career assessment and its role in enhancing career and personal development. The choice and use of career assessments can be based on three basic beliefs: (1) career development is an integral and inseparable part of learning and human development; (2) career guidance and career development programs should be a part of the total instructional program in schools, colleges, and training divisions of business and industry; and (3) all assessment enhances learning as well as career and personal development.

Uses of Career Assessment

With some foundational knowledge of how assessment in general and career assessment more specifically are conceptualized, it is important to consider how career assessments may be used in counseling. Herr, Cramer, and Niles (2004) identified four uses of career assessment: prediction, discrimination, monitoring, and evaluation. The first three of Herr et al.'s uses of assessment findings seek to improve the choices and career success of individuals; the fourth adds the dimension of program accountability to an individual focus by using assessment data in aggregate.

- *Prediction:* Career assessments may be used to predict future performance or attitudes in career-related tasks. Typically, prediction as a function refers to statistical prediction: what is the probability of a client's success in an educational program, occupation, or career?

- *Discrimination:* This function refers to distinguishing between a client's own abilities, interests, and values and those of a similar group, often on a continual basis. How similar is a client to those who are successful in a given program or occupation?

- *Monitoring:* Career assessments may serve to evaluate client progress or changes in abilities, interests, or values. Monitoring, thus, relates to career maturity and adaptability. What is the status of a client's career maturity, decision making, or planning skills?

- *Evaluation:* This final use refers to assessing how well career-related goals are met, at either an individual client and/or program level. How effective are career interventions or program activities? What is the success of a program in terms of client improvement or achieving the intended results or the program?

Mastie (1994) also noted four uses of career assessment: Compass, Credential, Process, and Empowerment.

- *Compass:* Career assessments as this function is the process of amassing information about a client in order to improve the accuracy of a decision. In light of the limitations of available assessment instruments, Mastie cautioned about the dangers of using such information to find a right career path.

- *Credential:* This use is seen as limiting access and opportunity for those assessed. If assessment is used to qualify clients for intended training opportunities and career paths, counselors must be aware of these hurdles and incorporate them into ongoing career development programs and provide intervention for clients to prepare for them.

- *Process:* The assumption underlying this purpose is that career development is an ongoing process, a series of choices. Thus, any particular career decision is merely a single instance in a lifetime of career choice points. Career assessment can assist clients to approach career choice points as times to reevaluate opportunities; to reassess their skills, interests, and values; to seek assistance if needed; and to use the information to create career path and initiate action. The emphasis is more on choosing wisely than on making wise choices.

- *Empowerment:* Career assessment as empowerment is based on the premise that career planning is the work of the client, and not the work of the counselor. Career assessments are seen as questions, not answers. Using assessment results helps clients take control of, inform, and enrich their own explorations of possible choices.

Whichever purpose(s) counselors cite as the reason for assessment, it is important to convey this to a client throughout the assessment process. Although there are distinctions between these two lists, there are collective assumptions about the use of career assessments: (a) career assessment is an important source of information about how clients are progressing in their career development; (b) it provides information on self-knowledge, career knowledge, and career-planning skills, all of which are necessary for clients to enhance their career development and career success; (c) it complements other assessments and instructional processes, and draws from these to enhance career development; and (d) it allows counselors to assess and improve program effectiveness. Career assessment, used properly, can provide form and focus to career development and to a career development program. Inappropriate, misused, or unconnected to other program efforts, it offers little and has the potential to interfere with career development and career success.

History of Career Assessment

As counselors consider how career assessments may be used across various settings, they should be familiar with key developments in the history of career assessment. The earliest record of assessment dates back to evaluating individuals for obtaining (and retaining) civil service positions in Ancient China in 2200 BC. Employees were tested in five areas to determine placement: civil law, military affairs, geography, agriculture, and revenue. While there is quite a long history of assessment, career assessment became significantly prominent during the Industrial Revolution, beginning in the late 1800s.

Career assessment developed in response to societal changes associated with this era, as Americans encountered new economic opportunities and often challenging social conditions such as relocation to city centers and an influx of immigrants seeking employment. Individuals needed assistance with identifying career options through testing and selecting from those options for appropriate job placement (Niles & Harris-Bowlsbey, 2013).

As there was increased attention to meeting the changing needs of adults entering or currently in the workforce, Frank Parsons articulated that adolescents needed assistance choosing a career that was congruent with their skills and interests. Parsons developed in 1908 the Boston Vocational Bureau, an agency that helped adolescents with career selection. Parsons' work evolved to create over 900 programs in high schools across the United States by 1918.

Parsons is known for his trait-and-factor approach to career assessment. The approach involves three tasks: know yourself, know the world of work, and consider the match between the two. More specifically, the first task referred to increasing one's self-awareness of abilities, interests, and values. The second task involved seeking occupational knowledge in a variety of ways (e.g., observing workers, reading vocation descriptions and requirements). Finally, the third task was to integrate the information about self-knowledge and vocational-knowledge to determine the best match for career choice (cf. Parsons, 1909). Parsons developed comprehensive descriptions of job requirements, as there was minimal information at that time (Niles & Harris-Bowlsbey, 2013). It is evident how Parsons' early work in vocational choice and matching individuals to jobs played an important role in future career theory and assessment.

In addition to Parsons' trait and factor assessments, some of the earlier vocational assessments were interest inventories. Miner (1922) is credited with the first formal interest inventory to assist high school students with career selection. Thorndike's (1912) work led to the development of several interest inventories such as the Carnegie Interest Inventory, the Strong Vocational Interest Blank (Strong, 1927), and the Kuder Preference Record and its revisions (see Kuder, 1934, 1966; Kuder & Diamond, 1979; Zytowski, 1985) based on work with 100 college students. Special aptitude tests were also developed for use in vocational counseling to test things such as mechanical, clerical, and artistic aptitudes. As aptitude tests evolved in vocational counseling, the need for multiple aptitude tests became more evident. For example, the Armed Services Vocational Aptitude Battery (ASVAB), the most widely used multiple aptitude assessment in the world, is used for military service qualification (Hays, 2013).

In addition to developments at the individual level, other developments in group testing occurred in intelligence and aptitude tests that had significant implications for career assessment. This began with World War I as the United States needed to screen over 1.5 million recruits for placement. Robert Yerkes developed the Army Alpha intelligence test and its nonverbal counterpart, Army Beta, to help with this process. With greater attention in education after World War I, ability testing flourished in public schools and higher education. The Army Alpha and Beta tests were released for public use and became the model for future ability tests. World War II with its more specialized careers (e.g., flight engineers, pilots, navigators), however, required more stringent selection for flight schools, and previous intelligence tests (i.e., Army Alpha, Army Beta) were not sufficient (Goslin, 1963).

Career assessment developments highlight the specific role counselors have played in the assessment world. That is, during the early days of the profession, counseling and testing were virtually synonymous. In fact, many of the counseling centers established during the 1930s and 1940s were called Counseling and Testing Centers (Hays, 2013). Since the early part of the 20th century, there have been several legislative actions taken and ethical guidelines developed based on societal changes that led to a greater emphasis on career assessment across settings. The next section will outline some of these key events.

Legal, Ethical, and Social Considerations

Today's users of career assessment instruments need to consider many more external factors than by those who pioneered the field. Very few laws existed 60 years ago when the post-World War II expansion of the use of tests in career counseling began. Since that time, both state and federal laws have been enacted that either govern, promote, or sometimes even require their use. Federal legislation that has promoted the use of tests for career counseling programs can be traced back to 1958 when the *National Defense Education Act* (NDEA) was passed with its emphasis on counseling and guidance in the public schools. NDEA was created as a means of facilitating talented youths' pursuit of math/science careers to make the United States more internationally competitive in the aeronautical/space field. This law was followed by *The Elementary and Secondary Education Act of 1965* and its later amendments that continued to promote school guidance and counseling activities, including testing and assessment.

A second stream of federal legislation that at first promoted vocational or career guidance and eventually required the use of tests in the public schools began with the *Vocational Education Act of 1963* and was expanded by its subsequent amendments in 1968 and 1976. The 1984 *Carl D. Perkins Vocational Education Act* included in section 204(c) a specific requirement for handicapped and disadvantaged students that stated:

> Each student who enrolls in a vocational education program and to whom subsection (b) applies shall receive (1) assessment of interests, abilities, and special needs of such student with respect to completing successfully the vocational education program.

The 1990s produced several pieces of federal vocational education legislation with implications for career assessment as part of guidance and counseling services. In 1990, the *Carl D. Perkins Vocational and Applied Technology Education Act* replaced the earlier Perkins act; eight years later it was superseded by the *Carl D. Perkins Vocational and Technical Education Act of 2006*. Although these acts have not explicitly required the use of career assessment instruments, they included extensive provisions for career guidance and counseling services. Both Perkins acts have also required performance standards that have increased the use of applied achievement assessments.

This increased attention to student achievement assessment was stimulated by the first SCANS report (U.S. Department of Labor, 1991). In the middle of the 1990s, Congress also enacted the *School to Work Opportunities Act of 1994*, which was intended to provide all students with salable skills upon leaving high school. The major focus of the act was to integrate school- and work-based learning using connecting activities that include many career guidance services.

Parallel to federal vocational education legislation, which has focused on public schools and community college/postsecondary institutions, were several acts directed at adults in the labor force who were unemployed or underemployed and who were economically disadvantaged. These include the *Manpower Development Training Act of 1962, Comprehensive Employment Training Act of 1973, Job Training Partnership Act of 1982,* and the recent *Workforce Investment Act of 1998.* Many of the programs developed by the states to implement these acts included various career counseling and assessment services.

Operating alongside federal vocational education legislation have been *The Education of All Handicapped Children Act of 1975* and its subsequent amendments, including *Individuals with Disabilities Education Act* (IDEA) in 1990 and the *Individuals with Disabilities Education Improvement Act of 2004* and its subsequent amendments. These laws have required the use of tests and other assessment devices as input to constructing Individualized Education Plans (IEPs) for individuals with disabilities through age 21 in the public schools. In addition, this legislation mandates transition services for all special education students including gathering information on a yearly basis regarding the students' vocational interests, aptitudes, strengths/limitations, and goals for the year after high school. Specifically transition planning is a required component of the IEP no later than by age 16, in order to enable students to participate "... in advanced placement courses or a vocational education program" [Sec. 614 (d) (1) (A) (vii)]. Because students with disabilities in the public secondary schools are served in vocational education programs, the development and use of tests targeted to this group have expanded greatly in quantity, if not in quality, over the past few decades and such tests are still a salient need to assist in successful transition planning.

Emerging over somewhat the same period as vocational education and disability legislation, the Career Education movement also contributed to the use of tests in career guidance and counseling. Beginning in 1971, this movement was promoted by separate legislation in 1974, 1976, and 1977. The major impact this movement had on career assessment was the development and use of instruments in the schools, including at the elementary and middle school level.

Although the above-described legislation promoted the use of assessment as part of the career guidance and counseling function of schools and agencies, other laws were passed that regulated its use. The U.S. Department of Health, Education, and Welfare's Office of Civil Rights issued federal *Vocational Education Programs Guidelines for Eliminating Discrimination and Denial of Services on the Basis of Race, Color, National Origin, Sex, and Handicap* (1979). These guidelines, based on three previous civil rights laws *(Civil Rights Act of 1964,* Title IX of the *Education Amendments of 1972,* and Section 504 of the *Rehabilitation Act of 1973),* prohibit the use of tests in ways that would limit a person's options to pursue training in vocational education programs. The 1974 *Family Educational Rights and Privacy Act* (The Buckley Amendment) and the National Institute of Education (NIE) (1978) *Guidelines for Assessment of Sex Bias and Sex Fairness in Career Interest Inventories* also govern or influence the use of tests.

Professional associations have provided guidance for the use of tests in career counseling as well as in other areas. The *Standards for Educational and Psychological Testing* (AERA, APA, & NCME, 1999) govern the development and use of all career assessment instruments. The National Board for Certified Counselors (NBCC) has also produced a code of ethics that included a section on Measurement and Evaluation.

In 1980, the American Personnel and Guidance Association (now the American Counseling Association [ACA]) published its policy statement *Responsibilities of Users of Standardized Tests* (RUST). This document, which contains much information relevant to the use of career assessment instruments, was revised in 2003. A similar publication, *Code of Fair Testing Practices in Education* (Joint Committee on Testing Practices [JCTP], 2004), involved six professional associations including ACA and Association for Assessment and Research in Counseling. This committee has also published *Rights and Responsibilities of Test Takers: Guidelines and Responsibilities* (JCTP, 1999). Web links to these documents are available at the NCDA webpage (http://www.ncda.org) as an online resource to this text.

In some ways, legislation has come somewhat full circle with the *America Creating Opportunities to Meaningfully Promote Excellence in Technology, Education, and Science (America COMPETES)* Act of 2007 and subsequent reauthorization (2010). This legislation is in some ways similar to the NDEA legislation with its intent to foster American advancement in space/aeronautics. While the America COMPETES legislation does not specifically address counselors and the use of career assessments, it would seem logical that developing student interests in science, technology, engineering, and mathematics (STEM) fields might benefit from career assessment instruments. Future reauthorizations would be wise to include such provisions.

Career Assessments in *A Counselor's Guide to Career Assessment Instruments*

The chapter thus far has outlined ways career assessments can be used in individual and group settings, and provided a brief historical context for their use and more recent ethical, legal, and social impacts. The sixth edition of *A Counselor's Guide to Career Assessment Instruments* contains 73 test reviews of 70 quantitative and 9 qualitative assessments. These are divided into nine chapters; Chapter 17 provides a comprehensive list of additional career assessment instruments. While the Preface of this text describes the general organization of the text, this chapter outlines additional information about the career assessment selection process itself.

How Assessments were Selected

The decisions as to which instruments to include for review were based on a review of the literature and major works on assessment, publisher websites, professional association's journals, and input from career development professionals. Specifically, the criteria for selecting career assessment instruments included the following:

- Commercially available instruments from U.S. publishers

- Buros Center for Testing Publications (i.e., *Mental Measurements Yearbooks, Tests in Print*)

- Innovative or promising career assessment instruments in an unaddressed area or for an underserved/under-researched population

- Instruments, not otherwise included, that could be used by employers to facilitate career development of employees and adults in career transitions

- Instruments or assessments that are available in non-traditional formats (e.g., qualitative assessments)

- Instruments included in the fifth edition of the text (that are still in commercial publication), revised using a new review format

Instrument Availability and Use

Trustworthy information about which career assessment instruments are most used for career counseling and related purposes can be difficult to obtain. The primary reason for this difficulty is that most users are familiar with only a few of the many available instruments. When users are asked to rate or rank the usefulness or applicability of a large number of instruments, they tend to place the ones they use at the top and then rank others by name recognition only somewhere below these choices. Several surveys conducted in the past have included instruments that are no longer available, yet they still received relatively large numbers of nominations for use, presumably because their names were familiar. In previous editions of *A Counselor's Guide,* the editors have reported such surveys conducted by others (Engen, Lamb, & Prediger, 1982; Kapes & Mastie, 1988; Kapes & Whitfield, 2001; Watkins, Campbell, & Nieberding, 1994; Zytowski & Warman, 1982). Given the dated and somewhat unreliable nature of this information, especially at the lower end of the rankings, these rankings were not included in the previous edition and are not included here.

Instruments in this edition are placed in the category which represents best their primary use. This does not mean that an assessment found in Chapter 12 (Interest and Values Instruments) may not be used with special populations, such as those listed in Chapter 15. It is possible that the reviewers or editors interpretation of an instrument's primary use may be different than the reader/consumer.

Sources of Information about Available Assessments

When the first edition of *A Counselor's Guide* was published in 1982, the only comprehensive source of information about career assessment instruments available was the Buros Center for Testing's publication, *Test in Print II* and its companion set of reviews, the *Eighth Mental Measurements Yearbook*. Since that time, Buros has published *Tests in Print III, IV, V, VI, VII;* and *VIII* (1983, 1994, 1999, 2002, 2006, 2011), and the *Ninth, Tenth, Eleventh, Twelfth, Thirteenth, Fourteenth, Fifteenth, Sixteenth, Seventeenth,* and *Eighteenth Mental Measurements Yearbook* (1985, 1989, 1992, 1995, 1998, 2001, 2003, 2005, 2007, 2010). Also, the Institute has established an online database through Bibliographic Retrieval Service (BRS) that makes reviews for subsequent yearbooks available as they are received.

The 175+ professional journals continue to publish reviews. Those likely to contain reviews or articles about the use of career assessment instruments are the *Journal of Counseling and Development, The Career Development Quarterly,* the *Journal of Career Assessment,* and the *Measurement and Evaluation in Counseling and Development* journal. Also, AARC, formerly the Association for Assessment in Counseling and Education (AACE), publishes test reviews in its organization newsletter, *NewsNotes,* many of which deal with career assessment instruments; these reviews are also available online (http://www.theaaceonline.com).

Those desiring additional information about the sources described here as well as other sources of information about testing and career assessment are encouraged to review Chapter 8 in this text as well as the online resources available for this text at the NCDA website (http://www.ncda.org).

Summary

This chapter presented an understanding of career assessment within the context of assessment as well as different conceptualizations of career assessment instrument purposes/uses. The development of career assessment was chronicled including the major historical and legislative influences and the impact of respective professional associations. Finally, we gave an overview of the selection of instruments and sources of information about career assessment instruments, including references to related chapters within this text.

Review Questions

1. What are the key assumptions about assessment? What is typically evaluated in career assessment? In what ways?

2. What are the major uses of career assessment presented in this chapter? How do Herr et al. and Mastie's conceptualization of career assessment use compare?

3. Identify the historical developments in career assessment.

4. What are the key legislative actions that have guided career assessment? Which acts most affect your specialty within the counseling profession?

5. Review the resources available online mentioned in this chapter (i.e., *RUST Statement, Code of Fair Testing Practices, Rights and Responsibilities of Test Takers: Guidelines and Responsibilities*). How might these reflect key legislative changes?

References

American Counseling Association. (2003). *Responsibilities of users of standardized tests* (3rd ed.). Alexandria, VA: Author.

American Educational Research Association, American Psychological Association, & National Council on Measurement in Education. (1999). *Standards for educational and psychological testing.* Washington, DC: AERA.

Engen, H. B., Lamb, R. R., & Prediger, D. T. (1982). Are secondary schools still using standardized tests? *Personnel and Guidance Journal, 60,* 287-290.

Goslin, D. A. (1963). *The search for ability.* New York, NY: Russell Sage Foundation.

Hays, D. G. (2013). *Assessment in counseling: A guide to psychological assessment procedures* (5th ed.). Alexandria, VA: American Counseling Association.

Uses of Career Assessment

Herr, E., Cramer, S. H., & Niles, S. G. (2004). *Career guidance and counseling through the lifespan: Systematic approaches* (6th ed.). Boston, MA: Pearson.

Joint Committee on Testing Practices. (1999). *Rights and responsibilities of test takers: Guidelines and responsibilities.* Washington, DC: American Psychological Association.

Joint Committee on Testing Practices. (2004). *Code of fair testing practices in education.* Washington, DC: American Psychological Association.

Kapes, J. T., & Mastie, M. M. (1988). *A counselor's guide to career assessment instruments* (2nd ed.) Alexandria, VA: National Career Development Association.

Kapes, J. T., & Whitfield, E. A. (2001). *A counselor's guide to career assessment instruments* (4th edition) Columbus, OH: National Career Development Association.

Kuder, G. F. (1934). *Kuder Preference Record — Vocational.* Chicago, IL: Science Research Associates.

Kuder, G. F. (1966). The Occupational Interest Survey. *Personnel and Guidance Journal, 45,* 72-77.

Kuder, G. F., & Diamond, E. E. (1979). *Occupational Interest Survey: General manual* (2nd ed.). Chicago, IL: Science Research Associates.

Mastie, M. M. (1994). Using assessment instruments in career counseling: Career assessment as compass, credential, process and empowerment. In J. T. Kapas, M. M. Mastie, and E. A. Whitfield (Eds.), *A counselor's guide to career assessment instruments* (3rd ed., pp. 31-40). Alexandria, VA: National Career Development Association.

Miner, J. (1922). An aid to the analysis of vocational interest. *Journal of Educational Research, 5,* 311-323.

Niles, S. G., & Harris-Bowlsbey, J. (2013). *Career development interventions in the 21st century* (4th ed.). Boston, MA: Pearson.

Parsons, F. (1909). *Choosing a vocation.* Boston, MA: Houghton Mifflin.

Strong, E. K., Jr. (1927). *Vocational interest blank.* Stanford, CA: Stanford University Press.

Thorndike, E. L. (1912). *Education: A first book.* New York, NY: Macmillan.

U.S. Department of Health, Education, Welfare, Office of Civil Rights. (1979, March 21). *Vocational education programs guidelines for eliminating discrimination and denial of services on the basis of race, color, national origin, sex, and handicap.* Washington, DC: 44 Fed. Reg. 6.

U.S. Department of Labor. (1991, June). *What work requires of schools: A SCANS report for America 2000.* Retrieved from http://wdr.doleta.gov/SCANS/whatwork/whatwork.pdf

Watkins, C. E., Jr., Campbell, V. L., & Nieberding, R. (1994). The practice of vocational assessment by counseling psychologists. *The Counseling Psychologist, 22,* 115-128.

Zytowski, D. G. (1985). *Manual supplement: Kuder DD Occupational Interest Survey.* Chicago, IL: Science Research Associates.

Zytowski, D. G., & Warman, R. E. (1982). The changing use of tests in counseling. *Measurement and Evaluation in Guidance, 15*(2), 147-152.

CHAPTER 2

TRENDS AND ISSUES IN CAREER ASSESSMENT

Edwin L. Herr

Spencer G. Niles

Department of Educational Psychology, Counseling, and Special Education
The Pennsylvania State University

Introduction

Since the beginning of the 20th century, policy makers, career theorists, and career counselors have viewed career assessment as important modality to achieve social, economic, and political goals, both at national and individual levels. In this sense, career assessment as a particular component of career intervention is often perceived to be an important sociopolitical instrument by which to achieve outcomes of significance to national aspirations. In oversimplified terms, goals to which career assessment is expected to contribute include such examples as the prevention of long-term unemployment; development of an effective workforce, and matching of workers and employers; adjustment by potential or active workers to rapidly changing requirements for employment or for retention; creation of individualized career plans for adolescents as well as persons considered marginally employable because of poor academic or technical skills, functional disabilities, interpersonal or other social problems, or discrimination; and provision of assistance to those who have become unemployed or underemployed as a result of industrial reorganization, outsourcing, or international economic competition.

These national goals have been reflected in a continuing stream of public policies and legislation, in the United States and other nations, affecting the form, substance, and purposes of career assessment, career counseling, career education, and other career interventions (Cedefop, 2011). Such policies and legislation have been direct responses to changing conditions in society at particular historical periods of recession, national defense, civil rights, war, technological effects on work processes or worker functions, skill shortages, or the consequences of the global economy. Embedded in each of these historical periods are assumptions about what types of assistance individuals need to develop the knowledge, skills, and attitudes that facilitate their transition through various stages of career development with primary emphases on choosing the particular type of work they wish to do, preparing for that work, being inducted into the work force, and adjusting to its requirements and changing conditions.

These goals, purposes, policies, and legislative actions related to work and to workers form an important backdrop against which career assessment and career interventions in general are developed, refined, and implemented. To be applicable within such evolving contexts, career interventions must be constantly examined as to the degree to which they are relevant for the contextual factors within which workers and potential workers must negotiate their career development, their career identity, and their employability. This is true not only in the United States, but in nations throughout the world as they come to terms with the reality that the major asset of any nation is not its wealth or its raw materials and natural resources; its major asset resides within a workforce that is competent in literacy, numeracy, communications ability, technological skills, and multiculturalism. Moreover, when workers with such competencies are also able to demonstrate the ongoing capacity to learn, to be flexible in order to adjust to evolving contexts, and are able to implement new knowledge and skills to advance work processes and products as they engage in work activities that they find satisfying, then the value of such workers to a nation cannot be overstated.

Nations tend to share many of the same goals for career interventions regardless of their specific cultural traditions (Organization for Economic Cooperation and Development [OECD], 2004). These goals include helping persons to distribute their abilities across the nation's occupational structure and to have equal opportunities for access to educational and occupational opportunities. More specifically, career interventions are "intended to assist people, of any age and at any point throughout their lives, to make educational, training and occupational choices and to manage their careers" effectively (OECD, p. 19).

Career assessment plays an integral role in achieving these goals and thereby contributes to making a positive impact on the individual and the society in which the individual lives. The assessment process can be defined as the use of any formal or informal technique or instrument to collect data about a client that can be useful in career planning and development (Niles & Harris-Bowlsbey, 2013). Most typically, career assessments are used to assist individuals in clarifying their current interests, skills, and/or values in order to identify their next educational or career choice in the sequence that makes up career development.

Niles and Harris-Bowlsbey (2013) noted that assessment instruments and techniques are commonly divided into two broad categories: informal and formal. Checklists, games, fantasies, forced-choice activities, card sorts, and structured interviews are examples of informal assessments. Informal assessments lack traditional psychometric evidence regarding their composition. They tend to be inexpensive and rely heavily upon the career counselor's competence relative to integrating them into the career intervention process.

Assessments labeled formal may be timed standardized tests or non-timed standardized inventories. It is common to call an instrument an inventory if it is assessing content areas in which there are no right or wrong answers and to call it a test if the items have right or wrong answers. Thus, an instrument measuring a person's interests is an inventory, whereas an instrument measuring a person's achievement in mathematics is a test. Formal assessments have been subjected to scientific rigor; that is, authors and publishers have performed research on the instrument in an effort to assure quality and to be able to know the properties that the instrument possesses. Demonstrating that a formal assessment is reliable and valid is essential for supporting its use (see Chapter 8).

As such, career assessments become fundamental stimuli to broadening the techniques employed in career intervention, to increasing the comprehensiveness of the persons and the settings served, and to increasing the range of individual needs and societal purposes addressed through career intervention processes. The result is that while still uneven in availability in many nations, career assessment, career counseling, career guidance, career education, and other career interventions have become worldwide phenomena. So much so that in most nations there is the recognition of the fact that "the nature and quality of private individual decisions are now a matter of considerable public importance, as are the extent and quality of the career services available to support them. Such services need to be widely accessible on a lifelong basis, to serve the needs of individuals, the economy and wider society" (European Centre for the Development of Vocational Training, 2009, p. 13).

These observations are not to suggest that the use of career assessments or other career interventions is the same from nation to nation. They are not! As we will discuss in the next section, there is an increase throughout the world in indigenous approaches to the delivery of career interventions that are compatible with the resources, cultural traditions, and policies of individual nations. In this sense, the theories and practices of career assessment do not exist in a vacuum; they are affected by economic, political, and social events that spawn new needs and goals for career assessment. In a continuous progression, visionaries, theorists, researchers, and practitioners emerge who can help to convert ideas related to career assessment into action.

Some Perspectives on Career Assessment

Career assessment originated in the United States primarily as an intimate adjunct to career counseling. Thus, in many cases, the contents of career counseling were seen as the scores and their interpretations that resulted from the administration of career assessments. Many professionals in the United States and in other countries continue to view career assessment as a part of the career counseling process, not as a separate intervention, even though the use of career assessments in self-directed, counselor-free, and computer-mediated career guidance systems have demonstrated their unique contributions as interventions in their own right.

A further way to view career assessment is as a bridge from career development theory to practice, a method of operationalizing theoretical constructs by incorporating them into career interventions and, in particular, into tests, inventories, and other measurements. This has been true in John Holland's theoretical constructs as these are embedded in the Vocational Preference Inventory, My Vocational Situation, and the Self-Directed Search; in the use of his theoretical framework (RIASEC) as the organizing and interpretive structure for the most recent iterations of the Strong Interest Inventory and for some of the informational and self-assessment components of computer-mediated career guidance systems; and the use of Holland's three-letter coding system of major personality types as a way of organizing U.S. government educational and occupational information through such sources as the Dictionary of Holland Codes (Holland, 1997).

In a similar fashion, Donald Super, from the beginning of his theory development, used assessment instruments to operationalize and evaluate his theoretical constructs (Super, 1990, 1994). Like Holland, he made his theoretical constructs accessible to researchers and to practitioners by using assessment to bridge theory and practice. Examples of the instruments that evolved from his theoretical propositions include the Career Development Inventory, the Adult Career Concerns Inventory, the Work Values Inventory, the Values Inventory, and the Salience Inventory. These instruments describe or measure such constructs as the individual's readiness for career decision making, career planfulness, knowledge and attitudes about career choice, intrinsic and extrinsic life-career values, and the relative importance of major life roles within a person's life structure. These instruments, then, are useful in defining goals for career counseling as well as for explicating and assessing particular types of content important to the decision making of individual clients. Super also developed models of career counseling, particularly the C-DAC Model (Osborne, Brown, Niles, & Miner, 1997), in which career assessment and career counseling are intimately interactive as interventions.

Other theorists also use assessments to translate theory into practice. Among them is John Krumboltz, who has developed several important theoretical concepts and innovative assessment devices that have emerged from his work in behaviorism, social learning, and cognitive behavioral theory. One example of such assessment that has linked his theoretical work to interventions is the Career Beliefs Inventory (Krumboltz, 1994), which is a counseling tool used to identify presuppositions and irrational beliefs that may block people from achieving their career goals. Similarly, Sampson, Peterson, Lenz, Reardon, and Saunders (1996) developed the Career Thoughts Inventory to help career counselors translate the Cognitive Information Processing theory to practice (Sampson, Reardon, Peterson, & Lenz, 2004).

Career Construction Theory developed by Savickas (2013) involves engaging the client in informal career assessment through the use of the Career Style Interview (CSI; Savickas, 2009). The CSI helps clients clarify and articulate the private meanings they attach to their career behavior. Through the use of questions eliciting client preferences for self-expression within life contexts, career construction counselors help clients remember their pasts in ways that fosters the construction of possible futures. In addition to asking clients to share three specific early life recollections, career construction counselors using the CSI ask the following questions to stimulate client consideration of their subjective career experience (i.e., the meaning-making process):

1. Who do you admire? Who would you like to pattern your life after?

    Who did you admire when you were growing up? Why?

2. Do you read any magazines regularly? Do you have any favorite television shows?

3. What do you like to do in your free time?

4. Do you have a favorite saying or motto?

5. What are/were your favorite subjects in school? What subjects do/did you hate?

Responses to these questions are connected to the life themes revealed in the early life recollections to help clients clarify the life projects that guide their career behavior. The CSI is discussed further in Chapter 16.

Although multiple theorists use career assessments (formal and standardized as well as informal and nonstandardized) within their theories, career counselors often lack fidelity to a singular theoretical model. Career assessment practices are often based upon a mixture of theory, research, professional experience, and local practices and habits, which collectively dictate which assessment instruments are used as well as how they are integrated into career counseling specifically.

The Changing Context for Career Assessment

These preliminary comments suggest the richness and the dynamic character of the history of career assessment. Obviously, the development of new career assessments and the refinements of older instruments are ongoing as new contextual and measurement challenges are addressed. Indeed, there are several trends emerging

Trends and Issues in Career Assessment

that will continue to spawn new types and uses of career assessments and adaptations of the old. In many cases, these trends include specific issues that require new career assessments or modified theoretical perspectives. Although it is not possible to be exhaustive in this brief chapter about such matters, there are several categories of trends and issues that exemplify the emerging pressures for new career assessments, new practices, and new theoretical perspectives. They include the changing nature of work; the development or adaptation of career assessment cross-nationally; the integration of technology and career assessment; and accountability, empirically supported treatments, and evidence-based practice. Each of these trends and issues will be discussed in the following sections.

The Changing Nature of Work

The ways in which work is done and organized are rapidly changing. There are multiple factors influencing such change and affecting the types of career assessments that will be required in the future. These factors include the pervasive use of advanced technology in the workplace and a global labor surplus, including a large number of highly educated and skilled workers seeking opportunities in whatever nation offers employment opportunities and economic security. As the migration of workers across national boundaries continues to take place and the ways in which work is organized and implemented are changing rapidly, the need arises for new definitions of workplace skills, personal attributes, and personal flexibility, and for the creation of career assessments to measure these competencies and behaviors.

In preparation for and adjustment to the workplaces now in transition, there is currently increased interest in assessing "soft skills" such as the ability to work in teams, work in diverse cultural environments, participate in decision making in the work place, be resilient in workplaces that are in a constant state of change, be teachable and adaptable as new products and processes are created and implemented in shorter intervals of time, and think in new ways about career planning that focuses on short time horizons (e.g., five years) rather than decades. Within such contexts, however one views work or career development in the 21st century, it will no longer be linear, or easily separated into sequential life stages of growth, exploration, advancement, maintenance, and disengagement. Very few individuals will remain in one job, one firm, one occupation throughout their working life; they are likely to be in career transition many times during their working life, susceptible to organizational changes occasioned by mergers and consolidations of workplaces leading to the shedding of redundant workers and the use of technology to stimulate productivity and reduce the costs of retaining workers who are not central to the particular goals of a given workplace. As workforces are reduced in size to only those workers who have the technical and managerial skills absolutely essential to the mission of the workplace, the workers terminated will, in many places, become members of the contingent, part-time work force, be self-employed, or be employed by outsourcing firms. In this scenario, developing competencies and comfort with transition experiences, managing job insecurity effectively, engaging in lifelong learning, and knowing how to network effectively become essential career competencies. Developing assessments to measure such competencies is important for the career planning and development process in the 21st century.

Knowledge Workers

In the United States, and in a growing number of other countries, the workplace has become more fully automated, applying more computer-driven lathes, robots, data analysis, diagnoses, design processes, telecommunications, and global supply chains of products and services. One result of these changes has been an increase in the educational requirements for many occupations. In essence, these changes have increased the need for knowledge workers, persons who know how (as well as why) they are implementing specific work processes. Now comprising over 60% of the U.S. workforce, knowledge workers must be able to adapt to rapid changes in work processes and problems, troubleshoot, solve problems, and apply new knowledge. As Drucker (Beatty, 1998) has contended, knowledge has replaced experience as the principal requisite for employment in most of the emerging occupations in the world.

Because of the need to link science and technology more fully to produce new products and services, more workplaces have become "learning organizations" (Senge, 1996) where assessing ideas and creativity are major elements in the continuous improvement of the content and processes being used (Florida, 2004). There are also workplaces where jobs as clearly defined, fixed sets of tasks, the principal way of organizing work, are giving way to new terms like boundaryless careers and multitasking. Some observers argue that "jobs" as a way of organizing work are social artifacts that have outlived their usefulness. Increasingly, employers are expecting workers to get work done that needs to be done regardless of the artificial boundaries that separate specific sets of tasks (Bridges, 1994). In such contexts, it is likely that emerging career assessments will emphasize individual initiative, creativity, problem solving skills, the ability to multitask, and the willingness to take risks.

Lifelong Learning

Embedded in the identification and preparation of knowledge workers in workplaces, where continuous learning is essential, is the fact that lifelong learning becomes a major part of one's ability to function effectively in the "new" workplace. For more and more workers, learning skills and achievements are major elements of individual career development. In a society of change, intense competition, creativity, and knowledge work, mastery of basic academic skills becomes a prerequisite for employability, for lifelong learning, and serves as a foundation for engaging in technical and occupational processes.

The World Bank (2003) reinforced the importance of lifelong learning, suggesting that the status quo for workers in a global economy is to be engaged in continuous learning and to feel constantly on edge and off balance, as they adjust and adapt to the ongoing transformation of work, a constant theme in the lives of workers engaged in a global economy. Essentially, the questions all workers need to ask themselves are: "Do I know what I need to know today and what is it that I need to learn to do that I may be asked to do tomorrow?" In response to such conditions, career assessments are likely to include more attention to individual ability to cope with ambiguity, stress, and resilience.

Some Implications from the Changing Nature of Work for Career Assessment

There is much more to be said about the changing nature of work, the global economy, and the changing nature of skills that workers will need to possess to function within a world-of-work that is in constant transition. Important implications of these factors are that today's worker must be his or her own career manager, keep his or her employability skills honed and attractive to employers, engage in continuous learning, and be attentive to trends that will affect his or her inventory of employable skills. Implicit in such perspectives is the view that although constancy, stability, and homeostasis, have frequently been cited in the psychological literature as desirable traits for individual growth and development, career planning and choices have become, and will continue to be, more spontaneous, values oriented, influenced by environmental and organizational flux, and unpredictable than they have been in the past.

The question relative to career assessment is this: Do our current instruments offer measures of personal flexibility, commitment to continuous learning, comfort with cultural diversity, ability to work in teams, willingness to engage in multitasking, self-initiative, ability to be creative, and motivation to be responsible for one's own career development? These are among the major competencies seen as essential to functioning well in a global economy. Minimally, it would seem useful to inventory our current career assessment instruments to determine to what degree there exist scales or subscales that measure such individual traits and abilities. If these measures do not exist, it will be necessary to construct them for these are the essential qualities required in 21st century workers.

The Development or Adaptation of Career Assessment Cross-Nationally

Although one can identify career assessments that include measures of particular competencies or abilities important in a changing world of work, or barring such availability, construct new assessments, it is also possible to adapt career assessments constructed in other nations. To an increasing degree, as career assessment and other career interventions have become worldwide phenomena, they have become more indigenous to their own nations' characteristics and to the career concerns of importance in that nation. Until recently, the adaptation of career assessment instruments has primarily focused on measurement instruments constructed in the United States or Western Europe and translated into the language of a nation interested in validating the instrument's suitability for use in that nation. While the principal adaptation of career assessments still tends to be from the United States or Western Europe to other nations, that trend may be less pronounced in the future. As the utility and comprehensiveness of career interventions, including career assessment, from nations around the world becomes increasingly accessible, provides culturally sensitive content, and procedures of relevance and high quality, the adaptation of indigenous instruments that measure skills, attitudes, or behaviors of interest to another nation will proceed rapidly. This process is already accelerating since many of the career assessments are now available through the Internet.

The importance of adapting accurately and validating thoroughly career assessments from another country is a growing issue. At the least, it requires knowledge of the methodological processes that led to the instrument being developed initially, its purposes, its psychometric properties in the country of origin, and the external and internal conditions that gave rise to the assessment instrument. To oversimplify the matter, then, its uses in a new culture and/or in a nation hoping to adapt the assessment must be validated, language standardized across cultures, reliability measured, and local or national norms developed. In professional terms, it is necessary for any adaptation of a test or assessment to adhere to copyright provisions, obtain the consent of the test's author and publisher, and observe the ethical standards that apply to test adaptation as provided by counseling or psychological associations located in some 80 countries around the world as well as the International Test Commission (Bartram, 2001).

Rossier (2004) compared the cross-cultural equivalence of several personality inventories frequently used in career counseling (e.g., 16PF, NEO-P1, Internal-External Locus of Control Scale). His very strong point is that when counselors use a translated instrument particular attention must be paid to its cultural validity or cultural replicability. Neglecting to do so can result in erroneous conclusions about the meaning of the scale scores. In addition to linguistic, conceptual, and scale equivalence, there also needs to be culture-specific normative equivalence if the scale is to be used in career counseling.

Duarte (2004) noted that adaptation of career assessment instruments from one nation to another is not simply a linguistic exercise. Rather, those who "translate" instruments from one language to another are obliged to do complete literature reviews related to the development of the instrument as well as to the meanings of the constructs assessed by the instrument. In the case of indigenous instruments being adapted from other nations to the United States, this will require U.S. researchers to become familiar with the published work in European, Asian, and other national journals and with the languages in which they are published (e.g., French, Japanese, Spanish, German). To the degree that such a trend intensifies, there will likely be a greater sensitivity in the United States to excellent research occurring in other nations and bring researchers to greater cooperation transnationally as they fashion instruments that are truly international in their concepts and content or adapt career assessments that are found to have high validity and reliability in many nations beyond their originating nation.

Technology and Career Assessment

One of the trends that will facilitate the cross-national development, adaptation, and use of career assessments is the pervasive use of the Internet for research, statistical analyses, management of data banks, and other tasks associated with the construction of career assessment instruments. As computers and available software continue to become more user friendly, comprehensive in their content, and less expensive to purchase and use, these tools will create conditions by which new measurement instruments will be made available.

In the past decade as the Internet achieved significant growth in websites that provided career advice, career information, job placement, and career assessments (Harris-Bowlsbey, 2003), research studies have indicated that the career assessment instruments in these websites vary from poorly constructed, locally used instruments to highly professional, standardized instruments with strong psychometric properties. Many of the latter were developed during the 1970s and 1980s when computer-based career guidance systems (e.g., DISCOVER, SIGI Plus) were being developed and integrated into state career-information delivery systems (CIDS) for use in schools, colleges, employment counseling agencies, and some workplaces. In many of these systems, career assessments have been prominent parts of the content as they help users clarify the status of their interests, values, abilities, and career goals and, based upon such information, refer users to relevant training and educational opportunities to explore (e.g., Kuder).

As computer-assisted career guidance systems and web-based systems became increasingly common in their use over the past several decades, the importance of career assessment as a complement to career counseling and other career interventions has been demonstrated empirically and in relation to the roles of career counselors. More specifically, multiple studies conducted over the past 25 years consistently indicate that such systems are more impactful when used in conjunction with career counseling rather than as standalone systems (e.g., Garis & Niles, 1990; Miller & Brown, 2013; Whiston, Brecheisen, & Stephens, 2003). It is, however, often the case that such systems and their related career assessments are not used in conjunction with career counselor contact. This is particulary problematic when so many web-based systems (including some rather popular ones) contain assessments that have either never been or are only minimally accompanied by psychometric evidence supporting their use. This is an ethical issue that the field needs to take a stronger stand against, in our opinion.

Indeed, when one thinks of interventions using computer-assisted career guidance systems or web-based systems, one can conceptualize the following scenarios: the career assessment itself as an intervention; the career assessment and the other elements of a computer-based system or website as an intervention; or the career assessment, other elements of a program or website, and a counselor as a career intervention. The results obtained tend to become more positive as these increments of interventions are added together in combination with the group or individual intervention of counselors (Herr, Cramer, & Niles, 2004; Niles & Harris-Bowlsbey, 2013).

To be fair, as computer-assisted career guidance systems and web-based systems have grown in number and use, ethical standards for the use of these interventions have been created by the National Board for Certified Counselors, National Career Development Association, Association of Computer-Based Systems for Career Information, and other groups (see Chapter 3). Even so, there are still ethical problems occurring in the use of these interventions, especially with regard to the psychometric value of the assessments such systems rely upon.

Thus, what has been said by a number of observers is that the Internet provides a huge array of websites which essentially offer a "smorgasbord of disjointed" information that is available to the public free of charge and without consumer protection (Harris-Bowlsbey, 2003; Niles & Harris-Bowlsbey, 2013). At the same time, however, the Internet provides enormous possibilities for high-quality occupational information, video, career assessments, portrayals of work environments and occupations, and online access to the best in professional literature, publications, summaries of research findings, cybercounseling, e-mail, chat rooms, text messaging, on-line discussions, e-learning, video conferencing, and telephone help lines with replies on-line (Offer, 2005). What is at issue, to an increasing degree, is a research base that analyzes material on the Internet to identify those items which meet quality standards and those career interventions, including career assessments, that are determined to be best practices, empirically supported, and evidence-based. Computer-assisted career assessment is discussed further in Chapter 4.

Evidence-Based Assessments, Empirically-Supported Treatments, and Accountability

As one uses terms like "best practices," "empirically-supported treatments," and "evidence-based," implicit, if not explicit, is the role played by assessments in achieving such outcomes. To an increasing degree, the whole range of interventions and the results they achieve individually and collectively are being questioned by legislators, policy makers, and institutional administrators (Vuorinen, 2008). They are asking: "What are we receiving for our investment of resources in career services?" "How do we know what interventions or combinations of them are the most effective?" "Do career services or interventions add value to the education of adolescents or college students, or to the purpose and productivity of adult workers?" "If so, how do we know?" "Why do we need counselors if counselor-free interventions are effective?" In one sense, the question is whether we can create a matrix that identifies problems presented in career counseling—stress, anxiety, indecision, indecisiveness, over commitment to work, under commitment to work, etc. – and the interventions and theories that have been found to affect these career concerns in positive and effective ways for different subpopulations under varying conditions. Essentially, these questions ask how does Intervention A compare with the effects of Intervention B or C or D vis-à-vis a particular presenting problem? What are the comparative costs of intervention A, B, C, or D in achieving the goals sought? How do we assure that the values achieved exceed the costs of the interventions? These are questions of accountability, of cost-benefit ratios, and of evidence-based or empirically-supported practices. Sampson, Dozier, and Colvin (2011) noted that such questions connect to social justice issues, as career practitioners must strive to ensure that effective career interventions, including career assessment, are readily available to all citizens. They acknowledged that achieving a satisfactory balance between effectiveness and access is challenging and requires the field to increase its understanding concerning the relationship between effectiveness and cost (the most effective intervention is not necessarily one that is

Trends and Issues in Career Assessment

available to all). This becomes an even more pressing social justice issue when budgets supporting the provision of career services are reduced, or even eliminated altogether.

One of the most important ways to examine accountability in the provision of career services for the future is cost-benefit analyses. Cost-benefit analyses tend to complete the circle from the creation, implementation, and evaluation of career assessments or other career interventions to their likely costs and benefits. Despite a clear set of philosophical assumptions about the value of career interventions and an enlarging research base that validates the importance of career interventions, it is fair to suggest that researchers and theorists in counseling, with the possible exception of those engaged in rehabilitation or in drug and alcohol research, have not systematically taken the next step of translating the available research findings into cost-benefit analyses. Even though one can make the over-simplified observation that every positive or negative correlation between a particular career intervention and a desired outcome carries with it economic costs and economic benefits, most theorists and researchers in career counseling and related career interventions have not focused on these issues (Sampson et al., 2011). There has not been the systematic examination of the costs of providing counseling or assessment to various populations for specific purposes compared to the economic and social benefits derived from such services. Nor have analyses accrued that have focused on the *added value* to an institution—school, university, employers, governments or society at large—of providing career services or to the individual who participates in career services.

Given limited economic resources available for counseling and competing human services, and rising demands for such resources, a strategic issue for the future will be the need to train counselors, theorists, and researchers in the mentality and methodology of cost-benefit analyses. Assessment strategies will be critical as they produce relevant measures of the added value of career interventions generally and career assessment in particular relative to the productivity of career counselors in different settings. Such approaches will be important tools in advocating to legislators and administrators policies that incorporate career counseling, career assessment, measurement, and evaluation as important assets in addressing major social and individual career goals.

These issues become critically important when one considers that there are now hundreds of career assessment instruments available, many of which have been studied at length in terms of their validity, reliability, and other psychometric properties, and others that have not. One issue is which of these instruments most likely measures most directly, effectively, and comprehensively the outcomes of most concern (e.g., career adaptability, information seeking, developmental status on necessary career tasks, personal flexibility) in comparing the impact of different interventions on the outcomes chosen.

To demonstrate accountability, there is also the need to reinvigorate career outcome research that assesses both single and comparative effects on the major career outcomes that are inherent in the most influential career theories in the field. Thus, it is concerning that Whiston et al. (2003) have reported that there has been a decrease in career outcome research even though there have been new techniques, including the Internet, and new career outcomes to be assessed. Although a series of meta-analyses and literature reviews have been conducted, most of these are now dated (Whiston & Buck, 2008) and, therefore, the need exists for current research related to career assessments and career intervention outcomes.

An issue related to accountability has to do with the consistency of the instruments used to assess the effects of career interventions on career outcomes. If different instruments are used to assess the same outcomes, unless it is clear that their contents are highly correlated, it becomes difficult to know what the obtained results mean. A further issue is that unless career-outcome research grows in its coverage and immediacy across a larger spectrum of career interventions, used singly and in combination, editors, practitioners, and researchers may conclude that approaches to career counseling, career education, career guidance, and other career interventions are not empirically supported or evidence-based practices.

While one can argue persuasively that, 'in the broadest or aggregate sense,' there is no longer a major question about the ability of career counseling and other career interventions to improve or change career behavior (e.g., Brown & Ryan Krane, 2000; Campbell, Connel, Boyle, & Bhaerman, 1983; Oliver & Spokane, 1988; Rounds & Tinsley, 1984; Whiston, 2003; Whiston et al., 2003; Whiston, Sexton, & Lasoff, 1998); the large array of research studies available have not really addressed accountability, empirically supported treatments, or evidence-based practice questions systematically. Meta-analyses and other research techniques have permitted researchers to summarize large numbers of studies and to determine the collective effect of research studies of

A COUNSELOR'S GUIDE TO CAREER ASSESSMENTS INSTRUMENTS

a particular process on different forms of behavior. In general, however, these studies have not compared the effects of Intervention A to that of Intervention B in relation to particular career-presenting problems. Nor have these studies essentially contrasted the utility of Theory A versus Theory B for understanding and intervening in specific career concerns. Increasingly, researchers and theorists are contending, as has Whiston (2003), that "there is not an established method or model for conducting career counseling that is consistently used in the field and evaluated by researchers. Hence, career counseling professionals do not have a clear understanding of precisely what is effective, nor has the field made great strides in comparing different approaches with different populations" (p. 40).

Unlike some other mental health emphases (e.g., psychotherapy), career counseling protocols or treatment manuals have not typically been developed to assure that practices being evaluated are standardized so that they can be examined relative to their efficacy in promoting particular types of behavior, reframing irrational thoughts, facilitating client decision making, or obtaining other desired outcomes. Without such standardization of practices, it is difficult to compare the implementation of Theory A versus Theory B. Nor can one deconstruct various approaches to career intervention into their components to assess which ingredients of that practice are essential and necessary or acceptable but not necessary (Wampold, 2001) as compared with other approaches. While such research approaches may not occur in the foreseeable future, pursuit of such goals would better enable the field to articulate differences among its major theoretical and intervention processes; allow practitioners to make intervention decisions regarding the use of career assessments more confidently; describe the importance of the contributions of career interventions to societal goals to policy makers, legislators, and administrators; improve the training of practitioners; and address cost-benefit ratios of career interventions.

Summary

This chapter has demonstrated that career assessment, both as a standalone career intervention and as an adjunct to career counseling and other career interventions, has sunk its roots deep into career development – related public policies, theory, and practice in the United States and beyond. Clearly, the purposes for which career assessment is expected to be a useful process have expanded and taken on new content, formats, and venues. Career assessments are now frequently available on the Internet as part of the growing presence of on-line career counseling and access to job information. Rather than adapting assessments developed in the United States, nations around the globe are increasingly creating career assessment instruments with content and procedures that are indigenous to their goals for career services for those choosing, preparing for, making the transition to, and adjusting to work.

As important as current career assessments are, the organization and substance of work itself is changing rapidly and qualitatively, as are the expectations of workers. Workers need to become their own career managers or investors of their time, talent, and effort systematically in the choices available to them. Since such career choices and career transitions will likely occur more often, workers will need to be personally flexible, able to cope with change, and engaged in continuous learning. The need to assess these types of competencies will grow and broaden the content of career assessments yet to be developed.

As the use of career assessments is worldwide, it is likely that major trends will include the development or adaptation of career assessments cross-nationally, the increased use of technologies (e.g., the Internet) to administer and interpret career assessments as counselor-free interventions or as the source of much of the content analyzed and discussed in the growing increase of online career counseling. Each of these trends will increasingly rely on the creation of new career assessments that address the changing nature of work and its reflection in career theory as well as providing measures of major dependent variables for purposes of accountability, empirically supported treatments, and evidence-based practices.

Review Questions

1. In what ways can career assessments be used as stimuli in career intervention?
2. Provide examples as to how career assessments can be used to bridge career theory and practice.
3. In what ways is research in career counseling and career assessment lacking?
4. What are the pro's and con's of computer-assisted career guidance systems as they relate to career assessment?
5. What are some concerns related to the growth of career assessments internationally?

References

Bartram, D. (2001). The development of international guidelines on test use: The international test commission project. *International Journal of Testing, 1(1),* 33-54.

Beatty, J. (1998). *The world according to Peter Drucker.* New York, NY: The Free Press.

Bridges, W. (1994, September). The end of the job. *Fortune, 130,* 62-74.

Brown, S. D., & Ryan Krane, N. E. (2000). Four (or five) sessions and a cloud of dust: Old assumptions and new observations about career counseling. In S. D. Brown & R. W. Lent (Eds.), *Handbook of counseling psychology* (3rd ed., pp. 740-766). New York, NY: Wiley.

Campbell, R. E., Connel, J. B., Boyle, K. K., & Bhaerman, R. (1983). *Enhancing career development: Recommendations for action.* Columbus, OH: The National Center for Research in Vocational Education, The Ohio State University.

Cedefop. (2011). *Lifelong guidance across Europe: Reviewing policy progress and future prospects.* Luxembourg: Publications Office of the European Union.

Duarte, M. E. (2004, June). *Assessment and cultural riches: Adaptation of psychological instruments and the global research village.* Paper presented at the symposium on International Perspectives on Career Development, San Francisco, CA.

European Centre for the Development of Vocational Training, (2009). *Professionalising career guidance.* Retrieved from http://www.cedefor.europa.ed/en/Files/5193_EN.PDF

Florida, R. (2004). *The rise of the creative class: And how it is transforming work, leisure, community and everyday life.* New York, NY: Basic Books.

Garis, J. W., & Niles S. G. (1990). The effects of two computer-assisted career guidance systems and a career planning class on undecided university students. *The Career Development Quarterly, 38,* 261-274.

Harris-Bowlsbey, J. (2003). A rich past and a future vision. *Career Development Quarterly, 52(1),* 19-25.

Herr, E. L., Cramer, S. H., & Niles, S. G. (2004). *Career guidance and counseling through the life span: Systematic approaches* (6th ed.). Boston, MA: Allyn and Bacon.

Holland, J. L. (1997). *Making vocational choices: A theory of vocational personalities and work environments* (3rd ed.) Odessa, FL: Psychological Assessment Resources.

Krumboltz, J. D. (1994). The career beliefs inventory. *Journal of Counseling and Development, 72,* 424-428.

Miller, M. J., & Brown, S. D. (2013). Counseling for career choice: Implications for improving interventions and for working with diverse populations. In S. D. Brown & R. W. Lent (Eds.), *Career development and counseling: Putting theory and research to work* (2nd ed., pp. 441-465). New York, NY: Wiley.

Niles, S. G., & Harris-Bowlsbey, J. (2013). *Career development interventions in the 21st century* (4th ed.). Saddle River, NJ: Pearson.

Obsorne, W. L., Brown, S., Niles, S. G., & Miner, C. (1997). *Career development assessment and counseling: Donald Super's C-DAC Model.* Alexandria, VA: American Counseling Association.

Offer, M. (2005, Summer). E-guidance: Can we deliver guidance by email and what issues does that raise? Recent research and evaluation in HE. *Career Research and Development, The NICEC Journal, 12,* 32-33.

Oliver, L. W., & Spokane, A. R. (1988). Career intervention outcome: What contributes to client gain? *Journal of Counseling Psychology, 35,* 447-462.

Organization for Economic Development and Cooperation (2004). *Career guidance and public policy: Bridging the gap.* Retrieved from http://www.oecd.org/dataoecd/33/45/34050171.pdf

Rossier, J. (2004, June). *An analysis of the cross-cultural equivalence of some frequently used personality inventories.* Paper presented at the Symposium on International Perspectives on Career Development, San Francisco, CA.

Rounds, J. B., Jr., & Tinsley, H. E. A. (1984). Diagnosis and treatment of vocational problems, In S. Brown & R. Lent (Eds.), *Handbook of counseling psychology* (pp. 137-177) New York, NY: Wiley.

Sampson, J. P., Jr., Dozier, V. C., & Colvin, G. P. (2011). Translating career theory to practice: The risk of unintentional social injustice. *Journal of Counseling & Development, 89,* 326-337.

Sampson, J. P., Jr., Peterson, G. W., Lenz, J. G., Reardon, R. C., & Saunders, D. E. (1996). *Career Thoughts Inventory.* Odessa, FL: Psychological Assessment Resources.

A Counselor's Guide To Career Assessments Instruments

Sampson, J. P., Jr., Reardon, R. C., Peterson, G. W., & Lenz, J. G. (2004). *Career counseling and services: A cognitive information processing approach.* Pacific Grove, CA: Brooks/Cole.

Savickas, M. L. (2009). Career-style counseling. In T. J. Sweeney (Ed.), *Adlerian counseling and psychotherapy: A practitioners' approach* (5th ed., pp. 183-207). New York, NY: Routledge.

Savickas, M. L., (2013). The theory and practice of career construction. In S. D. Brown and R. W. Lent (Eds.), *Career development and counseling* (2nd ed., pp. 42-70). Hoboken, NJ: Wiley.

Senge, P. M. (1996). Leading learning organizations: The bold, the powerful, and the invisible. In F. Hesselbein, M. Goldsmith, and R. Beckhard (Eds.), *The leader of the future, new visions, strategies and practices for the next era* (pp. 41-58). San Francisco, CA: Jossey-Bass.

Stricker, G. (2003). Evidence-based practice: The wave of the past. *The Counseling Psychologist, 31,* 546-554.

Super, D. E. (1990). A life-span, life-space approach to career development. In D. Brown & L. Brook (Eds.). *Career choice and development: Applying contemporary theories to practice* (pp. 197-261). San Francisco, CA: Jossey-Bass.

Super, D. E. (1994). A life span, life space perspective on convergence. In M. L. Savickas & R. W. Lent (Eds.), *Convergence in career development theories: Implications for science and practice* (pp. 63-74). Palo Alto, CA: CPP Books

Super, D. E., & Sverko, B. (1995). *Life roles, values, and careers.* San Francisco, CA: Jossey-Bass.

The World Bank. (2003). *Lifelong learning in the global knowledge economy, challenges for developing countries.* Washington D. C.: The author.

Vuorinen, R. (2008, September). *Rationale and added value of the European Lifelong Guidance and Policy Network.* Paper presented at Career Transitions and Lifelong Guidance: Building a European Response. Lyon, France.

Wampold, B. E. (2001). *The great psychotherapy debate: Models, methods, and findings.* Mahwah, NJ: Lawrence Erlbaum Associates.

Whiston, S. C. (2002). Application of the principles. *The Counseling Psychologist, 30,* 218-237.

Whiston, S. C. (2003). Career counseling: 90 years and yet still healthy and vital. *The Career Development Quarterly, 52,* 35-42.

Whiston, S. C., & Buck, I. M. (2008). Evaluation in career guidance programs. In J. A. Athanasou & R. V. Esbroeck (Eds.), *International handbook of career guidance* (pp. 677-694). New York, NY: Springer.

Whiston, S. C., Brecheisen, B. K., & Stephens, J. (2003). Does treatment modality affect career counseling effectiveness? *Journal of Vocational Behavior, 62,* 390-410.

Whiston, S. C., Sexton, T. L., & Lasoff, D. L. (1998). Career intervention outcome: A replication and extension of Oliver and Spokane (1988). *Journal of Counseling Psychology, 45,* 150-165.

22

CHAPTER 3

CAREER ASSESSMENT STANDARDS AND COMPETENCIES FOR PRACTIONERS

Janet E. Wall

President and Founder, Sage Solutions and CEUonestop.com

Introduction

Career practitioners serve students, clients, and customers. In order to do that well, they must act according to the expectations of the profession throughout the assessment process. That is, they are obliged to put aside their own interests, act with integrity, and maintain their competence in the field in which they work. This is particularly important in the area of assessment because the results are typically used for career decision-making, career planning and transition, life decisions, and often in gatekeeping for education and training programs. Assessment results can determine acceptance into certain educational programs, determine the receipt of certifications and licenses, channel individuals into one career over another, and affect the future quality of life for people.

As stated in a recent NCDA *Career Convergence* article (Wall, 2010),

Regardless of your title, career advisor, career navigator, career counselor, workforce development professional, etc., you are likely to employ some career assessments from your tool kit to help individuals move forward in their career choice and development. There are so many assessments now available, both in paper-pencil and online formats, that it is easy to forget to take proper care to use quality assessments with your students, customers, and clients. Using a poor quality instrument, one without strong technical characteristics or using an instrument in which you are not trained, can cause harm to your clients despite your genuine intent to do otherwise. (¶ 1)

Because assessment is important in practice for career practitioners, two ideas are paramount. First, they need to select the very best assessment for the purpose for which the assessment is being used. Second, and no less important, is the competency and qualifications to use the assessment in question. These two issues, test selection and practitioner competency, are key underlying themes of professional ethics and the reason that many assessment-related associations have crafted policies and professional and ethical standards.

Although there are many more ethical and professional standards as they relate to testing and assessment, this chapter reviews the many assessment standards and policies that have been developed that help define ethical and professional behaviors for career practitioners. Depending on specific professional affiliations, career practitioners are ethically bound to know, follow, and adhere to associated standards and competency statements and guidelines. Even if career practitioners are not affiliated with a professional association, they are morally bound not to cause harm to individuals by using substandard instruments or interpreting assessment results without the proper knowledge and competency in the field. The chapter provides a synopsis of the various ethical standards and policies that are pertinent to career counselors, facilitators, and practitioners. Specifically, standards are presented beginning with those pertinent to more general populations (i.e., assessment community, professional counselors) and then moving to standards more specific to career practitioners, including guidelines intended for specific uses. Then, standards developed for the test taker are presented. The chapter concludes with specific points that career practitioners should follow as they consider using assessments in their professional practice.

Standards Related to the Assessment Community in General

Producers of assessments, such as test publishers, states, and researchers, are guided by standards and best practices as outlined by the *Standards for Educational and Psychological Testing* (1999) and by the Association of Test Publishers.

Standards for Educational and Psychological Testing

These standards are crafted by the American Psychological Association, American Educational Research Association, and the National Council on Measurement in Education and are designed for use by individuals and organizations that create or administer tests and use the test results to draw conclusions about individuals or groups. Career practitioners who are interested in evaluating and selecting high quality and rigorously developed assessments, or are themselves creating assessments for use in career and workforce development, should use and adhere to these standards where they are applicable. These standards are considered by professionals in the assessment development field to be the definitive set of standards by which tests are developed, used, evaluated, selected, and interpreted. The standards are comprehensive, revised approximately every 10 years, and receive wide public reviews by organizations, associations, and individuals prior to final acceptance and publication. All credible test publishers adhere to these standards for the development and use of assessments to the extent that is psychometrically possible.

The latest version of the *Standards* presents reorganized material from the 1999 revision that includes the following sections: (a) foundational concepts such as reliability, validity, and test fairness; (b) operational or procedural information including test design and development, test administration, and scoring and reporting; and (c) application issues related to workplace testing, educational assessment, and policy implications. The latest version includes changes and updates in the areas of access, accountability, the use of technology in assessment, workplace assessment, and differing test formats.

Association of Test Publishers

The Association of Test Publishers is made up of publishers of assessments and services related to assessment, selection, screening, certification, licensing, educational, or clinical uses. Although the Association of Test Publishers does not have its own ethics statement, it is very instrumental in the quality of work and innovation in assessment by commercial test publishers. The association promotes adherence to the *Standards for Educational and Psychological Testing*, but it also has produced some specialized publications on assessment issues. These include *Operational Best Practices for Statewide Large-Scale Assessment Programs*, (Council of Chief State School Officers and Association of Test Publishers, 2010), *Model Guidelines for Preemployment Integrity Testing*, (Association of Test Publishers, 2010), and *Guidelines for Computer-Based Testing* (Association of Test Publishers, 2002). The association is also a source of knowledge on legal issues related to assessment and on copyright protection.

Standards Relevant to Professional Counselors

Professional counselors are also bound by competency standards and ethical statements associated with their specific discipline. These include the American Counseling Association (ACA) *Code of Ethics*, National Career Development Association (NCDA) *Code of Ethics*, the Council for Accreditation of Counseling and Related Educational Programs (CACREP) *2009 Standards*, and the National Board of Certified Counselors (NBCC) *Code of Ethics*.

ACA *Code of Ethics*

Members of the American Counseling Association (ACA) and professional counselors are bound by the ACA *Code of Ethics* (ACA, 2005). The ethics statements relate to assessment focused on the proper selection of technically solid assessments primarily, but not exclusively, in the areas of ability, personality, interests, intelligence, achievement, and performance. Not only are counselors responsible for their own actions, but they are charged to be aware of and be proactive in preventing the misuse of assessments by others. These ethics statements focus on the need for informed consent of the student, client, or customer; the competent interpretation by the counselors on assessments for which they are properly trained; and the release of results with the consent of the client and to persons who are qualified to interpret the results. The ACA *Code of Ethics* also addresses the proper selection of assessment instruments taking into consideration multicultural issues and diversity, proper test and assessment administration, and test security to include copyright protection.

NCDA *Code of Ethics*

The National Career Development Association (NCDA) *Code of Ethics* (NCDA, 2007a) is a modification of those produced by the American Counseling Association. The standards regarding assessment are virtually the same as those in the ACA document. These standards reinforce that career practitioners should follow appropriate assessment procedures.

CACREP Standards

The Council for Accreditation of Counseling and Related Educational Programs (CACREP) provide training standards, including those associated with assessment and career development as core areas (CACREP, 2009). From the professional identity point of view, CACREP expects counseling programs and counselors to have a solid understanding of assessment to include understanding basic assessment concepts such as various assessment techniques, standardized testing, non-standardized testing, performance assessment and psychological testing. On statistical issues, CACREP suggests that counselors know basic statistical techniques and the ideas behind and relationships between reliability and validity. Counselors should also take into consideration social and cultural factors related to assessment and evaluation. Programs should include content related to the ethical strategies for selecting, administering, and interpreting assessment and evaluation instruments and techniques in counseling. Specific to career counselors is the expectation that they know various assessment strategies related to career development and counseling, how to select appropriate assessments, how to identify bias in assessment, and how to properly administer, score, and report findings.

NBCC *Code of Ethics*

The National Board of Certified Counselors (NBCC) *Code of Ethics* (NBCC, 2005) applies to all those certified by NBCC regardless of any other professional affiliation. NBCC does cooperate with professional associations and credentialing organizations. Its ethics code and any violation of it apply to NBCC-certified counselors only. (ACA and NCDA have borrowed much from the NBCC *Code of Ethics*.)

The NBCC *Code of Ethics* emphasizes that certified counselors must limit their use of assessment to those areas for which they have been trained and that the training involves educational and psychological measurement concepts. Before using an assessment, the counselor should review its theoretical and technical characteristics and select the most appropriate assessment for the client while subsequently interpreting the results with appropriate caution and considering psychometric limitations.

Counselors are obligated to provide an orientation to an examinee about the assessment before and after the assessment to put the results in perspective. The client should be made aware of the use and purpose of the assessment being used. Further, counselors must maintain test security, administer the assessment according to specific directions, and honor the copyright. Finally, particular care and attention should be given to accurate and reliable computer test administration and score interpretation.

Standards Relevant to Career Counselors and Practitioners

This section presents standards specific to career counseling practices. These include the NCDA and Association for Assessment and Research in Counseling (AARC) *Career Counselor Assessment and Evaluation Competencies*, NCDA *Career Counseling Competencies*, and the Global Career Development Facilitator (GCDF) *Code of Ethics*.

NCDA/AARC *Career Counselor Assessment and Evaluation Competencies*

This set of statements has been produced by a joint committee composed of members of the Association for Assessment and Research in Counseling (AARC) and the National Career Development Association (NCDA &

AARC, 2010). Both associations endorsed these guidelines. These guidelines are directed to career counselors and the use of assessment by providing a description of the knowledge and skills that career counselors must demonstrate in the areas of assessment and evaluation. The competencies formulate a way for counselors to evaluate their own capabilities, and be a guide in assessing the quality of professional development programs as well as assessment and evaluation courses and requirements.

The guidelines describe the skills and competencies to be a competent career counselor in the areas of selecting the right assessment, types of assessment used in career counseling, proper administration and scoring, interpreting and reporting assessment results, use of assessments in decision making, proper analysis of test results, following professional ethics standards, and evaluating programs.

NCDA *Career Counseling Competencies*

NCDA has produced and revised career counseling competencies that include, in part, some guidelines related to assessment (NCDA, 2009). These relate primarily to the relationship between the counselor and the client. The competencies focus on assessing personal characteristics (such as aptitude, achievement, interests, values, personality traits, leisure interests, learning style, life roles, self-concept, career maturity, vocational identity, career indecision, work satisfaction) and the conditions of the work environment (such as tasks, knowledge and skill requirements, and qualities of the physical and social settings). The competencies also suggest that the counselor understand and be able to select appropriate assessments, score and interpret the results, and write accurate reports regarding the assessment results.

GCDF *Code of Ethics*

Career development facilitators are not required to possess competencies in counseling techniques. That said, the *Global Career Development* (GCDF) *Code of Ethics* (Center for Certification and Education [CCE], 2010) highlights the importance of certificate holders to recognize and abide by the limitations of their qualifications. They are asked to recognize the limitations of practice and qualifications, and provide services only when qualified and within the limits of their GCDF competencies based on "education, knowledge, skills, practice experience, credentials and other relevant considerations" (p. 2). The GCDF *Code of Ethics* cautions certificate holders not to use techniques harmful to clients and to inform clients about the purpose of the techniques they are using including the use of assessments and other similar strategies.

Standards Specific to Practitioner and Test User Competencies

This section highlights five sets of standards related to practitioner and test user competencies, which include applications to those who use career assessments. They include the *Competencies in Assessment and Evaluation for School Counselors, Ethical Standards for School Counselors, the RUST Statement, Code of Fair Testing Practices in Education,* and the *Standards for Qualifications of Test Users.*

Competencies in Assessment and Evaluation for School Counselors

School counselors must be professionally responsible when using assessment and evaluation practices and should act in accordance with the other codes of ethics and standards of practice. The *Competencies in Assessment and Evaluation for School Counselors* (AARC & ASCA, 1998) were developed to guide school counselors in sound assessment practices, including career assessment. Although the competencies are promulgated by the AARC, they were crafted by a committee that included members of the American School Counselor Association (ASCA).

In schools, it is generally the school counselor that is most knowledgeable about testing and assessment of youth. As a result, they must be skilled in selecting the best and most appropriate assessment strategy through an evaluation of the most commonly used instruments. They must be knowledgeable about the administration and scoring methods and be skilled in interpreting and reporting the results and the possibilities and limitations of using the results for decision making and the evaluation of school programs.

ASCA *Ethical Standards for School Counselors*

ASCA in its recently updated ethics statement (ASCA, 2010) calls upon school counselors to "adhere to all professional standards regarding selecting, administering, and interpreting assessment measures and only utilize the assessment measures that are within the scope of practice for school counselors and for which they are trained and competent" (A.9). School counselors must adhere to confidentiality, consider the developmental age and stage of the student, interpret results in a form that students can understand, and take reasonable steps to prevent others from misusing the results. Proper interpretations must include a consideration of the norms, particularly when certain populations may not have part of the norm group.

RUST Statement

AARC developed the *Responsibility of Users of Standardized Tests*, referred to as the *RUST Statement* (AARC, 2003) to promote the accurate, fair, and responsible use of standardized tests by the counseling and education communities. These standards were updated because of the influence of state testing mandates, the call for educational accountability and reform, and the emphasis on testing related to the No Child Left Behind legislation.

The guidelines and standards in this document focus on the qualifications of test users; technical knowledge about tests and assessment; proper test selection, administration, and scoring; interpreting tests results; and communicating test results to test takers and other interested persons. Appropriate test use when working with students and clients is a prime responsibility of the user of the instrument.

Code of Fair Testing Practices

The *Code of Fair Testing Practices* (Joint Committee of Testing Practices [JCTP], 2004) is a common language document to which nearly all professional testing companies have endorsed. Member associations of the Joint Committee include the American Counseling Association (ACA), the American Educational Research Association (AERA), the American Psychological Association (APA), the American Speech-Language-Hearing Association (ASHA), the National Association of School Psychologists (NASP), the National Association of Test Directors (NATD), and the National Council on Measurement in Education (NCME). Its strength results from the fact that all the Joint Committee associations have endorsed this document.

The *Code* provides guidance for both the test developer and the test user in the areas of developing and selecting appropriate tests, administering and scoring tests, reporting and interpreting test results, and informing test takers. As the document suggests, "States, districts, schools, organizations, and individual professionals are encouraged to commit themselves to fairness in testing and safeguarding the rights of test takers. The *Code* is intended to assist in carrying out such commitments" (p. 3). Such a commitment to fairness is also important to career practitioners.

Standards for Qualifications of Test Users

The *Standards for Qualifications of Test Users* (ACA, 2003) focuses on the skills and competency expectations for counselors who use tests and assessments. The standards emanate from the prime consideration that a counselor's ability to use assessments comes from their competence, which is obtained through education, training, and experience. The standards suggest that assessment should be integrated within the context of the theory and specialty areas within which the assessment will be used. Further, the standards consider it essential that test users have a thorough understanding of testing theory, test construction, and technical assessment characteristics such as reliability and validity. Test users should know sampling techniques, the construction and meaning of norms, and various statistical characteristics. Counselors should be able to select, administer, and interpret tests that have been reviewed carefully and determined to be appropriate for the specific students or clients while considering diversity issues.

Standards Relevant to Specific Uses or Populations

This section highlights four documents that are useful in specific settings. These include the *ACA Position Statement on High Stakes Testing, Standards for Multicultural Assessment, Pre-Employment Testing and the ADA*, and a guidebook from the U.S. Department of Labor, Education and Training Administration.

ACA *Position Statement on High Stakes Testing*

ACA developed a position statement on high stakes testing (ACA, 2004), recognizing the need for testing to assist in determining the effectiveness of our education system and the consequences for individuals when high stakes tests act as a gateway to various opportunities such as graduation, promotion, access to higher education and training programs. Among the principles addressed are the alignment of the assessment with the curriculum and instruction, the use of multiple rather than single measures to make important decisions, knowing the impact of any decision made using assessments, the goal that all youth have an equitable opportunity to learn material that will be evaluated with high stakes tests, the availability of remediation and resources to help ameliorate deficiencies, the use of high quality assessment, the need for assessment results that are understood by relevant parties, the appropriateness of assessment for diverse populations, and the implementation of policies and research that encourage the creation and use of high quality assessments that are meaningful to instruction and accountability.

Standards for Multicultural Assessment

This document was prepared by the Association for Assessment and Research in Counseling (AARC, 2012) in recognition of the increasing diversity of students and workers in American society. Specifically, "the mission and vision of AARC drives the continuing effort to create awareness of the importance of assessment and diagnostic techniques for an increasingly diverse population, to promote better training in the uses and development of assessments and to advocate for social justice concerns in counseling and educational assessment" (p. 1).

The document represents a review of related standards promulgated by various professional associations and places them in a single document focused on the multicultural test taker. Authors of this document have categorized various standards into five sections: advocacy, selection of assessments, administration and scoring of assessments, interpretation and application of assessment results, and training in the uses of assessments.

Pre-Employment Testing and the ADA (Americans with Disabilities Act)

This document was produced to emphasize the need for appropriate actions by test users including career practitioners and employers in the selection, modification, and interpretation of assessments that undergo changes in content, format, or administration to accommodate individuals with specific disabilities (AARC & ARCA, 2003). The ADA considers it discriminatory if an instrument screens out an employee based on a person's disability. Any assessment for selection into a job must be related to the job itself and the ability to do that job and not any other criteria.

The document reviews various common test accommodations and discusses its impact on the reliability, validity, and utility of the test results. Specifically test format, time limits, test content, and accommodations for specific disabilities are addressed. Test users are cautioned to be sure that accommodations do not change the nature of what is being measured (see Chapter 6).

Testing and Assessment: A Guide to Good Practices for Workforce Investment Professionals

Although not standards per se, this document published by the U.S. Department of Labor, Employment and Training Administration (2007), provides some good guidelines for persons using assessment in the workforce development field. The document summarizes pertinent laws regarding workforce development and assessment and suggests that workforce development professionals focus on the following assessment principles:

- Use assessment tools in a purposeful manner. It is critical to have a clear understanding of what needs to be measured and for what purpose.

- Use the whole-person approach to assessment. Do not rely too much on any one test to make decisions.

- Use only assessment instruments that are unbiased and fair to all groups.

- Use only reliable assessment instruments and procedures. In other words, use only assessment tools that provide dependable and consistent information.

- Use only assessment procedures and instruments that have been demonstrated to be valid for the specific purpose for which they are being used.

- Use assessment tools that are appropriate for the target population.
- Use only assessment tools that provide dependable and consistent information.
- Ensure that administration staff is properly trained.
- Ensure that testing conditions are suitable for all test takers.
- Provide reasonable accommodation in the assessment process for people with disabilities.
- Maintain assessment instrument security.
- Maintain confidentiality of assessment results.
- Ensure that scores are interpreted properly.

Standards Relevant to the Test Taker

This final section highlights a key document pertaining to the rights and responsibilities of test takers. *The Rights and Responsibilities of Test Takers: Guidelines and Expectations* (JCTP, 1999) is modeled to some extent after the Patient's Bill of Rights in the health care field. The rights of test takers include the following: to be informed of his or her rights; be treated with dignity and courtesy; be tested with appropriate assessments that meet professional standards; receive an explanation of the test and the use of test results prior to testing; know when the test will be administered and when the results will be available; be aware if there is a fee associated with the assessment; have the test administered by a trained individual who follows his or her professional standards; and know the consequences of not taking the assessment. Further, the test taker has the right to an explanation of the assessment results, have the results kept confidential, and have the right to present concerns about the process or the results.

Responsibilities of the test taker include listening to their rights and responsibilities, treating others with courtesy and respect, asking questions about the nature of the test and testing process, listening to the instructions, informing the administrator about any documented accommodation, paying for the test if that is required, appearing at the testing location ready to take the test, following instructions, representing themselves honestly, and presenting concerns about the testing process or conditions when appropriate.

Summary

The *National Career Development Guidelines* (NCDA, 2007b) promotes career development in three major domains: Personal/Social Development, Educational Achievement and Life Long Learning, and Career Management. In each of these domains, assessment plays a strong, and some might say, ubiquitous role for the career development professional and his or her students, clients, and customers. Assessment results are used in career decision making, educational planning, and career management, and transition. Assessment also helps determine the quality of the programs and techniques and provides indicators of ways that programs and services might be improved.

As a result, it is not surprising that many associations, committees, and organizations have developed aspirational standards for persons using assessment in their practice and employment. This chapter presented several sets of standards relevant to the assessment community as a whole, professional counselors, career practitioners, those needing standards for specific uses, as well as those developed for the test taker. If these various ethical standards and guidelines can be summed up in a few brief personal statements that carve out a course of action for career development professionals, they would be that career practitioners should:

- Understand that assessment results matter to individuals because they can enhance or block a person to a life path and the opportunities that affect his or her quality of life and happiness.
- When assessments are used for high stakes decisions, verify results and conclusions with multiple measures.
- Decide on the intended purpose for using an assessment and select only the theoretically and technically best instruments for that purpose.
- Review the technical characteristics of the instrument and how it was developed in order to better assure that the instrument is fair and interpretable for the intended student, clients, and customers.

Career Assessment Standards and Competencies for Practitioners

- Recognize the existence of various academic, cultural, experiential, and background differences of the assessment takers, and select instruments that will provide the most accurate and helpful information for educational and career decision making and planning.

- Only select, administer, and interpret the results of instruments for which appropriate professional training has been obtained.

- Acquire the academic and psychometric competencies necessary to interpret the results accurately and with the appropriate cautions and limitations.

- Orient the assessment taker to the purpose of the assessment, and provide and interpret the results in a timely manner.

- Keep individual assessment results private and available only to those who have a legitimate need to know the results.

- Uphold the security of the assessments and respect their copyright.

- Maintain the highest level of knowledge and expertise in all areas of the career development profession, particularly when using assessments.

- Never misrepresent abilities, training, credentials, or qualifications.

- Adhere to the professional standards and guidelines appropriate for the profession.

- Help others adhere to the highest standards of professionalism in the selection and use of assessment and assessment results.

- *Primum non nocere* – "First do no harm".

Career practitioners may also find the following related resources useful: American Psychological Association (http://www.apa.org/); Ericae.net: Clearinghouse on Assessment and Evaluation (http://www.ericae.net/); Buros Center for Testing (http://www.unl.edu/buros/); Buros Institute of Mental Measurements (http://buros.unl.edu/buros/jsp/search.jsp); Society for Industrial & Organizational Psychology, Inc. (http://www.siop.org/); National Council on Measurement in Education (http://www.ncme.org/); Institute for Credentialing Excellence (http://www.credentialingexcellence.org/); and Assessment Resources (http://www.assessmentresources.pbworks.com).

Review Questions

1. What are some of the important considerations for using an assessment with individuals or groups?

2. What ethical standard or guideline is most pertinent to professional counselors' use of career assessments?

3. What ethical standard or guideline do credible test publishers adhere to when developing their assessments?

4. Why should career practitioners using assessments take into consideration the education, cultural, and experiential background of their students, clients, and customers when using assessments?

5. What are some of the key activities career practitioners should do when engaging in the assessment process?

References

American Counseling Association. (2003). *Standards for qualifications of test users.* Retrieved from http://www.theaaceonline.com/standards.pdf

American Counseling Association. (2004). *ACA position statement on high stakes testing.* Retrieved from http://theaaceonline.com/High_Stakes.pdf

American Counseling Association. (2005). *Code of ethics.* Retrieved from http://www.counseling.org/Resources/CodeOfEthics/TP/Home/CT2.aspx

American Educational Research Association, American Psychological Association, & National Council of Measurement in Education (1999). *Standards for educational and psychological testing.* Washington, DC: American Education Research Association.

American School Counselor Association. (2010). *Ethical standards for school counselors.* Retrieved from http://www.schoolcounselor.org/files/EthicalStandards2010.pdf

Association for Assessment and Research in Counseling. (2003). *Responsibility of users of standardized tests.* Retrieved from http://theaaceonline.com/rust.pdf

Association for Assessment and Research in Counseling (2012). *Standards for multicultural assessment.* Retrieved from http://www.theaaceonline.com/multicultural.pdf

Association for Assessment and Research in Counseling and American School Counselor Association. (1998). *Competencies in assessment and evaluation for school counselors.* Retrieved from http://theaaceonline.com/competency.pdf

Association for Assessment and Research in Counseling and the American Rehabilitation Counseling Association. (2003). *Pre-employment and the ADA.* Retrieved from http://www.theaaceonline.com/employ.pdf

Association of Test Publishers (2010). *Model Guidelines for Preemployment Integrity Testing 3rd edition.* Washington, DC: Association of Test Publishers.

Association of Test Publishers (2002). *Guidelines for computer-based testing.* Washington, DC: Author.

Center for Credentialing and Education. (2010). *GCDF code of ethics.* Retrieved from www.cce-global.org/Downloads/Ethics/GCDFcodeofethics.pdf

Council for Accreditation of Counseling and Related Educational Programs. (2009). *CACREP 2009 standards.* Retrieved from http://www.cacrep.org/doc/2009%20Standards%20with%20cover.pdf

Council of Chief State School Officers and the Association of Test Publishers. (2010). *Operational Best Practices for Statewide Large-Scale Assessment Programs.* Washington, DC: Council of Chief State Officers and the Association of Test Publishers.

Joint Committee on Testing Practices. (1999). *Rights and responsibilities of test takers: Guidelines and expectations.* Retrieved from http://www.apa.org/science/programs/testing/rights.aspx

Joint Committee on Testing Practices. (2004). *Code of fair testing practices in education.* Retrieved from http://www.apa.org/science/programs/testing/fair-testing.pdf

National Board of Certified Counselors. (2005). *Code of ethics.* Retrieved from http://www.nbcc.org/Assets/Ethics/nbcc-codeofethics.pdf

National Career Development Association. (2007a). *Code of ethics.* Retrieved from http://associationdatabase.com/aws/NCDA/asset_manager/get_file/3395/code_of_ethicsmay-2007.pdf

National Career Development Association (2007b). *National career development guidelines framework.* Retrieved from http://associationdatabase.com/aws/NCDA/asset_manager/get_file/3384/ncdguidelines2007.pdf

National Career Development Association. (2009). *NCDA career counseling competencies.* Retrieved from http://associationdatabase.com/aws/NCDA/pt/sd/news_article/37798/_self/layout_ccmsearch/true

National Career Development Association and Association of Assessment and Research in Counseling. (2010). *Career counselor assessment and evaluation competencies.* Retrieved from http://theaaceonline.com/AACE-NCDA.pdf

U.S. Department of Labor, Employment and Training Administration. (2007). *Testing and assessment: A guide to good practices for workforce investment professionals.* Retrieved from http://www.onetcenter.org/dl_files/proTestAsse.pdf

Wall, J. (2010, September). Primum non nocere – First do no harm. *Career Convergence Magazine.* Retrieved from http://associationdatabase.com/aws/NCDA/pt/sd/news_article/32693/_self/layout_ccmsearch/false

CHAPTER 4

COMPUTER-ASSISTED CAREER ASSESSMENT

James P. Sampson, Jr.
Department of Educational Psychology and Learning Systems and
Center for the Study of Technology in Counseling and Career Development
Florida State University

Mary-Catherine McClain
The Career Center
Florida State University

Casey Dozier
The Counseling Center
University of Akron

Darrin L. Carr
Psychology and Behavioral Sciences
Tallahassee Community College

Jill A. Lumsden
Career Services
University of Phoenix

Debra S. Osborn
Department of Educational Psychology and Learning Systems
Florida State University

Introduction

There has been a proliferation of career information, online websites, and related assessments on the Internet as an increasing number of individuals seek career services (Hooley, Hutchinson, & Watts, 2010, Jerome et al., 2000; Tracey, 2010;). For example, a search engine generated more than 10,700,000 hits for "Internet-based career assessment." Computer-assisted career assessment, also referred to as Internet-based career assessment, has become an established feature of the delivery of career services. Although most computer-assisted assessments were initially simply computer versions of established paper-and-pencil measures, innovations in computer-assisted assessment have provided computer-based information and tools where you need it, when you need it, and in the form you need it. While access to assessments increased substantially, the availability of counseling support and the quality of assessments, however, decreased markedly. Practitioners have an ethical responsibility to learn about the benefits and limitations of computer-assisted career assessments and collaborate to improve the design and use of them (Osborn, Dikel, & Sampson, 2011).

Computer-assisted career assessment is used by a wide variety of persons with assistance provided by counselors. Persons seeking career assistance are categorized in this chapter as clients or individuals. *Clients* use career assessment within the context of a counseling relationship with a career counselor. *Individuals* use self-help assessments available on the Internet. For the sake of simplicity, both clients and individuals will be referred to as "persons," except when the content applies to only a client or individual.

A variety of practitioners (e.g., career development facilitators, psychologists, vocational rehabilitation specialists, teachers/faculty/academic advisors, librarians and media specialists, human resource specialists, social workers, practitioners-in-training, and student peer counselors) provide services to persons seeking help with career-related choices (Sampson, Reardon, Peterson, & Lenz, 2004). In this chapter the term *counselor* will be used to discuss considerations for computer-assisted career assessment, although considerations may apply to several practitioner types.

There are two types of career assessment: self-assessment and practitioner-assisted assessment. *Self-assessment* is designed to be used without help from a practitioner to select, administer, score, profile, and interpret the assessment. On the other hand, *practitioner-assisted assessment* is designed for use within the context of a helping relationship with a qualified practitioner (Sampson et al., 2004). Counselors should not limit their focus to only clients using practitioner-assisted career assessment. Clients have open access to assessments online and may have already used self-assessments on the Internet. As a result, this experience may influence client expectations for practitioner-assisted assessment, so counselors need to be generally aware of available self-assessment resources. The remainder of this chapter will outline computer-assisted career assessment roles, current trends in computer-assisted career assessment, benefits and limitations associated with these assessments, and future innovations in computer-assisted career assessment.

Computer-Assisted Career Assessment Roles

The ultimate effectiveness of computer-assisted career assessment is dependent upon making the optimum use of the capabilities of computers, counselors, and persons receiving assistance in making a career choice. With respect to the role of computers, computers are to be assigned tasks that best suit their capabilities as they are not an effective or appropriate replacement for the counselor in delivering career counseling (Whiston, Secton, & Lasoff, 1998; Zunker, 2011). They are best suited to perform computational and repetitive tasks, such as administering items, scoring tests, and constructing interpretive reports from predetermined algorithms. Computers are also particularly well suited to facilitating communication among clients and counselors, including distance counseling (Sampson, 2008). They can also be used to improve the quality of test instruments and procedures through the development of previously unavailable techniques. For example, computer technology has resulted in the development of adaptive devices that allow individuals with disabilities to complete assessments independently (McCarthy, Light, & McNaughton, 2007; Sampson, 2000a). In self-help situations, the computer can be programmed to suggest that the individual seek counseling when potential problems are identified by the user or the computer system (Jaeger, 2004; Offer & Sampson, 1999).

The role of the counselor is to ensure, to the best of his or her ability, that clients are given access to, or referred to, assessments that are valid and reliable for the purposes to which they are being used (American Educational Research Association [AERA], American Psychological Association [APA], & National Council on Measurement in Education [NCME], 1999; National Board for Certified Counselors [NBCC], 2012; National Career Development Association [NCDA], 2007). Additionally, counselors are best suited for cognitive, affective, and problem solving tasks, such as helping clients integrate assessment results from multiple sources into their existing knowledge about themselves and formulating a plan for action to meet their needs. Counselors must ensure the following: (a) assessments do not have any systematic bias with regard to gender, race, ethnicity, age, sexual orientation, or disability; (b) adequate steps are taken to maintain confidentiality of any client assessment records that are transmitted or stored on a computer; and (c) a lack of financial resources does not pose an unreasonable barrier for individuals to gain access to computer-assisted career assessments. Further, counselors are to explain the goals of utilizing computer-assisted career assessments prior to implementation, conduct regular evaluations to determine the effectiveness of the computer application in service delivery, that its implementation fosters a full realization of its potential benefits, and that a follow-up is executed with clients to enhance integration of all information (Campbell, 2000; Mastie, 1994; Reile & Harris-Bowlsbey, 2000; Sampson, McClain, Musch, & Reardon, in press; Sampson, 1998; Sampson, Peterson, & Reardon, 1989; Sampson & Pyle, 1983).

The role of persons includes the following: (a) seeking counseling assistance if prompted to do so by self-help career assessments; (b) following the directions provided by the counselor or the software to keep test use congruent with the standardization procedures that contribute to assessment reliability and validity; (c) responding to test items in an honest and complete manner; (d) confirming and expanding upon interpretations offered by the counselor based upon assessment data (Mastie, 1994); (e) evaluating whether the goals of assessment were accomplished (Campbell, 2000); (f) following through with the application of assessment results in developing a plan of action to meet their needs; and (g) being a self-advocate for good assessment by reporting fraudulent assessment practices associated with software and practitioners to appropriate regulating entities, such as states attorney offices, licensure boards, certification boards, and professional association ethics committees.

Current Trends in Computer-Assisted Career Assessment

Traditional face-to-face career counseling is often expensive and unavailable to individuals in the workforce needing external career support (Appana, 2008; Kleiman & Gati, 2004; Mayadas, Bourne, & Bacsich, 2009). The Internet provides an open access alternative, meaning that assessments and web-based career support can be available to anyone at any time. Larger assessment vendors appear to be implementing integrated, web-enabled delivery platforms through which they can deliver a variety of instruments from their portfolio of holdings using a common interface. Such platforms then allow for the centralized maintenance of client assessment records as well as easy purchase of additional test administrations. Integrated systems and delivery models often include career assessments or instruments as well as advising discussions, career planning forums, and online webinars for creating resumes (Khapova, Svennson, Wilderom, & Arthur, 2006). Some Internet-based career assessments allow links to websites that provide occupational information. Many Internet-based career assessments remain available at no cost, with the cost-recovery for development and delivery supported by on-screen advertising, made available by public sector organizations or through the government as a public good. Figure 1 shows the relationships among access options, quality, and cost recovery for development and delivery of career assessment, with the most common kinds of assessments shaded in gray.

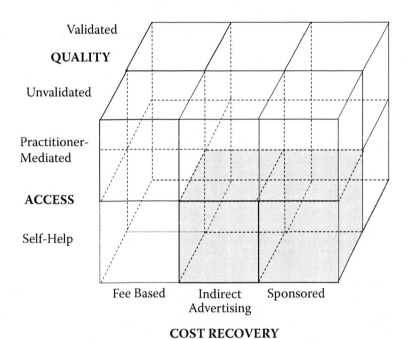

Figure 1. Organizational Schema for Internet-Based Career Assessments

A cursory review of the variety of websites suggests it could be difficult for the typical user to choose among competing sites with different agendas. Sites may pass the user to another website for a referral fee or encourage the purchase of additional products and services (e.g., a book or online degree) after offering a "career test." There are, however, websites with well-established career assessments with evidence of strong psychometric properties (Sampson & Lumsden, 2000). Unfortunately, some websites do not consistently provide test development information that already exists in print form. When information is available, it often uses terminology requiring a level of technical sophistication unlikely to be possessed by the average individual or even some counselors. It is important for those developing career assessments for the Internet to accurately describe the reliability, validity, standardization, and potential biases of their assessments in terms understandable to the general public.

Computer-assisted career assessment is widely available as one feature in career information delivery systems (CIDS). The three components of CIDS are (1) assessment of varying combinations of values, interests, skills, and employment preferences; (2) use of assessment data to identify potentially appropriate occupational information (e.g., entry requirements for occupations, wage data) or education options (e.g., description of educational programs and institutions); and (3) occupational and educational information delivery (Capuzzi & Stauffer, 2012). These three components are integrated so that the information from one component is used in completing another component. Examples of integration include using assessment results to search for occupations, or looking up educational programs for an occupation being researched. Three types of assessment that are used in CIDS include standardized tests administered online, standardized tests administered offline (and then input into the CIDS), and the sorting of self-assessment of variables (e.g., a checklist of values, interests, and skills) in order to expand and/or narrow down a client's occupational aspirations.

CIDS are available in almost all states and include occupational and educational information specific to each state as well as on a national basis (Capuzzi & Stauffer, 2012; Zunker, 2011). State-based CIDS typically provide more specific and detailed local data (e.g., financial aid, educational programs) and job information than national systems. Although many of these systems are used in self-help and practitioner-assisted modes, most schools, colleges, and agencies where the systems are available provide varying types of career services to help clients make effective use of the CIDS. Many CIDS are now available via the Internet. The design and use of these systems, including the assessments, is guided by voluntary standards originally established by the Association of Computer-Based Systems for Career Information (ACSCI) in 2005 and adopted in 2011 by the Alliance of Career Resource Professionals (ACRP 2013). Information on voluntary compliance of specific CIDS with ACSCI standards can be found at http://www.acrpro.org/aws/ACRP/pt/sp/home_page.

Benefits of Computer-Assisted Career Assessment

Computer technology has contributed to the reliability and validity of career assessment, provided opportunities for expanding the types of stimuli presented, improved client integration of assessment data in counseling, and enhanced staff efficiency and cost-effectiveness of career assessment (Sampson, 2000a; Olson-Buchanan & Drasgow, 1999). Additionally, clients are often actively engaged using this resource and experience higher levels of motivation (Sampson, 2000a). In the area of test administration, clients can input answers with fewer errors as compared to paper-and-pencil tests. Further, test scoring can be completed by the computer, providing quick and consistent results. The computer can often generate test score profiles customized for the client and the counselor, as well as narrative interpretive reports (e.g., Self-Directed Search; Reardon & PAR Staff, 2001). Clients can be provided with multimedia-based generalized test interpretations that review basic concepts and general test results before they receive a specific test interpretation from a counselor.

Computer-based test interpretation (CBTI) "uses information technology to integrate theory, practitioner judgment, and empirical evidence, as one source of data, to help practitioners and test takers better understand the meaning of test scores for the purpose of gaining insight and making decisions" (Sampson, Shy, & Purgar, 2003, p. 89). CBTI should be used in a consulting role, integrating a variety of data in creating an assessment (Sampson, 2000b). It should not be used to replace the practitioner (Garb, 2000) or as a standalone psychological report (Butcher, 1995). When an individual uses CBTI in a self-help situation, one of its roles is to indicate to the user the circumstances when counseling assistance may be needed (Sampson et al., 2003).

In comparison with traditional test interpretation, potential benefits of CBTI include: (a) the capability to process a greater number of complex variables (Snyder, 2000); (b) access to an expanded knowledge base as a result of the research data and practitioner judgment available (Sampson, 2000b); (c) the capability to organize and systematically access the extensive and rapidly growing databases related to popular measures (Krug, 1987); (d) being less affected by subjectivity (Butcher, 1995) and interpreter bias (Garb, 2000; Snyder, 2000); (e) increased consistency and reliability of interpretations (Butcher, 1995; Snyder, 2000); (f) rapid access to interpretative reports during preliminary stages of service delivery (Butcher, 1995; Snyder, 2000); and (g) rapid updating of interpretations as new research data become available (Krug, 1987).

Another benefit of CBTI is the improved access to career assessments. Access to Internet-based career assessment can be especially useful in counseling persons with disabilities, those living in remote locations, or those who have traditionally been reluctant to seek career services (Osborn et al., 2011; Robinson, Meyer, Prince, McLean, & Law, 2000; Sampson, 2000b; Sampson & Lumsden, 2000). The use of visual images may improve the effectiveness of career assessment for various multicultural groups (Clark, 2005; Sampson, 1990). Also, Internet-based career assessment has the capability for immediate updating of software, opportunity for immediate feedback, and reduction in scoring and interpretation variability due to these events occurring at a centralized location.

Limitations of Computer-Assisted Career Assessment

The benefits of using computer-assisted career assessment may be compromised by a variety of issues related to questionable quality of computer-assisted assessment, problems in the design of interpretive reports, lack of screening before using assessments, inappropriate access to career assessment, inadequate funding for the development of assessments, ethical issues, and confusion regarding the appropriate application of assessment standards. Similarly, as computers and technology continue to reach higher levels of power, autonomy, and speed, the potential for abuse, ethical violations, and misuse of assessment increases (Barros-Bailey & Saunders, 2010; Harvey & Carlson, 2003).

Questionable Quality of Computer-Assisted Assessment

The quality of career assessments available on the Internet varies in terms of validity and reliability (Olson-Buchanan & Drasgow, 1999). "Ethically and scientifically sound material coexists on the Internet with shoddy work that has not been evaluated at any level" (Clark, Horan, Tompkins-Bjorkman, Kovalski, & Hackett, 2000, p. 87). The Internet provides a point of access for many who might not otherwise use career assessments, but it also poses a problem when there is so little regulation about the credibility of the information being released (Barak, 2003).

Oliver and Zack (1999) completed a comprehensive review of career assessments available from 24 Internet sites that offered no-cost career assessments. Each site was then rated using a descriptive form covering ease of use, informative interpretation, fit of the assessment into a career planning schema, and the application of guidelines and standards. The results showed that few career assessment sites provided evidence of the psychometric quality of the assessments available. While the Oliver and Zack review occurred some time ago, a cursory review of Internet sites confirms that these problems remain.

Three distinct quality issues are associated with computer-assisted career assessment. First, new career assessments are being offered exclusively on computers and provide little or no evidence of quality. A likely assumption is that a "caveat emptor" (or "buyer beware") environment exists on the Internet similar to the magazine publishing environment that has regularly printed unvalidated psychological self-assessments in the guise of "quizzes" or "checklists." Further, computer-assisted assessment may measure examinee characteristics that are irrelevant to the construct being measured. This may include computer proficiency, computer platform and interface effects, speediness, and test anxiety (Huff & Sireci, 2001).

Second, test manuals and assessment websites often fail to provide evidence of the equivalency of the results obtained from traditional paper-and-pencil assessments that are subsequently available in computer-based versions. Enough evidence of score differences in administration modes for the same instrument exists to necessitate studies to establish the equivalence of paper-and-pencil and computer-based versions (Sampson, 2000b). Oliver and Chartrand (2000) stated, "no matter how well standardized, widely used, and highly regarded the instrument is, researchers and counselors cannot automatically assume that the measure will perform on a web site as it does in the usual environment for test administration" (pp. 98-99). The most recent *Standards for Educational and Psychological Testing* (AERA, APA, & NCME, 1999) require that developers provide evidence of the equivalence of various test administration modes (standards 4.10, 6.11, and 13.8). Prince, Chartrand, and Silver (2000) provided an example of how evidence of administration mode equivalency can be presented on career assessments developed both for paper-and-pencil delivery and for Internet delivery.

The third quality issue involves establishing the validity of a computer-based test interpretation as equally important to establishing the validity of the instrument itself. Even in cases where well-established instruments provide substantial evidence of the validity of the measure, little evidence is often provided on the validity of the computer-based test interpretation. It may be that a "halo effect" exists where counselors and clients assume that a "good" test must have a "good" interpretation. The *Standards for Educational and Psychological Testing* (AERA, APA, & NCME, 1999) requires that developers describe the basis of any interpretation (standard 5.11) and evidence supporting the interpretation given (standard 6.12).

Problems in the Design of Interpretive Reports

The provision of valid and useful narrative reports is crucial to the effectiveness of computer-based career assessment. Oliver and Zack (1999) found that the complexity of narrative interpretative reports varied for each assessment instrument on websites evaluated, and they construed three levels of increasing complexity: (a) *categorization* (e.g., labels such as "highly promotable" and screening suggestions such as "You would benefit from reading our book"); (b) *narration,* where the instrument generated a possible categorization with an additional narrative explaining the meaning of the categorization; and (c) *integration,* offering categorization, a narrative context, and referral to/guidance on additional information resources and services based upon specific user results. These three levels reside on a continuum of the clinical skills and functions performed by a counselor. It appears that the majority of Oliver and Zack sites resided on the lower end of this continuum. Furthermore, Oliver and Zack found interpretation to be "inadequate in many cases" (p. 330). Thus, even those assessments using the most complex interpretation scheme may need to be approached with caution by clients, individuals, and counselors.

The design and use of CBTI has several potential limitations: (a) a lack of appropriate qualifications of test developers, which may lead to poor quality interpretations (Carr, 1991); (b) the potential for inclusion of biased expert judgment in interpretations (Garb, 2000); (c) the perception of test users that test interpretations are more accurate when more nonspecific statements are used (Snyder, 2000); (d) the danger of CBTI lending itself to unrealistic credibility and assumptions of validity (Wetzler, 1990); (e) the possibility that overworked or inadequately trained counselors may become overly dependent on CBTI (Sampson & Bloom, 2001); and (f) the possibility that differences among CBTI reports exist for the same test generated from different software programs (Eyde & Kowal, 1987). An additional concern is the lack of validity evidence for CBTI. The validity of a CBTI is distinct from the validity of the test (Snyder, 2000), and it is possible to have an invalid interpretation of a valid test. Therefore, the validity of the test and the CBTI must be established independently (Sampson et al., 2003).

Given the Oliver and Zack (1999) data, it is not surprising that there is little evidence for Internet-based assessments that provide multimedia-based generalized test interpretation, despite the capability of the Internet to deliver this type of resource. Instead there appear to be many text-based interpretations that provide simple categorizations or narrations without reference to specific user needs. An example of multimedia-based generalized test interpretation would be a video presentation explaining the theoretical constructs that undergird an instrument (e.g., the Holland hexagon or the five factor model of personality) and where the person generally relates to these constructs. Generalized multimedia interpretations have several advantages: (a) the counselor is alleviated from routine communication of basic information, which may be perceived by the client as a counselor's boredom with the client's case; (b) interpretive information in different media (e.g., text, audio, and pictorial) allows a client to select a learning mode that best meets his or her needs; (c) presenting generalized interpretive information in a multimedia format can be beneficial to those clients with cognitive or sensory disabilities as more than one channel of communication is used; and (d) clients may come to the counselor better prepared to participate in a discussion about their assessment results, thus maximizing client-counselor time (Timmons, Podmostko, Bremer, Lavin, & Willis, 2004).

Lack of Screening before Using Assessments

The Joint Committee on Testing Practices states that test users should, "select tests through a process that includes persons with appropriate knowledge, skills, and training" (standard A.4; AERA, APA, & NCME, 1999). One problem with online assessments is that even when guidelines are clearly stated, people often disregard them, and take assessments without the adequate vocabulary level necessary for the assessment, which can then jeopardize the validity of the assessment (Barak, 2003).

Inappropriate Access to Career Assessment

The global nature of the Internet is simultaneously a strength and a weakness. Individuals worldwide can use career assessments, irrespective of ethnicity, culture, or language. This can become a problem, however, when individuals take tests that are intended to measure emic traits in a specific country, language, or culture that is not their own (Barak, 2003). This can cause difficulties because the norms used to interpret the results may not be applicable to them or because cultural differences may have a significant impact on test results (Anastasi & Urbina, 1997; Leong, Hardin, & Gupta, 2010). An additional consideration is to identify the norm population for an assessment and how that population compares to the client(s). Many assessments are developed according to White European assumptions, leaving minority populations underrepresented in norm samples. As a result, understanding the client and the norm group is important to consider when choosing and interpreting assessments (Flores & Heppner, 2002; Leong, Hardin, & Gupta, 2010). There is also concern that computer and Internet access are not readily available to all individuals or groups due to economic, social, or cultural reasons. This lack of equal opportunity, which is correlated with socioeconomic status, is a social justice concern because assessment cannot be offered equally to all individuals who need it (Barak, 2003; Osborn et al., 2011).

Inadequate Funding for the Development of Assessments

Although the cost of delivering career assessments on the Internet is relatively low, the cost of developing reliable and valid assessments and interpretive reports remains high irrespective of the delivery method. In the past, the costs associated with developing tests and interpretive reports were recovered through royalties paid to publishers by organizations delivering services or by clients receiving counseling. Oliver and Chartrand (2000) noted that numerous assessments are available at no charge on the Internet. It may be increasingly difficult to meet professional standards if adequate funding is not available for research and development (Harris-Bowlsbey, Riley-Dikel, & Sampson, 2002). Stable public and private sources of funding for developing Internet-based computer applications are needed to avoid a reduction in the quality of assessments available.

Ethical Issues

Numerous ethical issues have been raised related to computer-assisted assessment. In addition to the quality issues raised above, the confidentiality of assessment data stored and transmitted on servers, client devices, and computer networks can be compromised if appropriate security measures are not consistently followed. Individuals who need counseling along with using self-help computer software may be unaware of the potential value of counseling or they may be unable to locate an appropriate professional. Counselors may misuse or become dependent on computer-based test interpretation software as a result of being inadequately trained or overworked. Inadequate awareness of important location-specific circumstances may cause a counselor in a remote location to misinterpret client data or fail to recognize relevant issues. Clients with limited financial resources may have difficulty gaining access to computer resources, especially Internet-based resources. Also, gaining access to the Internet from a residence that is shared with other persons may not allow the auditory and visual privacy necessary for test administration and related counseling. It is also uncertain how state counselor licensure laws will apply to a counselor delivering career assessment and related counseling services across state and national boundaries (Bloom, 2000; Reile & Harris-Bowlsbey, 2000; Robinson et al., 2000; Sampson, 1998; Sampson & Lumsden, 2000).

Furthermore, Makela (2009) and Osborn et al. (2011) asserted that counselors asking clients to use online assessments should first assess the client's readiness or it would be inappropriate practice and a violation of ethical codes. Social networking sites create potential ethical issues in terms of both confidentiality and privacy concerns. Specific ethical standards for the use of social networking sites related to online assessment do not yet exist, although one can assume the same standards that apply to dual relationships apply in these situations (Osborn et al., 2011). Standards for Internet-based assessment are included in ethical statements of the Alliance of Career Resource Professionals (2013), Association for Assessment and Research in Counseling (2013), and the National Career Development Association (1997, 2007).

Confusion Regarding the Appropriate Application of Assessment Standards

The Joint Committee on Testing Practices established the *Standards for Educational and Psychological Testing* (AERA, APA, & NCME, 1999), which are the most often used standards in assessment (Baker & Linn, 2002). However, there may be confusion as to which assessments these standards apply. Although there appears to be general agreement that computer-based assessments from test publishers should abide by the standards, there is less agreement about Internet-based tests. One problem has to do with terminology. On the Internet, the terms test, instrument, scale, measure, questionnaire, and checklist appear to be used interchangeably. One position is that the standards only apply to assessments developed by members of the professional associations who approved the standards. Another position is that if individual items build to a scale, or if individuals rate themselves on a particular construct that leads to the development of insight, then assessment is taking place and the standards apply irrespective of the professional association membership of the authors.

In the first position, the focus is on the nature of the assessment developer, whereas in the second position the focus is on the outcome of using the assessment. In the second position, if it works like a scale, or a self-assessment of constructs, then it is assessment. We endorse this second position that focuses on the nature of assessment outcomes rather than the nature of the assessment developer. Providers and users of assessments need to become more aware of, and consistently apply, appropriate standards to ensure quality in computer-assisted career assessments.

Future Innovations in Computer-Assisted Career Assessment

Several future innovations have the potential of improving the quality and effectiveness of computer-assisted career assessment. These innovations include social media, synchronous and asynchronous communication, artificial intelligence, use of multimedia technology, improved assessment reviews, ubiquitous assessment, and mobile applications.

Social Media

Integrated and comprehensive career centers often implement social media resources to further facilitate assessment, connectedness, and overall engagement in the career development process (Osborn et al., 2011). Osborn and LoFrisco (2012) found that out of 78 career centers, 97% stated that they used social media to enhance and extend service delivery, on average using 2.7 social media venues. Although research on the use of social media and career assessments is limited, what is known is that millions of people subscribe and regularly use these sites. Social media can be used in a supportive role. Blogs, discussion forums, and wikis might provide a location for posting and discussing information about career assessment best practices, information, and resources (Osborn, 2012).

Also common with social media resources is the inclusion of quick surveys that predict, based on an answer to one or a few questions, personality, best type of mate, and career. Validity and reliability issues are a major concern with these types of quizzes or surveys. Several career inventories (e.g., Kuder, Self-Directed Search, and Strong Interest Inventory) are easily found through the search feature on Facebook; however, these are mostly "pages" that are used as a marketing tool, and are not providing the assessment via Facebook.

Synchronous and Asynchronous Communication

Integrating distance counseling into career services would make it easier to serve clients who have barriers to accessing career services, such as clients with disabilities or clients who live in geographically isolated areas (Sampson & Bloom, 2001). Synchronous communication via voice conferencing or videoconferencing allows clients the opportunity to discuss assessment results in a group, as well as facilitates interaction between counselors and clients. Telephone helplines have been shown to be effective in providing information and support to individuals who are making career choices (Watts & Dent, 2002). This type of distance support can be used to improve the effectiveness of career assessment for persons who might not otherwise receive the help they need. Asynchronous communication through a group listserv or e-mail would also facilitate discussion about assessment results among clients and counselors.

Artificial Intelligence

Advances in artificial intelligence such as the popularity of Apple's iPhone personal assistant Siri or the 2011 victory of IBM's Watson on the game show *Jeopardy* may lead us to fear the role of counselor will soon be obsolete (Apple Inc., n.d.; Tesauro, Gondek, Lenchner, Fan, & Prager, 2012). However, it is important to note that these systems are built for very limited tasks (e.g., scheduling an appointment or winning a trivia game show). To work, these systems must first recognize and "understand" the question, then make predictions about the best possible answers to these questions.

Siri excels at voice recognition, a technology which has been available for some time on personal computers for specific purposes (e.g., dictation). While this technology is useful to many persons, the benefits are substantial for persons with disabilities, who may have difficulty interacting with paper-and-pencil or standard keyboard assessments (Vuong, 2011). However, computer-assisted assessment developers must make the effort to integrate advances such as Siri into their resources.

Watson demonstrated the power of predictions (answers) that can be derived when amassing and integrating rule and data sets. On a smaller scale, assessment developers are beginning to create integrated assessment, the use of multiple measures of individual differences to make more powerful predictions and interpretations about vocational options (Betz & Borgen, 2010). For example, Betz and Borgen (2010) combined measures of vocational interest and career confidence to create an "integrative online system for college major exploration (p. 148)." Similarly, the Strong Interest Inventory, Myers-Briggs Type Indicator, and Skills Confidence Inventory have been combined in interpretive reports that have various degree of interpretive integration. Although telephones with high quality voice recognition and computers that answer questions are impressive, there are at least three reasons why such systems will play only a supportive role in career counseling. First, the technology, knowledge base, and problem-solving rules they work with must first be created by human experts. Second, this creation process is an expensive endeavor. Third, artificial intelligence may never truly "understand" the emotional nuance of the questions our clients ask because they cannot provide empathy. Siri and Watson are unlikely to provide career counseling anytime soon.

Use of Multimedia Technology

The availability of assessments that take advantage of multimedia technology to administer test items and present interactive interpretations remains elusive. The majority of current computer applications in career assessment are either computer versions of existing paper-and-pencil tests or simple assessments with limited interpretation of the results. Problems do exist in the use of videos, such as the validity of item presentation for various multicultural groups and the cost of video production. However, these challenges need to be weighed against the potential to create multimedia stimuli that more closely reflect reality as well as increasing the potential for persons to learn from interactive interpretations that combine text, sound, pictures, graphics, and video.

Improved Reviews of Computer-Assisted Career Assessment

The Internet provides numerous opportunities to design more effective self-assessments and counselor–assisted assessments in the delivery of career services. In order to innovate successfully, an in-depth and rigorous review of the current state of computer-assisted career assessment is necessary. Problems which might confront such a review would be: (a) how to select which assessments are described from the countless options available; (b) the rapid nature of change on the Internet; and (c) the timely compilation and distribution of information to practitioners and consumers given this rapid change. One option would be to adopt a comprehensive review model similar to that used by the Buros Center for Testing (2013). Counselors could access reviews of practitioner-assisted and self-help assessments in an adaptation of the current *Buros* format. The public could access brief reviews of self-assessments in a *Consumer Reports* format. To be effective, such a review for the general public would need to be featured prominently in any Internet search engine when terms such as "career tests" or "career assessment" are used. The information gathered from this effort could be provided to both practitioners and test publishers for a fee to recover costs, while consumers could access the information for free. However, obtaining adequate funding and identifying qualified practitioners to write the reviews will be a formidable challenge.

Ubiquitous Assessment

In their postmodern critique of assessment, Goodman and Carey (2004) used the term *ubiquitous assessment* to refer to assessment that is holistic and fully integrated into the learning and therapeutic process. For example, the popular instrument, The Self-Directed Search (SDS; Holland, Fritzsche, & Powell, 1994), can be conceptualized as a "simulated career counseling and planning activity" (Reardon & Lenz, 1998, p. 60) that immerses the client in both projective and objective assessment tasks. When taking the SDS, the client is clearly aware that assessment is occurring, but another kind of ubiquitous assessment is "evidenced-based stealth assessment" (Shute & Ke, 2012, p. 53). This assessment is occurring unknown to the client while he or she engages in another task, such as playing a game. Game playing supports not only content learning (e.g., What are duties of an accountant?) but development of more complex, competencies (e.g., How does an accountant solve problems?) through repetitive practice of behaviors that can be covertly measured and evaluated. For example, epistemic games like those developed by Shaffer (2008) work by helping clients to "... acquire and adopt knowledge, skills, values, and identities that are embedded within a particular discipline or professional community" (Shute & Ke, 2012, p. 50). Shute and Ke (2012) further noted that game playing requires iterative, goal-based, interactive problem solving that reinforces the metacognitive skill of self-control which have been suggested to be important components of effective career-decision making (Sampson, Reardon, Peterson, & Lenz, 2004).

In short, ubiquitous computing may lead to the ability to conduct ubiquitous "stealth" assessments, of targeted user behaviors that can be used to make inferences about that person's psychological characteristics. This could result in new "game-based" career assessments, but could also be derived from a record of your daily activities. For example, your Holland Code could probably be derived by integrating your respective watching, purchasing, and "liking" habits on Netflix, amazon.com, and Facebook via your tablet, work PC, and smart phone! While it would be unethical to conduct such assessments without a client's knowledge in a counseling relationship, there may be possible applications for such stealth assessment in classrooms and other settings where frequent or constant assessment is the norm.

Mobile Applications

Mobile phones have potential to further extend access to career resources and services (Vuorinen & Sampson, 2003). Application software, also known as "apps," represent a variety of interactive tools that can be used on multiple platforms, but are most commonly referenced with respect to smart phones, Blackberry devices, and tablet PCs. Apps can be educational, informational, or for entertainment, and can have application within the field of career counseling. While there are currently no apps that exist for well-established career inventories (e.g., Kuder, Self-Directed Search, or Strong Interest Inventory), several other possibilities emerge when typing in the term "career test." This may be due to the design purpose behind apps and career inventories, i.e., apps are designed to be accessed multiple times on a device, whereas most people will take a specific career inventory only once. For the time being, having a link to these assessments that can be accessed on multiple platforms might be the easiest way to go. However, the future will likely see the development of comprehensive apps might include not only the test, but also interactive tools that help the individual process and apply their results to their career concern.

Counseling Strategies for Computer-Assisted Career Assessment

No matter the assessment type used, it is important to employ these general strategies when working with clients and computer-assisted career assessments (Sampson et al., 2008):

1. Screening: Assess and determine the need for using computer-based assessments to facilitate the career problem-solving and decision-making process of clients. During this time, collaboratively setting goals is important as is establishing a good relationship with the counselor. Additionally, the client should have a better understanding of how the Internet could be useful while engaging in career problem solving (Capuzzi & Stauffer, 2012).

2. Recommending: Identify computer-assisted assessments that are appropriate and fit the clients' reported needs. One potential intervention is formulating a written plan for utilizing assessment resources, whereas an outcome could be achieving an understanding of how different assessments could meet personal and/or career needs.

3. Orienting: Foster effective use of a computer-assisted career assessment as well as discuss specific risks, benefits, or functions of technology. While orienting clients, practitioners may discuss how to distinguish high versus low quality websites and review certain website elements (e.g., privacy limits). Clients who can specify during this step a portion or portions of a website that may be helpful in addressing their needs could represent one potential outcome.

4. Follow-up: Ensure that previously identified needs have been met through selected computer-assisted assessments. Evaluating progress and demonstrating an understanding of content are potential client outcomes, whereas a counselor intervention could include reinforcing a client's information-seeking behavior.

Review Questions

1. What are some considerations for self-assessment as compared to practitioner-assessment when using computers?

2. What are the components of career information delivery systems and what role does computer-based career assessments play in those systems?

3. How might test interpretation be enhanced through computer-based career assessment? What are the potential limitations?

4. What are the quality issues in computer-based career assessment and how might counselors address them with clients?

5. How can the *Standards for Educational and Psychological Testing* be useful in addressing computer-based career assessment limitations?

Summary

Computer-assisted career assessment has undergone a substantial change in the evolution from personal computers to the Internet. The number of assessments now available has increased dramatically. The quality of assessments has always been a concern since the first tests were developed in the early 1900s. Evidence of the quality of Internet-based assessments is scarce at best. There is a probable chance that individuals will use the results from invalid assessments to make important decisions. Also, the distance counseling that could be used as an adjunct to self-help has limited availability. It is ironic that the Internet may provide clients and individuals with improved access to inferior assessments (Sampson, 1999). Counselors need to be proactive in using Internet websites to help individuals identify quality assessments and understand the role of assessment in making important decisions. Similarly, it is important for career development practitioners to ensure the quality of online assessments, that information generated by computer-assisted reports be integrated with other findings or factors (e.g., culture, socioeconomic status, gender), and to remain proactive in addressing ethical issues.

The Internet offers unique opportunities to improve test selection, orientation, administration, scoring, and interpretation. Career assessment is clearly still in a transition phase from being paper-and-pencil-based to being computer-based. This transition will accelerate as the costs of developing Internet-based assessment resources decline and as test developers gain more experience in developing computer-based assessments that take better advantage of computer capabilities.

Our success in developing and delivering cost-effective computer-assisted career assessments will depend on keeping the best of past psychometric rigor and counseling integration, while exploring future uses of multimedia and distance counseling to deliver quality assessments that provide clients with useful data, as well as provide new opportunities for promoting interaction among counselors and clients with social media. To achieve the potential of computer-assisted career assessment, the limitations identified in this chapter need to be carefully addressed. The Internet offers enormous potential to improve face-to-face and distance career assessment and counseling, as well as improve the quality of self-help career assessments. The opportunity to innovate and improve access to quality assessments is unprecedented.

References

Alliance of Career Resource Professionals (2013). *Standards Implementation Handbook*. Elletsville, IL: ACRP available from http://www,acrpro.org/aws/ACRP/pt/sp/standards

American Educational Research Association, American Psychological Association, & National Council on Measurement in Education. (1999). *Standards for educational and psychological testing.* Washington, DC: American Educational Research Association.

Anastasi, A., & Urbina, S. (1997). *Psychological testing* (7th ed.). Upper Saddle River, NJ: Prentice Hall.

Appana, S. (2008). A review of benefits and limitations of online learning in the context of the student, the instructor, and the tenured faculty. *International Journal on E-Learning, 7,* 5-22.

Apple, Inc. (n.d.). *Learn more about Siri.* Retrieved from http://www.apple.com/ios/siri/siri-faq/

Association for Assessment and Research in Counseling (2013, *Resources.* Available from http://www.theaceonline.com/resources.htm

Baker, E. L., & Linn, R. L. (2004). Validity issues for accountability systems. In S. Fuhrman and R. F. Elmore (Eds.), *Redesigning accountability systems for education* (pp. 47-72). New York, NY: Teachers College Press.

Barak, A. (2003). Ethical and professional issues in career assessment on the Internet. *Journal of Career Assessment, 11,* 3-21. doi:10.1177/106907202237457

Barros-Bailey, M., & Saunders, J. L. (2010). Ethics and the use of technology in rehabilitation counseling. *Rehabilitation Counseling Bulletin 53,* 255-259.

Betz, N., & Borgen, F. (2010). The CAPA integrative online system for college major exploration. *Journal of Career Assessment, 18,* 317-327.

Bloom, J. W. (2000). Technology and web counseling. In H. Hackney (Ed.), *Practice issues for the beginning counselor.* Needham Heights, MA: Allyn and Bacon.

Buros Center for Testing (2013). *Home page.* Retrieved from http://www.buros.org

Butcher, J. N. (1995). How to use computer-based reports. In J. N. Butcher (Ed.), *Clinical personality assessment: Practical approaches* (pp. 79-94). New York, NY: Oxford University Press.

Campbell, V. L. (2000). A framework for using tests in counseling. In C. E. Watkins, Jr. & V. L. Campbell (Eds.), *Testing and assessment in counseling practice* (2nd ed.). Mahwah, NJ: Lawrence Erlbaum Associates.

Capuzzi, D., & Stauffer, M. D. (2012). *Career counseling: Foundations, perspectives, and applications* (2nd ed.). New York, NY: Routledge.

Carr, A. C. (1991). Microcomputers and psychological treatment. In A. Ager & S. Bedall (Eds.), *Microcomputers and clinical psychology* (pp. 65-78). New York, NY: Wiley.

Clark, K. (2005). Serving underserved communities with instructional technologies: Giving them what they need, not what you want. *Urban Education, 40,* 430–445. doi:10.1177/0042085905276388

Clark, G., Horan, J. J., Tompkins-Bjorkman, A., Kovalski, T., & Hackett, G. (2000). Interactive career counseling on the Internet. *Journal of Career Assessment, 8,* 85-93. doi: 10.1177/2F106907270000800107

Eyde, L. D., & Kowal, D. M. (1987). Computerised test interpretation services: Ethical and professional concerns regarding U.S. producers and users. *Applied Psychology: An International Review, 36*(3/4), 401-417.

Flores, L. Y., & Heppner, M. J. (2002). Multicultural career counseling: Ten essentials for training. *Journal of Career Development, 28,* 181-202. doi: 10.1023/A:1014018321808

Garb, H. N. (2000). Computers will become increasingly important for psychological assessment: Not that there's anything wrong with that. *Psychological Assessment, 12,* 31-39. doi:10.1037/1040-3590.12.1.31

Goodman, G. S., & Carey, K. T. (2004). *Ubiquitous assessment: Evaluation techniques for the new millennium.* New York, NY: Peter Lang Publishers.

Harris-Bowlsbey, J., Riley-Dikel, M., & Sampson, J. P., Jr. (Eds.). (2002). *The Internet: A tool for career planning* (2nd ed.) (pp. 1-9). Tulsa, OK: National Career Development Association.

Harvey, V. S., & Carlson, J. F. (2003). Ethical and professional issues with computer-related technology. *School Psychology Review, 32,* 92-107.

Holland, J. L., Fritzsche, B. A., & Powell, A. B. (1994). *The Self-Directed Search technical manual.* Odessa, FL: Psychological Assessment Resources.

Hooley, T., Hutchinson, J., & Watts, A. G. (2010). *Careering through the Web: The potential of Web 2.0 and 3.0 technologies for career development and career support services.* London: UKCES.

Huff, K. L., & Sireci, S. G. (2001). Validity issues in computer-based testing. *Educational Measurement: Issues and Practice, 20*(3), 16-25. doi:10.1111/j.1745-3992.2001.tb00066.x

Jaeger, P. (2004). The social impact of an accessible e-democracy. *Journal of Disability Policy Studies, 15,* 19-26. doi:10.1177/10442073040150010401

Jerome, L. W., DeLeon, P. H., James, L. C., Folen, R., Earles, J., & Gedney, J. J. (2000). The coming age of telecommunications in psychological research and practice. *American Psychologist, 55,* 407-421. doi:10.1037//0003-066X.55.4.407

Khapova, S. N., Svensson, J. S., Wilderom, C. P. M., & Arthur, M. B. (2006). Usage of web-based career support. In M. Anandarajan, T. Teo & C. Simmers (Eds.), *Transformation of the workplace: The web and work in the 21st century.* Armonk, NY: M. E. Sharpe Inc.

Kleiman, T., & Gati, I. (2004). Challenges of Internet-based assessment: Measuring career decision-making difficulties. *Measurement and Evaluation in Counseling and Development, 37,* 41-55.

Krug, S. E. (1987). Microtrends: An orientation to computerized assessment. In J. N. Butcher (Ed.), *Computerized psychological assessment: A practitioner's guide* (pp. 15-25). New York, NY: Basic Books.

Leong, F., Hardin, E., & Gupta, A. (2010). A cultural formulation approach to career assessment and career counseling with Asian American clients. *Journal of Career Assessment, 37,* 465-486. doi: 10.1177/0894845310363808

Makela, J. P. (2009). *A case study approach to ethics in career development.* Broken Arrow, OK: National Career Development Association.

Mastie, M. M. (1994). Using assessment instruments in career counseling: Career assessment as compass, credential, process, and empowerment. In J. T. Kapes, M. M. Mastie, & E. A. Whitfield (Eds.), *A counselor's guide to career assessment instruments* (3rd ed.). Columbus, OH: National Career Development Association.

Mayadas, A.F., Bourne, J., & Bacsich, P. (2009). Online education today. *Science, 323,* 85-89.

McCarthy, J., Light, J., & McNaughton, D. (2007). The effects of internet-based instruction on the social problem solving of young adults who use augmentative and alternative communication. *Augmentative and Alternative Communication, 23,* 100-112.

National Board for Certified Counselors. (2013). *NBCC code of ethics.* Greensboro, NC: Author. Retrieved from http://www.nbcc.org/Code_of_Ethics/

National Career Development Association. (1997). *NCDA guidelines for the use of the Internet for provision of career information and planning services.* Broken Arrow, OK: Author. Retrieved from http://www.ncda.org

National Career Development Association. (2007). *NCDA code of ethics.* Broken Arrow, OK: Author. Retrieved from http://www.ncda.org

Offer, M., & Sampson, J. P., Jr. (1999). Quality in the content and use of information and communications technology in guidance. *British Journal of Guidance and Counselling, 27,* 501-516. doi:10.1080/03069889900760421

Oliver, L. W., & Chartrand, J. M. (2000). Strategies for career assessment research on the Internet. *Journal of Career Assessment, 8,* 95-103. doi:10.1177/106907270000800108

Oliver, L. W., & Zack, J. S. (1999). Career assessment on the Internet: An exploratory study. *Journal of Career Assessment, 7,* 323-356.

Olson-Buchanan, J. B., & Drasgow, F. (1999). Beyond bells and whistles: An introduction to computerized assessment. In F. Drasgow, & J. B. Olson-Buchanan (Eds.), *Innovations in computerized assessment* (pp. 1-5). Mahwah, NJ: Lawrence Erlbaum Associates.

Osborn, D. S. (2012). An international discussion about cross-cultural career assessment. *International Journal for Educational and Vocational Guidance, 12,* 5-16. doi:10.1007/s10775-012-9220-0

Osborn, D. S., Dikel, M. R., & Sampson, J. P. (2011). *The Internet: A tool for career planning* (3rd ed.). Broken Arrow, OK: National Career Development Association.

Osborn, D. S., & LoFrisco, B. (2012). How do career centers use social networking sites? *The Career Development Quarterly, 60,* 263-272.

Prince, J. P., Chartrand, J. M., & Silver, D. G. (2000). Constructing a quality career assessment site. *Journal of Career Assessment, 8,* 55-67. doi:10.1177/106907270000800105

Reardon, R., & PAR Staff. (2001). *Self-Directed Search Software Portfolio (SDS-SPTM) for Windows* [Computer program]. Odessa, FL: Psychological Assessment Resources, Inc.

Reardon, R., & Lenz, J. (1998). *The Self-Directed Search and related Holland career materials: A practioner's guide.* Odessa, FL: Psychological Assessment Resources, Inc.

Reile, D. M., & Harris-Bowlsbey, J. (2000). Using the Internet in career planning and assessment. *Journal of Career Assessment, 8,* 69-84. doi:10.1177/106907270000800106

Robinson, N. K., Meyer, D., Prince, J. P., McLean, C. & Law, R. (2000). Mining the Internet for career information: A model approach for college students. *Journal of Career Assessment, 8,* 37-54. doi:10.1177/106907270000800104

Sampson, J. P., Jr. (1990). Computer-assisted testing and the goals of counseling psychology. *The Counseling Psychologist, 18,* 227-239.

Sampson, J. P., Jr. (1998). The Internet as a potential force for social change. In C. C. Lee & G. R. Walz (Eds.), *Social action: A mandate for counselors* (pp. 213-225). Greensboro, NC: University of North Carolina at Greensboro, ERIC Clearinghouse on Counseling and Student Services.

Sampson, J. P., Jr. (1999). Effective design and use of Internet-based career resources and services. *IAEVG International Association for Educational and Vocational Guidance Bulletin, 63,* 4-12.

Sampson, J. P., Jr. (2000a). Computer applications. In C. E. Watkins, Jr. & V. L. Campbell (Eds.), *Testing and assessment in counseling practice* (2nd. ed), pp. 517-544. Hillsdale, NJ: Lawrence Erlbaum Associates, Inc.

Sampson, J. P., Jr. (2000b). Using the Internet to enhance testing in counseling. *Journal of Counseling and Development, 78,* 348-356. doi:10.1002/j.1556-6676.2000.tb01917.x

Sampson, J. P., Jr. (2008). *Designing and implementing career programs: A handbook for effective practice.* Broken Arrow, OK: National Career Development Association.

Sampson, J. P., Jr., & Bloom, J. W. (2001). The potential for success and failure of computer applications in counseling and guidance. In D. C. Locke, J. Myers, & E. L. Herr (Eds.), *The handbook of counseling* (pp. 613-627). Thousand Oaks, CA: Sage.

Sampson, J. P., Jr., Kolodinsky, R. W., & Greeno, B. P. (1997). Counseling on the information highway: Future possibilities and potential problems. *Journal of Counseling and Development, 75,* 203-212. doi:10.1002/j.1556-6676.1997.tb02334.x

Sampson, J. P., Jr., & Lumsden, J. A. (2000). Ethical issues in the design and use of Internet-based career assessment. *Journal of Career Assessment, 8,* 21-35. doi:10.1177/106907270000800103

Sampson, J. P., McClain, M. C., Musch, E., & Reardon, R. C. (in press). Variables affecting readiness to benefit from career interventions. *The Career Development Quarterly.*

Sampson, J. P., Jr., Peterson, G. W., & Reardon, R. C. (1989). Counselor intervention strategies for computer-assisted career guidance: An information processing approach. *Journal of Career Development, 16,* 139-154. doi:10.1007/BF01353007

Sampson, J. P., Jr., & Pyle, K. R. (1983). Ethical issues involved with the use of computer-assisted counseling, testing and guidance systems. *Personnel and Guidance Journal, 61,* 283-287.

Sampson, J. P., Jr., Reardon, R. C., Peterson, G. W., & Lenz, J. G. (2004). *Career counseling and services: A cognitive information processing approach.* Pacific Grove, CA: Brooks/Cole.

Sampson, J. P., Shy, J. D., & Cooley, J. (2008). *A four-step model for integrating counseling and web site use.* Tallahassee, FL: Florida State University, Career for the Study of Technology in Counseling and Career Development.

Sampson, J. P., Jr., Shy, J. D., & Purgar, M. P. (2003). Computer-based test interpretation in career assessment: Ethical and professional issues. *Journal of Career Assessment, 11,* 22-39. doi:10.1177/106907202237458

Shaffer, D. W. (2008). *How computer games help children learn.* New York, NY: Palgrave Macmillam.

Shute, V. J., & Ke, F. (2012). Games, learning, and assessment. In D. Ifenthaler, D. Eseryel, & Ge, X. (Eds.), *Assessment in game-based learning: Foundations, innovations, and perspectives* (pp. 43-58). New York, NY: Springer.

Snyder, D. K. (2000). Computer-assisted judgment: Defining strengths and liabilities. *Psychological Assessment, 12,* 52-60. doi:10.1037//1040-3590.12.1.52

Tesauro, G., Gondek, D., Lenchner, Fan, J., & Prager, J. (2012). Stimulation, learning, and optimization techniques in Watson's game strategies. *IBM Journal of Research and Development, 56 (3.4)* 1-11, doi: 10.1147/JRD.2012.2188931

Timmons, J., Podmostko, M., Bremer, C., Lavin, D., & Wills, J. (2004). *Career planning begins with assessment: A guide for professionals serving youth with educational & career development challenges.* Washington, D.C.: National Collaborative on Workforce and Disability for Youth, Institute for Educational Leadership. Retrieved from www.ncwdyouth.info/assets/guides/assessment/AssessGuideComplete.pdf

Tracey, T. J. G. (2010). Interest assessment using new technology. *Journal of Career Assessment, 18,* 336-344. doi:10.1177/1069072710374495

Vuong, A. (2011, October, 14). New iPhone a breakthrough for blind people. *The Denver Post.* Retrieved from http://www.denverpost.com/business/ci_19109321

Vuorinen, R., & Sampson, J. P. (2003). Using mobile information and communication technology to enhance counselling and guidance. In H. Kynaslahti, & P. Seppala (Eds.), *Mobile learning* (pp. 63-70). Edita, Finland: IT Press.

Watts, A. G., & Dent, G. (2002). Let your fingers do the walking: The use of telephone helplines in career information and guidance. *British Journal of Guidance and Counselling, 30*(1), 17-35. doi:10.1080/030698880220106492

Wetzler, S. (1990). Computerized psychological assessment. In D. Baskin (Ed.), *Computer applications in psychiatry and psychology* (pp. 43-56). New York, NY: Brunner/ Mazel.

Whiston, S. C., Secton, T. L., & Lasoff, D. L. (1998). Career-intervention outcome: A replication and extension of Oliver and Spokane (1998). *Journal of Counseling Psychology, 45,* 150-165. doi:10.1037//0022-0167.45.2.150

Zunker, V. G. (2011). *Career counseling: A holistic approach* (8th ed.). Independence, KY: Cengage Learning.

48

CHAPTER 5

MULTICULTURAL CONSIDERATIONS IN CAREER ASSESSMENT

Kathy M. Evans

Department of Educational Studies, Counselor Education
University of South Carolina

Introduction

Career assessment tools can be of great assistance with all clients if the counselor is culturally competent. Counselors have an ethical responsibility to understand and utilize multicultural counseling skills, including multicultural assessment skills (American Counseling Association [ACA], 2005). The United States is quickly fulfilling the census bureau's prediction that the ethnic minority population will grow faster than the White population. The 2010 Census puts the Latino/Latina population at 16.3%, African Americans at 12.6%, Asian/ Asian Americans at 4.8%, Native American/Alaska Natives at .9%, and multiracial individuals at 2.9% (U.S. Census Bureau, 2011). With the non-White population over 37%, an increasingly large population in the lower socioeconomic status and an uncounted number of sexual minority individuals, the reality is that counselors will encounter clients who are culturally different from them.

For the past four decades, the counseling profession has focused on training counselors on how to work with clients who differ from themselves. Increasingly, however, counseling is moving its multicultural efforts in the direction of social justice, advocacy, and social change. This shifts means that counselors need to do more than connect with all their clients; they need to become part of the solution to the oppression their clients experience in today's society (ACA, 2005).

Counselors have been given excellent guidance in the selection and use of tests from a culturally sensitive perspective from professional organizations (e.g., Association for Assessment and Research in Counseling [AARC], 2012). The ACA Code of Ethics (ACA, 2005) has an expectation that counselors will be culturally competent when conducting assessments of culturally diverse clients. Specifically, Standard E 8 states:

> Counselors use with caution assessment techniques that were normed on populations other than that of the client. Counselors recognize the effects of age, color, culture, disability, ethnic group, gender, race, language preference, religion, spirituality, sexual orientation, and socioeconomic status on test administration and interpretation, and place test results in proper perspective with other relevant factors.

Further, AARC outlined multicultural assessment competencies that speak to cultural competency and social advocacy considerations throughout the assessment process (AARC, 2012). The introductory section reads:

> Culturally competent professional counselors recognize the importance of social justice advocacy; they integrate understanding of age, gender, ability, race, ethnic group, national origin, religion, sexual orientation, linguistic background and other personal characteristics in order to provide appropriate assessment and diagnostic techniques. (p. 2)

Specifically, the standards on advocacy for assessment (AARC, 2012) ask that counselors immerse themselves in marginalized populations to understand them better, join with community leaders to address the needs of diverse clients, and address barriers that influence the assessment interpretation. Clearly a focus on multiculturalism is not going away and counselors are called to do more to advocate on behalf of their marginalized clients to ensure that assessment instruments are used in ways to eliminate oppression rather than foster it (Sampson, 2010; Wood & D'Agostino, 2010).

Further, the counseling accrediting bodies (i.e., the Council for the Accreditation of Counseling and Related Educational Programs [CACREP] and Council on Rehabilitation Education, [CORE]), emphasize that cultural and advocacy competencies be addressed in counselor training. CACREP (2009) states that the curriculum should cover: "counselors' roles in developing cultural self-awareness, promoting cultural social justice, advocacy and conflict resolution, and other culturally supported behaviors that promote optimal wellness and growth of the human spirit, mind, or body" (p. 11). CORE (2012) standards state:

> In particular, three elements integral to curricula in rehabilitation counselor education are ethical behavior, diversity or individual differences, and critical thinking. These three elements should be infused throughout all courses of the curriculum and rehabilitation counseling programs should be able to provide evidence these components are addressed appropriately. (p. 24)

Chapter 3 provides more detailed information on standards and competencies provided by counseling- and career-related associations/credentialing bodies.

Before counselors can become culturally competent in assessment techniques, they need to be culturally competent in general. ACA has endorsed multicultural competencies that value counselors' knowledge, awareness, and skills with regard to their own cultural heritage, their clients' worldview, and culturally appropriate interventions (Arredondo et al., 1996; Sue, Arredondo, & McDavis, 1992). Although there has been increased attention to as well as progress made in reducing cultural bias in the development of assessments, counselors must realize that assessments are only as culturally-sensitive as the person who selects, administers, and scores them. Counselors need to be keenly aware of their prejudices, biases, and values regarding assessment and assessment outcomes and work to deconstruct them. Equally important are counselors' knowledge and skills related to the characteristics and challenges of multicultural assessment when working with culturally diverse clients. Understanding clients from individualistic cultures that value competition is just as important as understanding collectivist cultures that value interdependence and cooperation. Counselors need to understand that within each cultural group, each person has his or her own perceptions of that culture. In addition, many individuals identify with several disenfranchised groups. For example, a client may be an African American lesbian with a disability. It would be important to explore her multiple identities and the multiple oppressions that go along with those identities when working with her on her career issues, including selection of assessment strategies (Schreier & Dudley Lassiter, 2010). In that same vein, counselors need to be aware of how clients have internalized oppression—the process by which individuals accept the oppression of their own group and believe negative stereotypes (Freire, 2007). It is believed that internalized oppression exists on a continuum and that all oppressed individuals have internalized oppression to some degree (Bailey, Chung, Williams, Singh, & Terrell, 2011). Being able to determine where on the continuum the client falls will help counselors choose instruments that build these clients' strengths rather than fuel self-hatred.

Career assessment can be a positive way to assist individuals in career decision making. Clients are often eager to take career instruments and use the information to learn more about their interests, values, personality, and abilities. However, when there are questions about whether or not the results of an instrument are applicable to a client because of his or her culture or experiences with oppression, using assessments can be a challenge in the counseling process. Research has shown that the assessments have some common problems with regard to individuals from ethnic and sexual minority groups (Worthington, Flores, & Navarro, 2005):

- The normative populations for many assessment instruments rarely represent the percentage of ethnic minority groups in the United States, although genuine steps are being taken to remedy this problem. The normative samples for sexual minorities, however, are nonexistent.

- Using instruments available only in English are problematic for those whose English proficiency is limited.

- Translation of instruments is difficult given dialects, and idioms may be specific to ethnic groups, regions, and even within an ethnic group.

- Misuse of tests for specific ethnic groups and for sexual minorities is possible if the counselor is not knowledgeable about the cultural incongruity that test has for that particular group.

This chapter will review the multicultural applications of career assessments (hereinafter referred to as *multicultural assessment*) that are commonly used, offer strategies for practitioners, discuss trends in multicultural assessment and suggest models of multicultural assessment for readers to consider.

Multicultural Issues across Career Assessment Categories

Counselors use a number of informal assessments to help clients with career planning but the most challenging for culturally diverse clients are the standardized assessments of abilities, interests, values, and personality. It is imperative that counselors use their knowledge of their clients' cultural background as well as information about any cultural issues associated with assessing their clients' cultural group when selecting, administering, and interpreting standardized measures. This section reviews four major categories of career assessment and highlights important considerations throughout the assessment process.

Assessments of Ability

Ability assessments are conducted to determine an individual's aptitude for a particular activity or his or her achievement in learning a particular skill or topic. Most ability tests are standardized. Some of the assessments of ability covered in this text are the following:

- Ability Explorer (Third Edition)
- Adult Basic Learning Examination (Second Edition)
- Armed Services Vocational Aptitude Battery Career Exploration Program (ASVAB)
- Highlands Ability Battery
- Motivational Appraisal of Personal Potential
- O*NET Ability Profiler
- Tests of Adult Basic Education (TABE 9&10)
- Wonderlic Basic Skills Test
- WorkKeys Assessments
- Workplace Skills Survey – FORM A

One of the concerns of multicultural career assessment is in respect to the importance our society places on ability testing and the negative effects poor scores may have on students from culturally diverse backgrounds (Wood & D'Agostino, 2010). Because of the societal focus on testing, some career decisions may be made for children before they have an opportunity to explore their options. The first time a child takes a standardized ability test, he or she risks being permanently labeled — gifted, developmentally delayed, learning disabled, below grade level, etc. Once labeled, society already has made some determinations about the career directions available for that individual. Labeling students with poor test scores and foreclosing their options is especially risky for students of color because their lower performance on ability testing has led to an overrepresentation of these students in special education (Losen & Orfield, 2002). According to Helms (2007), "In the worlds of education and employment, decision-makers have become overly dependent on tests of cognitive abilities, knowledge, or skills (CAKS) for making high-stakes decisions affecting the life opportunities of individual African American, Latino/Latina American, and Native American (ALANA) test takers" (p. 1083).

Tests of ability have been criticized in the past for being culturally biased because students of color have scored lower than White students on such tests (Aiken, 2003; Helms 2007; National Center for Educational Statistics, 2011a, 2011b; Rushton & Jensen, 2005), leading to a phenomenon referred to as the achievement gap. On average there is a 25-point gap in math and reading between African American and White students and a 20-point gap for Latino/a students. The gap does not hold for all students of color, however. As a group, Asians and Asian Americans usually score as high or higher than Whites on these assessments; this phenomenon is part of reason for the stereotype which labels them as the model minority. There are, however, Asian Americans who experience the achievement gap along with other individuals of color. Among Cambodians, Laotians, and Hmongs, only 40% have completed high school and only 14% have college degrees (U.S. Census Bureau, 2011).

Previous research has shown that tests of cognitive ability such as the Scholastic Assessment Test (SAT) and intelligence tests tend to be as predictive for African Americans, Latinos/as, and Native Americans as they are for Whites (Betz, 1992). In recent studies of the SAT, scores tended to be most predictive of the White male population. SAT scores, however, tend to overpredict first-year grade point averages (GPA) for African Americans, Native Americans, and Latinos/as and underpredict GPAs for women, and it was varied for Asian

Multicultural Considerations in Career Assessment

Americans (Mattern, Patterson, Shaw, Kobrin, & Barbuti, 2008; Young, 2001). Helms (2007) eloquently expressed the frustration with this problem of predicting success in college through standardized testing when she stated that social scientists "after more than 100 years of racial-groups testing, can consistently demonstrate racial-group differences in test scores but cannot provide empirically supportable explanations for why the difference occur" (p. 1083). The score differences and the underlying assumptions about their abilities, however, are known to clients of color and contribute to what has been called *stereotype threat* for those taking placement exams or other high stakes tests. Stereotype threat occurs when the test takers, fearful that the negative stereotypes about their cultural group's test scores are accurate, perform poorly on the assessment. Steele and Aronson (1995) found in a seminal study that African American student performance was negatively affected by the mere mention of the association between race and testing during test administration. Subsequent research has found similar patterns for Latinas and women in general (Cadinu, Maass, Rosabianca, & Kiesner, 2005; Gonzales, Blanton, & Williams, 2002).

Research indicates that African Americans and Latinos/as score lower than their White counterparts on popular objective instruments such as the ASVAB and O*NET Ability Profiler (Cioe, Bordieri, & Musgrave, 2010). As a result minorities (as well as White women) tend to be clustered or overrepresented in four areas of the armed services. When research was conducted on the reasons these populations were placed less frequently in other areas, it was discovered racial/ethnic minorities and women scored lower than White males for specialized areas of the armed services and thus were not qualified to enter those fields (Galing, 1991).

There is a long-standing debate in the social science, educational, and helping professions about the origins of score differences between Whites and racial/ethnic minority groups and why the achievement gap continues today. Some say that the gap is due to innate intellectual differences among racial groups, others believe that there is test bias or language barriers, while others contend that there is apparent inequity in education due to socioeconomic disadvantage (Evans 2008; Jordan, 2010; Ryan Krane & Tirre, 2005). According to Jordan (2010) and Helms (2007), there are obviously unaccounted for factors that contribute to the achievement gap, whether it is cultural background, school quality, or socioeconomic privilege. Because the reason for the differences has not been fully discovered and because adjusting scores for this imbalance is now illegal, use of testing to determine college admission, academic advancement, or job eligibility may be a social justice issue. In fact, the discussion of how to deal with differences has moved from test bias to one of fairness, which according to Worthington et al. (2005) is related to bias but also the equitable treatment of test takers.

Helms (2006) designed a complex quantitative fairness model to minimize the impact of race in multicultural assessment of cognitive abilities. Because there does not seem to be an identifiable reason for racial differences in assessment scores, rather than focusing the responsibility for the achievement gap on racial difference, Helms asserted that assessment of psychological constructs such as racial identity and stereotype threat should be part of the assessment process. Because racism and oppression figure into the life experiences and cultural socialization of ALANA students, they have to be taken into account when assessing client abilities and achievement. Racial identity measures of stereotype threat can be used to determine how these attributes are related to test items or scores within groups. Helms advocated that this information be used on an individual basis with clients to help move counselors out of a categorizing mode where ability tests are concerned.

Nowhere is the debate about the impact of ability assessment on the future careers of young people more important than the trend toward high stakes testing. Testing is considered *high stakes* when students' standardized test scores are used to make decisions about educational policies, student progress, teacher effectiveness, and school quality. In response to passage of the No Child Left Behind (NCLB) Act in 2001 that required K-12 schools to create a standards baseline that included measureable basic skills requirements in order to receive federal funding, many states quickly passed laws that linked student performance on standardized measures to student promotion, teacher employment, and/or school remediation. Today, all 50 states have some kind of high stakes testing laws (Nichols, 2007). The trouble with this kind of dependence on testing is that the careers of so many (students, teachers, administrators) rests on what might be flawed assessment instruments: those which clearly put racial/ethnic minorities (especially English Language Learners and low income students) at a disadvantage as compared to White middle-class students (Jordan, 2010). One goal for NCLB was to improve the chances for students in poor performing schools or who were performing poorly in school. Nichols (2007) reviewed the literature on high stakes testing since the inception of the NCLB legislation and found that, though there were some gains in test scores (most likely due to drilling or teaching to the test), there was no consistent evidence that these practices increase learning. Instead, Nichols reviewed evidence that the practice may have a negative effect for some students (e.g., increasing the dropout rate). Students who could not pass the high school exit exam or exams to move on to the next grade would drop out or age out of school.

ACA (n.d.) issued a statement regarding high stakes testing that recommends that tests "must be technically sound, free of gender, racial, and cultural bias and produce reliable, valid scores" (p. 2, para 6). It is questionable as to whether this kind of instrument currently exists. While publishers continue to pursue a truly culture fair test, counselors need to do all they can to ensure that ability test scores alone do not determine an individual's future career and to mediate the effects of high stakes testing. The ACA Advocacy competencies may be helpful to counselors when they attempt to achieve that goal. Wood and D'Agostino (2010) suggested that as advocates counselors can use ability assessments to the advantage of students by doing the following: (a) ensuring tests that are used for placement have an internal consistency and test-retest reliability scores of .80 or higher; (b) limiting the use of tests to those with manuals that give more than one measure of reliability; (c) looking for client strengths and identifying oppressive environmental and social factors that may positively or negative affect student outcomes; and (d) using data as a way of providing evidence of discrimination.

As previously mentioned, objective standardized ability assessments can result in negative consequences for clients of color and White women, such as stereotype threat and career foreclosure. From a multicultural perspective, instruments which assess self-estimates of ability may be preferable because they are not assessments of achievement or aptitude, and clients may approach them from a positive perspective. These assessments do not have right or wrong answers and are considered standardized because of their uniform procedures and reliability and validity of information.

Some of the standardized career assessments that are popular among career counselors include a number of self-estimates of abilities. For example, the Harrington O'Shea Career Decision-Making System and the Inventory of Work-Relevant Abilities (part of the ACT's Discover and Career Planning Survey) include self-estimates of abilities. In addition, there is the Self-Directed Search and the Campbell Interest and Skill Survey. Diverse clients may perceive these assessments positively because there is no stigma or stereotype about deficiencies associated with them.

On the other hand, research has shown that individuals tend to overestimate or underestimate their own abilities in comparison with measured abilities (Betsworth, 1999). This phenomenon is gender-specific. Women tend to underestimate their abilities and men tend to overestimate their abilities. As a result, each gender chooses occupations that reflect the respective beliefs about their abilities (Brown & Ryan Krane, 2000; Brown et al., 2003). Although career counselors are more likely to use self-assessments, it is important that they also understand the impact of objective standardized testing of abilities and achievement (AARC, 2012).

Interest Inventories

By far the most common career assessment is the assessment of interests (Hanson, 2005). The research on the applicability of these assessments toward racial/ethnic minorities, women, and other oppressed groups is somewhat similar to that of ability tests. Day and Rounds' (1998) research involving 49,000 participants was especially impressive for its large percentage of ethnic minority participants. They found that the structure of vocational interests were similar for Whites and all ethnic groups. Years later, similar results were found by Flores et al., (2006), Fouad and Mohler (2004), and Gasser, Larson, and Borgen (2007). These studies were based on Holland's theoretical model of career interests that is used in several interest inventories such as the Strong Interest Inventory (SII). The SII was updated in 2004 by increasing diversity in the normative samples. The sample for this revision included 10.3% African American females; 4.4% African American males, 6.2% Latinas, 3.8% Latinos; 4.3% Asian American females, and 2.4% Asian American males (Kelly, 2010). Kelly's (2010) critique of the new revision is that ethnic minority groups are still underrepresented in both the general themes and in the occupational scales, where the percentages were even lower.

According to Evans (2008), the interests of individuals from oppressed groups such as ethnic minorities, women, and sexual minorities are often limited due to discrimination, and gender socialization. Often individuals from these groups will gravitate toward "acceptable" occupations and careers, leaving them with a small range of career possibilities. Because of the narrowed interests of individuals from these groups, taking the SII or any interest inventory at face value is problematic. Typically individuals take an interest inventory, not only to see how strong their interests are, but also to narrow the choices down to the ones they feel most strongly about. However, when working with ethnic and cultural minority clients whose interests are already narrowed due to discrimination, socialization, and test inequities, it makes sense to use these inventoried results towards expanding their experiences and exposure to new areas—ones they have *not* chosen.

The culturally astute career counselor has to be aware of the narrowed interests of individuals socialized in groups who are oppressed in this society (Gainor, 2000). For example, African Americans tend to have interests in fields that are traditionally lower paying than those preferred by White men (Hamilton, Austin, & Darity, 2011). Using interest inventories that subscribe to the Holland code, Chung and Harmon (1994) found similar trends for gay men who scored higher on artistic and social occupations than heterosexual men. In fact, non-traditional careers choices are more common among gay men and lesbians than for their heterosexual counterparts (Croteau, Anderson, & Distefano, 2000). Finally, gender differences in interests is so pronounced that the SII has separate norms for men and women on all three scales (general occupational themes, basic interests, and occupational) (Harmon Hansen, Borgen, & Hammer, 1994).

The current trend is to use interest assessments with younger individuals. Often the results are used to find ways to introduce new experiences to them. Porfeli, Hartung, and Vondracek (2008) suggested counselors intervene with children because it is during childhood when they fixate on what they think are gender-appropriate career fields. However, interest inventories are also being used to narrow options with younger people with the same dangers as mentioned above with disenfranchised groups. Tracey and Sodano (2008) supported using interest inventories with individuals as young as those in the 8th grade, but not younger. The problem is with stability of interests, as interests are too unpredictable prior to the 8th grade and scores still seem to change even after that age. In fact, Tracy and Sodano found that there was a drop in interest scores for respondents when they enter middle school and again when they were about to enter the 12th grade, with girls' scores dropping more than boys'. Interest inventories should be used with younger clients to expand their interests rather than pinpointing specific careers for them.

Personality Assessment

Personality inventories used by career counselors are not usually employed to diagnose pathology. Instead these assessments help clients gain more information and better organize what they know about themselves already. One of the most widely used interest inventories is the Myers-Briggs Type Indicator (MBTI) (Sheperis, Perepiczka, & Limoges, 2011; Swanson & D'Achiardi, 2005; Whiston, 2012), which is most likely because of its ease of administering, understandability, and positive profiles (Johnson, Mauzey, Johnson, Murphy, & Zimmerman, 2001). It has been translated into a wide range of languages and used not only with career planning but also in building relationship and communication skills during marriage and couples counseling, college student-affairs programs, and management training in business and industry. Additional information about the MBTI may be found in Chapter 14 of this text.

McCaully and Moody (2008) stated that the MBTI has been effective with a number of cultures within the United States and in the international arena. However, when the instrument is translated, it is sometimes difficult to transfer the meaning of some idioms and some concepts. They report that "no truly stratified random sample exists for any group, so it is not yet possible to make a definitive comparison of type distributions in ethnic or national cultures." (p. 418). In general, the most common complaints about the instrument is not that it is culturally insensitive but the ipsative construction of the questions, lack of criterion-related validity, and its tendency to be a "feel good" instrument.

The Sixteen Personality Factor Questionnaire (16PF) is another personality assessment instrument that is popular with career counselors (see Chapter 14 for additional information). Clients learn how they compare with others on a number of personality factors. It was renormed in 1994; however, a reasoning test was added that resembles an IQ test. In fact, the reasoning test correlated highly with intelligence tests. The addition of the reasoning test yielded the same results with ethnic minority test takers as other IQ tests. Whites scored higher than African Americans, Native Americans, and Latinas/Latinos (Conn & Rieke, 1994). In the fifth edition, items that demonstrated racial and gender bias were removed, and research has shown that the 16 factors are applicable across countries (Rossier, 2005).

Multicultural Assessment Models

Multicultural assessment models may be useful to counselors as they consider cultural issues across assessment types and apply relevant competency standards. Two models are presented here to illustrate the inclusion of culture into all aspects of the assessment process.

Culturally Appropriate Career Assessment Model (CACAM)

The Culturally-Appropriate Career Assessment Model (CACAM; Flores et al., 2006) emphasizes the importance that counselors are culturally competent before applying the model for it to be effective. The model consists of four steps: (1) information gathering, (2) selection of instruments, (3) administration of career instruments, and (4) interpretation of career assessment results. Table 4.1 provides an example of how this model may be applied.

Step 1: Information Gathering. The information gathering step involves collecting data from the client using qualitative and/or quantitative assessment methods as appropriate. The assumptions in this model are that counselors can effectively assess client factors before or without the use of standardized tests and that discovering the client's worldview and cultural values are integral to the assessment process. According to Highlen and Sudarsky-Gleiser (1994), a qualitative assessment involves an interview as well as career stories, fantasies, guided imagery. In addition to the counseling interview, counselors may use intake forms, paper-and-pencil checklists, and other informal assessment to assist in the information gathering. A cultural interview should also include an exploration of racial, cultural, gender, feminist, and/or sexual identity. This assessment should help with understanding the salience of group memberships as well as knowing whether the client's identity is positive and working for the client or negative and contributing to internalized oppression or self-hatred.

Step 2: Selection of Instruments. When counselors want to use an assessment, it is important that they read the manual and other materials about its construction. This review should include information about reliability (more than one method should be reported) and validity. Using an assessment tool that does not give validity information can do a disservice to clients. A test must be able to measure what it purports to measure. Test manuals will usually give a description of content or construct validity, but criterion validity is preferable for career counseling because it is most helpful for predicting future performance. However, even when construct or content validity data are given, the instrument many not be appropriate for clients from groups that are oppressed in our society if they are not represented in the normative sample. Reviewing the normative groups used in standardized tests, therefore, is important.

According to Sheperis et al. (2011), counselors should ask "Does my examinee match the norming group for the test in age, gender, race, socioeconomic status, geographical location, education level, job or career type, and other relevant demographic characteristics?" (p. 157). Test manuals that may not give the racial or cultural breakdown of the normative sample make this question difficult to answer, and such tests should be avoided or, at the least, used with reservation. Additionally, counselors must seek out research on those instruments for the population of which their clients are members. If no research can be found, the counselor may decide to use the instrument and make certain when interpreting the results that the clients are aware of the limitations of that instrument, or look for an assessment instrument that includes that population or that is culturally sensitive. For example, a qualitative assessment of interests, abilities, values, and personality factors may be more suitable to provide clients with the opportunity to tell their stories and elaborate on their experiences as members of their diverse group. Being familiar with the research trends in ability, personality, and interest inventories will help counselors determine how much credence should be put into the scores their culturally diverse clients receive. Chapter 8 provides additional information about selecting career assessments.

Step 3: Administration of Career Instruments. Even when administering tests individually, test taking is a stressful experience. It is important, therefore, to help those taking the test to be as comfortable as possible. Almost all guidelines recommend comfortable seating and room temperature. However for ethnic minority

Multicultural Considerations in Career Assessment

clients, that comfort may need to be extended to the fact that they know and trust the examiner and that the examiner smiles and helps them relax with a kind word or humor to comfort them. When statewide testing is scheduled, this comfort is harder to achieve, but counselors need to do what is possible to achieve this goal. For example, some school counselors run motivational, stress reduction, and test-taking skills groups to help combat stereotype threat among their students (Bruce, Getch, & Ziomek-Daigle, 2009).

It is important to make sure that the clients have had adequate nutrition before taking the test. This information is important to obtain from test takers well in advance of test administration so that they can eat before taking the test if they have missed a meal. Often clients who come from low-income households also attend struggling schools, the combination which spells a recipe for disaster when students face ability or aptitude tests (Ryan Krane & Tirre, 2005). Counselors need to do all they can to minimize these barriers, such as by arranging for tutors from local high schools and colleges, applying for grants for tutoring software, or engaging in other activities that can boost student morale and perhaps student scores. Chapter 9 provides additional information on administration of career assessments.

Step 4: Interpretation of Career Assessment Results. The interpretation requires the understanding and knowledge of the clients' cultural background (including memberships in multiple disenfranchised groups) and individual characteristics. In addition, counselors should be knowledgeable about the group's history of oppression, stereotypes, and stigmas as well as discriminatory practices against that group(s). Because of all the accumulated knowledge, the counselor would be able to explain the nature of the assessment and the results so that the client has a clear understanding of the assessment and the results and what they mean to him or her. Chapter 9 provides additional information about interpretation of career assessments.

Table 4.1 — Case of Alejandria using the CACAM Model

Alejandria (Aleja) is a 14 year-old Puerto Rican adolescent of African descent. She is entering high school and is having trouble deciding what to do.

Step 1: Information Gathering

- Born in Puerto Rico, but moved to the continental United States when she was three years old.

- She is fluent in Spanish, but does not read or write the language. Spanish is her first language.

- Aleja identifies as Puerto Rican, but most of her friends are African American, not Latina. She says that the "Spanish girls treat her like garbage". She accepts people mistaking her for African American, but she knows she is Puerto Rican.

- Aleja is an average student, but makes an A in music.

- Aleja has excellent family support. Both parents attended a meeting where the school counselor informed them that Aleja had earned a spot in the local music magnet high school.

- Aleja hasn't thought about a career for herself, but both her mother and her older sister have good jobs as medical office assistants. According to Aleja, her father is a handyman.

- Aleja is reconsidering the music magnet high school. Her African American friends will attend the vocational technical school for either cosmetology or office assistant training, and no one else is going to the music school. Aleja thinks it would be a good idea to go with her friends because then she would know what she is going to do when she graduates from high school. Her brother is a trumpet player who spends more time out of work than he has with a musical job.

- Aleja wants to know what her options are; she is confused.

- The counselor explores with Aleja her feelings about being isolated from her friends, her interest in the office careers, and her thoughts about how her parents would make her change of mind. Although after the discussion, Aleja is more comfortable about attending a different school than her friends, she still seems confused about what to do about her future.

A Counselor's Guide To Career Assessments Instruments

Step 2: Selection of Instruments

- Knowing that the O*NET Interest Profiler and the O*NET Ability Profiler have been found to be, in some ways, as problematic for people of color as standardized aptitude tests and interest inventories, the counselor talks to Aleja about this option, and they decide to go on with the test because Aleja just wants to know what skills she is better at than others.

- To give her a more complete picture, the counselor works with Aleja using occupational, values and motivational card sorts. They discuss her choices and preferences before going on to complete the O*NET assessments.

Step 3: Administration of Career Assessments

- Aleja takes the O*NET assessment in the computer room at school after school hours so that she has few distractions from people or changing class schedules. She is familiar with the computers and is comfortable with them.

Step 4: Interpretation of Career Assessment Results

- The counselor and Aleja first discuss the card sort assessments and how she felt about them, and then the counselor reveals the results to Aleja. While she seemed to like the results from the interest profile—she thought it really reflected her interest and she felt solid about her music interests and abilities. Aleja was disappointed in the scores on the O*NET Ability Profiler because she thought she would be stronger on those skills needed for medical assistant or office manager. She liked the idea that she is artistic and that sometimes does not go well with organizational skills. The counselor and Aleja then discussed what steps she could take to make the most of her transition to a high school where she didn't know anyone.

Multicultural Assessment Process

Although not specifically a career assessment model, Ridley, Li, and Hill (1998) offered a systematic model that facilitates the incorporation of culture and environment into the assessment process. The multicultural assessment process (MAP) model has four phases that are somewhat similar to Flores et al. (2006) in that they focus on gathering cultural data and including it in the assessment process. The phases are the following:

Phase 1. Identify cultural data by using several methods: clinical interview, questionnaires, life history, and family history.

Phase 2. Interpret cultural data by developing a hypothesis based on distinguishing cultural data from idiosyncratic data, dispositional stress as opposed to environmental stress, and clinically significant data as opposed to clinically insignificant data.

Phase 3. Incorporate cultural data by using standardized assessments to test the hypotheses from Phase 2, not to generate new hypotheses.

Phase 4. Arrive at a sound assessment decision using the results of the hypothesis testing.

Collecting cultural data is important, but interpreting it is also an important step because the counselor tries to determine the significance of the cultural data to his or her specific client. The counselor may wish to explore the relevance of racial or cultural group membership to the client's culture or past decisions. The counselor would then come up with a working hypothesis about the client's career issue and use that hypothesis to decide on specific assessments to use during phase 3. While phase 4 seems more clinical in nature than career-related in that it hints at coming up with a diagnosis, in career counseling it would translate into coming up with or clarifying goals and exploring alternatives.

Counseling Strategies for Multicultural Assessment

It is imperative that counselors review the specific guidelines for multicultural assessment from AARC (2012) to ensure that they are using assessments ethically, effectively, and responsibly. Evans (2008, pp. 132-133) offered the following suggestions for practice as a starting point:

- Review the assessment procedures with clients to ensure that the assessments use will meet client needs.

Multicultural Considerations in Career Assessment

- If the assessment seems to meet client needs, investigate the assessment by reading all available information about its cultural inclusiveness (such as Manuals, *Mental Measurements Yearbooks,* research articles), including information on the language and reading levels.

- Pay special attention to the standardization sample. Ensure that diversity percentages are close to population numbers of diverse groups. If there are no ethnic minorities listed among the normative sample, justify the use of this particular assessment with a particular client (justifications might include that the client is highly acculturated or that local norms exist for the assessment).

- If the assessment utilizes ethnic minorities or other special populations in the normative sample, pay close attention to how close the ethnic population compares to that of the U.S. general population. Also, check to see if any analyses have been conducted comparing the responses of different cultural groups. If the ethnic minority population numbers are too small and/or there is no cultural comparison data, administration of the assessment needs to be justified, as in the item above.

- If there are data concerning testing differences between culturally different groups, note the data and make a decision as to whether or not to proceed with the assessment. If there are norms for your client's group, it is feasible to go ahead and use the assessment. If there are testing differences, but no norms for your client's cultural group, the information about the norming sample may still be used to interpret a client's test results. Determine how this information will be reported to the client.

- Always explain to clients any caveats before administering an assessment and again when you interpret the assessment for the client.

- Provide the best interpretation of the assessment results you can, taking into consideration the client's race, culture, and environment. Some lead-ins that may be helpful include the following:
  - We decided to use this assessment because ...
  - This assessment has limitation for you because ... What do you think?
  - A few of the things that are important to you as a _____ are ..., and this assessment _____ Am I right?
  - What all this means for you, according to what you have told me, is _____. Does that sound right to you?

Summary

Because of the growing diversity in the United States, multicultural assessment will soon be the norm rather than the exception. The requirements for completing a multicultural assessment are similar to the general multicultural requirements for career counselors. Counselors must be knowledgeable and positive about their own culture, their identities, their biases, and their values before they can effectively work with clients who differ from them. They need to be aware of the sociopolitical history and present-day issues that serve as the background for their culturally diverse clients' lives. In order to select and interpret assessments effectively, counselors must be willing and able to explore with the client the effects of the history, discrimination, and other painful topics. In addition, counselors need to be able to evaluate assessment instruments for their applicability to diverse clients. While test publishers are improving by reducing cultural bias in their tests, however, there are still unaccounted-for cultural differences in performance that impair test fairness. Finally, the field of counseling is looking beyond simple acceptance of cultural differences and requiring counselors to become advocates for change. It is this last trend that may make for some revolutionary changes in career assessment in the future.

Review Questions

1. What are some of the reasons that counselors need to be competent in multicultural assessment?

2. Discuss the rationale for high stakes testing and how you think it could be modified to be of assistance to more students.

3. A counselor's responsibility is to understand his or her own culture, prejudices, and biases. Discuss reasons why this would be as important to using assessments with clients who look like the counselor as it is to those who do not.

A Counselor's Guide To Career Assessments Instruments

4. Explain stereotype threat and the affect it can have on individual test takers.

5. Discuss the similarities and differences between the CACAM and MAP models.

References

Aiken, C. R. (2003), *Psychological testing and assessment.* Boston, MA: Allyn & Bacon.

American Counseling Association. (n.d.). *The American Counseling Association (ACA) position statement on high stakes testing.* Retrieved from http://www.theaaceonline.com/High_Stakes.pdf

American Counseling Association. (2005). *ACA code of ethics.* Retrieved from http://counseling.org/Files/FD.ashx?guid=ab7c1272-71c4-46cf-848c-f98489937dda

Arredondo, P., Toporek, M. S., Brown, S., Jones, J., Locke, D. C., Sanchez, J. and Stadler, H. (1996). *Operationalization of the multicultural counseling competencies.* Association of Multicultural Counseling and Development: Alexandria, VA.

Association for Assessment in Research and Counseling. (2012). *Standards for multicultural assessment: Fourth revision.* Retrieved from http://www.theaaceonline.com/AACE-AMCD.pdf

Bailey, T. M., Chung, Y., B. Williams, W. S., Singh, A. A., & Terrell, H. K. (2011). Development and validation of the Internalized Racial Oppression Scale for Black Individuals. *Journal of Counseling Psychology, 58,* 481-493. doi:10.1037/a0023585

Betsworth, D. G. (1999). Accuracy of self-estimated abilities and the relationship between self-estimated abilities and realism for women. *Journal of Career Assessment, 7*(1), 35-43.

Betz, N. E. (1992). Career assessment: A review of critical issues. In S. D. Brown & R. W. Lent (Eds.), *Handbook of counseling psychology* (2nd ed., pp. 453-484). New York, NY: Wiley.

Brown, S. D., & Ryan Krane, N. E. (2000). Four (or five) sessions and a cloud of dust: Old assumptions and new observations about career counseling. In S. D. Brown & R. W. Lent (Eds.), *Handbook of counseling psychology* (3rd ed., pp. 740-766). New York, NY: Wiley.

Brown, S. D., Ryan Krane, N. E., Brecheisen, J., Castelino, P., Budisen, I., Miller, M., & Edens, L., (2003). Critical ingredients of career choice interventions: More analyses and new hypotheses. *Journal of Vocational Behavior, 62,* 411-428.

Bruce, A. M., Getch, Y. Q., & Ziomek-Daigle, J. (2009). Closing the gap: A group counseling approach to improve test performance of African-American students. *Professional School Counseling, 12,* 450-457.

Cadinu, M., Maass, A., Rosabianca, A., & Kiesner, J. (2005). Why do women underperform under stereotype threat? Evidence for the role of negative thinking. *Psychological Science, 17,* 572–578.

Chung, Y. B., & Harmon, L. W. (1994). The career interests and aspirations of gay men: How sex-role orientation is related. *Journal of Vocational Behavior, 45,* 223-239.

Cioe, N., Bordieri, J., & Musgrave, J. (2010). Validity of the O*NET Ability Profiler for use in comprehensive vocational evaluations. *Vocational Evaluation and Career Assessment Professional Journal, 6,* 37-48.

Conn, S. R., & Rieke, M. L. (1994). *The 16PF Fifth Edition technical manual.* Champagne, IL: Institute for Personality and Ability Testing, Inc.

Council for Accreditation of Counseling and Related Educational Programs. (2009). *CACREP standards.* Retrieved from http://cacrep.org/doc/2009%20Standards%20with%20cover.pdf

Council on Rehabilitation Education. (2012). *Accreditation manual for master's level rehabilitation counselor education programs.* Retrieved from http://www.core-rehab.org/Files/Doc/PDF/COREStandardsPrograms.pdf

Croteau, J. M., Anderson, M. Z., & Distefano, T. M. (2000). Lesbian, gay, and bisexual vocational psychology: Reviewing foundations and planning construction. In R. M. Perez, K. A. DeBord, & K. J. Bieschke (Eds.), *Handbook of counseling and psychotherapy with lesbian, gay, and bisexual clients* (pp. 383-408). Washington, DC: American Psychological Association.

Day, S. X., & Rounds, J. (1998). Universality of vocational interest structure among racial and ethnic minorities. *American Psychologist, 53,* 728-736.

Evans, K. (2008). *Gaining cultural competence in career counseling.* Boston, MA: Lahaska Press.

Flores, L. Y., Berkel, L. A., Nilsson, J. E., Ojeda, L., Jordan, S. E., Lynn, G. L., & Leal, V. M. (2006). Racial/ethnic minority vocational research: A content and trend analysis across 36 years. *The Career Development Quarterly, 55,* 2-21.

Fouad, N. A., & Mohler, C. J. (2004). Cultural validity of Holland's theory and the Strong Interest Inventory for five racial/ethnic groups. *Journal of Career Assessment, 12,* 423-439.

Freire, P. (2007). *Pedagogy of the oppressed,* (30th anniversary ed.) New York: NY: Continuum.

Gainor, K. A. (2000). Vocational assessment with culturally diverse populations. In L. A. Suzuki, J. G. Ponterotto, & P. J. Meller (Eds.), *Handbook of multicultural assessment: Clinical, psychological, and educational applications* (2nd ed., pp. 169-189). San Francisco, CA: Jossey-Bass.

Galing, S. E. (1991) *Over-representation in the U.S. Army of minorities and women in career management fields.* Fort Sheridan, IL: U.S. Army Recruiting Command (USAREC SR 91-3).

Gasser, C. E., Larson, L. M., & Borgen, F. H. (2007). Concurrent validity of the 2005 Strong Interest Inventory: An Examination of gender and major field of study. *Journal of Career Assessment, 15,* 23-43.

Gonzales, P. M., Blanton, H. & Williams, K. J. (2002). The effects of stereotype threat and double-minority status on the test performance of Latino women, *Personality and Social Psychology Bulletin, 28,* 659–670.

Hamilton, D., Austin, A., & Darity, W., Jr., (2011). Whiter jobs, higher wages: Occupational segregation and the lower wages of black men. *Economic Policy Institute Briefing Paper #288,* 1-13.

Harmon, L., Hansen, J. I., Borgen, F., & Hammer, A. (1994). *Strong Interest Inventory: Applications and technical manual,* Palo Alto, CA: Consulting Psychologists Press.

Hanson, J. (2005). Assessment of interests. In S. D. Brown & R. W. Lent (Eds.), *Career development and counseling: Putting theory and research to work* (pp. 281-304). Hoboken, NJ: Wiley.

Helms, J. E. (2006). Fairness is not validity or cultural bias in racial-group assessment: A quantitative perspective. *American Psychologist, 61,* 845-859.

Helms, J. E. (2007). Implementing fairness in racial-group assessment of individuals. *American Psychologist, 62,* 1083-1085.

Highlen, P. S., & Sudarsky-Gleiser, C. (1994). A co-essence model of vocational assessment for racial/ethnic minorities: An existential approach. *Journal of Career Assessment, 2,* 304-329.

Johnson, W. L., Mauzey, E., Johnson, A. M., Murphy, S. D., & Zimmerman, K. J. (2001). A higher order analysis of the factor structure of the Myers-Briggs Type Indicator. *Measurement and Evaluation in Counseling and Development, 34,* 96-116.

Jordan, W. J. (2010). Defining equity: Multiple perspectives to analyzing the performance of diverse learners. *Review of Research In Education, 34,* 142-178.

Kelly, K. R. (2010). [Strong Interest Inventory (newly revised)]. In R. A. Spies, J. F. Carlson, & K. F. Geisinger, (Eds.), *The eighteenth mental measurements yearbook.* Lincoln, NE: Buros Center for Testing.

Losen, D. J., & Orfield, G. (2002). *Racial inequality in special education.* Cambridge, MA: Harvard Education Press.

Mattern, K. D., Patterson, D. F., Shaw, E. J., Kobrin, J. L., & Barbuti, S. M. (2008). Differential validity and prediction of the SAT. *Research Report No. 2008-4.* New York, NY: The College Board.

McCaully, M. H. & Moody, R. A. (2008) *Multicultural applications of the Myers-Briggs Type Indicator.* In L. A. Suzuki:, J. G. Ponterotto, & P. J. Meller (Eds.), *Handbook of multicultural assessment: Clinical, psychological, and educational applications (3rd ed.,* pp. 402-424 San Francisco, CA: Jossey-Bass).

Miller, M. J., & Brown, S. D. (2005). Counseling for career choice: Implications for improving interventions and working with diverse populations. In S. D. Brown & R. W. Lent (Eds), *Career development and counseling: Putting theory and research to work* (pp. 441-465). Hoboken, NJ: Wiley.

National Center on Education Statistics. (2011). *The nation's report card: Mathematics 2011 (NCES 2012–458).* Institute of Education Sciences, U.S. Department of Education, Washington, D.C.

National Center on Education Statistics. (2011a). *The nation's report card: Reading 2011 (NCES 2012–458).* Institute of Education Sciences, U.S. Department of Education, Washington, D.C.

Nichols, S. L. (2007). High-stakes testing: Does it increase achievement?. *Journal of Applied School Psychology, 23*(2), 47-64.

Pope, M., & Pangelinan, J. S. (2007). Using the ACA advocacy competencies in career counseling. In M. J. Ratts, R. L. Toporek, & J. A. Lewis, (Eds.), *ACA Advocacy Competencies: A Social Justice Framework for Counselors* (pp. 209-223). Alexandria, VA: ACA.

Pope, M., Barret, B., Szymanski, D. M., Chung, Y. B., Singaravelu, H., McLean, R., & Sanabria, S. (2004). Culturally appropriate career counseling with gay and lesbian clients. *Career Development Quarterly, 53,* 157-177.

Porfeli, E. J., Hartung, P. J., & Vondracek, F. W. (2008). Children's vocational development: A research rationale. *The Career Development Quarterly, 57*, 25-37.

Ridley, C. R., Li, L. C., & Hill, C. L. (1998). Multicultural assessment: Reexamination, reconceptualization, and practical application. *The Counseling Psychologist, 26*, 827-910.

Rossier, J. (2005). A review of the cross-cultural equivalence of frequently used personality inventories. *International Journal for Educational and Vocational Guidance, 5*, 175–188.

Rushton, J. P., & Jensen, A. R. (2005). Thirty years of research on race differences in cognitive ability. *Psychology, Public Policy, and Law, 11*, 235-294.

Ryan Krane, N. E. & Tirre, W. C. (2005). Ability assessment in career counseling. In S. D. Brown & R. W. Lent (Eds). *Career development and counseling: Putting theory and research to work* (pp. 330-352) Hoboken, NJ: Wiley.

Sampson, J. P., Jr. (2010). Quality, innovation, and social justice in career assessment. *Career Planning and Adult Development Journal, 25*, 8-13.

Schreier, B. A., & Dudley Lassiter, K. (2010). Competencies for working with sexual orientation and multiple cultural identities. In J. Cornish, B. A. Schreier, L. I. Nadkarni, L. Metzger, E. R. Rodolfa (Eds.), *Handbook of multicultural counseling competencies* (pp. 291-316). Hoboken, NJ: Wiley.

Sheperis, D., Perepiczka, M., & Limoges, C. (2011). Career assessment. In D. Capuzzi & M.D. Stauffer (Eds.), *Career counseling: Foundations, perspectives, and applications.* Upper Saddle River, NJ: Pearson.

Steele, C.M., & Aronson, J. (1995). Stereotype threat and the intellectual test-performance of African-Americans. *Journal of Personality and Social Psychology, 69*, 797-811.

Sue, D.W., Arredondo P., & McDavis R.J. (1992). Multicultural counseling competencies and standards: A call to the profession. *Journal of Counseling and Development, 70*, 477-486.

Swanson, J. L., & D'Achiardi, C. (2005). Beyond interests, needs/values, and abilities: Assessing other important career constructs over the life span. In: S.D. Brown & R.W. Lent (Eds.), *Career development and counseling* (pp. 353-381). Hoboken, NJ: Wiley.

Tracey, T. J. G. & Sodano, S. M. (2008). Issues of stability and change in interest development. *The Career Development Quarterly, 57*, 51-62.

U.S. Census Bureau. (2011). *Profile of general population and housing characteristics: 2010 demographic profile data.* Retrieved from: http://factfinder2.census.gov/faces/tableservices/jsf/pages/productview.xhtml?pid=DEC_10_DP_DPDP1&prodType=table

Whiston, S. C. (2012). *Principles and application of assessment in counseling* (4th ed.). Belmont, CA: Brooks/Cole.

Wood, C., & D'Agostino, J. V. (2010). Assessment in counseling: A tool for social justice work. In M. J. Ratts, R. L. Toporek, & J. A. Lewis, (Eds.), *ACA advocacy competencies: A social justice framework for counselors* (pp. 151-160). Alexandria, VA: ACA.

Worthington, R. L., Flores, L. Y., & Navarro, R. L. (2005). Career development in context: Research with people of color. In S. D. Brown & R. W. Lent (Eds). *Career development and counseling: Putting theory and research to work* (pp. 225-252). Hoboken, NJ: Wiley.

Young, J. W. (2001). *Differential validity, differential prediction, and college mission testing: A comprehensicve review and anaylsis* (College Board Research Report No. 2001-6). New York, NY: The College Board.

CHAPTER 6

ASSESSING YOUTH AND ADOLESCENTS WITH EDUCATIONAL AND CAREER DEVELOPMENT CHALLENGES

Mary Podmostko

Project 10: Transition Education Network
University of South Florida St. Petersburg

Joe Timmons, Christine Bremer, and Chris Opsal

Institute on Community Integration
University of Minnesota Twin Cities

Introduction

This chapter, adapted from material in the National Collaborative on Workforce and Disability for Youth (NCWD/Youth) publication *Career Planning Begins with Assessment* (Timmons, Podmostko, Bremer, Lavin, & Wills, 2005), addresses assessment strategies in career planning and development that can reduce or eliminate barriers to successful outcomes created by disability for youth and young adults ages 14-24. This chapter will discuss the four common domains of assessment, disability disclosure, the assessment process including accommodations and sources of assessment information (the Summary of Performance, Person Centered Planning, Situational Work Assessments, etc.), systemic challenges, and counseling strategies. Throughout this chapter, the value-neutral term *focus client* will be used to denote individuals who may need extra or modified assessment strategies and services. Understanding individual needs and developing an empathic approach to supporting these individuals are critical to individuals' attainment of desired outcomes.

Each focus client brings a unique set of characteristics (including one or more risk factors) and goals that will affect the career assessment process. By understanding the issues addressed in this chapter and ensuring that appropriate strategies are used, career counselors and other career development professionals can help individuals cope with and manage their risk factors and improve the quality of assessment services. Career assessment services provide a foundation for improving the lives of focus clients by helping them develop meaningful individualized career plans. For example, clients who receive services under the Individuals with Disabilities Education Act are required to develop plans based on "appropriate measurable postsecondary goals based upon age appropriate transition assessments related to training, education, employment, and, where appropriate, independent living skills" (Code of Federal Regulations, 300, D, 300.320, b, 1).

One of the issues affecting the career development of focus clients is their limited experience in career exploration and work-based activities. These limitations hinder accurate assessment and may prevent identification of skills, aptitudes, and interests that might appear after exposure and opportunity. In contrast, youth and adults who have had a wide range of positive experiences in school, community, and work, and who have had opportunities for leadership, generally have a better understanding of career development and can make more reasoned choices in many assessment activities (National Collaborative on Workforce and Disability for Youth, n.d.). Therefore, the ideal approach would be to administer assessment activities in a wide range of experiential settings or extended timeframes.

A key issue for many focus clients is that often their career planning process has not reflected the values of choice and self-determination. Many individuals with disabilities have been relegated to a passive role in their own career planning process, which typically results in

- very few options being recommended or offered,
- options that reflect the low expectations of advisors,
- options that feature perceived needs for protection and support, and
- options driven primarily by community availability rather than an individual's choices (Timmons et al., 2005).

Assessing Youth and Adolescents with Educational and Career Development Challenges

As a result, many focus clients have been guided into jobs that are neither motivating nor satisfying, and have not allowed them to use their skills, knowledge, and abilities to contribute to the workplace. Counselors during the career planning process can assist focus clients to identify their assets and then share this information with families, other professionals working with the focus clients, and potential employers. Effective assessment, both formal and informal, is the foundation upon which the career planning process rests.

The concept of Universal Design for Learning (UDL) is helpful in setting the context for discussing effective assessment practices. The goal of UDL is to create an environment in which the needs of clients and practitioners are met as simply and easily as possible. The Vocational Evaluation and Career Assessment Professionals (VECAP) position paper on Universal Design for career assessment, based on the work of Rose and Meyer (2002), describes how UDL guides effective practice and advances fairness and equity by providing the following:

- *multiple means of representation to give learners various ways of acquiring information and knowledge*—e.g., instructions for work performances and methods, such as work samples, standardized inventories, and situational assessments are available in a variety of formats;

- *multiple means of expression, to provide learners alternatives for demonstrating what they know*—e.g., individuals may use hands-on performances; oral, written, graphic, video, or computer-generated communication; or American Sign Language; and

- *multiple means of engagement, to tap into learners' interests, offer appropriate challenges, and increase motivation*—e.g., individuals may watch, listen, use their hands and bodies, or use digital platforms in the assessment process and help guide the process by selecting areas of interest or curiosity (Leconte, Smith, & Johnson, n.d., p. 1).

By considering UDL principles in choosing and administering assessments, practitioners can help to ensure valid and useful results.

Fairness and equity in assessment are also advanced by ensuring that career development professionals are aware of the obligations imposed by federal nondiscrimination statutes and regulations affecting testing and assessment. For example, policies and procedures should be in place to ensure nondiscrimination in the selection of tests, privacy and confidentiality of protected information such as disability and medical records, protected access to client (and employee) disability information, and appropriate documentation of the need for test accommodations.

Vocational assessments range from informal interest surveys that may be used simply to help the focus client start thinking about careers to comprehensive vocational evaluations conducted by trained and certified evaluators resulting in in-depth vocational profiles and recommendations. These assessments often need little or no modification for use with focus clients. Note that no assessment outcome stands alone and that assessment data from all four domains (see below), as well as information from observations, interviews, and record reviews, may be needed to assist the focus client in developing complete and well-documented career plans. Care should be taken to avoid duplicating assessment activities unnecessarily, and decisions should never be made on the basis of a single assessment.

Four Domains of Assessment

Career assessment addresses the range of interests, skills, knowledge, and expertise needed for success in work and life, such as those identified by the Partnership for 21st Century Skills (2009):

- Core subjects such as English, reading, or language arts; world languages; arts; mathematics, economics, and science; geography, history, government, and civics;

- Interdisciplinary themes such as global awareness; financial, economic, business, and entrepreneurial literacy; civic literacy; and health and environmental literacy;

- Learning and innovation skills such as creativity and innovation; critical thinking and problem solving; communication and collaboration;

- Information, media, and technology skills; and

- Life and career skills such as flexibility and adaptability; initiative and self-direction; social and cross-cultural skills; productivity and accountability; and leadership and responsibility.

Thorough career assessment for individuals with disabilities encompasses the knowledge/skills described above and covers four major domains: educational, vocational, psychological, and medical.

Career assessment instruments are used as part of an overall career assessment strategy selected by each client in collaboration with one or more career assessment professionals. These domains overlap, and assessment in one domain will often lead to useful information or understanding in another. Assessments in the educational domain and vocational domain are designed to measure achievement, aptitudes, skill levels, interests, physical and functional capacities, and cognition. These data are then used to help form educational, training, or employment plans specific to the client's situation.

For the psychological domain and medical domain, assessment for focus clients is typically conducted to identify or diagnose mental or physical problems that may impede an individual's academic progress, vocational growth, or career development; to develop treatment or therapy plans to alleviate these problems; and to identify appropriate accommodations for school, home, and workplace. These types of assessments are conducted by licensed physicians, psychologists, counselors, and other qualified professionals.

This chapter focuses primarily on supporting a focus client in the vocational domain, specifically using formal and informal vocational interest surveys that match a focus client's interests, goals, and values to potential career options; and vocational aptitudes and skills assessments that measure the focus client's ability or potential to learn or perform skills required in certain careers. (A third type of vocational assessment, occupation-specific certification tests, is usually administered by licensure boards, businesses, or workforce preparation programs to measure the ability to perform specific work compared to industry standards.)

Disability and Disclosure

It is not the career development professional's responsibility to diagnose disabilities. Because of the variety and high incidence of disabilities (up to 20% of the population according to the United States Census Bureau; Brault, 2012, p. 4), access to specialists (e.g., special educators, vocational rehabilitation counselors, healthcare professionals) who can evaluate potential focus clients and assist with individual assessment issues is needed. Career development professionals may work with clients with:

- physical or mental impairments affecting one or more of the following body systems: neurological, musculoskeletal, sense organs, respiratory (including speech organs), cardiovascular, reproductive, digestive, genito-urinary, hemic and lymphatic, skin, and endocrine;
- mental or psychological disorders (e.g., mental retardation, emotional or mental illness, specific learning disabilities); and
- undiagnosed or unidentified disabilities.

Focus clients may have previously received services or be currently receiving them via special education, vocational rehabilitation, or workforce development. They may have participated in career assessments and/or have an Individualized Education Program or Individualized Plan for Employment that includes employment and postsecondary education goals. In some cases, available medical or psychological records may be helpful. However, these documents are protected by privacy rules and may not be available to the career development professional.

Some focus clients have obvious disabilities (usually sensory or physical disabilities such as visual impairments, hearing loss, or orthopedic or neurological impairments). Others have somewhat less obvious but still recognizable cognitive disabilities (such as intellectual disabilities or autism). The majority of these individuals have had concrete interventions in school to alleviate the effects of the disability. Families often develop a good understanding of the dynamics of the focus client's disability, and odds are good that formal educational and vocational transition plans that include documentation of accommodations and supports needed for academic and career development have been developed.

Other focus clients have hidden or non-apparent disabilities or illness. Hidden disabilities include learning disabilities, Attention Deficit Hyperactivity Disorder (AD/HD), mental health or emotional problems (such as depression, anxiety disorders, or conduct disorders), and traumatic brain injuries (TBI). Because of the nature of hidden disabilities, identification and the provision of needed interventions and supports is more difficult. Families and professionals alike often have inadequate understanding of the nature of hidden disabilities, and

Assessing Youth and Adolescents with Educational and Career Development Challenges

some professionals may have no experience with transition planning. Most importantly, clients with hidden disabilities are less likely than others to disclose their disability because they wish to avoid being stigmatized or labeled. This means that clients with these disabilities may enroll and enter educational, training, and career development programs without communicating their disability or their needs for accommodations and special assistance.

Undiagnosed or unidentified disabilities may be suggested by a focus client's literacy levels, academic performance, vocabulary, behavior, assessment results, or interview responses. A screening process may be needed to determine whether further diagnostic assessment by a trained specialist should be provided. However, clients have the right to refuse screenings and diagnostic assessments.

Beyond disability, risk factors often come into play and also require consideration in career counseling settings. For example, many focus clients come from challenging family circumstances, have not finished high school, have been in foster care, have been involved in the justice system, or have a primary language other than English.

Some clients will choose not to disclose their specific diagnosis or prognosis or that they have previously qualified for or received disability-related accommodations or services. Adults often avoid disclosure because they wish to avoid being stigmatized or labeled as having a disability. Nondisclosure is an established right under the *Americans with Disabilities Act* (Public Law 110-325, Section 12112(d)(2)(A)). For the focus client, whether or not to disclose a disability or illness to prospective employers or others is an important decision that may have both short- and long-term ramifications. To help individuals understand the complex issues involved, the National Collaborative on Workforce and Disability for Youth (2005), has published *The 411 on Disability Disclosure*, a workbook to help individuals make informed decisions about disclosure and how these decisions can impact their education, employment, and social lives.

Career development and planning often involve a few false starts as individuals explore multiple options. Working with focus clients who have received or are receiving services from a number of agencies and programs may become confusing as they transfer from one program or service provider to another at various times. Each time a youth or adult begins working with a new program or a new career development professional, the need for assessment should be revisited since the purpose and form of assessment may vary by program and be affected by changing client goals. Also, throughout the interview and ongoing transition process, career development professionals will want to keep in mind that many focus clients have had limited or negative experiences with tests and testing which may impact validity and reliability in formal assessment.

Transition Services and the Summary of Performance

Focus clients who are adolescents or young adults (usually ages 14-24) are considered to be in "transition." This period can be particularly difficult for some individuals as they leave or prepare to leave the relative comfort of the public school system, where services tend to be centralized and familiar, and enter the adult service system, where they are just the opposite. Beyond the typical developmental issues of transition-age youth, focus clients may have added, more significant challenges relating to emotional well-being, self-esteem, personal relationships, and school engagement. These can affect the assessment context as well as the need for services and supports. Those who have hidden or non-apparent disabilities (e.g., learning disabilities, attention deficit disorder, mental health issues, and Asperger's syndrome) are more likely to be undiagnosed or have incomplete diagnoses. As a result, these individuals have a greater risk of invalid or unreliable findings in career assessment.

To help focus clients make the transition from secondary school to postsecondary education, employment, and independent living, federal special education law requires that students departing the public school system complete a Summary of Performance (SOP) with the assistance of their educational teams. The SOP may vary from school district to school district and is a legal document that details the student's present level of performance in as many as 12 cognitive, academic, and functional areas (National Transition Documentation Summit, 2005, pp. 3-6):

- Reading;
- Environmental Access/Mobility;
- Mathematics;

66

- General Ability and Problem Solving;
- Written Language;
- Attention and Executive Functioning;
- Learning Skills;
- Communication;
- Social Skills and Behavior;
- Self-Determination/Self-Advocacy Skills;
- Independent Living Skills; and
- Career-Vocational/Transition/Employment.

Additional information provided in the SOP may include the student's postsecondary academic and vocational goals, accommodations used in academic and vocational settings, and results from previous relevant assessments, including diagnostic assessments related to disability and health. The SOP can be a rich source of career assessment information for the career development professionals who are working with a focus client. For more information on the SOP requirements, visit http://www.nsttac.org/content/summary-performance-resources.

Transitioning to higher education is an additional consideration with this population. Until recently, most young people with significant disabilities had few opportunities to attend two- or four-year colleges. At the end of high school, options were often limited to sheltered workshops that paid less than minimum wage and provided no programming integrated with others without disabilities. Today, there are over 200 college and university programs across the country that include young people with intellectual and developmental disabilities. For example, the *Think College!* initiative at the University of Massachusetts/Boston promotes college programming and resources to support individuals with more significant disabilities. Its website at http://www.thinkcollege.net contains a searchable database of postsecondary programs in the United States.

Person-Centered Planning

For focus clients, assessment should support a consistent process for goal setting that includes person-centered planning—an approach in which the career planning process is driven by a client's needs and desires. In the context of career planning, person-centered planning focuses on a person's assets (e.g., interests, aptitudes, knowledge, and skills), not on his/her perceived deficits. Career development professionals who use person-centered planning seek to involve the people who are active in the life of an individual, such as family members, educators, employers, friends, and service providers. Although there is a natural tendency for focus clients to seek independence and rely less and less on parents and other family members, all participants in the process should understand that career planning is a process requiring flexibility and negotiation in which each focus client and family member(s) may have a part to play. Person-centered career planning will include multiple options, self-advocacy, bridging of academic and career needs, access to critical information, and professional assistance (Timmons et al., 2005).

Focus clients with more significant disabilities (including intellectual and developmental disabilities, neurological impairments, orthopedic impairments, some forms of autism, and traumatic brain injuries) will benefit from a person-centered planning process that includes record reviews, observations, interviews (particularly with parents), and formal and/or informal assessments (Timmons et al., 2005). The type of disability and its impact will determine whether clients can use an assessment "out of the box," with accommodations or modifications, or whether another assessment is a better match. Publisher and administrative guidelines should be followed closely in determining the appropriateness of assessments, with or without accommodations, for each person's use.

Clients with significant disabilities may need functional assessments of motor skills, communications skills, problem-solving abilities, self-care, social interactions, and other career-related skills and abilities. Situational assessments for career, educational, and independent living placements are often indicated. These assessments may be administered by counselors, psychologists, assistive technology specialists, speech therapists, occupational therapists, or other qualified professionals.

Assessing Youth and Adolescents with Educational and Career Development Challenges

Some clients with significant disabilities may benefit from in-depth functional vocational evaluations (FVEs) conducted by certified vocational evaluators or rehabilitation counselors. An FVE is a systematic assessment process used to identify practical useable career and employment-related information about an individual. It incorporates multiple formal and informal assessment techniques to observe, describe, measure, and predict vocational potential. A distinctive feature is that an FVE includes (and may emphasize) individualized experiential and performance-based opportunities in natural vocational or work environments (Castiglione, n.d.).

An example of an effective transition assessment process for students with significant disabilities can be found at http://www.rockingham.k12.va.us/RCPS_sped/transition/portfolio-SD.htm. Functional skills assessment forms, transition portfolio, and other resources are provided at this site and may be adapted for use as needed. Assessing independent living skills is another consideration during transitions. By late adolescence, many young people are making plans for living on their own. Skills needed for independent living are often taken for granted, but youth with disabilities or chronic illnesses may have physical or intellectual limitations that prevent them from engaging in adult activities without support or assistance. Additionally, independent living skills are closely related to the functional work skills discussed above. Assessment and instruction in activities of daily living (ADLs) are common in schools and rehabilitation programs serving youth with more significant disabilities. ADL assessment areas include: transportation and mobility; personal care (e.g., clothing, grooming, nutrition, medical); recreation and leisure; home maintenance; and communication skills. Specially trained teachers, trainers, counselors, and other qualified professionals can assess individuals in these and other areas.

Service providers often have specialty areas (e.g., vision loss, deafness, autism) and will work with individuals in the community, in schools, or in residential settings. In some cases, extensive longer-term training is required and is provided in rehabilitation centers found in many communities. This training is sometimes called prevocational because it may need to be completed prior to the individual's participation in vocational activities.

The Assessment Process

Often, the assessment process can be completed in less time and at lower cost by making use of the focus client's existing records, provided that permission to view and use these records has been obtained. To be useful, records containing background information, prior interviews and observations, histories, and testing must be up-to-date. Whether or not prior assessment results are considered current can often be determined from publishers' materials, which may specify a recommended interval between assessments, for example. New assessments may be needed if a focus client's situation has recently changed because of schooling, training, onset of a new disability, therapy, treatment, or other reasons. Records should be reviewed with an eye to assessing their value in supporting a focus client's future academic or career planning needs. If outdated or lacking validity, records may inappropriately limit a young person's options.

In more complex cases, it is good practice to have written plans with objectives and timelines, since some focus clients may require an extended process of supported planning and implementation. Deciding which formal tests should be administered and in what order is part of this process. Plans can be amended and updated based on testing outcomes, and the focus client's input should be considered as much as possible.

Streamlining the assessment process to eliminate unnecessary testing and activities can help to ensure that the most relevant assessments are completed and done well. However, interviews, histories, and other information-gathering activities should not be rushed. This is especially important when the focus client has a recently acquired disability. For example, special attention should be paid to those who have served in the military. According to research conducted at Harvard's John F. Kennedy School of Government, many veterans "suffer in isolation" after returning home; listening respectfully and nonjudgmentally to their stories and experiences creates an environment where "they can more easily give voice to what else they need—from practical help finding jobs ... to connection, creativity, and care" (Caplan, 2011).

Assessment Considerations

Prior to beginning formal or informal assessment or performance reviews, career counselors can gather much useful information through interviews. The initial interview establishes rapport with the client and his or her family and helps them develop a realistic understanding of what a career counselor has to offer. Personal information about health or disability issues may be part of the interview process and must be handled with tact and sensitivity. The ADA provides guidance and language in this regard. Privacy and confidentiality must be maintained, and securing information from other agencies, when appropriate, must be done ethically and legally, using signed consent forms when needed. Observation of the client at home, school, work, or other settings can also be useful in understanding and interpreting assessment results.

Helping focus clients make informed choices and achieve desired outcomes requires a structured, well-defined assessment process. The following principles should guide the assessment process:

- Self-determination based on informed choices should be an overriding goal of assessment;
- Assessment is a dynamic intervention process;
- Assessment facilitates self-discovery of talents, goals, strengths, and needs;
- The purposes and goals of assessment should be clear;
- Assessment should be integrated into a larger plan of person-centered planning and individualized services;
- Assessment should consider environmental factors affecting the individual;
- Formal assessment instruments should be carefully chosen with attention to their documented reliability and validity;
- Formal assessments should be administered and interpreted by qualified personnel;
- Assessment reports should be written in easily understandable language; and
- Assessment activities should be experienced as positive and should empower focus clients to communicate their goals to family members and others and to make decisions about next steps.

Assessment instruments are used to help determine a person's specific abilities, strengths, and challenges. The results of assessments should not be used merely to categorize an individual with a disability, but rather to develop strategies to help the individual reach desired goals. Assessments also help identify areas to probe in order to understand an individual's potential strengths and functional abilities in educational, vocational, and community settings.

New assessments and assessment approaches should be thoroughly researched prior to implementation. For example, work readiness assessments and certifications that assess potential employees based on the skills and knowledge required for specific jobs are becoming more common; triangulating work readiness profiles with other assessment results will ensure that focus client limitations or disabilities are not disproportionately emphasized.

Providing Accommodations

Accommodations are changes made in a classroom, work site, or assessment procedure that help people with disabilities learn, work, participate in assessment, or receive services. Accommodations are intended to do more than just comply with federal regulations and maximize the effectiveness of assessments; they are meant to alleviate the effects of a disability, not to lower expectations for performance. Common accommodations include allowing a focus client with a learning disability extra time to complete an assignment or a test, providing amplification equipment for a student with a hearing impairment in a classroom, or providing a special computer keyboard for someone with dexterity problems. The ADA and other federal laws provide for the use of appropriate testing accommodations for clients with disabilities for the purpose of increasing access and participation to public education and employment. Accommodations are often allowed when using criterion-referenced or norm-referenced instruments. The goal of providing accommodations is to change the way that a test is taken without changing the validity of the test results.

Sometimes a question arises about the reliability or validity of certain tests when accommodations are used. In such cases, the test publisher should be contacted for clarification. At no point should an individual be penalized or denied services because of unreliable or invalid test results. If a particular assessment cannot be conducted in a way that assures validity, other methods of assessment should be used. In general, accommodations come in four classes:

Assessing Youth and Adolescents with Educational and Career Development Challenges

- *Presentation format:* changes in how tests are presented, including accommodations like providing Braille versions of the tests or orally reading the directions to students;

- *Response format:* changes in the manner in which responses are given, including accommodations such as pointing to a response or using a computer for responding;

- *Setting of the test:* home, or in small groups, for example; and

- *Timing of the test:* including extending the time allowed, or providing more breaks during testing (Thurlow, House, Boys, Scott, & Ysseldyke, 2000).

Specific accommodations may affect the validity or fairness of individual tests. Familiarity with local practice is needed since states, local agencies, and school districts all have their own guidelines, and inconsistencies are widespread.

Career assessment of focus clients may lead to practical ideas for job accommodations in training programs and workplaces. Effective assessment can examine potential needs for accommodations that will enable an individual to perform the essential functions of a chosen job. On-site and off-site accommodations that might improve the job placement success of focus clients include modifications to a job, restructuring of tasks, use of job coaches to assist with training, or use of American Sign Language interpreters. The Job Accommodation Network (JAN) is a free consulting service that provides information about workplace accommodations, the ADA, and the employability of people with disabilities. JAN has information for employers and people with disabilities, including a Searchable On-line Accommodation Resource (SOAR), on its website: http://janweb. icdi.wvu.edu/.

Situational Work Assessments

Situational work assessments are contextualized assessments that focus on performance of tasks in realistic settings. Focus clients often benefit from this type of assessment of occupational skills. Work behaviors examined in situational work assessments may include capacities and competencies for performing essential job duties of specific competitive employment positions. For example, the measurement of a youth's keyboarding proficiency may be predictive of his or her ability to succeed in a job requiring a minimum speed for data entry or word processing. Allowing a client to try essential job functions of different jobs will help them decide if they really enjoy the work and if they have the stamina to meet work requirements.

Although the outcomes of occupational skills assessment are not entirely predictive of future success in a competitive job situation, they often can lead to job skills training, apprenticeships, or internships that help focus clients increase their competency and productivity. They can also lead to the development of creative, individualized job placement plans such as customized employment or "job carving" (a restructuring of job duties or tasks so that an individual with more significant disabilities can perform job functions of high interest). Typically, job carving is provided for people who, for a variety of reasons, cannot perform the entire job or the whole range of skills required (Griffin, 2005; Timmons et al., 2005).

In special education programs and community rehabilitation organizations, situational work assessments are also often used to study the "soft skills" needed in employment. They assess basic work behaviors and skills through practical hands-on work experiences. In particular, youth with identified behavioral disorders or learning disabilities can benefit greatly from situational work assessments. Many young people who struggle in the classroom flourish in work settings where hands-on activities better fit their learning styles.

Situational assessments may include ecological assessments, also known as environmental assessments, that examine the workplace context, which may contribute significantly to the success of an individual at work. Important aspects of the workplace context include availability of close supervision; style of supervision (e.g., casual vs. autocratic); physical building structures and layout of the learning or working environment; flow of product or service processes; effects of formal and informal rules; social interaction demands of others (e.g., co-workers, customers, classmates); sensory stimuli (e.g., noise, motion, temperature, air quality); work schedules and time requirements; opportunities for independence and decision making; performance expectations of authorities; and opportunities for self-correction. The client's temperament (e.g., preference for working with data, people, or things; preference for indoor vs. outdoor work; preference for working with others or alone) plays a large role in ecological assessments, since the fit of temperament to context can be of great importance in determining the success of an individual in a job.

Assessment results can be used to build a case for finding suitable employment opportunities for the focus client. Too often, individuals are not hired because prospective employers do not see how their needs will be met if they hire an individual with a disability, a chronic illness, or other perceived barriers. Assessment results can provide a communications tool for discussing with employers the actual capabilities of individuals with disabilities.

Functional skills (including transportation, communication, interpersonal skills, self-care, self-direction, and work tolerance) are critical to successful employment. Most people develop these skills over months or years and can discuss or demonstrate them in the course of a job interview. Focus clients with disabilities who have developed an understanding of their strengths and limitations can specifically address the concerns of employers, co-workers, and customers by explaining their compensatory strategies, including any needed accommodations or assistive technology. Because employers look for employees with two sets of skills—the functional skills that all workers need and the specific work skills to do a specific job—it is important that job seekers understand what these skills are and how to develop them if they are lacking.

Functional limitations refer to an activity or behavior that an individual cannot perform or performs with difficulty. Functional limitations may result from behaviors that the individual has difficulty performing with sufficient frequency, adequate intensity, in the appropriate manner, or under socially expected conditions, or from behaviors that occur too frequently, too intensely, last too long, or occur when and where they should not normally occur. Disability specialists in educational and vocational rehabilitation settings can suggest strategies to overcome work-related functional limitations.

Systemic Challenges

Focus clients who seek assistance from publicly-funded entities often find that they must navigate a complex maze of laws, regulations, and policies in order to access career assessment services. Institutional constraints include limited funding, lack of information on available assessment resources and expertise, privacy protections, and reporting and evaluation requirements. Federal legislation encourages collaborative, cross-agency cooperation (both statewide and in local communities) as a way to address systemic problems. Resource mapping, a type of environmental scanning, is a useful way for agencies and service providers to identify, record, and disseminate related resources and services that together comprise a delivery system. By detailing current capacities, needs, and expertise, an organization or group of organizations, both public and private, can begin to make strategic decisions about ways to efficiently broaden their collective assessment capacity and create an equitable and effective division of labor.

Resource mapping, sometimes referred to as *community asset mapping*, also allows states and communities to form partnerships and identify service gaps and service overlaps—information that is essential to aligning assessment services and strategic planning of multiple agencies and organizations. The resource mapping process may also reveal that some agencies or organizations have expertise in particular areas of need. For example, partners may wish to draw on the expertise of the state department of education in developing assessment accommodation guidelines that will ensure consistency across agencies.

Outcomes of the resource mapping process may include the following:

- list of assessment resources and available expertise;
- a common policy and release form for authorizing the receipt and sharing of confidential data or assessment information from focus clients, schools, family members, and partner agencies; and/or
- a division of labor for local assessment services such as academic assessments provided by the local public school system and/or community college, disability and functional evaluations provided by the vocational rehabilitation office, and vocational assessments provided by the local One-Stop Career Center (funded by the Workforce Investment Act) (Crane & Mooney, 2005; Griffin & Farris, 2010).

Assessing Youth and Adolescents with Educational and Career Development Challenges

Resource mapping and strategic planning processes are also useful in developing assessment services and aligning on-the-job supports for employers in the community.

Counseling Strategies for Assessing Youth and Adults with Career Development Challenges

Practitioners who integrate the following strategies into their work will reduce or eliminate barriers to successful outcomes and more effectively meet the assessment needs of individuals who have disabilities, chronic illness, or other at-risk factors:

- Ensure fairness and equity in assessment by employing a Universal Design for Learning approach and implementing policies and procedures that meet the obligations imposed by applicable federal nondiscrimination statutes and regulations.

- Provide effective career assessment that encompasses the four assessment domains (i.e., academic, vocational, psychological, and medical) and identify resources to support individuals with complex psychological or medical implications.

- Understand how independent living skills impact focus clients, such as barriers to career development and work created by housing, transportation, self-care, and time management challenges.

- Access specialists who can evaluate potential focus clients and assist with individual assessment issues as needed.

- Ameliorate disabilities and health issues of focus clients that can affect the selection and administration of career assessment strategies and instruments; base formal and informal accommodations on input from focus clients as well as family members and professionals who have provided support to them in the past.

- Understand the role of government and community support systems including those providing vocational rehabilitation, medical, mental health, financial, and independent living.

Summary

This chapter discussed a number of topics involved in the career assessment of youth and young adults, ages 14-24, who have diagnosed or undiagnosed disabilities and/or chronic health conditions. Contextual information for assessment includes Universal Design for Learning (UDL), the four domains of assessment, disability type and disclosure, special education transition services and the Summary of Performance, and systemic challenges. Descriptions are provided for client assessment processes such as person-centered planning, streamlining the assessment process, accommodations, situational work assessments, independent living skills assessments, and other assessment activities. Chapter information is summarized in seven strategies for career development professionals that will reduce or eliminate barriers to successful outcomes and more effectively meet the assessment needs of their transition-age clients.

Review Questions

1. What risk factors of focus clients may impact career assessment? What assessment strategies and activities may be employed to ameliorate them?

2. Why are equity and fairness important in the career assessment of clients with one or more risk factors? What assessment strategies support equity and fairness?

3. What sources of assessment information may be available for a focus client that may eliminate unnecessary or duplicative testing?

4. Describe the three assessment activities described in this chapter. How would you implement them with your clients?

5. What systemic challenges may impede effective career assessment? What strategies may be used to address them?

References

Brault, M. W. (2012, July). Current population reports. In U.S. Census Bureau, *Americans with disabilities: 2010.* Washington, DC: U.S. Department of Commerce. Available at http://www.census.gov/prod/2012pubs/p70-131.pdf

Caplan, P. J. (2011, November 4). Just by listening, civilians can help veterans heal. *The Washington Post.* Retrieved from http://www.washingtonpost.com/opinions/just-by-listening-civilians-can-help-veterans-heal/2011/11/01/gIQA7YYamM_story.html

Castiglione, S. (n.d.). *VECAP white paper on Functional Vocational Evaluation.* San Bernardino, CA: Vocational Evaluation and Career Assessment Professionals. Retrieved from http://www.vecap.org/images/uploads/docs/WhitePaperFunctionalEval.pdf

Crane, K. & Mooney, M. (2005, May). *Essential tools: Community resource mapping.* Minneapolis, MN: Institute of Community Integration, Inc. Retrieved from http://www.ncset.org/publications/essentialtools/mapping/NCSET_EssentialTools_ResourceMapping.pdf

Code of Federal Regulations, Title 34: Education, Subtitle B: Regulations of the Offices of the Department of Education (Continued), Chapter III: Office of Special Education and Rehabilitative Services, Department of Education, Part 300: Assistance to States for the Education of Children with Disabilities, Subpart D: Evaluations, Eligibility Determinations, Individualized Education Programs, and Educational Placements, 300.320, b, 1

Griffin, G. (2005). *Job carving: A guide for job developers and employment specialists.* Florence, MT, & Middletown, OH: Griffin-Hammis Associates. Retrieved from http://www.griffinhammis.com/publications/carving.pdf

Griffin, D., & Farris, A. (2010). School counselors and school-family-community collaboration: Finding resources through community asset mapping. *Professional School Counseling, 13*(5), 248-256.

Leconte, P., Smith, F. G., & Johnson, C. (n.d.). *VECAP position paper on universal design for career assessment.* San Bernardino, CA: Vocational Evaluation and Career Assessment Professionals. Retrieved from http://www.vecap.org/images/uploads/docs/vecap_udl_position_paper.pdf

National Collaborative on Workforce and Disability for Youth. (n.d.). *Guideposts for success* (2nd ed). Washington, DC: Institute for Educational Leadership. Retrieved from http://www.ncwd-youth.info/guideposts

National Collaborative on Workforce and Disability for Youth. (2005). *The 411 on disability disclosure: A workbook for youth with disabilities.* Washington, DC: Institute for Educational Leadership. Retrieved from http://www.ncwd-youth.info/411-on-disability-disclosure

National Transition Documentation Summit. (2005). *Nationally endorsed Summary of Performance template.* Retrieved from http://www.ldaamerica.org/aboutld/adults/post_secondary/print_sop.asp

Partnership for 21st Century Skills. (2009, December). *P21 framework definitions.* Tucson, AZ: Author. Retrieved from http://www.p21.org/storage/documents/P21_Framework_Definitions.pdf

Public Law 101-336 – Americans with Disabilities Act of 1990, as amended. Retrieved from http://www.ada.gov/pubs/ada.htm

Public Law 110-325 – Americans with Disabilities Act Amendments of 2008. Retrieved from http://www.ada.gov/pubs/adastatute08.htm

Rose, D. H., & Meyer, A. (2002). *Teaching every student in the digital age.* Alexandria, VA: Association for Supervision and Curriculum Development.

Thurlow, M., House, A., Boys, C., Scott, D., & Ysseldyke, J. (2000). *State participation and accommodation policies for students with disabilities: 1999 update* (Synthesis Report 33). Minneapolis, MN: University of Minnesota, National Center on Educational Outcomes. Retrieved from http://eric.ed.gov/PDFS/ED447611.pdf

Timmons, J., Podmostko, M., Bremer, C., Lavin, D., & Wills, J. (2005). *Career planning begins with assessment: A guide for professionals serving youth with educational and career development challenges (rev. ed.).* Washington, DC: Institute for Educational Leadership, National Collaborative on Workforce and Disability for Youth. Retrieved from http://www.ncwd-youth.info/career-planning-begins-with-assessment

74

CHAPTER 7

USING ASSESSMENT FOR PERSONAL, PROGRAM, AND POLICY ADVOCACY

Norman C. Gysbers
Department of Educational, School, and Counseling Psychology
University of Missouri–Columbia

Richard T. Lapan
Department of Student Development and Pupil Personnel Services
University of Massachusetts at Amherst

Sibyl Cato
Department of Counseling
Indiana University of Pennsylvania

Introduction

In this the first decade of the 21st century, Friedman (2007) declared that the "world is flat". Why is the world flat? According to Friedman the world is flat because of forces at work including the falling of the Berlin Wall, the introduction of Netscape, work flow software, open-sourcing, outsourcing, offshoring, supply-chaining, insourcing, in-forming, and finally, by something he called the steroids — digital processing.

As the power of these forces continues to unfold, they are causing substantial and long lasting changes in the occupational, industrial, and social structures of the United States, changes that are having dramatic impact on the workplace. Workplaces are becoming more global, characterized by technological change moving at near light speed. "More and more workers and the organizations in which they work are developing global identities" (Feller & Whichard, 2005, p. 23).

Societal structures and social and personal values also continue to change and become more diverse. People are on the move too, from rural to urban areas and back again as well as from one region of the country to another in search of economic, social, psychological, and physical security. Our population is also getting older and becoming increasingly more diverse (Shrestha, 2011).

All of these changes are creating substantial challenges for children, adolescents, and adults. A rapidly changing work world and labor force in a global economy; violence in the home, school, and community; divorce; teenage suicide; substance abuse; and sexual experimentation are just a few examples. These challenges are not abstract aberrations. These challenges are real, and they are having and will continue to have a substantial impact on the personal/social, career, and academic development of children, adolescents, and adults in the 21st century (Gysbers & Henderson, 2011).

Given societal changes such as these and the challenges they represent, what roles can assessment play in assisting individuals to respond directly and positively to them? We envision three roles. First, there is a *personal advocacy* role in which assessments can assist individuals to become personally empowered. Through the use of aptitude, achievement, interest, values, and personality and career development measures, valuable information can be provided as "tools of discovery," assisting them to explore, consider options, and make informed personal, academic, and career decisions. Second, there is a *program advocacy* role in which assessment instruments can be used to measure the effectiveness of guidance and counseling programs and their activities and services. In turn, such data can be used to advocate for and to expand, extend, and adjust these services and activities to the benefit of individuals of all ages and circumstances. Third, there is a *policy advocacy* role in which assessment data from personal advocacy and program effectiveness can be used to help formulate policy to provide direction for guidance and counseling programs at the national, state, and local levels.

The roles of personal, program, and policy advocacy parallel the American Counseling Association's (ACA) Advocacy Competencies (Lewis, Arnold, House, & Toporek, 2003). Advocacy competence is the "ability, understanding, and knowledge to carry out advocacy ethically and effectively" (Toporek, Lewis, & Crethar, 2009, p. 262). The Advocacy Competencies include three levels of advocacy: client/student *(personal)*, school/community *(program)*, and the public arena *(policy)* (Lewis et al., 2003). Additionally, the three levels have two domains: advocacy with and advocacy on behalf of the individual. The Advocacy Competencies give counselors "a means for determining when certain situations call for direct interventions, advocacy with or on behalf of an individual, and when interventions call for *microlevel* and *macrolevel approaches*" (Ratts & Hutchins, 2009, p. 270). This chapter focuses on the roles of personal, program, and policy advocacy as exemplifying the aforementioned Advocacy Competencies.

Personal Advocacy

Given the challenges of the 21st century, it is imperative that individuals of all ages and circumstances feel empowered by having purpose for and direction in their lives. Assessments, used as "tools of discovery," can improve the chances that all individuals will be able to create more satisfying career options, effectively respond to life's possibilities and challenges, take advantage of life's anticipated and unanticipated events (Goodman, Schlossberg, & Anderson, 2011), and find greater satisfaction in their life roles (Gysbers, Heppner, & Johnston, 2009). Used as "tools of discovery," assessments can empower individuals by providing them with vocabulary to describe themselves in various ways; then, they can use their new vocabulary to explore and gain insight into their personal, educational, and career options. The goal is to empower individuals with the knowledge and skills to become active and involved advocates for themselves.

The *client/student advocacy level* of the Advocacy Competencies (Lewis et al., 2003) occurs on the individual/ personal level in which counselor interventions are focused on the client/student or on the client/student's behalf. Counselor interventions focusing *on* the client/student are described as *client/student empowerment*, whereas counselor interventions *on behalf* of the client/student are described as *client/student advocacy*. Toporek et al. (2009) explained that it is possible that personal level empowerment and advocacy interventions could both be used when attempting to diffuse or challenge a systemic problem. Applying this level to assessments, counselors use assessments as a direct intervention to help clients and students carry out their personal, educational, and career goals. Counselors also could utilize assessments as interventions on behalf of the client or student to identify barriers to their personal, educational, and career goals, then working to eliminate the barriers impeding that individual's full participation in career development opportunities.

In addition to advocating on behalf of individuals, career development professionals using career assessment instruments also help clients/students become empowered to be self-advocates. What must individuals know and be able to do to become self-advocates? Lapan (2004, p. 25) recommended that individuals must be able to perform the following:

(a) interact with a sense of purpose and direction;

(b) orient themselves to valued opportunities and choices;

(c) act in agentic and empowered ways;

(d) exhibit a mature commitment to a self-defined direction;

(e) be hopeful, motivated, and optimistic about the present and the future;

(f) persevere and overcome obstacles, as well as turn unexpected events into positive opportunities;

(g) be creative and curious; and

(h) balance an ability to be entrepreneurial with the need to care for others and the environment.

What is required for individuals to acquire the knowledge and skills to become self-advocates? Lapan (p. 25) identified six primary constructs that promote self-advocacy development. They are:

(1) positive expectations, including self-efficacy beliefs and attributions;

(2) identity development through interrelated processes of career exploration and goal formation;

(3) an enhanced understanding of oneself, the world of work, and how best to fit or match this self-understanding to occupational possibilities;

(4) the pursuit of one's intrinsic interests and preferences;

(5) the ability to achieve academically and become a self-regulated, lifelong learner; and

(6) a range of complex social skills and work-readiness behaviors to be used in one's everyday interactions with others.

These constructs form the basis for guidance and counseling programs and services for individuals of all ages and circumstances because they are the knowledge and skill base that promotes positive development leading to self-empowerment. Assessments play a key role because as tools of discovery they expand and extend individuals' understanding of themselves, others, and their worlds. Assessments can open doors allowing individuals to see, explore, and consider new possibilities personally, educationally, and occupationally.

Assessments facilitate self-advocacy for individuals because they offer vantage points that highlight critical aspects of persons' experiences. These are perspectives that may be missed without the use of such assessments. As tools of discovery, assessments provide a medium though which critical issues can be identified, explored, and eventually reintegrated. They can empower individuals to make informed choices. In advocating for individuals, assessments can be used to measure the extent to which development of these six constructs is occurring and to identify barriers to such growth, such as the case of Carla (see Case Example 7.1).

Case Example 7.1

Carla is a high school senior who recently participated in a school-to-work evaluation study. She is a very strong student, ranking in the upper 10% of her class, and possesses a clear sense of efficacy about her ability to master a wide range of academic subjects. Unfortunately, her father died last year. In talking about her future plans, it was clear that she had a good sense of her talents and self-confidence. However, as she talked, her concerns about finances surfaced. She very articulately spoke of the financial challenges currently being faced by her mother. From her perspective, finances for her future educational and career plans would no longer be available. Finances had become a perceived barrier that she would not be able to overcome. Without an assessment procedure that took a "wide lens" in addressing the range of critical career constructs necessary for developing a more adaptive orientation to the world of work, these negative attributions would not have surfaced. The Advocacy Competencies describe that the counselor is able to identify these patterns through empowerment and advocacy at the individual or personal level (Lewis et al., 2003). Because of this assessment process, this young woman received emotional support from her school counselor enabling her to become an active and involved advocate for herself and for her goals and aspirations.

Program Advocacy

Today, the issue of program accountability is in the forefront of professional dialogue, although program accountability has been of concern since the work of counselors began in the early 1900s (Gysbers, 2004). As a result of the continued focus on accountability, counselors are increasingly being asked to assess the results of their work with children, adolescents, and adults (Astramovich, Coker, & Hoskins, 2005; Sink, 2009). Assessments are one of the major tools counselors use to evaluate the outcomes of their work and to advocate for their programs.

The role of counselors as advocates for effective programs based on evaluation data has significant consequences for both the assessments used and the assessment users (Gysbers & Henderson, 2011). For example, assessments used in program evaluation may face skeptical audiences. Policymakers and those who try to influence legislation, especially those who demand results-based program accountability, will ask critical questions of the evaluation results. Counselors will not be able to answer these questions adequately unless the assessments used address program content standards and meet rigorous psychometric standards. Counselors choosing tests to evaluate program outcomes may need to ask different questions about the psychometric adequacy of the tests than might typically be asked when working with individuals. A test-retest reliability question might focus on whether or not there is enough reliable variance in the range of possible test scores to show change over time. Some scales may be more vulnerable to ceiling effects that would create a restricted range of test scores, thus reducing variability and ultimately co-variability or possible mean changes over time. Finding significant differences may elicit a "so what" reaction from those who control the budget. Counselors will need to answer this validity question by demonstrating that changes measured by assessments robustly predict outcomes of concern to policymakers. Normative samples must include the perspectives of the diverse population living in the United States. Test makers will need to justify construct validity by demonstrating that their tests are not confounded by unmeasured background variables.

Some counselors may experience some anxiety in expanding their role to include program advocacy through evaluation (Perepiczka, Chandler, & Becerra, 2011). This reaction could be due to a number of factors. For example, graduate training programs for counselors have been criticized for not including rigorous evaluation training for counselors (Astramovich & Coker, 2007). Counselors may have been required to take introductory statistics courses, but such coursework likely did not instruct them in practical program evaluation strategies. From our experience counselors-in-training at the graduate level may experience a significant amount of anxiety in subject matter related to mathematics. Most counselors would identify with Holland's Social theme (i.e., wanting to promote individual growth and development by helping others) and not with the Investigative theme (i.e., analyzing and questioning) (Holland, 1997). These feelings and self-definitions may interact to make program evaluation appear much more daunting than is warranted.

The American School Counselor Association's (ASCA) framework for school counseling programs encourages school counselors to be well versed and familiar with program evaluation for the purposes of advocating for their school counseling programs. The accountability system component of the model suggests that school counselors conduct a yearly assessment or audit of their school counseling program with the use of data collection and data analysis in order to communicate the effectiveness of their programs to the appropriate stakeholders (ASCA, 2012).

To counteract the fear of evaluation, Missouri counselor educators, the Missouri Department of Elementary and Secondary Education, and the Missouri School Counselor Association set out to empower school counselors to conduct evaluation of their work without fear of data. The concept used is a train-the-trainer model called Program Results-Based Evaluation (PRBE). School counselors in Missouri are being trained to use and analyze local data to improve their work with students and their parents as well as to share results-based evaluation evidence with administrators, boards of education, teachers, the community, and with each other. The data they collect and analyze are used to improve the programming and services they provide as well as to provide data to advocate for the importance of their work with students and their parents (Gysbers, Lapan, & Stanley, 2006).

The *community/school level* of the Advocacy Competencies for counselors (Lewis et al., 2003) occurs through community collaboration and systems advocacy. Through the use of assessment, counselor interventions with community collaboration could be beneficial to create an awareness of common issues facing various aspects of the program, identify strengths of the group necessary for systemic change, as well as assessing the effectiveness of the counselor with the program (Lewis et al., 2003). With respect to systems advocacy, counselors can use assessment to devise a plan necessary to create changes in the program or system as outlined by the Advocacy Competencies. Through this lens, counselors are able to analyze data obtained through assessing the program, determine what change needs to happen, and develop a plan to create the changes. Case Example 7.2 provides an example of the role of career assessment in program advocacy.

Case Example 7.2

Anderson is a mental health counselor working at Waterside, a residential facility for young adults who struggle with homelessness. He developed a career development program at the agency more than one year ago and is interested in evaluating its effectiveness for fostering clients' career adaptability and job search skills. His ultimate goal is to ensure that the program is an affirmative experience for clients, whereas he is both empowering them and advocating on their behalf during the job search process. The program consists of Anderson facilitating group sessions, once per week, with clientele, administering a variety of quantitative and qualitative career assessments, placing clients with community stakeholders so that clients may learn various job skills while increasing their awareness of their interests and values, and gathering data related to job search outcomes and client self-awareness.

Each week Anderson collects feedback from participants on their experiences of the program, their ideas about how he can advocate more for the program within the residential agency and local community, and their plans for using career assessment findings to foster their career development. Further, he provides outcome data (e.g., career assessment results, job search outcomes) to the agency and various stakeholders to demonstrate the program's effectiveness and gathers feedback to bring back to program participants.

Policy Advocacy

A policy is "any plan or course of action adopted by a government, political party, business organization, or the like, designed to influence and determine decisions, actions, and other matters" (Morris, 1969, p. 104). Currently, there is no one national, state, or local policy that guides and directs counseling programs across the age span. Policies emanate from various sources. Federal and state agencies, professional associations, and many other groups shape and influence policy content and direction. As a result, there is a diffuse set of policies in operation that influence and determine decisions and actions regarding the nature, structure, and content of guidance and counseling programs and the activities and services they provide.

The *public arena level* of the Advocacy Competencies suggests that counselors advocate with interventions of public information and social/political advocacy (Lewis et al., 2003). "The ultimate goal of counselor intervention at this level is to increase public awareness, affect public policy, and influence legislation" (Lee & Rodgers, 2009, p. 285). With a variety of media outlets, the counselor has the ability to communicate and disseminate information to inform the public about concerns of issues of oppression as well as other barriers, and communicate a sense of urgency for change. In addition to utilizing public information, counselors carry out social/political advocacy by using assessment data to assist with political action; gathering supporters and allies for change, joining with other supporters for change, as well as lobbying for change. In order to be effective advocates at this level, Lee and Rodgers (2009) discussed certain characteristics counselors must possess. Counselors must be strong leaders with a vision for influencing social and political action. Counselors must be skilled at collecting and using data which speaks to the change they are wishing to implement. Finally, Lee and Rodgers asserted that the counselor must have courage to act as an advocate at this level.

Given our system of regulatory entities at the local, state, and national levels and the many and various groups vying for attention and influence, it is highly unlikely that there ever will be one overall policy at any level that will guide and direct guidance and counseling programs. This, however, should not stop us from using our professional expertise to influence and shape policy at all levels. Unfortunately, our profession has attended to this important area only sporadically. The professional counseling associations, working alone or in concert, have worked hard to develop and influence legislation at state and national levels. The American Counseling Association has created an Office of Public Policy and Legislation, and the American School Counselor Association has established an Office of Research (ACA, 2011). The ACA Public Policy and Legislative Agenda for the First Session of the 112th Congress in 2011 included a mission to "[i]ncrease support for professional counselors and their clients in all appropriate Federal and State laws, regulations, and legislation" (see ACA, 2011). These offices work to send information to members about current legislation, how to communicate with elected officials about significant counseling concerns, as well as how to get involved politically in order to advocate for the counseling profession. Various documents emphasizing preferred roles and functions of professional personnel including school counselors, career counselors, vocational rehabilitation counselors, and mental health counselors have been disseminated, as have professional association position statements on topics of national, state, and local importance.

Although efforts such as these by professional organizations and others have had some impact on shaping and influencing national, state, and local policy formulation and legislation, much more needs to be done. We propose that a concerted effort be made to gather and organize student/client assessment and program legislation at all levels. We further propose that policy briefs be developed for local, state, and national decision makers and policy analysts that make the connection between the effects of guidance and counseling programs on individuals of all ages and circumstances, and the needed policies and legislation that will promote and sustain such programs.

To accomplish these proposals will require that we "build a constantly evolving knowledge base about what works and what is promising" (Schorr, Sylvester, & Dunkle, 1999, p. 27). Unfortunately, much that counselors do still is fragmented and disconnected across the age span, as are the assessment data that they collect. Also, current "public policy often tends to segment problems artificially by age group or subject matter" (Research

Using Assessment for Personal, Program, and Policy Advocacy

and Policy Committee of the Committee for Economic Development, as cited in Herr & Gysbers, 2000). In addition to building a knowledge base, in part derived from assessment data, there is a need to connect and coordinate policies on guidance and counseling based on such data across all levels of government. As Herr and Gysbers (2000, p. 274) recommended:

> There is the need for co-ordination and integration of career services across settings and government levels. Public policy at the federal level must connect with public policy at state and local levels and vice versa. Similarly, as voids in public policy are identified and life-cycle approaches are considered, counselors must be made available and their services must be coordinated. In any locale, counselors in schools, employment services, rehabilitation agencies and other settings must take each other into account, and public policy must support the systematic integration of the skills each of these counselors have, rather than divide and isolate these professionals. In this regard, employers and workplaces need to be seen as part of a continuum of career guidance and counseling programs and services, not separate from and unrelated to such provisions.

Formulating and adopting coordinated policies for guidance and counseling programs and services across all levels of government, based in part on assessment data, require substantial and sustained work, but it is work that we must undertake. To begin, counselors can use currently available assessment data to develop policy briefs to be used with decision makers and legislators. A format for a two-page policy brief might look something like the following:

- *Statement of Need.* The career, personal/social, and academic development needs of a particular group or groups are described briefly.

- *A Response.* The work of professional counselors that responds to the needs is outlined. Assessment data and research studies that demonstrate the effectiveness of this work are highlighted.

- *The Keys.* The necessary organization, structure, resources, and staffing to carry out the effective guidance and counseling work are discussed briefly.

- *Problem.* Any problems in developing and implementing effective guidance and counseling programs are presented.

- *Recommendations.* Recommendations for policy formulation and legislation, if required, are presented.

Empowering the children, adolescents, and adults of our country to face the challenges of today and tomorrow requires the strongest overall system of guidance and counseling programs and services that our nation can provide. We believe this will occur only if policies that guide and direct guidance and counseling programs and services for individuals of all ages and circumstances are based in part on sound assessment data. Thus, we urge professionals to take assessment data beyond their offices in school buildings, public or private agencies, and colleges and universities into the world of policy makers at all levels. Only then will counselors realize that one of the most important but often neglected uses of assessment data is policy advocacy.

Integrating Personal, Program, and Policy Advocacy: Case of Shasta

We will now examine personal, program, and policy advocacy in the context of the ACA Advocacy Competencies (Lewis et al., 2003) in order to demonstrate counselor effectiveness, using the case of Shasta. Shasta is a 16-year-old, multiracial, high school student with aspirations of becoming a marine biologist. She lives in an urban environment with her twin brother, mother, and grandmother. At the end of last school year, she was at the top of her class, hoping to be the first in her family to attend college. Shasta's father died in an automobile accident over the summer, and for the last few months her grades have been declining, especially in her math and science classes. Her school counselor has administered to her various career interest and skills assessments and reflected with her on her academic goals. Further, Shasta has been participating in a small group with other students who have recently experienced loss. Additionally, her school counselor referred Shasta and her family to a community agency for support to address issues pertaining to the grief and loss of her father. Unfortunately, the agency is located quite a distance from her family residence, and Shasta's mother does not drive and the nearest bus lines have been eliminated due to recent budget cuts. The family insurance does not cover counseling, so this expense would be out of pocket.

Personal Advocacy (Client/Student)

Acting with Shasta in individual counseling, the school counselor helps Shasta to recognize her strengths as a student, as highlighted using various assessments, that have allowed her to be at the top of her class. Her strengths include perseverance, courage, determination, and passion. Additionally, the school counselor helps Shasta to identify various economic and social class systems of support which can assist her in her development.

In addition to these things, the school counselor works in collaboration with Shasta to help her identify specific career goals and assess Shasta's level of college readiness. After identifying these, the school counselor uses assessments to identify Shasta's perceived barriers to achieving these goals. Additionally, the school counselor assists Shasta with accessing post-secondary options, which includes gathering college information and accessing financial resources. The school counselor, Shasta, and Shasta's mother together complete scholarship and FAFSA application forms. The school counselor also writes a separate letter to a college financial aid office outlining the unique circumstances of Shasta's current situation.

Program Advocacy (Community Collaboration and Systems Advocacy)

As a result of Shasta's situation, the school counselor became aware of a few recurring themes: access to public transportation for her students and families was becoming an increasing problem, along with access to affordable counseling services within the community. Looking specifically at access to affordable counseling services, the school counselor consulted with other school counselors in her district and mental health counselors in the community. The school counselor developed a group of counselors devoted to establishing a plan to create a system of more affordable and accessible mental health services in this urban community. Other stakeholders were invited to take part in this change effort, including doctors, lawyers, educators, and law enforcement officers dedicated to the community.

For systems advocacy, the network of stakeholders established a needs assessment which was distributed to community members inquiring about their interpretation of the need and access of mental health services in the community. The data were analyzed and, based on this, the counselors established a vision for expanding accessible and affordable mental health services in the community. This step-by-step plan included examining budgets, applying for local, state, and federal grants and other government assistance, along with enhancing collaboration and communication with insurance companies about extending their benefits packages to include better coverage for mental health services. Additionally, the network of stakeholders examined the local organizations which provide service and education to specific populations. Culturally grounded organizations such as the NAACP and the United Negro College Fund promote education and could potentially help individuals like Shasta with their college and career goals. Finally, minority student affairs offices at local colleges and universities were included in the consultation process. These offices could also help with college and career related goals, in addition to providing the possibility of a mentoring relationship with students like Shasta.

Policy Advocacy (Public Arena)

The network of stakeholders established communication via the Internet and e-mail to communicate results of the needs assessment and data about what other communities have done nationwide to establish affordable mental health care services to communities like this one. Additionally, members of the network collaborated with the local and state chapters of professional counseling associations in order to strengthen the message being communicated about affordable access to mental health services.

The network of stakeholders contacted elected officials, presenting their data, and their plan for change. They identified legislators and other policy makers who believed in their cause and who were willing to work with them to create change. The network also identified others in the legislative assembly who were familiar with this type of change process regarding mental health services in order to learn from their process of effective change.

Counseling Strategies for Personal, Program, and Policy Advocacy

The following are tips for how counselors can use the career assessment process to engage in personal, program, and policy advocacy in their work with clients/students:

Using Assessment for Personal, Program, and Policy Advocacy

- As the world of work continues to become more global, recognize the importance of incorporating technology in the career assessment process to assist in advocacy efforts.
- Understand the basic principles of the ACA Advocacy Competencies and how they relate to the career assessment process.
- Examine the counselor role in various environments (e.g., school, clinical mental health) and determine concrete ways the career assessment process might be enhanced.
- Identify the unique needs of the population served by the counselor to apply appropriate implementation strategies for the career assessment process.
- Identify barriers which may deter success of the career assessment process for the population served by the counselor and devise a plan to address such barriers.
- Remain current on career assessments. This includes understanding revised versions of assessments and research conducted on career assessments, and be aware of assessments which target specific populations.
- Consult, collaborate, and coordinate with local organizations and political forces. Garner such support to enhance the career assessment process for the client/student.
- Research program accountability literature, examine current program accountability data, and collect program accountability data which can be used to improve the career assessment process in the counseling program.

Summary

In these challenging and turbulent times assessments can play key roles in personal, program, and policy advocacy, especially when used in conjunction with the Advocacy Competencies for counselors (Lewis et al., 2003). Assessments can facilitate individuals' positive growth and development by providing them with critical information that can empower them to make informed decisions about potential life-work choices. Counselors use the Advocacy Competencies at the client/student level to enhance client/student empowerment and influence client/student advocacy. Assessments also can assist career practitioners to be accountable and to evaluate their work with their clientele. This will ensure they are providing their clientele with the best possible guidance and counseling programs and services. The community/school Advocacy Competencies include the use of community collaboration and influence systems advocacy. Finally, practitioners can inform policy makers at all levels as they seek to create sound policies to guide the development and implementation of sound guidance and counseling programs and services. The public-arena Advocacy Competencies includes using public information and enhancing social/political advocacy. Given these important roles and competencies, it is time to use assessments and assessment data to the fullest for personal, program, and policy advocacy.

Review Questions

1. What is advocacy competence?

2. In terms of personal advocacy, what must an individual know and be able to do to become self-advocates?

3. The ACA Advocacy Competencies (Lewis et al., 2003) include three levels which increase from the micro to the macro level. What are these three levels?

4. Why might counselors find it difficult to conduct program advocacy and what have training programs done to combat this?

5. How can counselors be policy advocates in the public arena?

References

American Counseling Association. (2011). *American Counseling Association Public Policy and Legislative Agenda for the First Session of the 112th Congress, 2011.* Retrieved from http://www.counseling.org/PublicPolicy/2011_ACA_PPL_Agenda.pdf

American School Counselor Association. (2012). *The ASCA national model: A framework for school counseling programs (3rd ed).* Alexandria, VA: Author.

Astramovich, R. L., & Coker, J. K. (2007). Program evaluation: The accountability bridge model for counselors. *Journal of Counseling & Development, 8*(2), 162–172.

Astramovich, R. L., Coker, J. K., & Hoskins, W. J. (2005). Training school counselors in program evaluation. *Professional School Counseling, 9,* 49-54.

Feller, R. W., & Whichard, J. (2005). *Knowledge nomads and the nervously employed: Workplace change and courageous career choices.* Austin, TX: Pro-Ed.

Friedman, T. L. (2007). *The world is flat: A brief history of the twenty-first century 3.0.* New York, NY: Farrar, Straus and Geroux.

Goodman, J., Schlossberg, N. K., & Anderson, M. L. (2011). *Counseling adults in transition: Linking practice with theory* (4th ed). New York, NY: Springer.

Gysbers, N. C. (2004). Comprehensive guidance and counseling programs: The evolution of accountability. *Professional School Counselor, 8,* 1-14.

Gysbers, N. C., & Henderson, P. (2011). *Developing and managing your school guidance and counseling program* (5th ed.). Alexandria, VA: American Counseling Association.

Gysbers, N. C., Heppner, M. J., & Johnston, J. A. (2009). *Career counseling: Process, issues, and techniques* (3rd ed.). Boston, MA: Allyn & Bacon.

Gysbers, N. C., Lapan, R. T., & Stanley, B. (2006). No fear results evaluation: The Missouri story. *ASCA School Counselor, 43,* 35-37.

Herr, E. L., & Gysbers, N. C. (2000). Career development services and related policy issues; The U.S. experience. In B. Hiebert & L. Bezanson (Eds.) *Making waves: Career development and public policy.* Proceedings from the international symposium, May 2-4, 1999. Ottawa, Canada: Canadian Career Development Foundation.

Holland, J. L. (1997). *Making vocational choices: A theory of vocational personalities and work environments* (3rd ed.). Odessa, FL: Psychological Assessment Resources.

Lapan, R. T. (2004). *Career development across the K-16 years: Bridging the present to satisfying and successful futures.* Alexandria, VA: American Counseling Association.

Lee, C. C. & Rodgers, R. A. (2009). Counselor advocacy: Affecting systemic change in the public arena. *Journal of Counseling & Development, 87,* 284-287.

Lewis, J., Arnold, M., House, R., & Toporek, R. (2003). *American Counseling Association advocacy competencies.* Retrieved from http://www.counseling.org/resources/competencies/advocacy_competencies.pdf

Morris, W. (Ed.). (1969). *The American dictionary of the English language.* Boston, MA: Houghton Mifflin.

Perepiczka, M., Chandler, N., & Becerra, M. (2011). Relationship between graduate students' statistics self-efficacy, statistics anxiety, attitude toward statistics, and social support. *The Professional Counselor: Research and Practice, 1,* 99-108.

Ratts, M. J. & Hutchins, A. M. (2009). ACA advocacy competencies: Social justice advocacy at the client/student level. *Journal of Counseling & Development, 87,* 269-275.

Schorr, L., Sylvester, K., & Dunkle, M. (1999). *Strategies to achieve a common purpose: Tools for turning good ideas into good policies.* Washington CD: Institute for Educational Leadership.

Shrestha, L. B. (2011). *The changing demographic profile of the United States.* Washington DC: Congressional Research Service, The Library of Congress.

Sink, C. A. (2009). School counselors as accountability leaders: Another call for action. *Professional School Counseling, 13,* 68-74.

Toporek, R. L., Lewis, J. A., & Crethar, H. C. (2009). Promoting systemic change through the ACA advocacy competencies. *Journal of Counseling & Development, 87,* 260-268.

84

CHAPTER 8

SELECTING CAREER ASSESSMENT INSTRUMENTS

F. Robert Wilson
Mei Tang
School of Human Services, College of Education
University of Cincinnati

Cornelia R. Wilson
College of Nursing
University of Cincinnati

Introduction

Assessment of both individuals and the environment in which they live and work is an important part of career counseling, as the keystone of career counseling is, according to Frank Parsons, to help clients find a correspondence between individuals and their environments. Parsons encouraged practitioners "to objectify interests, values and abilities through use of standardized assessment to guide people in identifying where they fit within the occupational structure" (Niles & Harris-Bowlsbey, 2013, pp. 18-19). Decades later, assessment still plays a critical role in career intervention.

The role of assessment in providing career counseling is multifaceted. First, high quality assessment can provide information about individual characteristics of clients, necessary for counselors to gain understanding of clients' needs. Secondly, the assessment process itself can facilitate self-exploration and self-awareness of clients that is very critical in career counseling. Further, assessment, used properly, can help clients expand unknown territories, and therefore, provide alternative options and choices that clients may need in their career pursuit. From an ecological perspective, behavior is contextualized, meaningful and interactional (Cook, 2012). An individual's choice of career is the same. Career development is influenced by a multitude of personal attributes and contextual, environmental, and situational factors. How an individual makes meaning of the interaction of self and environment is critical to career choice and career success. Since the dawn of trait and factor theory, assessment of individual attributes, work environments and the interactional relationship between the two has become a key focus of career assessment, assessing fitness for, satisfaction with, and likely sustainability of their career choice. Postmodern career assessment based on constructivism expanded the trait and factor model by focusing attention on empowering clients to make meaning of their own experiences and construct their own journey. From this postmodern perspective, the conducting of a thorough assessment is, in itself, a career intervention for the client.

Since World War II, testing has become a booming business in the United States and elsewhere. Multiple tests have been produced for a wide variety of assessment applications. Practitioners face a challenge in selecting the best possible tests for their clients. To help career counselors select tests, this chapter will review critical elements in selecting a career assessment instrument and present an organized process to help counselors decide what tests should be chosen. The chapter also provides sources of information for assessment, including a guide to the test reviews included in this book, and discusses practical issues which arise in selecting an instrument. Although this chapter focuses primarily on selecting quantitative assessments, many considerations listed may apply to qualitative assessment tools.

Factors to Consider in Selecting a Career Assessment Instrument

In choosing a career assessment tool, multiple factors need to be considered in order to best serve clients' needs. These factors are critical because if these factors are neglected or not addressed appropriately, the assessment could be, at minimum, failing to accomplish its mission to help clients, or, at worst, even harmful to clients. Therefore, when choosing a career assessment it is important for counselors to carefully evaluate its purpose, client and counselor factors related to the instrument, technical quality of the test, and the limitations of the testing context/environment.

Purpose for the Assessment

The purposes for using assessment in the career counseling process are varied and depend on the goals that counselors and clients have identified for their work. There are four important considerations to understanding the purpose of career assessment. First, it is necessary to consider whether assessment could assist clients to meet their goals for seeking help. For instance, high school students might need assessment to increase self-understanding and to facilitate exploration of career options. On the other hand, a laid-off worker may benefit from career assessment to plan for reemployment. Secondly, it is ethically imperative to consider the client's welfare when making a decision about career assessment (American Counseling Association [ACA], 2005). Thirdly, counselors should follow the principle of nonmaleficence and ensure that administration of a career assessment instrument would not cause harm to the client's psychological wellbeing. Finally, it is important to consider the quality of the assessment tool chosen. In other words, counselors should not give a test to clients unless the test has reasonable scientific merit (a detailed discussion of evaluating the scientific merit of an assessment tool will be presented later in this chapter) (Niles & Harris-Bowlsbey, 2013). In sum, the purpose of using assessment needs to be carefully evaluated before taking actions to select and administer the tests.

Once the use of tests is determined helpful, counselors need to review existing assessment tools and find the instrument or inventory that matches the purposes identified jointly with clients. It is important to keep in mind that data generated from the testing process should provide the information that clients need to know in their career exploration. If no acceptable formal tests are appropriate to provide the information needed for a specific career exploration task, alternative informal assessment tools may be most beneficial.

Client Factors

Whether the selected instrument or assessment tool can adequately generate the desired information depends, in part, on the degree to which (a) the client approaches the task with a constructive test taking attitude, (b) understands the instructions and the item content, and (c) responds to the questions completely, consistently, and accurately. While all three are important, perhaps the most important is client attitude.

Assessment efforts succeed when clients approach the test with an attitude of openness and intent to do well. With assessments of aptitude, knowledge, and skill, this means the client puts forward their best effort; with assessments of personal characteristics and traits, it means that the client answers the test's self-disclosure questions openly and honestly. To help clients approach the test with constructive attitude, building rapport is paramount and, during the administration of the test, counselors should observe whether the client is alert, attentive, and concentrating on the assessment tasks at hand.

But even with a constructive attitude, to succeed, the client must understand the instructions and be able to read and comprehend the test's items. Counselors should carefully walk clients through the instructions, testing comprehension of the instructions to insure the client really understands how to take the test. It is of equal importance for the counselor to assess whether the client can read and comprehend the items of the test given the language in which the test is written, given the reading level at which it is pegged, and given the client's cultural experience. As Leong and Hartung (2000) and Flores, Spanierman, and Obasi (2003) have noted, with the increasing cultural diversity of our clients, close attention to the meaning clients derive from test items and the meaning they make of test results is critical regardless of whether the assessment instrument measures personal characteristics or aptitudes and abilities. In order to select an assessment tool that accommodates the client's educational and cultural background, counselors need to carefully evaluate the constructs and psychometric properties of tests by conducting a thorough review of the test manual and relevant published research articles. Only by close study of the test's purpose and physical and psychometric properties can a counselor determine whether the test is a good fit to the age, cultural background, and reading ability of the intended clients.

If the client approaches the task with a constructive attitude and the test is a good fit with the client's needs, abilities, and cultural background, it is likely that the client will be able to respond to the test questions completely, consistently, and accurately. Completeness is easily tested by scanning the client's answer sheet for blank items. Obviously, for any given scale, unanswered items lower the maximum score the client can earn on the scale. With aptitude and achievement tests, the consequence is obvious. With scales measuring personality traits or clinical symptoms, depending on whether higher scores mean greater health or greater disturbance, unanswered items may make a client appear to be more healthy or more disturbed. Conscientious counselors also use whatever information is available to judge whether the client has answered the questions consistently and accurately. Sophisticated measures of psychological characteristics often include scales to assess consistency and truthfulness. For tests that do not provide such validity scales, counselors may make inferences from knowledge they have about the context of testing (e.g., might the client see it as being to his or her advantage to fake being more unhealthy or incompetent than he or she really is) or from observations of the client's behavior while he or she was taking the test.

Counselor Factors

But successful assessment does not rest solely on the characteristics of the client. Assessment is based in the interpersonal relationship between client and counselor; thus counselor factors are equally important. In choosing to conduct career assessment with clients, counselors must attend scrupulously to the client's welfare. From test selection, to test administration, to test interpretation, the counselor must assess goodness of fit between the assessment tools and process with the client's experience and meaning-making. For the counselor, it begins with his or her own training and mindset. Providing a guiding structure to help clients understand the purpose for assessment and to help the client make meaning from their experience is easiest when the counselor has developed a clear, coherent theoretical approach to career assessment and career guidance. While the specific procedures selected for assessment depend on the purposes of intervention, they also depend on the counselor's theoretical orientation and conceptual framework (Lonborg & Hackett, 2006; Lowman & Carson, 2000, p. 125). Naturally, framing one's theoretical orientation is a developmental process. Through coursework and continuing education, counselors build their framework and keep abreast of current developments in the career assessment and guidance field.

For the counselor, career assessment can become a routine activity. One may learn a *patter*, a scripted speech one makes when introducing and explaining an assessment tool. The benefit of a scripted speech is that important information is not forgotten. The risk is that one may not be psychologically present to the client and may miss cues necessary for evaluating the client's alertness, attention, and attitude. While career assessment may be routine for the counselor, it is a new and perhaps frightening experience for the client. Out of caring for the welfare of the client, counselors must monitor themselves to insure the establishment and maintenance of rapport and psychological presence with the client while also maintaining technical competence in administering the assessment.

Perhaps the most important of the counselor factors is the counselor's ability to help the client make meaning from the assessment experience. As with test administration, one may develop a scripted patter by which one describes the outcomes of the assessment. While it is important to be technically accurate in reporting and making inferences from test scores, it is even more important to explore with the client the meaning they make from the interpretation. Active listening and empathy are crucial. Test findings may confirm what the client has always thought, awaken frightening realizations, dash cherished dreams, or awaken hope for a brighter future. Psychological presence is required to hear accurately the meaning being made by the client and help the client profit from the assessment experience.

Technical Quality of the Test

To ensure that an assessment tool will serve the intended purpose, critical evaluation of the technical quality of tests is crucial. While in training, counselors may have been introduced to the theory and process of test construction and validation, but may now require additional training in psychometrics to advance their skills in critical evaluation. Just as it is important for counselors to constantly update their knowledge of career development theory and techniques, continuing education and professional development in test evaluation is part of a counselor's ethical responsibility. As with so many issues in counseling, consultation with other professionals who have expertise in test evaluation is encouraged. Key elements in judging the technical quality of career assessment tools will be described later in this chapter.

Limitations of the Testing Context and Environment

When selecting a career assessment tool, one must insure that its use is feasible given the the context in which the test is to be used and the resources necessary for its purchase and administration. Among the existing assessment tools, counselors need to find a test that can serve the intended purpose and at the same time is available, accessible and affordable. Can both the counselor and the clients afford the time required to administer the test? Does the counselor have access to the kind of testing environment required by the test? If the test is designed for group administration, will the counselor be able to gain access to naturally occurring groups in which to administer it or will the counselor have to choreograph the group administration? If, however, the test is to be individually administered, are qualified personnel available to administer it? An excellent instrument acclaimed by the reviewers may not necessarily be the best for a particular client for a variety of reasons (e.g., not matching the purpose of assessment for this client, not providing the information needed for this client's career exploration, or requiring reading skills that are beyond client's ability). Further, although for some assessment purposes, there are free tests available, most tests cost money. Whether the agency or the clients can afford the costs associated with testing and whether the potential benefits warrant the costs should be carefully considered before making clients take the tests. It is again unethical to coerce or make clients to take a test without their informed consent. It is the responsibility of counselors to find an assessment tool that satisfies as many as possible of the requirements for good practice in testing.

Resources for Information for Assessments

Formal and Informal Assessment in Career Counseling

Historically, career assessment has concentrated on four domains: (a) individual preferences to career related attributes such as interests and values; (b) individual aptitudes and abilities or skills; (c) individual personality traits; and (d) characteristics pertaining to career decision-making (e.g., style, beliefs, barriers, and self-efficacy) (Gati & Asullin-Peretz, 2011). As career development theories expand to address the impact of our ever-changing social and economic structures, career assessment should strive to be a continual and expanding effort to evaluate fit between individuals and career contexts (Lock & Hogan, 2000).

In addition to formal career assessment tools, career counselors may also use informal assessment tools that lack the psychometric properties and characteristic of standardized assessments but could contribute to a client's personal meaning-making (Niles & Harris-Bowlsbey, 2013). For example, career counselors may use checklists, game play, career fantasy exercises, interviewing, or card sorts to stimulate conversation with their clients. Some informal assessment tools have been shown to have positive impact on clients' increased self-understanding and meaning-making (Schultheiss, 2005; Whiston & Rahardja, 2005). Unlike formal assessments in which clients' responses are compared to normative groups, informal assessments tend to focus on meaning-making and facilitating clients' self-understanding through interviews or constructing narratives. The process for selection of these types of tests is similar to that taken in selecting formal assessments: evaluating the degree of fit with the purpose of the assessment, the client being assessed, the counselor's skill in using the approach, and the feasibility of its use. Informal assessments (e.g., qualitative assessment, card sorts) are discussed later in the text.

Sources of Information

There are a variety of resources available to help counselors locate tests, test reviews, and research on test psychometrics. Key publishers of educational, career, and psychological tests include: Consulting Psychologists Press, Educational Testing Services, Psychological Assessment Resources, Pearson Assessments, and Western Psychological Services. Counselors may obtain the information via the publishers' websites or catalogs.

Another source for either published or non-published tests is the host of scholarly journals in the fields of assessment and measurement which provide test reviews and application guides (Drummond & Jones, 2010). For example, *Measurement and Evaluation in Counseling and Development, Educational and Psychological Measurement, The Career Development Quarterly,* and *The Journal of Career Assessment* are rich sources of current research on career and other test instruments. Similarly, scholarly databases such as PsychInfo, ERIC, and Psychological Abstracts can help with locating tests, test reviews, and psychometric research as well. Professional organizations such as the Association for Assessment and Research in Counseling, the National Career Development Association, and Society of Vocational Psychology publish newsletters that offer up-to-date information related to new test development and test reviews.

The most comprehensive clearinghouse of test information is the *Mental Measurements Yearbook,* published by Buros Institute of Mental Measurement. It provides descriptive information, expert reviews, and recent research on a wide variety of tests. The yearbook's online version provides a flexible search function to ease user access. *Tests in Print,* another comprehensive list of available tests, provides basic information about tests, but does not provide detailed reviews as does the *Mental Measurements Yearbook.*

Technical Information on Assessments for Practitioners

As stated in the ACA *Code of Ethics* (ACA, 2005), "the primary purpose of educational, psychological, and career assessment is to provide measurements that are valid and reliable in either comparative or absolute terms. These include, but are not limited to, measurements of ability, personality, interest, intelligence, achievement, and performance" (Section E.1.a., p. 12). Counselors using such measurements are responsible for all aspects of test selection and use. In charging counselors with this responsibility, the ethical code describes the scope of responsibility broadly: "Counselors are responsible for the appropriate application, scoring, interpretation, and use of assessment instruments relevant to the needs of the client, whether they score and interpret such assessments themselves or use technology or other services" (Section E.2.b., p. 12).

Regardless of circumstance or ecological level assessed (c.f. Bronfenbrenner, 1977), counselors are responsible for the consequences of their testing. Whether using a test to guide or make decisions about an individual client, using testing to assess family, peers, or siblings in the client's microsystem, using test results to describe or influence institutional policy or behavior in exosystemic environments, or using test results to influence laws or socioeconomic conditions within the macrosystem, a counselor's responsibility remains the same: "Counselors responsible for decisions involving individuals or policies that are based on assessment results [must] have a thorough understanding of educational, psychological, and career measurement, including validation criteria, assessment research, and guidelines for assessment development and use" (ACA, 2005, Section E.2.c., p. 12).

Measurement, according to Stevens (1959), "is the assignment of numerals to events or objects according to rule" (p. 25). At the most concrete level, when a counselor administers a test to a client, the counselor gets a set of scores in return. Before attempting to imbue those numbers with meaning, the counselor must have first investigated the psychometric properties of the test being used to determine what valid inferences can be made from the test's scores. As the ACA *Code of Ethics* (ACA, 2005) states, "counselors carefully consider the validity, reliability, psychometric limitations, and appropriateness of instruments when selecting assessments" (Section E.6.a., p. 12).

Reliability

Evaluating whether a test is suitable for a counselor's purposes begins with study of the reliability of its scores. When a test yields a single score, as is true for the Beck Depression Inventory and other "single-trait" symptom and attitude scales and "single-ability" aptitude and achievement tests, it is easy to think of its reliability coefficient as being a measure of test reliability. Thompson (2003) has argued that reliability coefficients are always an estimate of score reliability and should not be referred to as reflecting test reliability. Thus, with tests that assess multiple dimensions, reliability should be reported for each separate score produced by the test.

Classical quantification of reliability. For a score to be a valid measure of a given property of an entity in a given context, the score must first be reliable. Grounded in the classical theory of true and error scores, reliability has traditionally been studied in four ways: the stability of a test's scores across repeated measurement; the equivalence of a test's scores to test scores produced by measurement with a parallel test administered concurrently; the equivalence of a test's scores to test scores produced by a parallel test administered at a later time; and the homogeneity of the items which comprise the test (Allen & Yen, 1979). *Stability* of test scores is typically studied by measuring a group of individuals and then retesting them after a suitable lapse of time (i.e., test-retest reliability). The correlation between the two sets of measurements reflects the degree to which

Selecting Career Assessment Instruments

the scores have been stable. The law of entropy suggests that test scores will be less stable over longer time intervals. In selecting a test to be used in a test-retest situation, a counselor should seek evidence that scores produced by the test being evaluated have sufficient stability over the counselor's intended time-lapse interval. Score equivalence is assessed when a test has been designed to have equivalent forms (referred to as parallel tests) which are expected to yield equivalent means, equivalent variances, high correlation with one another, and equivalent correlations with other measures. Rules for whether tests are truly parallel tests are exacting (c.f. Allen & Yen, 1979). Studies of *equivalence* and *stability* combine examination of form equivalence with assessment of score stability over time to yield a very stringent estimate of alternate test forms, *Homogeneity* or internal consistency of a test's items, most useful when the test has been rationally constructed to measure a specific criterion or well-defined theoretical construct, reflects the degree to which the items of the test may be judged to be measuring a single underlying construct. Methods for assessing item homogeneity include the split-half method, the Kuder and Richardson (1937) formulas, Hoyt's (1941) analysis of variance method, and Cronbach's (1951) coefficient alpha. Modern methods for the study of test performance include generalizability theory; Cronbach, Rajaratnam's, and Gleser (1963) extension of classical theory; and Rasch based generalizability theory (Bond & Fox, 2007).

Equally important, a counselor selecting a test for decision making must consider the reliability of decisions made from the test's scores. For tests being used to render dichotomous classification of clients (e.g., pass-fail, admit-reject, retain-dismiss), the reliability of the decision is of greater importance than the reliability of the test scores which underpin the decision. The counselor should seek evidence of the test's *sensitivity*—its ability to identify the presence of a property and its *specificity*—its ability to identify the absence of the property (Loong, 2003). Examination of the area under the receiver operating curve or AUROC is helpful in determining the consequences of choosing various cut-scores (McFall & Treat, 1999).

Interpreting reliability coefficients. The interpretation of a reliability coefficient depends on (a) the degree of stability we expect in the capacity, aptitude, ability, or trait being measured; and (b) the kind of reliability being assessed. Some human characteristics, such as intelligence, are conceptualized as highly stable traits, showing little variance over variability from time to time and situation to situation. Other characteristics, such as state anxiety and state depression, appear to be more context-dependent and show more variance over time or across situations. In general, we expect career assessment scales to evidence high internal consistency reliability (item homogeneity) because we expect that all items in a scale to be measuring the same underlying construct. Likewise, we expect alternate forms reliability (form equivalence) to be high as we compare scale to scale across forms because the logic underlying the construction of alternate forms requires that all alternate forms of a scale measure the same underlying construct. Test-retest reliability (score stability), however, is a volatile measure of reliability. High values for test-retest reliability arise when the property being measured has high inherent stability and when the persons being assessed are not being affected by external influence; low values for such estimates of stability are expected when the underlying property is unstable and when the clients are influenced by powerful external forces known to affect the property being assessed. Thus, we expect greater score stability in controlled conditions over short time intervals than in uncontrolled conditions over longer time intervals.

Since the magnitude of a score's reliability sets a ceiling for assessment of its validity (Sechrest, 1984), one wants scores with high reliability reflecting a relative absence of error variance. When comparing groups, a value of .70 is commonly thought to be a minimally acceptable estimate of item homogeneity for measures of personality variables, with a more stringent value of .80 being minimally acceptable for measures of aptitude or ability (DeVellis, 1991). Naturally, even more stringent standards must be applied when a test is being used for making decisions about individual clients.

Reliability is defined as the proportion of total score variance which is true score variance. Since under classical true-score test theory, a test score presumed to be the sum of a true plus an error component and thus total test variance is equal to true score variance plus error variance, its estimate is approached by first getting an estimate of the size of the error variance and then calculating: R_{xx} = (Total Variance − Error Variance) / Total Variance (Sechrest, 1984). That the reliability coefficient is a "proportion of variance" statistic is most obvious when Cronbach's alpha is used to estimate the item homogeneity of a scale, but it is equally true when a correlation coefficient is calculated to assess test-retest stability or alternate-forms equivalence. Since a reliability coefficient reflects the proportion of true score variance in a test score, it is inappropriate to square a reliability coefficient and interpret this value as a coefficient of determination.

Validity

Validity is a property of argument, not a property of scores. The basic question is, "Is it valid to infer that when measured in this context, a client of this kind has this property to this degree?"

The property. The common and woefully understated definition for validity is that the test assesses what it claims to assess; e.g., that a test labeled as an anxiety scale actually measures anxiety. Three key approaches have been developed for demonstrating that it is valid to argue that a particular test yields scores that measure the intended property: content validity, criterion-related validity, and construct validity. Content validity is studied by employing a panel of subject matter experts to review the items of a test and judge the degree to which each item in the test is essential for measuring the property to be measured. These subject matter experts may also be employed to determine whether the items in the test constitute a representative sampling of the sorts of items the test should have included. Since Lawshe (1975) first proposed a method for quantifying subject-matter expert judgments of *content validity,* it is common for researchers to report summary statistics and their statistical significance for claims of a test's content validity. In some high stakes testing situations, non-expert judges are used to evaluate its face validity to determine whether the test looks like it ought to measure what it claims to measure. Although the judgment of non-expert judges cannot be used as evidence for making valid inference from scores, information from studies of face validity may be helpful in choosing from among tests yielding equivalent expert-judgment content validity to minimize risk of litigation in high stakes testing situations. In situations where there is an identifiable criterion measure for the property to be measured, studies of criterion-related validity may be conducted.

Criterion-related validity is established by studying the statistical relationship between scores from the test in question and a criterion measure. These studies may look at concurrent measurements *(concurrent validity)* or measurements with a lapse of time between measurement by the test and collection of the criterion measure *(predictive validity).* The careful counselor will note whether the time lapse in the validation studies corresponds to the time lapse expected between measurement with the predictor test and collection of the criterion measure in the counselor's real-world measurement situation. When there is no appropriate criterion measure available, a test validator must rely on amassing evidence that the test's scores change according to the theory of the construct the test was created to assess.

Construct validity is never confirmed by a single study; it is demonstrated by repeated evaluation of whether the test scores conform in the direction and in the magnitude of association predicted by the theory of the construct. Such studies may be associational studies of the relationship between the test's scores and scores from tests to which the experimental test should be related *(convergent validity)* or should not be related *(divergent validity).* They may also involve comparisons of groups theoretically expected to differ in their possession of the property to be assessed or experimental studies of differences between experimental groups in which change in the level of the property has been theoretically induced by the experimental conditions and control groups not experiencing the experimental manipulation. Analysis of internal structure of a test is also employed to confirm that the items within an instrument cluster in the manner predicted by theory *(factorial validity).*

The client. Clients differ in a multitude of ways. "Counselors are cautious when selecting assessments for culturally diverse populations to avoid the use of instruments that lack appropriate psychometric properties for the client population" (ACA, 2005, E.6.c., p. 12). Part of a counselor's responsibility in test selection is assuring that the test to be used has been studied in the population from which the counselor's client arose. Well-publicized questions have been raised about whether various tests evidence racial, cultural, socioeconomic, and gender bias. A counselor may find research evidence that a test score has predictive value when assessing the career interests of white youth from middle and upper income level families but has little value in assessing such interests among black youth who grew up in impoverished circumstances. Careful examination is required to ferret out evidence that the arguments made from the test scores are valid for the kind of clients the counselor intends to test.

The context. The ethical counselor recognizes that a test must be administered in a manner consistent with the context in which the validity of test score inferences was studied and the procedures followed during its administration. The ACA *Code of Ethics* (ACA, 2005) is specific: "Counselors administer assessments under the same conditions that were established in their standardization (E.7.a., p. 12). The standards continue, "When assessments are not administered under standard conditions, as may be necessary to accommodate clients with disabilities, or when unusual behavior or irregularities occur during the administration, those conditions are noted in interpretation, and the results may be designated as invalid or of questionable validity" (E.7.c., p. 12). In some testing contexts, clients may be motivated to present themselves as more knowledgeable, skilled, or healthy than they are (referred to as *under-reporting* or *faking good);* in others, clients may present themselves as more uninformed, unskilled, or unhealthy (referred to as *over-reporting* or *faking bad).* High stakes testing situations in which a person stands to gain (e.g., gain entry to a desired opportunity, earn a concrete reward) or lose (e.g., be refused entry to a desired opportunity, fail to get a concrete reward, or lose a benefit already obtained) according to test performance amplify client tendencies to present themselves differently than they truly are. In any assessment battery, note should be taken as to whether the battery's scales include scales for detecting lack of completeness, client unreliability, or client invalidity in responding.

Interpreting validity coefficients. Studies of validity fall into two broad categories: (a) studies of the degree to which a scale's score correlates well with those variables to which theory suggests it should be related (or fails to be correlated with those variables to which theory suggests it should not), and (b) studies of the degree to which groups of people who by virtue of known differences between them or by virtue of experimental manipulations done to them evidence score differences consistent with theoretical expectation. To interpret correlation coefficients, one examines magnitude, direction, and likelihood of a correlation of the magnitude observed having arisen by chance. Interpretation of the magnitude of a correlation is aided by computing the coefficient of determination (accomplished by squaring the correlation). For example, the coefficient of determination for a correlation of .70 is .49, indicating that the two variables share 49% common variance.

Assessment experts view validity coefficients as being on a continuous scale and, although higher coefficients are more desirable, setting an absolute level for acceptability is not possible (Aamodt, 2007). In its guidebook on testing and assessment, the U.S. Department of Labor, Employment and Training Administration (2000) suggests that validity coefficients above .35 (12% shared variance) are deemed "very beneficial", whereas those below .11 (1% shared variance) are "unlikely to be useful." As with reliability, the greater the potential adverse impact, especially on individual clients, the more stringent should be one's standard for the acceptability of a validity coefficient.

The direction of a correlation is indicated by its sign. A correlation bearing a plus (+) sign indicates direct correlation (increase in the value of one variable is associated with increase in the value of the other). A correlation bearing a minus (–) sign indicates an inverse correlation (increase in the value of one variable is associated with decrease in the value of the other). Thus, in a group of people standing in a room with a ceiling, the people's weight in pounds will be directly (positively) related to their height measured as the distance from the floor to the top of their heads, but inversely (negatively) related to their height measured as the distance from the top of their head to the ceiling.

Finally, the likelihood that a correlation of the magnitude observed could have arisen by chance is assessed by statistical test. Formulas for testing the statistical significance of a correlation and tabled values for such tests are presented in most popular statistics texts. As a general rule, correlations of larger magnitude are less likely to have arisen by chance than those of smaller magnitude but weak correlation may be found statistically significant while correlations of large magnitude may fail to achieve significance. It all depends on sample size. With smaller samples, coefficients of larger magnitude are required to achieve significance than is true with larger samples. In the social sciences, the typical level of significance chosen is .05. However, in high risk or high stakes situations one might insist on a more stringent criterion for significance, such as .01, .005, or .001. Thus, in summary, to judge the value of a validity coefficient, one must determine whether the coefficient is of sufficient magnitude to be significant at an acceptable level of confidence, has directionality consistent with expectation, and represents sufficient common variance to be educationally or psychologically meaningful given the context of the testing.

Interpreting studies of group difference relies on the same logic as is used in interpreting correlations between variables: one is concerned with the direction and magnitude of the group differences and the likelihood that such difference could have arisen by chance. Thompson (2003) has pointed out that three different views of significance must be examined: "statistical" significance, "practical" significance, and "clinical" significance. Did the groups being compared differ in the direction suggested by one's theory of the property being measured? What is the likelihood that a difference of that magnitude could have arisen by chance? Is the difference observed of sufficient magnitude to be educationally or psychologically meaningful? Did the change observed reflect movement from a state of deficit or ill health to a state of completeness or health? Once again, sample size is critical.

Statistical significance. With large samples, small differences may be "statistically" significant at one's chosen level of confidence and yet so small as to be essentially meaningless. With very small samples, a difference of sufficient magnitude to be meaningful may not be large enough to exceed chance expectations. It is all a matter of statistical power, a measure of the ability to detect true difference, and power is a function of sample size, the size of the difference one wishes to detect, and the level of confidence deemed acceptable for the study. The most useful studies are those in which the groups to be compared are comprised of sufficient people to have the power to detect differences of a clinically meaningful size.

Practical significance. Once assured that the differences observed exceed chance expectation, the next step is to determine whether they are of sufficient magnitude to have real-world impact. Examination of effect sizes (e.g., Cohen's d, η^2, ω^2) can assist in evaluating the "practical" significance of group differences and a single group's change over time.

Clinical significance. Clinicians in the health care professions are concerned with whether change in individuals and groups can be judged to be "clinically" significant—that treatment has rendered them indistinguishable from normal individuals for those characteristics for which they were receiving treatment (Kendall, 1999). By extension, "clinically" significant thresholds can be established for tests of knowledge and skill. To determine "clinical" significance, one computes a Reliable Change Index (RCI) to determine whether a score has changed sufficiently to be considered reliable change and then examines whether the score also crossed a pre-established threshold for health or competence. ACORN, a collaborative outcomes resource network, has prepared an Excel utility which may be accessed from their website to calculate the RCI and clinical cutoff score for any outcome measure (http://www.psychoutcomes.org/bin/view/OutcomesMeasurement/ReliableChangeIndex).

Norms

Test scores, especially those arising from educational, psychological, and career assessments, rarely provide absolute measures of the property being assessed. However, they do provide a basis for judging relative performance—the person's standing relative to others. Although in some testing settings (for example, ability and achievement testing), the individual's performance is compared to a priori criteria for performance. In the fields of career and mental health counseling, a person's performance is typically judged by comparing it to test norms (scores yielded by testing groups of individuals drawn from relevant reference groups), which enables the counselor to determine client's relative performance compared to the norm group. Depending on the type of test, norms may be established for estimating a client's global level of functioning, developing a descriptive profile across facets of client functioning (as in interest and personality assessment), or evaluating the client's rate of development in a specific domain of functioning (MacCluskie, 2009). As with studies of validity, in evaluating a test's norms, a counselor must attend to whether the norms are relevant and representative.

Relevance. In evaluating a test's norms, the counselor must consider whether the test was normed by studying the test's performance in a population that is relevant to the counselor's purposes. If a counselor wants to know how an African American client's career interests differ from other African Americans, the counselor will need norms based on a sample of African Americans. Whether drawn from the test's manual or from published research, using norms that do not adequately represent the population to which the test selector wishes to compare the client will result in giving the client misleading feedback (Murphy & Davidshofer, 1988). Before making a norm based interpretation of a client's scores, the counselor must evaluate whether the normative sample was drawn from a relevant population.

Representativeness. Even if the normative population is the correct one for a user's purposes, the sample drawn from that population could be inadequate. While the science of sampling has evolved and now may involve highly sophisticated techniques, even novice professionals can form a judgment about whether the sample drawn from the population of interest is likely to be representative. How large is the sample compared to the size of the population? Was the sample assembled by random selection or was the sample based on cooperativeness and convenience of the participants? Were relevant variables (e.g., age, gender, ethnicity, socioeconomic status, geographic locale) considered in assembling the sample? Even good norms can become stale. While a counselor's clients evolve with unfolding changes in their surrounding social world, test norms do not change unless intentionally re-developed. Norming is an expensive, exhausting process; developers of even the most widely used educational, psychological, and career development tests, re-norm tests only infrequently (Murphy & Davidshofer, 1988). In selecting tests, it is the ethical responsibility of the counselor to evaluate the relevance and representativeness of test norms.

Test Review Structure

In subsequent chapters of this book, test reviews will be provided for a wide variety of career assessment instruments. These reviews are structured to provide pertinent information and resources to assist with the assessment selection process. Additional information about the assessment (e.g., publisher/author name and contact information, publication dates, available forms, computer software options, costs) is presented before each test review.

Test reviews include four major sections: Description, Technical Considerations, General Utility and Evaluation, and References and Additional Resources. For the Technical Considerations section, quantitative and qualitative assessment reviews provide different types of information given their respective characteristics.

Description. The test review will identify the purpose of the instrument and describe the physical characteristics of the test including (a) the stated purpose for which the test was designed and use for which it was intended; (b) a description of the test, its content, the design of its items, and the scores which it yields; (c) the practical features of the test including the legibility, attractiveness, convenience, and durability of the test, and its administrative and timing requirements; (d) the age and grade levels for which the test was constructed; (e) languages into which the test has been translated; and (e) the use to which counselors might put the test.

Technical considerations. The description section is followed by the core of the test review. For quantitative assessment reviews, a thorough analysis will be provided of indicators of the reliability and validity of the scores yielded by the test and, when available, the nature of and quality of the test norms. For qualitative assessment reviews, the theory driving the development of the tool in addition to evidence of its rigor based on qualitative assessment criteria (McMahon, Patton, & Watson, 2003) are presented.

General utility and evaluation. Finally, the test review will provide an evaluation of the general utility of the test, including discussion of (a) the usefulness of the manual, and (b) comments made by other reviewers of the test, concluding with a global evaluation of the test. Occasionally, the test reviewer may provide additional comments about unique qualities of the test, its construction, or its psychometrics.

References and additional resources. References are provided to document sources and assist the counselor in pursuing investigation of original sources cited in the review. Additionally, supplemental resources such as helpful texts or websites may be included.

Practical Issues in Selecting an Instrument

Searching for and selecting an assessment instrument is a crucial step in successful assessment. A counselor must determine that a test is valid for the counselor's intended purposes. Practical considerations include identifying the purpose and context for the assessment; identifying the skill level of the professionals and staff who are to administer the instrument and interpret the scores produced by the assessment; identifying the budget for the assessment, including monetary and non-monetary cost ceilings; surveying the field of plausible instruments and developing a short list of likely candidates; obtaining sample copies of the tests and their user's manuals and conducting a thorough review of their documentation of quality; and finally selecting the instrument to use. Guidelines for test selection may be found in the *Code of Fair Testing Practices in Education* (Joint Committee on Testing Practices, 2004). Certain practical problems in selection deserve greater detail.

Identifying Purposes for Testing

Counselors are to identify the purpose for the assessment including the sorts of people who are to be assessed, the setting in which the assessment is to be conducted, and the specific uses to be made of the test results. Is the test to be used in a high-stakes situation where decisions will be made about people on the basis of their test performance? Is the test to be used in educational or counseling situations to diagnose problems and plan for formative or remedial interventions? *The purposes should drive the test selection; the tests available should not drive the creation of purpose.*

Ensuring Test Use is Within One's Scope of Practice

Before selecting a test, a counselor must be sure that use of the test is within the scope of practice of those who will be ultimately responsible for using it. Identify the skill level of the staff members who will be administering and interpreting the tests. As evidenced by the level system used by many test publishers to control access by prospective test users to assessment instruments, individually administered tests of intelligence and personality typically require more extensive training and supervised experience than group administered tests. Test publishers often categorize tests according to the training required to purchase and use them. Typically, requirements are set for level of academic degree held and amount of specific training in psychological assessment completed. In some instances permission for use of a test is extended to individuals who will be working under the direct supervision of a professional who has the appropriate level of education and training. Counselors must also be familiar with state regulations regarding use of tests in counseling. In some states, counselors face severe limitations on which tests, if any, they may purchase or use. The National Fair Access Coalition on Testing (FACT) monitors restrictions placed on the use of tests by counselors and advocates for employing demonstrated competency in assessment and testing rather than guild membership as the criterion for test use (c.f., http://www.fairaccess.org).

Ensuring the Test Fits the Counselor's Purpose

Counselors are required to evaluate the quality of instruments used in assessments. A useful strategy is to first survey available instruments and methodologies that address the intended assessment purpose, create a short list of candidate instruments, and then exercise due diligence by thoroughly reviewing available literature. Then, it is critical to attend to whether the published psychometric studies were produced only by the test's author or accompanied by studies produced by researchers with no vested interest in the product. In addition to this guide to career assessment instruments, standard references include the *Mental Measurements Yearbook* series published through the Buros Center for Testing, now in its 19th edition (Carlson, & Geisinger, 2012), and *Tests in Print* (Murphy, Spies, & Plake, 2006).

Ensuring that the Test is "Within Budget"

The expense of a test can be measured by several metrics: time and staff required to administer the test; time required to score and interpret the test; financial cost associated with storing materials, administering, scoring, interpreting, and communicating the test's results; and the impact on the nature of the client/counselor relationship. A test with excellent psychometrics may have to be removed from consideration if it takes too long to administer, score, and interpret; if it is cost prohibitive by the institution or the clients who will have to pay for it; or if its use changes the client/counselor relationship in unacceptable ways.

Issues of Internet-Based Assessment

With the widespread Internet use and advanced media technology, online testing in a variety of forms becomes increasingly accessible to a large number of individuals. While online testing certainly has advantages such as easy and timely access, cost effectiveness, and reports available to clients in quick and visual friendly fashion, there are several concerns about use of Internet-based career assessment. One issue is the questionable psychometric qualities found in some Internet available tests, especially self-help online assessments. The other issue is confidentiality (Sampson & Lumsden, 2000). To reject use of online testing is simply not realistic in the context of the digitalized world of today. Rather, more research should be conducted to improve the quality of Internet-based assessment and to provide best practice models (Oliver & Whiston, 2000). Meanwhile,

Selecting Career Assessment Instruments

counselors should educate themselves to expand knowledge about available online testing tools and integrate clients' self-help assessment results into career counseling intervention. As Gati and Asulin-Peretz (2000) argued, online career assessment ought to complement not compete with face-to-face assessment. The same principles of selecting assessment in traditional format should apply to choosing an online test. The additional consideration is that counselors need to ensure that clients have the computer and internet accessibility to utilize the online testing. Internet-based career assessment was discussed in Chapter 4 in this text.

Counseling Strategies for Selecting Career Assessment Instruments

In summary, the following are some brief suggestions to help you in preparing for assessment, conducting assessment, interpreting the results of assessment, and evaluating an assessment program. These tips were drawn from the American Psychological Association (2012), the Joint Committee on Testing Practices (2004), and Krieshok and Black (2009).

Preparing for Assessment

- Know the legal, ethical, and professional standards for conducting career assessments. Know and comply with your scope of practice.
- Study both theories of career development and theories of normal and abnormal personal/social development.
- Develop a clear, coherent theoretical framework for your career counseling.
- Keep current with the literature on career and personal/social counseling; obtain advanced training and supervised experience when necessary.
- Keep current on the standards and technical skills necessary for evaluating the psychometric properties of assessment tools.
- Develop a clear statement of purpose for your use of career assessment instruments within your counseling practice.
- Conduct a thorough environmental scan to determine the kind of assessment procedures that will fit with the clients and the resources and limitations of your assessment environment (e.g., types of clients to be assessed; relevant information available in client files; level of support for testing in your assessment environment; skill level of potential test administrators; resources available to support the purchase, administration, scoring, and interpretation of tests).
- Conduct a thorough search for assessment tools that will accomplish your purpose and fit within the resource limitations imposed by your assessment environment.
- Select assessment tools that provide the best fit.
- Become an expert on the assessment tools chosen—read test manuals; read the literature on the tools chosen; rehearse administering, scoring, and interpreting the scores produced.

Conducting Assessment

- Attend to the client (e.g., be aware of verbal and non-verbal cues to attitude and affect).
- Be sensitive to diversity (e.g., gender, ethnicity, developmental level, culture, first language, reading skill, handicapping or special needs conditions).
- Build rapport with the client (e.g., respond to client attitude, affect, and needs with understanding and empathy; establish clear structure and provide clear explanation of the assessment process; encourage questions and provide clear answers, ask for feedback).
- Ensure that the tests are administered according to the instructions given by the test author. If modifications of standard procedures are necessary due to special client circumstances or handicapping conditions, take careful notes on the nature of the modifications made.
- Provide time for post-assessment processing of the client's experience during the assessment. Encourage questions, provide answers, elicit feedback.

Interpreting Assessment Results

- Know your assessment tool(s) thoroughly.

- Know the recommended way to interpret each client's score(s).

- Integrate the findings across the instruments into a coherent interpretation consistent with your theoretical framework for career and personal/social counseling.

- Interpret assessment findings in language the client will understand; relate the results to the world of work.

- Balance highlighting of client strengths and discussion of client deficits or challenges.

- Facilitate the client's process of meaning-making. Encourage the client to put your interpretation into his or her own words; encourage the client to own his or her strengths and to view revealed limitations as opportunities to improve; encourage questions; seek feedback.

- Write reports that are clear, concise, coherent, and integrated. Provide accurate descriptions of findings and concrete recommendations.

Evaluating the Assessment Program

- Provide opportunities for clients to evaluate their satisfaction with their assessment experience.

- Collect follow-up evaluations of the impact the assessment experience on the client's life.

- Conduct scheduled reviews of collected evaluation data to monitor whether the assessment program is satisfying the purpose for which it was established.

Summary

Selecting an instrument for career assessment is a collaborative process requiring both counselors and clients to understand the factors that might influence the use of assessment in career counseling. It is the ethical responsibility of counselors to consider clients' welfare in decision making related to whether tests should be administered or not. It is also counselors' ethical obligation to select a reliable and valid instrument that serves the purposes of assessment in career intervention. Counselors should follow the test review structure recommended in this chapter in the selection of assessment tools to optimize the opportunity of finding a trustworthy instrument. Counselors need to be mindful of clients' welfare from test selection, to administration of the test, to interpretation of the test results. After all, clients are the changing agent and, therefore, their meaning-making of the assessment process cannot be ignored.

Review Questions

1. Explain your ethical responsibility as a test user. For what are you responsible?

2. What are the factors that counselors need to consider in selecting a career assessment?

3. What is test score reliability? What is test score validity? Explain why counselors must use these psychometric properties in choosing a test to use in counseling with clients.

4. Explain why it is important to review a test's technical information and psychometrics before using an educational, career, or psychological test in counseling with a client?

5. Name and describe strategies that you will use to ensure your selected instrument is the best possible test for your purpose.

References

Aamodt, M. (2007). Beauty may be in the eye of the beholder, but is the same true of a validity coefficient? *Assessment Council News.* Retrieved from http://www.ipacweb.org/acn/acn_0710.pdf

Allen, M. J., & Yen, W. M. (1979). *Introduction to measurement theory.* Monterey, CA: Brooks/Cole.

American Counseling Association. (2005). *ACA code of ethics.* Alexandria, VA: Author.

American Psychological Association. (2012). *Rights and responsibilities of test takers: Guidelines and expectations.* Retrieved from http://www.apa.org/science/programs/testing/rights.aspx

Bond, T. G., & Fox, C. M. (2007). *Applying the Rasch model: Fundamental measurement in the human sciences* (2nd ed.). New York, NY: Psychology Press.

Bronfenbrenner, U. (1977). Toward an experimental ecology of human development. *American Psychologist, 32*, 513-531.

Carlson, J. F., & Geisinger, K. F. (Eds.). (2012). *The nineteenth mental measurements yearbook.* Lincoln, NE: Buros Center for Testing.

Cook, E. P. (Ed.). (2012). *Understanding people in context: the ecological perspective in counseling.* Alexandra, VA: American Counseling Association.

Cronbach, L. J. (1951). Coefficient alpha and the internal structure of tests. *Psychometrika, 16*, 297-334.

Cronbach, L. J., Rajaratnam, N., & Gleser, G. C. (1963). Theory of generalizability: A liberalization of reliability theory. *British Journal of Statistical Psychology, 16*, 137-163.

DeVellis, R. F. (1991). *Scale development.* Newbury Park, NJ: Sage.

Drummond, R. J., & Jones, K. D. (2010). *Assessment procedures for counselors and helping professionals* (7th ed). Upper Saddle River, NJ: Pearson Merrill Prentice Hall.

Flores, L. Y., Spanierman, L. B., & Obasi, E. M. (2003). Ethical and professional issues in career assessment with diverse racial and ethnic groups. *Journal of Career Assessment, 11*, 76-95.

Gati, I., & Asulin-Peretz, L. (2011). Internet-based self-help career assessments and interventions: Challenges and implications for evidence-based career counseling. *Journal of Career Assessment, 19*, 259-273. doi: 10.1177/1069072710395533

Hoyt, C. (1941). Test reliability estimated by analysis of variance. *Psychometrika, 6(2)*, 153-160.

Joint Committee on Testing Practices. (2004). *Code of fair testing practices in education.* Washington, DC: Author.

Kendall, P. C. (1999). Clinical significance. *Journal of Consulting and Clinical Psychology, 67*, 283-284.

Krieshok, T. S., & Black, M. D. (2009). Assessment and counseling competencies and responsibilities: A checklist for counselors. In E. A. Whitfield, R. W. Feller, & C. Wood, *A counselor's guide to career assessment instruments,* (5th ed., pp. 61-68). Broken Arrow, OK: National Career Development Association.

Kuder, G. F., & Richardson, M. W. (1937). The theory of the estimation of test reliability. *Psychometrika, 2*, 151-160.

Lawshe, C. H. (1975). A quantitative approach to content validity. *Personnel Psychology, 28(4)*, 563–575.

Leong, F. T. L., & Hartung, P. J. (2000). Cross-cultural career assessment: Review and prospects for the new millennium. *Journal of Career Assessment, 8*, 391-401.

Lock, J. D., & Hogan, R. (2000). Expanding the focus of career assessment. *Journal of Career Assessment, 8*, 411-417.

Lonborg, S. D., Hackett, G. (2006). Career assessment and counseling for women. In W. B. Walsh & M. J. Heppner (Eds.), *Handbook of career counseling for women* (2nd ed., pp. 103-166). Mahwah, NJ: Lawrence Erlbaum.

Loong, T-W. (2003). *Understanding sensitivity and specificity with the right side of the brain.* Retrieved from http://www.bmj.com/content/327/7417/716.full

Lowman, R. L., & Carson, A. D. (2000). Integrating assessment data into career counseling. In D. Luzzo (Ed.), *Career counseling of college students: An empirical guide to strategies that work* (pp. 121-136). Washington, DC: American Psychological Association.

MacCluskie, K. C. (2009). Norms. In American Counseling Association (Ed.), *The ACA encyclopedia of counseling,* (pp. 370-371). Alexandria, VA: American Counseling Association.

McMahon, M., Patton, W., & Watson, M. (2003). Developing qualitative career assessment processes. *The Career Development Quarterly, 51(3)*, 194-202.

McFall, R. M., & Treat, T. A. (1999). Quantifying the information value of clinical assessments with signal detection theory. *Annual Review of Psychology, 50*, 215-241.

Murphy, K. R., & Davidshofer, C. O. (1988). *Psychological testing* (4th ed.). Upper Saddle River, NJ: Prentice-Hall.

Murphy, L. L., Spies, R. A., & Plake, B. S. (Eds.). (2006). *Tests in print VII.* Lincoln, NE: University of Nebraska Press.

Niles, S. G., & Harris-Bowlsbey, J. (2013). *Career development interventions in the 21st century* (4th ed.) Upper Saddle River, NJ: Pearson Merrill Prentice Hall.

Oliver, L. W., & Whiston, S. C. (2000). Internet career assessment for the new millennium. *Journal of Career Assessment, 8,* 361-369.

Sampson, J. P., & Lumsden, J. A. (2000). Ethical issues in the design and use of Internet-based career assessment. *Journal of Assessment, 8,* 23-35.

Schultheiss, D. E. P. (2005). Qualitative relational career assessment: A constructivist paradigm. *Journal of Career Assessment, 4,* 381-394.

Sechrest, L. (1984). Reliability and validity. In A.S. Bellack & M. Hersen (Eds.), *Research methods in clinical psychology* (pp. 24-54). New York, NY: Pergamon Press.

Stevens, S. S. (1959). Measurement, psychophysics and utility. In C. W. Churchman & P. Ratoosh (Eds.), *Measurement: Definitions and theories.* New York, NY: John Wiley.

Thompson, B. (2003). Understanding reliability and coefficient alpha, really. In B. Thompson (Ed.), *Score reliability: Contemporary thinking on reliability issues.* Thousand Oaks, CA: Sage.

U.S. Department of Labor, Employment and Training Administration. (2000). *Testing and assessment: An employer's guide to good practices.* Retrieved from http://www.onetcenter.org/dl_files/empTestAsse.pdf

Whiston, S. C., & Rahardja, D. (2005). Qualitative career assessment: An overview and analysis. *Journal of Career Assessment, 13,* 371-380.

CHAPTER 9

TEST ADMINISTRATION, INTERPRETATION, AND COMMUNICATION

Susan C. Whiston
Ciemone S. Rose

Department of Counseling and Educational Psychology
Indiana University

Introduction

The administration, scoring, and interpretation of career assessments are key to the career counseling process and critical as an assessment strategy. When a counselor selects a career assessment, it is usually to gather information about a client's characteristics, such as interests, abilities, values, or personality. Key to gathering accurate assessment information is appropriate administration of an instrument and accurate scoring. Once an instrument is correctly scored, the results need to be precisely interpreted, and then communicated in an understandable manner to the client. This chapter discusses in more detail the appropriate administration of career assessments, scoring issues, various approaches to the interpretation of career assessments, and communicating assessment results to clients. The chapter concludes with a discussion of multicultural issues related to administration, interpretation, and communication with a focus on issues of gender and race/ethnicity.

Administration

Before administering any career assessment, a career counselor must ensure that they are competent in the use of the identified instrument. The National Career Development Association's (2007) *Code of Ethics* states in standard E.2.a that career professionals use only those assessments for which they have been trained and are competent. Moreover, in Competency 1.f from the *Career Counseling Assessment and Evaluation Competencies* (National Career Development Association [NCDA] & Association for Assessment and Research in Counseling [AARC], 2010) requires career counselors to use only those assessments for which they are properly and professionally trained. Therefore, the assessment process starts before the administration of an instrument begins, when the career counselor is selecting an instrument in which they are competent to use. Competent use of a career assessment requires an understanding of psychometric measurement issues and training in using the specific instrument. For some career assessments, career counselors will need to attend training workshops, whereas other assessments training can be accomplished by thoroughly studying the instrument's manual.

Before administering a career assessment, career counselors must ensure that they have clients complete an appropriate informed-consent document (see standard E.3 in the NCDA *Code of Ethics*). Informed consent frequently involves a form which is signed by the client or the client's legal representative, but it can occasionally be done verbally in certain circumstances. In the informed consent, the nature, purposes, and specific uses of the assessment are explained to the client in a language that he or she can easily understand. In developing an informed consent document, a career counselor considers the client's personal and cultural context and the client's level of understanding of the assessment results. The informed consent also includes information on who will be the recipient of the results and how those results will be used. The informed consent will also specify privacy issues and how the release of information may occur with proper signatures and to individuals who have the appropriate training to understand the results. Hence, career counselors should be familiar with the NCDA *Code of Ethics* before they begin to administer a career assessment. They also should be familiar with the *Career Counselor Assessment and Evaluation Competencies* (NCDA & AARC, 2010).

Test Administration, Interpretation, and Communication

The significance of test administration is emphasized in the *Standards for Educational and Psychological Testing* (American Educational Research Association [AERA], American Psychological Association [APA], & National Council on Measurement in Education [NCME], 1999), which is an important guidebook for all types of assessments. According to the *Standards,* the usefulness and the interpretability of any test score require that a test be administered according to the developer's instructions. Therefore, counselors will need to be well acquainted with the instrument manual and the instructions for administration. Career assessments will vary in terms of degree of detail in administrative instructions. For some career assessments, the client will simply read the instructions that are at the beginning of the career assessment. For other career assessments (e.g., aptitude tests), there may be detailed pre-testing procedures and administrative instructions that must be precisely followed. For example, the assessment administrator may need to arrange the room in a certain manner to avoid cheating or be prepared to time each subtest. With certain instruments, the administrator must read specific instructions to the client. In all circumstances, the administrator must read the manual concerning the administrative protocol and follow the instruction provided in the manual.

When administering any career assessment, a counselor should consider the testing environment. As indicated above, there are instruments in which the administrative environment is specified, but frequently with career assessments, the counselor will be instructed to administer the assessment in a conducive environment. A conducive environment is one that has adequate lighting, ventilation, and space that allows the client to feel comfortable in completing the career assessment. As many career assessments are now administered using a computer, career counselors also need to consider both the client's comfort level with computers and the physical location of the computer. As Barak (2003) suggested, Internet-based career assessment now plays a predominant role in the field. Barak advised that career counselors prescreen clients before having them take an Internet-based career assessment because issues of age and social class may influence one's familiarity with computers. Another issue with computer-based or Internet-based assessment is the location of the computer and the degree to which that computer is monitored and secure. There may be situations where a computer that is used for assessment is located in an unmonitored location (e.g., a career library), which could be problematic as unauthorized persons might be able to retrieve confidential assessment information. The testing environment, whether it be computer-based or not, is important and counselors should consider issues of confidentiality, comfort, and accessibility for all clients. Accessibility is a particularly important issue as it relates to clients with disabilities and the need to adapt testing conditions in order to accommodate those with disabilities. For an expanded discussion of these topics, please see Chapters 4 and 6 in this text.

Although a good working alliance during the administration of a career assessment is probably important for all clients, Flores, Spanierman, and Obasi (2003) asserted that it is particularly salient with culturally diverse clients. In considering issues of culture, counselors should also consider a client's familiarity with the English language. In reviewing research related to test accommodations with English Language Learners, Abedi, Hofstetter, and Lord (2004) advised against using a one-size-fits-all approach in making accommodations to the administration of the assessment. For example, for some English Language Learners, a Spanish version of an interest inventory may be appropriate, whereas for other clients the use of a dictionary may be more appropriate (Abedi et al., 2004). For some instruments, any modifications to standardized test administration procedures will need to be documented. Career counselors should be discouraged from simply having someone translate the career assessment for an English Language Learner, however, as ensuring that translated version of instruments are comparable to the original version of the assessments is a complicated process. With clients from diverse backgrounds, career counselors should check the instrument's manual and related professional literature for recommendations on how to adapt the administration of the assessment for the client.

In conclusion, the most important part of administering a career assessment is to be prepared and to administer the assessment consistently with the instructions contained in the instrument's manual or other trusted source. A client could receive erroneous results if they do not understand the instructions of a career assessment; therefore, ensuring that the instrument is administered properly is a crucial step in the assessment process. Proper administration involves being knowledgeable about the process from the manual and also ensuring that the testing environment is appropriate for the situation.

Scoring

After a career assessment is administered and before the results can be interpreted and communicated to the client, the instrument must be scored. Accurate scoring of an instrument is key to the career assessment process. Some career assessments are hand scored (e.g., the Self-Directed Search) as compared to machine scored, and research indicates that hand scoring is more prone to errors (Whiston, 2013). Therefore, in cases of hand scoring, the career counselor may need to double check the scoring to ensure that a scoring error has not occurred.

Computer scoring, as compared to hand scoring, is often more accurate, rapid, and can be more complex. Furthermore, computers tend not to be biased and will not unintentionally consider factors such as race or gender in scoring. Computer scoring, however, is not infallible because computers are programmed by humans who can make mistakes. To ensure accurate scoring, the *Standards* (AERA, APA, & NCME, 1999) calls for the instruments' publishers to document the procedures they use when scoring an instrument.

With certain types of career assessments, such as qualitative assessments, there is subjectivity in the scoring. In qualitative career assessment, the goal is typically to identify themes and find meaning, and often information is elicited by having the client tell stories with the counselor listening to narrative. Examples of qualitative career assessments are autobiographies, card sorts, life lines, and genograms (see Chapter 16 for reviews of qualitative assessments). With qualitative career assessments, the counselor works collaboratively with the client to construct these new meanings; hence, a good working alliance is necessary. The career counselor does not calculate a numerical score as the goal is to facilitate learning and generate new meanings. Consequently, there is less objectivity in the scoring and interpretation of qualitative career assessments than more traditional career assessment (e.g., interest inventories). To use qualitative career assessments, a counselor needs to understand the philosophical underpinnings (see Blustein, Kenna, Murphy, DeVoy, and DeWine (2005).

Interpretation

The interpretation of career assessment results is one of the more critical steps in the assessment process. An instrument is considered neither valid nor invalid, for as the *Standards* (AERA, APA, & NCME, 1999) state: "[V]alidity refers to the degree to which evidence and theory support the interpretations of test scores entailed by proposed uses of tests" (p. 9). Therefore, validation evidence is directly related to the interpretation of results rather than something that is characteristic of the instrument itself. A counselor cannot interpret the results of any career assessment without thorough knowledge of the validation evidence. Most career assessment manuals will include substantial information about the validity of an instrument, and it is important that a career counselor wade through this information in order to conduct proper interpretations. Validation evidence will often include information on the construction of the instrument, how well the instrument correlates with related constructs, and other relevant research results. The type of validation information will vary, however, depending on the type of career assessment.

Norm-Referenced and Criterion-Referenced Assessment

One of the first steps in interpreting a score on a career assessment concerns determining whether the assessment is a norm-referenced or criterion-referenced. A *norm-referenced* instrument involves comparing the individual's performance to other people who have taken the assessment. The term *norm* refers to a group of individuals who have taken the assessment to which others' scores are then compared. A norming group for instruments can be small or it can be quite large (e.g., thousands of participants). In general, a counselor can have more confidence in comparing the performance of a client to a larger norming group. Not only is it better to have a large norming group, but it is also better to have one that is representative of the population being served. In the NCDA (2007) *Code of Ethics,* career counselors are instructed to "use, with caution, assessment techniques that were normed on populations other than that of the client" (p. 24).

With *criterion-referenced* instruments, the client's performance is not compared to other people, but rather to a standard or a criterion. With criterion-referenced assessments, there is a predetermined standard that is set before the client takes the assessment and the score is interpreted based on that standard. A major question with criterion-referenced instruments concerns how the standard or criterion is determined. The standard or criterion is often determined by previous research, the opinion of experts, or based on professional standards, such as national curriculum standards.

An interest inventory can serve as an example to distinguish between norm-referenced and criterion-referenced assessments. With a criterion-referenced instrument, the instrument developers would set a standard or criterion for what constitutes high interest in an area. Hence, the developers may decide that indicating an interest in 8 out of 10 items merits a rating of high interest. With a norm-referenced interest inventory, the instrument would be given to the norming group and then the client's score would be compared to the norming group's scores. As an example, a counselor may find that the client's score in the interest area is higher than 68% of norming group.

Norm-Referenced Interpretation

With norm-referenced instruments, it is usually helpful to know the mean and the standard deviation of the instrument in order to interpret the score. This can be particularly true if the score falls into a normal distribution or a normal curve. This is the bell shaped curve in which approximately 68% of the norming group will fall between one standard deviation below the mean and one standard deviation above the mean, 95% of the norming group will fall between two standard deviations below the mean and two standard deviations above the mean, and 99.5% will fall between three standard deviations below the mean and three standard deviations above the mean. Hence, if the scores have a normal distribution, then the counselor will know that a score that is three standard deviations above the mean signifies that the client scored better than the vast majority of clients.

In interpreting the results from a norm-referenced instrument, a counselor should be familiar with certain types of scores that are frequently used. Often in career assessments, instrument developers will use percentile scores. *Percentile scores* or *percentile ranks* indicate the percent of people who score at or below a certain score. Therefore, if a client score placed them in the 83rd percentile, this would be interpreted that 83% of the norming group having scored at or below the client's score. Percentiles should not be confused with the common scoring method of indicating the percentage of items answered correctly as they always indicate the percentage of people who scored at or below a certain level. Percentile scores can be very helpful in interpreting career assessments, as low percentile scores indicate very few people in the norming group scored below the client; whereas, high percentile scores indicate that most of the people in the norming group scored below the client.

In using career assessments, it is sometimes difficult to remember all of the various means and standard deviations for the different instruments. For example, a counselor would need to remember both the mean and the standard deviation of an instrument to determine that a client's score is one standard deviation below the mean. Therefore, many instrument developers will convert their raw scores to standard scores. *Standard scores* are converted scores so that they always have a set mean and standard deviation, which makes them easy to understand. For example, if an instrument developer decides to use z-scores, the counselor will know that the mean is always 0 and the standard deviation is 1. Therefore, if a client z-score is -1.00, a counselor would automatically know that the client's score is one standard deviation below the mean. Another commonly used standard score are T-scores, which have a fixed mean of 50 and a standard deviation of 10. The advantage of T-scores is that there are no negative numbers like there are with z-scores. Hence with T-scores, a score of 40 would indicate that the client is one standard deviation below the mean. Although there are other standard scores, z-scores and T-scores are the most commonly used standard scores in career assessment.

Another psychometric concept that counselors should be familiar with in interpreting scores is the standard error of measurement. *Standard error of measurement* is based on reliability and provides a range of where the client's "true score" would fall if the client were to take the assessment multiple times. Standard error of measurement is based on the premise that when individuals take a test multiple times, the scores will fall into a normal distribution, and the standard error of measurement provides the range of where the true score would fall approximately 68% of the time, 95% of the time, and 99.5% of the time. For example, if a client's score was 50 on a career assessment and the standard error of measurement was 2, then 68% of the time we would expect the clients true score to fall between one standard error of measure below the score to one standard error of measurement above the score (i.e., 68% of the time the clients true score would fall between 48 and 52). To interpret where a client's score would fall 95% of the time, a counselor then uses two standard error of measurements around the score. Hence, with our example of a score of 50 and a standard error of measurement of 2, we would expect that 95% of the time a client's true score would fall between 46 and 54. To interpret where a true score might fall 99.5% of the time, a counselor would use three standard error of measurement. With our example, a counselor would expect that this client's score would fall 99.5% of the time between 44 and 56. Sometimes on career assessment scoring profiles, the range of score is provided and the counselor needs to understand that this range represents the standard error of measure. Therefore, when a counselor is interpreting the results of a career assessment and sees a range of scores, they need to understand whether the true score would fall 68%, 95%, or 99.5% of the time. For those who would like more information on standard error of measurement, please see Whiston (2013).

Once a counselor has examined the results of career assessment and understands the scores and the possible range of scores, the counselor should next go to the instrument's manual to understand precisely what the scores mean. For example, an interest inventory may indicate that the client is interested in social science occupations, but the counselor needs to understand how social science occupations were defined by these instrument developers and which occupations are included in their definition. As indicated previously, the validation information informs the counselor on how to interpret the assessment results and, therefore, a counselor must be thoroughly familiar with the validation evidence before he or she can begin to communicate the results to the client.

Communication of Results

In the career assessment process, communicating the assessment results to the client is an important stage. The miscommunication of career assessment results could influence a client's career direction, which could have a substantial negative impact on a client's job satisfaction and career success. Therefore, the communication of career assessment results should be done carefully with attention to interpreting the results in an accurate and understandable manner. In particular, a counselor should consider how to communicate the results in a manner that corresponds to the client's developmental level and understanding of the career constructs. For example, some younger clients may perceive that the results of an interest inventory are informing them of "what they should be" rather than simply providing a reflection of their interests. Also important to consider in the communication of career assessments is that, like any type of assessment, the results provide only a piece of information and should never be considered as providing a complete picture of the client. For this, a counselor needs to look outside of the assessment for other relevant information, including but not limited to contextual variables. Career assessments can be used as supplements to other types of information, or may serve as a basis for gathering additional information at times. This should be clearly communicated to clients. Although the communication of assessment results is a critical part of the career assessment process, there is surprisingly little research on the topic. Whiston (2002) found that most of the studies on interpretation and communication of career assessments were published before 1985. In a meta-analysis of counseling interventions, Oliver and Spokane (1988) found an effect size of .62 for individual test interpretation and an effect size of .76 for group test interpretation. This means that those who received a test interpretation were more than two thirds of a standard deviation higher on the outcome measures used than those who did not receive interpretations. The finding that group test interpretation is slightly more effective than individual test interpretation does not indicate that all career assessment results should be communicated in a group setting as the effect sizes are not substantially different and these results are based on only six studies. Furthermore, with all types of assessments, Goodyear (1990) found that clients prefer to receive assessment results individually.

Hanson, Claiborn, and Kerr (1997) investigated two styles of test interpretation and communication in career counseling. The interpretations of the career assessments were delivered with very little client interaction or results were communicated in a manner that encouraged client interaction. In the interactive style, the counselor would describe the career construct being measured and then ask the client to provide one or two behavioral examples of the construct. The counselor would then affirm the behavioral examples if they were consistent with the manual or modify the behavioral example so it more adequately fit the career construct. Hanson et al. found that the participants evaluated the interactive style as compared to the more directive style as having more depth. Clients in the interactive condition also perceived the counselor as being more trust-

Test Administration, Interpretation, and Communication

worthy, expert, and interpersonally attractive as compared to clients in the more directive group. Therefore, this study would indicate that counselors should attempt to communicate results in an interactive manner and encourage client discussion in the process.

Many times in counseling, a counselor will use personality assessments (Swanson & D'Achiardi, 2005) and there is a growing body of research related to using Therapeutic Assessment (Finn, 2007) with personality assessments. Although much of Therapeutic Assessment is geared toward psychologists who do assessment batteries, it has some applicability to counselors conducting career assessments. In Therapeutic Assessment, there is an emphasis on creating a collaborative relationship with the client, and feedback is given in a sequential manner. At the beginning of the process of providing test feedback, Level 1, the counselor should focus on results that correspond to how clients already think about themselves. The counselor then moves to providing Level 2 feedback in which the focus is on reframing or increasing the clients' views of themselves. Finally, if the process is going well, the counselor moves to Level 3 findings in which the assessment results are more discrepant or are in conflict with the usual way the clients view themselves. Poston and Hanson (2010) did a meta-analysis of 17 studies in which psychological assessments were used as a therapeutic intervention that focused on creating a collaborative environment when providing assessment feedback. Poston and Hanson found an effect size of .42 when they compared the results of those who received a therapeutic feedback approach to those who received no assessment or a more traditional feedback session. An effect size of .42 means that those who received the therapeutic feedback approach were almost a half of a standard deviation above those who did not receive therapeutic feedback on the outcome measures. Although this line of research is not specific to career assessment, it does indicate that a collaborative and therapeutic approach to assessment feedback can produce more positive outcomes than a more traditional approach.

Specific to career assessment, Hartung (2005) argued that career assessment and counseling should be an integrative process and that counseling means more than simply taking "the test." He also asserted that career assessments have tended to focus on matching individuals to work environments, which is consistent with a logical positivist epistemology. Hartung further contended that counselors should take a postmodern position in which the goal of an integrative career assessment and counseling approach is to generate meaning for the client. A postmodern approach emphasizes exploring clients' subjective, qualitative, and personal career realities (Hartung, 2005). Once again, this is accomplished through a collaborative relationship between the client and the counselor with a focus on meaning making. The postmodern approach suggested by Hartung may involve traditional career assessments, but also stories, narratives, and qualitative career assessments that are focused on identifying life patterns and themes. A postmodern or a constructivist approach will also involve issues of social class, gender, and race or ethnicity, which are discussed in the next section of this chapter.

In concluding this section on communicating career assessment results to client, it should be emphasized that the content of the communication should be guided by the instrument's manual, other key resources, and related validation evidence. Validation evidence indicates how assessment results can be interpreted and, thus, guides the content of what is communicated to clients. Certainly, clients should be encouraged to ask questions as the results are communicated and the counselor should attempt to answer these questions in a manner that is understandable and respectful of the client. Finally, when the counselor has concluded reporting all of the results to the client, he or she should summarize and re-emphasize major points so that the client hears the important assessment results once again.

Multicultural Considerations

As Hartung (2005) mentioned, issues related to gender, socioeconomic status, and race and ethnicity are often pertinent in career assessment and counseling. The following section will focus on issues gender and race/ethnicity as very little research has focused on career assessment and socioeconomic status.

Gender

In interpreting the results of career assessments, it is important that counselors examine not just the overall reliability coefficients but also the reliability estimates for both men and women. An instrument that may be quite reliable for men may not be as reliable for women. The same can be said about examining the validation evidence and differences in terms of validity of an instrument for men and women. It may be with certain instruments that a counselor may need to be more cautious when interpreting the results with women as there may be more validation evidence for men or vice versa.

One of the major concerns related to career assessment with men and women has centered on the identification of nontraditional interests. There is research that indicates men and women tend to have different interests. In a recent meta-analysis of gender differences in interests, Su, Rounds, and Armstrong (2009) found that men showed stronger interests in Realistic and Investigative areas whereas women showed stronger Artistic, Social, and Conventional interests (Holland, 1997). They also found that men were more interested than women in engineering, science, and mathematics. Therefore, an important question is how does a counselor identify a woman with Realistic interests or a man with Social interests?

One of the ways to identify non-traditional career interests in an interest inventory is to use same-sex norms as it facilitates the identification of nontraditional interests that would often be obscured if the interests were being compared to both men and women (Whiston & Bouwkamp, 2003). With same-sex norms, females' interests would be compared with those of other females. For example, a female who is interested in a number of Realistic activities may receive a score of moderately high interest in this area when compared with other females, but her score may appear only as average or even below average if half of the norming group is male. Therefore, the use of same-sex norms may help in the identification of nontraditional interests. Betz (2005) proposed that in addition to using same-sex norms, counselors have a responsibility to assist women in broadening their experiences, particularly in areas such as the sciences, mathematics, engineering, and technology.

Concerning career assessment with women, Betz (2005) also recommended that counselors both formally and informally assess self-efficacy beliefs. For example, with formal assessments, a counselor could consider using either the *Skills Confidence Inventory* (Betz, Borgen, & Harmon, 1996) or the *Expanded Skills Confidence Inventory* (Betz et al., 2003). In particular, counselors should be sensitive to women's propensity to underestimate their capabilities in certain areas such as mathematics. When assessing women's self-efficacy beliefs in areas such as science, mathematics, engineering, and technology, a counselor should explore whether these self-efficacy beliefs are resulting in self-imposed limitations that will restrict career choices and directions. In addition to self-efficacy, Betz proposed that counselors assess client outcome expectations. Women considering non-traditional careers may have concerns about the extent to which these nontraditional careers will lead to desired rewards and outcomes.

Race and Ethnicity

A counselor should also be sensitive to issues of race and ethnicity in career assessment. In a meta-analysis, Fouad and Byars-Winston (2005) found that while racial/ethnic minorities did not differ from Whites in terms of their career aspirations, they did differ from Whites in terms of their perceptions of fewer occupational opportunities and greater career barriers. A growing body of research has drawn attention to the complex interaction of the perception of barriers to career interests and career decision-making (Lease, 2006; Luzzo, 1993; Luzzo & McWhirter, 2001), highlighting additional issues for counselors to consider. Consequently, a counselor must be sensitive to these perceptions when conducting career assessments and knowledgeable about the existing literature related to career assessment with racial/ethnic minorities.

Flores et al. (2003) developed a culturally sensitive model of career assessment for ethnically diverse clients. In their assessment model, general counseling skills, multicultural counseling competencies, and counseling competencies are the foundational skills that are needed throughout the process. The first phase in this model is *information gathering that is culturally encompassing.* As information gathering is the primary role of career assessment, these researchers emphasized that data gathering should assist in identifying the presenting career issues and understanding the client as a cultural being. This culturally encompassing information gathering will then inform the selection and administration of assessments, the interpretation of the assessment results, and inform future career interventions. These authors asserted that "assessing cultural variables that may be related to the client's career issue is a critical and necessary component of culturally competent career assessment" (p. 84).

The second phase of the Flores et al. (2003) model is the *culturally appropriate selection of instruments.* Within this phase, the counselor considers scale development and the degree to which racial/ethnic groups are represented in the scale development process. Also within this phase, the counselor should consider measurement issues and the amount of information that is provided regarding differing groups. In considering measurement issues, the model calls for the counselor to examine both cultural validity and cultural specificity. According to Leong and Hartung (2000), cultural validity concerns the degree to which instruments developed within a predominantly Eurocentric cultural perspective transfer or measure the same constructs for those from non-European groups. Comparatively, cultural specificity concerns the extent to which variables such as worldview, racial or ethnic identity, language, or other culturally relevant variables influence the career assessment process. Similarly, when selecting a career assessment, Flores et al. indicated that the counselor should consider the degree to which the instrument is equivalent across different ethnic groups (i.e., the validation evidence indicates it measures the same construct for different groups).

The third phase of Flores et al.'s (2003) model of culturally sensitive career assessment involves *culturally appropriate administration.* Flores et al. asserted that a strong therapeutic alliance is critical with culturally diverse clients and is important regardless of the type, form, or context in which the instrument is administered. They also suggested that familiarizing the client with the purpose of the career assessment and how the information will be used may contribute to the client's level of comfort. When administering the assessment, the counselor may also want to consider locations (e.g., schools, community centers) where the client may feel more comfortable as compared to a practitioner's office

The final phase of Flores et al.'s (2003) model concerns *culturally appropriate interpretation of assessment data* in which all of the information from the previous steps is coalesced and synthesized in order to inform future steps within the counseling process. The authors emphasized that counselors should use caution when interpreting the assessment results from culturally diverse clients, particularly when there is limited normative data for the assessment. If possible, they advised counselors to use the norms that are appropriate for the group to which the client belongs. In the interpretative process, it is also important to integrate relevant cultural information obtained from interviewing the client, which could entail information pertaining to acculturation, worldview, and racial identity. Particularly important during this process is for the counselor to examine their own cultural beliefs and be attentive to any possible biases or assumptions about specific cultural groups. Results and interpretations must be communicated to clients in a manner which is understandable and culturally sensitive. Flores et al. suggested that practitioners encourage client participation with an understanding of cultural differences in regards to deference to authority. Finally, they accentuated that the career assessment process should be culturally affirming to the client.

In conclusion, many of the recommendations provided by Flores et al. (2003) apply to working with all clients as issues of culture are frequently germane. Furthermore, their model includes appropriate assessment protocols and, therefore, has applicability in most career assessment situations.

Counseling Strategies for Administration, Scoring, and Interpretation

In summary, the following are some brief suggestions for use during the career assessment process.

- Ensure competence in using an career assessment before administering it to a client.

- Have a client or an appropriate representative sign an informed consent document before administering the career assessment.

- Read the administrative procedures that are typically in the instrument's manual carefully.

- Make necessary preparations for the administration (e.g., arrange the room appropriately).

- Be sensitive to multicultural issues in planning for the administration of the assessment.

- Answer appropriately any questions the client may have about taking the career assessment.

- Administer the career assessment according to the procedures outlined in the instructions and the instrument's manual.

- Score or have the instrument scored correctly.

A Counselor's Guide To Career Assessments Instruments

- Examine the reliability and validity evidence in order to begin the interpretation process.
- Consider multicultural issues in interpreting the results of the career assessment.
- If the instrument is criterion-referenced, review the information on setting the criterion.
- If the instrument is norm-referenced, review the information on the norming group.
- Return to the instrument manual to interpret all score values (e.g., percentiles, standard scores).
- Prepare to communicate the results of the career assessment in a manner the client will find understandable.
- Establish a collaborative relationship with the client before communicating results.
- Be sensitive to multicultural aspects in communicating results.
- Encourage client to ask questions as the results are discussed.
- Summarize and re-emphasize important results before concluding the communication of the assessment results.

Summary

In conclusion, the administration, scoring, interpretation, and communication of career assessment results are all important aspects of the career assessment process. In order to accomplish these tasks effectively, the counselor must have studied the instrument's manual thoroughly. Most manuals will have instructions for administration and the counselor should follow these instructions closely. If the assessment is administered by computer or over the Internet, the counselor should ensure the client feels comfortable using a computer. Most instrument manuals will also include pertinent information on scoring and how scores should be interpreted. Critical to the interpretation of assessment results is the validation evidence, which will dictate what conclusions can be drawn from the assessment results. In interpreting the results from career assessments, counselors should consider the attributes of the client and the construct being measured. There is some research that indicates that a counselor should have an interactive style when communicating assessment results. Certainly, the communication of the assessment results should be guided by the validation evidence. Issues regarding gender and race/ethnicity should be considered before an assessment is administered and continued to be taken into account during the scoring, interpretation, and communication of results. In terms of issues related to gender, a counselor should be particularly sensitive to issues of identifying nontraditional interests. Regarding race or ethnicity, Flores et al. (2003) recommended a culturally sensitive model of career assessment in which the counselor first gathers information that is culturally encompassing. The second and third phases of Flores et al.'s model concern the culturally appropriate selection of instruments and the culturally appropriate administration of career assessments. The final phase of Flores et al.'s model is culturally appropriate interpretation of assessment data. Finally with all clients, a counselor should answer any questions or concerns that a client may have in the career assessment process.

Review Questions

1. How might personal and cultural characteristics (e.g., language, age, physical or mental ability, social status) of the client impact some of the considerations that need to be made with regard to the testing environment during the administration of a career assessment?

2. What are some of the advantages and disadvantages with the use of hand-scored versus computer-scored career assessments?

3. What are the differences between criterion-referenced versus norm-referenced career assessments?

4. In what ways are the concepts of standard scores, percentiles, and standard error of measurement useful in career assessment interpretation?

5. When communicating assessment results to clients, what multicultural factors are important to consider?

References

Abedi, J., Hofstetter, C. H., & Lord, C. (2004). Assessment accommodations for English language learners: Implications for policy-based empirical research. *Review of Educational Research, 74*, 1-28. 10.3102/00346543074001001

American Educational Research Association, American Psychological Association, and National Council on Measurement in Education. (1999). *Standards for educational and psychological testing.* Washington, DC: American Educational Research Association.

Barak, A. (2003). Ethical and professional issues in career assessment on the internet. *Journal of Career Assessment, 11*, 3-21. doi:10.1177/106907202237457

Betz, N. E. (2005). Women's career development. In S. D. Brown & R. W. Lent (Eds.), *Career development and counseling: Putting theory and research to work* (pp. 253–277). Hoboken, NJ: Wiley.

Betz, N. E., Borgen, F. H., & Harmon, L. W. (1996). *Skills Confidence Inventory: Applications and technical guide.* Palo Alto, CA: Consulting Psychologists Press.

Betz, N. E., Borgen, F. H., Rottinghaus, P., Paulsen, A., Halper, C. R., & Harmon, L. W. (2003). The Expanded Skills Confidence Inventory: Measuring basic dimensions of vocational activity. *Journal of Vocational Behavior, 62*, 76-100. doi: 10.1016/S0001-8791(02)00034-9

Blustein, D. L., Kenna, A. C., Murphy, K. A., DeVoy, J. E., & DeWine, D. B. (2005). Qualitative research in career development: Exploring the center and margins of discourse about careers and working. *Journal of Career Assessment, 13*, 351-370. doi:10.1177/1069072705278047

Finn, S. E. (2007). *In our clients' shoes: Theory and techniques of therapeutic assessment.* New York, NY: Taylor & Francis.

Flores, L. Y., Spanierman, L. B., & Obasi, E. M. (2003). Ethical and professional issues in career assessment with diverse racial and ethnic groups. *Journal of Career Assessment, 11*, 76-95. doi:10.1177/106907202237461

Fouad, N. A., & Byars-Winston, A. (2005). Cultural context of career choice: Meta-analysis of race/ethnicity differences. *The Career Development Quarterly, 53*(3), 223-233. doi:10.1002/j.2161-0045.2005.tb00992.x

Goodyear, R. K. (1990). Research on the effects of test interpretation: A review. *The Counseling Psychologist, 18*, 240-257. doi:10.1177/0011000090182006

Hanson, W. E., Claiborn, C. D., & Kerr, B. (1997). Differential effects of two test-interpretation styles in counseling: A field study. *Journal of Counseling Psychology, 44*(4), 400-405. doi:10.1037/0022-0167.44.4.400

Hartung, P. J. (2005). Integrated career assessment and counseling: Mindsets, models, and methods. In W. B. Walsh & M. L. Savickas (Eds.), *Handbook of vocational psychology* (3rd ed., pp. 371-395). Mahwah, NJ: Erlbaum.

Holland, J. L. (1997). *Making vocational choices* (3rd ed.). Odessa, FL: Psychological Assessment Resources, Inc.

Lease, S. H. (2006). Factors predictive of the range of occupations considered by African American juniors and seniors in high school. *Journal of Career Development, 32*(4), 333-350. doi:10.1177/0894845305283003

Leong, F. T. L., & Hartung, P. J. (2000). Cross-cultural career assessment: Review and prospects for the new millennium. *Journal of Career Assessment, 8*(4), 391-401. doi:10.1177/106907270000800408

Luzzo, D. A. (1993). Ethnic differences in college students perceptions of barriers to career development. *Journal of Multicultural Counseling and Development, 21*(4), 227-236. doi:10.1002/j.2161-1912.1993.tb00233.x

Luzzo, D. A., & McWhirter, E. H. (2001). Sex and ethnic differences in the perception of educational and career-related barriers and levels of coping efficacy. *Journal of Counseling & Development, 79*(1), 61-67. doi:10.1002/j.1556-6676.2001.tb01944.x

National Career Development Association. (2007). *Code of ethics.* Broken Arrow, OK: Author.

National Career Development Association and Association for Assessment and Research in Counseling. (2010). *Career counselor assessment and evaluation competencies.* Retrieved from http://ncda.org/aws/NCDA/asset_manager/get_file/18143/aace-ncda_assmt_eval_competencies

Oliver, L. W., & Spokane, A. R. (1988). Career-intervention outcome: What contributes to client gain? *Journal of Counseling Psychology, 35*(4), 447-462. doi:10.1037/0022-0167.35.4.447

Poston, J. M., & Hanson, W. E. (2010). Meta-analysis of psychological assessment as a therapeutic intervention. *Psychological Assessment, 22*(2), 203-212. doi.org/10.1037/a0018679

Su, R., Rounds, J., & Armstrong, P. I. (2009). Men and things, women and people: A meta-analysis of sex differences in interests. *Psychological Bulletin, 135*(6), 859-884. doi:10.1037/a0017364

Swanson, J. L., & D'Achiardi, C. (2005). Beyond interest, needs/values, and abilities: Assessing other important career constructs over the life span. In S. D. Brown & R. W. Lent (Eds.), *Career development and counseling: Putting theory and research to work* (pp. 353-381). Hoboken, NJ: Wiley.

Whiston, S. C. (2002). Application of the principles: Career counseling and interventions. *The Counseling Psychologist, 30*(2), 218-237. doi:10.1177/0011000002302002

Whiston, S. C. (2013). *Principles and application of assessment in counseling* (4th ed.). Belmont, CA: Brooks/Cole Cengage.

Whiston, S. C., & Bouwkamp, J. C. (2003). Ethical implications of career assessment with women. *Journal of Career Assessment, 11*(1), 59-75. doi:10.1177/106907202237460

112

PART II

CAREER ASSESSMENT
INSTRUMENTS

114

CHAPTER 10

APTITUDE AND ACHIEVEMENT MEASURES

- Ability Explorer, Third Edition

- Adult Basic Learning Examination, Second Edition

- Armed Services Vocational Aptitude Battery Career Exploration Program

- The Highlands Ability Battery

- O*NET Ability Profiler

- Tests of Adult Basic Education

- Wonderlic Basic Skills Test

- WorkKeys Assessments

- Workplace Skills Survey

ABILITY EXPLORER, THIRD EDITION
Joan C. Harrington, Thomas F. Harrington, and Janet E. Wall

JIST Publishing, Inc.

875 Montreal Way
St. Paul, MN 55102

http://www.jist.com

Target Population: Adolescents, young adults, and adults; Grade 8 reading level.

Statement of the Purpose of the Instrument: The Ability Explorer (AE) provides information designed to facilitate enhanced self-awareness of work and career-related abilities and any self-efficacy issues related to the abilities in order to aid individuals with the process of educational and career exploration and career preparation.

Titles of Subtests, Scales, Scores Provided: Twelve abilities: (1) Artistic, (2) Clerical, (3) Interpersonal, (4) Language, (5) Leadership/Persuasive, (6) Manual/Technical, (7) Musical/Dramatic, (8) Numerical/Mathematical, (9) Organizational, (10) Scientific, (11) Social, (12) Spatial.

Forms and Levels Available, with Dates of Publication/Revision of Each: Ability Explorer, Third Edition Assessment (2012), Ability Explorer Professional Resources CD-ROM (2012), Ability Explorer User's Guide (2012), Hand-scorable survey booklet 2012.

Date of Most Recent Edition of Test Manual, User's Guide, Etc.: 2012.

Language in Which Available: English only.

Time:

Actual Test Time: 30-45 minutes.

Total Administration Time: 30-45 minutes.

Norm Group(s) on Which Scores Are Based: The AE was normed on middle school students, high school students, postsecondary students, and adults.

Manner in Which Results Are Reported for Individuals: The numbers for each ability score represent raw scores that will be converted to percentiles and then the results are reported as high (67 to 99 percentile), medium (34 to 66 percentile), or low (1 to 33 percentile). Assessment is self-scored and self-interpreted.

Report Format/Content for Group Summaries: Not available.

Machine Scoring: Not available.

Hand Scoring: Hand scored by counselee.

Computer Software Options Available: Not available.

Cost of Materials: Due to possible price changes since publication date, be sure to check the publisher's website.

Specimen Set: A free sample is available from the publisher's website.

Counselee Materials: Package of 25 Ability Explorer Assessment Booklets, $53.95; Package of 10 Ability Explorer Assessment Booklets, $49.95.

Published Reviews of the Instrument in the Last 15 Years: Not available. See the "References and Additional Resources" section in the test review that follows for reviews of previous editions.

ABILITY EXPLORER, THIRD EDITION

Reviewed by:

Wei-Cheng J. Mau

College of Education
Wichita State University

Description

The Ability Explorer, third edition (AE; J. C. Harrington, T. F. Harrington, & J. Wall, 2012), a self-report inventory, assesses 12 work-related abilities congruent with skill areas identified by the U.S. Department of Labor. The AE is a 2012 revision of a previously published instrument (J. C. Harrington & T. F. Harrington, 1996, 2006) designed to "help individuals identify their highest ability and use those results, along with other information, to identify promising career paths" (J. C. Harrington et al., 2012, p. 1). In general, the intent of the AE is to provide information designed to facilitate enhanced self-awareness of work and career-related abilities and any self-efficacy issues related to the abilities in order to aid individuals with the process of educational and career exploration and career preparation. The AE is a self-report measure designed to provide middle school/ junior high, high school, and postsecondary students, as well as adults with information about their abilities as they directly relate to the world of work and to educational and career planning.

There are 12 work-related abilities:

- Artistic
- Clerical
- Interpersonal
- Language
- Leadership/Persuasive
- Manual/Technical
- Musical/Dramatic
- Numerical/mathematical
- Organizational
- Scientific
- Social
- Spatial

Test takers respond to the questions in the AE items on a 6-point Likert scale ranging from *very good* to *very poor*. Hand scoring involves summing responses for each column and transferring the summed scores to a summary sheet. Only raw scores are provided in the booklet. Users must refer their raw scores to a table in order to understand how they compare to other people's scores in terms of "high," "medium," or "low." Percentiles and *T* scores are available from a separated document in a professional manual.

The assessment is divided into four steps: (1) Rate abilities, (2) Understand scores, (3) Identify careers that match abilities, and (4) Research the careers. In Step 1, the individual is instructed to rate 120 ability statements using the 6-point Likert scale. Statements measuring the same ability are presented in every sixth item in the sequence. The scoring boxes of the items measuring the same ability are located in the same column, which make it easier to add up the subtotals. In Step 2, look-up tables showing "High", "Medium", and "Low" ability ranges are presented. Definitions on each ability scale are provided for interpretation purposes. In Step 3, the test taker is asked to examine occupations that match his or her two highest-rated abilities. Instructions on how to match top abilities with occupations listed in the Abilities-to-Careers Finder are provided. The Abilities-to-Careers Finder is color coded, making it easier for the individual to locate the matching occupations. The occupations listed in the Abilities-to-Careers Finder are classified by the primary, secondary, and tertiary ability relevant to that line of work. Occupations are also coded by educational level. In Step 4, tips and resources for further exploration of promising careers are presented.

There is no time limit required for completing the booklet. Directions for administration are clearly stated and easy to follow step-by-step. No special training is needed. In general, the font sizes and styles of assessment questions and instructions are clear enough to read. The shading and color-coded columns and sections add attractiveness and hold the user's attention. It also makes interpretation easier with clearly delineated steps that move people through the assessment process.

Ability Explorer, Third Edition

Several obvious improvements have been made to this edition. The AE uses 20 fewer items than the previous editions in order to shorten the administration and scoring time required. This edition also focuses more on career planning with an "Abilities-to-Careers Finder" that matches takers' results to 400 occupations with a bright outlook, including a special emphasis on STEM (Science, Technology, Engineering, Math) careers.

The AE is written at an eighth-grade reading level. The test was designed to be taken by two age groups in the first edition: adolescent and adult. The third edition provides only one assessment age group: Grade 7 through adult.

The AE can be used in conjunction with an interest inventory to compare and contrast results. The information obtained from the AE can become an integral part of the career portfolio. "Just as the individual should use a career portfolio to record what is best about him or her, so the Ability Explorer profile report is a record of what the person considers his or her strongest abilities" (J. C. Harrington et al., 2012, p. 23). Further, counselors could use AE to help their clients develop a functional-based resume, at least in part, on abilities. The individual's highest rated abilities can be highlighted in the resume, perhaps as a section heading in the body of the resume.

The AE could be used as a tool when practicing for job or informational interviews. "The counselor or teacher can extend this further by allowing the individual to reflect upon his or her AE results during a counseling session. This encourages the student or adult client to articulate his or her best strengths, a skill that can certainly make for successful interviews. The individual's peers and/or parents or guardians could also be encouraged to participate in 'interviews' focused on his or her Ability Explorer results" (J. C. Harrington et al., 2012, p. 24).

Technical Considerations

The inventory items were developed through writing initial statements and reviewed by experts, field tests, and an item analysis procedure. A panel of minority experts reviewed all statements in all three parts of the AE, as well as the directions. The second edition used the standardization groups established in the previous edition. The norm group for the AE contains 4,837 cases, including 3,532 middle/junior high and high school students and 1,305 college students and adults. The normative sample is representative of the U.S. population, although the African American group is overrepresented.

The AE uses a single, large, norm group. It does not break down information by grade level, sex, or race, although data show that there are differences among groups. The authors argued that "The focus of the Ability Explorer is on what abilities are needed to perform an occupation, not the abilities for males performing an occupation or females performing the same occupation. The source of the questions on the instrument was job analysts' findings. These job analysts looked at the abilities and skills needed to do a job, as opposed to whether a male or female, Black or Hispanic, etc., used the same abilities to do the same job" (J. C. Harrington et al., 2012, p. 29). Although separate norms for each grade level are provided in the professional manual, a single norm table is used for interpretation in the test booklet.

The AE has good internal consistency reliability for the norm group. The median coefficient for abilities is .87, with a range of .84 to .89. No gender differences for the coefficients were noted. The median Standard Error of Measure (SEM) is 3.48. Further, the AE appears to be a fairly stable measure for college students. The test-retest reliability, based on 73 college students over a two-week period, averaged .84 for skill scales and .75 for activity scales. The authors did not provide estimates of score stability based on middle/high school students. One should not automatically infer that AE can be stably measured for middle or high school students.

The median scorer reliability, provided in the professional manual was .98. This high correlation is indicative that the AE has accurate self-scoring capability. However, despite the high correlation indicating an index of agreement, 8% of the total sample made errors that would have changed their results. Although this percentage is small, administrators would need to exercise some caution when calculating the scores for interpretation.

With respect to validity, there are little new validity data provided by authors in the third edition of the professional manual. The validity evidence summarized here is largely from the second edition of the professional manual. The authors did a nice job of providing content validity, and the evidence appears to be fairly adequate. Inter-correlations among ability subscales were used to provide partial evidence of construct validity. In general, most of the scales are moderately correlated, which show that the scales are distinct yet measure a similar construct.

Evidence of criterion-related validity was shown by the correlations with measures of career-related aptitude tests. However, the provided evidence tends to be low. For example, the correlations with the Differential Aptitude Test (DAT) are low to moderate, ranging from .08 (clerical) to .46 (numerical). Correlations with the G score of the General Aptitude Test Battery (GATB) also tend to be low, ranging from .01 (manual) to .33 (numerical/mathematical). Correlation with SAT aptitude test language is .27 and with the numerical/mathematical scale is .25.

Another criterion-related validity evidence was based on comparisons of 14 ability-scale profiles of eight college majors against the skills required on the job based on the U.S. Department of Labor job analysts' data reported in the Guide for Occupational Exploration (GOE). Results indicated that there was a 73% match between students' self-rated abilities and job analysts' data reported in the GOE.

The authors also reported validity evidence inferred from Harrington and O'Shea's (2000) study, which compared ability profiles of the Career Decision-Making System (CDM) based on five college majors and four employed-worker samples. Findings showed that 67% matched. The CDM and the first edition of AE each have 14 ability scales, and 12 of the abilities have similar names. Another study by Harrington and Schafer (1996) examined the concurrent validity inferred from a comparison of the CDM self-reported abilities and the GATB Occupational Aptitude Pattern Structure (OAP) abilities. The authors concluded that the self-reported work abilities of employees are generally consistent with the GOE.

Although the new edition of the Ability-to-Careers Finder is an improvement, it is unclear how the primary and secondary codes were developed. The rationale of using knowledge instead of abilities or skills used in O*NET is not very clear. The process of assigning AE abilities to O*NET knowledge is not fully explained. Empirical studies are needed to provide validity evidence of these alignments.

General Utility and Evaluation

The third edition of AE has made some improvements over the previous versions in that it attempts to shorten the instrument as well as adds the Abilities-to-Careers Finder. The reduction of items from 140 to 120 makes it possible for more time to fit interpretations within a single administrative session. The Abilities-to-Careers Finder connects the assessed abilities with bright outlook occupations listed in the O*NET database.

Not retained in the third edition are the suggested courses and enrichment activities one might pursue to cultivate the assessed abilities (Steps 5, 6, 7, and 8 in the second edition). Instead, these activities are now only available in the professional manual, which makes this assessment less self-directed and more dependent on counselors' intervention. The publisher also provides a user's guide and professional manual that are very helpful.

Borman (2001) and Mau (2001, 2009) have reviewed the previous editions of the AE. Both have commented on the limited information on validity, especially in the area of predictive validity and construct validity. Although some initial evidence of construct validity has been substantiated by the literature and theoretical/logical reasoning, more direct evidence for validity is needed (Mau, 2001, 2009). Most of the criterion-related evidence of validity was drawn from college students or adults. The validity of AE for middle/high school students remains questionable. Some of the validity data is questionable, especially comparing results to traditional aptitude tests (Borman, 2001). The authors have toned down the value of predictive validity of the instrument and stressed the importance of its guidance purpose. The authors believe that "an individual's wide range of potential talents needs to be identified and explored before a prediction of success or failure is made" (T. Harrington & J. C. Harrington, 1996, p. 8). Although some improvements and enhancements have been made to the new edition, no new validity data were added to the third edition. Perhaps users of AE should place more emphasis on using the assessment results for personal awareness and self-efficacy intervention rather than for prediction of occupational obtainment or job satisfaction.

A common problem shared by many self-assessment tests is rating bias. Raters tend to either overestimate or underestimate their abilities, depending on the difficulty of the tasks or subject matter. Users should be aware the potential biases of self-reported measures and the limited validity evidence of the assessment in predicting career choices. Nevertheless, the AE provides career counseling practitioners with a cost-effective assessment tool especially in promoting clients' self-awareness and developing their desired abilities.

References and Additional Resources

Borman, C. (2001). [Ability Explorer.] In J. Kapes & E. Whitfield (Eds.), *A counselor's guide to career assessment instruments* (4th ed., pp. 74–81). Columbus, OH: National Career Development Association.

Harrington, T., & Harrington, J. C. (1996). *Ability Explorer.* Itasca, IL: Riverside Publishing.

Harrington, T., & Harrington, J. C. (2006). A new generation of self-report methodology and validity evidence of the ability explorer. *Journal of Career Development, 9* 41–48.

Harrington, J. C., & Harrington, T. F., & Wall, J. E. (2012). *Professional manual, Ability Explorer* (3rd ed.). Indianapolis, IN: JIST Publishing.

Harrington, T., & Schafer, W. (1996). A comparison of self-reported abilities and occupational ability patterns across occupations. *Measurement and Evaluation in Counseling and Development, 28* 180-190.

Harrington, T., & O'Shea, A. (2000). *The Harrington-O'Shea Career Decision-Making System Revised.* Circle Pines: MN: American Guidance Service.

Mau, W. C. (2001). [Ability explorer.] *Newsnotes.* Retrieved from www.theaaceonline.com

Mau, W. C. (2009). [Ability Explorer.] In E. A. Whitfield, R.W. Feller, & C. Wood. (Eds.). *A counselor's guide to career assessment instrument,* (5th ed., pp. 82-88). Broken Arrow, OK: National Career Development Association.

Adult Basic Learning Examination, Second Edition
Bjorn Karlsen and Eric F. Gardner

Pearson Assessments

EA Customer Service
P.O. Box 599704
San Antonio, TX 78259

http://www.pearsonassessments.com
EDAssessments@pearson.com

Target Population: Adults with fewer than 12 years of formal schooling.

Statement of the Purpose of the Instrument: The Adult Basic Learning Examination (ABLE) is designed to measure the educational achievement of adults who may or may not have completed 12 years of schooling. It is also useful in evaluating efforts to raise the educational level of these adults.

Titles of Subtests, Scales, Scores Provided: There are six subtests available: (1) Vocabulary, (2) Reading Comprehension, (3) Spelling, (4) Language, (5) Number Operations, and (6) Problem Solving. A Total Language composite score is available for subtests 3 and 4, and a Total Mathematics composite score is available for subtests 5 and 6.

Forms and Levels Available, with Dates of Publication/Revision of Each: There are three levels available: Level 1 (adults with 1-4 years formal education), Level 2 (adults with 5-8 years formal education), and Level 3 (adults with 8 or more years formal education). Two equivalent forms (Forms E and F) and a screening battery (Level C). 1986.

Date of Most Recent Edition of Test Manual, User's Guide, Etc.: 1986.

Languages in Which Available: English: English and Spanish (ABLE Screening Edition).

Time:

Actual Test Time: Approximately 3 hours.

Total Administration Time: Complete Battery: Varies, although approximately 3 hours. Vocabulary (all levels): 20 minutes; Reading Comprehension: Level 1—30 minutes, Level 2 & 3—35 minutes; Spelling: Level 1—15 minutes, Level 2 & 3—20 minutes; Language: No Level 1, Level 2 & 3—20 minutes; Number Operations: Level 1—30 minutes, Level 2 & 3—35 minutes; Problem Solving (all levels): 35 minutes.

Norm Group(s) on Which Scores Are Based: Adults in GED programs and prison populations (Levels 1 and 2) and adults in vocational/technical high school programs (Level 3).

Manner in Which Results Are Reported for Individuals: A profile/score form is provided (item-response summary report is optional). Types of scores include grade equivalents, stanines, and percentile ranks. A group record is completed by counselor. The same scores as on individual reports can be accommodated.

Report Format/Content for Group Summaries: Not available.

Machine Scoring: Not available.

Hand Scoring: Hand scored by counselor in 10 minutes.

Computer Software Options Available: Not available.

Cost of Materials: Due to possible price changes since publication date, be sure to check the publisher's website.

Specimen Set: ABLE Examination Kit: $60.00 (includes Level 1, 2, and 3 test booklets; Form E), Directions for Administering (Level 1, and Levels 2 and 3), Group Record (Level 2), Hand-Scorable Answer Sheet (Level 2), Ready Score Answer Sheet (Level 2), and SelectABLE Ready Score Answer Sheet.

Counselee Materials: Test booklet and answer sheet.

Published Reviews of the Instrument in the Last 15 Years:

Geisinger, K. F. (2009). [ABLE, second edition.] In E. A. Whitfield, R. W. Feller, & C. Wood (Eds.), *A counselor's guide to career assessment instruments* (5th edition, pp. 90-93). Broken Arrow, OK: National Career Development Association.

ADULT BASIC LEARNING EXAMINATION, SECOND EDITION

Reviewed by:

Kurt F. Geisinger

Director, Buros Center for Testing
University of Nebraska — Lincoln

Description

The Adult Basic Learning Examination, second edition (ABLE), authored by Bjorn Karlsen and Eric F. Gardner, is a battery of tests designed to measure basic levels of educational achievement or functional academic skills and abilities among adults. It was developed originally as an instrument for adults who may have quite varied levels of formal education. The current edition was published in 1986. Three levels of the test are available: Level 1 (one to four years of education), Level 2 (five to eight years of education), and Level 3 (at least eight years of education). An untimed screening test composed of items measuring verbal and numerical concepts takes from 15 minutes to an hour to complete and may be used in determining which level to administer to a client.

All three levels of the ABLE include five subtests: Vocabulary, Reading Comprehension, Spelling, Number Operations, and Problem Solving. Each level has material that increases in difficulty. Level 1 includes Vocabulary, Reading Comprehension, Spelling, Number Operations, and Problem Solving subtests. Some of these items at Level 1 (Vocabulary and Spelling as well as the first five questions on the Number Operations subtest) are dictated to the test taker (rather than given in writing). Levels 2 and 3 contain the same five subtests at a more advanced level, and a Language subtest that covers grammar, capitalization, and punctuation is also generated. No items are dictated for Levels 2 and 3. All answers are made on answer sheets. The administration manuals for the tests are very explicit with regard to the required procedures. Subtests may be administered separately or together. Each level of the examination takes approximately 2 hours, 40 minutes to administer, but none of the tests are timed. Two new forms have been developed, labeled Forms E and F. This reviewer was provided only Form E by the publisher. A previous form, Form C, is apparently also still available.

The publisher's website indicates that a Spanish form of the instrument is available, although no information was presented to this reviewer to consider regarding this form, its development, or the psychometric basis for using it; the website provides essentially no psychometric information on the measure. The Spanish form was developed in 1989; it appears that the same form continues to be employed and is intended to be appropriate for adults with 5 to 8 years of schooling.

This measure could be used in a career counseling setting with individuals who have limited academic history (the target user market) but who are considering educational and vocational options. The measure is not as vocationally oriented as some of its competitors, such as the Test of Adult Basic Education (TABE) (Geisinger, 1998). ABLE is appropriate for use with adults in a variety of contexts, including adult education programs, which was its intended market, and the various levels are appropriate for pre-kindergarten through post-high school. Level 3 would be most appropriate within GED programs, and Levels 2 and 3 are likely appropriate in various technological education programs. ABLE could be used to help adults decide whether to pursue a GED.

The norms of the measure are adequate enough to permit a counselor to assess the academic skills of a stu-

A Counselor's Guide To Career Assessments Instruments

dent who is pondering assorted vocational possibilities. The measure is reasonably non-threatening and could be used, for example, with adults who have been out of the workforce but are considering rejoining. It also could be used in a variety of institutional education programs as well (such as in prisons) to help individuals decide their possible options once released.

A Handbook of Instructional Techniques and Materials (Karlsen & Gardner, 1986a) is available for teachers of classes of adult learners and is enhanced by a *Reading Supplement* (Karlsen & Gardner, 1986b). Both can be used in helping instructors to design instruction for the appropriate level and are available from the test publisher.

Technical Considerations

The norm sample was used to derive norms in terms of percentile ranks, stanines, and normal curve equivalents. The norming population for Levels 1 and 2 included adults in GED and prison education programs, whereas at Level 3 or it was composed of adults in vocational/technical high school programs (Fitzpatrick, 1992). All populations were described in terms of their age, race, and geographical breakdowns. Grade equivalents are also available through analyses that linked scores on the ABLE with those of the Stanford Achievement Test series.

The internal consistency reliability of the measures was evaluated using the standard Kuder-Richardson formulations, equivalent to coefficient alpha when items are scored as correct and incorrect as they are in ABLE. Subtest values range from the high .70s through the low .90s. In the opinion of this reviewer, these values are probably acceptable for the low stakes purposes for which it is used, especially for the evaluation of adult educational programs. One previous reviewer characterized these coefficients as approaching acceptable reliability (Williams, 1992). Some indication of temporal stability would also be useful.

Correlations between one of the experimental forms of the ABLE and a form of the Stanford Achievement Tests were respectable, although these correlations were achieved using an experimental form of the ABLE (Fitzpatrick, 1992). The contents of the two tests do not overlap highly, however, and one concern might be that to some extent the ABLE assesses general developed mental ability (or intelligence) rather than educational attainments per se. This correlation is found, of course, in most or all tests of academic achievement.

The test is also supported primarily by arguments of content validity. Although the materials provided to this reviewer did not permit the assessment of evidence of content validity, it is possible to differentiate two aspects of content validation. It is clear that the items well represent the domains for which they were written, although one might assert, as has Fitzpatrick (1992), that the Level 1 Vocabulary subtest is really a test of "auditory comprehension." The authors of the test, are both exceedingly well experienced in test construction. However, one might question the choice of some of the scales. Perhaps tests of spelling and vocabulary are not the best way to assess a person's verbal ability, especially with examinees who have been out of the educational process for some time or who have had little formal education. Moreover, vocabulary is a strong component/correlate of intelligence and may represent a sense that the test is measuring general developed mental ability as well as educational development. On the other hand, such scales may be less threatening for individuals lacking significant formal education than tests of critical reading or business writing.

Some evidence of fairness and appropriateness for use with ethnic minorities and individuals with disabilities would greatly enhance the value of the measure to counselors.

General Utility and Evaluation

The ABLE is one of the better tests for use toward its intended purpose. A key component of score interpretation is based upon the last grade completed by individuals in the norming reference population (Fitzpatrick, 1992). The measure should probably be used in conjunction with a measure of interests, so that a counselor can assess not only one's educational attainments but also the nature of his or her interests. It should also be used with an interview, so that the counselor can determine just how much the individual has been using his or her academic skills. It is possible that a person who once succeeded adequately in school some time ago has let these skills lie fallow; perhaps in such circumstances, a brief refresher could enhance them substantially. Validity evidence indicates that the TABE scores match GED performance better than the ABLE, an argument

Adult Basic Learning Examination, Second Edition

for the TABE competitor battery (Monsaas, 2007; the TABE review may be found later in this chapter).

The measurement of language use has moved beyond assessments of spelling and vocabulary, even though they are economical techniques for assessing verbal ability quickly. One problem is that measures of vocabulary are so highly related to intelligence rather than academic achievement per se. Nevertheless, this measure has a satisfactory purpose, one that it meets at least adequately and perhaps substantially better than other less well-constructed measures. Some mention of its use with language minorities and those with disabilities is needed, and neither such statements were provided to this reviewer. The measure appears professional and is attractive and well made.

References and Additional Resources

Fitzpatrick, A. R. (1992). [Adult Basic Learning Examination, Second Edition]. In J. J. Kramer & J. Close Conoley (Eds.), *The eleventh mental measurements yearbook* (pp. 19-21). Lincoln, NE: Buros Center for Testing.

Geisinger, K. F. (1998). [Tests of Adult Basic Education Work-Related Foundation Skills]. In J. C. Impara & B. S. Plake (Eds.) *The thirteenth mental measurements yearbook* (pp. 1086-1088). Lincoln, NE: Buros Center for Testing.

Karlsen, B., & Gardner, E. F. (1986a). *Handbook of instructional techniques and materials.* San Antonio, TX: Harcourt.

Karlsen, B., & Gardner, E. F. (1986b). *Reading supplement.* San Antonio, TX: Harcourt.

Monsaas, J. (2007). [Tests of Adult Basic Education, forms 9 & 10.] In K. F. Geisinger, R. A. Spies, J. F. Carlson, & B. S. Plake (Eds.), *The seventeenth mental measurements yearbook.* Lincoln, NE: Buros Center for Testing.

Williams, R. T. (1992). [Adult Basic Learning Examination, second edition]. In J. J. Kramer & J. Close Conoley (Eds.), *The eleventh mental measurements yearbook* (pp. 21-23). Lincoln, NE: Buros Center for Testing.

ARMED SERVICES VOCATIONAL APTITUDE BATTERY CAREER EXPLORATION PROGRAM

U.S. Department of Defense Personnel Testing Division

U.S. Department of Defense

Defense Manpower Data Center Monterey Bay
400 Gigling Road
Seaside, CA 93955
http://www.asvabprogram.com

Target Population: Adolescents and young adults; high school sophomores, juniors, seniors, and post-secondary students.

Statement of the Purpose of the Instrument: The Armed Services Vocational Aptitude Battery Career Exploration Program (ASVAB CEP) is a comprehensive career exploration and planning program that includes a multiple-aptitude test battery, an interest inventory based on Holland's theory, and various career planning tools designed to help students learn about themselves and the world of work and gain confidence in making career decisions.

Titles of Subtests, Scales, Scores Provided: There are eight subtests: General Science, Arithmetic Reasoning, Word Knowledge, Paragraph Comprehension, Mathematics Knowledge, Electronics Information, Mechanical Comprehension, and Auto and Shop Information. There are three Career Exploration Score composites: Verbal Skills, Math Skills, and Science and Technical Skills. The Military Entrance scores (AFQT) are for students interested in the military. The Find Your Interests (FYI) inventory yields six RIASEC scores: Realistic, Investigative, Artistic, Social, Enterprising, and Conventional.

Forms and Levels Available, with Dates of Publication/Revision of Each: Exploring Careers: The ASVAB Career Exploration Guide, 2012; ASVAB Career Exploration Program Overview Guide, 2010.

Date of Most Recent Edition of Test Manual, User's Guide, Etc.: The ASVAB Career Exploration Program: Technical Summary, 2012; ASVAB Counselor Guide, 2012; Career Cluster Connection, 2011; Theoretical and Technical Underpinnings of the Revised Skill Composites and OCCU-Find, 2010; and ASVAB Norms for the Career Exploration Program, 2004. The online official site of the ASVAB contains various technical reports on the ASVAB battery, including a technical bulletin on the development of the paper-based forms used in the ASVAB CEP. During 2011-2012 an Internet-delivered, computer adaptive version of the ASVAB (i.e., iCAT) was piloted in high schools. The plan is to transition to iCAT testing in high schools potentially during the School Year 2013-14. As a result, more of the technical information on the Official Site of the ASVAB will be of interest to counselors and educators.

Language in Which Available: English only.

Time:

Actual Test Time: 136 minutes.

Total Administration Time: Paper-based Administration: 170 minutes, add 15-20 minutes more for group administration;

Internet-Computer Adaptive ASVAB: approximately 90 minutes.

Norm Group(s) on Which Scores Are Based: ASVAB norms are based on the Profile of American Youth (PAY97) project by the U.S. Department of Defense and the U.S. Department of Labor. Two nationally representative samples were obtained. The norms for 10th, 11th, and 12th grade students are based on 4,700 youth who expected to be enrolled in grades 10, 11, and 12 as of the fall of 1997. The norms for post-secondary students are based on approximately 6,000 American youth ages 18-23 as of June, 1997. FYI norms are based on the results of a national sample of 1,958 high school students from 19 high schools. The schools were randomly selected and the resulting sample was weighted to be nationally representative.

Manner in Which Results Are Reported for Individuals: Students are provided with norm-based standard scores and percentile scores for the eight ASVAB subtests and three Exploration Score composites. Standard scores are provided based upon norms for the same grade, combined sex group. The same grade standard scores are also presented graphically with error bands to pictorially show strengths and weaknesses. Norm-based percentile scores are provided as follows: same grade/same sex, same grade/opposite sex, and same grade/combined sex. The paper-and-pencil version of the FYI is self-scored. Students determine their top three RIASEC codes based on gender combined norms. An additional scoring step allows students to determine gender-based results. The online FYI takes 5-8 minutes to complete. Students are provided with their top three RIASEC codes based on both gender-combined and gender-based norms.

Two copies of the ASVAB Summary Results (ASR) are provided, one for the student and one for the counselor. The ASR reports scores, provides definitions of each scale and composite, and provides a brief summary of the meaning of the scores. All participants receive a post-test interpretation from trained CEP personnel. During the interpretation, the ASVAB scores are explained; students have an opportunity to ask questions; students take and self-score the Find Your Interests (FYI) inventory; learn about the role of work-related values; learn about the OCCU-Find; and how to explore careers via the CEP website. On the ASR, participants are provided with an access code to the website that will allow them access to take the FYI online and use an expanded OCCU-Find with links to the Occupational Outlook Handbook, O*NET, and http://www.careersinthemilitary.com. The students have access to this website for up to two years.

Schools can elect to have students complete the interpretation session in a computer lab using their access codes from the ASR. This allows students to take the FYI electronically in approximately 8 minutes. Students are presented with both combined group and gender specific RIASEC codes. The online OCCU-Find facilitates career exploration providing students with immediate information on occupations of interest.

Report Format/Content for Group Summaries: Counselors are provided with a copy of each student's ASVAB Summary Results sheet as well as a group summary.

Machine Scoring: There are no costs either to participating schools or students. There is a 2-week turnaround time for scoring and returning.

Hand Scoring: Hand scoring of the ASVAB is not available. Students can take the FYI inventory and self-score it or take it online and have it scored electronically.

Computer Software Options Available: Students can use both the FYI inventory and OCCU-Find online.

Cost of Materials: Free.

Specimen Set: Not available.

Counselee Materials: FYI Inventory or online access to instrument.

Published Reviews of the Instrument in the Last 15 Years:

Patrick, J., Blosel, C. W., & Gross, C. L. (2009). [Armed Services Vocational Ability Battery Career Exploration Program.] In E. Whitfield, R. Feller, & C. Wood (Eds.), *A counselor's guide to career assessment instruments* (5th ed., pp. 94-104). Broken Arrow, OK: National Career Development Association.

Rogers, J. E. (2001). [Armed Services Vocational Aptitude Career Exploration Program.] In J. T. Kapes & E. A. Whitfield (Eds.), *A counselor's guide to career assessment instruments* (4th ed., pp. 93-101). Columbus, OH: National Career Development Association.

ARMED SERVICES VOCATIONAL APTITUDE BATTERY CAREER EXPLORATION PROGRAM

Reviewed by:

John Patrick

Jeff Samide

Deidre L. Muth
Department of Counselor Education
California University of Pennsylvania

Nikki S. Comito
English and Philosophy Programs
California University of Pennsylvania

Christi L. Gross
Department of Sociology
Kent State University

Description

The ASVAB Career Exploration Program (ASVAB-CEP) is a comprehensive print and web-based career exploration and planning program that has been developed and maintained by the U.S. Department of Defense and is comprised of the ASVAB (a multiple aptitude battery), an interest inventory, and other structured career-related activities designed to assist high school (grades 10-12) and post-secondary students in exploring the world of work and making career decisions (U.S. Military Entrance Processing Command, 2005a). There is no cost incurred by an individual utilizing the ASVAB-CEP.

The purpose of the ASVAB-CEP is "to give students the opportunity to explore a variety of careers using knowledge they have gained about their interests and skills through assessment components and structured activities" (ASVAB, 2005, p. 1). Additionally, the ASVAB-CEP is also used by the U.S. Military Services to identify students who may qualify for entry into the military and the assignment of qualified individuals to specific military occupational training programs (U.S. Military Entrance Processing Command, 1999). The results of the ASVAB-CEP may help students to evaluate their aptitudes and interests, explore occupations congruent with their interests and skills, and discern potential careers.

The ASVAB-CEP has undergone extensive revisions and is now comprised of the following components:

- The paper-and-pencil version of the ASVAB (P&P-ASVAB), a general multiple aptitude test battery;

- The *Find Your Interest* (FYI) occupational interest inventory;

- ASVAB Summary Results, a score report provided to students that describes their standard and percentile scores on individual ASVAB tests, Career Exploration Score composites, and military entrance score;

- *Exploring Careers: The ASVAB Career Exploration Guide* designed to assist students in understanding and using their ASVAB scores with the OCCU-Find, a list of over 400 occupations grouped by the six John Holland RIASEC interest areas or by 16 Career Clusters;

- http::/www.asvabprogram.com, the program website that contains the online FYI Inventory and OCCU-Find and has links to the Occupational Outlook Handbook, O*NET Online, http://www.careerclusters.org, and http://www.careersinthemilitary.com;

- *Military Careers,* a publication that offers a broad overview of career opportunities in the military;

- http://www.careersinthemilitary.com, a website that provides extensive information on approximately 140 military occupations;

- *My Educational and Career Plans,* an activity for students to assist them in making future educational and career plans;

- *Coursework Planner,* a worksheet to help students plan remaining high school courses based on tentative career choices; and

- *Idea Sheets,* a series of guided exercises and activities that educators can use to incorporate career exploration activities into the classroom.

The three primary components of the program that will be reviewed here include the ASVAB, FYI Inventory, and the OCCU-Find feature found on the program website (http://www.asvabprogram.com).

The ASVAB itself is recognized as one of the most widely used multiple aptitude test batteries in the world. The test is administered in one of two forms: (1) the P&P-ASVAB, and (2) a computerized version (CAT-ASVAB) that is used solely at a Military Entrance Processing Station (MEPS) or a Military Entrance Test (MET) site. Military applicants' CAT-ASVAB results are used to determine enlistment eligibility and to assign applicants to specialized military occupational training, while high school and post-secondary students take the P&P-ASVAB that is used primarily to aid students in career exploration. Military eligibility is also assessed with the P&P-ASVAB (Pommerich, Segall, & Moreno, 2009). The ASVAB tests primarily measure Verbal, Math, Science and Technical, as well as Spatial domains.

The P&P-ASVAB (Forms 23/24) consists of 200 items, requires nearly three hours to complete, and is administered as a paper-and-pencil test. The eight subtests are (1) *General Science* (GS/25 items), measuring knowledge of biological and physical sciences; (2) *Arithmetic Reasoning* (AR/30 items), measuring the ability to solve basic arithmetic word problems; (3) *Word Knowledge* (WK/35 items), measuring the ability to understand the meaning of words through synonyms; (4) *Paragraph Comprehension* (PC/15 items), measuring ability to obtain information through written material; (5) *Mathematics Knowledge* (MK/25 items), measuring knowledge of mathematical concepts and applications; (6) *Electronics Information* (EI/20 items), measuring knowledge of electrical current, circuits, devices, and electronic systems; (7) *Auto and Shop Information* (AS/25 items), measuring knowledge of automotive maintenance and repair, and wood and metal shop practices; and (8) *Mechanical Comprehension* (MC/25 items), measuring knowledge of the principles of mechanical devices, structural support, and properties of materials. The eight subtests are power tests, which allow for generous time limits to complete the test battery.

In addition to eight subtest scores, three *Career Exploration* composite scores are yielded. *Verbal Skills* is a general measure of vocabulary and reading skills covered in the WK and PC tests. *Math Skills* is a general measure of mathematical ability covered in the MK and AR test results. Similarly, *Science and Technical Skills* is a general measure of science and technical skills covered in the GS, EI, and MC subtests. These three composite scores are reported as standard scores normed on a national sample of youth ages 18 to 23. A fourth composite score, the *Military Entrance Score,* also known as the Armed Forces Qualification Test (AFQT) score, is derived from the AR, MK, PC, and WK subtests and is the score used in determining military career fields an individual may qualify for. The AFQT score is reported as a percentile score between 1 and 99. ASVAB results are reported both to students and counselors on the *ASVAB Summary Results sheet.* This report shows grade-specific, gender-specific, and combined standard scores and score bands for all eight subtests and the three Career Exploration Scores. It also provides students with percentile-based interpretations of those scores.

The CAT-ASVAB Forms 5-8 were introduced in 2008. The CAT-ASVAB is comprised of 145 items and takes approximately two and a half hours to complete. It is an automated test administration system that displays questions sequentially on a computer screen, without the ability to backtrack and change previously submitted answers. This system will score and record answers, score ASVAB subtests, compute the military entrance score (AFQT) and all composite scores, as well as allow for flexible start times and self-paced responding (Pommerich et al., 2009). Pommerich et al. (2009) also reported that an Internet version of the CAT-ASVAB is in development for use in both military and civilian testing.

The CAT-ASVAB subtests measures the same abilities as the P&P-ASVAB, with the primary difference being that the P&P-ASVAB Automotive and Shop Information subtest is broken into separate subtests in the CAT-ASVAB but are combined into one single score (AS). This test is adaptive in that it adapts to the examinee's ability level so as to maximize the precision of the CAT-ASVAB based on the examinee's responses to previous questions. If the examinee performed well on a test item of medium difficulty, the examinee would be presented next with a more challenging question. Conversely, if the examinee performed poorly, a less difficult item would be presented. This pattern will continue until the test has been completed; only answering questions that are appropriate to the examinee's ability level. The CAT-ASVAB has been equated with the P&P-ASVAB, therefore CAT-ASVAB scores have the same meaning as its paper-and-pencil equivalent (ASVAB, 2012).

The FYI Inventory is an interest inventory based on John Holland's theory of career choice and can be taken online at http://www.asvabprogram.com or as a paper-and-pencil self-scoring version. The FYI assesses an individual's correspondence to each of the six RIASEC (Realistic, Investigative, Artistic, Social, Enterprising, and Conventional) types. The FYI consists of 90 items, usually requires about 15 minutes to complete, and employs a 3-point scale of *Like* ("I would like to do this activity"), *Indifferent* ("I don't care one way or the other"), and *Dislike* ("I would not like to do this activity") for each item. In scoring the FYI, a *Like* receives a score of 2, an *Indifferent* is scored as a 1, and *Dislike* is assigned a 0. Raw scores range from 0 to 30, with higher scores reflecting higher interest in that domain (ASVAB, 2005).

The OCCU-find feature found on the program website organizes close to 500 occupations by RIASEC interest codes or by 16 career clusters (i.e., Agriculture, Food & Natural Resources, Education and Training) developed by the U.S. Department of Education, Office of Vocational and Adult Education, so that individuals can rapidly discover occupations that match their own interests, skills, and abilities. Individuals are provided with comprehensive occupational information and links from O*NET online, the Occupational Outlook Handbook, and http://www.careersinthemilitary.com

Technical Considerations

The ASVAB is one of the most highly developed and researched aptitude test batteries of its kind (Jensen, 1988; Rogers, 2001). P&P-ASVAB Forms 23/24 were equated with ASVAB Form 8(a), thus ensuring that percentile scores on all test forms can be interpreted in the same way. Anchor norms for the current forms were derived from aptitude test data collected as part of the Profile of American Youth (PAY97) project. This large-scale research project was sponsored by the U.S. Department of Defense in cooperation with the U.S. Department of Labor to update current national norms for the ASVAB. The norming samples for the current forms of the P&P-ASVAB were drawn to be representative nationally of two groups of American youth. The first norming sample was comprised of approximately 6,000 American youth, ages 18 to 23 as of June 1, 1997, with oversampling of Latino and Non-Latino Black youth. Norms for students in post-secondary schools (two-year colleges) were obtained from this data. The second norming sample was comprised of approximately 4,700 youth who were matriculated in grades 10, 11, and 12 as of Fall 1997. The norming samples were drawn based on a stratified clustered random sampling design and are considered generally representative of the U.S. population for grades 10, 11, and 12 and post-secondary students (Sims & Hiatt, 2004).

Reliability estimates for the P&P-ASVAB are based on item response theory. The reliability estimates across grades for the ASVAB composite scores range from .88 to .91, while estimates for the eight individual tests range from .69 to .88. Because the P&P-ASVAB is primarily used by the military for the effective classification of recruits, numerous criterion-related studies have been conducted that indicate the ASVAB is a valid predictor of success in military training and entry-level job performance (Welsh, Kucinkas, & Curran, 1990). However, there have been only a few studies that have examined the criterion-related validity of the ASVAB in predicting success in civilian occupations (Holmgren & Dalldorf, 1993; Hunter, Crosson, & Freedman, 1985). Holmgren and Dalldorf (1993) found significant correlations between ASVAB composite and individual test scores and measures of success with 8 of 11 popular civilian occupations. Hunter (1983) noted that the General Aptitude Test Battery (GATB), a multiple aptitude test battery used by the U.S. Employment Service, is psychometrically equivalent to the ASVAB. Because the GATB has long been recognized in the literature as a predictor of job performance in the civilian sector, Hunter concluded that the ASVAB also predicts performance in civilian occupations. Since psychometrically equivalent tests share similar validity coefficients with external data, Hunter et al. (1985) determined that the ASVAB was a valid predictor of military and civilian job performance. Given the paucity of research as to the efficacy of using the ASVAB to predict civilian job performance, counselors should exercise some caution in using the ASVAB for this purpose. Additional studies are needed in order to make a conclusive determination if the ASVAB can be used alone as a predictor of success in civilian occupations. However, use of the ASVAB in conjunction with the FYI and other components of the ASVAB-CEP are

Armed Services Vocational Aptitude Battery Career Exploration Program

superior to use of the ASVAB alone in facilitating career exploration and planning of civilian occupations because it also incorporates interests and work values into the career exploration program. The ASVAB is considered to have sufficient content and construct validity (Welsh et al., 1990).

The CAT-ASVAB was normed utilizing a sample from test data collected from the National Longitudinal Survey of Youth 1997 (NLSY97) conducted by the U.S. Department of Labor in collaboration with the U.S. Department of Defense (The Ohio State University, Center for Human Resource Research, 2003). A sample of 7,127 NLSY97 respondents completed the CAT-ASVAB and was comprised similarly to the P&P-ASVAB norming samples in that the NLSY97 sample was representative of American youth between the ages of 17 and 23 with an oversampling of Latino and Non-Latino Black youth.

Reliability estimates for the CAT-ASVAB (Forms 5-9) are also based on item response theory. Reliability estimates for the individual tests ranged from .85 to .91 and met or exceeded test-retest reliability estimates of the P&P-ASVAB (Defense Manpower Data Center, 2008). Wolfe, Moreno, and Segall (1997) reported that the CAT-ASVAB had been demonstrated to be equivalent or superior to the P&P-ASVAB in terms of ability constructs measured and relationships to military job training performance. Moreno and Segall (1997) collected data from 1,470 male Navy recruits in which their results indicated that the CAT-ASVAB measured the same traits as the P&P-ASVAB, with equal or greater precision with threats to validity minimal or nonexistent.

The other testing instrument included in the ASVAB-CEP is the FYI Inventory. The FYI Inventory is based on John Holland's theory of career choice and assesses an individual's resemblance to each of the six RIASEC types. More than 1,000 items were initially written and administered to more than 5,000 high school students in 48 randomly selected schools. The best performing 120 items were selected for further review in a second large scale study (N = 1,958) that was roughly equal in the number of males and females, exhibited ethnic diversity, and was weighted to be nationally representative, so as to identify the best 90 items that would comprise the final version of the FYI. The ASVAB Career Exploration Program Counselor Manual (U.S. Military Entrance Processing Command, 2005a) indicates that the internal consistency of the six RIASEC scales as assessed by coefficient alpha ranged from .92 to .94. The manual also makes reference to additional evidence that was obtained from 259 students who took the FYI Inventory on two occasions over a two to two and one-half week period. Test-retest correlations ranged from .89 (Enterprising) to .93 (Artistic) indicating stability of scores over time. Initial reliability studies of the FYI indicate that the inventory is reliable (U.S. Military Entrance Processing Command, 2005a).

The U.S. Military Entrance Processing Command, (2005a) also reported that initial validity information for the FYI Inventory was obtained from two types of analysis: (1) FYI Inventory item and scale interval relationships, and (2) relationships between FYI Inventory scales and the various scales in the 1994 version of the Strong Interest Inventory. The results of these analyses indicate that the FYI Inventory has substantial evidence for the construct validity of the FYI at the item level. Multidimensional scaling techniques were used to assess the degree to which the FYI Inventory scales fit the RIASEC hexagonal pattern hypothesized by John Holland. This analysis indicated that the FYI had an excellent goodness of fit and exhibited the same type of hexagonal shape as other RIASEC-based interest inventories. Other data presented in the ASVAB-CEP counselor manual suggests that the FYI Inventory has content and criterion validity also.

Gender and diversity concerns have been raised with previous editions of the ASVAB and FYI. The authors have taken considerable time and effort to update current national norms for the ASVAB so that individual scores are compared to a nationally representative sample of youth at their particular grade level (Sims & Hiatt, 2004). Complete information on the gender and racial/ethnic composition of the reference sample will be provided in the next revised technical manual for the ASVAB-CEP. A primary issue with the ASVAB is how the test scores are used in predicting future educational and career outcomes. U. S. Department of Defense research personnel and civilian review panels have investigated the ASVAB thoroughly and have concluded that the test is as free of bias as possible (U.S. Military Entrance Processing Command, 2005a). Wise et al. (1992) concluded after the most recent wide-scale investigation of the ASVAB that the test is a sensitive predictor of training and performance for all applicant groups. According to the ASVAB-CEP Counselor Manual (U.S. Military Entrance Processing Command, 2005a) a variety of statistical decision rules and statistical analyses were employed to help select items for the FYI that minimized gender differences and did not favor one applicant group from another.

As the core component of the ASVAB-CEP, the ASVAB continues to be used as the admissions and placement test for entering the Armed Services. However its use has been expanded so that it can also be used as a career exploration and planning assessment tool for counseling students in the 10th grade and higher about military as well as civilian job and training opportunities (Erford, 2007). More specifically, the ASVAB-CEP can be employed by counselors to aid high school and post-secondary students in learning more about themselves through interest and aptitude skills assessment (ASVAB and FYI Inventory) and explore occupations by engaging in specific structured career planning activities such as the *OCCU-Find, Career Clusters, My Educational and Career Plans,* and *Coursework Planner.* A key feature of the ASVAB-CEP is the ability to assist students in identifying high school courses that will increase their skills and readiness for future employment and post-secondary education. Additionally school counselors may find the ASVAB-CEP helpful when initiating career exploration and planning programming consistent with provisions of the No Child Left Behind Act.

General Utility and Evaluation

The materials that comprise the ASVAB-CEP are of exceptional professional quality. The test booklets, manuals, and other ASVAB publications are well-designed, easy to read, and attractive to the user (Rogers, 2001). The ASVAB Career Exploration Program Counselor Manual (U.S. Military Entrance Processing Command, 2005a) provides school counselors with comprehensive information on program components, ASVAB and FYI test content, reliability, validity, and norms, as well as sections on ASVAB and FYI test administration and interpretation. This manual is currently under revision and will be released on the official ASVAB website upon completion. The ASVAB Career Exploration Program Guide (U.S. Military Entrance Processing Command, 2005b) provides an overview of the ASVAB-CEP and provides answers to the most frequently asked questions about the program. A practice test comprised of sample ASVAB test questions from each subtest is included in the program guide. Another publication, the ASVAB Exploring Careers: The ASVAB Career Exploration Guide (U.S. Military Entrance Processing Command, 2005c) assists students through the interpretation of their ASVAB and FYI scores and how to use the OCCU-Find to interpret their test results.

Students are provided with their ASVAB test results on the ASVAB Summary Results Sheet. This report shows grade-specific standard scores and score bands for all eight tests as well as the three Career Exploration Scores. Students also receive a Military Entrance Score (also known as the Armed Forces Qualifying Test [AFQT] score) that determines if they have met entrance requirements for military service (U.S. Military Entrance Processing Command, 2005a). Counselors also receive a copy of the summary results for each student tested.

The ASVAB is administered by the U.S. Department of Defense or U.S. Office of Personnel Management employees so as to ensure test security. Test administration times and dates are usually arranged by making contact with a military recruiter or an Education Services Specialist at a local Military Entrance Processing Station. Schools are responsible for scheduling ASVAB test sessions, making necessary arrangements for proctors, and providing facilities for test administration (U.S. Military Entrance Processing Command, 2005a).

It should be noted that ASVAB testing is exempt from the provisions of the Family Educational Rights and Privacy Act of 1974 and does not require a signed parental release statement (U.S. Military Entrance Processing Command, 2005a). Participation by students remains voluntary. It is important to note though that unless a student takes the ASVAB, he or she will not be able to obtain an access code that will enable full access to the ASVAB career exploration program website. School officials must also inform the military prior to testing which of the eight options they select to provide ASVAB test results to military recruiters. Only options 7 and 8 forbid the release of ASVAB test results to military recruiters. This is perhaps the component of the ASVAB-CEP that draws the most criticism and remains an impediment to wider civilian use of the ASVAB-CEP. If schools make the decision to release test information to military personnel, then the testing data provided can be used by military recruiters to make contact with students in the 11th grade and higher. This may warrant unsolicited contact by military recruiters for some students.

As the ASVAB-CEP continues to evolve, the ease of use of this career exploration and planning program, as well as its relevance to the field of counseling, continues to grow. The reviewers agree with Rogers (2001) that the materials comprising the ASVAB-CEP are of excellent quality, and include visually appealing test booklets, a logical approach to design and layout, and text that are readable for the test taker. The ASVAB-CEP has also

Armed Services Vocational Aptitude Battery Career Exploration Program

been enhanced with the recent revisions to the ASVAB and FYI Inventory that appear to have reduced gender and diversity bias to the extent possible. Both versions of the ASVAB and FYI Inventory represent the state of the art in test construction. The ASVAB functions exceptionally well as the admissions and placement examination for the armed services, but its predictive validity when applied to civilian occupations are questionable. This can be attributed to the paucity of research examining how predictive the ASVAB is to job performance among civilian occupations. Hopefully this can be addressed in the near future with further research.

The ASVAB-CEP also provides an exceptionally professional comprehensive website well designed for use by both students and counselors. Along with general program information, the site includes assessments that students can use to identify strengths, work values, and vocational interests, as well as structured activities to explore nearly 400 occupations. The website also offers the OCCU-Find to assist students with researching the educational and skill requirements, projected outlook, and expected salary range for specific occupations. Additionally, the site provides helpful information for interested educators, counselors, and parents. The website is easily navigable and very informative, and serves to enhance the overall ease of use and relevance of the ASVAB-CEP. The ASVAB-CEP is a good choice for aptitude and interest assessment as well as career exploration and planning for its intended audience.

References and Additional Resources

ASVAB Official Website: http://www.official-asvab.com

ASVAB. (2005). *Armed Services Vocational Aptitude Battery.* New York, NY: Simon & Schuster.

ASVAB. (2012). *The CAT-ASVAB.* Retrieved from http://official-asvab.com/catasvab_rec.htm

Defense Manpower Data Center. (2008). *CAT-ASVAB forms 5 - 9* (Technical Bulletin No. 3). Seaside, CA: Author. Retrieved from http://official-asvab.com/docs/asvab_techbulletin_3.pdf

Erford, B. T. (2007). *Assessment for counselors.* New York, NY: Lahaska Press.

Holmgren, R. L., & Dalldorf, M. R. (1993, October). *A validation of the ASVAB against supervisors' ratings in the General Aptitude Test Battery (GATB).* Washington, DC: United States Employment Service.

Hunter, J. E. (1983). *The prediction of success in the military: A preliminary report.* Rockville, MD: Research Applications.

Hunter, J. E., Crosson, J. S., & Friedman, D. H. (1985). *The validity of the Armed Services Vocational Aptitude Battery (ASVAB) for civilian and military job performance.* Washington, DC: Office of the Assistant Secretary of Defense (Force Management and Personnel).

Jensen, A. R., (1988). [Armed Services Vocational Aptitude Battery.] In J. T. Kapes & M. M. Mastie (Eds.) *A counselor's guide to career assessment instruments* (2nd ed., pp. 59-62). Alexandria, VA: National Career Development Association.

Moreno, K. E., & Segall, D. O. (1997). Reliability and construct validity of CAT-ASVAB. In W. A. Sands, B. K. Waters, & J. R. McBride (Eds.), *Computerized adaptive testing: From inquiry to operation* (pp. 169-174).Washington, DC: American Psychological Association.

Patrick, J., Blosel, C. W., & Gross, C. L. (2009). [Armed Services Vocational Ability Battery Career Exploration Program.] In E. Whitfield, R. Feller, & C. Wood (Eds.), *A counselor's guide to career assessment instruments* (5th ed., pp. 94-104). Broken Arrow, OK: National Career Development Association.

Pommerich, M., Segall, D.O., & Moreno, K. E. (2009). The nine lives of CAT-ASVAB: Innovations and revelations. In D. J. Weiss (Ed.), *Proceedings of the 2009 GMAC Conference on Computerized Adaptive Testing.* Retrieved from http://www.psych.umn.edu/psylabs/CATCentral/

Rogers, J. E. (2001). [Armed Services Vocational Aptitude Career Exploration Program.] In J. T. Kapes & E. A. Whitfield (Eds.), *A counselor's guide to career assessment instruments* (4th ed., pp. 93-101). Columbus, OH: National Career Development Association.

Sands, W. A., Waters, B. K., & McBride, J. R. (Eds.) (1997). *Adaptive testing: Inquiry to operation.* Washington, DC: American Psychological Association.

Sims, W. H. & Hiatt, C. M. (2004). *Description of student testing program norms.* Alexandria, VA: The CNA Corporation.

The Ohio State University, Center for Human Resource Research. (2003). *A guide to the rounds 1-5 data national longitudinal study of youth 1997.* Retrieved from http://www.bls.gov/nls/97guide/rd5/nls97ugall.pdf

A Counselor's Guide To Career Assessments Instruments

U.S. Military Entrance Processing Command, (1999). *Technical manual for the ASVAB 18/19 career exploration program.* North Chicago, IL: Author.

U.S. Military Entrance Processing Command. (2005a). *ASVAB career exploration program counselor manual* (DD Form 1304-SCM). North Chicago, IL: Author.

U.S. Military Entrance Processing Command. (2005b). *ASVAB career exploration program overview guide* (DD Form 1304-5OV). North Chicago, IL: Author.

U.S. Military Entrance Processing Command, (2005c). *ASVAB exploring careers: The ASVAB career exploration guide* (DD Form 1304-5WB). North Chicago, IL: Author.

Welsh, J. R., Kucinkas, S. K., & Curran, L. T. (1990). *Armed Services Vocational Aptitude Battery (ASVAB): Integrative review of validity studies* (AFHRL-TR-90-22). Brooks Air Force Base, TX: Air Force Human Resources Laboratory.

Wise, L., Welsh, J., Grafton, F., Foley, P., Earles, J., Sawin, L., & Divgi, D. R. (1992). *Sensitivity and fairness of the Armed Services Vocational Aptitude Battery (ASVAB)* technical composites (DMDC Technical Report 92-002). Monterey, CA: Defense Manpower Data Center.

Wolfe, J. H., Moreno, K. E., & Segall, D. O. (1997). Evaluating the predictive validity of CAT-ASVAB. In W. A. Sands, B. K. Waters, & J. R. McBride (Eds.), *Computerized adaptive testing: From inquiry to operation* (pp. 175-179). Washington, DC: American Psychological Association.

134

THE HIGHLANDS ABILITY BATTERY
Robert McDonald (Paper-and-Pencil Version and CD Version)
and Lazar Emanuel (CD Version and Online Version)

The Highlands Company

1328 Boston Post Road
Larchmont, NY 10538

http://www.highlandsco.com
http://www.highlandslifeandcareercenter.com
CD version: http://www.highlandscd.com
Online version: http://www.abilitybattery.com

Target Population: Adolescents, young adults, and adults; ages 15 and older.

Statement of the Purpose of the Instrument: The purpose of the The Highlands Ability Battery (tHAB) is to compare the client's scores on each of 19 work samples with the scores of all users who have completed the Battery in the same format (CD or online). Further, the purpose is to conduct feedback with clients either individually or in groups (e.g., corporate groups, student groups). Each work sample measures a different innate ability by requiring the client to respond on his or her keyboard to visual and aural stimuli. In this way, the tHAB measures whether the client is a specialist or a generalist, and whether he or she is an introvert or an extrovert. It also measures the client's orientation to time management, as well as to the following abilities: classification, concept organization, idea productivity, spatial relations (abstract and structural), verbal memory, tonal memory, image memory, kinesthetic memory, number memory, pitch discrimination, observation, visual speed, visual accuracy, and vocabulary. Results are adjusted to compensate for ranges in typing speed. Instructions are given both on screen and aurally.

Titles of Subtests, Scales, Scores Provided: The Battery consists of 19 work samples or subtests:

- Generalist/Specialist
- Extrovert/Introvert
- Time Frame Orientation
- Classification (Inductive Reasoning)
- Concept Organization (Analytical Reasoning)
- Time Frame (Foresight)
- Idea Productivity (Ideaphoria)
- Spatial Relations Visualization (Structural)
- Spatial Relations Theory (Abstract)
- Design Memory

- Verbal Memory (Associative Memory)
- Observation
- Tonal Memory (Auditory Memory)
- Pitch Discrimination
- Rhythm Memory
- Number Memory
- Visual Speed
- Visual Accuracy
- Vocabulary Level

All the subtests have scores in the range of 5 to 99. The client receives a separate score for each subtest, measured on the following scale: Low 5-34; Mid-Range 35-64; High 65-99. tHAB is scored during the assessment process. A report is available to the client immediately upon completion of the assessment. The report contains 32 pages of text and graphics.

Forms and Levels Available, with Dates of Publication/Revision of Each: CD version, 2000; Online version, revised in 2006.

Date of Most Recent Edition of Test Manual, User's Guide, Etc.: Test Manual, 2006. Instructions for registration and technical support are supplied to each user. Directions for completing the subtests are contained within the CD itself and within the online version.

Languages in Which Available: English only.

The Highlands Ability Battery

Time:

> **Actual Test Time:** Approximately three hours.

> **Total Administration Time:** Approximately three hours.

Norm Group(s) on Which Scores Are Based: Norms were based originally on all clients who completed the paper-and-pencil version of the Battery. The norms were tested and confirmed by Dr. C. L. Holland in 1994. In 2002, the Chauncey Group, an Educational Testing Service (ETS) subsidiary, examined 4,307 CD reports. The Chauncey Group computed sample sizes, means, standard deviations and complete norms tables for each of the 23 CD-based scores for four groups of examinees ages 15-21, 22-30, 31-39, and 40 and older. Also, examination of the frequency distributions among the four age groups show consistent similarities for scores at the different percentiles regardless of age group. Those differences in scores by age group that did exist were consistent across the different age groups.

Since completion of the Chauncey Group report, The Highlands Company has been collecting additional data in an online data bank based upon the test results of each client. Norms based on the CD results are computed by age and sex and are compared with the paper-and-pencil results to assure reasonable conformity. Since the introduction of the online version, a separate set of data has been maintained for it. These are also distributed by sex and age. The age range is 15-21, 22-30, 31-39, 40-55, and 56+. Data are also maintained by sex. Each subdivision of age and sex is separately normed.

Manner in Which Results Are Reported for Individuals: A score expressed in percentile ranking is issued for each work sample. A 32-page report is issued to each client. The report contains a bar chart showing the client's score on each work sample. The results and their significance are explained in narrative form, as well as graphically. Sample reports may be found at the publisher's website. After the report is issued and analyzed by a user and an affiliate of the company, an individual feedback conference lasting two hours is conducted. During the conference, the results are explained to the client. In some situations, as with corporate teams or a class of students, feedback can be accomplished effectively in group feedback sessions lasting 4 to 8 hours. The Battery is used in many corporate and student settings for training in individual development, team building, and leadership.

Report Format/Content for Group Summaries: For each type of group, there is a facilitator's manual and a participant manual. Manuals are available in Personal Development, Team Building, and Leadership. Before each program, a Group Profile showing the distribution of scores among the participants is prepared and issued. This enables the affiliate to focus on the strengths and challenges of the group as a whole, as well as of the individual participants.

Cost of Materials: Due to possible price changes since publication date, be sure to check the publisher's website.

> **Specimen Set:** The Battery and the two-hour individual feedback are treated as one integrated service, approximately $450.00. The Highlands Company pays one or another of its affiliates for conducting the individual feedback. When they deal with their own clients, affiliates of the company are permitted to establish their own prices for the Battery and feedback. When group programs are substituted for individual feedback, the cost varies depending on the size of the group, the nature of the program, and the length of the program. Clients in a group feedback are charged approximately $50.00 each for the Participant's Manual.

> **Counselee Materials:** Various manuals and instruction sheets.

> **Machine Scoring:** All scores are computed and stored electronically in a common database housed on the company's own server. Scores are collected and scored immediately. Scoring is done online as a work sample is completed.

Hand Scoring: Not available.

Local Machine Scoring: Not available.

Computer Software Options Available: Computerized adaptive administration. The software was designed, implemented, and is copyrighted by The Highlands Company.

Additional Comments of Interest to Users: The Highlands Company employs a full-time technician who is available to answer any questions relating to the CD version and the online version.

A Counselor's Guide To Career Assessments Instruments

Published Reviews of the Instrument in the Last 15 Years:

Ratts, M. J. (2009). [The Highlands Ability Battery.] In E. A. Whitfield, R. W. Feller, & C. Wood (Eds.), *A counselor's guide to career assessment instruments* (5th ed., pp. 155-162). Broken Arrow, OK: National Career Development Association.

Werner, W. L. (2011). Make the right move: Career assessment tools. *Law Practice: The Business of Practicing Law, 37* (4), 54-55.

The Highlands Ability Battery

Reviewed by:

Manivong J. Ratts

Julian R. McCullough

Department of Counseling and School Psychology
Seattle University

Description

The Highlands Ability Battery (tHAB) is based on the initial work of Johnson O'Connor, a research scientist devoted to studying innate abilities. O'Connor (1928) theorized that individuals are born with certain natural abilities developed from infancy and can be measured upon maturation, usually by age 14. tHAB was developed primarily for use in career counseling with high school students, college students, and for working adults in career transition. The publisher, The Highlands Company, offers the tHAB in paper-and-pencil (1992), CD (2000), and online (2004) formats (Tavantzis, 2007). The paper-and-pencil version can be administered in individual or group formats. tHAB CD and online versions may be taken in one sitting or in intervals.

tHAB consists of a series of 19 timed work samples. Each work sample (scale) measures a particular ability and is categorized under one of the following sections (subscales in parentheses): (1) Personal Style Assessment (Generalist-Specialist, Introvert-Extrovert Scale, and Time Frame Orientation); (2) Driving Abilities (Classification, Concept Organization, Idea Productivity, Spatial Relations Theory, and Spatial Relations Visualization); (3) Specialized Abilities (Design Memory, Observation, Verbal Memory, Tonal Memory, Rhythm Memory, Pitch Discrimination, Number Memory, and Visual Speed and Accuracy); and (4) Vocabulary (Vocabulary). Sample reports, which include examples of work samples, are available on The Highlands Company website. Each report includes descriptions of each work sample as well as an explanation of an individual's score on that work sample. Individual scores for each work sample are expressed as percentiles of all persons who have completed that work sample. Individual scores are categorized as low, medium, or high percentile scores.

Each work sample is timed to determine the ease with which an individual is able to complete a particular task. The paper-and-pencil and CD versions take approximately 3 hours to complete, while the online version can be completed in 2 hours and 30 minutes. Both tHAB CD and online versions include written and voice-recorded instructions. All three versions of the Battery provide examples of how to complete each work sample and offer test takers practice work samples.

Results of both tHAB CD and online versions are available immediately in electronic format upon completing the Battery. The report includes a detailed 30-page summary of each work sample compiled in a personal profile and bar chart to illustrate ability patterns and how certain abilities cluster. A copy of the results is also automatically transmitted via the Internet to a trained and certified Highlands affiliate. Affiliates are available live or via phone for 2 hour (individual or group) interpretation of results. Live interpretations can also be recorded on a CD-ROM and mailed to test takers.

The Highlands Ability Battery

Individual reports vary depending on whether the test taker is a student or an adult. A report issued in 2007 relates natural abilities to the functions of leadership. Certified affiliates who consult with students are likely to explore college choices, college curriculum, college majors, and college selection. Affiliates working with adults may address career changes, career transitions, career exploration, career services, and leadership.

Interpretation of results by a trained affiliate is required for all versions by The Highlands Company. Certified Highlands affiliates are individuals who have participated in *The Highlands Company Affiliate Training Program*, who are either employed through The Highlands Company or one of the more than 250 trained and certified consultants from around the world (e.g., United States, United Kingdom, Singapore, and Canada). Affiliates are able to explain results, provide meaning to the Battery, and discuss future steps in individual and group formats. An application is required for consideration to be a trained Highlands affiliate. The training consists of completing tHAB, receiving live feedback on the results, and participating in eight 2-hour telephone-based training sessions. Face-to-face training is also available. Affiliate training is offered via tele-classes up to 10 times per year and in person a minimum of two times per year. Customized corporate training is also an option. Affiliates are also trained to offer individual and group feedback and required to provide two practice feedback reports and two practice feedback conferences.

The Highlands Company made a significant contribution to their knowledge of law and the skills and talents lawyers possess. *The Highlands Ability Battery and the Lawyers' Report* (Emanuel, 2011) was released in August 2011. This report was designed to guide all law practitioners and law students in various stages of their careers. Additionally, the release of a new Career Supplement to provide abilities-based career exploration for students is planned for 2013 (D. Stiles, personal communication, November 13, 2012).

tHAB is intended to be used to help individuals better understand their natural abilities and how these relate to career development and planning for high school-aged students, college and university students, and adults. Counselors may also find the Battery useful in helping students understand their learning styles as one section of the instrument measures learning styles (Tavantzis, 2007). The Battery is also used to assist individuals who are in career transition, to help businesses restructure their workforce according to employee abilities, employee team building and development, employee training needs and leadership. Counselors refer clients to a Highlands affiliate to take the instrument, and it is common for clients to share the results of their scores with their counselor. When appropriate, and with client's signed permission, counselors will communicate directly with a Highlands affiliate.

Technical Considerations

A summary of psychometric properties (e.g., reliability and validity measures) of tHAB is available on The Highlands Company website. A convenience sample from previous test takers is used to determine psychometric properties. Age and gender differences are considered in this sample. Racial differences are not considered. The Highlands Company asserts that the minimum reliability scores required for all 19 work samples of the Battery is $r = .80$. Holland (1994) revealed that the 19 work samples have reliability scores ranging from .83 to .95. Reliability scores were obtained from a convenience sample of 298 Highlands test takers ranging in age between 15 to 66 and included 146 males and 152 females. Adults over 25 were mainly college graduates, and those under 25 were either in college or former college students (Holland, 1994).These scores suggest the 19 work samples are highly reliable and useful for comparison purposes. Updated reliability and re-norming data for the tHAB, conducted by independent psychometrician Andrew Neiner, Ph.D., will be available in 2013. Included in the analysis will be a sample of more than 11,000 test takers who have completed an online version of the tHAB since 2007 (D. Stiles, personal communication, November 13, 2012).

In 2002, The Highlands Company contracted with the Chauncey Group, a subsidiary of the Educational Testing Service (ETS), to conduct a statistical audit of the CD version of the Battery (Breyer, Katz, & Duran, 2002). This study computed sample sizes, means, standard deviations, and provided norms tables for test takers in the following age categories: (1) 15-21, (2) 22-30, (3) 31-39, and (4) 40 and older. The researchers concluded that the CD version yielded 23 separate scores on the 19 work samples and that each score on the Battery correlated sufficiently, thus deeming them reliable for interpretation purposes.

Validity studies have also been conducted. Holland (1994) concluded that there was adequate evidence of both convergent and divergent validity when assessing individual work samples. That is, abilities that were expected to be related (e.g., typing speed and visual speed) were related. Similarly, those abilities that should not be related (e.g., time frame and writing speed) showed little relationship. This seems to suggest strong initial evidence of validity on tHAB. No studies beyond Holland have been conducted to date. However, The Highlands website does provide access to a Technical Manual (McDonald, 1995), which highlights Holland's research and provides psychometric properties.

General Utility and Evaluation

tHAB assesses natural abilities through completion of timed objective tasks. This can be helpful in assisting students with career decisions, adults who are in the midst of a life transition, and those interested in understanding how their abilities relate to leadership qualities. A key strength of tHAB relates to the multiple formats available. Offering CD and online versions of the Battery allows test takers freedom to take the instrument at their convenience as long as they have access to a computer and reliable Internet access. Both CD and online formats use voice-recorded instruction, which can be an added benefit for those who are auditory learners. Instructions, both on the screen and in the voice recording, are simple, clear and comprehensive. Test takers using the CD version need to complete the Battery on the same computer because scores are stored on the computer's hard drive. Receiving results immediately upon completion of the Battery is also an added feature. It is important to note that the CD version of the tHAB will soon be phased out to enable better access to ongoing research and test updates.

Although technology has increased to provide additional formats, test takers who are not computer proficient or do not have access to a computer and/or the Internet are still able to use the paper-and-pencil test. Further, Highlands affiliates are professional and helpful in their interpretation of results for any format.

The time (2.5 hours to 3 hours) required to complete the tHAB is consuming when compared to other inventories. A mitigating factor of the lengthy time required is that tHAB may be taken in one sitting or in intervals. The information provided is in-depth and can be useful for those in the midst of career exploration and decision making. Another limitation is that tHAB CD is not compatible with Apple computers. However, Apple computer users have the option of using the Internet version of the Battery – which is the most popular among the two versions (D. Stiles, personal communication, November 13, 2012).

This instrument is only available in English. The lack of multiple language versions is unfortunate because it leaves out important cultural groups that may benefit from taking this instrument. The Highlands Company states that it presently administers the instrument in other countries where English is either the primary or secondary language: Kazakhstan, Australia, Canada, France, India, Singapore, Switzerland, Thailand, United Kingdom, and Germany (D. Stiles, personal communication, November 13, 2012). This instrument is appropriate for a variety of age groups (e.g., adolescents to late adulthood) and is applicable for use with males and females.

There are several resources available for applying findings for tHAB (see References and Additional Resources). Further, the Highlands Company has a Facebook page.

References and Additional Resources

Breyer, F. J., Katz, J., & Duran, M. (2002). *A report on the statistical characteristics of The Highlands Ability Battery CD.* Princeton, NJ: The Chauney Group.

Brown, C., Harvey, S., & Stiles, D. (2011). Using a natural abilities battery for academic and career guidance: A ten year study. *Journal of Veterinary Medical Education 2011, 38*(3), 270-7.

Emanuel, L. (2011). *The highlands ability battery and the lawyers' report.* Highlands Forum. Retrieved from http://www.highlandslifeandcareercenter.com/highlands-forum.php?authid=54

Holland, C. L. (1994). *Research proposal: The highlands ability battery.* Atlanta, GA: Georgia State University.

Martin, L. H., & Danelo, K. T. (2006). *Highlands the right choice: Matching your abilities with college and career.* Leesburg, VA: Highlands Consulting Group.

McDonald, R. D. (1995). *The highlands ability battery technical manual.* Larchmont, NY: The Highlands Company.

McDonald, B., & Hutcheson, D. E. (2005). *Don't waste your talent: The 8 critical steps to discovering what you do best.* Larchmont, NY: The Highlands Company.

O'Connor, J. (1928). *Born that way.* Baltimore, MO: The Williams & Wilkins Company.

Tavantzis, T. N. (2007). *A report on the organization, function, reliability, and validity of the Highlands Ability Battery (tHAB).* Saint Joseph's University.

The Highlands Company Facebook page: https://www.facebook.com/TheHighlandsCompany.

The Highlands Company website: http://www.highlandsco.com

A COUNSELOR'S GUIDE TO CAREER ASSESSMENTS INSTRUMENTS

O*NET ABILITY PROFILER
U.S. Department of Labor, Employment and Training Administration

Employment & Training Administration
USDOL, FPB Mail Stop S4231
200 Constitution Avenue, NW
Washington, DC 20210
http://www.doleta.gov/programs/onet
http://www.onetcenter.org/AP.html
o-net@dol.gov

Target Population: Individuals seeking to identify their work-related abilities and use them to explore careers: high school and post-secondary students as well as adults. Age 16 or older with a minimum sixth-grade English reading level.

Statement of the Purpose of the Instrument: The O*NET Ability Profiler was designed as part of a whole-person assessment approach. The instrument enables users to identify their ability profile to use this information to identify their Occupational Information Network (O*NET) system at http://online.onetcenter.org, the nation's leading source of occupational information. The instrument measures nine abilities: Verbal, Arithmetic Reasoning, Computation, Spatial Ability, Form Perception, Clerical Perception, Motor Coordination, Finger Dexterity, Manual Dexterity. The first six of these abilities are measures through six paper-and-pencil subtests, and the remaining three are measured by five psychomotor subtests. The instrument is appropriate for a variety of users including students, first-time job seekers, and those individuals in occupational transition. After taking the Ability Profiler, counselees receive a customized score report, which not only presents their ability profile, but presents concepts about career exploration that users will be able to use throughout their working lives.

Titles of Subtests, Scales, Scores Provided: Percentile and raw scores for nine abilities: Verbal, Arithmetic Reasoning, Computation, Spatial Ability, Form Perception, Clerical Perception, Motor Coordination, Finger Dexterity, and Manual Dexterity. There are 11 subtests: Arithmetic Reasoning, Computation, Vocabulary, Three-Dimensional Space, Name Comparison, Object Matching, Mark Making, Place, Turn, Assemble, and Disassemble.

Forms and Levels Available, with Dates of Publication/Revision of Each: 2001.

Date of Most Recent Edition of Test Manual, User's Guide, Etc.:

Instrument Materials: O*NET Ability Profiler, Form 1 (2002), Using your O*NET Ability Profiler Results (2002), Part 7 Mark Making Answer Sheet (2002).

Administration Materials: Administration Manual (2002), User's Guide (2011), Record of Apparatus Scores (2002), Three-Dimensional Space Cutouts (2000).

Scoring Materials: Scoring Program User's Guide (2011), O*NET Ability Profiler Envelope-Premarked Response Sheets for Scoring Calibration (2000), Ability Profiler Data Entry Program (2011), Ability Profiler Data Entry Help Files (2011).

Training Materials: Administration Training Manual (2002), Administrator Training Overhead Masters (2000), Administrator Training Overhead Masters (2000), Administrator Training Participants Guide (2002).

Languages in Which Available: English and Spanish.

Time:

Actual Test Time: 60 minutes

Total Administration Time: There are three administration options:

1. Administer the 11 separately timed exercises (approximately 2-1⁄2 hours and may require some additional apparatus set-up time). This option provides the most information to the examinee about his or her abilities and how they relate to all occupations. This option should be selected if information is needed about all occupations, including those that require psychomotor abilities.

141

O*NET Ability Profiler

2. Administer the 7 paper-and-pencil exercises (Parts 1 through 7; approximately1-1⁄2 to 2 hours). With this option, information about some occupations that require psychomotor abilities may not be available to the examinee. This option should be selected if information is NOT needed about occupations that require manual dexterity or finger dexterity.

3. Administer the 6 non-psychomotor exercises (Parts 1 through 6; approximately1-1⁄2 to 2 hours). With many occupations, scores on the psychomotor exercises are not needed. This option should be selected if information is NOT needed about occupations that require motor coordination, manual dexterity, or finger dexterity.

Norm Group(s) on Which Scores Are Based: General working population ages 18 to 54. Supplemented with high school samples, ages 16 to 18.

Manner in Which Results Are Reported for Individuals: Counselee receives a customized generated 16-page score report. The score report, designed for self-interpretation, includes the following: (1) definitions of the abilities measured; (2) percentile and number correct scores for each of nine abilities; (3) graphical display of an individual's ability profile; (4) an exercise to select a job zone (amount of training, education, work experience the counselee currently has or wishes to pursue); (5) a set of steps describing using your ability profile and job zone to explore careers; and (6) five lists of occupations developed using the client's ability profile and each one of the five job zones. The score report also instructs the counselee in exploring occupations on his or her occupational lists in the U.S. Department of Labors' O*NET system, the nation's leading source of occupational information.

Report Format/Content for Group Summaries: Not available.

Machine Scoring: Not available.

Hand Scoring: Not available.

Local Machine Scoring: There are two options for scoring:

1. O*NET Ability Profiler Scoring Program (APSP). This program enables the use of answer sheets which are machine scanned. The scanned results are downloaded to a computer which produces the printed customized individual score report. Instructions and materials for using the APSP and scanner equipment are provided for free download at www.onetcenter.org/AP.hmtl

2. O*NET Ability Profiler Data Entry Program. This program enables data entry of clients' item responses and the creation of a file which can be downloaded to a computer. The downloaded file produces the client's customized score report. The data entry program and instructions for use are provided for free download at http://www.onetcenter.org/AP.hmtl

Equipment/configurations necessary for the O*NET Ability Profiler Scoring Software is as follows: Personal computer with at least an Intel Pentium family central processing unit (CPU) running at 200 MHz, 32 MB of random access memory (RAM), about 30 MB of free disk space, CD-ROM or DVD drive, and screen resolution of 800 × 600 or higher; printer; support software — Windows, Word 97 or later; recommended scanning equipment and software — scanner models: OpScan 2, 3, 4, 4xp, 5, 6, 7, 8, or 10; Windows ScanTools software version 1.6 or higher or Windows ScanTools II software version 1.0 or higher; connection cable between scanner and CPU.

Note: Although the system will run correctly with the minimum configuration, it may not execute very quickly. The program relies on advanced object linking and embedding (OLE) technology that is very resource intensive. For reasonable speed you should be running at least a Pentium II 233MHz CPU and have at least 64 MB of RAM. Other scanner models may also work correctly but have not been tested. If you need to use other models, confirm that the scanner is reading the data in a manner compatible with APSP. System on p. 12). There are many configurations of hardware and software on the market that can be used to automatically scan the examinee response sheets and place the information in a computer file in the layout expected by the scoring program. At this time, the scanners above along with ScanTools software are supported. These particular types of scanning equipment and software are not required to use the APSP. However, if a different scanner and/or scanning software is used, someone with computer programming skills may be needed to create a new examinee test-response-sheet definition file that will allow your scanner to read the examinee response sheets.

A Counselor's Guide To Career Assessments Instruments

Cost of Materials: Due to possible price changes since publication date, be sure to check the publisher's website. All materials (instrument, demonstration version of the instrument, user guides for counselors, technical development reports) are available free to download at www.onetcenter.org/AP.hmtl. You can purchase the machine-scorable answer sheets for $43.00 (100 each package).

Specimen Set: Not available.

Counselee Materials: O*NET Ability Profiler Instrument, Form 1 Ability Profiler machine-scorable answer sheet.

Published Reviews of the Instrument in the Last 15 Years:

Kinnier, R. T., & Gorin, J. (2009). [O*NET Ability Profiler.] In E. A. Whitfield, R. W. Feller, & C. Wood (Eds.), *A counselor's guide to career assessment instruments* (5th ed., pp. 180-187). Broken Arrow, OK: National Career Development Association.

O*NET Ability Profiler

Reviewed by:

Richard T. Kinnier
Division of Psychology
Arizona State University

Joanna Gorin
Educational Testing Service

Description

The O*NET Ability Profiler is one of three O*NET assessment tools that provides clients with career-related information that can serve to facilitate career choice. The Ability Profiler focuses on the extent to which the test taker has (or can learn) the knowledge and skills required by numerous occupations. The Ability Profiler, developed by the U.S. Department of Labor, was derived from Forms E and F of the General Aptitude Test Battery (GATB of the U.S. Employment Service). Following considerable efforts to improve the scales qualitatively and quantitatively (e.g., a reduction of the number of items and subtests, the reduction of item bias, aesthetic and clarity improvements), those forms were the basis for the development of the Ability Profiler Forms 1 and 2.

The Ability Profiler consists of 11 separately timed sections: 7 are paper-and-pencil tests of which 6 are non-psychomotor and one is psychomotor, and 4 sections involve the manipulation of pegs and rivets. The tests are combined to measure nine basic abilities: Arithmetic Reasoning (18 items), Verbal Ability (19 items), Spatial Ability (20 items), Computation (40 items), Clerical Perception (90 items), Form Perception (42 items), Motor Coordination (drawing lines within squares), Manual Dexterity (placing and turning pegs), and Finger Dexterity (assembling and disassembling rivets).

The manual states that the results can be used on a "stand alone" basis or with other O*NET career exploration tools or with other assessments. Test results are presented in two ways: (1) scores expressed as percentiles (derived from large national norms) for each of the nine ability scales, and (2) a list of occupations that "match" the examinee's ability profile. Examinees can also search for their "matches" within five specific Job Zones. Zones refer to levels of preparation needed to enter a particular job. Zones range from "little or no preparation" needed (Zone 1) to "extensive preparation" needed (Zone 5).

As with all tests in career counseling, the results of any test should be used in conjunction with other test results and the "raw data" derived from the client's life experiences and self-assessment activities. The results from the Ability Profiler can be a rich data source providing a profile of a client's abilities and a list of promising occupations. Certainly the two other O*NET tests (as well as other well-respected values and interest inventories) could further enhance the test taker's self-knowledge.

O*NET Ability Profiler

The Ability Profiler results should rarely, if ever, be used to definitively rule in or out any specific occupation for a client. Rather, high scores can inform the client that he or she may possess a talent for succeeding in specified occupations, while low scores might serve as a warning that challenges loom ahead if he or she chooses to pursue any of those occupations. That information should be considered along with other criteria relevant to career success and satisfaction such as interests, values, levels of motivation, and family-related issues. In our opinion, the most important benefit to be derived from using the Ability Profiler (and other tests) is how the derived information is likely to inspire the client to seek more career-related information. Clients are likely to want to find out more about occupations identified as good "matches" for them. The O*NET system also provides extensive information about those and other occupations that clients might be interested in reading about.

Technical Considerations

The O*NET Ability Profiler was derived from the already highly regarded GATB. Impressive attempts were made to improve the GATB scales both qualitatively and quantitatively (see Segall & Monzon, 1995; *Ability Profiler User's Guide*, U.S. Department of Labor, 2002a). Qualitative revisions included aesthetic and clarity improvements as well as improvements in item wording and scoring procedures. Quantitatively, item and scale properties were evaluated with several impressive statistical analyses. Item response theory (IRT) was used to assist in the equating of the nonspeeded forms, to select optimally discriminating items, as well as to reduce cultural bias of any items. The final versions of the scales provide the most reliable information for the middle of the ability distribution. The dimensionality analyses used, which employed the most modern nonlinear factor analytic techniques, supports the hypothesized structure of most of the ability scales.

Reliability was estimated by alternate-form correlations. The alternate-form reliability coefficients for the Profiler (*Range* = .78 to .92) were higher than the coefficients for the GATB forms. Validity was evaluated by correlating scores between the GATB scales and the Ability Profiler scales, which are highly correlated. Also, nonlinear factor analysis supported the structural validity of the scores. In our opinion, reliability and validity of the individual Profiler scales have been well established. Validity would be further enhanced if future studies performed correlational analyses on the scales with external measures of job performance and success.

The procedures by which the authors established "matching" test-taker score profiles with numerous occupations were psychometrically complex and ambitious (see Allen, Tsacoumis, & McCloy, 2011; McCloy, Campbell, Oswald, Rivkin, & Lewis, 1999). In essence, based on GATB score profiles for numerous Dictionary of Occupational Titles (DOT) occupations and job analysis information, prediction equations were developed for the nine abilities of the Profiler. Profile scores for about 11,500 occupations (labeled, O*NET occupations) were standardized (M = 100, SD = 20), allowing test-takers' profiles to be correlated with occupational profiles. This information is translated into a list of occupations that the test taker's pattern of abilities "match" (i.e., occupations that the test taker has the requisite skills to perform successfully). Allen et al. (2011) described a study in which new occupational ability profiles were computed. Using correlational analyses, cluster and discriminant function analyses, and expert ratings, the authors concluded that the results "suggest that linking O*NET Ability Profiler results to occupational ability profiles is beneficial to individuals identifying occupations as potential careers" (p. 2).

Although the procedures and analyses employed to establish match profiles for test takers and occupations is impressive, we were not able to find some information that would give us more confidence that the score profile matches are clearly valid. Based on the available information, the psychometric and statistical data reduction procedures applied likely resulted in appropriate job profiles, though evidence specifically addressing this issue would be useful. For example, originally regression equations were established for ability estimates of the DOT occupations and some O*NET occupations combined numerous DOT occupations. Their regression equations were based on "representative" DOT occupations. In our earlier 2009 review, we questioned to what extent these are valid representatives. Recent research, however, has resulted in all occupations being formulated from within the constantly growing O*NET database, according to David Rivkin (personal communication, June 12, 2012), one of the developers of the O*NET Ability Profiler. Because of the ongoing and extensive research on the measure, we think that the O*NET Ability Profiler probably ranks it as one of the most valid psychological tests in existence.

According to Rivkin (personal communication, March 27, 2007), test takers record their answers for the paper-and-pencil portions of the instrument on a machine-scanable answer sheet. Administrators record raw scores on answer sheets for the psychomotor portions of the instrument. The psychomotor portions are optional. Answer sheets are scanned and a data file is created which is read by a scoring software program. The scoring software produces a customized score report for each individual test taker. If scanning equipment is not available, administrators can enter in the test taker's answers into a data entry program which then produces the customized score reports.

General Utility and Evaluation

The O*NET Ability Profiler is an impressive test. Its predecessor measure, the GATB, was a widely used and well-established test. The Ability Profiler is an improvement of an already excellent test. For test-takers, the items and instructions are clear and straight-forward. The 2½-hour test yields much data on the test taker's career-related abilities. The psychometric procedures, including the use of IRT based methods, used to improve the test and establish reliability and validity are ambitious and impressive. Future external validity studies on the individual scales and a clearer establishment of the validity on all of the occupational matches will improve an already excellent measure. In the meantime, counselors should feel confident that their clients' scores are basically valid. Ability Profiler results (like all test results) are best used in conjunction with other assessment information to guide further self-exploration and occupational information seeking. Given that perspective, we highly recommend the O*NET Ability Profiler as one excellent career counseling tool.

References and Additional Resources

Allen, M. T., Tsacoumis, S., & McCloy, R. A. (2011). *Updating occupational ability profiles with O*NET content model descriptors*. (Vol. 1). Raleigh, NC: National Center for O*NET Development.

McCloy, R., Campbell, J., Oswald, F., Rivkin, D., & Lewis, P. (1999). *Generation and use of occupational Ability Profiles for exploring O*NET Occupational units* (Volumes I and II). Raleigh, NC: National Center for O*NET Development.

Segall, D. O., & Monzon, R. I. (1995). *Equating forms E and F of the P&P-GATB*. San Diego, CA: Navy Personnel Research and Development Center.

U. S. Department of Labor. (2002a). *O*NET Ability Profiler user's guide*. Washington, DC: Author.

U.S. Department of Labor. (2002b). *O*NET Ability Profiler administrator training manual*. Washington, DC: Author.

U. S. Department of Labor. (2002c). *O*NET Ability Profiler administration manual*. Washington, DC: Author.

TESTS OF ADULT BASIC EDUCATION

CTB/McGraw-Hill

CTB/McGraw-Hill
20 Ryan Ranch Road
Monterey, CA 93940
800-538-9547
http://www.ctb.com

Target Population: Tests of Adult Basic Education (TABE 9 & 10) can be used with a wide range of audiences: high school equivalency or General Equivalency Degree (GED) programs; vocational programs; certain community college programs; welfare-to-work programs; occupational or military advancement programs; alternative educational programs; and English for speakers of other languages (ESOL) programs, which may include basic education, vocational, and life skills assessment.

Statement of the Purpose of the Instrument: TABE is an assessment product designed to measure basic skills commonly found in adult basic education curricula and instructional programs. TABE is most commonly used to assess adults for placement in education, training, or employment programs as well as determining readiness for the GED exam.

Titles of Subtests, Scales, Scores Provided: Reading, Math Computation, Applied Math, Language, Language Mechanics, Vocabulary, and Spelling.

Forms and Levels Available, with Dates of Publication/Revision of Each: TABE 9&10, both forms 2003. 5 levels — Limited Literacy, Easy, Medium, Difficult, and Advanced.

Date of Most Recent Edition of Test Manual, User's Guide, Etc.: Teacher's Guides (2005); Test Directions (2003).

Languages in Which Available: English and Spanish.

Time:

Actual Test Time:

Locator Test	Complete Battery of Items	Estimated Testing Time *	Survey No. of Items *	Estimated Testing Time *
Reading	50	0:50	25	0:25
Mathematics	40	0:24	25	0:15
Computation Applied	50	0:50	25	0:25
Mathematics Language	55	0:55	25	0:25
Language Mechanics	20	0:14	---	---
Vocabulary	20	0:15	---	---
Spelling	20	0:10	---	---
Total	225	3:34	100	1:30

Please note that these times are used as guidelines only. Allow 10 minutes for instruction, recording names on answer sheets, etc. Note that the Spelling test is optional and does not contribute to total Battery scores.

Total Administration Time: About 2 hours.

Norm Group(s) on Which Scores Are Based: TABE was normed on a population age 14 years and older. TABE is a viable option to current norm-referenced tests for high school levels. Although TABE items were specifically designed for adults, TABE scale scores are linked statistically to the California Achievement Tests, Fifth Edition (CAT/5), created for K–12 students.

Manner in Which Results Are Reported for Individuals: Grade equivalent, scale scores, number correct, national percentile, NCE, national stanine, % mastery, predicted GED score, NRS (National Reporting System) Level. Customer scored is the only option for TABE 9&10. CTB does not provide scoring (Basic Service). Online scoring and reporting is available with TestMate TABE Software. Hand scoring option is available with scoring stencils or by using the self-scoring Scoreze answer sheets.

Report Format/Content for Group Summaries: Student Test Report—offers a skill-by-skill report for each individual student; Student Pre- and Post-Test Report—provides a pre- and post-test summary for each individual student; Student Prescriptive Report—shows individual performance by skill, then refers each student to specific lessons in the books and software available in your organization; Rank List Report—presents (in roster listing) students in selected score order; Group List Report—presents a class roster, listing each student's grade equivalent, national percentile, and additional scores; Group Report—gives a summary of pre- and post-test scores for all students in a group, plus average scores for the group selected; and Item Analysis Report—presents item-by-objective results for an individual.

Machine Scoring: Not available.

Hand Scoring: Scored by counselor.

Local Machine Scoring: Provisions/conditions/equipment required: OMR scanners used for scoring sit on a desk, but are different from the image scanners that are commonly attached to a desktop computer. OMRs can scan both sides of a 48-column answer sheet at the same time. The scanner captures each student's responses and transmits them to TestMate TABE in order to generate reports. These scanners can typically scan 100 sheets in five minutes, which makes the scoring process much faster than scoring manually.

Computer Software Options Available: Standard online administration.

Ways In Which Computer/On-Line Version Differs: Computer version has real-time scoring and reporting and is administered completely online.

Cost of Materials: Due to possible price changes since publication date, be sure to check the publisher's website.

> **Specimen Set:** Includes test books for each level for Complete Battery and Survey and test directions.

> **Counselee Materials:** Materials come in sets of 25. TABE Complete Battery test books, $129.25; Survey test books, $129.25; Practice Exercise/Locator Test, $71.65; Word List, $33.05; SCOREZE answer sheets for Locator Test, Complete Battery, and Survey, $45.95 each; Compuscan answer sheets, $40.20; Scoring stencils for Locator Test $26.50, Complete Battery and Survey, $53.05 each. Additional pricing information for accessories is available at the publisher website.

Published Reviews of the Instrument in the Last 15 Years:

Monsaas, J. A. (2007). [Tests of Adult Basic Education Forms 9&10.] In R. A. Spies, B. S. Plake, & K. F. Geisinger (Eds.), *The seventeenth mental measurements yearbook.* Lincoln, NE: Buros Center for Testing.

Piccone, J. E. (2006). Administering the Test of Adult Basic Education at intake: A biased marker of offender ability. *Journal of Correctional Education, 57,* 239-248.

Prins, E. (2009). [Tests of Adult Basic Education Forms 9 &10.] In E. A. Whitfield, R. W. Feller, & C. Wood (Eds.), *A counselor's guide to career assessment instruments* (5th ed., pp. 202-208). Broken Arrow, OK: National Career Development Association.

TESTS OF ADULT BASIC EDUCATION

Reviewed by:

Andrew M. Burck

Department of Counseling
Marshall University

Description

The Tests of Adult Basic Education Forms (TABE) 9&10 assesses achievement of skills that are familiar and important to adults such as life skills, work, and education. These skills are "basic skills commonly found in adult basic education curricula taught in high school and adult instructional programs" (CTB/McGraw Hill, 2008, p. 2). The objective of the TABE is to assess what adults should know and their ability to demonstrate their knowledge in real life settings.

The TABE has two test-length choices: a complete battery and a survey-based version. The complete battery takes approximately 3½ hours while the survey-based version is about 2 hours. For each choice, the TABE measures Reading, Mathematics Computation, Applied Mathematics, and Language for four test levels of increasing difficulty. The Reading scale, (complete battery = 50 items, survey = 25 items), depending on test level, measures concepts such as recognizing letters, interpreting graphic information, information recall, and construct information. The Mathematics Computation scale (complete battery = 40 items, survey = 25 items) assesses multiplying whole numbers, fractions, percentiles, and algebraic operations. Applied Mathematics (complete battery = 50 items, survey = 25 items) measures number operations, reasoning, computation, estimation, and measurement. The Language scale (complete battery = 55 items, survey = 25 items) evaluates usage, punctuation, writing conventions, usage, and sentence formation. Sample items for the Reading and Mathematics Computation sections are provided on the publisher's website (CTB/McGraw-Hill, 2012).

The TABE also includes an optional test that measures Vocabulary, Language Mechanics, and Spelling and can be used with either test-length choice. The optional test contains 20 items; it takes individuals 14 minutes to complete the Vocabulary and Language Mechanics sections and 10 minutes for the Spelling section. The Vocabulary Test assesses understanding of word meanings and multi-meaning words, while Language Mechanics measures understanding of sentence, phrases, clauses, and writing conversations. Spelling assesses the ability to identify misspelled words and use of spelling in everyday life.

Advanced-level tests assess higher level knowledge in the areas of Science, Social Studies, Algebra/Geometry, and Writing. Science reviews life concepts, physical science, and earth and space science, while the Social Studies area assesses geography, economics, and civics. The Algebra area measures variables, expressions, operations, linear equations, inequalities, lines, angles, triangles, polygons, and circles. The Writing Test provides an opportunity to understand the individual's ability to ingest information, process it, and then write out a cohesive answer.

The TABE is comprised of a multilevel method to assess individuals at their current level of knowledge. Examinees have 37 minutes to complete a Locator Test to determine their appropriate test level: L (Limited Literacy – Pre-Reading), E (Easy), M (Medium), D (Difficult), and A (Advanced). Examinees also complete a practice exercise that provides examples of TABE test items. The practice exercise requires 20 minutes to complete. Once the examinee has completed the TABE Locator Test and practice exercise, a counselor provides the TABE test instructions for the respective level. The test manual provides exact phrasing for the counselor to verbalize including common questions when administering the instrument. The test materials are very clear, concise, and follow a logical flow based on how the material is presented and how it is explained.

The TABE can be hand scored, computer scored (i.e., TABE PC 9&10 and TestMate TABE), or scored by the test publisher. TABE-PC 9&10 is an automated version of the TABE 9&10 and will provide immediate scoring of the instrument, while the TestMate TABE is scanning software used with pencil-and-paper responses.

The TABE has many uses such as a pretest-posttest evaluation of instruction; as a screening tool for employment, clients, and children; and as a predictor of readiness on the General Equivalency Degree (GED). For example, a school counselor may consult with teachers about changes in TABE scores to determine additional resources a student may need. A career counselor may administer the TABE to assess foundational skills in clients and use this information in assisting them with the job search process. It is important for counselors across specialty areas to be familiar with TABE tests to assist students or clients to develop or maximize skill areas.

Technical Considerations

The normative sample for the TABE involves a diverse population from 495 institutions that include 34,676 adult examinees from 46 states and locations such as adult basic education centers, alternative high schools, vocational and technical colleges, and correctional institutions. The educational background of the sample includes individuals from adult basic education institutions, alternative high schools, vocational/technological colleges, and correctional institutions. The norming of the TABE is provided for the ABE-All and the ABE-Juvenile that includes individuals ages 14 to 20. The ABE-Juvenile is a subsample of the ABE-All sample for those counselors that need norming information for adolescents. The majority of the ABE-All sample was male ($n = 24,892, 71\%$), African American, ($n = 13,660, 39\%$) and were in Adult Corrections ($n = 17,124, 49\%$). Although the authors state that the norming of the TABE 9&10 is representative of the population (CBT/McGraw-Hill, 2004a), the U.S. Department of Education (2011) reported a smaller percentage of African Americans are in Adult Education ($n = 456,249$; 20% of total adult education population) when compared to the TABE data set.

The validity and the reliability of the TABE have been established based on the research of the publishers and professional publications. Content validity was established with adult educators about their success, concerns, and goals in education. The authors also reviewed current curricula and standards, identified specific areas of emphasis in educational material, and observed changes in adult education and legislation as well as functions of adult, vocational, and academic programs (CBT/McGraw-Hill, 2004a, 2008). The authors also summarized goals of adult education programs and reviewed current research on the TABE and the GED. To provide evidence of construct validity, the authors compared the TABE with the GED. Correlations between similar and dissimilar scales on the TABE 7 Tests, Total Battery, and the 2002 GRE scores were provided to demonstrate convergent and divergent validity. The correlations ranged from .39 (Total Mathematics to Reading) to .58 (Total Battery to Math). However, no significance levels are provided in the information. Ritchey (2000) stated that the strength of these relationships is classified as moderately weak positive to moderate strong positive (CBT/McGraw-Hill, 2004a). With respect to criterion-related validity, previous research has found that the TABE, when compared to other similar assessment instruments, is more effective in the placement of students in adult literacy classes (Venesky & Bristow, 1997) and as a measure of current reading ability (Greenberg, Levy, Rasher, Kim, Carter, & Berbaum, 2010).

The technical report (CBT/McGraw-Hill, 2004a) indicates evidence of strong internal consistency and acceptable standard error of measurement estimates as indices of reliability. The standard error of measurement was calculated for both versions of both forms. Table 1 provides KR-20 estimates and SEM calculations for the TABE forms.

Table 1
KR-20 and SEM Estimate Ranges for TABE 9&10

Form	Level	KR–20	SEM
	L	.88 – .90	1.40 – 1.97
	E	.93 – .95	2.12 – 3.19
9 (Complete)	M	.89 – .93	2.17 – 3.14
	D	.87 – .91	2.62 – 3.14
	A	.88 – .92	2.67 – 3.10
	L*	–	–
	E	.86 – .90	1.73 – 2.13
9 (Survey)	M	.77 – .89	1.75 – 2.16
	D	.76 – .81	2.07 – 2.23
	A	.78 – .84	1.98 – 2.21

A Counselor's Guide To Career Assessments Instruments

	*	.79 – .88	1.35 – 2.00
	E	.92 – .95	2.19 – 3.33
10 (Complete)	M	.90 – .93	2.25 – 3.07
	D	.87 – .92	2.59 – 3.17
	A	.90 – .94	2.59 – 3.17
	L	–	–
	E	.83 – .92	1.75 – 2.22
10 (Survey)	M	.81 – .87	1.81 – 2.12
	D	.74 – .84	2.05 – 2.15
	A	.83 – .87	2.05 – 2.20

* = These values are not provided in the manual.

General Utility and Evaluation

The TABE test directions, Locator Test, practice exercises, and the tests themselves are written in a clear and direct manner that provides verbatim administration instructions. Similarly, Monsaas (2007) stated that the TABE was well-developed and easy to score, administer, and interpret. The TABE (2004b) provides a brief review of the provided data and explains in a clear manner the importance of the data and how these data are to be read. The technical manual provides a detailed review of the TABE. Although it is clear in the descriptions of the material, the order and the flow of the material in the manual is less clear, causing a reader to navigate to various locations in the various manuals to locate similar information. The TABE can be administered using Braille, audio, and large print versions. The TABE can be administered to individuals needing accommodations; guidelines are provided in the scoring process (CBT/McGraw-Hill, 2004a).

There are some available studies on the TABE. Piccone (2006) stated that TABE scores for the prison population, specifically men and young adults, improved one year after admission to the correctional setting. Further, Priccone noted that psychological factors related to incarceration were associated with lower pre-test scores; however, specific reasons are not clear. Changes were also reported in TABE Reading and Math scores over time in an alternative high school based on faculty, program design, and interaction between faculty and program development (Duggar & Duggar, 1998).

Even with documented changes in TABE scores for these populations, other scholars have noted limitations. Prins (2009) expressed concern about the inability of the items on the TABE to adequately assess individuals in naturalistic settings. The TABE items, comprised of specific, sterilized questions that have a right or wrong answer, are incongruent with real-world settings that involve complex problem-solving (Prins, 2009). There is also concern about the insufficient amount of data on the validity and the reliability of the TABE. The information that is provided on the TABE is inconclusive, and the information is not explained clearly so the reader can interpret the TABE (Prins, 2009). Finally, the use of Object Mastery levels is unclear. The technical report provides the cutoffs for each of the levels and then provides statements about the ineffectiveness of these cutoffs (Monsaas, 2007).

References and Additional Resources

CBT/McGraw-Hill. (2004a). *TABE 9&10: All levels. Technical report.* Monterey, California: Author.

CBT/McGraw-Hill. (2004b). *TABE norm book. Complete battery and survey. Form 9&10 all levels.* Monterey, California: Author.

CBT/McGraw-Hill (2008). *Discover TABE 9&10.* Monterey, California: Author.

CBT/McGraw-Hill. (2012). TABE overview. Retrieved from http://www.ctb.com/ctb.com/control/productFamilyView Action?p=products&productFamilyId=608

Duggar, J. M., Duggar, C. W. (1998). An evaluation of a successful alternative high school. *The High School Journal, 81*(4), 218-228.

Greenberg, D., Levy, S. R., Rasher, S., Kim., Y., Carter, S. D., & Berbaum, M. L. (2010). Testing adult basic education students for reading ability and progress: How many tests to administer? *Adult Basic Education and Literacy Journal, 4,* 96-103.

Henson, R. K. (2001). Understanding internal consistency reliability estimates: A conceptual primer on coefficient alpha. *Measurement and Evaluation in Counseling and Development, 34,* 177-189.

Monsaas, J. A. (2007). [Tests of Adult Basic Education Forms 9&10.] In R. A. Spies, B. S. Plake, & K. F. Geisinger (Eds.), *The seventeenth mental measurements yearbook.* Lincoln, NE: Buros Center for Testing.

Piccone, J. E. (2006). Administering the Test of Adult Basic Education at intake: A biased marker of offender ability. *Journal of Correctional Education, 57,* 239-248.

Prins, E. (2009). [Tests of Adult Basic Education Forms 9&10.] In E. A. Whitfield, R. W. Feller, & C. Wood (Eds.), *A counselor's guide to career assessment instruments* (5th ed., pp. 202-208). Broken Arrow, OK: National Career Development Association.

Ritchey, F. (2000). *The statistical imagination: Elementary statistics for the social sciences.* Boston, MA: McGraw-Hill.

U.S. Department of Education. (2011). *Adult Education and Family Literacy Act of 1998: Annual report to Congress 2007-08.* Retrieved from http://www2.ed.gov/about/offices/list/ovae/resource/nrs-rtc-2007-08.pdf

Venezky, R. L., & Bristow, P. S. (1997). When less is more: Methods for placing students in adult literary classes. *Adult Basic Education, 7*(1), 3-22.

WONDERLIC BASIC SKILLS TEST

Eliot R. Long, Victor S. Artese, and Winifred L. Clonts

Wonderlic, Inc.

400 Lakeview Parkway
Suite 200, Vernon Hills, IL 60061
877.605.9496
http://www.wonderlic.com

Target Population: Adolescents, young adults, and adults.

Statement of the Purpose of the Instrument: The Wonderlic Basic Skills Test (WBST) is a short-form measure of adult language and math skills for job or school training readiness.

Titles of Subtests, Scales, Scores Provided: Verbal Skills and Quantitative Skills; Scores: Test of Verbal Skills (Word Knowledge, Sentence Construction, Information Retrieval, Total). Test of Quantitative Skills (Explicit Problem Solving, Applied Problem Solving, Interpretive Problem Solving, Total). Composite score.

Forms and Levels Available, with Dates of Publication/Revision of Each: V1, V2, Q1, and Q2, 1994.

Date of Most Recent Edition of Test Manual, User's Guide, Etc.: 1999.

Languages in Which Available: English only.

Time:

    Actual Test Time: 20 minutes per test (Timed test).

    Total Administration Time: 5 minutes for per test.

Norm Group(s) on Which Scores Are Based: Students in high schools, junior colleges, vocational schools, and adults in work settings (manufacturing, financial services, fast food services, oil drilling, truck assembly, highway/construction).

Manner in Which Results Are Reported for Individuals: Scale score, percentile distribution, GED scale, and grade level are provided. Scoring of the WBST can be through the use of a PC and the WBST Scoring Program diskette or through the Wonderlic Reporting Service. The WBST Scoring Program can provide the following reports, which can be printed: Individual Summary Report, Individual Detailed Report, Summary Listing, and Interpretation Guide. The Wonderlic Reporting Service will score and run diagnostic analyses to evaluate individual assessments. The Wonderlic Reporting Service also provides quarterly reports.

Report Format/Content for Group Summaries: Alphabetical listing date, test scores, and local vs. national norms are available.

Machine Scoring: Cost of basic service per counselee: $55.00 per quarter.

Hand Scoring: Not available.

Local Machine Scoring: Paper-and-pencil administration—computer diskette scoring.

Cost of Materials: Due to possible price changes since publication date, be sure to check the publisher's website.

    Specimen Set: Sample tests available at no charge.

    Counselee Materials: Verbal (package of 25): $95.00; Quantitative (package of 25): $95.00; Composite (package of 25): $130.00.

Published Reviews of Instrument in the Last 15 Years:

Donlon, T. F. (1998). [Wonderlic Basic Skills Test.] In J. C. Impara and B. S. Plake (Eds.), *The thirteenth mental measurements yearbook.* Lincoln, NE: Buros Center for Testing.

Hanna, G. S. (1998). [Wonderlic Basic Skills Test.] In J. C. Impara and B. S. Plake (Eds.), *The thirteenth mental measurements yearbook.* Lincoln, NE: Buros Center for Testing.

Hanna, G. S., & Hughey, K. F. (2001). [Wonderlic Basic Skills Test.] In J. T. Kapes and E. A. Whitfield (Eds.), *A counselor's guide to career assessment instruments.* Columbis, OH: National Career Development Association.

Power, S. J. (2009). [Wonderlic Basic Skills Test.] In E. A. Whitfield, R. W. Feller, & C. Wood (Eds.), *A counselor's guide to career assessment instruments* (5th ed., pp. 209-213). Broken Arrow, OK: National Career Development Association.

WONDERLIC BASIC SKILLS TEST

Reviewed by:

Sally J. Power

Management Department
University of St. Thomas

Description

The Wonderlic Basic Skills Test (WBST) is two short, multiple-choice tests that determine basic levels of quantitative and verbal skills. The test is designed for those with a high school education or less and is focused on the lower three levels of the six-level General Educational Development (GED) scale. The verbal skills tested are word knowledge, sentence construction, and information retrieval. The qualitative skills tested are explicit, applied (word questions), and interpretative (using tables, charts, and figures). Each test takes 20 minutes.

This test is used primarily by employers to determine job readiness for entry level positions. It can also be used to identify jobs for which an individual might have the basic skills and/or an individual's readiness for vocational training. Finally, it is approved by the U.S. Department of Education (2006) for use in assessing Title IV "ability to benefit" Federal financial aid (see FR Doc. E6-7682, 5/18/06).

Example questions available on the Wonderlic website include the following:

1. Choose the verb that correctly completes the sentence.

    Have you _____ the painting yet?

    A. finish   B. finishes   C. finishing   D. finished

2. If there is an error in one of the <u>underlined</u> sections below, choose the letter below the line as your answer. Otherwise, choose D.

    Because <u>they were feeling</u> sick,   maybe tomorrow <u>they will be feeling</u>
              A   C
    <u>I don't send</u> them to school today;   better. <u>No error.</u>
              B   D

3. Choose the word that best completes the sentence.
    We waited downstairs for 10 minutes. At last, the _____ arrived, and we rode it up to the tenth floor.
    A. bus   B. package   C. elevator   D. neighbors

4. Choose the answer that most nearly means the same as the <u>underlined</u> word.
    An <u>inaccuracy</u> is a
    A. mistake   B. type of medicine   C. prison   D. chance happening

5. $56 \div 4 =$
    A. 16   B. 9   C. 14   D. 23

6. The 5:15 train takes 2 hours and 10 minutes to get to Graystone. Today the train will be 15 minutes late. What time will it get to Graystone?

    A. 7:15   B. 7:05   C. 7:25   D. 7:40

7. Use this chart for the following question:

Population: Selected Cities & Villages	
Ashdown	5,150
Batesville	9,187
Crosett	6,282
Herber Springs	5,628
Pocahontas	6,151
Wynne	8,817

About 2/5 of the people in Ashdown were watching the Ashdown Athletes last Friday. How many people watched the Athletes on Friday?

    A. 206   B. 248   C. 2,480   D. 2,060

The test results are reported in an easy to read format specialized for educators (focusing on GED levels and what skills could be improved or need review) or for businesses (focusing on the individual's results in comparison to GED levels needed for the work of a specific job description as specified by the O*NET).

The test can be administered untimed for examinees that are unlikely to have a fair assessment of their skills using the 20-minute time limit. It will indicate when the pattern of answers on the test suggests the examinee may have been skipping questions, guessing, or making careless mistakes; retesting is then suggested. Finally, the test results will indicate when the individual's GED level is above the assessment range of the test. There are two versions of each type of test available. They are nicely printed and come with answer sheets and a PC-compatible disk for on-site scoring. The text questions have been reviewed and analyzed statistically by independent experts to assure that the questions would be equivalent for all subgroups and free of content bias (Long, Artese, & Clonts, 2001). Hanna (1998) reported that the test items are well-written, varied, and clearly relevant to the world of work without being job specific, gender specific, or subculture specific.

The questionnaire can also be taken on-line and scored within minutes. Another scoring option is to contract with Wonderlic Reporting Service. This will provide more sophisticated analysis of individual results as well as quarterly reports of testing done at your site with comparisons to Wonderlic's national database by job title, education level, demographic classification and recruiting source.

Finally, if the test will be used to provide Title IV "ability to benefit" validation for Federal financial aid, the Wonderlic company must be informed. Additional systems and manuals are required (Long, 2007). A 2010 version of the manual is available as a PDF file online.

The WBST could be very useful for career counseling with individuals who have been out of school for some time, have a high school education or less, and are seeking an entry level job and/or additional vocational training. It would give quick information concerning the general levels of the basic language, math, and reasoning skills in a form that can be used to identify types of jobs clients might want to pursue. Because the test also reports its results in terms of grade level, it could be used to identify the level of training materials individuals could use successfully.

One table in the *User's Manual* may be particularly useful for career counselors who are focusing on facilitating job searches. This table reports the median WBST scores by job title and training program for jobs where Wonderlic has data from 50 or more individuals. This data were collected either in the original field studies done with the test or in their work with commercial customers (Long, 2007). If one assumes that employers are likely to hire applicants with better scores, this data provides information about levels of scores needed for likely employment in specific jobs while *The Dictionary of Occupational Titles* and O*NET report minimum requirements. The table contains 86 jobs or training programs.

Technical Considerations

The WBST used item response theory (IRT) heavily during the development of its items. IRT's guiding assumption is that only one dominant factor is being measured — in this case, basic verbal and quantitative skills. Items were tested to make sure that each progressive item was more difficult than those before and that all items have comparable capacity to separate examinees into their appropriate skill levels. Finally, the IRT methodology allows for comparing the reliability of test items (Long et al., 2001). Test reliability was measured by doing test-retest studies with various time periods. The reliability coefficients in this series of tests are reported for the same form (ranging from .83 to .91 for the quantitative skills test and from .84 to .90 for the verbal skills test) and for parallel forms (ranging from .83 to .89 for the quantitative skills test and from .89 to .93 for the verbal skills test). Finally, internal consistency was measured by calculating Cronbach alphas for all subscales comparing timed and untimed tests. The Cronbach alphas for the separate tests ranged from .77 to .90 and showed not only that all content domains were measured reliably but that the 20-minute time limit is sufficient for the tests. Hanna and Hughey (2001) noted that, although the variety of reliability testing is highly commendable, the samples in these studies did not include means or standard deviations and thus were difficult to interpret.

The prime method for determining validity of the tests has been through content validity. Test content was developed by subject matter experts in line with the GED levels, and the manual shows correlations with students in grades 6-12, which indicates that the test does, in fact, measure basic verbal and quantitative skills. As has been pointed out by other reviewers, however, the evidence of the validity of this test would be stronger if studies showing it's predictive validity had been done (Donlon, 1998; Hanna, 1998). Furthermore, no testing has shown the possible effects of "test wiseness" or sensitivity to coaching (Hanna, 1998).

General Utility and Evaluation

The WBST is a very good test of basic verbal and quantitative skills. It could be particularly useful when working with adults with a high school education or less who have been out of school for a number of years. Using the educational report, counselors can work with a client to determine options for improving specific quantitative and/or verbal skills. Another potential strength is that the analysis of its commercial use which Wonderlic has made available via the table on median scores for occupations. This provides counselors with information regarding the level of basic skills possessed by people who are likely to be hired for particular jobs.

References and Additional Resources

Donlon, T. F. (1998). [Wonderlic Basic Skills Test.] In J. C. Impara and B. S. Plake (Eds.), *The thirteenth mental measurements yearbook.* Lincoln, NE: Buros Center for Testing.

Hanna, G. S. (1998). [Wonderlic Basic Skills Test.] In J. C. Impara and B. S. Plake (Eds.), *The thirteenth mental measurements yearbook.* Lincoln, NE: Buros Center for Testing.

Hanna, G. S., & Hughey, K. F. (2001). [Wonderlic Basic Skills.] In J. T. Kapes and E. A. Whitfield (Eds.), *A counselor's guide to career assessment instruments* (4th ed.). Columbus, OH: National Career Development Association.

Long, E. G. (2007). *Wonderlic Basic Skills Test user's manual.* Vernon Hills, IL: Wonderlic, Inc.

Long, E. G., Artese, V. S., & Clonts, W. L. (2001). *Wonderlic Basic Skills Test.* Vernon Hills, IL: Wonderlic, Inc.

Power, S. J. (2009). [Wonderlic Basic Skills Test.] In E. A. Whitfield, R. W. Feller, & C. Wood (Eds.), *A counselor's guide to career assessment instruments* (5th ed., pp. 209-213). Broken Arrow, OK: National Career Development Association.

U.S. Department of Education. (2006, May 19). *Update notice, Federal register.* Vol. 71, no. 97 pp. 29135-29137. Retrieved from http://www.gpo.gov/fdsys/pkg/FR-2006-05-19/html/E6-7682.htm

Wonderlic website: http://www.wonderlic.com

WorkKeys Assessments
Act, Inc.

Act, Inc.
500 ACT Drive
P.O. Box 168
Iowa City, Iowa 52243-168
http://www.act.org/workkeys

Target Population: Adolescents (grade 9+), young adults, and adults; current or potential job seekers.

Statement of the Purpose of the Instrument: WorkKeys assessments are part of a job skills assessment system that links education and the workforce, offering a common language to enhance communication about job skill requirements needed to develop employees and build a better workforce. "Real world" skills that employers believe are critical to job success are measured, including communication, problem solving, critical thinking, and personal and interpersonal skills.

Titles of Subtests, Scales, Scores Provided: (8 foundational skills and 3 soft skills assessments)

Applied Mathematics: level scores 3-7; scale scores 65-90. Extended version available (level scores 1-2).

Applied Technology: level scores 3-6; scale scores 65-90.

Business Writing: level scores 1-5; analytic scores for sentence structure, mechanical, grammatical, word usage, style/tone/language, organization, and development.

Listening for Understanding: level scores 1-5; scale scores 50-90.

Locating Information: level score 3-6; scale scores 65-90.

Workplace Observation: level scores 1-5.

Reading for Information: level scores 3-7; scale scores 65-90. Extended version available (level scores 1-2).

Teamwork: level scores 3-6; scale scores 65-90.

WorkKeys Fit (fit between individual interests and values to the work environment), WorkKeys Performance (measure of general work attitudes and risk-taking behaviors), and WorkKeys Talent (measure of various personality facets), percentile rankings, and categorical descriptors.

Individuals can receive a National Career Readiness Certificate by taking the WorkKeys Applied Mathematics, Locating Information, and Reading for Information exams.

Forms and Levels Available, with Dates of Publication/Revision of Each: See content areas and levels above. The website (http://www.act.org/workkeys/assess/glance.html) outlines the following available formats per exam type: paper-based, Internet-based, express score, Spanish paper-based, practice or prep tests, and whether the test includes audio or video components. Applied Mathematics, Locating Information, Reading for Information, Applied Technology are all 55 minutes for Internet version, 45 minutes for paper-based version, and 55 minutes for the Spanish version. Business Writing is 30 minutes for Internet format, and 30 minutes for paper-based version. Listening to Understand is 45 minutes for Internet version. Teamwork is 64 minutes for the paper-based version, and Workplace Observation is 55 minutes for Internet format. Fit, Performance, and Talent are offered as Internet versions between 15 and 35 minutes in length. Express Score is offered for Applied Mathematics, Applied Technology, Locating Information, Reading for Information, and Teamwork.

Date of Most Recent Edition of Test Manual, User's Guide, Etc.: Supervisor's manual (2012). Technical manuals for each content area (2008).

Languages in Which Available: All content areas are available in English. The Applied Mathematics, Locating Information, Reading for Information, and Applied Technology are also available in Spanish.

Time:

Actual Test Time: 55 minutes for Applied Mathematics, Locating Information, Reading for Information, Workplace Observation & Applied Technology; 30 minutes for Business Writing; 45 minutes for Listening to Understand; 64 minutes for Teamwork; and 15-35 minutes for Fit, Performance, & Talent exams.

Total Administration Time: Collection of demographics, tutorials, and reading directions take up to 15 minutes.

Norm Group(s) on Which Scores Are Based: WorkKeys assessments are criterion based, except for Performance, Talent, and Fit exams.

Manner in Which Results Are Reported for Individuals: See above for most WorkKeys assessments and percentile ranks and descriptors for Performance, Talent, and Fit. Individual score reports, with description of current skills and recommendations for raising scores. Comparisons of individual score with "profile" of job requirements.

Report Format/Content for Group Summaries: Basic Service: Roster Report. Data export for sorting and filtering by demographic and other categories. Comparison of group scores (by individual and aggregate) with "profile" of job requirements.

Machine Scoring: Cost of basic service per counselee: cost is per content area, averaging $5.00 to $20.00 per assessment. Paper-and-pencil materials shipped for scoring 10 days from arrival to score.

Hand Scoring: Not available.

Local Machine Scoring: Local scoring available through ACT contractual arrangement.

Provisions/conditions/equipment Required: Online testing available for many content areas (see below); paper-and-pencil delivered materials on-site scoring requires license (Express score) and specified scanning equipment and software.

Computer Software Options Available: Standard administration online.

Ways in Which Computer/online Version Differs: Additional 10 minutes for test taking on all assessments except Teamwork. Teamwork is the only assessment not available online.

Cost of Materials: Due to possible price changes since publication date, be sure to check the publisher's site. Applied Mathematics, Applied Technology, Locating Information, and Reading for Information practice tests are available for $5.00 each.

Specimen Set: Website examples of all assessments.

Counselee Materials: Practice tests available.

Published Reviews of the Instrument in the Last 15 Years:

Osborn, D. S. (2009). WorkKeys. In E. A. Whitfield, R. W. Feller. & C. Wood (Eds.), *A counselor's guide to career assessment instruments* (5th ed., pp. 214-222). Broken Arrow, OK: National Career Development Association.

WORKKEYS ASSESSMENTS

Reviewed by:

Debra S. Osborn

Department of Educational and Psychological Learning Systems
Florida State University

Description

WorkKeys (ACT Inc., 2012a) is a job skills assessment system intended to compare an individual's current skill set with the skills required for specific positions within a company. WorkKeys serves several potential purposes, including informing hiring and promotion decisions, creating training solutions, and offering specific skills certifications and the National Career Readiness Certificate. Eleven assessments are included on the WorkKeys website (ACT, Inc., 2012a) ranging in test-taking time from 30 to 64 minutes each. There are eight "foundational skills assessments" (Applied Mathematics, Applied Technology, Business Writing, Listening for

A Counselor's Guide To Career Assessments Instruments

Understanding, Locating Information, Workplace Observation, Reading for Information, and Teamwork), and three "soft skills" assessments (Talent, Performance, and Fit). Descriptions of the assessments, skills measured and sample items are provided for each assessment on the WorkKeys website. Tests can be used beginning with students in grade 9 to help plan a high school curriculum.

The *Applied Mathematics* test measures mathematical reasoning, critical thinking, and problem-solving strategies individuals apply to problems in the workplace. Questions are designed to be taken with a calculator and represent five difficulty ranges. While formulas are provided on a separate sheet, the test taker must choose the correct formula and then set up and solve the problem with the information given. A sample level 3 item for this assessment is:

> Quik Call charges 18¢ per minute for long-distance calls. Econo Phone totals your phone usage each month and rounds the number of minutes up to the nearest 15 minutes. It then charges $7.90 per hour of phone usage, dividing this charge into 15-minute segments if you used less than a full hour. If your office makes 5 hours 3 minutes worth of calls this month using the company with the lower price, how much will these calls cost?

There are five possible answers: $39.50; $41.48; $41.87; $54.00; and $54.54. The *Locating Information* test consists of four levels of questions and measures how well people use graphics such as charts, tables, flowcharts, and instrument gauges to make workplace decisions. The test taker must either locate or place information into a graphic. For example, the examinee might be asked to look at a gauge and be given the following question: "You regularly check the pressure gauge on a large tank. According to the gauge shown, what is the current pressure (in PSI)?" with these answers as options: 30, 35, 40, 45, and 100. The *Reading for Information* test consists of five difficulty levels and measures a person's reading skills with respect to performing job duties. This may include interpreting memos, directions, policies, regulations, directions, and the like. For example, the examinee might be shown a notice and given this question: "You are a cashier. According to the notice shown, what should you write on a store employee's receipt?" Respondents choose a correct answer from the following: the employee's identification number, the employee's department number, the amount of sales tax, the 20% discount price, or your initials. These three tests form the basis for the National Career Readiness Certificate Program.

There are five assessments that evaluate additional foundational skills. The *Applied Technology* test consists of four difficulty levels and emphasizes reasoning and problem solving skills with machines and workplace equipment, and basic principles within electricity, mechanics, fluid dynamics, and thermodynamics. A sample item might include a diagram of a truck with the following information and question:

> Your industrial services company has been hired to deliver a small but heavy gearbox. The container is too small to justify renting a large truck and too heavy for the company's pickup truck. You decide to rent a heavy-duty utility trailer and pull it with the pickup truck. At which spot, labeled 1 – 5, on the trailer shown should you place the container to pull the load most easily and safely?

The respondent would choose an answer option (1, 2, 3, 4 or 5). The *Business Writing* test consists of five levels, requires about 30 minutes to complete and examines an individual's ability to communicate clearly, in a grammatically correct way, and without errors. A sample prompt would be the following:

> At your office, employees are allowed to skip their morning and/or afternoon breaks to take longer lunch breaks. However, the personnel manager says that employees have been taking too much time on their lunch breaks as a result of this policy. She wants to require all employees to take their morning and afternoon breaks and the standard lunch break. Write a letter to the personnel manager explaining whether or not you are in favor of this proposal and why.

The *Listening for Understanding* test is an auditory test that measures a person's ability to hear, correctly interpret, and follow workplace directions. A sample item might be about a woman who has questions about her flight itinerary. The respondent would listen to a dialogue between a flight attendant and the woman, in which specific details are given about the itinerary. Following the dialogue, the respondent is presented with a multiple choice question about the conversation, such as "At what time is Ms. Ramirez to be at the reception desk?" with possible answers of 7, 8, 9 and 11 o'clock. The *Teamwork* test consists of four difficulty levels, requires 64 minutes to complete, and uses video to present 12 scenarios involving teamwork. A sample item would include a detailed scenario followed by a question such as:

As a member of this team, the stocker could best support the team and get the work task accomplished by: (1) having the new employee help her stock shelves as she explains store procedures; (2) having the new employee learn by just watching the other employees; (3) telling the cashier to take care of training the new employee so the stocker can get her work done; or (4) telling the manager that nothing is going right and that she doesn't have time to train the new employee.

The individual must select the best response for a team. The *Workplace Observation* test uses both audio and video and measures a person's ability to focus, observe, follow, remember, and evaluate workplace demonstrations and procedures. For example, a respondent might watch a video on how to wash hands thoroughly, and then answer a multiple choice question such as "After scrubbing your hands with soapy lather, the next step is to: (a) dry your hands with paper towels; (b) rinse your hands with warm water; (c) turn off the water taps; or (d) use paper towels to grasp the door handle."

WorkKeys also has three soft skills assessments. The *Fit* test determines the degree of match between the interests and values between the work environment and the individual. Sample values are precision, physical activity, influencing others, and autonomy. Sample interest items include calculating the interest on a loan, plan work for other people, or help someone make an important decision. The *Performance* test alerts the employer that an individual may tend to have unsafe attitudes towards and be more apt to engage in unsafe behaviors at work, such as theft, substance abuse, anger outbursts, and absenteeism. For example, a respondent might be asked to provide a rating from strongly disagree to strongly agree for this item: "I sometimes resent my coworkers and/or my supervisor." The *Talent* test is designed to measure an individual's attitudes and behaviors related to work, with the aim of predicting how a person will perform beyond basic work skills. For example, an examinee might be asked to rate on a scale from strongly disagree to strongly agree an item such as this: "I usually stay calm, even in stressful situations."

WorkKeys consists of three basic steps, including job profiling, assessments, and training. During job profiling, which identifies the skills necessary to perform a specific job, the employer has the option to use the database of over 18,000 profiled job titles or to go through the job profiling process specific to the company, which might consist of the WorkKeys Estimator (a fast way of estimating skill level requirements for jobs) or a more intensive Job Profiling and its associated 7-week training in which a person learns how to profile a job. The second step is the assessment of an individual's current level of skills, which may include some or all of the 11 assessments and compares the results to job titles within the company or the WorkKeys database in which an individual can compare her or his results with occupations at the WorkKeys website (ACT, Inc., 2012a).

The third step would be training, which is designed to narrow the gap between the skills required for the job and a person's actual skills. WorkKeys offers several training options. The first, KeyTrain, is an interactive, targeted curriculum to help individuals develop career readiness skills as measured by the WorkKeys assessments. Career Ready 101 is a career training course, and Key Train Career Skills is a soft skills curriculum designed to enhance employability skills and improve work habits.

The WorkKeys system has many possible counseling related uses within the career planning process, such as enhancing self and occupational knowledge, identifying skill gaps, creating a plan to address those gaps, job searching, and career advancement planning. For self-knowledge, the assessment results can provide valuable evidence of existing skills, which could be used in the initial career decision-making process to generate options. The WorkKeys Occupational Profiles can be a useful tool to help clients gain specific occupational information. If the person has completed similar tests as those in the database, this would allow for a comparison between the individual's skills and the skills required of desired occupations. If a gap is noted, a plan could be developed that would include training or volunteer experiences to help the person gain skills. During the job search process, the assessment results could be used as a way to document skills, thus helping in resume and portfolio building. Another potential use would be for career advancement planning. An employee who is wanting to progress in a company but unsure how her or his personal skills match with higher level positions, could compare her or his test results to those of the higher positions. Similarly, an employer who anticipates the development of new positions and wants to promote from within, but is unsure which employees have more of the required skills or could have the skills with a little training could compare the job profile with the profiles of existing employees. Helping identify transferable skills and relate those skills to specific jobs can be of great use to individuals who are needing or wanting to explore new career options.

A COUNSELOR'S GUIDE TO CAREER ASSESSMENTS INSTRUMENTS

Technical Considerations

ACT provides detailed technical manuals on the specific WorkKeys assessments. In reviewing several of the manuals, it appears that there has been much energy devoted into developing valid and reliable assessment tools within the WorkKeys system. With so many different assessments making up the WorkKeys system, the psychometric properties of each range from adequate to outstanding. The detail provided in the manuals is excellent; however, a review of the literature yielded no recent empirical studies on any of the assessments or a review in the *Mental Measurements Yearbook*. These types of publications would be valuable as ongoing evidence of the applicability of WorkKeys to different settings.

ACT provides separate manuals for the WorkKeys assessments, which provide substantial information on reliability and validity. KR 20s for the *Applied Mathematics* test (ACT, Inc., 2008a) was .92 for two high school groups, with standard error of measurements mostly fewer than 2 points. An examination of construct validity demonstrated correlations between the number correct score and scale scores for the Applied Math test and the ACT Mathematics test as ranging from .71 to .81. Significant gender and racial/ethnic differences were found, with males and Asian American/Pacific Islanders scoring highest.

The technical manual for the *Reading for Information* (RFI; ACT, Inc., 2008b) test reports KR 20s of .82 and .90, based on two samples of approximately 120,000 high school students each, with standard error of measurements mostly fewer than 2 points. In one example of validity information, the manual reports a 71-79% accuracy rate between employees' job performance classification and their classification as indicated by this test for several organizations. Correlations between the RFI and ACT Reading and English scores were approximately .65, indicating moderately high concurrent validity. Statistically significant differences are reported between genders and across race/ethnicities, with males and Whites scoring higher than females and racial/ethnic minorities. The authors suggest that employers ensure that employment decisions are based on clear indications of an individual's ability to perform tasks critical to the job.

On the *Locating Information* test (ACT, Inc., 2008c), KR 20s for three forms ranged from .79 to .83. No gender differences were found, but significant differences were found for racial/ethnic groups, with Whites scoring significantly higher than non-majority persons. Score consistency for the *Business Writing* test (ACT, Inc., 2008b) was examined by comparing human scoring to computer scoring of test takers' responses. In one study they found perfect agreement 51% of the time, and within one point or less 95% of the time. Detailed information is provided on how validity evidence was documented. No information was provided on gender and racial/ethnic scores.

The *Workplace Observation* manual provides details about how test items were defined and structures through the use of a taskforce, career clusters, a test blueprint, prototype testing, field test studies, and revisions. Reliability coefficients for both forms were found to be .78 and .77, with generalizability coefficients at .8 for both forms. The *Applied Technology technical manual* (ACT, Inc., 2012b) reports internal consistency coefficients of .85 and reliability-like coefficients of .85 for rank-ordering test results and .84 judging performance levels. No specific information is provided on demographic group differences in scores or on validity, although the authors provide a very detailed section in the manual on how items were developed, suggesting strong content validity. The manual for the *Listening for Understanding* assessment was in process of being completed at the time of the review, and the *Teamwork* assessment was in the process of being revised with an accompanying new technical manual.

Technical manuals also exist for the soft skills assessments. The *Fit Assessment user and technical guide* (ACT, Inc., 2007a) reports internal consistencies as ranging from .77 to .85. The authors also describe measures taken to decrease fakeability (i.e., answering questions in a way to make a match to a specific occupation), in that in order to do this, a person must create a profile that matches across 24 specific measures. There were no significant differences in scoring across different demographic groups. To examine validity, the researchers utilized a Fit Index, and reported observed validity correlations of .11-.16 for anticipated tenure, and .26-.37, for job commitment. The *Performance Assessment* manual (ACT, Inc., 2007b) reported internal consistencies ranging from .89 to .90. For predictive validity, a median correlation of .27 was found with supervisor ratings of job performance. In their examination of adverse impact, they found small ($r < .15$, $p < .05$) significant differences for gender, ethnicity, and education, with women, Whites, and those who have more education obtaining higher scores. As a follow-up on the ethnic differences, the researchers compared performance index scores using Chi-square and found no significant differences. Finally, the *Talent Assessment* manual (ACT, Inc., 2009) reports a median reliability of .85 and reports that the assessment measures themes similar to other personality measures, and predicts work-related behaviors such as performance, productivity, and citizenship. No significant adverse impacts were found with this assessment.

General Utility and Evaluation

The WorkKeys test manuals provide substantive information about each test and are on, average, about 80 pages each. WorkKeys is a comprehensive system with strong evidence of reliability and validity. Of concern are the noted gender and racial/ethnic scoring differences on several of the WorkKeys assessments (i.e., *Reading for Information, Applied Mathematics,* and *Locating Information*). This needs to be addressed through additional studies and continued evaluation and improvement of the tests to decrease the likelihood of adverse outcomes for non-majority individuals. An earlier critique (Osborn, 2009) also noted that due to the comprehensive nature of the WorkKeys system, the process of determining which portion(s) such as specific assessments or job analysis are most relevant can be overwhelming. The last review of the WorkKeys system was in 2009. However, empirical articles on the use of WorkKeys are lacking.

On the positive side, a counselor can feel confident in the background work behind the WorkKeys tests, as well as the quality of work devoted to developing the job analyses results through the extensive job profiling process. If the counselor wants to work in a consulting role with larger employers, incorporating a system such as WorkKeys can help the counselor provide the employer with solid information about current employees' skills and potential areas for training. Test centers, practice tests, and other resources are also available. In summary, WorkKeys is a comprehensive system with a great deal of supporting documentation and possibilities for use.

References and Additional Resources

ACT, Inc. (2007a). *Fit Assessment User and technical guide.* Iowa City, IA: Author.

ACT, Inc. (2007b). *Performance Assessment user and technical guide.* Iowa City, IA: Author.

ACT, Inc. (2008a). *Applied Mathematics technical manual.* Iowa City, IA: Author.

ACT, Inc. (2008b). *Reading for Information technical manual.* Iowa City, IA: Author.

ACT, Inc. (2008c). *Locating Information technical manual.* Iowa City, IA: Author.

ACT, Inc. (2008d). *Business Writing technical manual.* Iowa City, IA: Author.

ACT, Inc. (2009). *Talent Assessment user and technical guide.* Iowa City, IA: Author.

ACT, Inc. (2010). *Workplace Observation technical manual.* Iowa City, IA: Author.

ACT, Inc. (2012a). *WorkKeys.* Retrieved from http://www.act.org/workkeys/index.html

ACT, Inc. (2012b). *Applied Technology technical manual.* Iowa City, IA: Author.

Osborn, D. S. (2009). [WorkKeys]. In E. A. Whitfield, R. W. Feller. & C. Wood (Eds.), *A counselor's guide to career assessment instruments* (5th ed., pp. 214-222). Broken Arrow, OK: National Career Development Association.

WorkKeys Resources: http://www.act.org/workkeys/resources.html

WORKPLACE SKILLS SURVEY

Industrial Psychology International Ltd.

Industrial Psychology International Ltd.
4106 Fieldstone Rd.
P.O. Box 6479
Champaign, IL 61826-6479
http://www.metritech.com
ipi@metritech.com

Target Population: Adolescents, young adults, and adults; job applicants and employees for the Original form and students in school-to-work and vocational programs for Form E.

Statement of the Purpose of the Instrument: The Workplace Skills Survey (WSS) is designed to provide information regarding basic work ethics and employment skills (Original form). The WSS on Form E is designed to assess students' work place readiness and employment skills.

Titles of Subtests, Scales, Scores Provided: Communication; Adapting to Change; Problem Solving; Work Ethics; Technological Literacy; Teamwork (Original form). Career Planning; Job Attainment; Communication; Adapting and Coping with Change; Problem Solving; Work Ethics; Technological Literacy; Teamwork; Workplace Readiness Skills (Form E). A total score and scores for eight areas are provided.

Forms and Levels Available, with Dates of Publication/Revision of Each: Original form, 1998; Student Form (Form E), 1998.

Date of Most Recent Edition of Test Manual, User's Guide, Etc.: 1998 (Original Form), 1998 (Form E).

Languages in Which Available: English only.

Time:

  Actual Test Time: Varies.

  Total Administration Time: 20 minutes (Original form) and 50 minutes (Form E).

Manner in Which Results Are Reported for Individuals: Standard scores.

Report Format/Content for Group Summaries: Not available.

Machine Scoring: Form E is machine scored only. Scoring services are provided by Metritech.

Hand Scoring: Available only for the Original form. The WSS uses a self-scoring answer sheet, hand-scored by test taker or counselor in approximately 10 minutes.

Computer Software Options Available: Not available.

Cost of Materials: Due to price changes since publication date, be sure to check the publisher's website. Original form prices: $47.00 for 5 reusable test booklets, 20 answer/score sheets, and manual. Please contact Industrial Psychology for Form E pricing.

  Specimen Set: Introductory kit available for initial orders. Answer sheets and test booklets (for reorders). For reorders: Test booklet (reusable) 10 for $22.00, Answer sheets (not reusable) 20 for $36.00.

  Counselee Materials: Test booklet and self-scoring answer sheet (Original); Test booklet (Form E).

Published Reviews of the Instrument in the Last 15 Years:

Kirnan, J. (2007). [Workplace Skills Survey.] In R. A. Spies, B. S. Plake, K. Geisinger, & J. Carlson (Eds.), *The seventeenth mental measurements yearbook.* Lincoln, NE: Buros Center for Testing.

Sauser, W. (2007). [Workplace Skills Survey.] In R. A. Spies, B. S. Plake, K. Geisinger, & J. Carlson (Eds.), *The seventeenth mental measurements yearbook.* Lincoln, NE: Buros Center for Testing.

WORKPLACE SKILLS SURVEY
Reviewed by:
Erika Raissa Nash Cameron
Department of School, Family, and Mental Health Professions
University of San Diego

Description

The Workplace Skills Survey (WSS) provides critical information regarding basic work ethics and employment skills across industries and job levels (Industrial Psychology International, 1998a). Test takers respond to items related to workplace scenarios and common business information. The test items measure work skills such as the appropriate use of company time and resources, telephone etiquette, the proper way to resolve on-the-job conflicts, and essential skills related to success in the workplace. This information may be useful to the test taker in selecting future careers or in interviewing with employers. Test takers can include their score report in a career portfolio, indicate results on a resume, or use it to highlight their strengths in an interview.

The WSS consists of 48 multiple-choice items, many of which present a scenario describing a realistic workplace situation, problem, or issue, followed by a series of questions. Other items require test takers to interact with workplace materials, such as memos, forms, and charts.

WSS provides test-takers with a profile of relative strengths in six areas: communication, adapting to change, problem solving, work ethics, technological literacy, and teamwork. These areas correspond to competencies identified as necessary work skills by the U.S. Department of Labor (U.S. Department of Labor, 1991). Written at a sixth-grade reading level, WSS items are presented in a reusable test booklet. Test takers respond on a pull-apart answer sheet that automatically transfers their responses onto a scoring key. The WSS has a self-scoring system (Industrial Psychology International, 1998b), which was designed to reduce the risk of error. When test-takers have completed the survey, they separate the scoring page from the answer sheet. A diamond indicates correct answers and each of the six areas are indicated by a different color. Raw scores are calculated by counting one point for each diamond circled within a single color group. The raw scores rank people in terms of what the six areas WSS measures. A more effective approach to using the scores is by converting them into either a stanine or T-score. The stanine score has a mean of 5 and standard deviation of 2. The general interpretation of stanine scores is below average (1-3), average (4-6), above average (7-9). The manual states that for research purposes the stanine score may not be as useful. In that case, users can transform the raw score into a standard score, by utilizing Table 2 in the WSS Manual (Industrial Psychology International, 1998b). The T-score norm has a mean of 50 and a standard deviation of 10.

In addition to the WSS, Industrial Psychology International developed the WSS Form E in 1998. This version of the WSS is geared towards high school students and measures their knowledge and use of essential skills related to success (non-academic workplace skills) in the workplace. It consists of 56 multiple-choice items that include examining realistic scenario and authentic workplace materials, followed by a series of questions.

In addition to a total test score, results are reported with respect to eight areas. Six of these areas are recommended by the U.S. Department of Labor (1991) (communication, adapting to change, problem solving, work ethics, technological literacy, and teamwork), and two areas were added to help high school students focus on career planning and job attainment. There is no information or rationale given as to why these two additional areas have been added to Form E other than that the target population would need to focus on these two areas.

The WSS takes 20 minutes to complete, requires a specific answer sheet and can be easily scored in about 10 minutes after completion. The WSS Form E takes 50 minutes to complete and requires a specific answer sheet that must be returned to the publishing company to be scored. Counselors will need to collect the answer sheets and complete the Order for Scoring Services (OSS) to be shipped to MetriTech. [Please note that on MetriTech website there is no information listed for the WSS Form E, but if you call customer service, the assessment is available for purchase and scoring services are available.] The answer sheet has to be submitted to the publisher for scoring, which may not provide feedback to the test taker in a timely manner. The WSS Form

E Administrator's Manual provides a specific script for giving directions (Industrial Psychology International, 2000a). For both WSS and WSS Form E, the overall appearance and readability of the assessments and manuals are clearly stated, organized, and easy to use.

Both the WSS and WSS Form E are suitable to be administered by high school counselors, college counselors, and career counselors working with any individual 16 years of age and older. Both the surveys were developed to assess the test taker's minimum knowledge and skills required to obtain and maintain employment and not just the academic skills needed to be successful in the workplace. The test taker's scores provide counselors with discussion points on the test taker's ability to work effectively with others, understand time management techniques, interact with technology, show up for work, follow instructions, and demonstrate a host of non-technical skills that make a difference between success and failure on the job. Many first-time workers or unemployed individuals may not realize the necessary skills needed to obtain or maintain a job. They both allow test takers to holistically look at their employability and ability to be successful in the workplace. The WSS Form E goes a step beyond the WSS, by providing items on career planning and job attainment in addition to the WSS's six areas for high school students.

Technical Evaluation

According to the WSS Manual, "the normative sample for the WSS consisted of 472 community college students with an internal consistency reliability of approximately 0.90" (Industrial Psychology International, 1998b, p. 2). In addition, the WSS Manual states that it cannot "summarize in a few coefficients or studies" the test score validity (p. 2). The WSS Manual does describe the developers' field-testing of 120 items on a sample of 764 community college students. The results led to the selection of 48 discriminating items of appropriate difficulty. Item Response Theory was used to analyze the items and generate norms (e.g., a typical high school graduate would obtain a stanine scale score of 5 or a T-score of 50 and a typical graduate from a two- or four-year program would obtain a stanine score of 6 or 7 or a T-score between 55 and 60).

The WSS Form E has no information printed about its reliability and validity. The only information that is provided is that the WSS Form E was normed on 135,840 high school students. According to the WSS Form E Summary Report (Industrial Psychology International, 2000b), a panel of educators and business leaders set the passing score to be a 54 (scales score), equating that a test taker has the minimum knowledge and skills in the areas tested required to obtain and maintain employment. A student that receives a scaled score lower than 54 would have not yet met the standards of the assessment. To be clear, a passing score is defined for the test as a whole, not for individual content areas as does the WSS.

General Utility and Evaluation

The WSS manual is very useful in describing the items and scoring procedures. It is easy to use with clearly outlined administration instructions. Further, the manual provides information on the test's development and background. Overall, the manual makes proctoring very simple without a lot of directions or instructions. The WSS Form E manual does not offer information on the test's development or background as does the WSS Manual. However, it provides a detailed script for test administration. Just like the WSS, the manual is clearly written and is easy to use when proctoring the assessment. It is unfortunate that both the WSS and WSS Form E lack a thorough description of technical data in their respective manuals because of the tests's unique and necessary scope of assessment. Both instruments are attempting to capture information that can help test takers analyze and reflect on their abilities and understanding of basic work ethics and employment skills needed to be successful in the workplace. The lack of technical data could leave one wondering if it is actually a useful assessment and able to be used with diverse populations.

Although there is nothing available in academic literature on about either assessment, both are interesting surveys that can be used to provide a quick assessment to help individuals assess the skills needed to be successful employees. It is a practical tool in that it assesses work success skills rather than technical skills that would need updating with technological advances. It is recommended that to be helpful and efficient the publisher should considered creating an electronic format of the WSS Form E to be administered by counselors, so that the results can be received instantly. In addition, providing more technical data to the manual could give more creditability to the assessment, and it might be used more by test takers, counselors, and researchers.

References and Additional Resources

Industrial Psychology International, Ltd. (1998a). *Workplace Skills Survey.* Champaign, IL: Author.

Industrial Psychology International, Ltd. (1998b). *Workplace Skills Survey administrator manual.* Champaign, IL: Author.

Industrial Psychology International, Ltd. (2000a). *Workplace Skills Survey manual.* Champaign, IL: Author.

Industrial Psychology International, Ltd. (2000b). *Workplace Skills Survey summary report.* Champaign, IL: Author.

Kirnan, J. (2007). [Workplace Skills Survey.] In R. A. Spies, B. S. Plake, K. Geisinger, & J. Carlson (Eds.), *The seventeenth mental measurements yearbook.* Lincoln, NE: Buros Center for Testing.

MetriTech. (2012). *Workplace Skills Survey.* Retrieved from https://www.metritech.com/catalog_product.aspx?ID=3&ptype=6

Sauser, W. (2007). [Workplace Skills Survey.] In R. A. Spies, B. S. Plake, K. Geisinger, & J. Carlson (Eds.), *The seventeenth mental measurements yearbook.* Lincoln, NE: Buros Center for Testing.

U.S. Department of Labor. (1991). *What work requires of schools. A SCANS (Secretary's Commission on Achieving Necessary Skills) Report for America 2000.* Washington, DC: Author.

CHAPTER 11

COMPREHENSIVE OR COMBINED MEASURES

- Career Interests, Preferences, and Strengths Inventory

- CareerScope: Career Assessment and Reporting System, Version 10

- COPSystem Career Guidance Program

- Differential Aptitude Tests for Personnel and Career Assessment and the Career Interest Inventory, Fifth Edition

- Employability Competency System Appraisal Test

- EXPLORE and PLAN

- Kuder Career Planning System

- Occupational Aptitude Survey and Interest Schedule, Third Edition

- World of Work Inventory

CAREER INTERESTS, PREFERENCES, AND STRENGTHS INVENTORY
Gary Clark, Katherine Synatschk, James Patton, and Lawrence Steel

Pro-Ed, Inc.

8700 Shoal Creek Blvd.
Austin, TX 78757-6897
http://www.proedinc.com
info@proedinc.com

Target Population: Adolescents and potentially young adults; Students ages 11-22, grades 5-12.

Statement of the Purpose of the Instrument: The Career Interests, Preferences, and Strengths Inventory (CIPSI) examines interests, preferences, and strengths and aligns those with the 16 Career Clusters and hundreds of careers.

Titles of Subtests, Scales, Scores Provided: Careers and U.S. Department of Education Career Clusters aligned with strengths, interests, and general preferences are used. There are four surveys included in the CIPSI: (1) Personal Interests Survey, (2) Strengths Survey, (3) General Preferences Survey, and (4) Careers Survey. Percentages are computed based on number of items endorsed on each of the four surveys. These percentages correspond with Career Clusters.

Forms and Levels Available, with Dates of Publication/Revision of Each: Computerized and paper-and-pencil versions available. 2012.

Date of Most Recent Edition of Test Manual, User's Guide, Etc.: 2012.

Languages in Which Available: English only.

Time:

    Actual Test Time: Varies.

    Total Administration Time: 15-30 minutes, typically 20 minutes.

Manner in Which Results Are Reported for Individuals: Careers and U.S. Department of Education Career Clusters aligned with their strengths, interests, and general preferences are presented.

Machine Scoring: Available.

Hand Scoring: Not available.

Computer Software Options Available: Available.

Cost of Materials: Due to price changes since publication date, be sure to check the publisher's website.

    Specimen Set: $125.00 for CD-ROM and 56-page manual.

    Counselee Materials: Can complete through computer program or printout from program.

Published Reviews of the Instrument in the Last 15 Years: Not available.

CAREER INTERESTS, PREFERENCES, AND STRENGTHS INVENTORY

Reviewed by:

Maria I. Kuznetsova
Department of Psychology
University of Wyoming

Shawn Powell
School of Social and Behavioral Sciences
Casper College

Description

The Career Interests, Preferences, and Strengths Inventory (CIPSI), designed for individuals in Grades 5 through 12, "offers a system to help students examine their personal interests, strengths, and general preferences in relation to Career Clusters" (Clark, Synatschk, Patton, & Steele, 2012, p. 4). It consists of four surveys: (1) Personal Interests Survey (69 Yes/No questions); (2) Strengths Survey (88 Yes/No questions); (3) General Preferences Survey (19 three-point Likert scale questions); and (4) Careers Survey (65 Yes/No questions). Scores for each survey provide percentages of endorsed items for each of the Career Clusters, which are provided by the U.S. Department of Education.

Students can complete all four surveys on a computer in 20 to 40 minutes depending on their reading skills. The computerized version is user-friendly and easy to follow. It provides immediate results in the form of a computer-generated report upon the student's submission of the responses. The programming allows a counselor to print separate reports for each of the four surveys or one summary report based on all four surveys. The results are linked to the O*NET Code connector, which allows for more in-depth explorations of careers using the U.S. Department of Labor occupational groupings and codes. These worksheets enable career counselors and educators to help students identify careers that align with their personal interests.

CIPSI can be used in career and educational counseling. Counselors can use the CIPSI for initial exploration of career interests with a student. The worksheets provided with the manual can assist counselors in working with students to explore career options. The reports can also help counselors develop plans on how students can transition into their chosen career(s) after graduation. Counselors or other educators can relay their students CIPSI results individually or in group formats. If the CIPSI was administered to younger students, it could be considered an initial career guide. When administered to older students it could be used to assist in choosing vocational training and higher education programming to align with a student's self-reported interests.

Technical Considerations

No normative data are available for the CIPSI as the instrument was developed to match U.S. Department of Labor and U.S. Department of Education's pre-established groupings. The results of the surveys are linked to the U.S. Department of Education's Career Clusters and U.S. Department of Labor occupational groups.

No evidence of the reliability of this instrument is provided in the administration manual. In addition, the CIPSI lacks validity evidence. There is some evidence, however, of face validity as the inventory's questions are linked to 16 Career Clusters. Questions were reviewed by general education teachers, teachers of students with disabilities, transition specialists, career counseling professionals, and professional school counselors.

General Utility and Evaluation

The CIPSI could be used for initial career interest exploration. The manual provides a good explanation for how the CIPSI can be used and how the questions were developed. It addresses the needs of typically developing students and of students with special education needs. The CIPSI can be used to fulfill requirements of Individuals with Disabilities Education Act (IDEA) for students who receive special education services to have

Career Interests, Preferences, and Strengths Inventory

transitional/career guidance prior to graduating from high school.

As there is no evidence of its psychometric properties, it is not possible to determine if this assessment instrument is reliable or valid. The administration manual has worksheets students can complete to further their career exploration based on their inventory results. It is an excellent tool for those who do not know where to start with career exploration. It also allows students who complete this inventory on a computer with Internet access to immediately learn more about the careers for which they endorsed most of the items.

Reference

Clark, G. M., Synatschk, K. O., Patton, J. R., & Steel, L. E. (2012). *Career Interests, Preferences, and Strengths Inventory.* Austin, TX: PRO-ED, Inc.

A Counselor's Guide To Career Assessments Instruments

CAREERSCOPE: CAREER ASSESSMENT AND REPORTING SYSTEM, VERSION 10
Vocational Research Institute

Vocational Research Institute
1845 Walnut Street – Suite 660
Philadelphia, PA 19103
800.874.5387
http://www.vri.org
info@vri.org

Target Population: Adolescents, young adults, and adults, reading at or above the 4th grade level and able to use a computer.

Statement of the Purpose of the Instrument: The CareerScope Assessment and Reporting System establishes career interest and aptitude score profiles and occupational clusters in which the consumer can experience work activity and satisfaction and probable success in occupational training.

Titles of Subtests, Scales, Scores Provided: CareerScope Interest Inventory; CareerScope Aptitude Battery: General Learning Ability, Verbal Aptitude, Numerical Aptitude, Spatial Aptitude, Form Perception, Clerical Perception.

Interest Inventory — Scale percentile ranks as compared to total age appropriate norm group and as graphically displayed and statistically analyzed as standardized idiographic 12-scale profile.

Aptitude Battery — Reported as standardized scores, as numerical percentile ranks and as a composite profile histogram display.

Forms and Levels Available, with Dates of Publication/Revision of Each: Version 10, published in 2010. The instrument offers several accommodation options including instructions in audio format, Spanish administration, and some assessments can be untimed for users who have reading difficulties. CareerScope Online is the web-based version of the CD-based CareerScope; Spanish and audio formats are included at no additional cost for CareerScope Online. Version 11 is under development.

Date of Most Recent Edition of Test Manual, User's Guide, Etc.: 2010.

Languages in Which Available: English and Spanish.

Time:

Actual Test Time: Interest Inventory — Untimed (typically 15 minutes); Aptitude Battery — 25 minutes.

Total Administration Time: 45-60 minutes.

Norm Group(s) on Which Scores Are Based: Please review the Research Briefs (Vocational Research Institute, 2006a, 2006b, 2006c, 2006d) referenced in the review for details.

Manner in Which Results Are Reported for Individuals: The consumer's Assessment Profile includes interest and aptitude score tables and graphic displays, with supporting narrative text, and career cluster recommendations (with descriptions of general work activities). The Counselor Report presents raw scores, corresponding percentile ranks, and standardized scores and viable career clusters in a concise tabular format. The Summary Report provides a one-page graphical overview of Interest Results, Aptitude Results, and Work Group or Career Clusters/Pathways Recommendations. Assessment Profile career recommendations can be founded upon the synthesis of interest and aptitude results; career recommendations can be presented in formats consistent with the Guide for Occupational Exploration/Dictionary of Occupational Titles (GOE/DOT), O*NET, or U.S. Department of Education's Career Cluster/Pathway system; illustrative high-growth/high-replacement-rate occupations can be included/excluded.

Report Format/Content for Group Summaries: The CareerScope system supports local configurations and generation of group summary reports that identify examinees with specific score or recommendation outcomes.

Machine-Scoring Service: Not available. The assessment is self-scored and the license owner generates reports on a local/network printer or can save reports in PDF format.

Hand Scoring: Not available.

Local Machine Scoring: Not available.

Computer Software Options Available: CareerScope with audio, CareerScope English w/Spanish; these options are available at an additional cost. For examinees with reading difficulties, Numerical Reasoning and Word Meanings can be offered as an untimed assessments to provide additional time for these subtests that require reading comprehension.

Cost of Materials: Due to possible price changes since publication date, be sure to check the publisher's website. Examinees are to contact a representative through the website for the most updated pricing.

Specimen Set: Two pricing plans are available: the Licensed Plan and the Metered Plan. A single-user license is $3000.00. This license entitles the user to administer the assessment to an unlimited number of test users on a single computer. Multiple workstation and site licenses are also available. The Metered Plan is a "pay by the administration" plan that allows users to use CareerScope on an unlimited number of computers at a single address. The initial software license costs approximately $500.00 (one-time cost), plus the cost of administrations (ranging from $5.00 to $14.00 per administration, depending on the quantity purchased).

For CareerScope Online, one portal fee is $299.00, with additional portals at $199.00 each. Cost per administration varies based on quantity ordered: $16.00 each (49 or fewer), $12.00 each (50 to 149), $11.00 each (150-299), $9.00 (300 to 499), and $7.00 (500 or more).

Counselee Materials: All assessment questions are administered on the computer workstation, and test user responses are automatically stored on the computer. Therefore, no consumable test forms or answer sheets are necessary. Additional materials required are scratch paper and pencil, which should be provided to each test user for completion of tasks involving numerical operations.

Published Reviews of the Instrument in the Last 15 Years:

Boylan, M. (2009). [CareerScope Career Assessment and Reporting System]. In E. A. Whitfield, R. W. Feller, & C. Wood (Eds.), *A counselor's guide to career assessment instruments* (5th ed, pp. 112-118). Broken Arrow, OK: National Career Development Association.

Brown, C. D. (2001). [CareerScope Career Assessment and Reporting System]. In J. T. Kapes & E. A. Whitfield (Ed.), *A counselor's guide to career assessment instruments* (4th ed.). Columbus, OH: National Career Development Association.

CAREERSCOPE ASSESSMENT AND REPORTING SYSTEM, VERSION 10

Reviewed by:

Gabriel I. Lomas

Department of Education and Educational Psychology
Western Connecticut State University

Description

The CareerScope Career Assessment and Reporting System (CareerScope) is published by the Vocational Research Institute (VRI), a division of JEVS Human Services. The first version of CareerScope was published in 1997 (Boylan, 2009); Version 10, published in 2010, is available in a CD-ROM or an online administration format (i.e., CareerScope Online). Changes to Version 10, as compared to prior versions, include a Group Clusters Report and Updated Occupational Databases. The updated Group Clusters Report allows counselors to easily identify clients in either group or individual administrations with assessment profiles that are aligned with designated career clusters. The updated occupational databases are aligned with the most up-to-date information from the U.S. Department of Labor's O*NET database (Version 14), as well as the latest update

A COUNSELOR'S GUIDE TO CAREER ASSESSMENTS INSTRUMENTS

to the Standard Occupational Classification (SOC) taxonomy. CareerScope is categorized as a career interest inventory and aptitude test to help counselors identify and measure the client's attraction to the U.S. Department of Labor's interest areas. Interest areas include the following: Artistic, Plants/Animals, Mechanical, Business Detail, Accommodating, Leading/Influencing, Scientific, Protective, Industrial, Selling, Humanitarian, and Physical Performing. These interest areas also correspond with the U.S. Department of Labor's General Aptitude Test Battery (GATB): General Learning Ability, Verbal Aptitude, Numerical Aptitude, Spatial Aptitude, Form Perception, and Clerical Perception.

By means of a computer, CareerScope clients are presented with statements about tasks from a variety of occupations and must rate them by indicating their like for, dislike of, or lack of knowledge about the task. The CareerScope Interest Inventory takes about 15 minutes to complete and is comprised of three parts: (1) general instructions, (2) practice, and (3) administration of the inventory items. The CareerScope Aptitude Battery consists of seven aptitude tasks in the following areas: object identification, abstract shape matching, clerical matching, pattern visualization, computation, numerical reasoning, and word meanings. Clients first complete practice items, then complete the tasks, each requiring between one and seven minutes. At the end of each task, the clients is offered an optional rest time of 90 seconds.

Upon the completion of the test, CareerScope provides clients and counselors three reports: 1) the Assessment Profile, 2) the Counselor Report, and 3) the Summary Report. The Assessment Profile is comprised of three parts: Interest Results, Aptitude Results, and Recommendations. Interest Results are presented in both a graphic display and in a tabulated configuration. Aptitude Results are reported in both standard score and percentile score formats. Both scores offer a comparison of the test user with others in the normative group at the same developmental level. Finally, users and counselors are provided Recommendations in three available formats: Guide for Occupational Exploration/Dictionary of Occupational Titles (GOE/DOT), O*NET, and U.S. Department of Education Career Cluster/Pathway recommendations. The Counselor Report is a three-page document that offers the counselor a summary of the most important information in a variety of tables. The Summary Report is a graphical overview of the assessment information in a one to two page format.

The latest version of CareerScope is up to date with Version 14 of the O*NET career information database as well as the latest update to the Standard Occupation Classification (SOC) taxonomy. The publisher has also placed an informational video on its website to orient clients and counselors to the purpose and use of the instrument.

Technical Considerations

Technical information regarding CareerScope is not available in the manual that accompanies the software, nor is it publicly available on their website. However, VRI makes technical reports available to individuals upon request. Standardization of the Aptitude Battery was done on 115 employed individuals (i.e., 74% female, 79% White, and 16% African American). No date was provided for the norming studies of the Aptitude Battery. The CareerScope Research Brief #1 (VRI, 2006a) reported the results of a concurrent validity study on 97 employed individuals from Philadelphia, Pennsylvania. The participants were primarily female (74%) and White (79%). Correlations with the General Aptitude Test Battery (GATB) were moderate on two of the subtests (Clerical Perception = .52 and Form Perception = .59) but high (ranging from .71 - .82) on the remaining four subtests. Research Brief #2 (VRI, 2006b) reports test-retest reliability for the CareerScope Aptitude Battery. The report indicated the study was done in 1998 with 307 students in 7th through 12th grades, all in a single Louisiana parish. Slightly more than half of the population was female (57%), and most (75%) were White. Retest reliabilities were all acceptable as results ranged from a low of .70 (Spatial Ability, Form Perception) to a high of .80 (General Learning Ability).

Standardization of the CareerScope Interest Inventory was done with a vocational sample of 525 individuals from nine sites (locations were not reported), with demographics that represent many large U.S. urban areas (46.7% White, 21.6% African American, 23.4% Hispanic/Latino, 4.7% Asian, 3.6% Other; 62% female). The prevocational sample was comprised of 856 individuals from nine sites (locations were not reported), with demographics that represent many large U.S. urban areas (58.5% White, 16.8% African American, 18.1% Hispanic/Latino, 1.8% Asian, 4.8% Other; 49.9% female). The 12 scales of the instrument were validated against

CareerScope: Career Assessment and Reporting System, Version 10

corresponding scales of the Department of Labor's USES Interest Inventory. Correlational studies conducted with a sample of 573 individuals revealed Pearson product-moment correlations between corresponding scales ranging from a low of .70 to a high of .96, which is acceptable. CareerScope Research Brief #3 (VRI, 2006c) reported retest reliability of the Interest Inventory scales. The report indicated the study was done in 1998 with 307 students in 7th through 12th grades, all in a single Louisiana parish. Slightly more than half of the population was female (57%), and most (75%) were White. Test-retest reliabilities were all acceptable as results ranged from .73 (Industrial, Accommodating) to .87 (Physical Performing). Based on this report, the CareerScope Interest Inventory appears to be a reliable measure for secondary school students.

CareerScope Research Brief #4 (VRI, 2006d) reported the internal consistency of the Interest Inventory scales based on a study of 97 employed individuals from Philadelphia, Pennsylvania. The participants were primarily female (74%) and White (79%). Alpha coefficients for each of the 12 interest scales ranged from .81 to .91, with a median of .89. These findings demonstrate good internal consistency for all scales of the Career-Scope Interest Inventory.

General Utility and Evaluation

The Startup Guide that accompanies the CD version of CareerScope is brief and straightforward (VRI, 2010). It is designed to aid purchasers in loading the software onto a workstation or network. The full User Guide (close to 200 pages), which is available to counselors via the CareerScope Management System, provides detailed explanations of the CareerScope assessment, Management System features, and report output, as well as a guide to report interpretation and an appendix with supplemental resources. Customer support is available, with direct phone lines for regional representatives as well as the centralized office support and technical support listed on their website. Available adaptations for special populations outlined earlier in this test review are helpful in the administration to diverse individuals.

Technical information, provided upon request, leaves counselors with a mixed review. Strengths for the Aptitude Battery include good test-retest reliability and several scales demonstrating high concurrent validity with the GATB. Weaknesses for the Aptitude Battery include a small normative group (115 individuals) and a validity study with only 97 participants which were mostly White females from a single geographic area. Strengths for the Interest Inventory include a sizable vocational sample ($N = 525$) and prevocational sample ($N = 856$), with both samples representative of the current demographics of the United States. Both studies reporting test-retest reliability and internal consistency reported acceptable properties for the Interest Inventory. Like the Aptitude Battery, weaknesses with the Interest Inventory include a small normative group that lacked the diversity of current U.S. demographics.

The test itself is beautifully presented using a computerized workstation and can be used on a network for administration with larger groups. The instrument offers audio instructions and an opportunity to practice prior to testing. CareerScope can be completed in a single sitting and is engaging enough to keep the attention of users. The results provided by the instrument can be a powerful tool in helping both school counselors and students identify career strengths and aptitudes to assist with post-secondary decision making. It can also be used with adults making decisions related to education, vocational rehabilitation, and career development.

According to Boylan (2009), one benefit of CareerScope is that it is able to combine one's interests with one's aptitude in a single assessment and in one report. This is clearly an attractive attribute as many other instruments are designed to measure only one of these two constructs, requiring the use of two instruments. The cost of the instrument is affordable for most school systems, career counseling centers, and public and private agencies that focus on career assessment. Finally, the 4th-grade reading level and the relative ease of navigation of the system make CareerScope widely accessible to nearly all high school-aged individuals and adults, including most individuals with disabilities.

References and Additional Resources

Boylan, M. (2009). [CareerScope Career Assessment and Reporting System]. In E. A. Whitfield, R. W. Feller, & C. Wood (Eds.), *A counselor's guide to career assessment instruments* (5th ed., pp. 112-118). Broken Arrow, OK: National Career Development Association.

Brown, C. D. (2001). [CareerScope Career Assessment and Reporting System]. In J. T. Kapes & E. A. Whitfield (Eds.), *A counselor's guide to career assessment instruments* (4th ed.). Columbus, OH: National Career Development Association.

Vocational Research Institute. (2006a). *Concurrent validity of the CareerScope aptitude battery* (Research Brief #1). Philadelphia, PA: Author.

Vocational Research Institute. (2006b). *Retest reliability of the CareerScope aptitude battery* (Research Brief #2). Philadelphia, PA: Author.

Vocational Research Institute. (2006c). *Retest reliability of the CareerScope interest inventory* (Research Brief #3). Philadelphia, PA: Author.

Vocational Research Institute. (2006d). *Internal consistency of the CareerScope interest inventory* (Research Brief #4). Philadelphia, PA: Author.

Vocational Research Institute. (2010). *CareerScope: Career Assessment and Reporting Software Start Up Guide.* Philadelphia, PA: Author.

176

COPSystem Career Guidance Program:
Career Occupational Preference System Interest Inventory
Career Ability Placement Survey
Career Orientation Placement and Evaluation Survey
Robert R. Knapp, Lila F. Knapp, and Lisa Knapp-Lee

EdITS/Educational and Industrial Testing Service

P.O. Box 7234
San Diego, CA 92167
http://www.edits.net
customerservice@edits.net

Target Population: Children, adolescents and adults; grade 4 and up.

Statement of the Purpose of the Instrument: The COPSystem instruments (Career Occupational Preference System Interest Inventory [COPS], Career Ability Placement Survey [CAPS], and Career Orientation Placement and Evaluation Survey [COPES]) are designed to provide individuals with coordinated measures of interest, abilities, and work values in terms of eight major career clusters. Scores on the combination of the assessments provide a starting point for career exploration.

Titles of Subtests, Scales, Scores Provided: All assessments are keyed to 14 COPSystem Career Clusters: Science Professional, Science Skilled, Technology Professional, Technology Skilled, Consumer Economics, Outdoor, Business Professional, Business Skilled, Clerical, Communication, Arts Professional, Arts Skilled, Service Professional, and Service Skilled. CAPS subtests include: Mechanical Reasoning, Spatial Relations, Verbal Reasoning, Numerical Ability, Language Usage, Word Knowledge, Perceptual Speed and Accuracy, and Manual Speed and Dexterity. The COPES scales are the following: Investigative vs. Accepting, Practical vs. Carefree, Independence vs. Conformity, Leadership vs. Supportive, Orderliness vs. Flexibility, Recognition vs. Privacy, Aesthetic vs. Realistic, and Social vs. Reserved.

Forms and Levels Available, with Dates of Publication/Revision of Each: COPS (1995), COPS Professional Level (COPS-P, 2002), COPS Form R (COPS-R, 2008), COPS Intermediate Inventory (COPS-II, 2003), COPS Picture Inventory (COPS-PIC, 2007), Spanish COPS (SPOC, 1995), Spanish CAPS (1976), Career Ability Placement Survey (CAPS, 1976), and Career Orientation Placement and Evaluation Survey (COPES, 1995). COPS, COPS-R, CAPS, and COPES were re-normed in 2007.

Date of Most Recent Edition of Test Manual, User's Guide, Etc.: COPS Technical Manual (1990, 2007, in press); CAPS Technical Manual (1992); COPES Technical Manual (1995).

Languages in Which Available: English, Spanish, and nonreading. Some translations of directions for the COPS-PIC, CAPS, and COPES are available in Spanish, Hmong, Russian, Croatian, Laotian, and Vietnamese.

Time:

Actual Test Time: COPS: 20-30 minutes; CAPS: 40 minutes; COPES 20 minutes.

Total Administration Time: 2 hours: COPS: 25-35 minutes; CAPS 50 minutes; COPES: 30-50 minutes.

Norm Group(s) on Which Scores Are Based: Junior high, high school, and community college/college norms.

Manner in Which Results Are Reported for Individuals: Raw scores, Percentiles, Stanines, and Verbal Labels are included COPSystem scores keyed to 14 COPSystem Clusters as described in the interpretive booklet. The interpretive booklet provides information about each cluster including: a definition of each career cluster, related courses of study, sample occupations, related college majors, necessary skills and abilities, activities for experience, career planning worksheet, educational planning worksheet, and local job interview sheet.

COPSystem Career Guidance Program

Options available include self-scoring and machine-scoring through EdITS, local onsite machine scoring or online results. Machine scoring provides individual printouts.

Report Format/Content for Group Summaries: Summary of Interest shows the percent of times one of the 14 Career Clusters was chosen by examinees as one of their top three areas of interest; Needs Assessment Summary provides a summary of student responses to a career planning questionnaire; Examinees by Interest Area is a listing of students interested in one of three top Career Clusters. Basic List Report is a condensed summary of student responses to the COPS, CAPS, and COPES. Record Labels have the same information as basic list on self-adhesive labels. Data may be summarized by any grouping and is available electronically for the machine scoring version.

Machine Scoring: Machine-scoring service is available for all assessments at $1.80 per assessment; time required for scoring and returning is typically no more than: 10 business days.

Hand Scoring: Hand scored by counselee, clerk, or counselor in approximately 15-20 minutes.

Computer Software Options Available: The COPSystem 3C is available at the publisher's website.

Cost of Materials: Due to possible price changes since publication date, be sure to check the publisher's website.

Specimen Set: COPS, CAPS, and COPES specimen sets range from $9.00 to $37.50 and include one copy of all forms and manuals. COPSystem Career Guidebook — $219.75 (package of 25).

Counselee Materials: All materials are consumable, and prices are based on machine-scored or self-scored format. Each assessment may be used as a stand-alone instrument. COPS machine-scored format: Test Booklets and Answer Sheets — $18.00 (package of 25), $63.00 (package of 100), and $296.50 (package of 500). COPS self-scored format: Test Booklets — $17.50 (package of 25), $62.75 (package of 100), and $292.25 (package of 500); Self-Interpretation Profile and Guide — $17.00 (package of 25), $59.25 (package of 100), and $275.50 (package of 500). CAPS machine-scored format: Test Battery set (8 tests per set) — $59.25 (25 sets), $199.25 (100 sets), and $942.00 (500 sets); Test Forms — $16.25 (25 tests), $174.50 (500 tests). CAPS self-scored format: Test Battery set — $100.25 (25 sets), $371.75 (100 sets), and $1254.25 (500 sets); Self-Interpretation Profile and Guide — $17.00 (package of 25) and $275.50 (package of 500). COPES machine-scored format: Test Booklets and Answer Sheets — $18.00 (package of 25), $63.00 (package of 100), and $296.50 (package of 500). COPES self-scored format: Test Booklets — $17.50 (package of 25), $62.75 (package of 100), and $292.25 (package of 500); Self-Interpretation Profile and Guide — $6.75 (package of 25), $16.75 (package of 100), and $79.00 (package of 500). The publisher's website offers additional support materials for the COPSystem.

Published Reviews of the Instrument in the Last 15 Years:

Bullock, E. E., & Madson, M. B. (2009). [COPSystem Career Guidance Program (COPS, COPES, and CAPS).] In E. A. Whitfield, R. W. Feller, & C. Wood (Eds.), *A counselor's guide to career assessment instruments* (5th ed., pp. 119-126). Broken Arrow, OK: National Career Development Association.

Wickwire, P. N. (2001). [COPSystem (COPS, CAPS, and COPES).] In J. T. Kapes & E. A. Whitfield (Eds.), *A counselor's guide to career assessment instruments* (4th ed., pp. 210-217). Columbus, OH: National Career Development Association.

COPSystem Career Guidance Program:
Career Occupational Preference System
Interest Inventory
Career Ability Placement Survey
Career Orientation Placement
and Evaluation Survey

Reviewed by:

Emily Bullock-Yowell and Lauren K. Osborne

Department of Psychology
University of Southern Mississippi

Description

The Career Occupational Preference System (COPSystem; Knapp, Knapp, & Knapp-Lee, 1990) includes three coordinated instruments that are designed to assess career interest, abilities, and values. The purpose of these instruments is to increase self-awareness in junior high students, high school students, college students, and adults engaging the career decision-making process. All instruments include test booklets and examiner's manuals for interpretation and reference. Surveys instructions are clearly printed, easily understood and legible. Materials are durable and answers are reported by test takers directly on the survey materials and lend to convenient hand or machine scoring. Online administration and scoring is advertised on the publisher's website (EdITS, 2012a)

The three instruments within the COPSystem are the Career Occupational Preference Interest Inventory (COPS), Career Ability Placement Survey (CAPS), and the Career Orientation Placement and Evaluation Survey (COPES). The development and revision of these instruments has a strong theoretical and research basis. Original versions of these instruments appeared between 1975 and 1981, and the latest normative data were gathered between January 2004 and June 2007.

The COPS has multiple versions to meet the needs of the test administrator and potential test takers. The standard version of the COPS is for use with junior high students, high school students, college students, or adults. The COPS-P is specifically designed for college students and adults. The COPS-R is for use with those in the 6th grade through high school. The COPS II was designed for use with those in 4th grade through high school and with special education populations. Any of the versions of the COPS can be ordered for use with the COPES and CAPS. There are Spanish versions of the COPS and CAPS with norms composed of Spanish-speaking students from the United States combined with a Spanish-speaking sample from Mexico (EdITS, 2012a).

The Career Occupational Preference Interest Inventory (COPS) is a measure of job activity preference in relation to 14 clusters of related occupations. It takes 20 to 30 minutes to respond to the 168-item inventory. The items are composed of activities associated with specific work environments such as "care for patients in a hospital" and "arrange flower displays." Test takers respond to items using the response choices of *like very much, like moderately, dislike moderately,* or *dislike very much* (Knapp et al., 1990).

Results are presented in percentiles that represent a comparison of the examinee's scores to the normative sample. The results provide the test taker information relative to the strength of his or her interests in relation to 14 Career Clusters. The Professional and Skilled distinctions reflect differences in level of training and responsibility for occupations within that cluster. The 14 Career Clusters include the following:

Science Professional	Outdoor	Science Skilled	Clerical
Business Professional	Technology Professional	Business Skilled	Communication
Technology Skilled	Consumer Economics	Service Professional	Arts Professional
Service Skilled	Arts Skilled		

COPSystem Career Guidance Program

The CAPS is a battery of eight ability tests grouped into these categories:

Mechanical Reasoning	Language Usage
Spatial Relations	Word Knowledge
Verbal Reasoning	Perceptual Speed and Accuracy
Numerical Ability	Manual Speed and Dexterity

Each test is administered by recorded instructions and has a five-minute time limit. The total administration of the CAPS takes about 50 minutes. Each item on the CAPS requires the test taker to complete a task relevant to the ability category. For example, in Word Knowledge the test taker must choose the best one-word definition for the term "synchronize" (Knapp, Knapp, & Knapp-Lee, 1992).

The CAPS can be used and interpreted as a stand-alone measure of vocationally oriented ability by interpreting the resulting percentile and stanine scores relative to the eight ability tests. As recommended, it can also be used and interpreted within the COPSystem by interpreting the resulting percentile scores relative to the 14 Career Clusters. The reported scores represent a comparison between the examinee's scores and the normative sample. Through extensive factor analytic research, the eight CAPS abilities have been keyed to the 14 Career Clusters to help examinees identify within which career clusters his or her abilities best match (Knapp et al., 1992).

The COPES is a measure of vocational values. There is a self-scoring form (128 items) and a machine scoring form (160 items) of the COPES, and each take 30 to 50 minutes to complete. Each item allows the test taker to choose one of two statements that best reflect his or her values by completing the sentence, "I value activities or jobs in which I ..." To complete the sentence test takers can, for example, mark either "team up with others "or "work on my own." The items were written with consideration of the 14 Career Clusters and numerous previous factor analytic studies of values (Knapp & Knapp-Lee, 1996).

Results are reported in percentile scores that represent a comparison between the test taker's scores and the normative sample. Interpretation of COPES results begins by identifying the three most salient or highest percentile values for the examinee. The COPES results can then be used in the interpretation of the full COPSystem. Extensive research aided in determining which COPES values fit best with the occupations represented in each of the 14 COPS Career Clusters. The work values measured by the COPES are composed of eight work values dichotomies:

Investigative vs. Accepting	Orderliness vs. Flexibility
Practical vs. Carefree	Recognition vs. Privacy
Independence vs. Conformity	Aesthetic vs. Realistic
Leadership vs. Supportive	Social vs. Reserved

Currently, the COPSystem is available in paper-and-pencil versions and online versions. The test taker can score all three COPSystem inventories by hand (Knapp et al., 1990). Machine scoring that provides a summary of the entire battery's results is available through EdITS. Computer administration is available at the publisher's website, and scoring software is available with the Integrated Reporting and Interpretation System (IRIS), allowing on-site, immediate score feedback. Time to score and interpret the instruments within the COPSystem will vary depending on clinician choice of how to use it (e.g., self-scoring, in groups) and what support tools to incorporate.

The COPSystem is a set of coordinated career assessment instruments composed of separate measures of interest, ability, and values for use with junior high students, high school students, college students, and adults. It appears the COPS serves as the anchor instrument within the system. The results of the COPS communicate the level of a test taker's interest in 14 Career Clusters, which are composed of occupations with similar job activities. Knapp et al. (1992) stated that the results of the ability and values measures are best used when interpreted in light of the 14 Career Clusters as an integrated COPSystem battery. The eight scales of the CAPS (ability) and the eight scales of the COPES (values) have been keyed to the 14 Career Clusters through extensive factor analytic research.

A Counselor's Guide To Career Assessments Instruments

The COPSystem Technical Manual (Knapp et al., 1990) outlines several ways and environments in which it is appropriate to use the coordinated inventories. Environments such as schools, businesses, and private practice counseling settings are all suggested. In the school system, the COPSystem can be used for career planning, self-awareness, or early career awareness programming. Relevant norm groups make the COPSystem appropriate for use at the junior high, high school, and college levels. The use of the COPSystem may be lead by a school counselor or individual teachers through a group or individual interpretation format. In business and industrial settings, the COPSystem may serve as a tool for personal development, increased self-awareness, and selection and placement (Knapp et al., 1990). Knapp and Knapp-Lee (1996) cited the COPES as being especially useful in counseling settings when the therapist is working with an adult in career transition.

Technical Considerations

Updated normative data were collected for the COPSystem in five geographic regions between January 2004 and June 2007. The data consisted of a sample of 22,691 seventh through twelfth grade students and an additional sample of 1,898 college students. Because there is a significant difference in the manner in which males and females respond to the COPS items, gender-based norms are provided. The collected normative sample appears to adequately represent each gender (EdITS, 2012b). Reliability data for each instrument is reported in the technical manual (Knapp et al., 1990). Reliability and validity information are presented below for each test. It should be noted that some of the reliability and validity data reported do not use the most recent normative data collected.

Reliability coefficients ranging from .86 to .92 are reported for the scales of the COPS (EdITS, 2012b). Based on the 1974 version of the instrument, a one-year interval test-retest procedure yielded coefficients ranging from .62 to .80 for all scales of the interest inventory (Knapp, Knapp, & Knapp-Lee et al. 1990). Numerous studies supporting the validity of the COPS are reported. In a study including the Kuder scales and the COPS, correlations between similar scales ranged from .21 to .49. Eighty-nine percent of those sampled in this study chose at least one of same top three interest areas on both instruments. Correlations between similar scales of the COPS and the Vocational Preference Inventory ranged from .5 and .7. Concurrent validity was indicated in a study reporting that 71% of the sample declared college majors that aligned with interests measured on the COPS. In support of predictive validity, a study demonstrated that 64% of the sample was in a job or college major that aligned with their COPS interest areas one to seven years after being assessed (EdITS, 2012b).

The development of the CAPS focused on creating a reliable measurement of cognitive ability that would fit into the typical time allotted for cognitive assessment within a career battery. This task was pursued with the understanding that a shorter instrument would result in lower reliability. In a sample of 90 high school students, test-retest reliability coefficients ranging from .70 to .95 were yielded after a two-week interval. Alternate form reliability was measured during the test development process and ranged from .70 to .89 for all CAPS scales. Numerous studies citing the intercorrelations among CAPS scales, other measures of ability, and career choice support the criterion and construct validity of the CAPS (Knapp et al., 1992).

Internal consistency reliability coefficients ranged from .71 to .89 for the COPES scales. Concurrent validity evidence is based on moderate correlations among the 1977 version of the COPES scales and similar scales on other values inventories. A predictive validity study involving a 1 to 4 year follow-up with 9th through 12th graders concluded that 89% of those that responded to the follow-up survey were currently pursuing a career congruent with their original COPES results (Knapp & Knapp-Lee, 1996). In addition, Knapp and Knapp-Lee (1996) cited the theoretical factor structure of the items that was confirmed through factor analytic research as evidence for the construct validity of the instrument.

General Utility and Evaluation

Manuals for the COPS, COPES, and CAPS are available for reference. Each manual provides detailed descriptions of the COPSystem interest clusters and background regarding development of the overall testing system. Individual instrument manuals also provide details regarding different sections of the tests, orientation, administration, and scoring of all materials. References for interpretation are also provided with example cases, profile sheets, and survey summaries for test takers. Each manual reports reliability, validity, and norm development information for individual surveys. Information regarding the newly released IRIS scoring software is not currently included in the manuals. An IRIS software user guide is available for PDF download online through the publisher's website. Overall, the manuals provide useful and practical information for test takers regarding understanding, administering, and interpreting all instruments in the system.

A variety of supportive materials can be ordered to supplement the interpretation or use of the COPSystem results. Support materials for purchase from the publisher's website include Career Brief Kits, Career Clusters Booklets Kit, and Career Clusters Charts. Career Brief Kits are composed of 485 color-coded cards that explain one occupation in detail. The Career Cluster Booklets Kit is composed of booklets that detail information on each career cluster found throughout the COPSystem. Career Cluster Charts serve as wall or pocket sized visuals of how the Career Clusters and associated occupations are organized (EdITS, 2012a).

The COPSystem is a uniquely coordinated career development assessment battery composed of a measure of interest, values, and skills. The foundation for the development of each of the instruments is based in well-established theory, 30 years of sound research, and confirmed factor analysis. The psychometric properties of each instrument appear adequate for making decisions about individuals. Reports of the psychometric properties of the instruments were confusing at times due to the use of different versions of the instruments for the establishment of reliability and validity. Further, caution needs to be exercised in relation to the new norms and psychometrics as the results were not peer reviewed and were provided by the publishers.

There are a variety of versions and supportive materials that allow for tailoring the COPSystem to a variety of client populations. Yet, the presentation of inventory materials, manuals, and support materials can be confusing to one unfamiliar with the system. A manual or webpage that provides an overall explanation of the system, it's possible uses, support materials, and various versions would be helpful in understanding how the COPSystem could be integrated into potential test administrators' environments.

Overall, the COPSystem is an impressive and intriguing set of coordinated instruments. As stated in previous reviews (Bullock & Madson, 2009; Wickwire, 2001), the COPSystem is suggested for consideration by counselors in primary schools, secondary schools, colleges, businesses, and private practice settings.

References and Additional Resources

Bullock, E. E., & Madson, M. B. (2009). [COPSystem Career Guidance Program (COPS, COPES, and CAPS).] In E. A. Whitfield, R. W. Feller, & C. Wood (Eds.), *A counselor's guide to career assessment instruments* (5th ed., pp. 119-126). Broken Arrow, OK: National Career Development Association.

EdITS (2012a). *COPSystem: Career measurement package.* Retrieved from http://www.EdITS.net/products/copsystem.html.

EdITS (2012b). *Brief summary of the reliability and validity of the COPSystem assessments.* Retrieved from http://www. EdITS.net/component/content/article/22/63-EdITS-supplemental-test-information-and-resources-copsystem-reliability-and-validity.html

Knapp, L., & Knapp-Lee, L. (1996). *Manual: COPES: Career Orientation Placement & Evaluation Survey, 1995 ed.* San Diego, CA: EdITS.

Knapp, L., Knapp, R. R., & Knapp-Lee, L. (1992). Career Ability Placement Survey (CAPS): *CAPS technical manual.* San Diego, CA: EdITS.

Knapp, R. R., Knapp, L., & Knapp-Lee, L. (1990). *COPSystem technical manual.* San Diego, CA: EdITS.

Wickwire, P. N. (2001). [COPSystem (COPS, CAPS, and COPES).] In J. T. Kapes & E. A. Whitfield (Eds.), *A counselor's guide to career assessment instruments* (4th ed., pp. 210-217). Columbus, OH: National Career Development Association.

DIFFERENTIAL APTITUDE TESTS
FOR PERSONNEL AND CAREER ASSESSMENT, FIFTH EDITION, AND CAREER INTEREST INVENTORY
George K. Bennett, Harold G. Seashore, and Alexander G. Wesman

---

Pearson Assessments

19500 Bulverde Road
San Antonio, TX 78259
800.627.7271
http://www.pearsonassessments.com

Target Population: Adolescents, young adults, and adults; ages 16 and older. Level 1: grades 7-9; Level 2: grades 10-12 and adult.

Statement of the Purpose of the Instrument: The purpose of the Differential Aptitude Tests (DAT) for Personnel and Career Assessment (DAT) are to assist students with career guidance and school-to-career transition as well as help organizations with selection of individuals on the basis of basic skills. The DAT is a battery of eight tests designed to measure students' ability to learn or to succeed in a number of different areas. The DAT is designed to be used alone or in conjunction with the Career Interest Inventory (CII), a career guidance instrument designed to provide information about students' educational goals, interest in a variety of school subjects and activities, and interest in fields of work. When the DAT is used in conjunction with the CII, a complete profile of students' interests and aptitudes can be developed.

Titles of Subtests, Scales, Scores Provided: There are three major clusters: (1) General Cognitive Abilities (Verbal Reasoning and Numerical Ability); (2) Perceptual Abilities (Abstract Reasoning, Mechanical Reasoning, and Space Relations); and (3) Clerical and Language Skills (Spelling, Language Usage, and Clerical Speed and Accuracy).

Forms and Levels Available, with Dates of Publication/Revision of Each: 1990. Two levels of the DAT and CII are available. Level 1 is designed to be used with students in Grades 7-9, Level 2 is designed to be used with students in Grades 10-12. Both levels of the DAT can be used with adults. However, it is recommended that only the Level 2 of the CII be used with adults.

Date of Most Recent Edition of Test Manual, User's Guide, Etc.: 1992.

Languages in Which Available: English and Spanish.

Time:

Actual Test Time: Sections may be completed in 6 to 20 minutes; the partial and complete batteries take approximately 1.5 and 2.5 hours, respectively.

Total Administration Time: Approximately 196 minutes for complete DAT battery; CII is 30 minutes and untimed.

Norm Group(s) on Which Scores Are Based: DAT norms for each Grade 7-12, males, females, and combined gender; DAT norms for four groups of adults. See norms booklets.

Manner in Which Results Are Reported for Individuals: Percentile ranks, stanines, and scaled scores are presented separately for males and females, as well as combined.

Report Format/Content for Group Summaries: Group summary is available upon request (listing of students and scores and/or total group scores).

Machine Scoring: Can be scored within 21 days. Contact publisher for pricing.

Hand Scoring: Hand scored by counselee (CII only) or counselor (DAT) within 10 minutes.

Computer Software Options Available: DAT/CII Scoring Assistant helps produce computer reports for results from hand-scored instruments.

Cost of Materials: Due to possible price changes since publication date, be sure to check the publisher's website. Technical manuals: $21.00 to $83.00.

Specimen Set: DAT with CII Examination Kit (includes Level 1 Test Booklet, Level 2 Test Booklet, Directions for Administering, Level 1 and Level 2 Answer Documents with Career Interest Inventory, Perceptual Speed and Accuracy-Part 1 Answer Sheet, Practice Test, and Directions for Administering Practice Test): $53.00. DAT Partial Battery Examination Kit (includes Type 1 Level 1 Answer Documents for CII, Type 1 Level 2 Answer Documents for CII, DAT Partial Battery Level 1 Test Booklet, DAT Partial Battery Type 2 Answer Document, and DAT Partial Battery Directions): $53.00. CII Examination Kit (includes Level 1 CII Machine-Scorable Answer Document, Level 2 CII Hand-Scorable Booklet, Directions for Administering, and Student Profile): $27.55.

Counselee Materials: Individual test books (package of 25 for $177.00 each for DAT; $88.00-$93.30 for CII) for each subscale; Answer documents (package of 50 for $137.00 each for DAT and $88.00 for CII) for each subscale; Scoring keys ($90.00 each) for select subscales.

Published Reviews of the Instrument in the Last 15 Years:

Brown, L. L. (2003). [Differential Aptitude Tests, Australian and New Zealand Editions, Forms V and W.] In B. S. Plake, J. C. Impara, R. A. Spies (Eds.), *The fifteenth mental measurements yearbook.* Lincoln, NE: Buros Center for Testing.

Gebart-Eaglemont, J. E. (2003). [Differential Aptitude Tests, Australian and New Zealand Editions, Forms V and W.] In B. S. Plake, J. C. Impara, & R. A. Spies (Eds.), *The fifteenth mental measurements yearbook.* Lincoln, NE: Buros Center for Testing.

Kelley, K. N. (2009). [Differential Aptitude Tests and Career Interest Inventory.] In E. A. Whitfield, R. W. Feller, & C. Wood (Eds.), *A counselor's guide to career assessment instruments* (5th ed., pp. 127-136). Broken Arrow, OK: National Career Development Association.

Schafer W. D. (1998). [Career Interest Inventory.] In J. C. Impara and B. S. Plake (Eds.), *The thirteenth mental measurements yearbook.* Lincoln, NE: Buros Center for Testing.

Zedeck, S. (1998). [Career Interest Inventory.] In J. C. Impara and B. S. Plake (Eds.), *The thirteenth mental measurements yearbook.* Lincoln, NE: Buros Center for Testing.

DIFFERENTIAL APTITUDE TESTS FOR PERSONNEL AND CAREER ASSESSMENT, FIFTH EDITION, AND CAREER INTEREST INVENTORY

Karl N. Kelley

Department of Psychology
North Central College

Description

In the 1940s George K. Bennett, Harold G. Seashore, and Alexander G. Wesman (Bennett, & Wesman, 1947; Bennett, Seashore, & Wesman, 1948; Seashore, 1950) argued that individual aptitudes predict career and academic success. They defined an aptitude as the capacity of an individual to learn. Thus, aptitude assesses an individual's ability to learn specific skills and acquire knowledge. Rather than advocating a single aptitude to learn (similar to the "g" intelligence), these researches viewed aptitudes as a collection of different factors. The challenge became to identify and assess the key aptitudes in predicting career and academic performance. First published in 1947, the Differential Aptitude Tests (DAT) were designed to empirically demonstrate the relationship between aptitudes and performance. The four revisions of this test (the most current being in 1990) have continually refined these measures and expanded the normative basis for the test.

A Counselor's Guide To Career Assessments Instruments

The DAT was originally developed and marketed by the Psychological Corporation, which was eventually purchased by Harcourt Brace and Company. In 2008, this test (along with Harcourt Brace Assessments) was purchased by Pearson Assessments, and the test was renamed The Differential Aptitude Tests for Personnel and Career Assessment. It has broadened the scope of the test from primarily high school counseling to more organizational uses. If used in selection, Pearson Assessments claims the test is designed to assist in determining an applicant's general cognitive and perceptual abilities as well as clerical and language skills.

The current version of the DAT consists of eight specific tests (Verbal Reasoning, Numerical Reasoning, Abstract Reasoning, Perceptual Speed & Accuracy, Mechanical Reasoning, Space Relations, Spelling, and Language Usage) that can be conceptually organized around three global aptitude dimensions (Cognitive, Perceptual, and Clerical/Language). Each specific test is linked to courses of study and career fields. For example, high scores on the Verbal Reasoning scale are correlated with success in general academics classes and occupations including business, law, education, journalism, and the sciences. The global aptitude dimensions are linked to skills that are more general. The global aptitude dimensions are:

- Cognitive — Contains tests of Verbal Reasoning and Numerical Ability. These tests measure the ability to learn from books and manuals, self-instruction, or trainers/teachers.

- Perceptual — Contains tests of Abstract Reasoning, Mechanical Reasoning, and Space Relations. Assesses aptitudes in understanding things, rather than people or words.

- Clerical/Language — Contains tests of Spelling, Language Usage, and Clerical Speed/Accuracy. Tests skills necessary to perform various types of clerical skills.

The test consists of 510 items and takes 2.5 hours to complete the full battery. All items are presented in a multiple-choice format and responses are recorded on machine-scorable optical-scan forms.

This test is designed to assist high school students (and to a lesser degree young adults and adults) in selecting appropriate courses and exploring career paths. Counselors can administer this test in group or individual sessions. The tests can be returned to the publisher for machine scoring or can be scored by the counselor or student.

Reports include raw score, percentile, and stanine information. With some training, students and parents should be able to understand their scores. However, individual sessions with students may be beneficial since there are multiple scales to interpret and students, particularly in the earlier grades, may become confused. To assist in this interpretation process, the publisher also provides 10 supplemental publications for understanding and using scores. Some of these publications directly address student and parent concerns whereas others are focused on the questions for professional counselors. All of these materials are well written and easy to read. They do not get bogged down in technical considerations. Technical manuals are available for those who are interested in the test psychometrics. In addition to the interpretative materials, practice tests are available to students so that they can become familiar with the types of test items and requirements for the various subtests.

It is important to note that the interpretative materials stress that although these tests can provide useful information, they should be interpreted with caution. The test results provide clues and the first steps in the career development process. Counselors are encouraged to seek converging evidence with other information including actual academic performance, results from other tests, and the student's interests. For career planning and selection, each subscale is linked to a specific career skill and occupation.

The Career Interest Inventory (CII) is an easy to use self-report test for helping students explore a variety of academic and career choices. The results of the test are linked to the DAT scores to allow students to understand the convergence (or divergence) of their interests and aptitudes. The test presents participants with a set of tasks/jobs (such as draw pictures for books; work in a hotel; raise dogs to sell) and has them rate each one on a 5-point scale from liking the activity very much to disliking the activity a great deal. There are two levels of this test corresponding to the DAT levels. Responses to the job/activity statements are organized into 15 career clusters as described in the U.S. Department of Labor Dictionary of Occupational Titles (e.g., sales, fine arts, legal services, building trades).

Differential Aptitude Tests and the Career Interest Inventory, Fifth Edition

Technical Considerations

The DAT has been in print since 1947 and is currently in its fifth revision (1990). The most recent Technical Manual (published in 1992) contains a wealth of information about the development of the test and appropriate psychometrics. The CII was published in 1990 and is standardized with the latest edition of the DAT.

The basic structure of the DAT has remained stable over time, measuring the same basic aptitudes. The current version has made several substantial revisions in the content of the items. The first major change was to divide the test into two levels: a basic level for Grades 7 to 9 and a more advanced version for Grades 10 to 12 (and young adults). All of the items (with the exception of the Perceptual Speed and Accuracy [PSA] tests) are new in this version. Over 4000 new items were developed and refined into the final 310 items (not including the 200 items from the PSA sections).

Test developers carefully screened DAT items for readability and bias. They defined readability as adhering to the guidelines established by Taylor's (1989) research on core vocabulary. Bias was addressed by establishing a nine-member panel of subject matter experts (SME) who reviewed each item for potential gender and racial stereotypes or the existence of demeaning or offensive terms.

The normative base for the DAT included 84,000 students who participated in the National Item Tryout Program in 1988. These students were from over 150 school districts varying in socioeconomic status, enrollment, and region. The Technical Manual lists all participating school districts and provides basic demographic information. Norm tables provide descriptive information including stanine and percentile ranks for females, males, and combined sex. Same-sex interpretation is suggested for mechanical reasoning, space relations, and perceptual speed and accuracy scales. The developers recommend using combined-sex norms for all other scales.

The test developers assessed internal reliability using Kuder-Richardson 20 (KR-20) analyses. All scales yield high internal consistency (coefficients ranging from .82 to .95). These statistics are not computed for the Perceptual Speed and Accuracy Tests, which is appropriate. In addition, the standard error of measurement (SEM) is computed for each scale for each grade tested (including separate analyses for males, females, and combined sex). These SEMs range from 2.6 to 5.5 for individual scales.

The DAT makes the theoretical argument that there are multiple discrete aptitudes. In order to establish the validity of this claim, intercorrelations among the scales are presented. The only two scales showing consistently high correlation are the verbal reasoning and numerical reasoning scales (with correlations around .70). These correlations do not vary substantially between sexes or across grade levels. Other scales are moderately interrelated.

Construct validity of the DAT is supported by a multitrait matrix which includes a collection of correlations with other tests of aptitude and achievement. In general, specific scales on this test demonstrate logically consistent correlations tests such as the Otis-Lennon School Ability Test, the American College Testing Program Battery, and the Armed Services Vocational Aptitude Battery. The criterion-related validity of the test is established by correlating test scores with student grade point averages (GPAs). As could be expected, the combination of verbal and numerical reasoning (VR + NR) yields the highest correlations with GPAs (correlations range from .36 to .84 with a median correlation of .66). Other scales do not yield correlations as high or as consistent as the VR and NR scales.

With respect to the CII, the normative sample included approximately 100,000 participants representing a reasonable cross-section of the population in terms of geographic region, socioeconomic status, urban classification, and ethnicity. Items were linked logically (as opposed to empirically) to the 15 DOT career fields. Items were retained for this test if they exhibited good item-scale correlations. After the initial item scaling, internal consistency reliability coefficients were computed and ranged from .82 to .94 for Level 1 and .87 to .94 for Level 2. Construct validity was established by linking items to the DOT career fields and correlations with matched scales from the Ohio Vocational Interest Survey, Second Edition. Correlations were generally strong.

General Utility and Evaluation

The DAT has been in use since 1947 and has been a popular test among high school career counselors. With the recent acquisition by Pearson Assessments, it is making its way into new areas including organizational

A Counselor's Guide To Career Assessments Instruments

selection. This instrument brings many strengths to the table including a comprehensive set of tests covering conceptual, perceptual, and clerical/language skills. Broad-based normative data provide a sound reference point for interpreting scores. In addition, the test publisher provides clear and helpful interpretation materials. The technical manual provides support for the internal reliability of the test and evidence for construct validity. Content validity is strong with particular attention being paid to avoiding unfair item bias and offensive content. The readability and the face validity of the test are also strengths.

The DAT has been around for a long time, but it has not inspired much recent research and there are many important unanswered questions. One of the major drawbacks in using this test in career development is the lack of predictive validity studies in areas beyond GPA. Additional research needs to be conducted to establish this important area. Counselors need to be very cautious in making recommendations without this information. In addition, more research should be conducted to more firmly establish the construct validity of the test and test-retest reliability.

It should be noted that the DAT is an instrument in transition. The materials purchased from Pearson Assessments included some with the Pearson logo and others with the Harcourt Brace & Company logo. With the recent scope expansion into organizational selection, more research needs to be conducted on the predicative validity of this test. Future revision of this test should also link results to U.S. Department of Labor's O*NET resources.

Another caution in using this test is the length. The full test required more than two hours of testing time, and younger students could lose interest and motivation. However, since individual subtests can be purchased and used, administrators can selectively focus on the most relevant scales. More research needs to be conducted in this area.

Although there are some important cautions in using this test, it does provide a sound starting point for helping students consider their academic lives while helping them plan for a career. It should be noted, that this test is a starting point and is not giving specific directions. With a new publisher, it remains to be seen if there is a planned update or revision of this test in the works.

For the CII, counselors will find it is an easy to use and understandable test for assisting students with career development plans. Reports and summary information from the publisher are clear and helpful. This test will be most valuable when used in conjunction with the DAT, and the publisher does a good job of linking the results of these two tests.

References and Additional Resources

Bennett, G. K., & Wesman, A. G. (1947). Industrial test norms for a southern plant population. *Journal of Applied Psychology, 31*, 241-246.

Bennett, G. K., Seashore, H. G. & Wesman, A. G. (1948). *Validation of the Differential Aptitude Tests.* San Antonio, TX: Psychological Corporation.

Brown, L. L. (2003). [Differential Aptitude Tests, Australian and New Zealand Editions, Forms V and W.] In B. S. Plake, J. C. Impara, R. A. Spies (Eds.), *The fifteenth mental measurements yearbook.* Lincoln, NE: Buros Center for Testing.

Gebart-Eaglemont, J. E. (2003). [Differential Aptitude Tests, Australian and New Zealand Editions, Forms V and W.] In B. S. Plake, J. C. Impara, & R. A. Spies (Eds.), *The fifteenth mental measurements yearbook.* Lincoln, NE: Buros Center for Testing.

Hattrup, K. (1995). [Differential Aptitude Tests, fifth edition.] In J. C. Conoley and J. C. Impara (eds.), *The twelfth mental measurements yearbook.* Lincoln, NE: Buros Center for Testing.

Kelley, K. N. (2009). [Differential Aptitude Tests and Career Interest Inventory.] In E. A. Whitfield, R. W. Feller, & C. Wood (Eds.), *A counselor's guide to career assessment instruments* (5th ed., pp. 127-136). Broken Arrow, OK: National Career Development Association.

Schafer W. D. (1998). [Career Interest Inventory.] In J. C. Impara and B. S. Plake (Eds.), *The thirteenth mental measurements yearbook.* Lincoln, NE: Buros Center for Testing.

Differential Aptitude Tests and the Career Interest Inventory, Fifth Edition

Schmitt, N. (1995). [Differential Aptitude Tests, fifth edition.] In J. C. Conoley and J. C. Impara (Eds.), *The twelfth mental measurements yearbook*. Lincoln, NE: Buros Center for Testing.

Seashore, H. G. (1950). Understanding the individual through measurement. *American Council on Education Studies, 14,* 41-51.

Taylor, S. E. (1989). *EDL core vocabularies in reading, mathematics, science, and social studies.* Columbia, SC: Educational Development Laboratories.

Zedeck, S. (1998). [Career Interest Inventory.] In J. C. Impara and B. S. Plake (Eds.), *The thirteenth mental measurements yearbook*. Lincoln, NE: Buros Center for Testing.

A Counselor's Guide To Career Assessments Instruments

Employability Competency System Appraisal Test
(ECS Appraisal Form 120 and Form 130)

Comprehensive Adult Student Assessment Systems (CASAS)

5151 Murphy Canyon Rd., Ste. 220
San Diego, CA 92123-4339
1.800.255.1036
858.292.2900
http://www.casas.org

Target Population: Individuals age 16 and older in Adult Basic Education. Grade level equivalents are 4th–9th grade (Form 120) and 4th–12th grade (Form 130).

Statement of the Purpose of the Instrument: "[T]he intended purpose of the Employability Competency System (ECS) Reading [Math] Assessments, which include forms from the Workforce Learning System (WLS) Reading [Math] Assessments, is to measure the NRS [National Reporting System] educational functioning levels of members of the youth and adult education population in the content domain of reading/math" (Comprehensive Adult Student Assessment System, 2008a, p. 1; 2008b, p. 1). The ECS Appraisal Test, on the other hand, is a paper-and-pencil instrument used to determine which ECS assessments are most appropriate to administer as well as assist in decision-making about placement.

The test items of the ECS Appraisal Test address competencies needed in a work environment. Scores from the ECS Appraisal Forms 120 or 130 determine an individual's skill level in reading comprehension and math. These appraisal forms "provide a quick, general indicator of reading, math, or listening abilities" (see http://www.casas.org). The results of the appraisal aid instructors or administrators in determining a test taker's program, educational placement, and pre-test. The complete ECS System includes assessments of Adult Basic Education learners' reading and math skills from beginning to advanced levels. Many adult education programs, human service agencies and labor agencies use the ECS (Mellard, Patterson, & Prewett, 2007).

Titles of Subtests, Scales, Scores Provided: (1) Reading, (2) Math. Scores include raw scores (the number of items correct) which are converted to scaled scores. Form 120, Reading Test, 20 items, scale scores 197-228; Form 120, Math Test, 20 items, scale scores 197-228. Form 130, Reading Test, 25 items, scale scores 200-245; Form 130, Math Test, 25 items, scale scores 200-245. Both forms include two additional optional test items in critical thinking and 12 skills in pre-employment and work maturity (purchased separately).

Forms and Levels Available, with Dates of Publication/Revision of Each: Both Form 120 and 130 have paper-and-pencil test booklets. Form 130 can also be administered via computer. CASAS has published various forms and levels of the ECS tests in 1988, 1996, 2001, and 2003. The ECS Appraisals Forms 120 and 130 (provided to this reviewer) were published in 1994 and 2004. The second edition of the ECS Appraisal Test Administration Manual: Form 120, Form 130 (CASAS, 2002) provided to this reviewer was published in 2002.

Date of Most Recent Edition of Test Manual, User's Guide, Etc.: ECS Appraisal Test Administration Manual, 2002; Technical Manuals for the Reading Assessments and Math Assessments of the Employability Competency System/Workforce Learning Systems, 2008.

Languages in Which Available: English only.

Time:

Actual Test Time: There is no required time limit for students to complete the tests. However, Form 120 usually takes about 20 minutes each (for Reading and for Math) and Form 130, 25 minutes each test. This equates to a total time of 40 minutes (Form 120) and 50 minutes (Form 130).

Total Administration Time: Varies based on accommodation needs.

Norm Group(s) on Which Scores Are Based: The normative samples presented in the ECS Reading and Math Technical Manuals do not address the norming samples used for the ECS Appraisals, nor is this information included in the ECS Appraisal Administration Manual. However, there is extensive, although at times obtuse, data on the norming samples used for the assessments in the ECS.

Employability Competency System Appraisal Test

Manner in Which Results Are Reported for Individuals: Scores are reported on a common numerical scale that is divided into five instructional skill levels, A through D. Raw scores are the number of multiple-choice test items answered correctly. This is converted to a scaled score related to the basic skill levels. Raw scores range from 1 to 25 on Form 130 for both Reading and Math and from 1 to 20 on Form 120. Accurate scaled scores range from 200 to 245 for Form 130 (raw scores 4 to 21). Accurate scaled scores for Form 120 range from 197 to 228 (raw scores 4 to 16). The extreme raw scores at the upper and lower end may not accurately assess the test taker's ability.

Administrators, and in some cases students, score Form 120 or 130 with a self-scoring answer sheet, computer scored with TOPSpro, or with answer keys and a conversion chart. If Form 130 is taken by computer, the appraisals are automatically scored.

Report Format/Content for Group Summaries: The CASAS Tracking of Program and Students (TOPSpro) produces group summaries.

Machine Scoring: Not available.

Hand Scoring: Hand scored by counselee, counselor, or clerk in approximately 1 minute per form (Schafer, 2009).

Local Machine Scoring: Sites implementing CASAS, including the ECS, use the software program TOPSpro. This allows for computer scoring.

Cost of Materials: Due to price changes since publication date, be sure to check the publisher's website. The administration of the regular ECS assessments requires training and certification by CASAS. Because they typically are used in educational settings, school districts or organizations typically cover the cost. There is no cost to the test taker. A potential test administrator (or buyer) should verify the current cost with a test representative or by consulting the CASAS website. Form 130 (Employability Competency System Appraisal for Reading and Math) costs $77.00 for the Administration Manual, $70.00 for a set of 25 test-booklets, $35.00 for a set of 25 self-scoring answer sheets (or $52.50 for a set of 100 TOPSpro answer sheets).

Specimen Set: A test administration manual, directions, samples of Forms 120 and 130, and a self-scoring sheet for each form. The reviewer received a specimen set of the ECS Appraisals, which includes the ECS Appraisal Manual with instructions for administering the tests, sample test booklets for Forms 120 (Reading and Math) and 130 (Reading and Math), and self-scoring answer sheets.

Counselee Materials: Test booklet and self-scoring answer sheet.

Published Reviews of the Instrument in the Last 15 Years:

Flowerday, T. (2005). [Comprehensive Adult Student Assessment System (CASAS)]. In R. A. Spies & B. S. Plake (Eds.), *The sixteenth mental measurements yearbook* (pp. 256-258). Lincoln, NE: Buros Center for Testing.

Gorman, D., & Ernst, M. L. (2004). Test review: The comprehensive adult student assessment system (CASAS) life skills reading tests. *Language Assessment Quarterly, 1,* 73-84.

Parke, C. S. (2005). [Comprehensive Adult Student Assessment System (CASAS)]. In R. A. Spies & B. S. Plake (Eds.), *The sixteenth mental measurements yearbook* (pp. 258-261). Lincoln, NE: Buros Center for Testing.

Schafer, W. D. (2009). [Employability Competency System Appraisal Test (ECS Appraisal)]. In E. A. Whitfield, R. W. Feller, & C. Wood (Eds.), *A counselor's guide to career assessment instruments* (5th ed.) pp. 137-143. Broken Arrow, OK: National Career Development Association.

A Counselor's Guide To Career Assessments Instruments

EMPLOYABILITY COMPETENCY SYSTEM APPRAISAL TEST

Reviewed by:

Marie F. Shoffner

Counselor Education Department
Virginia Commonwealth University

Description

The Comprehensive Adult Student Assessment Systems (CASAS) involve assessments based on the CASAS Content Standards. The CASAS Competencies directly relate to the basic skills listed in the Secretary's Commission on Achieving Necessary Skills (SCANS; U.S. Department of Labor, Education and Training Administration, 2009). The CASAS tests assess adults with low skill levels in reading, writing, and math competencies by measuring attainment of specific competencies related to workplace and survival needs, such as reading technical manuals, tax forms, or prescription labels (Mellard, Paterson, & Prewett, 2007). The Employability Competency System (ECS), part of CASAS, is a series of reading and math assessments focused on work-related basic skills. Instructors use pre- and post-tests to monitor student progress and to identify needed skills for workplace success. The ECS includes four pre-and post-test levels from beginning literacy to adult secondary level. The ECS Appraisals are used to assess reading and math basic skills, placement levels, and pre-test forms. This review will only address the ECS Appraisal, including technical properties and uses of Forms 120 and 130.

The specimen set for the ECS Appraisals includes test booklets, bubble sheets, and the ECS Appraisal Test Administration Manual (CASAS, 2002). The administration manual includes basic statistics, score conversion information, and other critical information for the administration of the appraisals.

Form 120 is used for test takers at the A (beginning literacy) or B levels. Form 130 is for higher-level test takers at the high-B, C, or D (high school) levels and can be used to determine if test takers are ready for the GED. CASAS offers Form 130 in both pencil-and-paper and computer formats. These Appraisals are not meant for learners with low English proficiency. (The appropriate forms for these learners are part of the ESL Appraisal group.)

Counselors can use test booklets that include self-scoring answer sheets, use the CASAS TOPS answer sheet and TOPSpro software, or use answer keys and charts in the Test Administrator's manual with a general answer sheet. Scoring is automated when using the computer administration of Form 130. The charts provide information on how to convert a raw score (the number of correctly answered items) to a scaled score. For all CASAS tests, there is a range outside of which the test taker's score may not be an accurate measure of his or her actual ability. The manual contains information and options for retesting if the test takers score is in the inaccurate range. Accurate scale scores are 197-228 for Form 120 and 200-245 for Form 130.

Counselors, instructors, or administrators can use the ECS to determine adults' basic skill levels in reading, mathematics, writing, and listening. Required free implementation training can be completed through a free online self-paced module or free face-to-face training using Adobe Connect (both offered by CASAS). CASAS is currently one of the primary assessments used in Adult Basic Education and is used in multiple states. The ECS Appraisals are used for adult basic skills education referral, program placement, and selection of pre- and post-tests.

Technical Considerations

Technical manuals for the ECS Reading series (CASAS, 2008a) and the ECS Math series (CASAS, 2008b) describe in detail the following: the processes of item writing, pilot-testing, field-testing, item calibration, and assignment to forms; fairness and sensitivity test results; publishing dates; validation of score comparability across forms; security procedures; history of the assessments; procedures for determining cut scores and their standard errors of measurement; modifications for persons with disabilities; reliability estimates and classification consistency; the measured competencies; qualifications of content experts; and information on content and construct validity. Further, the technical manuals delineate test specifications design, the results from classical item analyses, and results based on the one-parameter Rasch measurement model.

Employability Competency System Appraisal Test

However, there is less information available about the ECS Appraisals themselves in either the ECS Technical Manuals (CASAS, 2008a, 2008b) or the ECS Appraisal Administration Manual (CASAS, 2002). It appears that the publishers believe the test administrators will assume that much of the information related to the ECS applies to the ECS Appraisals as well. However, because this is not explicitly stated, it remains unclear to this reviewer. Therefore, the technical information included in this section applies only to the ECS Appraisals.

The ECS Appraisal Test Administration Manual (CASAS, 2002) presents the psychometric properties of the ECS appraisals. The Kuder Richardson KR-20 estimates for Form 120 are .88 (Reading) and .92 (Math). The reliability estimates for Form 130 are .84 for both Reading and Math. Using point bi-serial correlation coefficients, the average item-total correlations are .56 (Reading) and .63 (Math) for Form 120 and .63 (Reading) and .44 (Math) for Form 130 (CASAS, 2002). It might be that the norming samples used to estimate these properties are the same as those used for the ECS itself. However, CASAS does not state this explicitly.

The CASAS ECS Assessments indicate strong content and construct validity. For content validity, CASAS ECS Reading and Math items are closely associate with content of the NRS Educational Functioning Levels and the CASAS content standards and competencies. Construct validity has been indicated with significant comparisons between CASAS ECS assessments and other assessments designed to assess educational gain for similar populations (CASAS, 2008a, 2008b). CASAS investigates the validity of these instruments in an ongoing manner and presents detailed validity evidence in the two ECS Technical Manuals. The ECS Appraisal information in the ECS Appraisal Administration Manual does not include validity estimates.

General Utility and Evaluation

The administration directions appear to leave much room for interpretation. The administration manual (CASAS, 2002) includes "Suggested Verbal Instructions" (p. 11) and there is no time limit, although an hour is recommended. Therefore, counselors may use different instructions and may allow more or less time.

The two ECS technical manuals (CASAS, 2008a, 2008b) for the full set of tests in the ECS Reading and Math series are complex, but clear. The information in the ECS Administration Manual is clearer and less complex. As mentioned by Schafer (2009), the technical manuals do not provide information about the selection of field test takers or of the experts used to evaluate items. However, these manuals do include information about the positions of these experts. The administration manual for the ECS Appraisals does not include this information, so perhaps the administrator can assume the experts are the same, and that the ECS Appraisal items are chosen from the test bank of items used for the ECS Reading and Math Assessments. It is unfortunate that CASAS does not include a paragraph in the ECS Appraisals Administration Manual that explicitly states whether this is the case. It would make the determination of the psychometric properties of the appraisals much easier.

As implied above, the Test Administration Manual for the ECS Appraisals (Forms 120 and 130) is clear, concise, and easy to follow. Score interpretation is well explained. This reviewer thinks that after the required free training, scoring and score interpretation would be straightforward. The Test Administration Manual also includes detailed information about the CASAS competencies addressed by the items in Forms 120 and 130. However, the manual does not include information on the validity of the ECS Appraisals or information about the items themselves (e.g., were they drawn from the same item bank?).

Diverse populations are considered in all psychometric investigations related to the ECS. There is important information missing from the technical manuals, however. Previous critiques of CASAS and ECS have mentioned this. The manuals present information about the norming populations, but do not address how these populations are similar in demographic characteristics from the actual adult education population for whom the appraisals and assessments are designed. In addition, CASAS does not provide cross tabulation of demographic information.

The QuickSearch Online database is very helpful in determining the resources needed for instruction. The database can searched by competency, series, skill, type of program, or publication (Shafer, 2009). However, a search for the ECS Appraisals resulted in a failed search. These resources appear to be primarily for use with the varying CASAS assessments themselves, rather than the appraisals. This would make sense, because the appraisals are used to determine placement and pre-test scores.

Gorman and Ernst (2004) criticized the CASAS for not providing evidence of construct or concurrent validity for the CASAS life skills reading tests. This series of tests is similar to the ECS series, although somewhat different in terms of its focus. At the time of this review, the ECS manuals did provide evidence for construct validity. They also provided evidence of concurrent validity, although their choice of parallel measures could have been stronger. There is no information on predictive validity and if the skills assessed relate to future success in the workforce. The National Reporting System does collect data on the outcomes of Adult Education, and CASAS is used in a large number of the U.S. states and territories to assess progress (NRS, n.d.). However, CASAS does not provide predictive validity information for the ECS Appraisals, and these tests are not part of the NRS.

This reviewer agrees with Gorman and Ernst (2004) regarding the complete lack of biased or offensive content in the ECS series. There are no references to race, gender, ethnicity, or sexual orientation in either Form 120 or 130 of the ECS Appraisals. However, the reports of differential performance by test taker groups are difficult to decipher. The CASAS series (which include the ECS) are used as standardized assessments in many adult education programs across the U.S., as well as in human service agencies and labor/workforce agencies (Mellard et al., 2007). Gorman and Ernst, after their careful review of the CASAS Life Skills Series (similar to the ECS) noted these assessments as the best community adult assessment system available. In fact, in a search through the 2009-2010 State-By-State Tabulation of Assessment Test Use for Adult Learners presented (NRS, n.d.), CASAS assessments were used by more than half (30) of the 57 U.S. states and territories (Virgin Islands assessments were not available) to track the progress of adult learners (NRS, n.d.).

References and Additional Resources

Comprehensive Adult Student Assessment System. (n.d.). *TOPSpro Enterprise: Assess. Learn. Achieve.* Retrieved from https://www.casas.org/docs/product-brochures/topsprobrochure.pdf?sfvrsn=2

Comprehensive Adult Student Assessment System. (2002). *ECS Appraisal Test administration manual.* San Diego, CA: CASAS.

Comprehensive Adult Student Assessment System. (2008a). *Technical manual for use in the National Reporting System (NRS) Workforce Investment Act: Reading Assessments—Employability Competency System/Workforce Learning Systems.* San Diego, CA: CASAS.

Comprehensive Adult Student Assessment System. (2008b). *Technical manual for use in the National Reporting System (NRS) Workforce Investment Act: Math Assessments—Employability Competency System/Workforce Learning Systems.* San Diego, CA: CASAS.

Comprehensive Adult Student Assessment System. (2010). *Accommodation guidelines.* Retrieved from https://www.casas.org/training-and-support/testing-guidelines/accommodations-guidelines

Comprehensive Adult Student Assessment System. (2012). *Catalog 2012.* Retrieved from https://www.casas.org/docs/newsroom/Catalog.pdf?Status=Master

Flowerday, T. (2005). [Comprehensive Adult Student Assessment System (CASAS)]. In R. A. Spies & B. S. Plake (Eds.), *The sixteenth mental measurements yearbook* (pp. 256-258). Lincoln, NE: Buros Center for Testing.

Forum on Educational Accountability. (August, 2007). *Assessment and accountability for improving schools and learning: principles and recommendations for federal law and state and local systems.* Retrieved from http://www.edaccountability.org/AssessmentFullReportJUNE07.pdf

Gorman, D., & Ernst, M. L. (2004). Test review: The comprehensive adult student assessment system (CASAS) life skills reading tests. *Language Assessment Quarterly, 1,* 73-84.

Mellard, D., & Paterson, M. B., & Prewett, S. (2007). Reading practices among adult education participants. *Reading Research Quarterly, 42*(2), 188-213.

National Reporting System. (n.d.). *Home page.* Retrieved from http://www.nrsweb.org

Parke, C. S. (2005). [Comprehensive Adult Student Assessment System (CASAS)]. In R. A. Spies & B. S. Plake (Eds.), *The sixteenth mental measurements yearbook* (pp. 258-261). Lincoln, NE: Buros Center for Testing.

Schafer, W. D. (2009). [Review of Employability Competency System Appraisal Test (ECS Appraisal)]. In E. A. Whitfield, R. W. Feller, & C. Wood (Eds.), *A counselor's guide to career assessment instruments* (5th ed.; pp. 137-143). Broken Arrow, OK: National Career Development Association.

U.S. Department of Labor, Employment and Training Administration. (2009). *Secretary's Commission on Achieving Necessary Skills.* Retrieved from http://wdr.doleta.gov/SCANS/

A Counselor's Guide To Career Assessments Instruments

EXPLORE
ACT, Inc.

ACT, Inc.

500 ACT Drive
P.O. Box 168
Iowa City, Iowa 52243-0168
http://www.act.org

Target Population: Adolescents; Grades 8 and 9.

Statement of the Purpose of the Instrument: The EXPLORE program is designed to help 8th and 9th graders investigate a broad range of options for their future. EXPLORE prepares students not only for their high school coursework, but for their post—high school choices as well. It marks an important beginning for a student's future academic and career success. EXPLORE can serve as an independent program or as the entry point into ACT's Educational Planning and Assessment System (EPAS). Both 8th and 9th grade norms are available for EXPLORE.

Titles of Subtests, Scales, Scores Provided: The EXPLORE program includes the following components:

1. Four multiple-choice tests of academic achievement:
   * English (providing a total test score and two subscores: Usage/Mechanics and Rhetorical Skills)
   * Mathematics (providing a total test score)
   * Reading (providing a total test score)
   * Science (providing a total test score)
   * A Composite score (average of four test scores)
2. UNIACT Interest Inventory (an interest inventory score is provided)
3. Needs Assessment
4. Plans and Background Information.

Forms and Levels Available, with Dates of Publication/Revision of Each: 2010.

Date of Most Recent Edition of Test Manual, User's Guide, Etc.: 2010.

Languages in Which Available: English and Spanish.

Time:

Actual Test Time: 120 minutes (30 minutes per academic test).

Total Administration Time: Approximately 3 hours (135 minutes for test component and 50 minutes for non-test components including the Interest Inventory, Needs Assessment, Plans, and Background Information).

Norm Group(s) on Which Scores Are Based: Norms are reported as "percents at or below" (cumulative percents) on EXPLORE reports. They indicate the percent of examinees in the Fall 2005 norming study who received the same scale score or a lower scale score. For example, if a student has a percent at or below 75, it means that 75 percent of the examinees in the norm group received the same score, or a lower score, than the student. Norms are provided for the following three groups: Fall Grade 8 (those who test August through January), Spring Grade 8 (those who test February through July), and Grade 9.

Manner in Which Results Are Reported for Individuals: World-of-Work Map career areas and regions for UNIACT are presented. Scale Score (1-25) are presented for each academic achievement test. Scale Score (1-12) for each subscore reported for the English Test. Composite score, which is the average of the four achievement test scores. Estimated PLAN composite score range. Percents at or above for each scale score reported for the achievement tests based on the national representative norms. Results and follow-up materials are shipped to the school three weeks after test materials are received at ACT's scoring center. Routine score reports include two copies of the Student Report including color highlighting of UNIACT results on World-of-Work map graphic and career areas. College Readiness Standards, statements of skills and knowledge that the student are likely to know and be able to do based on the student's scores, are provided on the back of the student report.

EXPLORE and PLAN

Report Format/Content for Group Summaries: Results and follow-up materials are shipped to the school three weeks after test materials are received at ACT's scoring center. Student roster (includes self-reported career plans, self-reported educational plans for high school and beyond, scale scores, and both national and local percentiles); profile summary report; early intervention roster (helps identify students needing extra attention); and presentation packet. Additional supplemental reports are available (see publisher's website).

Machine Scoring: $8.50 per processed answer document. See publisher's website for additional scoring services.

Hand Scoring: Not available.

Local Machine Scoring: Not available.

Computer Software Options Available: Not available.

Cost of Materials: Due to possible price changes since publication date be sure to check the publisher's website.

   Specimen Set: Not available.

   Counselee Materials: Included in cost of scoring. Using Your EXPLORE Results—interpretive guide for students (reusable); Student Score Report (not reusable); http://www.explorestudent.com—interpretive website for students and parents.

Additional Comments of Interest to Users: ACT offers Braille test books, audiorecordings, CDs, reader's scripts, large-print test booklets, and large-print worksheets for EXPLORE.

Published Reviews of the Instrument in the Last 15 Years:

Loew, S. A., (2001). [EXPLORE]. In B. S. Plake & J. C. Impara (Eds.), *The fourteenth mental measurements yearbook.* Lincoln, NE: Buros Center for Testing.

Taber, B. J., & Splete, H. H. (2009). [EXPLORE/PLAN]. In E. A. Whitfield, R. W. Feller, & C. Wood (Eds.), *A counselor's guide to career assessment instruments* (5th ed., pp. 144-154). Broken Arrow, OK: National Career Development Association.

A COUNSELOR'S GUIDE TO CAREER ASSESSMENTS INSTRUMENTS

PLAN
ACT, Inc.

ACT, Inc.

500 ACT Drive
P.O. Box 168
Iowa City, Iowa 52243-0168
http://www.act.org

Target Population: Adolescents; Grades 10.

Statement of the Purpose of the Instrument: The PLAN program helps 10th graders build a solid foundation for future academic and career success and provides information needed to address school districts' high-priority issues. It is a comprehensive guidance resource that helps students measure their current academic development, explore career/training options, and make plans for the remaining years of high school and post-graduation years. PLAN can help all students—those who are college-bound as well as those who are likely to enter the workforce directly after high school. As a "pre-ACT" test, PLAN is a powerful predictor of success on the ACT. At the same time, many schools recognize the importance of PLAN testing for all students, as it focuses attention on both career preparation and improving academic achievement.

Typically, PLAN is administered in the fall of the sophomore year.

Titles of Subtests, Scales, Scores Provided: The PLAN Program includes the following components:

1. Four multiple-choice tests of academic achievement:

    • English (providing a total test score and two subscores: Usage/Mechanics and Rhetorical Skills)

    • Mathematics (providing a total test score and two subscores: Pre-Algebra/Algebra and Geometry)

    • Reading (providing a total test score)

    • Science (providing a total test score)

    • A Composite score (average of the four total test scores)

2. UNIACT Interest Inventory (an interest inventory score is provided)

3. Needs Assessment

4. High School Course/Grade Information

5. Plans and Background Information.

Forms and Levels Available, with Dates of Publication/Revision of Each: A new form is provided every year and released to the students after administration.

Date of Most Recent Edition of Test Manual, User's Guide, Etc.: 2011.

Languages in Which Available: English and Spanish.

Time:

   Actual Test Time: 115 minutes.

   Total Administration Time: Approximately 3.5 hours (135 minutes for test component plus 60-75 minutes for non-test components including the Interest Inventory, Needs Assessment, High School Course/Grade Information, Plans and Background Information).

Norm Group(s) on Which Scores Are Based: Norms are reported as "percents at or below" (cumulative percents) on PLAN reports. They indicate the percent of examinees in the Fall 2005 norming study who received the same scale score or a lower scale score. For example, if a student has a percent at or below 75, it means that 75 percent of the examinees in the norm group received the same score, or a lower score, than the student. Norms are provided for the following groups: Fall Grade 10 (those who test August through January) and Spring Grade 10 (those who test February through July).

197

EXPLORE and PLAN

Manner in Which Results Are Reported for Individuals: World-of-Work Map career areas and regions for UNIACT are presented. Scale Score (1-32) for each academic achievement test. Scale Score (1-16) for each subscore reported for the English and Mathematics Test. Composite score, which is the average of the four achievement test scores. Estimated ACT composite score range. Percents at or above for each scale score reported for the achievement tests based on the national representative norms. Student report includes Test Scores, course plans compared to core, college readiness indicators, profile for success regarding their career area preference, career information based on their Interest Inventory results, their item response information for each question, and narrative statements for suggestions on improving their skills based on their scores. Results and follow-up materials are shipped to the school three weeks after test materials are received at ACT's scoring center. Routine score reports include two copies of the Student Report.

Report Format/Content for Group Summaries: Results and follow-up materials are shipped to the school three weeks after test materials are received at ACT's scoring center. High School List Report (includes self-reported career plans, self-reported educational plans for high school and beyond, scale scores, and national percentiles); Score labels; Profile Summary Report; Early Intervention Roster (helps identify students needing extra attention); Presentation Packet. Additional supplemental reports are available (see publisher's website).

Machine Scoring: $11.25 per processed answer document. See publisher's website for additional scoring services.

Hand Scoring: Not available.

Local Machine Scoring: Not available.

Computer Software Options Available: Not available.

Cost of Materials: Due to possible price changes since publication date be sure to check the publisher's website.

    Specimen Set: Not available.

    Counselee Materials: Included in cost of scoring. Using Your PLAN Results—interpretive guide for students (reusable); Student Score Report (not reusable); http://www.planstudent.com—interpretive website for students and parents.

Additional Comments of Interest to Users: ACT offers Braille test books, audio recordings, CDs, reader's scripts, large-print test booklets, and large-print worksheets for EXPLORE.

Published Reviews of the Instrument in the Last 15 Years:

Blackwell, M., & Hening Stout, M. (1995). [PLAN]. In J. C. Impara, & J. Conoley (Eds.), *The twelfth mental measurements yearbook.* Lincoln, NE: Buros Center for Testing.

Taber, B. J., & Splete, H. H. (2009). [EXPLORE/PLAN]. In E. A. Whitfield, R. W. Feller, & C. Wood (Eds.), *A counselor's guide to career assessment instruments* (5th ed., pp. 144-154). Broken Arrow, OK: National Career Development Association.

EXPLORE AND PLAN

Reviewed by:

Linda H. Foster

Department of Counseling and Psychology
Troy University Montgomery

Description

EXPLORE is designed to assess academic progress of students at the eighth- or ninth-grade level in English, mathematics, reading, and science. PLAN evaluates these four areas for tenth grade students. EXPLORE and PLAN also collect information about interests, needs, plans, and background characteristics to be used in guidance and planning activities. They provide information about how well a student performs in relation to other students. Based on the ACT's College Readiness Standards, EXPLORE and PLAN can be used to determine if students are prepared for college.

A COUNSELOR'S GUIDE TO CAREER ASSESSMENTS INSTRUMENTS

EXPLORE and PLAN each contains four multiple choice tests in English, mathematics, reading, and science designed to measure curriculum-related knowledge and to assess students' cognitive skills deemed to be important for post-secondary plans (i.e., college or work). The English test for EXPLORE contains 40 items and allows 30 minutes for completion, while PLAN includes 50 items for the same time allotment. This subject test measures standard written English (e.g., punctuation, grammar and usage, and sentence structure). The English test also assesses rhetorical skills such as strategy, organization and style. The usage is based on students' ability to read and write at a middle or secondary school level, and uses several prose passages accompanied by multiple-choice questions. This subtest measures Usage/Mechanics (based on 25 items for EXPLORE and 30 items for PLAN) and Rhetorical Skills (based on 15 items for EXPLORE and 20 items for PLAN).

The Mathematics test contains 30 items and allows 30 minutes for completion for EXPLORE and 40 items within 40 minutes for PLAN. The content areas for EXPLORE include the following: Pre-Algebra, Elementary Algebra, Geometry, and Statistics/Productivity. Basic quantitative reasoning is emphasized and uses problems encountered at the middle or junior high school level. The content areas for PLAN include the following: Pre-Algebra, Elementary Algebra, Coordinate Geometry, and Plane Geometry. Each test evaluates four cognitive levels: knowledge and skills, direct application, understanding concepts, and integrating conceptual understanding. Specific sections of the Mathematics test allow usage of a calculator, and test administrators are given specific directions in the supervisor's manual. Two subscores are reported for the PLAN: Pre-Algebra/Algebra based on 22 items and Geometry based on 18 items.

The Reading test contains 30 items and allows 30 minutes for completion for EXPLORE and 25 items with a 20-minute time allotment for PLAN. This section measures the student's level of reading comprehension by deriving meaning from several sections of text. Students are asked to use referral and reasoning skills to perform the following: determine main ideas; locate and interpret significant details; sequence events; make comparisons; understand cause and effect; understand context-dependent words, phrases, or statements; generalize; and analyze the voice of author or narrator. This is accomplished by presenting three prose passages from middle and junior high school curricula in the areas of social science, fiction, or humanities. Each of the three passages is labeled and includes a set of multiple-choice test items. The publisher states that this section focuses on complementary and mutually supportive skills "across a range of subject areas."

The Science test contains 28 items and allows 30 minutes for completion for EXPLORE and 30 items within 25 minutes for PLAN. Scientific reasoning skills acquired up to the eighth grade for EXPLORE (and tenth grade for PLAN) are measured using six sets of scientific information through multiple-choice test items. Three formats are used: data represented by graphs, tables, etc.; summaries of research; or conflicting viewpoints. Students must be able to understand the information and concepts; examine relationships in the information presented; and generalize to demonstrate new information, draw conclusions, or make predictions. Depending on the test, this section is based on a typical eighth-grade or tenth-grade curriculum in the areas of life sciences, earth/space sciences, and physical sciences (eighth grade); and biology, earth/space sciences, chemistry, and physics (tenth grade).

The supervisor's manual, available for download from the publisher's website, contains all policies and procedures for test administration, including accommodations and timing details. The publisher has included guidelines for creating standardized procedures, test security, and Standards for Fair Testing Practices. The supervisor's manual is very clear and presents an array of guidelines regarding timing before, during, and after test administration. Additionally, directions for verbal administration and post-test activities are included.

The format of EXPLORE and PLAN is excellent. The publisher produces a sample test booklet and answer folder to familiarize students with the content, format, and testing procedures. ACT also publishes a student booklet with scoring instructions so that students can score their sample test and review their performance. The directions for self-scoring are straightforward and actually show students how to transfer raw scores into scaled scores for comparison to national norms. Both of these booklets are legible and appear durable.

EXPLORE and PLAN are used to assess educational achievement and assist in developing plans for further education and work. As a part of the assessment process PLAN explores students career and education options based on their skills, interests, and ambitions.

Technical Considerations

The technical manual outlines the norming procedures and includes sampling information for the 2010 Norming Study. For EXPLORE, data were collected from the following: the group of schools that used the EXPLORE test during the Fall of 2010, nonuser schools that participated in the 2010 EXPLORE equating study, and a sample of schools from among the nonusers of EXPLORE drawn specifically for the norming. Samples included both eighth and ninth graders, and the publisher reports that 960,460 examinees participated in a stratified cluster sample. For PLAN, data were collected from the following: the group of schools that used the PLAN test during the Fall of 2010, and a sample of schools from among the nonusers of PLAN. Samples included both tenth and eleventh graders, and the publisher reports that 977,197 examinees participated in the weighted sample.

The technical manual includes a comprehensive description of the analyses performed to derive reliability and standard error of measurement scores. Reliability coefficients for composite scores on EXPLORE, including all four subtests, ranged from .93 to .95. Standard error of measure for composite scores ranged from .79 to .81. Reliability coefficients for composite scores on PLAN for tenth graders, including all four subtests, ranged from .80 to .95 and from .81 to .95 for eleventh graders. Standard error of measure for composite scores was estimated at .95 for both tenth and eleventh graders.

The technical manual for each test includes a section on validity. The content validity for EXPLORE was determined by a detailed analysis of instructional objects for Grades 6-9 nationwide, review of approved textbooks for Grades 6 through 8, and review by subject matters experts (educators from secondary and postsecondary levels). Additionally, ACT also conducted an analysis of correlations between EXPLORE test scores and subscores which indicated that examinees scoring well on one test tended to score well on another. Finally, ACT also analyzed correlations between EXPLORE scores and course grades, high school grade point averages and has compared EXPLORE scores with ACT scores. The test publisher conducts a rigorous analysis of the EXPLORE to determine validity in measuring educational achievement.

The content validity for PLAN was determined by a detailed analysis of instructional objectives for Grades 7-12 nationwide, a review of approved textbooks for Grades 7-12, and a review by subject matters experts (educators from secondary and postsecondary levels). Additionally, ACT also conducted an analysis of correlations between PLAN test scores and subscores which indicated that examinees scoring well on one test tended to score well on another. Finally, ACT also analyzed correlations between PLAN scores and course grades, and high school grade point averages, and has compared PLAN scores with EXPLORE and ACT scores. The test publisher conducts a rigorous analysis of the PLAN to determine validity in measuring educational achievement.

General Utility and Evaluation

The quality of the materials included in the EXPLORE and PLAN assessment program is exceptional. The test publisher provides a comprehensive technical manual outlining the entire EXPLORE or PLAN program and the connection to ACT's College Readiness Standards and College Readiness Benchmarks. The technical manual provides a thorough analysis of the scaling and norming procedure associated with the 2010 Norming Sample. Reliability and validity information is presented in a clear and easily understandable manner. Also included in the technical manual is a section on relating the EXPLORE or PLAN interest inventory to the World-of-Work Map (WWM) making this a valuable tool and resource for counselors.

The supervisor's manual is also exceptional in content and readability. Policies and procedures are clearly outlined and detailed instructions are provided for pre-planning for test administration. A comprehensive section on testing students with accommodations provides very clear directions with options for accommodations. Test administration policies are also presented in a clear and detailed way providing instructions ranging from situations such as defective materials to prohibited student behaviors. The supervisor's manual is a well prepared and informative document.

EXPLORE was originally normed in 1992 with more than 4,000 eighth-grade students. Loew (2001) noted discrepancies in the original norming group in 1992, noting a discrepancy in 1995 and again in 1999 regarding the underrepresentation of racial and geographic demographic characteristics. Demographic information from the 2010 Norming Sample appears to be more equally distributed in racial/ethnic origin and in geographic region. Loew also noted that the interest inventory seemed to be an afterthought by the test developer rather

A COUNSELOR'S GUIDE TO CAREER ASSESSMENTS INSTRUMENTS

than a valuable career exploration tool. The latest version offers an entire chapter in the technical manual to the EXPLORE Interest Inventory resulting in a stronger focus on post–high school planning.

PLAN was originally normed in 1988 with both tenth and twelfth grade students. Blackwell and Henning Stout (1995) mentioned the underrepresentation in the norming sample when compared to the U.S. Census demographic information. Information from the publisher regarding 2010 Norming Sample attempts to address underrepresentation by weighting the sample. The publisher reports that the weighted sample appears to be reasonably representative of the national population of interest at .95.

The ACT webpage (http://www.act.org/plan/) contains a wealth of resources for educators, administrators, and general public. More importantly, there is particular information specifically designed for students (http://www.act.org/planstudent/). From this website, students can gain familiarity with the entire ACT system; specifics about the PLAN and what their scores mean, and can PLAN their future career options. There is also a webpage specifically designed for parents (http://www.act.org/path/parent/tests/plan.html). From this page, parents can gain valuable information about the PLAN and college planning. ACT has created an assessment system to measure academic progress beginning with PLAN and continuing throughout high school promoting college and career planning.

References and Additional Resources

ACT, Inc. (2012). EXPLORE features. Retrieved from http://www.act.org/explore/features.html

ACT, Inc. (2012). *EXPLORE resources for educators. Student materials and general program materials.* Retrieved from http://www.act.org/explore/downloads.html

ACT, Inc. (2012). *College and career readiness workshops EXPLORE. Test materials, reports and supporting materials, student materials, and general program materials.* Retrieved from http://act.org/ccrw/resources/explore.html.

ACT, Inc. (2012). *It's time to EXPLORE.* Retrieved from http://www.act.org/explorestudent/

ACT, Inc. (2000). *EXPLORE.* Retrieved from http://web.ebscohost.com/ehost/detail?vid=3&hid=113&sid=9b8dfe5b-8d07-486c-b349-90a90df054fd%40sessionmgr114&bdata=JnNpdGU9ZWhvc3QtbGl2ZQ%3d%3d#db=loh&AN=15012572

ACT, Inc. (2012). *PLAN features.* Retrieved from http://www.act.org/PLAN/features.html

ACT, Inc. (2012). *PLAN resources for educators.* Student materials and general program materials. Retrieved from http://www.act.org/PLAN/downloads.html

ACT, Inc. (2012). *College and career readiness workshops PLAN. Test materials, reports and supporting materials, student materials, and general program materials.* Retrieved from http://act.org/ccrw/resources/PLAN.html

ACT, Inc. (2012). *It's time to PLAN.* Retrieved from http://www.act.org/PLANstudent/

ACT, Inc. (2012). *PLAN.* Retrieved from http://web.ebscohost.com.proxy.mercer.edu/ehost/detail?vid=3&hid=7&sid=856dc60e-a7ce-437d-a29f-830284a67a75%40sessionmgr15&bdata=JnNpdGU9ZWhvc3QtbGl2ZQ%3d%3d#db=loh&AN=12011349

Blackwell, M., & Henning Stout, M. (1995). [PLAN]. In J. C. Impara & J. Conoley (Eds.), *The twelfth mental measurements yearbook.* Lincoln, NE: Buros Center for Testing.

Loew, S. A., (2001). [EXPLORE]. In B. S. Plake & J. C. Impara (Eds.), *The fourteenth mental measurements yearbook.* Lincoln, NE: Buros Center for Testing.

Taber, B. J., & Splete, H. H. (2009). [EXPLORE/PLAN.]. In E. A. Whitfield, R. W. Feller, & C. Wood (Eds.), *A counselor's guide to career assessment instruments* (5th ed., pp. 144-154). Broken Arrow, OK: National Career Development Association.

KUDER CAREER PLANNING SYSTEM:
KUDER CAREER INTEREST ASSESSMENT,
KUDER SKILLS CONFIDENCE ASSESSMENT,
AND KUDER WORK VALUES ASSESSMENT

KUDER CAREER INTERESTS ASSESSMENT

JoAnn Harris-Bowlsbey, Spencer Niles, Donald Zytowski, Jack Rayman, and Jerry Trusty

---

Kuder, Inc.

302 Visions Parkway
Adel, Iowa, 50003
http://www.kuder.com
info@kuder.com

Target Population: Students (grades 7 and higher), young adults, and adults.

Statement of the Purpose of the Instrument: The aim of the Kuder Career Interests Assessment (KCIA-32) is to determine the relative level of interest a respondent has in each of the six Holland areas of interests. These six interest scores are then used to identify the O*NET occupations and 16 national career clusters and pathways that best match the respondent's self-efficacy, based on the value of a Euclidean distance similarity index.

Titles of Subtests, Scales, Scores Provided: The KCIA-32 presents scores primarily in two manners; either by occupational scales of the 16 Career Clusters and pathways or Holland clusters (RIASEC codes). In addition, Kuder provides scores on other career cluster systems as requested by customers both domestically and internationally.

Forms and Levels Available, with Dates of Publication/Revision of Each: The KCIA-32 is one of three assessments included in the Kuder Career Planning System, 2012. The assessments are available for middle school through adult levels; it is Internet-based, as an assessment instrument in the Kuder Navigator and Kuder Journey. The Internet-based online Kuder Navigator and Kuder Journey are career planning systems that provide research based assessments, occupational and school databases, education plans, job-seeking tools and searches, Free Application for Federal Student Aid (FAFSA) completion, and connection to parents/administrators.

Date of Most Recent Edition of Test Manual, User's Guide, Etc.: 2012.

Languages in Which Available: English, Spanish, Arabic, Korean, and Chinese.

Time:

    Actual Test Time: Approximately 9 minutes.

    Total Administration Time: 15-25 minutes including registration.

Norm Group(s) on Which Scores Are Based: To ensure that the KCIA-32 scores reliably and validly reflect interests in the six Holland areas with efficiency and without bias, a number of psychometric research and development activities were undertaken prior to its release. These activities involved the use of (a) an initial pool of 168 items arranged in 56 triadic sets, (b) a panel of five incontrovertible international leaders in career counseling and guidance for various formal judgmental exercises, (c) item-by-item response data from a national sample of 958 workers who were engaged in a large variety of occupations, and (d) item-by-item response from a sample of 142 ninth- and twelfth-grade students. To date, three sets of analytic activities addressing three aspects of reliability and validity have been undertaken and additional research and analyses are currently planned and continuing.

Manner in Which Results Are Reported for Individuals: Bar graphs with Low, Medium, High scales as well as verbal labels of top five pathway results or Holland code are provided. Kuder provides an Interest results report as well as a composite report comparing Interests and Skills, and a one-page summary report. Scoring of the KCIA-32 is instantaneous on completion of the last item.

Report Format/Content for Group Summaries: Group summaries are sorted on several variables that may be accessed at the administrator's site.

Machine Scoring: Instantaneous scoring after completion of assessment.

Hand Scoring: Not available.

Local Machine Scoring: Not available.

Computer Software Options Available: Standard administration online.

Cost of Materials: Due to possible price changes since publication date, be sure to check the publisher's website. Standard pricing is based on an annual site license for a number of licensed uses. This includes the cost of the Kuder Administrative Database Management System, for counselors and administrators. Minimum orders are 25 units for Kuder Navigator and 50 units for Kuder Journey to have access to the Administrative Database Management System. Volume discounting is provided, so it is best to contact Kuder for specifications. Individual user accounts may be purchased online for $29.95 and $34.95, respectively.

Additional Comments of Interest to Users: The ADMS has an updated design, new reports, and more tools to provide administrative users with everything they need to manage use of the Kuder system.

New Person Matches sketches are presented in a Q&A type format. There are interviews with individuals who have similar interests as the test taker. The intent of this feature on the interest assessment is to trigger further exploration of a career by providing a real-world look at career stories from adults. There are continued navigation improvements to provide a more user-friendly experience. Users are able to start an assessment for the first time or complete unfinished assessments directly from their Kuder home page. Users also have the capability of sharing their assessment results from within the system via Facebook, Twitter, and email.

Published Reviews of the Instrument in the Last 15 Years: Not available.

KUDER SKILLS CONFIDENCE ASSESSMENT
AND KUDER SKILLS CONFIDENCE ASSESSMENT—ADULT
JoAnn Harris-Bowlsbey, Spencer Niles, Donald Zytowski, Jack Rayman, and Jerry Trusty

Kuder, Inc.

302 Visions Parkway, Adel, Iowa, 50003
http://www.kuder.com
info@kuder.com

Target Population: Students Grades 7 and higher for the Kuder Skills Confidence Assessment (KSCA-16); young adults and adults ages 18 and older for the Kuder Skills Confidence Assessment—Adult (KSCA-A).

Statement of the Purpose of the Instrument: The aim of the KSCA-16 and KSCA-A is to determine the relative self-efficacy of the respondent in each of the six areas of the respondent's Holland profile. These self-efficacy scores are then used to identify the O*NET occupations, and 16 national career clusters and pathways, that best match the respondent's self-efficacy, based on a Euclidean distance similarity index.

Titles of Subtests, Scales, Scores Provided: The KSCA-16 presents scores primarily by occupational scales of the 16 national career clusters and pathways. The KSCA-A presents scores primarily by occupational scales of the Holland cluster (RIASEC) codes. In addition, Kuder provides scores for both versions on other career cluster systems as requested by customers both domestically and internationally.

Forms and Levels Available, with Dates of Publication/Revision of Each: The KSCA-16/KSCA-A is one of three assessments included in Kuder Navigator/Kuder Journey, 2012.

Date of Most Recent Edition of Test Manual, User's Guide, Etc.: 2012.

Languages in Which Available: English, Spanish, Arabic, Korean, and Chinese.

Time:

Actual Test Time: Approximately 7 minutes for each version.

Total Administration Time: Approximately 15-25 minutes for each version.

Norm Group(s) on Which Scores Are Based: To ensure that the KSCA-16 scores reliably and validly reflect self-efficacy in the six Holland areas with efficiency and without bias, a number of psychometric research and development activities were undertaken prior to its release. These activities involved the use of (a) an initial pool of 175 potential Likert-type items aimed at measuring self-efficacy in the six Holland areas, (b) a panel of five incontrovertible national leaders in career counseling and guidance for various formal judgmental exercises, and (c) item by item response data from a national sample of 2,100 respondents for various statistical analyses.

To ensure that the KSCA-A scores reliably and validly reflect self-efficacy in the six Holland areas with efficiency and without bias, a number of psychometric research and development activities were undertaken prior to its release. These activities involved the use of (a) an initial pool of 170 potential Likert-type items aimed at measuring self-efficacy in the six Holland areas; (b) a panel of five incontrovertible international leaders in career counseling and guidance for various formal judgmental exercises, and (c) item-by-item response data from a national sample of 2,000 respondents for various statistical analyses.

Manner in Which Results Are Reported for Individuals: Bar graphs with Low, Medium, High scales as well as verbal labels of top five pathway results are provided. Kuder provides a Skills results report as well as a composite report comparing Interests and Skills, and a one-page summary report.

Report Format/Content for Group Summaries: Group summaries are sorted on several variables that may be accessed at the Administrator's Site.

Machine Scoring: Scoring for both versions is instantaneous on completion of the last item. The test taker is able to view the score after administration.

Kuder Career Planning System

Hand Scoring: Not available.

Local Machine Scoring: Not available.

Computer Software Options Available: Standard administration online. The Internet-based online Kuder Navigator is a career-planning system that provides research-based assessments, occupational and school databases, education plans, job seeking tools and searches, FAFSA completion, and connection to parents/administrators.

Cost of Materials: Due to possible price changes since publication date, be sure to check the publisher's website. Standard pricing is based on an annual site license for a number of licensed uses. This includes the cost of the Kuder Administrative Database Management System (ADMS) for counselors and administrators. Minimum orders for the KSCA-16 are 25 units and for the KSCA-A are 50 units with inclusion of the ADMS. Volume discounting is provided, so it is best to contact Kuder for specifications. Individual purchases are available online for $29.95 (KSCA-16) and $34.95 (KSCA-A).

Additional Comments of Interest to Users: The ADMS has an updated design, new reports, and more tools to provide administrative users with everything they need to manage use of the Kuder system. New Person Matches sketches are presented in a Q&A type format. There are interviews with individuals who have similar interests as the test taker. The intent of this feature on the interest assessment is to trigger further exploration of a career by providing a real-world look at career stories from adults. There are continued navigation improvements to provide a more user-friendly experience. Users are able to start an assessment for the first time or complete unfinished assessments directly from their Kuder home page. Users also have the capability of sharing their assessment results from within the system via Facebook, Twitter, and email.

Published Reviews of the Instrument in the Last 15 Years: Not available.

KUDER WORK VALUES ASSESSMENT
JoAnn Harris-Bowlsbey, Spencer Niles, Donald Zytowski,
Jack Rayman, and Jerry Trusty

Kuder, Inc.

302 Visions Parkway, Adel, Iowa, 50003
http://www.kuder.com
info@kuder.com

Target Population: Students (Grades 7 and higher), young adults, and adults.

Statement of the Purpose of the Instrument: The Kuder Work Values Assessment (KWVA) was formerly labeled Super's Work Values Inventory-revised (SWVI-r) Version 1.2. The previous version of the KWVA contained 72 items designed to measure 12 work values. Based on an evaluation of item contents and results of a series of factor analyses, it was determined that the items could be made to measure a more parsimonious set of five particular work values effectively: Workplace, Innovation, Accomplishment, Income, and Prestige. Therefore, the aim of the revision was to identify the subset of work values items that are optimally efficient, while meeting or exceeding the latest technical standards of reliability, validity, and fairness set forth by the American Psychological Association, the American Educational Research Association, and the National Council on Measurement in Education (Standards, 1999).

Titles of Subtests, Scales, Scores Provided: The KWVA presents rank-order scores of five work values: Workplace, Innovation, Accomplishment, Income, and Prestige.

Forms and Levels Available, with Dates of Publication/Revision of Each: The KWVA is one of three assessments included in the Kuder Career Planning System, 2012. The assessments are available for middle school through adult levels; it is Internet-based as an assessment instrument in the Kuder Navigator and Kuder Journey.

Date of Most Recent Edition of Test Manual, User's Guide, Etc.: 2012.

Languages in Which Available: English, Spanish, Arabic, Korean, and Chinese.

Time:

    Actual Test Time: Approximately 4 minutes.

    Total Administration Time: Approximately 15-25 minutes.

Norm Group(s) on Which Scores Are Based: To ensure that the final KWVA scores reliably and validly reflects the five work values, with efficiency and without bias, a number of psychometric research and development activities were undertaken prior to its release. These activities involved the use of (a) an initial pool of 72 SWVI-r Version 1.2 items, (b) a panel of five incontrovertible international leaders in career counseling and guidance for various formal judgmental exercises, and (c) item-by-item response data from a national sample of 4,000 respondents for various statistical analyses. To date, five sets of analytic activities addressing five aspects of reliability, validity, and fairness have been undertaken and additional research and analyses are currently planned and continuing.

Manner in Which Results Are Reported for Individuals: Bar graphs with Low, Medium, High scales as well as labels of top five work values in rank order are provided. In Kuder Journey, a personality report is presented that includes interests, skills, and work values results.

Report Format/Content for Group Summaries: Group summaries are sorted on several variables that may be accessed at the administrator's site.

Machine Scoring Service: Scoring for the KWVA is instantaneous on completion of the last item. The test taker is able to view the score after administration.

Hand Scoring: Not available.

Local Machine Scoring: Not available.

Computer Software Options Available: Standard administration online. The Internet-based online Kuder Navigator is a career-planning system that provides research-based assessments, occupational and school databases, education plans, job seeking tools and searches, FAFSA completion, and connection to parents/administrators.

Cost of Materials: Due to possible price changes since publication date, be sure to check the publisher's website. Standard pricing is based on an annual site license for a number of licensed uses. This includes the cost of the KuderAdministrative Database Management system for counselors and administrators. Minimum orders are 25 units for Kuder Navigator and 50 units for Kuder Journey to have access to the Administrative Database Management System. Volume discounting is provided, so itis best to contact Kuder for specifications. Individual user accounts may be purchased online for $29.95 and $34.95, respectively.

Additional Comments of Interest to Users: The ADMS has an updated design, new reports, and more tools to provide administrative users with everything they need to manage use of the Kuder system. New Person Matches sketches are presented in a Q&A type format. There are interviews with individuals who have similar interests as the test-taker. The intent of this feature on the interest assessment is to trigger further exploration of a career by providing a real-world look at career stories from adults. There are continued navigation improvements to provide a more user-friendly experience. Users are able to start an assessment for the first time or complete unfinished assessments directly from their Kuder home page. Users also have the capability of sharing their assessment results from within the system via Facebook, Twitter, and email.

Published Reviews of the Instrument in the Last 15 Years: Not available.

Kuder Career Planning System:
Kuder Career Interest Assessment, Kuder Skills Confidence Assessment, and Kuder Work Values Assessment

Reviewed by:

Melinda M. Gibbons

Department of Educational Psychology and Counseling
University of Tennessee, Knoxville

Description

The newly revised (2012) Kuder Career Planning System is based on original career assessments created by Frederic Kuder in 1938, and is currently published by Kuder, Inc., founded in 1997. According to the Kuder website, the System is "designed to help students and adults with career and educational planning." The System is Internet-based and provides customizable career and educational information based on interests, skills, and work values assessments. System users create personal portfolios that save their test scores and other information researched on the website. Kuder provides multiple levels of career programming, including the Kuder Galaxy for Pre-K and elementary school, Kuder Navigator for middle and high school, and Kuder Journey for postsecondary students and adults. The three main assessments, Kuder Career Interest Assessment (2012), Kuder Skills Confidence Assessment (2012), and Kuder Work Values Assessment (2012), are available through the Navigator and Journey sections.

Kuder Career Interest Assessment

The Kuder Career Interest Assessment (KCIA-32; Kuder, Inc., 2012) is an interest inventory formerly referred to as the Kuder Career Search. According to the website, the KCIA takes approximately 9 minutes to complete. It contains 32 triads of interest items that are ranked by preference and correspond with Holland's types. For each page listing three activities, test takers are asked to decide their *most preferred, second most preferred,* and *third most preferred.* Each ranking can only be used once per triad of activities. The same version of the assessment, available in both English and Spanish, appears in both Navigator and Journey. A bar graph appears on the screen showing how much of the assessment has been completed.

In the Navigator version, the results indicate level of interest in specific pathways based on the 16 national career clusters. Pathways are described as "sub-groups of occupations" (Kuder, Inc., 2012) within larger career clusters. Students can then explore related occupations, view sample plans of study, or read interviews of people from various careers who had similar interests to those they chose. In the Journey version, a Holland code is provided along with a brief description of each letter in the code. Again, related occupations and person match are available, along with related majors based on interest code results.

Kuder Skills Confidence Assessment

The Kuder Skills Confidence Assessment (KSCA; Kuder, Inc., 2012), formerly referred to as the Kuder Skills Assessment, is available in two versions: KSCA-16 for Navigator and the KSCA-A for Journey. Fifty-six skills are included in the KSA-16 and 52 skills are in the KSA-CA. Both versions are available in English or Spanish and each is estimated to take about 7 minutes to complete. Again, a bar graph appears on the screen showing how much of the assessment has been completed.

The KSCA-16 asks test takers to estimate their current self-efficacy for a variety of skill areas that correspond with the Holland profiles. Students are asked to respond to each item by indicating the level to which they currently do the task on a 5-point Likert-type scale (*I have done this task well* to *I haven't done this task, and it would be hard for me to learn*). Eight items are provided per page. As with the KCIA-32, results are presented using career pathways based on the 16 national career clusters.

The KSCA-A is similar, but test takers are asked to rate their current level of confidence in performing a variety of tasks, again on a 5-point scale (*cannot do at all* to *completely certain I can do*). Results are instead presented using Holland codes, with majors and related occupations easily accessible for review.

Kuder Work Values Assessment

Twenty-five work-related values make-up the Kuder Work Values Assessment (KWVA), formerly labeled Super's Work Values Inventory (Kuder, Inc., 2012). The KWVA takes approximately 4 minutes to complete, and the instructions ask test takers to rate the level of importance of various values on a 5-point Likert-type scale, from *not important at all in job selection* to *crucial, would not consider a job without it*. KWVA is available in both English and Spanish, and a bar graph helps test takers identify how much of the instrument they have completed. The results page provides a list of the five values that were ranked as most important, and definitions of each value are provided. Related occupations can be searched based on values.

Use in Counseling

The Kuder Career Planning System is a useful, completely interactive online program that provides career planning for clients from ages 4 and older. The Navigator and Journey systems each include three career assessments to help clients learn more about themselves as they plan for the future. Navigator focuses on middle and high school students while Journey is targeted for college students and adults. The assessments have been recently updated and shortened, making them user-friendly. In addition, the extensive research conducted on each assessment demonstrates strong evidence of reliability, validity, and attempts for cultural fairness.

A highlight of the website is its ease of use. Test results are immediately available and saved in a portfolio. Clients create their personal portfolio where they are able to track and compare their test results, explore occupations, plan for education and work, and find a job. Careers can be explored by career clusters or by assessment results, and career information is based on O*NET information. Education and work planning includes a variety of options, based on level of education desired and activities needed to successfully apply for a job. Much of the information can be interpreted without a professional counselor, but for maximum results, clients should work with a school or career counselor as they proceed through the website.

Technical Considerations

All of the instruments associated with the Kuder Career Planning System have been newly updated. It appears, based on technical reports (Suen, 2012), that the instruments were all shortened, with extensive reli-

Kuder Career Planning System

ability and validity testing completed as part of the shortening process. The KCIA-32 began with 168 possible items (56 triads); item analyses and content validity by an expert panel of five leaders in career and guidance led to the shortened version containing 96 items, or 32 triads. The last version of the KCIA-32 (i.e., Kuder Career Search) included 60 triads (Schenck, 2009), so this new version has been substantially reduced. Two national sample groups, one with 958 working adults and the other with 142 high school students, completed the longer instruments to help the expert panel determine items that maximized reliability and item discrimination. Coefficient alpha reliability for each of the six Holland scales ranged from .73 - .86 for the adult sample and .74 - .87 for the high school sample (Suen, 2012).

The KSCA-16 and KSCA-A (2012) underwent similar revisions, with the KSCA-16 being shortened from 175 to 56 items and the KSCA-A reducing from 170 to 52 items (Suen, 2012). Again, this is a reduction from the last versions of the KSCA (i.e., Kuder Skills Assessment), which included 90 to 175 items, depending on the format used (Schenck, 2009). The KSCA-16 was reviewed by an expert panel and included a complete item analysis based on a national sample of 2,100 participants. Reliability coefficient alphas ranged from .74 to .91, and factor analyses provided evidence for its relationship to the Holland model. The KSCA-A also was reviewed by the same expert panel and the item analysis and reliability information was based on a national sample of 2,000 participants. Reliability coefficient alphas ranged from .85 - .93, and factor analyses again demonstrated high relatedness to the Holland model (Suen, 2012).

The KWVA (Kuder, Inc., 2012) was reduced from 72 to 25 items based on a national sample of 4,000 participants. The same expert panel reviewed the results and completed factor analyses, item analysis, and reliability testing. Reliability coefficient alpha values ranged from .83 to .89, and factor analyses demonstrated evidence or relatedness to the Holland model (Suen, 2012).

General Utility and Evaluation

The Kuder Career Planning System and its collection of career assessments appear to be a sound and valid way to help clients of all ages explore career-related information. A recent study of the impact of the System on middle school students (Kuder, Inc., 2009) found the majority of the 735 participants believed the system helped them learn about their interests, skills, and values, and most noted it helped in finding career-related information. For these students, the System in general and the assessments in particular, were found to be helpful in thinking about career planning. One limitation of the Kuder System is the difficulty in finding a technical manual. Brief technical reports are available upon request, but are not easily accessible on the website. In addition, the technical reports mention the use of a national sample, but no specific information about the cultural or regional groups represented in the samples is available.

It seems to this reviewer that Kuder would be especially helpful when working with pre-K–16 students because it provides a one-stop location for many items related to career development. The instruments are easy to take, demonstrate strong evidence of validity and reliability, and provide instant results that can be saved in an online personal portfolio. The instruments can be used with individuals or in a group setting, making them adaptable as well. Finally, research demonstrates a strong attempt at cultural fairness through representative sampling and multicultural item analysis. The Kuder Career Planning System and its career instruments represent a well-researched and easy-to-use one-stop career planning service.

References and Additional Resources

Kuder, Inc. (2009). *Kuder Career Planning System technical brief.* Adel, IA: Author.

Kuder, Inc. (2012). *About Kuder.* Retrieved from http://www.kuder.com.

Schenck, P. M. (2009). [Kuder Career Planning System.] In E. A. Whitfield, R. W. Feller, & C. Wood (Eds.), *A counselor's guide to career assessment instruments* (5th ed, pp. 168-173.). Broken Arrow, OK: National Career Development Association.

Suen, H. K. (2012). *Kuder technical summaries; Kuder Career Search with Person Match 2012, Kuder Skills Confidence Assessment-16 2012, Kuder Skills Confidence Assessment-A 2012, Kuder Work Values Assessment 2012.* Adel, IA: Kuder, Inc.

OCCUPATIONAL APTITUDE SURVEY AND INTEREST SCHEDULE, THIRD EDITION

Randall M. Parker

PRO-ED Inc.
8700 Shoal Creek Blvd.
Austin, TX 78757-6897
http://www.proedinc.com
info@proedinc.com

Target Population: Adolescents (Grades 8-12), young adults, and adults.

Statement of the Purpose of the Instrument: The Occupational Aptitude Survey and Interest Schedule—Third Edition (OASIS-3) was developed to assist individuals in their career search by providing them with information regarding their relative strengths in several aptitude areas related to the world of work. By using the OASIS-3 and related materials, students and adults may identify a list of jobs to help focus the search for further job information.

Titles of Subtests, Scales, Scores Provided: (1) Vocabulary, (2) Computation, (3) Spatial Relations, (4) Word Comparison, and (5) Making Marks. Scores provided include raw scores, percentiles, and stanines.

Forms and Levels Available, with Dates of Publication/Revision of Each: OASIS-3 Aptitude Survey (2002); OASIS-3 Interest Schedule (2002); and OASIS-3 (AS/IS) Interpretation Workbooks (2002).

Date of Most Recent Edition of Test Manual, User's Guide, Etc.: 2001.

Languages in Which Available: English only.

Time:

    Actual Test Time: Varies.

    Total Administration Time: 30-45 minutes.

Norm Group(s) on Which Scores Are Based: Eighth to twelfth-grade public school students and adults in post-secondary educational settings.

Manner in Which Results Are Reported for Individuals: Scoring form/Student Profile.

Report Format/Content for Group Summaries: Not available.

Machine-Scoring: Special forms must be purchased/used when administering the test. The completed machine-score forms are then shipped to PRO-ED to scan. The assessment can be machine scored and returned to the counselor in less than a week.

Local Machine Scoring: Not available.

Hand Scoring: Hand scored by counselor in 5-10 minutes.

Computer Software Options Available: Not available.

Cost of Materials: Due to possible price changes since publication date, be sure to check the publisher's website.

    Specimen Set: OASIS-3:AS Machine-Scorable Kit (package of 10) $67.00, and OASIS-3: IS Machine Scorable Kit (package of 10) $67.00.

    Counselee Materials: The OASIS-3 materials are priced as follows:

    OASIS-3: AS Occupational Aptitude Survey and Interest Schedule—Third Edition $191.00

    OASIS-3: AS Answer Sheets (50) $51.00

    OASIS-3: AS Machine-Scorable Kit (10) $58.00

    OASIS-3: AS Examiner's Manual $67.00

    OASIS-3: AS Profile Sheets (50) $31.00

    OASIS-3: AS Scoring Keys $0.00

OASIS-3: AS Student Test Booklets (10) $51.00

OASIS-3: IS Occupational Aptitude Survey and Interest Schedule—Third Edition $206.00

OASIS-3: IS Examiner's Manual $67.00

OASIS-3: IS Machine Scorable Kit (10) $58.00

OASIS-3: IS Scoring Forms (50) $31.00

OASIS-3: IS Student Answer Sheets (50) $31.00

OASIS-3: IS Student Profile Sheets (50) $31.00

OASIS-3: IS Student Test Booklets (25) $51.00

The Examiner's Manual, Student Booklets, Scoring Keys are reusable for both versions.

Published Reviews of the Instrument in the Last 15 Years:

Akos, P., & Spangler, R. (2009). [Occupational Aptitude Survey and Interest Schedule—third edition]. In E. A. Whitfield, R. W. Feller, & C. Wood (Eds.), *A counselor's guide to career assessment instruments* (5th ed.; pp. 189-194). Broken Arrow, OK: National Career Development Association.

Bunch, M. B. (2005). [Occupational Aptitude Survey and Interest Schedule, third edition]. In R. A. Spies & B. S. Plake (Eds.), *The sixteenth mental measurements yearbook* (pp. 715-720). Lincoln, NE: Buros Center for Testing.

Michael, W. B. (2005). [Occupational Aptitude Survey and Interest Schedule, third edition]. In R. A. Spies & B. S. Plake (Eds.), *The sixteenth mental measurements yearbook* (pp. 713-715). Lincoln, NE: Buros Center for Testing.

OCCUPATIONAL APTITUDE SURVEY AND INTEREST SCHEDULE, THIRD EDITION

Reviewed by:

A. Stephen Lenz

Department of Counseling, Educational Psychology, and Research
The University of Memphis

Description

The Occupational Aptitude Survey and Interest Schedule, (OASIS-3) consists of two instruments — the OASIS-3 Aptitude Survey and the OASIS-3 Interest Schedule — that are designed to "encourage self-exploration, vocational exploration, and career development" (Parker, 2002a, p. 1). Originally designed to assist individuals in grades 8 through 12, the third edition of the OASIS reflects a decade of research prior to its publication that extended the normative sample of the instrument to include individuals in post-secondary education settings as well. This extension of the normative sample is congruent with the author's intention to provide the OASIS-3 as an instrument that can help individuals throughout their lifespan pursue educational development, training, and exposure to the world of work.

Items on the OASIS-3 Aptitude Survey (AS) were developed with the assumption that aptitude consists of cognitive abilities across many distinct domains including the following: spatial relations, numerical calculation, verbal reasoning, memory, and speed. Consequently, the AS yields a considerable amount of information related to an individual's strengths in a number of areas within the world of work. The AS is composed of a General Ability scale and five subscales: Vocabulary, Computation, Spatial Relations, Word Comparison, and Making Marks, each with different item quantities and time limits for completion.

The first AS subtest is Vocabulary which requires individuals to review lists of words and identify the two that are either synonyms or antonyms. Each of the 40 items on this subscale consists of four words (e.g., Fast,

A Counselor's Guide To Career Assessments Instruments

Cold, Rapid, and Humid) requiring individuals to choose the correct combination (e.g., Fast and Rapid are synonyms) within a 9-minute time limit. Next, the Computation subtest requires individuals to solve arithmetic and algebra problems (e.g., 4 + 2) mentally or using scratch paper. Each of the 30 items provides five response options (e.g., 4, 2, 6, 8, none of these) and must be completed within the 12-minute time limit for this section. The Spatial Relations subtest gives individuals 8 minutes to review 20 items that depict two-dimensional figures with lines indicating possible folding points. For each two-dimensional figure, individuals are presented four choices of three-dimensional illustrations and are to select the object that could be constructed by folding along the marked lines. The fourth subtest, Word Comparison, requires individuals to evaluate sets of symbols that include names, letters, and numbers to determine whether they are the same or different. Individuals are given five minutes to determine whether the 100 items (e.g., 12345 West Ave. – 12354 West Ave.) are the same or different. Finally, the Making Marks subtest requires individuals to draw as many asterisks within a set of squares within two 30-second rounds. Each of the AS subtests provides two practice prompts and an opportunity to clarify the task prior to beginning the timed portion.

The OASIS-3 Interest Schedule (IS) was developed to increase knowledge about preferences, traits, and capacities by stimulating self-exploration through purposeful inventorying of an individual's interests and experiences. The results of the IS are intended to help individuals make informed choices that positively influence their future educational and vocational goals. The OASIS-3 Interest Schedule (IS) is untimed and has 240 items that ask test takers to rate preferences *(like, neutral,* and *dislike)* regarding specific careers and vocational activities. Each of the items is assigned to 1 of 12 scales composed of 20 items; of the 20 items, 10 reflect occupational titles (e.g., Chemist) and 10 depict job activities associated with those titles (e.g., Develop new chemical products) drawn from research conducted by the U.S. Employment Service which led to the development of the *Guide for Occupational Exploration,* now in its third edition (Farr, Ludden, & Shatkin, 2001). The occupational domains of the 12 scales include the following: Artistic (ART), Scientific (SCI), Nature (NAT), Protective (PRO), Mechanical (MEC), Industrial (IND), Business Detail (BUS), Selling (SEL), Accommodating (ACC), Humanitarian (HUM), Leading-Influencing (LEA), and Physical Performing (PHY).

Parker (2002a, 2002b) in the AS and IS manuals emphasized that precise administration and scoring of the instrument protocols are imperative to sustaining the reliability and validity of the results. Parker recommended that test users have adequate knowledge and skills related to assessment practices obtained through training and supervision. In addition to general assessment knowledge and skills, counselors using the OASIS-3 should be knowledgeable about the world of work (i.e., vocational titles and associated duties), variables that promote the fit between person and work environments, and theories of adolescent and adult human development. The OASIS-3 can be administered in an individual or group format with the recommended ratio not to exceed 30 individuals per proctor. Although the AS has specific time limits for each section, the IS is untimed and both include scripted instructions for administrators, procedural instructions for completing practice prompts, and recommendations for answering test taker questions. Counselors are also recommended to ensure that the test taking environment be conducive to optimal performance by controlling for lighting, ventilation, noise, and other distractions that may inhibit performance.

A proctor or counselor provides each test taker with two pencils, a piece of scratch paper, an AS and IS Student Booklet, and respective answer sheets. The Student Booklets are printed using large font, format, and spacing that promote legibility and clarity of the items; answer sheets use a complementary format, are relatively self-explanatory, and easy to complete in a paper-and-pencil format. Both the AS and IS can be scored by machine or manually using the clear plastic scoring templates provided with the OASIS-3 kits. Whether using the machine or manual scoring format, each protocol requires the test administrator to spend between three and five minutes per individual to review answer sheets for stray marks and incomplete items. Each AS subtest and IS scale yields a raw score that is converted to percentiles and stanines using the normative tables included in the Examiner's Manuals. Both the AS and IS kits include a Student Profile that depicts an individual's demographic information as well as the raw score, percentile score, and stanine for each subtest (AS) and scale (IS). Overall, the time requirements for test administration (about 60 minutes), scoring (10-15 minutes), and transferring scores to the Student Profiles (10-15 minutes) requires at least one-and-a-half hours.

The OASIS-3 provides counselors with a rich depiction of an individual's vocational strengths, abilities, aptitudes, experiences, and interests that can be used to promote self-exploration, decision making, and

Occupational Aptitude Survey and Interest Schedule, Third Edition

planning with clients. Counselors working in secondary and post-secondary education settings can use the OASIS-3 to help individuals explore and evaluate their work-related strengths, interests, and experiences using a system designed to assist in setting goals, making decisions, and planning for careers after graduation. Parker (2002a, 2002b) noted unequivocally that the OASIS-3 should not be used by counselors to prescribe a vocation to individuals; on the contrary, it is an instrument that can facilitate a individual's enthusiasm, motivation, and personal commitment to a subjectively meaningful career path. Additionally, because the OASIS-3 can be administered in both individual and group formats, this instrument can by utilized across settings by professionals working in secondary schools, college counseling and individual affairs capacities, community agencies, private practice, and vocational guidance.

The raw score, percentile, and stanine values included on the Student Profile may be only minimally useful to clients without a context with which to make meaning of them; therefore, counselors are encouraged to provide test takers with a verbal interpretation in either an individual or group format. A thoughtful, developmentally appropriate interpretation can facilitate clients breathing life into the numbers and graphs and provide a forum for addressing the development of the profound subjective meaning associated with a vocational identity that is both authentic and fulfilling.

Parker (2002a, 2002b) suggested that counselors implement the following guidelines to promote meaningful understanding of the OASIS-3 AS and IS results by clients:

1. Convey to individuals that the AS and IS are not predictive assessments, but rather a resource for organizing their search for occupational information. Also, individuals should be informed that the results are not static and can change over time as they become more knowledgeable about the world of work or have more life experiences.

2. Solicit the individual for their initial impressions about the process of taking the test and make note of their attitudes about testing and feelings about themselves.

3. Provide individuals with a copy of their profile and ample time for them to review and consider their results making sure to observe their responses to the data.

4. Educate individuals about the comparison (norm) group and discuss the meaning of confidence intervals and percentile scores without jargon and using relevant examples.

5. Be sensitive when including the individual to actively participate in the interpretation process.

6. Do not defend the results of the inventories and facilitate the individuals' expression of affect, even if it is negative.

7. Make an effort to provide a positive interpretation that stimulates positive self-exploration and environmental exploration by the individuals while emphasizing that the OASIS-3 is designed to broaden self-perspective rather than limit it.

8. Near the end of the interpretation session, counselors should facilitate the individuals' verbal discussion regarding their personal understanding of the results making sure to clarify any distortions and process the general meaning associated with their experience with the assessment process.

Although the guidelines provided by Parker are similar to the standard procedures for interpreting most tests, the AS and IS Interpretation Workbooks are useful resources that may facilitate vocational and guidance counseling objectives. Moreover, the information included in the interpretative materials could be used in conjunction with other information sources such as O*NET (www.onetonline.org), state career information systems, or career information/exploration texts that are designed to help individuals develop an understanding about the knowledge, skills, work tasks, and compensation associated with certain professional activities and while investigating potential job markets.

Technical Considerations

Both the AS and IS Examiner's Manuals include extant information regarding the technical and psychometric characteristics of the OASIS-3 including information about standardization, norming, gender bias, reliability, and validity. Parker (2002a, 2002b) indicated that the OASIS-3 was standardized and normed with a sample of 2,005 individuals from 8th to 12th grades ($N = 1,505$; 752 boys, 753 girls) as well as adults in post-secondary education settings (N = 500; 220 men, 280 women). The author implemented quota and purposive sampling methods across several regions of North America to obtain a nationally representative sample based on U.S. Census and U.S. Department of Education data. Differences in the norms between the secondary and post-secondary education groups were detected during analysis and are reflected in separate norming scales to reduce gender bias.

The OASIS-3 Examiner's Manuals provide detailed reporting of the reliability of the AS and the IS scales. Alpha coefficients, split half, and alternate forms reliabilities for the AS are provided for the normative sample. For individuals in 8th through 12th grades, alpha coefficients for the AS General Ability scale ranged from .89 to .90 with a median of .90. Median reliability estimates for this subgroup of individuals in grades 8-12 are as follows: .88 (Vocabulary, alpha coefficient), .84 (Computation, alpha coefficient), .78 (Spatial Relations, split-half), .90 (Word Comparison, alternate forms), and .89 (Making Marks, alternate forms). These estimates indicate that the reliability of the AS General Ability and Making Marks subscales are within the excellent range (> .90), with Vocabulary, Computation, and Word Comparison falling within the good range (.80-.89), and Spatial Relations within the acceptable range (.70-.79). For the second subgroup of the normative sample (adults in post-secondary education), reliability metrics were calculated for gender and ethnic groups. For each individuals in post-secondary settings AS subtest (Vocabulary, Computation, Spatial Relations, Word Comparison, and Making Marks) reliability information is reported in association with the related aptitude factors (Verbal, Numerical, Spatial, Perceptual, and Manual Dexterity) rather than the subtest. The General Ability alpha coefficients for this normative sample ranged from .90 to .93 with a median of .91. Alpha coefficient reliability estimates for this subgroup of individuals are as follows: .90 (Verbal), .83 (Numerical), .70 (Spatial), .89 (Perceptual), and .91 (Manual Dexterity). Similar to the adolescent data, while General Ability, Verbal, and Manual dexterity scales are within the excellent range and Numerical and Perceptual subscales are fairly robust, the Spatial Relations subtest yielded the lowest reliability coefficients within the acceptable to debatable range.

Alpha and test-retest reliabilities are included for the 12 scales in the IS Examiner's Manual. For individuals in 8th through 12th grades, the reported alpha coefficients ranged from .78 to .94 with scale values typically above the mid- .80s. Specifically, alpha reliability estimates for this subgroup are as follows: .89 (ART), .90 (SCI), .94 (NAT), .91 (PRO), .92 (MEC), .90 (IND), .91 (BUS), .89 (SEL), .85 (ACC), .89 (HUM), .88 (LEA), and .90 (PHY). Test-retest reliabilities obtained for a 2-week interval and computed from a sample of 54 junior high and high school individuals revealed a similar range of values for the IS scales (.72 to .90). Reliability coefficients for each scale are as follows: .91 (ART), .77 (SCI), .75 (NAT), .81 (PRO), .72 (MEC), .75 (IND), .88 (BUS), .66 (SEL), .89 (ACC), .82 (HUM), .86 (LEA), and .90 (PHY). For adults in post-secondary education, alpha coefficients ranged from .84 to .96 with similar values detected between genders and ethnicities, indicating a high level of internal consistency of scale items. Specifically, reliability estimates for this subgroup are as follows: .91 (ART), .91 (SCI), .95 (NAT), .93 (PRO), .95 (MEC), .96 (IND), .92 (BUS), .93 (SEL), .89 (ACC), .92 (HUM), .84 (LEA), and .95 (PHY). Test-retest reliabilities obtained with a 2-week interval and computed from a sample of 44 college individuals were generally stronger when compared to the adolescent sample and also revealed that the values obtained by the IS scales ranging from .82 to .91 remain stable over time. These reliability coefficients for each scale among college individuals are: .90 (ART), .91 (SCI), .91(NAT), .87 (PRO), .85 (MEC), .84 (IND), .88 (BUS), .95 (SEL), .88 (ACC), .90 (HUM), .87 (LEA), and .89 (PHY).

Evidence for the construct validity of the OASIS-3 was obtained through examining intercorrelations and factor analyses for AS subscales and IS scales. For the AS, intercorrelations between subtests are low with the exception of those between Vocabulary and Computation (.51; 26% shared variance) and between Computation and Word Comparison (.40; 16% shared variance), indicating that each of the subtests is measuring a separate dimension of vocational aptitude. The AS intercorrelation matrix was factor analyzed using the principal axis technique with iterated communalities that yielded two factors accounting for 63.2% of the shared variance. The first factor included Vocabulary, Computation, and Spatial Relations, and was labeled as a general ability factor. The second factor composed of Word Comparison and Making Marks was labeled a perceptual motor factor. Concurrent validity for the AS was examined through comparison of the AS subtests with the *Iowa Tests of Educational Development* (ITED; Feldt, Forsyth, Ansley, & Alnot, 1994), the SRA Achievement Series (SRA; Naslund, Thorpe, & Lefever, 1978), and the General Aptitude Test Battery (GATB; U.S. Department of Defense, 1993). The results of these analyses revealed that the AS subtests provide the expected convergent and

Occupational Aptitude Survey and Interest Schedule, Third Edition

discriminate correlations with subtests purported to measure similar and dissimilar constructs, as the ITED, SRA, and GATB subtests.

For the IS, convergent validity evidence was based upon moderate (r > .45) and significant intercorrelations between the 12 IS scales and Holland's six Self-Directed Search (SDS) classifications that revealed correspondence between the two measures and supportive evidence for the constructs underlying the OASIS-3 scores (Parker, 2001). For example, the SDS Investigative scale correlated significantly with the IS Scientific subscale (r = .50). Additional validity evidence for the IS is reported from several other studies (Jorjorian, 1986; Levinson, Parker, Barker, & Emery, 1998; Green & Parker, 1989; Michele, 2003; Parker, 2001; Parker & Green, 1987, 1988) suggesting that the individuals score higher on scales associated with their eventual college majors among adults and congruence between self-ratings and tested interest scores among adolescents.

General Utility and Evaluation

The OASIS-3 provides counselors with an instrument that is an alternative to other available measures and is supported by psychometric data grounded in a sound theoretical framework. The AS and IS Examiner's Manuals are well organized and written in a style that promotes understanding of necessary material by individuals with a specialization in assessment; however, test users should have an understanding of quality test administration and interpretation practices before adopting this instrument for use. The quality of the administrative, interpretive, and technical manuals are developmentally appropriate for test takers, well made, and durable. The inclusion of a normative sample for individuals in post-secondary settings is a timely enhancement to this instrument given the increasing emphasis on completing a college education to promote access to the job market in North America. Furthermore, the instrument's author does not overestimate the utility of the OASIS-3 and instead introduces all activities and concepts as an exploratory tool rather than a predictive solution for career development concerns.

Although the OASIS-3 is in general a useful instrument for increasing self-awareness and self-exploration among adolescents and adults in post-secondary settings, some limitations are worth noting. Foremost, although the OASIS-3 may be a briefer alternative to other career aptitude and interest assessments, the overall time for administration, scoring, and interpretation can take well over two hours, which may not be practical for practitioners or researchers in some settings. In addition to time requirements, the OASIS-3 may not be as cost-effective for counselors in some educational and community-based settings when compared to other open source inventories; however, many open-source or free materials do not provide the depth of technically supported information that is produced by the OASIS-3. As noted in other reviews (Bunch, 2005; Michael, 2005) some racial/ethnic minority groups are underrepresented in the normative sample. This may make interpretation of results for Asian, Hispanic/Latino, and Native American subgroups less valid when compared to individuals identifying with African American and White/Caucasian categories. Finally, much of the item development and normative data included in the OASIS-3 was developed throughout the 1990s. Although several of the occupational titles and activities are contemporarily relevant, the OASIS-3 does not reflect the prominent expansion of careers associated with technology skill sets during the last 20 years. As web-based and cloud-based commerce and communication continue to expand, it will be important for counseling professionals to have access to resources that promote development within occupations associated with internet network maintenance; program writing using Java, Oracle, and C languages; cloud-based computing, development of applications for smart phones; graphics design; and web page administration. Finally, although some individuals have used the OASIS-3 as an assessment for conducting vocational and guidance research (Green, Snell, & Parimanath, 1990; Su, Rounds, & Armstrong, 2009), the OASIS-3 was designed as a practical instrument and may be best used to this end.

The OASIS-3 is a well-conceptualized and technically evaluated instrument that may provide a valuable resource for counselors across settings to provide support and guidance to their clientele. The strengths and convenience of the OASIS-3 outweigh its modest limitations if counselors are vigilant about recognizing the importance of this assessment to encourage self-exploration that can inform decision making. Counselors intending to implement career assessment practices with large populations of individuals may elect to take advantage of the electronic scoring and interpretation options for this instrument. In all, the OASIS-3 may be practical addition to the counselor's toolkit.

A COUNSELOR'S GUIDE TO CAREER ASSESSMENTS INSTRUMENTS

References and Additional Resources

Akos, P., & Spangler, R. (2009). [Occupational Aptitude Survey and Interest Schedule—third edition]. In E. A. Whitfield, R. W. Feller, & C. Wood (Eds.), *A counselor's guide to career assessment instruments* (5th ed., pp. 189-194). Broken Arrow, OK: National Career Development Association.

Bunch, M. B. (2005). [Occupational Aptitude Survey and Interest Schedule—third edition]. In R. A. Spies & B. S. Plake (Eds.), *The sixteenth mental measurements yearbook* (pp. 715-720). Lincoln, NE: Buros Center for Testing.

Farr, J. M., Ludden, L., & Shatkin, L. (2001). *Guide for occupational exploration* (3rd ed.). Indianapolis, IN: JIST Works.

Feldt, L., Forsyth, R., Ansley, T., & Alnot, S. (1994). *Teacher, administrator, and counselor manual, Iowa Test of Educational Development.* Chicago, IL: Riverside.

Green, D. W., & Parker, R. (1989). Vocational and academic attributes of individuals with different learning styles. *Journal of College Individual Development, 30,* 395-400.

Green, D. W., Snell, J. C., & Parimanath, A. R. (1990). Learning styles in assessment of individuals. *Perceptual and Motor Skills, 70,* 363-369. doi:10.1177/0013164496056005007

Jorjorian, S. (1986). Preparing for the world of work: A study of adolescents with learning disabilities. *Dissertation Abstracts International, 47,* 4357A.

Levinson, E., Parker, R., Barker, W., & Emery, J. (1998). Empirical exploration of the crosswalk between the Guide for Occupational Exploration's 12-factor interest model and Holland's 6-factor interest theory. *Vocational Evaluation and Work Adjustment Bulletin, 31,* 67-70.

Michele, T. (2003). A criterion-related validation study of the Oasis-3 Interest Schedule. *Dissertation Abstracts International: Section B. Sciences and Engineering, 64*(2-b), 4217.

Michael, W. B. (2005). [Occupational Aptitude Survey and Interest Schedule—Third Edition]. In R. A. Spies & B. S. Plake (Eds.), *The sixteenth mental measurements yearbook* (pp. 713-715). Lincoln, NE: Buros Center for Testing.

Naslund, R. A., Thorpe, L. P., & Lefever, D. W. (1978). *SRA Achievement Series.* Chicago, IL: Science Research Associates.

Parker, R. M. (2001). *Correlations of self-ratings of interests and tested interests.* Unpublished manuscript.

Parker, R. M. (2002a). *Occupational Aptitude Survey and Interest Schedule, third edition, Aptitude Survey examiner's manual.* Austin, TX: Pro-Ed Incorporated.

Parker, R. M. (2002b). *Occupational Aptitude Survey and Interest Schedule, third edition, Interest Schedule examiner's manual.* Austin, TX: Pro-Ed Incorporated.

Parker, R. M., & Green, D. (1987). Construct validity of the OASIS Interest Schedule. *Educational and Psychological Measurement, 47,* 755-757.

Parker, R. M., & Green, D. (1988). Construct validity of the OASIS Interest Schedule: A replication. *Educational and Psychological Measurement, 48,* 459-462.

Parker, R. M., & Levinson, E. (1998). *Concurrent validity indices for the OASIS Interest Survey and the Self-Directed Search.* Unpublished manuscript.

Su, R., Rounds, J., & Armstrong, P. I. (2009). Men and things, women and people: A meta-analysis of sex differences in interests. *Psychological Bulletin, 135,* 859-884. doi:10.1037/a0017364

U.S. Department of Defense. (1993). *ASVAB 18/19 technical manual.* North Chicago, IL: U.S. Military Entrance Processing Command.

218

World of Work Inventory

Robert E. Ripley, Gregory P. M. Neidert, and Nancy L. Ortman

World of Work, Inc.

410 W. 1st Street, Suite 103
Tempe, AZ 85281-2874
http://www.wowi.com/
info@wowi.com

Target Population: Adolescents, young adults, and adults; ages 13 to 65+.

Statement of the Purpose of the Instrument: The World of Work Inventory (WOWI) is designed to assist individuals in identifying occupations most compatible with their unique combination of job-relevant abilities, interests, and personality. It is used for career counseling, vocational rehabilitation, employee selection and development, student guidance, and adult/career education classes.

Titles of Subtests, Scales, Scores Provided: Career Interest Activities (17 scores: Public Service, The Sciences, Engineering & Related, Business Relations, Managerial, The Arts, Clerical, Sales, Service, Primary Outdoor, Processing, Machine Work, Bench Work, Structural Work, Mechanical & Electrical Work, Graphic Arts, Mining); Job Satisfaction Indicators (12 scores: Versatile, Adaptable to Repetitive Work, Adaptable to Performing Under Specific Instructions, Dominant, Gregarious, Isolative, Influencing, Self-Controlled, Valuative, Objective, Subjective, Rigorous): Career Training Potentials (6 scores: Verbal, Numerical, Abstractions, Spatial-Form, Mechanical/Electrical, Organizing Skill).

Forms and Levels Available, with Dates of Publication/Revision of Each: The WOWI Long Form is comprised of 516 items and is no longer available electronically or in print. It has been entirely replaced by the WOWI Short Form, which has superior psychometric properties. The WOWI Short Form is comprised of 330 items and is available in a number of versions and reading levels. A version of the WOWI is also available for the visually impaired.

Date of Most Recent Edition of Test Manual, User's Guide, Etc.: Interpretation Manual for the World of Work Inventory (5th Edition) was last revised and published in 2001. An interpretation guide, quick reference sheet, and numerous detailed help menus are available to test administrators on the website. These online test administration and interpretation resources were last revised in 2009.

Languages in Which Available: North American English, British English, Australian English, and Spanish.

Time:

Actual Test Time: Career Interest Activities (10-15 minutes), Career Training Potentials (30-40 minutes), and Job Satisfaction Indicators (8-10 minutes).

Total Administration Time: (48-65 minutes).

Norm Group(s) on Which Scores Are Based: The norms are based on a national cross section of 169,436 individuals, including corporate executives, managers, line-level employees, displaced and injured workers, students (high school, college, and graduate), welfare recipients, inmates at correctional facilities (federal, state, and local), etc. New norms will be published in 2013 (see http://www.wowi.com).

Manner in Which Results Are Reported for Individuals: All of the measured scales of the WOWI provide both a numerical score and graphical representation of each score on the Profile Report. A written description and interpretation of each score is provided in the Interpretive Report (see below). The Career Interest Activities and Job Satisfaction Indicator subscales are idiographic by design and are therefore expressed only as raw scores, between −60 and +60. The Career Training Potentials (formally named the Vocational Training Potentials) subscales are nomothetic by design and are therefore both expressed as raw and standardized scores [in standard deviation units], with separate comparisons of the test taker with those of the same age and education level.

All test takers receive a 3-page Profile Report, which provides both numerical scores and graphical representation of individuals' assessment results. In addition, a 2-3 page Summary Report provides the test taker with a brief narrative description of each measured scale. The Summary Report concludes with a listing of job recommendations that have at least an 85% match with the test takers results. The jobs are organized by levels of educational attainment and represent occupations that are stable or growing in demand.

In addition, a 6-8 page Interpretive Report provides the test taker with a narrative description and interpretation of each measured scale of the assessment. The Interpretive Report concludes with a listing of job recommendations that have at least an 85% match with the test takers results. The jobs are organized by levels of educational attainment and represent occupations that are stable or growing in demand. For test takers in the United States, each recommended job title has direct links to its O*NET Online, Occupational Outlook Handbook (OOH), and optionally Dictionary of Occupational Titles (DOT) descriptions. For test takers in Canada, Australia, and the United Kingdom, each recommended job title has direct links to its description in each country's respective online occupational resource.

Report Format/Content for Group Summaries: Not available.

Machine Scoring: WOWI Online – Profile Report with Summary Report (1-4) $25.00 each, (5-19) $19.00 each, (20+) $15.00 each. WOWI Online – Profile Report with Summary and Interpretive Report (1-4) $27.00 each, (5-19) $21.00 each, (20+) $17.00 each. There are substantial discounts for non-profit organizations.

Hand Scoring: Not available.

Local Machine Scoring: Not available.

Computer Software Options Available: Standard administration online.

Cost of Materials: Due to possible price change since publication date, be sure to check the publisher's website.

Specimen Set: Complimentary WOWI Online assessment provided to qualified workforce, rehabilitation, and career professionals.

Counselee Materials: Online Site License (one-time fee) $189.00. Additional Site Licenses within the same organization are $50.00 each. Account upgrades are available: email notification (one-time fee) $50.00, Client View Feature (one-time fee) $50.00.

Published Reviews of the Instrument in the Last 15 Years:

Jenkins, J. (2005). [The World of Work Inventory.] In R. A. Spies & B. S. Plake (Eds.), *The sixteenth mental measurements yearbook* (pp. 1172-1174). Lincoln, NE: Buros Center for Testing.

Sheehan, E. (2005). [The World of Work Inventory.] In R. A. Spies & B. S. Plake (Eds.), *The sixteenth mental measurements yearbook* (pp. 1174-1176). Lincoln, NE: Buros Center for Testing.

Sheehan, E. (2009). [World of Work Inventory.] In E. A. Whitfield, R. W. Feller, & C. Wood (Eds.), *A counselor's guide to career assessment instruments* (5th ed., pp. 223-228). Broken Arrow, OK: National Career Development Association.

WORLD OF WORK INVENTORY

Reviewed by:

Eugene P. Sheehan

College of Education and Behavioral Sciences
University of Northern Colorado

Description

According to its webpage, "The World of Work Inventory (WOWI) is a comprehensive career assessment instrument, which has been carefully constructed to help a client learn the most about him or herself in relation to the wide variety of occupations available" ("The World of Work Inventory," 2012). The WOWI collects information about the test taker's occupational interests, inclination to perform certain job tasks, aptitude in different vocational areas, and job temperament factors; compares this information against normative groups, and provides clients with a Profile Report, an Interpretive Report, and a Summary Report. These reports provide clients with information on their career interests, job-related temperament factors, aptitude for learning, and academic achievement. This information is matched to occupational characteristics and with a list of specific job recommendations provided in the Interpretive Report.

There are several parts to the WOWI. Test takers first indicate their choice, from a list of 12, of two general occupational areas in which they would like to work. Also from a list of 12, they select their two best-liked academic subjects.

The major and most time consuming parts of the WOWI are the Career Interest Activities (CIAs); Career Training Potentials (CTPs); and Job Satisfaction Indicators (JSIs). The CIAs section contains 136 items in which respondents specify whether or not they would like, dislike, or are neutral about performing a job-related activity (e.g., "planning TV commercials"; "determining how much a loan company should lend an applicant"; writing an article for the newspaper") for at least six months or more. The Interpretation Manual (Neidert & Ortman, 2001) states the "CIAs measure what job duties people like (and dislike), and how much they like (or dislike) engaging in them" (p. 44). These responses are linked to the respondent's interest in 17 Basic Occupational Areas, as identified by the U.S. Department of Labor: public service, the sciences, engineering and related, business relations, managerial, the arts, clerical, sales, service, primary outdoor, processing, machine work, bench work, structural work, mechanical/electrical work, graphic arts, and mining. The Profile Report provides a scale score on each of these occupational areas.

The CTPs section covers a range of areas that are either aptitude or achievement based. There are six subsections: verbal, numerical, mechanical/electrical, spatial-form, clerical, and abstractions. There are 98 total items on this portion of the inventory: 28 on the verbal and 14 on each of the others. Each of the subsections contains fairly standard types of items. For example, in the verbal section, there are items that cover vocabulary and word reasoning. The numerical section contains items that deal with addition, decimals, metrics, and series. Other items include cog direction and electrical diagramming. The Report Profile allows respondents to compare their performance on each area of the CTPs with others of the same age and others of the same education.

The JSI section measures temperament factors that relate to job satisfaction and work motivation. This scale contains 96 items to which respondents indicate if they would like, dislike, or are neutral about performing job-related tasks such as "keeping things orderly and systematic," "doing work involving fine accuracy," or "facing physical dangers." Responses to these items result in a scale report along 12 job satisfaction/temperament dimensions: versatile, adapt to repetitive work, adapt to performing under specific instructions, dominant, gregarious, isolative, influencing, self-controlled, valuative, objective, subjective, and rigorous.

Administration of the WOWI is quite straightforward. It can be administered via an assessment booklet or online. Last time I reviewed the WOWI, I took the online version of the inventory and found the webpage easy to navigate and the test directions easy to follow. Completion of the inventory took under an hour, with most of the time devoted to the CTPs section (respondents need time to solve the numerical reasoning and series questions). My 17-year old took the WOWI this time and had a similar experience as me: directions were easy to follow and it took about an hour to complete.

Respondents receive three WOWI reports: a Profile Report, an Interpretive Report, and a Summary Report. The Profile Report summarizes the areas in which the respondent has demonstrated high training potential (e.g., numerical and mechanical/electrical, self-selected occupational areas (e.g., mathematics and science) and best-liked subjects (e.g., social studies or history), high measured job satisfaction indicators (e.g., subjective), and high measured career interest activities (e.g., the sciences). As mentioned earlier, this report also permits respondents to compare their performance on the CTP section with others of the same age and others of the same education. Scaled score profiles of the Job Satisfaction Indicators and the Career Interest Activities round out this report.

The Interpretive Report is a narrative explanation of the respondent's inventory profile. It goes through all of the various scales on which the respondents had high scores and provides an outline of the meaning of each dimension and the application of that dimension to work situations. The interpretive report ends with a list of career recommendations. With the online report, each of the jobs listed comes with an active link to further information. Interestingly, in my case, several of the jobs on my list were jobs I had performed prior to entering the academy. In the case of my son, the results were very much in line with discussions he is having with his

World of Work Inventory

parents and with his school counselor. The areas in which he has expressed a strong vocational interest, science and engineering, were the areas identified on the WOWI. Additionally, he has shown academic strength in numeric and verbal reasoning—two of several areas in which he scored highly. His overall impression of the inventory and the results was that it made him think about jobs and parts of jobs. Additionally, the results were extraordinarily accurate for him.

As outlined on its webpage, the WOWI provides several advantages over its competitors. A primary advantage is that the WOWI is the only instrument that combines measures of career interests, work styles, and skills in a single measure. Thus, it is more comprehensive than similar assessments. Additionally, the WOWI has the advantage of linking directly to the Department of Labor Occupational Outlook Handbook and to the Department of Labor O*NET. Respondents can therefore quickly move from a review of their results to job exploration in a nationwide database.

Information on the webpage also has an international flavor. There are links to information about jobs and working in the United States, Australia, and Canada. For example, the webpage allows individuals to link to a page titled "Working in Canada," which permits an active search of available jobs in Canada. Similar resources are available for the United States and Australia.

The inventory and the three reports can provide a career counselor and a client with a good deal of information to provoke discussion about job-related strengths and weaknesses along with information about career interests, job temperament, and satisfaction factors as well as a list of potentially relevant jobs. In the hands of a competent counselor, this wealth of information could be put to good use assisting a client identify a career focus. There are many vocational inventories such as this and, in general, from a face validity perspective, the WOWI stands up well.

Technical Considerations

Two reviews in *The Mental Measurement Yearbook,* including one by this reviewer, have questioned some of the psychometric data supporting the WOWI (Jenkins, 2005; Sheehan, 2005). Both the manual and the website contain information on the development of the WOWI. The process of test development adhered to commonly accepted standards. Proper item-analysis procedures were followed, including the use of judges to assist in item selection.

The test authors indicate the WOWI is normed on a large sample of 169,436 individuals. However, as both Jenkins (2005) and Sheehan (2005) point out, no descriptive data beyond gender, age, and education are provided. As mentioned in the 2005 review, critical information such as occupation and norming procedures is not provided, making use of the scales questionable.

Reliability and validity data are detailed. Coefficient alphas are provided for each scale, and the data are favorable, with alphas for all scales above .81. For 28 of the 35 scales, alphas are .85 or higher. Data on test-retest reliabilities, taken at one-week, six-week, and two-year intervals, are also favorable. For example, the one-week reliabilities are .92 for the CIAs, .89 for the JSIs, and .70 for the VIPs.

As mentioned earlier, the face validity of the instrument is strong. To a respondent, it is very clearly a psychometric device to be used in career guidance. Measured validity data are positive, with inter-item correlations at appropriate levels of significance and in anticipated directions. Comparisons with other career counseling instruments reveal expected results.

General Utility and Evaluation

The WOWI is a comprehensive instrument designed to assist in the career guidance process. It provides information on a wide range of job-related variables that a respondent and counselor would find invaluable in the career counseling process. Test administration and scoring are easy and straightforward. The three reports provided are very helpful, with the interpretive report providing useful information in narrative format. Norming notwithstanding, the psychometric information on the WOWI indicates the instrument is constructed in a sound manner and has solid data to support its use as a career counseling tool.

References and Additional Resources

Jenkins, J. (2005). [The World of Work Inventory.] In R. A. Spies & B. S. Plake (Eds.), *The sixteenth mental measurements yearbook* (pp. 1172-1174). Lincoln, NE: Buros Center for Testing.

Neidert, G., & Ortman, N. (2001). *Interpretation manual for the World of Work Inventory.* Tempe, AZ: World of Work Inc.

Sheehan, E. (2005). [The World of Work Inventory.] In R. A. Spies & B. S. Plake (Eds.), *The sixteenth mental measurements yearbook* (pp. 1174-1176). Lincoln, NE: Buros Center for Testing.

Sheehan, E. (2009). [World of Work Inventory.] In E. A. Whitfield, R. W. Feller, & C. Wood (Eds.), *A counselor's guide to career assessment instruments* (5th ed., pp. 223-228). Broken Arrow, OK: National Career Development Association.

The World of Work Inventory. (2012). *WOWI homepage.* Retrieved from http://www.wowi.com/geninfo/intro/description.php

224

CHAPTER 12

INTEREST AND VALUES INVENTORIES

- Campbell Interest and Skill Survey

- Career Directions Inventory, Second Edition

- Career and Life Explorer, Third Edition

- Expanded Skills Confidence Inventory

- Hall Occupational Orientation Inventory, Fourth Edition

- Harrington-O'Shea Career Decision-Making System - Revised

- Jackson Vocational Interest Survey, Second Edition

- O*NET Interest Profiler and Computerized O*NET Interest Profiler

- O*NET Work Importance Profiler and Work Importance Locator

- Self-Directed Search, Fourth Edition, and Career Exploration

- Strong Interest Inventory and Skills Confidence Inventory

- Study of Values, Fourth Edition

- Values Preference Indicator

- Wide Range Interest and Occupation Test, Second Edition

CAMPBELL INTEREST AND SKILL SURVEY
David Campbell

Pearson Assessments

5601 Green Valley Drive
Bloomington, MN 55432
http://www.pearsonassessments.com

Target Population: Adolescents, young adults, and adults; age 15 and older.

Statement of the Purpose of the Instrument: The Campbell Interest and Skill Survey (CISS) helps assess an individual's interest in occupational areas and provide a comparison to people who are happily and successfully employed in those fields. In addition, the CISS adds parallel skill scales that present an estimate of the individual's confidence in his or her ability to perform various occupational activities.

Titles of Subtests, Scales, Scores Provided: Orientation Scales, which cover seven broad themes of occupational interests and skills; Basic Interest and Skill Scales, which are detailed subscales of the Orientation Scales; and Occupational Scales, which compare an individual's interest and skill patterns with those of workers in a range of occupations.

- Orientation Scales: Influencing, Organizing, Helping, Creating, Analyzing, Producing, and Adventuring.
- Basic Interest and Skill Scales: The Orientation Scales are divided into 25 categories, each with a parallel interest and skill scores.
    - Influencing: Leadership, Law/Politics, Public Speaking, Sales, Advertising/Marketing
    - Organizing: Supervision, Financial Services, Office Practices
    - Helping: Adult Development, Counseling, Child Development, Religious Activities, Medical Practice
    - Creating: Art/Design, Performing Arts, Writing, International Activities, Fashion, Culinary Arts
    - Analyzing: Mathematics, Science
    - Producing: Mechanical Crafts, Woodworking, Farming/Forestry, Plants/Gardens, Animal Care
    - Adventuring: Athletics/Physical Fitness, Military/Law Enforcement, Risks/Adventure
- Occupational Scales: There are 60 Occupational Scales that correspond with the Orientation Scales.

Forms and Levels Available, with Dates of Publication/Revision of Each: 1992.

Date of Most Recent Edition of Test Manual, User's Guide, Etc.: 1992.

Languages in Which Available: English and Spanish.

Time:

Actual Test Time: Approximately 25 minutes.

Total Administration Time: Approximately 25 to 35 minutes.

Norm Group(s) on Which Scores Are Based: The normative sample included 5,225 employed men and women representing a wide array of occupations and ethnic backgrounds.

Manner in Which Results are Reported for Individuals: Standard scores. There is a narrative report with an optional report summary.

Report Format/Content for Group Summaries: Not available.

Machine Scoring: 1-4 administrations: $17.20 per administration; 5-49 administrations: $13.15 per administration; 50-99 administrations: $12.65 per administration; 100-249 administration: $12.15 per administration. Additional discounts are available based on volume. Specially designed answer sheets may be mailed to Pearson Assessments for processing within 24 to 48 hours of receipt and returned via regular mail.

Hand Scoring: Not available.

Local Machine Scoring: Q Local scoring and reporting software required (available from Pearson Assessments).

System Requirements:

- Pentium II Processor
- 350 MHz
- 128 MB RAM
- 400 MB of free hard disk space
- Operating System—

Windows XP Professional, SP2	Windows XP Home, SP2
Windows NT Workstation 4.0 SP6a	Windows NT Server 4.0 SP6a
Windows NT Server 4.0 Enterprise SP6a	Windows 98SE
Windows 2000	Windows ME
Windows 2003, SP1	

Microsoft Desktop Edition (MSDE) 2000 sp3 installed with the Q Local installation. If you have a different version installed, you will have to upgrade to sp3 or sp3a

Computer Software Options Available: Standard administration online.

Cost of Materials: Due to possible price changes since publication date, be sure to check the publisher's website.

Specimen Set: Q Local or CISS Mail-In Starter Kit with Profile Reports (includes CISS manual, 3 CISS Career Planners, Interest/Skill Pattern worksheets, and 3 mail-in answer sheets with test items included, i.e., all the materials necessary to generate 3 reports using the mail-in scoring service): $69.55. The Q Local Starter Kit does not include the Q-Local software. CISS Main-In Profile Reports, Q Local CISS Answer Sheets, CISS Individual Profile Q Local Reports: pricing based on volume.

Counselee Materials: CISS Interest/Skill Pattern Worksheets (package of 50): $14.50; CISS Career Planner: $2.70 per unit for 250 or fewer units, volume discounts available.

Published Reviews of the Instrument in the Last 15 Years:

Pugh, R. C. (1998). [Campbell Interest and Skill Survey.] In J. C. Impara & B. S. Plake (Eds.), *The thirteenth mental measurements yearbook.* Lincoln, NE: Buros Center for Testing.

Roszkowski, M. J. (1998). [Campbell Interest and Skill Survey.] In J. C. Impara & B.S. Plake (Eds.), *The thirteenth mental measurements yearbook.* Lincoln, NE: Buros Center for Testing.

Severy, L. E. (2009). [Campbell Interest and Skill Survey.] In E. A. Whitfield, R. W. Feller, & C. Wood (Eds.), *A counselor's guide to career assessment instruments* (5th ed., pp. 235-242). Broken Arrow, OK: National Career Development Association.

CAMPBELL INTEREST AND SKILL SURVEY

Reviewed by:

Lisa E. Severy

Director of Career Services & Assistant Vice Chancellor of Student Affairs
University of Colorado at Boulder

Description

The Campbell Interest and Skill Survey (CISS) is one of three Campbell Development Surveys published by Pearson Assessments. The instrument helps individuals discover how their interests and perceived skill levels compare with the world of work (Campbell, 2002). The CISS was developed by Dr. David Campbell after his split with the publishers of the Strong-Campbell Interest Inventory in 1987. He first released the new instrument, including self-perception of skill, in 1989.

Campbell Interest and Skill Survey

The CISS contains 200 interest and 120 skill items and takes about 25 minutes to complete. Respondents are asked to rate their level of interest or skill on 6-point scales. Pairs of interest and skill scores are graphically reported in the results profile providing guidance as to where the user might find satisfaction and success in the world of work. The CISS also provides an Interest/Skill Pattern worksheet to expand the client's understanding by helping them to engage the results in future planning.

The CISS results include five sections: 7 Orientation Scales, 29 Basic Interest and Skill Scales, 58 Occupational Scales, 3 Special Scales, and Procedural Checks. To make the results easier to explain, the scoring scales are reported as *T* scores, normed so that the average of each scale is 50 with a standard deviation of 10 (Campbell, Hyne, & Nilsen, 1992).

The Orientation Scales reflect the interest content domain well established by theorists such as E.K. Strong and John Holland. Campbell believed that the titles for these categories were confusing to clients and sometimes rejected due to associated values, so he updated them for the new inventory (Campbell et al., 1992). He also expanded the original six interest categories by dividing the Realistic construct into two different categories (see Campbell, 2002). The Campbell Orientation Scales include the following:

Scale	Interests
Influencing (I)	Leadership, Law/Politics, Public Speaking, Sales, Advertising/Marketing
Organizing (O)	Supervision, Financial Services, Office Practices
Helping (H)	Adult Development, Counseling, Child Development, Religious Activities, Medical Practice
Creating (C)	Art/Design, Performing Arts, Writing, International Activities, Fashion, Culinary Arts
Analyzing (N)	Mathematics, Science
Producing (P)	Mechanical Crafts, Woodworking, Farming/Forestry, Plants/Gardens, Animal Care
Adventuring (A)	Athletics/Physical Fitness, Military/Law Enforcement, Risks/Adventure

Counselors familiar with John Holland's codes will recognize the similarities:

Holland's Codes	Campbell's Codes
Realistic	Adventuring & Producing
Investigative	Analyzing
Artistic	Creating
Social	Helping
Enterprising	Influencing
Conventional	Organizing

As with other interest inventories, the Orientation Scales on the CISS are reported in terms of a one-, two-, or three-letter code designed to reflect interest profiles. By comparing individual letter codes with occupational codes, clients can explore occupational areas where they are more likely to feel satisfied and confident (Campbell et al., 1992).

The Basic Interest and Skill Scales cover specific topic areas like law/politics, writing, mathematics, or animal care and are arranged according to their inter-correlations, with those having the most in common next to each other. The Occupational Scales represent 58 specific occupations like attorney, financial planner, realtor, or media executive to which individual scales are compared. The scales reflect a sample of workers from each occupation self-described as satisfied and successful. Therefore, an individual's score on an Occupational Scale signifies the degree of similarity between that individual's preferences and satisfied workers in a particular occupation (Campbell et al., 1992).

The CISS also provides measures for three Special Scales. These scales represent interest preferences and perceived skills in Academic Focus (intellectual, scientific, and literary activities), Extraversion (attraction to and confidence in outgoing activities), and Variety (the number of diverse tasks within an occupation). The Variety Scales are experimental and are, therefore, not graphically reported on the results profile (Campbell et al., 1992).

Finally, the Procedural Checks are reported to give the user the ability to detect problems in the test administration or processing. These include the Response Percentage Check (unusual patterns to responses), Inconsistency Check (correlations between similar items), and Omitted Items Check (how many items were skipped).

Clients are encourage to PURSUE areas that indicate both a High Interest and a High Skill confidence, DEVELOP any areas that indicate a High Interest but Low Skill confidence, EXPLORE possibilities in areas with Low Interest but High Skill confidence, and AVOID areas with both a Low Interest and Low Skill confidence.

The CISS is widely used by counselors helping clients seeking information about their occupations interests and skills, making educational or career plans, or for group activities such as team building (Campbell et al., 1992). The 13-page report that describes and explains the results is geared towards the client rather than the counselor, making the report easy to understand and interpret. After reviewing results in an individual session or within a group session, clients are encouraged to take the report home for further review. With both paper and online versions of the instrument, the CISS is simple to administer, take, and interpret.

It is important for both counselors and clients to understand that the skills assessment included in the CISS is not an actual assessment of skill but rather a rating of level of self-confidence in that skill. As such, the skill assessment may be more useful if considered a measure of self-efficacy related to a particular skill. Profiles that include low self-estimates of skill may be indicative of self-efficacy problems that should be explored further (Campbell et al., 1992).

When utilizing assessments based on RIASEC constructs, counselors should also be aware of significant differences between individual instruments. Savickas and Taber (2006) found that individuals responding to different inventories received significantly different RIASEC results. These differences were attributed to variations in test construction and the notion that different inventories measure different aspects of the RIASEC types. Counselors should attend to these differences when selecting appropriate inventories.

Technical Considerations

The CISS is referenced to a norm base of self-described *satisfied* and *successful* employees spread out over 58 occupations. The norm sample, collected in 1989, consisted of 1,790 women and 3,435 men, and was subsequently weighted to provide equal gender representation (Campbell et al., 1992). Unlike other similar inventories, the CISS compares individuals to the norm sample collectively rather than divided by gender. Practitioners should be aware that 7 of the 29 Basic Interest and Skill scales reflected a gender gap in terms of employment areas that they are attracted to and in which they feel confident (Campbell et al., 1992). Women scored higher on Child Development and Fashion, while men scored higher in Financial Services, Mechanical Crafts, Woodworking, Military/Law Enforcement, and Risk/Adventure. As this gender gap occurs in almost one-quarter of the Basic Scales, those interpreting results should examine these categories closely and be aware of ways in which an individual's interest and/or skill reports may be overemphasized or underemphasized due to gender. Some researchers, including Betz (1993) recommend that counselors use a combination of same-sex normed inventories and sex-balanced inventories (such as the CISS) in order to balance the gender influence on interest inventory results.

Campbell Interest and Skill Survey

The manual for the CISS includes reports on reliability and validity (Campbell et al., 1992). Campbell (2002) resisted the concept of *statistical significance* and, as such, focuses instead on measures of magnitude, consistency, and replication (Campbell et al., 1992). Excellent estimates of reliability and validity have also been reported by independent researchers (Hansen & Leuty, 2007; Rottinghaus, Larson, & Borgen, 2003).

As noted earlier, the Interest portion of the CISS is designed to measure the construct of interests also measured by numerous other instruments. Savickas, Taber, and Spokane (2002) examined whether a collection of interest inventories that claim to measure the same construct actually produce scores that correspond. As a popular and well-researched instrument, the CISS was one of the instruments included. Results indicated that the scales correlated moderately and demonstrated convergent and discriminant validity. In looking specifically at the CISS, however, Savickas et al. (2002) found that the CISS Adventure scale correlated significantly with the Social scale in two of the instruments and the Enterprising scale in two others. In other words, the Adventure scale seemed to have more in common with seemingly unrelated scales than with the Realistic scale as the CISS developers purport (Savickas et al., 2002). Similar problems were found with the Organizing scale. Thus, although five of the seven CISS Orientation Scales demonstrated validity in correlation with Holland's codes, the Adventuring and Organizing Scales did not (Savickas et al., 2002). While these discrepancies do not change the validity of the test itself, practitioners should be aware of these discrepancies when interpreting the CISS using Holland's constructs or when referring clients to subsequent materials such as the Holland Dictionary of Occupational Codes.

General Utility and Evaluation

The CISS is a widely-used and accepted measure of interest preferences and self-reported skills. Whether in the paper-and-pencil version or online application, it is easy to administer and easy for clients to engage. The generated Individual Profile Report provides both appropriate narrative explanation and graphic illustrations that make the results easy to understand. Both practically and historically, it is a well-built inventory with an established base of users. As with other career inventories, careful interpretation is necessary when reviewing the specific career titles as clients must understand those titles are representative of a diverse range of jobs. There is always some danger of clients taking these results too literally and selecting exact job titles based upon these results. In addition, because only about one third of the variance in interests can be attributed to self-efficacy (Betz & Rottinghaus, 2006), further research should explore other factors including external and contextual factors.

While careful attention has been paid to item bias and sensitivity to the issues of diversity with the CISS, this has mainly focused on the avoidance of potentially-offensive language. In that significant differences were found between genders within the norm group, it is reasonable to assume that some ethnic or racial gaps would also be found within some items. Lauver and Jones (1991) found ethnic and gender differences in various measures of self-efficacy, especially with Native American respondents. As not much information is readily available regarding the CISS and ethnicity directly, counselors must take extra care in interpreting results for clients whose backgrounds may be significantly different from the norm sample. Future research should focus on the demographics of the original norm sample as well as any significant differences in item responses.

References and Additional Resources

Betz, N. E. (1993). Issues in the use of ability and interest measures with women. *Journal of Career Assessment, 1,* 217-232.

Betz, N. E., & Rottinghaus, P. J. (2006). Current research on parallel measures of interests and confidence for basic dimensions of vocational activity. *Journal of Career Assessment, 14*(1), 56-76.

Campbell, D. P (2002). The history and development of the Campbell Interest and Skill Survey. *Journal of Career Assessment, 10*(2), 150-168.

Campbell, D. P., Hyne, S. A. & Nilsen, D. L. (1992). *Manual for the Campbell Interest and Skill Survey (CISS).* Minneapolis: NCS Pearson, Inc.

Hansen, J-I. C., & Leuty, M. E. (2007). Evidence of validity for the Skill Scale scores of the Campbell Interest and Skill Survey. *Journal of Vocational Behavior, 71,* 23-44.

Lauver, P. J., & Jones, R. M. (1991). Factors associated with perceived career options in American Indian, White, and Hispanic rural high school students. *Journal of Counseling Psychology, 38,* 159-166.

Rottinghaus, P. J., Larson, L. M., & Borgen, F. H. (2003). The relations of self-efficacy and interests: A meta-analysis of 60 samples. *Journal of Vocational Behavior, 62,* 221-236.

Savickas, M. L. & Taber, B. J. (2006). Individual differences in RIASEC profile similarity across five interest inventories. *Measurement and Evaluation in Counseling and Development, 38,* 203-210.

Savickas, M. L., Taber, B. J., & Spokane, A. R. (2002). Monograph: Convergent and discriminant validity of five interest inventories. *Journal of Vocational Behavior, 61,* 139-184.

CAREER DIRECTIONS INVENTORY, SECOND EDITION
Douglas N. Jackson

SIGMA Assessment Systems, Inc.
P.O. Box 610757
Port Huron, MI 48061-0757
http://www.sigmaassessmentsystems.com

Target Population: Adolescents, young adults, and adults. It is useful for the following settings: schools, colleges, university counseling services, employment offices and agencies, business and industry, vocational rehabilitation, adult counseling centers.

Statement of the Purpose of the Instrument: The Career Directions Inventory (CDI) is designed to facilitate educational and career exploration. It matches an individual's interests with related career and academic paths. The CDI is suitable for a wide spectrum of the population, not only for those who are headed for post-secondary school or a professional career.

Titles of Subtests, Scales, Scores Provided: The 15 Basic Interest Scales include the following: Administration, Assertive, Food Service, Health Service, Personal Service, Sales Systematic, Writing, Art, Clerical, Industrial Art, Outdoors, Persuasive, Science, and Teaching/Social Service.

Forms and Levels Available, with Dates of Publication/Revision of Each: 2003. The first edition was published in 1986.

Date of Most Recent Edition of Test Manual, User's Guide, Etc.: 2003 and republished in 2009 (LiveCareer, Ltd.).

Languages in Which Available: English and French.

Time:

    Actual Test Time: 30 minutes.

    Total Administration Time: 30 minutes, although the manual indicates 50 minutes is more useful.

Norm Group(s) on Which Scores Are Based: Norms are based on a sample of 2,320 individuals (1,169 men and 1,151 women). Separate norms are available for males and females and for six age groups (15 years or younger, 16 to 17 years, 18 to 19 years, 20 to 30 years, 31 to 40 years, and 41 or older).

Manner in Which Results Are Reported for Individuals: Percentiles. The CDI Extended Report includes a basic interest profile, a profile for seven general occupational themes, scores of similarity to 27 broad occupational clusters with narrative summaries of the three most similar clusters, sample occupations and a lengthy profile of similarity to more than 100 educational/occupational groups. Lists of sample occupations are included with the O*NET or NOC codes for each given occupation. The Extended Report is available online at www.SigmaTesting.com as well as through mail-in scoring and software scoring. The report can also be purchased for online scoring and administration at http://www.livecareer.com.

Report Format/Content for Group Summaries: Not available.

Machine Scoring: The cost to complete the CDI at the Sigma Testing website (http://www.sigmatesting.com/nformation/prices.htm) is $8.00. According to the technical manual, the CDI can also be completed at the LiveCareer website (http://www.livecareer.com/), which stated "comprehensive free results" for career tests, although the CDI was not mentioned specifically at the website. The CDI is used as part of a comprehensive career planning solution at LiveCareer.com, and is the exclusive career interest test used to deliver career related information.

The cost to score a package of 10 reports via the mail-in scoring service is $10.50. The report can be returned by email or regular mail. The time required for scoring is 48 hours, excluding mailing time.

Hand Scoring: Not available.

Local Machine Scoring: The cost is $150.00 for the software installation package, including 10 coupons. The cost to score an extended report using software coupons is $13.80 per report. Volume discounts are available.

Computer Software Options Available: Software administration; standard administration online at http://www.Live Career.com.

Cost of Materials: Due to possible price changes since publication date, be sure to check the publisher's website. CDI manual: $24.00.

Specimen Set: Examination kit (CDI manual [CD-ROM] and one mail-in extended report): $30.00.

Counselee Materials: Question-answer booklet or computer with Internet access, depending on the format used.

Published Reviews of the Instrument in the Last 15 Years:

Goldman, B. A. (2007). [Career Directions Inventory (2nd ed.).] In K. F. Geisinger, R. A. Spies, J. F. Carlson, & B. S. Plake (Eds.), *Seventeenth mental measurements yearbook*. Lincoln, NE: Buros Center for Testing.

Hughey, K. F., & Carlstrom, A. H. (2009). [Career Directions Inventory.] In E. A. Whitfield, R. W. Feller, & C. Wood (Eds.), *A counselor's guide to career assessment instruments* (5th ed., pp. 243-249). Broken Arrow, OK: National Career Development Association.

Maddux, C. D. (2007). [Career Directions Inventory (2nd ed.).] In K. F. Geisinger, R. A. Spies, J. F. Carlson, & B. S. Plake (Eds.), *Seventeenth mental measurements yearbook*. Lincoln, NE: Buros Center for Testing.

CAREER DIRECTIONS INVENTORY, SECOND EDITION

Reviewed by:

Aaron H. Carlstrom
Department of Psychology
University of Wisconsin-Parkside

Kenneth F. Hughey
Department of Special Education, Counseling, and Student Affairs
Kansas State University

Description

The Career Directions Inventory, Second Edition (CDI) is an interest inventory "designed to identify areas of greater or lesser interest from among a wide variety of occupations," and is for use in educational and career counseling, planning, and decision making, and for research where "vocational interests, job satisfaction, and personnel classification" is examined (Jackson, 2003/2009, p. 1). It consists of 100 forced-choice triads of statements associated with job-related activities. For each of the triads, respondents are to select both the activity most liked and the one least liked. The CDI items are written at a sixth-grade reading level (Jackson, 2003/2009).

Percentile scores are reported for three reference groups: males, females, and combined. Scores are provided for 15 Basic Interest Scales (BIS), seven General Occupational Themes (GOT), a comparison of one's scores to people in 27 job groups and educational programs (Job Clusters), and a profile showing the similarity of one's interests to those of students in 100 educational fields (Educational Specialty Groups). In addition, the following Administrative Indices are provided to assess inconsistent or problematic responding: Percentage of Scorable Responses, Infrequency Score, Incorrect Items, and Reliability Index. The BIS (e.g., Administration, Clerical, Science, Writing, Assertive) scores "are indicative of the degree to which respondents will be interested in activities within the domain of each of the named basic interests" (Jackson, 2003/2009, p. 38). The GOT are similar to Holland's (1997) types. Based on research for the CDI, a seventh theme, Serving, is included. Although the Holland type names are used (e.g., Realistic/Practical), the order of the themes, in the manual and the report, varies from Holland's work.

The amount of time required to administer the CDI is not prohibitive and is consistent with other interest inventories. Some individuals may not like the use of forced-choice triad items, and so it is important to inform them prior to their starting the CDI of this feature and the reason this format is used. The availability of both

A Counselor's Guide To Career Assessments Instruments

paper-and-pencil and computer administered formats allows counselors flexibility in administration. Also, the availability of online and computer software scoring allows for results to be quickly obtained.

According to Jackson (2003/2009), "[t]he CDI is appropriate for a very wide spectrum of the general population, not only those headed for a university education or a professional career" (p. 2). At the publisher's website, it is noted that the CDI can be used with high school, college, and university students, and adults. The CDI can be used in career exploration, planning, decision making, and counseling. The publisher's website highlights that it can be used with students in high school through university for the purposes of educational and career counseling, with adults who are making career transitions, and in corporate restructuring.

Technical Considerations

Jackson (2003/2009) stated that in standardizing the CDI a "broad representation from a wide geographic area, diverse specialty groups, and a wide sampling of educational institutions" (p. 77) was sought. To develop the "initial normative sample," 12,846 individuals (roughly equal numbers of males and females) were drawn from "several appropriate occupationally-oriented programs" (p. 77) that offered the different educational specialty groups identified. A subsample of 1,000 individuals (500 males, 500 females) was selected from the original group and used to develop the original norms for the first edition of the CDI. A new sample of 2320 individuals (1169 males, 1120 females), drawn from the United States and Canada, was used to develop the profiles for the current CDI. The new norms were presented in six age groups: 15 years and younger, 16-17 years, 18-19 years, 20-30 years, 31-40 years, and 41 years and older. No rationale was provided for the age groupings.

It is commendable that the new sample was drawn from both the United States and Canada and included age groupings. However, age (for the new norm group) and gender is the only demographic information provided. Other demographic information relevant to career development (e.g., race/ethnicity, socioeconomic status, and region beyond reporting that the new norm group was sampled from both the United States and Canada) was not reported. Based on the information presented in the manual, it would be challenging for counselors to assess the relevance of the norm sample for the individuals and groups with whom they work. Additionally, the ability to assess the representativeness of the norm sample to any external population is limited. This is a concern since CDI scores are presented as percentiles; without the ability to assess the relevance of the norm group, percentiles lack meaning.

Means and standard deviations for the 15 BIS are provided for the age groups for the new norms, and for gender and total sample for both the new and old norms. However, no mean comparison data are provided regarding potential differences by age, norm group, or gender.

Reliability and validity evidence does not appear to have been updated for the second edition of the CDI. Test-retest reliability and internal consistency reliability are reported for the various scales. Test-retest reliability coefficient ranges were the following: (a) .72 to .94, with a median coefficient of .87 for the BIS; (b) .86 to .95, with a median coefficient of .90 for the GOT; (c) .76 to .92, with a median coefficient of .88 for the Occupational Clusters; and (d) .67 to .96, with only 10 reliability coefficients falling below .80 for the Educational Specialty Groups. These reliability coefficients are satisfactory to good; however, the test-retest reliability is based on a sample of 70 high school students, with a time between sessions that averaged four weeks. Having test-retest reliability data representative of all groups targeted by the CDI would be helpful and informative.

Internal consistency reliability evidence is based on a sample of 1,000 individuals from the original norm sample. Internal consistency reliability coefficient ranges were the following: (a) .62 to .91 (median = .80) for the BIS; (b) .85 to .91 (median = .87) for the GOT; (c) .74 to .91 (median = .86) for the Occupational Clusters; and (d) .62 to .92, with only 8 reliability coefficients falling below .70 for the Educational Specialty Groups.

Jackson's (2003/2009) description of the construction of the CDI indicates techniques (e.g., factor analysis, item analysis) were used that are associated with building valid tests. From this description, it also appears that items of the BIS are relevant and representative. Furthermore, Jackson (2009) noted that the use of the forced-choice format removes a significant response bias associated with interest measures and, thus, contributes to increased discriminant validity.

Career Directions Inventory, Second Edition

Additional validity evidence for the CDI was assessed by comparing "people in general" (i.e., the 1,000 individuals from the original norm group) to individuals in different specialty groups (i.e., individuals in relevant specialty groups from the original sample of 12,846 not included in the 1000 person norm group). Comparisons were made between the groups on the distribution of scores of educational specialty group scales and cluster scales. For example, individuals in the Electrical Engineering Technology specialty group were compared with "people in general" on the Electrical Engineering Technology Scale and the Electronic/Technology Cluster Scale. A greater percentage of people in the Electrical Engineering Technology specialty group had higher scores on both of the scales than "people in general"; this appeared to be offered as concurrent validity evidence for those two scales. Additionally, a comparison of cumulative percentiles for the Electrical Engineering Technology Scale and Electronic/Technology Cluster Scale between "people in general" and persons in the Electrical Engineering Technology specialty group was provided. As predicted, the same score was associated with a lower cumulative percentage of individuals in the specialty group, which again demonstrated that the specialty group had greater interest in areas connected with their specialty than people not in their specialty group.

Validity evidence was not provided for every Educational Specialty Group or Occupational Cluster. Additionally, validity evidence was presented graphically and a descriptive narrative was also provided in pages 82-93 of the manual. Potential significance of group mean differences was not reported. No evaluation of concurrent validity with other interest inventories was reported in this version of the manual. Some concurrent validity evidence is provided in Shermer and MacDougall (2011).

General Utility and Evaluation

The CDI technical manual (Jackson, 2003/2009) is well-organized and useful. The five chapters cover descriptions of the general characteristics of the CDI, the administration procedures and scoring options, interpretation issues, the process and procedures of constructing the CDI, and the psychometric properties. For example, in the administration and scoring chapter, clear instructions for completing the paper-and-pencil form are provided, and general procedures for introducing individuals to career assessment are covered.

In the interpretation chapter, a sample report is available and five case studies are provided. The case studies address important issues in interest assessment, including career dissatisfaction, high school non-completion, and discrepancies between reported and inventoried interests; however, four of the case studies are of high school students and one is of an adult. It would be helpful to have case studies that reflect the full spectrum of individuals with whom the CDI is reported to be appropriate for use. The interpretation section also addresses difficult cases, such as individuals with no high or low scores, and discrepancies between interests and aptitudes. However, there is not a specific section that addresses diversity issues related to the use of interest inventory results, although the issue of gender-traditional occupations is addressed in one of the case studies.

Based on feedback from graduate students and colleagues who completed the CDI and our review of the CDI, we believe it can be useful in facilitating students' career exploration and planning. Thoughtful, professional interpretation and integration of the results are strongly recommended to maximize the usefulness of the CDI. The utility of the CDI for various groups may vary, depending on their career development and educational status.

In terms of the interpretation of the item format used (forced-choice triad), Jackson (2003/2009) noted that this has the advantage of preventing individuals from marking "like" to all items, which can occur with other interest inventories. The assumption, it seems, is that respondents are able to differentiate equally between the three options for each item. Jackson (2003/2009) stated, "Low scale scores on the CDI represent rejected activities" (p. 11), and added that these are likely activities that are disliked or detested. We concur with Sabers (1994) who stated, " A more accurate statement, because of the forced-choice nature of the task, is that these are relatively less attractive activities for the individual" (p. 153). From our perspective, taking into account both high and low CDI scores is important.

There are limitations to the information provided about the psychometric properties of the CDI with implications for interpretation of results. First, the description of the normative sample lacks clarity, which can lead to interpretive difficulties when using norm-referenced scores. Related to this point is the lack of a description of the racial/ethnic composition of the normative samples. Second, we concur with Goldman (2007) that "With the exception of new norms from which little technical data are compiled, the addition of four new job clusters,

A Counselor's Guide To Career Assessments Instruments

and the division of one job cluster into two, the second edition of the CDI and its accompanying manual appears to be identical to the first edition, which was published in 1986." Including a section in the manual that clarified the enhancements in the second edition of the CDI would have been helpful. Furthermore, we echo Sabers' (1994) comment that there is not a lack of validity data, but that the validity evidence is of poor quality. Also, Maddux (2007) noted that validity of the CDI "has not been satisfactorily established." Suggestions for future research with the CDI are presented in the chapter on psychometrics. We concur with Schermer and MacDougall (2011) that because there is little published research on the CDI, it is important that future research examine the relation between the CDI and other interest inventories; this could improve the validity evidence of the CDI.

An in-depth computerized extended report is available, which is 21 pages in length. There is also a two-page Counselor's Summary Report. The CDI report is presented in an organized, informative manner. We believe the applicability and relevance of CDI results for respondents' career and educational planning are enhanced with solid interpretations by knowledgeable counselors/professionals. Included are the CDI results relating to 15 BIS, seven GOT scales, and 27 Job Cluster scales. The extended report also includes the 100 Educational Specialty Group scales, and the Counselor's Summary Report also includes the Administrative Indices.

The CDI report also includes a list of resources (i.e., O*NET listings, Suggested Readings, Organizations, Activities) for three job clusters that most closely match respondents' interest pattern. The use of O*NET is commendable, and the Occupational Outlook Handbook was noted as a resource in the manual. Under the final set of activities intended to help students explore their career options, however, it would seem helpful to include the involvement of parents and school counselors in career and educational planning.

Jackson (2003/2009) stated, "Many jobs will combine the expression of two or more of these occupational themes" (p. 18; p. 4 of the sample CDI report); however, this idea does not seem to be developed for respondents' use with their results.

References and Additional Resources

Goldman, B. A. (2007). [Career Directions Inventory (2nd ed.).] In K. F. Geisinger, R. A. Spies, J. F. Carlson, & B. S. Plake (Eds.), *Seventeenth mental measurements yearbook.* Lincoln, NE: Buros Center for Testing.

Holland, J. L. (1997). *Making vocational choices: A theory of vocational personalities and work environments* (3rd ed.). Odessa, FL: Psychological Assessment Resources.

Hughey, K. F., & Carlstrom, A. H. (2009). [Career Directions Inventory.] In E. A. Whitfield, R. W. Feller, & C. Wood (Eds.), *A counselor's guide to career assessment instruments* (5th ed., pp. 243-249). Broken Arrow, OK: National Career Development Association.

Jackson, D. N. (2003/2009). *Career Directions Inventory technical manual.* Port Huron, MI: Sigma Assessment Systems; LiveCareer Ltd.

Maddux, C. D. (2007). [Career Directions Inventory (2nd ed.).] In K. F. Geisinger, R. A. Spies, J. F. Carlson, & B. S. Plake (Eds.), *Seventeenth mental measurements yearbook.* Lincoln, NE: Buros Center for Testing.

Sabers, D. L. (1994). [Career Directions Inventory.] In J. T. Kapes, M. Moran Mastie, & E. A. Whitfield (Eds.), *A counselor's guide to career assessment instruments* (2nd ed., pp. 151-155). Alexandria, VA: National Career Development Association.

Schermer, J. A., & MacDougall, R. (2011). The Jackson Career Explorer in relation to the Career Directions Inventory. *Journal of Career Assessment, 19,* 442-451.

238

CAREER AND LIFE EXPLORER, THIRD EDITION
Michael Farr

JIST Publishing

875 Montreal Way
St. Paul, MN 55102
http://jist.emcpublishingllc.com/page-jist/
educate@emcp.com

Target Population: Adolescents; middle and high school students.

Statement of the Purpose of the Instrument: The Career and Life Explorer (CLE) is designed to explore with students their career interests, values, and goals.

Titles of Subtests, Scales, Scores Provided: The CLE is an exploratory tool for personal growth, and there are no scales and scores. The CLE is a paper-and-pencil learning tool with open-ended, rank-ordered, and checklist items.

Forms and Levels Available, with Dates of Publication/Revision of Each: 2011.

Date of Most Recent Edition of Test Manual, User's Guide, Etc.: 2011.

Languages in Which Available: English only.

Time:

> **Actual Test Time:** Varies.

> **Total Administration Time:** 20-30 minutes, but can take longer depending on the the administration format (i.e., group versus individual; single versus multiple sessions).

Manner in Which Results Are Reported for Individuals: The CLE is a self-exploration tool to end with a career plan not scores. It may be self-guided, self-scored, and self-interpreted.

Report Format/Content for Group Summaries: Not available.

Machine Scoring: Not available.

Hand Scoring: Interpreted by counselee throughout the test-taking process itself.

Local Machine Scoring: Not available.

Computer Software Options Available: Not available.

Cost of Materials: Due to possible price changes since publication date, be sure to check the publisher's website.

> **Specimen Set:** $45.00 per 25 instruments, with a reduced rate for bulk purchases. The Administrator's Guide is available for download at no cost.

> **Counselee Materials:** 6 panel paper-and-pencil instruments (not reusable).

Published Reviews of the Instrument in the Last 15 Years: Not available.

CAREER AND LIFE EXPLORER, THIRD EDITION

Reviewed by:

Tara Hill

Department of Counseling and Human Services
Old Dominion University

Description

The third edition of the Career and Life Explorer (CLE; Farr & JIST Publishing, 2011) is a learning tool available for use with middle and high school students (Grades 6-10) to identify their career interests, values, and abilities. The purpose of this learning tool is to provide respondents with an avenue to examine the intersection of the influences of desires, skills, and career interests on possible career routes. The Administrator's Guide, available online as a free download, provides an overview of the instrument, theoretical basis, and information on techniques for administration. The CLE can be administered, scored, and interpreted by each user through a self-directed approach; includes clusters of career options with a variety of occupations that relate to those groups; encourages youth to think of important factors such as their values, educational attainment, and necessary skills that are part of the career decision making process; and provides an opportunity for students to begin making steps in long-term career planning.

The CLE is a career exploratory tool developed on several empirically sound evidenced-based theoretical research findings conducted by the U.S. Department of Labor (DOL), the Holland Typology, and Crystal's Career Planning. More specifically, the first two steps in the CLE are based on two career assessments: the O*NET Work Importance Locator and the O*NET Interest Profiler. Both of these DOL assessments were modified for usefulness with the CLE's targeted youth users (Farr & JIST Publishing, 2011). The Holland codes (Realistic, Investigative, Artistic, Social, Enterprising, and Conventional; Holland, 1959) are used in the CLE to help youth match their personality type with occupations. With respect to Crystal's Career Planning, John Crystal was a pioneer in career counseling and the first to apply a holistic approach to career planning by taking into consideration an individuals' skills, traits, and educational level among other characteristics. Steps 1 and 4 of the CLE utilize Crystal's approach and concepts such as skill identification and analysis.

The CLE may be completed individually or in a group in one or multiple sessions. Although the instrument can be completed in 20 to 30 minutes, various administration method options may require additional administration time. According to the Administrator's Guide, the instrument can also be used with adults for whom reading and comprehension may be a concern. The CLE is an attractive, colorful, tri-fold, six panel, paper-and-pencil learning tool with open-ended, rank-ordering, and checklist items. The instrument can be self-administered as the instructions are clear and very easy to follow.

The CLE involves five steps: *(1) Discover Your Career Clues, (2) Identify Your Interests, (3) Match Your Interests to Your Career, (4) Discover Your Ideal Job,* and *(5) Take the Next Step.* The first step, Discover Your Career Clues is designed to assist students with identifying factors that contribute to their potential career path. On the CLE the factors of personal heroes, work values, preferred pastimes and mastered skills, anticipated educational or training levels, and preferred working environment, policies, and activities are referred to as "clues" for consideration in the first step of career exploration and planning. The five clues are individually arranged in colorful boxes with open-ended and checklist items.

Identifying interests (Step 2) involves selecting 3 of the 6 descriptions of interest areas which are based on the Holland Codes. Each description includes a discussion of several qualities, preferred occupational activities, and two adjectives used to illustrate the characteristics of a person who shares that interest area. Next to each description is a listing of occupations for the particular interest area. In Step 3, students indicate the occupations that they find interesting, beginning with, but not limited to, the three interest areas identified in Step 2. In Step 4, all of the information is combined onto one colorful page in specific boxes. In the middle of these boxes is the statement, "Your ideal job includes as many of these things as possible!" (Farr & JIST Publications, 2011, p. 5). The final step of the CLE guides the student through creating a career action plan by posing four

240

reflective open-ended questions for further exploration regarding high school courses to take, hobbies or other extracurricular activities, and possible volunteer and summer jobs available for the student. A final question encourages students to list some things that can be done in the next few months to learn more about the jobs, training, and educational opportunities for the identified occupations of interest.

The CLE has been used in a number of school counseling career programs, although there is a dearth of published literature examining the clinical use of the CLE. The CLE has been specially identified for use as a career activity for middle school students by New York's Lakeshore School District Guidance Plan (Lakeshore School District's School Counseling Department, 2009). In addition to using a career portfolio, school counselors administer the CLE to middle school students to "relate their interests to possible careers for the future" (p. 27).

The CLE has also been used in an extracurricular and summer education program in Louisiana, the LA GEAR UP program (Beer, 2009). The LA GEAR UP program focuses on academics, behavior and leadership, college preparation and career exploration, and service to the school and community for middle and high school low-income students. Depending on the grade level of the student participant, other career activities (e.g., career portfolio, career exploration workbook) are introduced. Beer (2009) found that students who participated in the program had significantly higher grade point averages and scores on the English/Language Arts and Social Studies sections of the standardized graduation exit exam. Beer surmised that for the participants in the LA GEAR UP program, a combination of the cultural capital gained as a result of the positive peer influence regarding attaining a college education, a focus on career exploration, and attainment of higher GPAs and test scores lead to these students being more likely to enroll and be successful in postsecondary education. However, to date, no follow-up studies have been published to verify this assertion.

Further, in a study exploring the career development of ninth-grade girls with disabilities, Lusk and Cook (2009) reported using the CLE and other career-related activities (i.e., career portfolio, Self-Directed Search, worksheets, interviews with professionals, homework assignments, small group discussions). After eight sessions, Lusk and Cook found that program participants had "a much improved self-appraisal of their overall abilities in decision-making and career exploration" as compared to a control group (p. 151).

Although the above sources do not clearly document the method in which the CLE was used for each of the programs, the Administrator's Guide offers instructions and detailed interactive assignments and activity ideas as prompts for professionals. Whether the instrument is being used with one individual, a group, in one session or over the course of several meetings, the Guide provides examples of activities ranging from small group discussion, presentations, field visits, and action activities such as researching a particular occupation using the U.S. Department of Labor website, the O*NET classification system, and interviews with professionals. Included in the Guide is a worksheet for students to record information about potential occupations of interest. This worksheet can be very beneficial as an ongoing record of their research as students develop a portfolio. Additionally, counselors may break up and assign only particular portions of the CLE as dictated by time and content restraints.

Best practices dictate that counselors should be well versed on the tool and instrument prior to using it with clients and students. The Administrator's Guide suggests that for one session administration counselors should start with Step 2 and continue to Step 3, which are the Holland code descriptors and occupation groups. When limited in time, carefully crafted questions to assist an adolescent in reflecting on which grouping best describes him or her and accurately mirrors his or her interests may enhance the experience. However, utilizing the CLE in a group experience with adolescents allows deep thoughtful discussion. Group participants can be divided into small groups for each part of Step 1. Counselors can schedule a career discussion day. At this event professionals from each group (Step 2 category) will be invited to participate in a panel interview conducted by the students. Again, small group breakouts matching the student's interest with the professional from the specific grouping is another option. This may be particularly beneficial for agencies and schools that have social, policy, or budgetary restrictions limiting field trips or preventing excused absences for career development for students.

Technical Considerations

The CLE is an instrument that is used for individuals to develop personal insight and apply that information to a plan of action. Because of this, no information is available about a normative sample or reliability and

Career and Life Explorer, Third Edition

validity. While the author of the Administrator's Guide touts the CLE's face validity, stating that users of the instrument can easily recognize that the items are directly related to career exploration, face validity does not offer any psychometric confidence to administrators. The publishers do not purport to measure a construct or offer any prediction as to the future career path of respondents. Further, there is no information provided concerning reliability or a normative sample.

General Utility and Evaluation

The CLE is best used as an activity of career self-exploration or intervention to assist adolescent middle and high school students explore and process their career interests, values, and abilities. The CLE should not be used as a career test, assessment, or data collection instrument. However, with the use of quality counseling skills in individual or group settings, individuals responding to the CLE may gain fruitful personal insights and career knowledge, and establish future career-related goals based on the intersection of their interests, values, and abilities. The CLE is designed for youth; however, for those with difficulty learning or reading special assistance may be required. Although there is no statistical information on the use of this instrument with diverse populations a face validity assessment shows the instrument appears to be suitable for multicultural populations.

References and Additional Resources

Beer, G. S. (2009). *The impact of summer/academic year learning projects on the academic achievement of student participants.* Dissertation, Louisiana Tech University.

Farr, M. & JIST Publishing (2011). *Career and Life Explorer Administrator's Guide* (3rd ed.). Indianapolis, IN: JIST Publishing.

Holland, J. L. (1959). A theory of vocational choice. *Journal of Counseling Psychology, 6,* 35-45.

Lakeshore Central School District's School Counseling Department. (2009). *Lakeshore Central School District's comprehensive K-12 school counseling programs.* Retrieved from http://www.nyssca.org/docs/Lakeshore_School_District_Guidance_Plan.pdf

Lusk, S. L., & Cook, D. (2009). Enhancing career exploration, decision making and problem solving of adolescent girls with disabilities. *Journal of Vocational Rehabilitation, 31,* 145-153. doi: 10.3233/JVR-2009-0484

A Counselor's Guide To Career Assessments Instruments

Expanded Skills Confidence Inventory
Nancy Betz, Fred Borgen, and Lenore Harmon

Nancy Betz

The Ohio State University
240b Lazenby Hall
1827 Neil Avenue Mall
Columbus, OH 43210
614-292-4166
betz.3@osu.edu

Target Population: Adolescents, young adults, and adults; age 15 or older.

Statement of the Purpose of the Instrument: The Expanded Skills Confidence Inventory (ESCI) is designed to measure a client's perceived level of confidence in performing skills related to the six General Occupational Themes.

Titles of Subtests, Scales, Scores Provided: Levels of Skills Confidence by RIASEC Themes.

Forms and Levels Available, with Dates of Publication/Revision of Each: 2004

Date of Most Recent Edition of Test Manual, User's Guide, Etc.: Not available.

Languages in Which Available: English only.

Time:

　　Actual Test Time: Varies.

　　Total Administration Time: 20 minutes.

Manner in Which Results Are Reported for Individuals: Standard scores.

Report Format/Content for Group Summaries: Not available.

Machine Scoring: Not available.

Hand Scoring: Hand scored by counselor or counselee.

Local Machine Scoring: Not available.

Computer Software Options Available: Not available.

Cost of Materials: Contact Nancy Betz for purchase information: betz.3@osu.edu.

Published Reviews: Not available.

Expanded Skills Confidence Inventory
Reviewed by:
Jacqueline M. Swank

School of Human Development and Organizational Studies in Education
University of Florida

Description

The Expanded Skills Confidence Inventory (ESCI) was developed by Nancy Betz, Fred Borgen, and Lenore Harmon in 2003. This 186-item, paper-and-pencil self-report instrument is designed for adults and has been adapted to use with high school students (ESCI-HS; Betz & Wolfe, 2005). The ESCI is available by contacting the first author, Nancy Betz, at betz.3@osu.edu. There is no manual available; however, technical information is discussed within this review and described in greater detail within the resources listed at the end of this review.

Expanded Skills Confidence Inventory

The ESCI was created under the presupposition that both interest and self-efficacy (confidence) are needed in order to successfully choose a career within a specific domain. Betz and colleagues (Betz et al., 2003) wanted to "develop measures of self-efficacy or confidence with respect to basic dimensions of vocational activity analogous to the Basic Interest dimensions of the Strong Interest Inventory" (p. 79). The ESCI has 17 Basic Confidence Scales (BCSs) that correspond with changes in the workforce and that are applicable to various occupations (Betz et al., 2003). Additionally, the Skills Confidence Inventory (SCI; Betz, Borgen, & Harmon, 1996), which measures confidence regarding Holland's six occupational themes, is also embedded within the ESCI. Additional information about the SCI may be found in Jeffrey Jenkins' review of the Strong Interest Inventory (SII) and SCI later in this chapter.

The 17 BCSs include the following: using technology, mechanical, mathematics, science, creative production, writing, helping, teaching, cultural sensitivity, public speaking, sales, leadership, organizational management, data management, office services, teamwork, and project management. Directions instruct respondents to indicate their level of confidence in performing a task or completing a course using a 5-point Likert scale ranging from *no confidence at all* to *complete confidence*. The scoring key designates the items grouped within each of the 17 BCSs, and the items encompassed within the six Holland themes from the SCI. The scores are rank ordered and reflect the individual's confidence, and thus, possible willingness to attempt tasks, courses, and majors. Scores above 3.5 suggest a willingness to attempt the task or course. Thus, a person interpreting the test may suggest interventions to improve confidence levels when a high interest in an area is indicated, but confidence in that area is low. The ESCI measures confidence in career domains to assist with career decision making. Within the college environment, career resource centers and academic advisors may use the instrument to assist college students in making decisions about choosing a college major and occupation. Additionally, counselors may use the ESCI in career planning with adults at various stages in their life (e.g., a client who has the desire to pursue a different career but uncertain about the specific area). High school counselors can also use the adapted ESCI-HS to help high school students in the career decision-making process (e.g., course selection to prepare for technical training or college admission). Thus, the ESCI is useful in a variety of counseling settings to assist clients and students in making career-related decisions.

Technical Considerations

In developing the ESCI, Betz et al., (2003) created 250 items to combine with the 91 items used for developing the SCI. The new items were administered to 302 psychology students at two Midwestern universities. The authors then met to construct the 17 BCSs, selecting items to enhance scale homogeneity and validity, while reducing gender differences. They constructed the scales to contain 12-14 items, giving preference to items included within the SCI, with the goal of having 10 items in each final scale.

The experimental version of the assessment containing 194 of the 341 items was then given along with the SCI (containing 60 items) to two groups of introductory psychology undergraduate students at a large Midwestern university (N = 934). The first group (n = 627) included 346 females (55.2%) and 277 males (44.2%), with a mean age of 18.74. The reported racial/ethnic makeup was 80% White, 9% African American, 6% Asian American, 2% Latino/Hispanic, 1% Native American, and 1% multiracial. Regarding year in school, 80% reported being freshmen, 13% sophomores, 5% juniors, and 1.4% seniors. The second group (n = 320; 223 females [69.7%] and 97 males [30.3%]) had a mean age of 18.2. The race/ethnicity of this group was reported as 83% White, 7% African American, 3% Asian American, 3% Latino/Hispanic, and 0.3% Native American. After conducting factor analyses, the final scale contained 186 items and 17 BCSs, and included the six 10-item General Confidence Scores of the SCI.

The 186-item ESCI was then given to a sample of employed adults (N = 972) who had served as the norming group for the SII. Of the participants reporting demographic information, 600 (~62%) were female and 366 (~38.%) were male. Race/ethnicity was reported as 88% White, 3% multiracial, and 2% each for African American, Asian American, Pacific Islander, and Latino/Hispanic. Participants' occupations included primarily geographer (10%), computer scientist (9%), ESL instructor (9%), recreation therapist (8%), regional planner (8%), technical support specialist (7%), chiropractor (6%), administrative assistant (5%), editor (5%), computer systems administrator (3%), and firefighter (3%).

A Counselor's Guide To Career Assessments Instruments

Internal consistency reliabilities for the 17 BCSs were high overall with a median value of .90 in both samples (college students and employed adults). The coefficient α reliabilities for the college sample ranged from .84 to .94, and the reliabilities for the adult sample ranged from .80 to .94. Test-retest reliability was examined by Robinson and Betz (2004) among a sample of college students enrolled in an introductory psychology class ($N = 160$). The three-week test-retest mean reliability coefficient was .85 and the coefficients for the 17 BCSs ranged from .77 to .89, which represents acceptable values.

Construct validity was assessed by Betz et al. (2003) by conducting a factor analysis to explore the relationship between the 17 BCSs with the General Confidence (Holland) Themes. The correlations are too vast to discuss here in detail; however, the lowest and highest correlations were .12/-.04 and .95/.96, respectively, for college students/employed adults (Betz et al., 2003). Betz et al. noted that the correlations between the BCSs and Holland themes were rational conclusions and that, interestingly, the smallest and largest correlations were similar among both samples. The researchers also examined concurrent validity of the 17 BCSs for the eight largest occupational groups within the employed adult sample. The occupational groups were selected by having at least 50 participants, with at least 25% encompassing the less represented gender. In summarizing the concurrent validity findings, Betz et al. found large differences across the occupational groups with the value of λ overall as .14, accounting for 69% to 86% of the variance within occupations, which in comparing this predictive efficacy with prior probabilities implies greater prediction using the 17 BCSs.

Robinson and Betz (2004) further examined concurrent validity, using two samples of college students enrolled in an introductory psychology course ($N = 203$). The researchers explored the relationship between ESCI and Holland themes represented by choice of college major using the C-index (i.e., a measure of interest congruence based on Holland's code, which was developed by Brown and Gore [1994] to distinguish between differences in the person-environment congruence). The mean C-index was 10.1 for the first sample ($n = 134$) and 11.1 for the second sample ($n = 69$). These findings suggested evidence for confidence-choice fit based on both values exceeding the theoretical population parameter of 9.0.

Rottinghaus, Betz, and Borgen (2003) evaluated predictive validity to determine whether the BCSs of the ESCI could predict college students' ($N = 715$) choice of major and occupation. They found that the concurrent use of the BCSs of the ESCI and the BIS (Basic Interest Scales) of the SII lead to a better prediction than either set of scales used alone. When used together, the scales accounted for a total variance ranging from 60% (educational aspirations) to 96% (career plan clusters).

In summarizing the assessment of the psychometric properties of the ESCI, the normative group appears to be relatively current (within the last 10-12 years), representative of the population for which the instrument was designed for, and has an adequate sample size. Gender representation does not appear to be a concern; however, the vast majority of participants (at least 80%) in each sample were White/Caucasian. Additionally, the college sample in Betz et al. (2003) was obtained from a single university in the Midwest with all students encompassing those taking an introductory psychology course. The geographical location of the employed adult sample in Betz et al. (2003) is unknown. Therefore, future research may focus on examining the instrument with a sample representing a greater portion of diverse racial/ethnic groups (e.g., African American, Asian American, Latino/Hispanic, Native American) and representing various geographical regions. In regards to evidence of reliability and validity, the findings presented by Betz et al. (2003), Robinson and Betz (2004), and Rottinghaus et al. (2003) indicate strong evidence in both areas, supporting the utilization of the ESCI with college students and employed adults.

General Utility and Evaluation

There is no technical or administrative manual for the ESCI. However, a search in academic research databases yielded nine results regarding the examination or use of the ESCI in scholarly articles and dissertations, some of which are discussed in this review. Nevertheless, no information is provided regarding special populations or diversity considerations. Additionally, no reviews of the ESCI are provided within the *Mental Measurements Yearbook* database.

In summary, the ESCI is grounded in research and career decision-making models. Additionally, the instrument was developed using a vigorous process, which yielded evidence of strong reliability and validity for the

Expanded Skills Confidence Inventory

both the college student and employed adult samples encompassed within the norming group. The scholarly articles describe the development and use of the ESCI; however, a technical and administrative manual would promote accurate and appropriate use of the assessment. Furthermore, an expansion on the use of the ESCI with diverse populations would also be beneficial for appropriately using the instrument with these individuals. Nevertheless, in considering the information available regarding the development and use of the ESCI, it appears to be a useful, appropriate instrument for assessing self-efficacy (confidence) within vocational areas during the career decision-making process.

References and Additional Resources

Bertz, N. E., Borgen, F. H., & Harmon, L. W. (1996). *Skills Confidence Inventory.* Mountain View, CA: CPP, Inc.

Betz, N. E., Borgen, F. H., Rottinghaus, P., Paulsen, A., Robinson, C. H., & Harmon, L. W. (2003). The Expanded Skills Confidence Inventory: Measuring basic dimensions of vocational activity. *Journal of Vocational Behavior, 62,* 76-100. doi: 10.1016/S0001-8791(02)00034-9

Betz, N. E., & Wolfe, J. B. (2005). Measuring confidence for basic domains of vocational activity in high school students. *Journal of Career Assessment, 13,* 251-270. doi:10.1177/1069072705274951

Brown, S. D., & Gore, P. A. (1994). An evaluation of interest congruence indices: Distribution characteristics and measurement properties. *Journal of Vocational Behavior, 45,* 310-327. doi:10.1006/jvbe.1994.1038

Robinson, C. H., & Betz, N. E. (2004). Test-retest reliability and concurrent validity of the Expanded Skills Confidence Inventory. *Journal of Career Assessment, 12,* 407-422. doi:10.1177/1069072704266671

Rottinghaus, P. J., Betz, N. E., & Borgen, F. H. (2003). Validity of parallel measures of vocational interests and confidence. *Journal of Career Assessment, 11,* 355-378. doi:10.1177/1069072703255817

HALL OCCUPATIONAL ORIENTATION INVENTORY, FOURTH EDITION

Lacy G. Hall

Scholastic Testing Service, Inc.
480 Meyer Road
Bensenville, IL 60106-1617
http://www.ststesting.com

Target Population: Adolescents, young adults, and adults.

Statement of the Purpose of the Instrument: The purpose of the Hall Occupational Orientation Inventory (HALL) is to provide career, leisure, and lifestyle planning assistance. The HALL also provides a verbal picture of one's interests, work values, and needs for satisfaction in one's chosen career instead of prescribing what a person should choose as a career.

Titles of Subtests, Scales, Scores Provided: Provides a rating scale so that test takers can determine their fields of greatest interest from 22 different areas of interest, needs, and values.

Forms and Levels Available, with Dates of Publication/Revision of Each: Form II (2000) and Young Adult/College/Adult Form (2000).

Date of Most Recent Edition of Test Manual, User's Guide, Etc.: 2000.

Languages in Which Available: English only.

Time:

    Actual Test Time: Varies, although typically fewer than 45 minutes.

    Actual Administrative Time: Approximately 60 minutes.

Norm Group(s) on Which Scores Are Based: Not available.

Manner in Which Results Are Reported for Individuals: The HALL allows for interpretation based on reviewing the overall responses on 22 different scales, and then reviewing each sentence that was marked for the interests, needs, and work values. The verbal labels include areas such as need for security, risk, and relationships toward people, data, or things. Individuals take the inventory and mark on a self-marking, self-scored response sheet. Once the response sheet is complete, directions are provided to profile the interests, needs, and work values of the individual.

Report Format/Content for Group Summaries: Not available.

Machine Scoring: Not available.

Hand Scoring: Hand scored by counselee or counselor.

Local Machine Scoring: Not available.

Computer Software Options Available: Not available.

Cost of Materials: Due to possible price changes since publication date be sure to check the publisher's website. Inventory booklets (package of 20): $36.90 (Form II) or $41.30 (Young Adult/College/Adult Form); Response Sheets (package of 20): $25.60 (Form II) or $28.00 (Young Adult/College/Adult Form); Self-Interpretive Digests (package of 20): $108.35 (Form II) or $29.35 (Young Adult/College/Adult Form); and Professional Manual: $18.05 (Form II) or $20.10 (Young Adult/College/Adult Form). Additional items are available at the publisher's website.

    Specimen Set: Each set includes 1 Inventory Booklet, 1 Response Sheet, and 1 Self-Interpretive Digest.

    Counselee Materials: Inventory booklet, response sheets, and self-interpretive folder. *The Counselor/User's Manual* and *Choosing Your Way* are reusable.

Hall Occupational Orientation Inventory, Fourth Edition

Published Reviews of the Instrument in the Last 15 Years:

Dik, B., & Eldridge, B. (2009). [Hall Occupational Orientation Inventory.] In E. A. Whitfield, R. W. Feller, & C. Wood (Eds.), *A counselors' guide to career assessment instruments* (5th ed., pp. 257-261). Broken Arrow, OK: National Career Development Association.

Geisler, J. S. (2005). [Hall Occupational Orientation Inventory.] In R. A. Spies & B. S. Plake, Eds.), *The sixteenth mental measurements yearbook.* (pp. 425-429) Lincoln, NE: Buros Center for Testing.

Law, J. G. (2005). [Hall Occupational Orientation Inventory.] In R. A. Spies & B. S. Plake, Eds.), *The sixteenth mental measurements yearbook.* (pp. 427-428) Lincoln, NE: Buros Center for Testing.

HALL OCCUPATIONAL ORIENTATION INVENTORY, FOURTH EDITION

Reviewed by:

Bryan J. Dik

Department of Psychology
Colorado State University

Description

The Hall Occupational Orientation Inventory, Fourth Edition (Hall, 2000) a is a self-report instrument consisting of 150 items (for Form II) or 175 items (for the Young Adult/College/Adult Form). This review focuses on the latter form. According to the *Counselor/User's Manual*, the HALL, first published in 1968, "was designed to provide client and counselor with a self-administered, self-scored, and self-interpreted humanistic, nonnormative vocational counseling tool that would be an alternative to the trait-factor, computer scored, predictive vocational inventories that dominated vocational counseling at that time" (Hall, 2000b, p. 1).

Testing materials for the HALL include a reusable item booklet, a one-time use response sheet, a self-interpretive profile booklet to assist in scoring, a companion booklet *CHOOSING: YOUR WAY, A Supplementary Career Reader* (Hall, 2000c), designed to assist in self-interpretation of results, and a *Counselor/User's Manual*. All materials appear somewhat dated in appearance, but are sensibly organized and highly readable. The HALL reports scores for 35 homogenous scales arranged into five categories (scales in parentheses):

(1) Needs-Values (Creativity-Independence, Information-Knowledge, Belongingness, Security, Aspiration, Esteem, Self-Actualization, Personal Satisfaction, and Routine-Dependence), based on Anne Roe's theory of occupational choice and Abraham Maslow's personality-need theory;

(2) Career Interests (People-Social-Accommodating, Data-Information, Things-Physical, People-Business-Influencing, Ideas-Scientific, and Aesthetic-Arts);

(3) Abilities (same labels as the Career Interest scales), derived from a model of interests analogous to Holland's RIASEC types, but adapted by Hall from the 12 interest areas in the U.S. Department of Labor's 1979 *Guide for Occupational Exploration*;

(4) Job Characteristics (Geographic Location, Abilities, Monetary Compensation, Workplace, Coworkers, Time, Qualifications, and Risk), and

(5) Choice Styles (Subjective External Authority; Objective External Authority; Subjective Internal Authority; Shaping, Autonomy and Self-Empowerment; Interdependent; and Procrastination), derived from Hall's career choice model, which posits that decision-making progresses in stages that correspond loosely to those in Jean Piaget's and Lawrence Kohlberg's models of cognitive and moral development.

A variety of continuous and weighted response formats are used for items on the HALL. For Needs-Values, Career Interest, and Job Characteristics scales, item anchors are 4 = *Most Desirable*, 3 = *Desirable*,

2 = *Not Important,* 1 = *Undesirable,* and 0 = *Very Undesirable.* Ability scales use 4 = *Strong,* 3 = *Above Average,* 2 = *Average,* 1 = *Weak,* and Choice Style scales use 4 = *Very Like Me,* 2 = *Like Me,* 1 = *Not Like Me.* In the inventory booklet, these options are presented using single-letter abbreviations of the anchor descriptions (e.g., *Most Desirable* = M). These are converted to numeric values and summed to produce raw scores that are transferred to a self-interpreted profile sheet, which classifies raw scores as Low, Average, or High. This booklet also contains written interpretations for the 35 scales and urges respondents to use the *CHOOSING: YOUR WAY* booklet for further assistance in interpreting scores.

The HALL can be used in both individual and group counseling settings, although group procedures are described in much greater detail in the *Counselor/User's Manual.* Clients are encouraged to make use of self-interpretation tools on their own time, allowing group sessions to focus on in-depth application of scores. The *Manual* provides recommendations for using the HALL with various age groups, beginning with junior high students. With high school seniors and college students, the inventory is described as useful in assisting with the crystallization of life goals, the identification of major and career possibilities, and with building self-efficacy for various tasks in the career choice process. For adults considering a career change, counselors are encouraged to use the HALL as an aid in reexamining values, needs, interests, and other occupational concerns. Finally, Hall proposes that the non-threatening nature of the results presented on the HALL makes the inventory useful in teambuilding and conflict resolution interventions in organizations.

Technical Considerations

The HALL originated with a pool of more than 1,000 items, which was reduced by first retaining only those items that correlated higher with their own scale than any other scale, with a magnitude of at least $r = .55$. Items were then selected according to the extent to which they had "a singular and logical relationship to the one scale for which it was written" (Hall, 2000b, p. 5), and yielded a response distribution that approximated a normal curve. The HALL was designed to report raw scale scores for use in ideographic interpretation; thus, no normative data are available.

Evaluating evidence for reliability and validity of scale scores on the HALL is difficult, given the extremely limited scope of psychometric information reported in the *Manual.* A survey of 2,200 individuals for the purpose examining the item response distribution is reported, but no demographic data for the sample are cited and no reference is cited to help the reader gather more detailed evaluative information. Similarly, brief descriptions of results from surveys of 225 college students, 288 workers from various occupations, 75 professional counselors, and an unspecified number of college seniors were reported. These results were described as providing evidence of validity using traditional criteria (e.g., "comprehensiveness" or content validity, "relevancy" or predictive validity, and "occupational differences" or concurrent validity) and unconventional criteria (e.g., attitudes toward taking the inventory, evidence of appropriate use by practitioners, the latter of which, although interesting, is not useful for evaluating the psychometric support for the instrument). All descriptions of these studies lack critical information (e.g., sample characteristics, methods, statistics, publication references). Limited validity data are available in the form of correlations among Hall's interest types, which generally varied in expected directions based on their relative degrees of similarity. Finally, results from an experimental study of 160 college freshmen found that participants in a group counseling intervention incorporating the HALL reported a larger increase in levels of self-awareness than did participants in a group counseling intervention incorporating the Strong Vocational Interest Blank (SVIB), but no information about the study design, sample demographics, or effect size was reported. The author states that because the characteristics measured by the HALL are dynamic and continually changing, traditional benchmarks for assessing reliability are not relevant. Thus, reliability data reported in the *Manual* consists only of item-scale correlations for each of the inventory's 175 items. By design, these are all larger than .55. Unfortunately, psychometric information for the HALL is even more limited in sources other than the *Manual;* a literature search using PsycINFO indicated that no available research studies have used the HALL since 1980.

General Utility and Evaluation

In the 5th edition of *A Counselor's Guide to Career Assessment Instruments,* the review of the HALL (Eldridge, 2009) was generally unfavorable. This appraisal remains the same for the 6th edition. Some users may find the HALL a useful vehicle for conversation with clients, and the inventory's basis in a humanistic career-choice model makes it somewhat unique. Yet, the HALL continues to suffer from the considerable limitations identified in earlier reviews. Most notably, very little data are reported from the scale development efforts, and evidence supporting the reliability and validity of scale scores is extremely limited. The test author reports that the HALL is not subject to the standards of traditional reliability criteria because the inventory measures dynamic personality variables that are constantly changing. However, strong evidence exists to suggest a high level of stability in at least some of the constructs (e.g., vocational interests) measured by the HALL. The test author reiterates at several points in the *Manual* that the inventory is designed for exploration, not prediction, yet when assessment information is used to inform career decisions that potentially have long-term implications, evidence for predictive validity always is relevant. The nonnormative, nonpredictive model on which the HALL was based is described by the author as a "new psychometric paradigm" that "has perhaps become a preeminent standard used throughout the United States and numerous foreign countries" (Hall, 2000b, p. xi). I am aware of no evidence that supports this claim.

References and Additional Resources

Dik, B., & Eldridge, B. (2009). [Hall Occupational Orientation Inventory.] In E. A. Whitfield, R. W. Feller, & C. Wood (Eds.), *A counselors' guide to career assessment instruments* (5th ed., pp. 257-261). Broken Arrow, OK: National Career Development Association.

Eldridge, B. (2009). [Hall Occupational Orientation Inventory.] In E. A. Whitfield, R. W. Feller, & C. Wood (Eds.), *A counselors' guide to career assessment instruments* (5th ed., pp. 257-261). Broken Arrow, OK: National Career Development Association.

Hall, L. G. (2000a). *Hall Occupational Orientation Inventory* (4th ed.). Bensenville, IL: Scholastic Testing Service.

Hall, L. G. (2000b). *Counselor/user's manual for the HALL Occupational Orientation Inventory* (4th ed.). Bensenville, IL: Scholastic Testing Service.

Hall, L. G. (2000c). *CHOOSING: YOUR WAY, A supplementary career reader for the HALL Occupational Orientation Inventory* (4th ed.). Bensenville, IL: Scholastic Testing Service.

Geisler, J. S. (2005) [Hall Occupational Orientation Inventory]. In R. A. Spies & B. S. Plake (Eds.), *The sixteenth mental measurements yearbook* (pp. 425-427). Lincoln, NE: Buros Center for Testing.

Law, J. G. (2005). [Hall Occupational Orientation Inventory]. In R. A. Spies & B. S. Plake (Eds.), *The sixteenth mental measurements yearbook* (pp. 427-428). Lincoln, NE: Buros Center for Testing.

Scholastic Testing Service, Inc. website: http://www.ststesting.com/h04a.html

Author Note: Brandy M. Eldridge, University of New Mexico, contributed to the review of this instrument in the fifth edition of the *A Counselor's Guide to Career Assessment Instruments*. Portions of her work have been retained in this review.

HARRINGTON-O'SHEA CAREER DECISION MAKING SYSTEM – REVISED

Arthur J. O'Shea and Rich Feller

Pearson Assessments

5601 Green Valley Drive
Bloomington, MN 55437
http://www.pearsonassessments.com

Target Population: Adolescents, young adults, and adults.

Statement of the Purpose of the Instrument: The Harrington-O'Shea Career Decision-Making System-Revised (CDM-R) is used to assist career planners identify occupational interests, values, and abilities, and match these dimensions to career options.

Titles of Subtests, Scales, Scores Provided: Level 1 identifies career interest areas (Crafts, Scientific, The Arts, Social, Business, Office Operations) as organized into 18 career clusters. Level 2 includes five categories: career clusters, school subjects, work values, abilities, and future plans.

Forms and Date of Publication: CDM-R Level 1 (Grades 7 through 10; lower reading levels), 2000; CDM-R Level 2 (senior high school through adult), 2000; CDM-R Internet, 2008.

Date of Most Recent Test Manual, Test Booklets, etc.: 2000.

Languages in Which Available: English and Spanish.

Time:

Actual Test Time: Level 1: Fewer than 30 minutes; Level 2: 20-40 minutes.

Total Administration Time: Level 1: Fewer than 30 minutes; Level 2: 20-40 minutes.

Norm Group(s) on Which Scores Are Based: Students in high schools, junior colleges, vocational schools and adults in work settings (manufacturing, financial services, fast food services, oil drilling, truck assembly, highway/construction).

Manner in Which Results Are Reported for Individuals: For Level 1, job charts for the six CDM-R career interest areas that are organized into 18 career clusters are included; Level 2 provides two high scores in the six interest areas to suggest three or four relevant career clusters for exploration.

Report Format/Content for Group Summaries: Not available.

Cost of Materials: Due to possible price changes since publication date, be sure to check the publisher's website. CDM 2000 Manual: $37.30; CDM 2000 Audiocassette: $19.70; and CDM DVD: Tour of Your Tomorrow (3rd edition): $125.00.

Specimen Set: None.

Counselee Materials: Level I Booklets – hand-scored edition (English and Spanish): (25 booklets per package): 1-3 pkgs $71.05; 4-18 pkgs $67.95; 19+ pks $64.30; Level 2 Booklet and Interpretive Folder (25 per pkg): 1-3 pkgs $71.05; 4-18 pkgs $67.95; 19+ pkgs $64.30. CDM Level 1 Classroom Set includes CDM Level 1 Booklets (25); BCES Workbooks (25), Teacher's Guide, and Tour of Your Tomorrow Video Series $480.00. CDM Level 2 Classroom Set includes CDM Level 2 Booklet and Instruction Folders (25), CES Workbooks (25), Teacher's Guide, and Tour of Your Tomorrow Video Series $480.00. Pricing is the same for Spanish Editions of Level I and Level II Booklets. CDM Internet Vouchers: 1-99 administrations ($4.95 per administration); 100-499 administrations ($2.45 per administration); 500+ ($1.99 per administration).

Published Reviews of the Instrument in the Last 15 Years:

Campbell, V. L., & Raiff, G. W. (2001). [Harrington-O'Shea Career Decision-Making System, Revised.] In J. T. Kapes & E. A. Whitfield (Eds.), *A counselor's guide to career assessment instruments* (4th ed., pp. 262-267). Columbus, OH: National Career Development Association.

Campbell, V. L., & Raiff, G. W. (2009). [Harrington-O'Shea Career Decision-Making System Revised.] In E. A. Whitfield, R. W. Feller, & C. Wood (Eds.), *A counselor's guide to career assessment instruments* (5th ed., pp. 262-267). Broken Arrow, OK: National Career Development Association.

Kelly, K. R. (2005). [Harrington-O'Shea Career Decision-Making System Revised.] In R. A. Spies & B. S. Plake (Eds.), *Sixteenth mental measurements yearbook.* Lincoln, NE: Buros Center for Testing.

Pope, M. L. (2005). [Harrington-O'Shea Career Decision-Making System Revised.] In R. A. Spies & B. S. Plake (Eds.), *Sixteenth mental measurements yearbook.* Lincoln, NE: Buros Center for Testing.

Harrington-O'Shea Career Decision Making System-Revised

Reviewed by:

Vicki L. Campbell

QuaVaundra A. Perry

Department of Psychology

University of North Texas

Description

The 2000 Career Decision-Making System-Revised (CDM-R) guides individuals towards effective career decision making by surveying "not only interests, but also stated career choices, school subjects, work values, abilities, and future training plans" (Harrington & O'Shea, 2000, p. 1). The interest survey is based on John Holland's theory of career choice, and provides six interest areas (Crafts, Scientific, The Arts, Social, Business, Office Operations) that correspond with Holland's six personality types (Realistic, Investigative, Artistic, Social, Enterprising, Conventional).

The CDM-R is a valuable tool for junior high and high school students, individuals planning to enter or reenter the workplace, or those seeking a career change. Level 1 introduces younger students (Grades 7 through 10) or individuals with lower reading levels (Grade 4) to the career exploration process. The Level 1 booklet is colorful with simple directions for answering the 96 interest items. Scoring and interpretation are conveniently included in the survey booklet.

Level 2 assists high school individuals and adults in deciding on a college major or selecting career training or occupations. The Level 2 booklet has participants select preferences from lists in five categories: career clusters, school subjects, work values, abilities, and future plans. Users then complete a 120-item gender neutral interest survey that is scored within the booklet. Administration time for Level 1 is 20 minutes and for Level 2 approximately 30 to 45 minutes. The CDM-R may be administered in both individual and group settings.

The CDM Internet is a new option developed in 2008 for individuals age 12 and older (O'Shea & Feller, 2008). Users complete the 120-item interest survey online in 20 to 25 minutes and receive a summary profile and interpretive report. A bonus of this version is that each job in the interpretive report links to an occupational profile with a job description, required tasks and skills, necessary education and training, wages, occupational outlook, and a list of similar jobs. The CDM Internet offers flexibility in that it may be administered at school, home, or wherever the Internet is available. It adds convenience since users may print their interpretive report or log-in to review their results as often as they like.

The CDM-R provides many options for school counselors, career counselors, or teachers to assist students and adults with the career development process. Interest survey results provide individuals with their top three career clusters for further exploration. The Level 1 summary page and the Level 2 interpretive folder guide users through steps illustrating the multiple factors important in arriving at a career decision. The materials provide

A COUNSELOR'S GUIDE TO CAREER ASSESSMENTS INSTRUMENTS

a large amount of information about jobs in each career cluster including a number-letter code that indicates occupational outlook and required education and training with biennial updates. The interpretive folder directs users to resources such as the video series, *Tour of Your Tomorrow,* and the Occupational Outlook Handbook. Both the CDM Internet and http://www.CDMCareerZone.com link to additional career planning resources (e.g., frequently asked questions, finding a college at the College Board site, resume-writing skills, job interview tips). Although the CDMCareerZone.com site says "Locate career opportunities near you," only the CDM Internet had links to this option at the time of this review.

Although the CDM-R can be used alone, it may be especially useful as part of a career development curriculum. The Career Exploration System (CES; Stone & McCloskey, 1993a, 1993b) provides a curriculum that facilitates career exploration, planning, and decision making for individuals who are at least 14 years old or on a sixth-grade reading level. A Beginning Career Exploration System (BCES) is available for younger participants or individuals with lower reading levels. The CES is suited for use in a classroom setting or workshop format, and may be implemented by high school teachers, adult education teachers, and career counselors. Leaders are given a step-by-step guide on how to administer and interpret all levels and formats of the CDM-R. The manual and CES leader's guide include case studies and helpful suggestions for complex issues such as working with individuals with unrealistic career goals or who lack confidence, and maintaining awareness of possible gender stereotyping. Counselors may also educate parents/guardians about the CDM-R so that they may use the interpretive report to generate effective career conversations with their children.

Technical Considerations

The majority of information about psychometric properties of the CDM-R used the 1981 and 1991 editions of the CDM-R. In the 1981 edition, normative data for Level 1 was gathered from 9,650 students in 7th through 12th grade. Level 2 was normed on college students and adults in government training programs. Levels 1 and 2 of the 1991 edition of the CDM-R were normed on junior high and high school students. The manual provides percentile ranks for all standardization samples. However, the authors recommend the use of raw scores, citing ease of score interpretation and reduced distortion from gender-specific norms (Harrington & O'Shea, 2000).

The CDM-R has excellent internal consistency (α = .90 for Level 1; α = .93 for Level 2). The Spanish edition of the CDM-R also demonstrated good internal consistency (α = .85 to .89; median .87). The only test-retest reliability was gathered for Level 1 in a group of 45 unemployed adults one month after the initial administration. Coefficients ranged from .74 to .87 with a median of .79 (Harrington & O'Shea, 2000). The stability of self-reports was assessed for high school and first-year college students. Percentages of agreement show general consistency over a five-month period. The current version of the CDM-R relies heavily on psychometric data from the CDM, and analyses support the equivalence of forms.

Evidence for the validity of the CDM-R is also based on the original instrument. Studies offer evidence of construct validity for the English and Spanish versions, showing expected correlations between the interest scales of the CDM and Holland's six personality types (Harrington & O'Shea, 2000). A study comparing CDM codes and the code found in the Dictionary of Holland Occupational Codes found a close match for 2,330 individuals representing 53 occupational groups. Another indicated a close match between CDM code and current academic major for students in vocational and college settings (Harrington & O'Shea, 2000; Kelly, 2005). CDM scores in Grade 9 were found to be good predictors of students' occupational preferences in Grade 12 (Harrington & O'Shea, 2000). Additional evidence of predictive validity comes from individuals who completed the CDM in 1986 and were contacted 20 years later (Harrington, 2006). Hit rates indicated significant agreement between individuals' current occupation and their original CDM interest code.

A recent equivalency study compared the CDM Internet with the hand-scored edition of the CDM-R (Level 2) (Carlson, 2011). Four hundred thirty-four high school students (9th and 10th grade) took both versions. Overall, this study suggests that both versions will produce comparable outcomes, with the greatest similarity for post-secondary plans, interest scores, and career clusters (Carlson, 2011).

General Utility and Evaluation

In summary, the CDM-R is a comprehensive career exploration, planning, and decision-making system that offers several benefits. It is an easy and attractive method of exposing individuals to the world of work and psychometric properties are comparable to other interest inventories. The system has been developed and updated with attention to gender and minority opportunities, and the *Tour of Tomorrow* DVD focuses on challenging gender stereotypes. The technical manual and CES Leader's Guide are well-written and offer teachers and counselors excellent information on implementing a career development program. Because the CDM-R is a system for career exploration, not simply an interest inventory, it teaches concepts and skills to help users make informed career decisions. O'Shea and Harrington (2003) illustrated the utility of the CDM-R for developing many career development competencies established by the National Standards for School Counseling Programs.

The main criticism of the CDM-R is the limited research supporting the system's goals of teaching the components of career development and encouraging career exploration, although that is not unique to this measure. Previous reviews of the CDM-R cite the lack of evidence for "exploration validity" (Campbell & Raiff, 2001) or consequential validity (Kelly, 2005). Although the CDM-R is described as an intervention for career development used by "millions of people to make successful career choices" (Career Planning Associates, Inc., 2008), more information about the effects of using the system would be helpful. The instrument was normed with a variety of cultural and socioeconomic status groups; however, the applicability and impact on current groups from diverse cultures and backgrounds remains unclear.

References and Additional Resources

Campbell, V. L., & Raiff, G. W. (2001). [Harrington-O'Shea Career Decision-Making System, Revised.] In J. T. Kapes & E. A. Whitfield (Eds.), *A counselor's guide to career assessment instruments* (4th ed., pp. 262-267). Columbus, OH: National Career Development Association.

Campbell, V. L., & Raiff, G. W. (2009). [Harrington-O'Shea Career Decision-Making System Revised.] In E. A. Whitfield, R. W. Feller, & C. Wood (Eds.), *A counselor's guide to career assessment instruments* (5th ed., pp. 262-267). Broken Arrow, OK: National Career Development Association.

Career Planning Associates, Inc. (2008). *CDM Internet.* Retrieved from http://www.cdminternet.com

Carlson, L. A. (2011). *Technical report for exploration of the psychometric equivalence of the hand-scored version and the Internet version of the Career Decision-Making System Revised, Level 2.* Needham, MA: Career Planning Associates.

Harrington, T. F. (2006). A 20-year follow-up of the Harrington-O'Shea Career Decision-Making System. [Special issue]. *Measurement and Evaluation in Counseling and Development, 38*(4), 198-202.

Harrington, T. F., & O'Shea, A. J. (2000). *The Harrington-O'Shea Career Decision-Making System-Revised Manual.* Circle Pines, MN: American Guidance Service.

Kelly, K. R. (2005). [Harrington-O'Shea Career Decision-Making System Revised.] In R. A. Spies & B. S. Plake (Eds.), *Sixteenth mental measurements yearbook.* Lincoln, NE: Buros Center for Testing.

O'Shea, A. & Feller, R. (2008). *The Harrington-O'Shea Career Decision Making System Revised Internet Version.* Minneapolis, MN: Pearson.

O'Shea, A. J., & Harrington, T. F. (2003). Using the Career Decision-Making System-Revised to enhance students' career development. [Special issue]. *Professional School Counseling, 6*(4), 280-286.

Pope, M. L. (2005). [Harrington-O'Shea Career Decision-Making System Revised.] In R. A. Spies & B. S. Plake (Eds.), *Sixteenth annual mental measurements yearbook.* Lincoln, NE: Buros Center for Testing.

Stone, W., & McCloskey, L. (1993a). *Beginning career exploration system.* Circle Pines, MN: American Guidance Service.

Stone, W., & McCloskey, L. (1993b). *Career exploration system.* Circle Pines, MN: American Guidance Service.

A COUNSELOR'S GUIDE TO CAREER ASSESSMENTS INSTRUMENTS

JACKSON VOCATIONAL INTEREST SURVEY, SECOND EDITION

Douglas N. Jackson

SIGMA Assessment Systems, Inc.

P.O. Box 610984
Port Huron, MI 48061-0984
http://www.SigmaAssessmentSystems.com

Target Population: Adolescents, young adults, and adults; age 14 and older. Useful in schools, colleges, university counseling services, employment offices and agencies, business and industry, vocational rehabilitation, and adult counseling centers.

Statement of the Purpose of the Instrument: The Jackson Vocational Interest Survey (JVIS) was developed to create an efficient hand or machine-scorable vocational interest measuring device to appraise the interests of males and females along a common set of dimensions. Aid in vocational counseling and decision making. The format and scales for the JVIS were designed to combine an optimal amount of information relevant to vocational interests with ease of interpretation.

Titles of Subtests, Scales, Scores Provided: There are 34 scales for the JVIS:

The Arts
1. Creative Arts
2. Performing Arts

Science and Mathematics

3. Mathematics
4. Physical Science
5. Engineering
6. Life Science
7. Social Science

Practical, Outdoor Activities
8. Adventure
9. Nature-Agriculture
10. Skilled Trades

Service Activities
11. Personal Service
12. Family Activity

Medicine and Health
13. Medical Service

Interpersonal and Job-Related Work Styles
14. Dominant Leadership
15. Job Security
16. Stamina
17. Accountability

Teaching and Social Welfare Activities
18. Teaching
19. Social Service
20. Elementary Education

Business, Administrative, and Related Activities
21. Finance
22. Business
23. Office Work
24. Sales
25. Supervision

Legal, Professional, Persuasive Work Roles
26. Human Relations Management
27. Law
28. Professional Advising

Literary, Academic
29. Author Journalism
30. Academic Achievement
31. Technical Writing

Work Styles Related to Job Activities
32. Independence
33. Planfulness
34. Interpersonal Confidence

Forms and Levels Available, with Dates of Publication/Revision of Each: 1999.

Date of Most Recent Edition of Test Manual, User's Guide, Etc.: 1999.

Languages in Which Available: English, French, and Spanish.

Time:

Actual Test Time: 45 minutes.

Total Administration Time: 55 minutes.

Norm Group(s) on Which Scores Are Based: The most recent normative sample of JVIS profiles was collected in 1999. These consist of the responses of 1,750 males and 1,750 females from Canada and the U.S. This sample of 3,500 individuals includes the responses of 2380 secondary school students (1,190 males and 1,190 females) and 1,120 adults (560 males and 560 females). The adult sample consists of university and college students as well as adults seeking career interest assessment. The total sample of 3500 profiles is used to generate the JVIS Extended and Basic Reports as well as the profile sheets for hand scoring.

Manner in Which Results Are Reported for Individuals: Raw scores and percentiles are provided. The JVIS Basic Report contains the basic interest scales profile and data similar to the Extended Report but with preprinted interpretative information rather than the personalized narrative summaries. The JVIS Extended Report includes the basic interest profile, a profile for 10 general occupational themes, a profile of similarity to 17 educational major field clusters, a ranking of 32 occupational group clusters, validity scales, an academic satisfaction score and other information. A narrative summary of the 3 highest-ranked educational and occupational clusters is particularly useful. The Basic Report is only available through mail-in scoring. The Extended Reports are available online at http://www.SigmaTesting.com or http://www.JVIS.com, as well as through mail-in scoring.

Report Format/Content for Group Summaries: Not available.

Machine Scoring: JVIS Extended Reports and Basic Reports are available from a mail-in answer sheet and laser printed report. There is a 48-hour turnaround time (excluding mail time).

Hand Scoring: Hand scored by clerk or counselor in approximately 10 minutes.

Local Machine Scoring: Not available.

Computer Software Options Available: Computerized adaptive administration; standard administration online.

Cost of Materials: Due to possible price changes since publication date, be sure to check the publisher's website.

Specimen Set: JVIS Examination Kit includes manual on CD, JVIS Applications Handbook, JVIS Occupations Guide, machine scorable answer sheet for Extended Report, reusable test booklet, hand-scorable answer sheet, profile sheet, and website password, $95.00.

A COUNSELOR'S GUIDE TO CAREER ASSESSMENTS INSTRUMENTS

Additional Comments of Interest to Users: Marc Verhoeve, author of the JVIS Applications Handbook, offers a free, 90-minute teleconference discussing the best practices in counseling and how to get the most out of the JVIS. Upcoming dates are listed on the website.

Counselee Materials: Answer sheet and test booklet or password.

Published Reviews of the Instrument in the Last 15 Years:

Sanford, E. E. (2003). [Jackson Vocational Interest Inventory (1999 Revision).] In B. S. Plake, J. C. Impara, & R. Spies (Eds.), *The fifteenth mental measurements yearbook.* Lincoln, NE: Buros Center for Testing.

Sanford-Moore, E. E. (2009). [Jackson Vocational Interest Survey.] In E. A. Whitfield, R. W. Feller, & C. Wood (Eds.), *A counselor's guide to career assessment instruments* (5th ed., pp. 268-273). Broken Arrow, OK: National Career Development Association.

JACKSON VOCATIONAL INTEREST SURVEY, SECOND EDITION

Reviewed by:

Eleanor E. Sanford-Moore

Senior Vice-President for Research and Development
MetaMetrics, Inc.

Description

The Jackson Vocational Interest Survey, Second Edition (JVIS; Jackson, 1999) can be used to interpret career transition points that range from career starters (e.g., adolescents completing high school) to career transitioners (e.g., adults considering job changes, promotions, job loss, or retirement) to blended career-pathers (e.g., dual professional spouses) to team management in the work place. With research for the JVIS beginning in 1969, the second edition is a result of renorming the instrument, conducting additional studies with the instrument (reliability, validity, and other areas of research), and revising and updating reports and interpretative materials. The JVIS booklet consists of 289 pairs of statements describing occupational activities that are used to represent interests (work roles) and preferences (work styles) relevant to work. Regardless of ability, the respondent is asked to determine which of the two statements he or she prefers.

The JVIS reports the following scores: 34 Basic Interest Scales that examine work roles and work styles, 10 Occupational Themes, an Academic Satisfaction Scale, similarity to 17 clusters of educational majors, similarity to 32 job groups, and 3 administrative indices (number of unscorable responses, Response Consistency Index, and the Infrequency Index). Once converted to percentiles, the scores are used to develop a profile of the respondent's vocational interests and preferences.

The JVIS can be administered either individually or in a group setting by paper-and-pencil, on the computer (using the *SigmaSoft JVIS for Windows* computer software), and over the Internet. The JVIS will take the respondent about 45 to 60 minutes to complete, and it may be scored by hand or by computer.

If the JVIS is scored by computer, the report contains a comparison of the individual's profile with various educational groups and occupational clusters. The JVIS website contains information and links for students, parents, school counselors, and career changers. Information is provided about the assessment and basic interpretive frameworks (with suggestions to discuss the results with a career counselor). The information comes in various forms including a Career Exploration Guide, a University Exploration Guide, and a career links section. Each section contains practical information, case studies, and links to numerous websites with specific information.

Before interpreting the JVIS profile, the results from the three administrative indices should be examined to determine the validity of the situation and examine the respondent's test-taking behavior. The respondent's profile can be interpreted in relation to combined norms or gender-specific norms. The manual suggests that gender-specific norms are more appropriate for some scales (e.g., Engineering, Elementary Education) because the use of separate norms can encourage the diminishment of traditional occupational roles.

Jackson Vocational Interest Survey, Second Edition

The assessment manual provides extensive information and case studies to help counselors and other test administrators interpret the results of the JVIS. There is a section that describes recurring counseling problems and situations with suggestions and solutions: a flat JVIS Basic Interest profile, measured interests that are discrepant with career plans, abilities and interests appear to conflict, low reliability index for an individual machine-scored profile, Basic Interest Scales appear to conflict with Similarity to Job Groups, and the client is considering an occupation which appears unrelated to any of the 32 job groups. In addition, the JVIS Applications Handbook (Verhoeve, 2000) provides extensive case studies that can be used during training.

The JVIS Applications Handbook (Verhoeve, 2000) presents a methodology to interpret the results of the JVIS based on over 20 years of interpretation and analysis of profiles and the tracking of career paths of these individuals. Verhoeve (2000) presented the Career Constellation Model to work with clients to "explain the stress of career transition, and for dramatically improving the power of the Jackson Vocational Interest Survey as a computerized career snapshot" (p. 11). This model consists of eight dimensions that describe a person's career: education, fitness, religion, personal space, community activities, hobbies, family, and job (at the center). This model can be used during the interpretation of JVIS profiles to help the client understand how the various aspects of his or her life impact career choices.

To help clients better understand the General Occupational Themes, Verhoeve (2000) presented a more dynamic method — the Career Ergonomic Decagon. This model portrays the relationship of the individual with the environment by examining the personality fit between the person and the job environment. Verhoeve has found that this model facilitates more discussion with the client about the whole person and shows how the General Occupational Themes are interrelated. This model also works very well in partner and team-management situations where the individuals can see how the skills of the various people can complement each other.

Technical Considerations

The JVIS has undergone an extensive development process. The conceptual foundation of the JVIS is related to the work of David Campbell (1971) with the Strong Vocational Interest Blank (SVIB). The SVIB examined the relationship of vocational interests to specific occupations. Jackson departed from this way of thinking to instead relate vocational interests to work roles and work styles (occupational clusters). Thus, the focus of the results is more for career exploration and planning (examining many occupations), rather than seeing how well an individual's interests match a specific occupation. Jackson began by identifying a large set of work roles and work styles and then selecting dimensions within these work roles and work styles to measure.

Initially more than 3,000 statements were developed and administered in multiple forms to 2,203 respondents. The results were examined by first suppressing response bias resulting from the initial item format (the respondent was asked to indicate whether he or she "liked" or "disliked" the activity in the statement). The residual score matrix was then factor analyzed to identify statements that were related to each of the Basic Interest Scale dimensions. Based on these results, the final items were selected for each scale such that the relationship of the item to other items on the scale was maximized and the relationship of the item to other scales for which it was not related was minimized.

The JVIS was renormed in 1999 with 3,500 secondary school students and adults. The sample was equally split between males and females. Raw score means and standard deviations and percentiles are provided for each scale for males, females, secondary students, adults, and the combined sample.

In the JVIS manual, test-retest and coefficient alphas are presented for the Basic Interest scales (generally in the mid .70s to low .80s) and for the General Occupational Themes (generally in the mid to upper .80s).

The internal structure of the JVIS is examined by correlating the scales. Generally, the scales are independent for samples of females and males ($N = 1250$ in each sample) with the mean interscale correlation coefficient of .28 for males and .24 for females. In another study, a factor analysis was conducted with 1,163 male and 1,292 female high school students. Two conclusions were drawn from the results of the factor analysis: (1) there are characteristic patterns of JVIS scores and the counselor can expect to see these patterns, and (2) the emergence of the patterns permitted the development of the 10 Occupational Themes for reporting results. Also, the manual (Jackson, 1999) contains studies showing how the JVIS can be used in other areas of research:

A COUNSELOR'S GUIDE TO CAREER ASSESSMENTS INSTRUMENTS

relationship to academic major, genetic and environmental influences on career interests, choice of academic college, classification of occupational groups, structure of interests, and the career assessment of groups of individuals—individuals with disabilities, women, minorities, and different age groups.

General Utility and Evaluation

The JVIS takes a different approach to the assessment of vocational interests by examining the relationship of interests and preferences to occupational clusters. By focusing on occupational clusters rather than specific occupations, respondents are more likely to explore careers that they may not have considered previously. The respondent can then take into consideration other information related to career choice: the availability of opportunities, interest in higher education or training, individual abilities and interpersonal skills, and individual values in relation to work satisfaction. The JVIS is a well-developed test for examining occupational interests for career planning and has adequate validity and reliability for this use. The JVIS website provides information that can be tailored to the informational needs of each examinee.

References and Additional Resources

Campbell, D. P. (1971). *Handbook for the Strong Vocational Interest Blank.* Stanford, CA: Stanford University Press.

Campbell, D. P., Borgen, F. H., Eastes, S. H., Johansson, C. B., & Peterson, R. A. (1968). A set of basic interest scales for the Strong Vocational Interest Blank for men [monograph]. *Journal of Applied Psychology, 52*(6), 1-64.

Jackson, D. N. (1999). *Jackson Vocational Interest Inventory: Manual.* Port Huron, MI: SIGMA Assessment Systems, Inc.

Sanford, E. E. (2003). [Jackson Vocational Interest Inventory (1999 Revision).] In B. S. Plake, J. C. Impara, & R. Spies (Eds.), *The fifteenth mental measurements yearbook.* Lincoln, NE: Buros Center for Testing.

Sanford-Moore, E. E. (2009). [Jackson Vocational Interest Survey.] In E. A. Whitfield, R. W. Feller, & C. Wood (Eds.), *A counselor's guide to career assessment instruments* (5th ed., pp. 268-273). Broken Arrow, OK: National Career Development Association.

Verhoeve, M. A. (2000). *JVIS applications handbook.* London, ON: Research Psychologists Press Division, SIGMA Assessment Systems, Inc.

A COUNSELOR'S GUIDE TO CAREER ASSESSMENTS INSTRUMENTS

O*NET INTEREST PROFILER AND
COMPUTERIZED O*NET INTEREST PROFILER
U.S. Department of Labor, Employment and Training Administration

---

Employment & Training Administration
USDOL, FPB S4231
200 Constitutional Avenue, NW
Washington, DC 20210
http://www.doleta.gov/programs/onet
http://www.onetcenter.org
o-net@dol.gov

Target Population: Adolescents, young adults, and adults. Individuals seeking to identify their work related interests and use them to explore careers. High school and postsecondary students and adults; age 14 years and older with a minimum sixth-grade reading level.

Statement of the Purpose of the Instrument: The O*NET Interest Profiler (IP) and Computerized O*NET Interest Profiler (CIP) were developed as self-assessment instruments as part of a whole person assessment approach. The instrument and its computerized form were designed to help individuals identify their work related interests and use them to explore the world of work. They are appropriate for a variety of users including students, first time job seekers, and those individuals in occupational transition. In addition to receiving a list of occupations based on their results, the O*NET system is located at http://online.onetcenter.org, the nation's leading source of occupational information.

Titles of Subtests, Scales, Scores Provided: Realistic, Investigative, Artistic, Social, Enterprising, and Conventional (RIASEC). A numerical raw score is provided for each interest area.

Forms and Levels Available, with Dates of Publication/Revision of Each: 2001.

Date of Most Recent Edition of Test Manual, User's Guide, Etc.: 2001.

Language in Which Available: English only.

Time:

Actual Test Time: 20-60 minutes for the O*NET IP; 15-30 minutes for the CIP.

Total Administration Time: Varies.

Norm Group(s) on Which Scores Are Based: The O*NET IP and CIP are not norm referenced; however, piloting and validity/reliability information was collected from more than 2,000 subjects from across the country. Participants included high school students, college students, workers in transition, and employed and unemployed workers. Additionally, during the pilot of the O*NET IP, the Interest Finder — a well-established interest measure — was also administered to compare the psychometric characteristics of the instruments.

Manner in Which Results Are Reported for Individuals: For the O*NET IP, clients receive a 24-page preprinted score report. Clients transfer their six numerical interest scores from the instrument to the first page of the score report. The score report walks the client through several phases that enables the client to use his/her primary and/or secondary interest score to explore careers: (1) the score report defines the interest area for the client, (2) the client selects a job zone (level of education, training, and work experience they have now or wish to pursue) which they will use to help select occupations to explore, (3) six steps are presented that enable the client to use his or her top interest areas and job zone to select occupations to explore, or (4) if the client is not satisfied with their results, alternatives are presented to help the client continue his/her career exploration, and (5) lists of occupations are from the U.S. Department of Labor's O*NET system at http://online.onetcenter.org, the nation's leading source of occupational information. Additionally, clients are directed towards expanded lists of occupations to explore.

For the CIP, the counselee is presented information on several screens. In addition to viewing the results, counselees can print out their six score interest profiles, definitions of the six individual interest areas, and the definitions of the job zone (level of education, training, and work experience they have or wish to pursue)

261

they selected to use to help determine occupations to explore. These occupations may be found in the O*NET system. The client is also presented with several screens that explain the next steps in career exploration; these screens can be printed out.

Report Format/Content for Group Summaries: Not available.

Machine Scoring: Not available.

Local Machine Scoring: Not available.

Hand Scoring: The O*NET IP is scored by counselee in fewer than 5 minutes. Counselee counts number of "Ls" (i.e., work activities they would like to perform) marked for each of the six interest areas measured (RIASEC). Counselee records each of the six scores on the instrument.

Computer Software Options Available: Standard administration online.

A computerized version of the instrument, the O*NET Computerized Interest Profiler (CIP) is available for download, free of charge. The User Guide and the software can be downloaded at www.onetcenter.org/CIP.hmtl . The items presented in the CIP are the same as those presented in the paper-and-pencil version. The CIP scores the instrument for the client, and uses all six RIASEC scores the client received and the job zone the client selected to identify occupations to explore.

Cost of Materials: Print shop files of all materials can be downloaded free of charge on the website.

Specimen Set: O*NET Interest Profiler, O*NET Interest Profiler Score report, O*NET Interest Profiler User's Guide.

Counselee Materials: O*NET Interest Profiler, Score Report, Occupations Master List, Occupations Combined List or O*NET Computerized Work Importance Profiler.

Published Reviews of the Instrument in the Last 15 years:

Brown, M. B. (2005). [O*Net Interest Profiler.] In R. A. Spies & B. S. Plake (Eds.), *The sixteenth mental measurements yearbook.* Lincoln, NE: Buros Center for Testing. [Electronic Version]

Eggerth, D. E., Bowles, S. M., & Andrew, M. E. (2005). Convergent validity of the O*NET Holland code classifications. *Journal of Career Assessment, 13,* 150-158.

Michael, W. B. (2005). [O*Net Interest Profiler.] In R. A. Spies & B. S. Plake (Eds.), *The sixteenth mental measurements yearbook.* Lincoln, NE: Buros Center for Testing. [Electronic Version]

Pope, M. (2005). Review of the O*NET Career Interests Inventory: Based on the O*NET Interest Profiler developed by the U.S. Department of Labor. In R. A. Spies & B. S. Plake (Eds.), *The sixteenth mental measurements yearbook.* Lincoln, NE: Buros Center for Testing. [Electronic Version]

Pope, M. (2009). [O*NET Interest Profiler]. In E. A. Whitfield, R. W. Feller, & C. Wood (Eds.), *A counselor's guide to career assessment instruments* (5th ed, pp.279-285). Broken Arrow, OK: National Career Development Association.

O*NET INTEREST PROFILER
AND COMPUTERIZED O*NET INTEREST PROFILER

Reviewed by:

Stephanie A. Crockett

Department of Counseling
Oakland University

Description

In 2000, the U.S. Department of Labor Employment and Training Administration published five O*NET Career Exploration Tools (i.e., Interest Profiler, Computerized Interest Profiler, Ability Profiler, Work Importance Locator, and Work Importance Profiler) to assist individuals with the career exploration process. This

A Counselor's Guide To Career Assessments Instruments

review focuses on two of the O*NET Career Exploration Tools: O*NET Interest Profiler (IP) and Computerized Interest Profiler (CIP).

The IP is a career exploration tool that assists individuals in determining work-related activities and occupations that are of interest to them. The instrument aims to help users identify their vocational interests and further explore the world of work. IP developers also sought to develop an unbiased assessment that was applicable to and met the needs of individuals from diverse ethnic backgrounds and socioeconomic statuses; create an assessment that reliably and accurately measures vocational interest profiles within Holland's (1985) RIASEC construct; provide individuals, who have diverse vocational interests and goals, with an assessment that represents the entire world of work through the provision of a wide range of work-related activities; and empower clients in making career exploration decisions by developing an assessment that can be self-administered and self-scored (Lewis & Rivkin, 1999).

The IP is a self-administered and self-interpreted paper-and-pencil interest inventory that can be administered independently or in conjunction with the other four O*Net Career Exploration Tools. To assist users, the U.S. Department of Labor Employment and Training Administration (2000) published a score report, user guide, and O*NET Occupations Master List. The IP, score reports, user guide, and master list can be downloaded free of charge from the O*NET Resource Center website (http://www.onetcenter.org). These materials can also be purchased from the Government Printing Office.

The computerized version (i.e., CIP) allows for flexibility in the assessment's delivery mode. The CIP has an identical format and uses the same scoring method as the IP. It is offered free of charge from the O*NET Resource Center website. An alternate, shortened form of the O*NET Interest Profiler is now available for users. The O*NET Interest Profiler Short Form (Rounds, Su, Lewis, & Rivkin, 2010) is a web-based assessment. It is also available from the O*NET Resource Center website free of charge. The Interest Profiler is not a timed test, but takes approximately 20 to 60 minutes to complete; the CIP takes 30 to 60 minutes to complete. The IP Short Form takes users approximately 10 minutes to complete.

The IP is comprised of 180 items that describe work activities associated with a wide range of occupations and vocational training levels. Specifically, the instrument measures vocational interests across six 30-item scales that are compatible with Holland's (1985) RIASEC typology. The scales are realistic (R), investigative (I), artistic (A), social (S), enterprising (E), and conventional (C). Example work activity items include the following: fix a broken faucet (R scale), investigate crimes (I scale), direct a play (A scale), teach a high school class (S scale), sell automobiles (E scale), and operate a calculator (C scale). Users are asked to mark whether they Like (L), Dislike (DL), or are Unsure (?) about each of the 180 work activities. The IP encourages test takers to focus on whether they would like or dislike an activity rather than the salary or educational level associated with each activity. To score the inventory, users assign one point for every work activity marked with an L; dislike and unsure answers receive no points. Scores are then summed for each of the six scales. Accordingly, the inventory yields six scale scores that can range from 0 to 30 points. The highest score across all six scales is referred to as a primary interest area; the second and third highest scores are called secondary interest areas and are used to assist the client in exploring more career options.

If using the paper-and-pencil version of the assessment, test takers are referred to the provided score report to learn more about their work-related interests. The score report is a 30-page booklet that assists users in exploring their primary career interests across a variety of job zones. Job zones are clusters of occupations that require different levels of education and training for job entry. The score report also walks users through several options to consider if they do not agree with their IP results. Nearly 20 pages of occupations are included in the score report, and users are invited to explore the occupations that fall into their specified interest area and work zone. For a more extensive list of occupations users are referred to the O*NET Occupations Master List, a 20-page booklet containing more than 700 occupations that are classified according to interest area and job zone.

The O*NET IP Short Form consists of 60 work activity items across the six RIASEC scales. Each of the six scales includes 10 items and, similar to the long form, users are given three response item choices — Like (L), Dislike (DL), or are Unsure (?) — for each of the 60 work activities. Scale scores range from 0 to 10 and are calculated by summing the number of Like responses. The Interest Profiler Short Form has also been adapted for computer-based use. The computerized short form utilizes a five-point response format for work activities:

0 = strongly dislike, 1 = *dislike,* 2 = *unsure,* 3 = *like,* and 4 = *strongly like.* Scale scores range from 0 to 40 and are calculated by summing all responses.

One of the most practical features of the IP is its flexibility in format and administration. The IP is readily available to users in two formats. Administration time for both full-length versions is reasonable, and users can opt for the short form if needed. The IP and CIP can be administered individually or in a group guided by a counselor/career professional. The instrument can also be self-administered, giving users the freedom to complete the IP outside of a counseling setting. The IP and CIP can be administered free of charge, making it accessible to a diverse population of users. Lastly, the IP and CIP results can be directly linked to the O*NET Online, which has vocational information for more than 900 occupations.

The IP's test format and scoring is straightforward. The test and scoring instructions are clear and easy to understand. Users receive detailed instruction regarding the nature and purpose of the test, the career exploration process, and how to explore occupations using test scores. For added convenience, the U.S. Department of Labor, Employment and Training Administration provides a score report, extensive user guide, and O*NET Occupations Master List to assist users in understanding and applying their scores to the career exploration process. The IP requires an eighth-grade reading level to adequately comprehend test items and related materials (Brown, 2005). Lewis and Rivkin (1999) stated that the IP was developed for persons age 14 and older; they estimate that the instrument can be used as early as junior high school.

The CIP is not a web-based assessment but can be downloaded in a Windows format (.exe) from the O*NET Resource Center website; a MAC version of the CIP is not available. The computerized interface is user-friendly and the testing instructions are written clearly and are detailed enough to guide a user who is unfamiliar with computers successfully through the assessment. The CIP's computerized format is very flexible, providing users the option to return to previous pages, change their answers prior to scoring, and restart the assessment where they previously left off. Scores are electronically calculated and presented to the user in a one-page summary. A two- four- sentence summary of each RIASEC scale is provided. Lastly, the CIP conveniently allows users to select their job zone and generates a list of potential occupations based on the users' primary interests scores and chosen job zones. Users can then electronically explore careers that match their primary interest area and job zone through the O*NET.

The primary use of the IP in counseling is to assist clients with career exploration and planning. Specifically, counselors should use the IP to help clients identify their work-related interests and understand the role of these interests in identifying a satisfying occupation.

Counselors can use this assessment with adolescents and young adults who are making initial educational and occupational decisions as well as with adults considering a mid-life career transition or those re-entering the workforce as a means for exploring and identifying potential occupations. The IP's compatibility with Holland's (1985) RIASEC typology makes it easy for the counselor to combine the assessment with additional career exploration tools. It should be noted that IP results are not intended to be used in the hiring process. The User's Guide (U.S. Department of Labor, Employment and Training Administration, 2000) clearly indicates that a client's IP results, "should not be used for employment or hiring decisions. Employers, education programs, or other job related programs should not use [the client's] results as part of a screening process for jobs or training" (p. 3).

Technical Considerations

The IP underwent a thorough eight-phase process of development. The first seven steps of the development process are detailed the User's Guide (U.S. Department of Labor, Employment and Training Administration, 2000; for an exhaustive review, see Lewis & Rivkin, 1999). These include the following: (1) review of existing DOL interest instruments; (2) identification of existing test items that could potentially be used; (3) development of the underlying item taxonomy; (4) organization of retained items within the taxonomy and creation of new items; (5) screening of new items; (6) item analysis, development of preliminary subscales, and determination of initial psychometric properties; and (7) format design for administration and scoring. The resulting instrument included six scales reflecting work activities across each of Holland's (1985) RIASEC constructs. It is important to note that test developers strove to reduce the presence of gender and racial/ethnic bias in the IP's items. During stage six, Lewis and Rivkin (1999) evaluated the extent to which items were restrictive to a particular gender

A Counselor's Guide To Career Assessments Instruments

or racial/ethnic group. Results revealed that items on all subscales, with the exception of the Realistic scale, were gender balanced. Racial/ethnic balance was also achieved on the majority of subscales. African Americans indicated a stronger preference for Enterprising items than White/Non-Latinos, and Latinos were more likely to prefer items on the Social scale than their White/Non-Latino counterparts. Lewis and Rivkin concluded that "the dissimilar[ities] may reflect cultural differences of the two subgroups" than racial/ethnic bias (p. 14).

The eighth and final step of development for the IP was a validation study conducted by Rounds, Walker, Day, and Hubert (1999). Rounds, Walker, et al. (1999) used a diverse sample of 1,061 individuals to evaluate the instrument's validity and reliability. Participants were solicited from four regions across the United States (Michigan, New York, North Carolina, and Utah) at data collection sites, which included employment service offices, junior colleges, trade schools, and other government agencies. More than half of all participants were female (58.8%). Participant age varied widely, with nearly half (47.8%) of participants being 23 to 40 years of age. The majority (58.4%) of participants identified as White, 24.9% as African American, 10.1% as Latino, 2.66% as Native American, 1.51% as Asian or Pacific Islander, and 1.60% as Other. Most participants (58.5%) did not hold a bachelor's degree and the majority were unemployed (62.0%). Eighty three participants were high school students, and 228 were enrolled an institution of high education or vocational school.

The IP is a reliable and valid measure. The internal consistency estimates across all six RIASEC scales is high, ranging from .93 to .96 (Rounds, Walker, et al., 1999). A one-month test-retest analysis revealed high reliability estimates, ranging from .81 to .92 (Rounds, Walker, et al.,1999), indicating the IP is stable over time and consistently identifies user vocational interests over multiple administrations of the test within a short time period. Rounds, Walker, et al. (1999) also found the IP and the Interest-Finder (Wall & Baker, 1997), a comparable scale that measure vocational interests, share a similar factor structure. Corresponding scales on both instruments were highly correlated, providing evidence of convergent validity for the IP. Correlations with Holland's RIASEC scales, however, suggest a problem with the IP's Enterprising scale. Specifically, the Enterprising scale correlates too closely with the Artistic scale, and not high enough with the Social scale. Rounds, Walker, et al. concluded that the problematic Enterprising scale was most likely the result of a "low-prestige-problem" (p. 9). In an attempt to serve the needs of a diverse clientele, developers of the IP included many lower-level jobs that were not included in Holland's (1985) original RIASEC model; the introduction of this variability into the Enterprising scale may account for the loss in conceptual validity. The User Guide (U.S. Department of Labor, Employment and Training Administration, 2000) notes that these results are solely based on comparisons with the Interest-Finder (Wall & Baker, 1997) and that differing results may occur if the IP was compared with another RIASEC instrument.

Two sample populations were used to evaluate the validity and reliability of the CIP. A total of 588 participants from across the four regions of the United States provided data for a comparability and test-retest study. Most participants in both the comparability and test-retest samples were female. Minority participants were over-represented in the comparability study (see Rounds, Mazzeo, Smith, & Hubert, 1999, for detailed information regarding participant characteristics). The CIP was found to be a reliable measure with stability in participant score over time. Specifically, Rounds, Mazzeo, et al. (1999) reported very high internal consistency scores across all RIASEC subscales ranging from .93 to .96, as well as high test-retest reliability ranging from .82 to .92 over a one-month time frame. Based on these results Rounds, Mazzeo et al. concluded that the computerized form of the IP had little impact on the instrument's stability over time and reliability of scores. The CIP also demonstrated evidence of criterion-related validity, convergent validity, and structural validity. Overall, Rounds, Mazzeo's et al. validation study supported the use of the CIP as a reliable and valid measure of vocational interests, highly comparable to the paper-and-pencil IP.

The IP Short-Form was developed and normed using the sample ($N = 1,060$) from the initial IP validation study (see Rounds, Walker, et al., 1999). In a validation study (Rounds, Su, Lewis, & Rivkin, et al., 2010), an additional stability sample of 132 was used to evaluate the short form's psychometric properties. Rounds et al. found that the IP Short-Form demonstrated high reliability and stability over time. Cronbach's alpha across the RIASEC subscales ranged from .78 to .87, and test-retest reliability ranged from .78 to .86 (time interval unknown). Evidence for convergent and discriminant validity was supported in Rounds et al.'s validation study by the correlations between the short form and the Interest-Finder (Wall & Baker, 1997). It should be noted that gender differences in the RIASEC scales were found to exist between the short form and long form of the IP. When compared to the long form, men were more likely to be favored on the Realistic scale of the short form and women were moderately favored on the short form's Social scale (Rounds et al., 2010).

General Utility and Evaluation

The IP User Guide (U.S. Department of Labor, Employment and Training Administration, 2000) is extensive in nature and includes information related to administering and interpreting the IP, as well as details regarding the development and psychometric properties of the IP. Detailed instructions for administering and scoring the IP are provided to both users and career development professionals. The administration section outlines guidelines for administering the IP to individuals and groups. The User Guide also walks users through the IP, provides an overview of Holland's (1985) RIASEC constructs, offers an explanation of the score report and how it is used to interpret IP results, and outlines possible challenges that the user might face in taking, scoring, and interpreting the IP. The development section of the User Guide outlines the eight IP developmental phases, as well as the instrument's reliability and validity. The User Guide does not provide any demographic information for the norming sample and lacks specific information regarding the evidence for validity and reliability. Career development professionals must obtain this detailed information from Lewis and Rivkin's (1999) validation study. The User Guide (U.S. Department of Labor, Employment and Training Administration, 2000) does, however, discuss gender and race/ethnic bias with regard to the IP and describes measures taken to "reduce the likelihood of the [IP] leading to restrictive career options for particular subgroups" (p. 39). Overall, the User Guide is well-written and logically organized; it provides sufficient information for guiding users in self-administration and career development professionals who desire to administer the test to individuals or groups.

A user guide is also available for the CIP on the O*NET Resource Center website (http://www.onetcenter.org). The CIP User Guide closely parallels the IP User Guide, but includes information unique to using the interest profiler's computerized format. Specifically, the User Guide addresses issues related to the installation of the CIP, navigating the CIP test screens, and saving client data files. The information in the CIP User Guide is clear and easy to understand. The guide contains detailed step-by-step instructions, including graphics of the CIP screens, that allow users with varying levels of computer literacy to successfully navigate the electronic assessment.

The IP is a well-developed instrument with several strengths. Specifically, the IP is a free/low cost assessment that measures career interests in the context of Holland's RIASEC framework and, unlike similar interest assessments, the IP does not include user self-estimates of competencies. Such characteristics make the IP a better quality measure than many of the comparable interest assessments available (e.g., Self Directed Search; Pope, 2009). The IP has, however, received criticism for using single Holland codes rather than a combination (Brown, 2005). Users are instructed to use their primary interest area to explore potential careers in the Master Occupations List instead of using their top three interest areas. Exploring one primary interest area may significantly narrow a user's career options, when the point of career exploration tools such as the IP is to broaden vocational possibilities.

Another key strength of the IP is the sound psychometric properties (Brown, 2005; Michael, 2005). Great care was taken in the development of the IP and subsequent validation studies to ensure the construction of a valid and reliable interest assessment that serves diverse users. However, the normative data are not extensive or readily available to users in the user's guide. In a review of the IP, Michael (2005) pointed out the need for the "creation of extensive and easy-to-read normative data" (Summary section, para. 1). Additionally, it is important to note that evidence of convergent validity for the IP has only been established with the Interest Profiler. Accordingly, Michael and Pope (2009) recommended that follow-up validation studies using a diverse sampling group are needed to provide additional evidence of such validity. Pope (2009) further suggested that test-retest reliability needs to be established over longer intervals of time (e.g., 6 months, 1 year) to provide evidence for the instrument's stability over time.

The CIP greatly enhances the accessibility and utility of the interest profiler. Although, as Pope (2009) noted, the CIP is only available for download in a Windows format; there is not currently a MAC version. The downloadable Windows version is not without problems. The version was developed in 2000 and has not been updated to accommodate newer, wide-screen monitors. For example, some of the text on the instruction screens is unreadable, and images appear in inadvertent locations on the many of the screens. In lieu of the downloadable CIP, it is recommended that an online version of the assessment be developed. An online version would eliminate existing operating system compatibility issues and potentially allow users to access the assessment on any computing device with a web browser (e.g., smart phones, tablets). Additionally, users could be directly linked to the O*NET for further career exploration through an online version of the CIP. In summary, the IP an attractive, well-constructed, and versatile assessment of career interests that can be used to facilitate the career exploration process with a variety of clients.

References and Additional Resources

Brown, M. B. (2005). [O*Net Interest Profiler.] In B. Plake & R. Spies (Eds.), *The sixteenth mental measurements yearbook*. Lincoln, NE: Buros Center for Testing.

Eggerth, D. E., Bowles, S. M., & Andrew, M. E. (2005). Convergent validity of the O*NET Holland code classifications. *Journal of Career Assessment, 13,* 150-158.

Holland, J. L. (1985). *Making vocational choices: A theory of vocational personalities and work environments* (2nd ed.). Englewood Cliff, NJ: Prentice Hall.

Lewis, P., & Rivkin, D. (1999). *Development of the O*NET Interest Profiler.* Raleigh, NC: National Center for O*NET Development.

Michael, W. B. (2005). [O*Net Interest Profiler]. In B. Plake & R. Spies (Eds.), *The sixteenth mental measurements yearbook*. Lincoln, NE: Buros Center for Testing. [Electronic Version]

O*NET Resource Center website: http://www.onetcenter.org

Pope, M. (2009). [O*NET Interest Profiler]. In E. A. Whitfield, R. W. Feller, & C. Wood (Eds.), *A counselor's guide to career assessment instruments* (5th ed, pp. 279-285). Broken Arrow, OK: National Career Development Association.

Pope, M. (2005). Review of the O*NET Career Interests Inventory: Based on the O*NET Interest Profiler developed by the U.S. Department of Labor. In R. A. Spies & B. S. Plake (Eds.), *The sixteenth mental measurements yearbook*. Lincoln, NE: Buros Center for Testing. [Electronic Version]

Rounds J., Mazzeo, S. E., Smith, T. J., & Hubert, L. (1999). *O*NET Computerized Interest Profiler: Reliability, validity, and comparability.* Raleigh, NC: National Center for O*NET Development.

Rounds, J., Su, R., Lewis, P., & Rivkin, D. (2010). *O*NET Interest Profiler Short Form Psychometric Characteristics: Summary.* Raleigh, NC: National Center for O*NET Development.

Rounds, J., Walker, C. M., Day, S. X., & Hubert, L. (1999). *O*NET Interest Profiler: Reliability, validity, and self-scoring.* Raleigh, NC: National Center for O*NET Development.

U.S. Department of Labor, Employment and Training Administration. (2000). *O*NET Interest Profiler user's guide.* Raleigh, NC: Author.

Wall, J. E., & Baker, H. E. (1997). The Interest-Finder: Evidence of validity. *Journal of Career Assessment, 5,* 255-273.

A Counselor's Guide To Career Assessments Instruments

O*NET Work Importance Profiler and Work Importance Locator
U.S. Department of Labor, Employment and Training Administration

---

Employment & Training Administration
USDOL, FPB S4231
200 Constitutional Avenue, NM
Washington, DC 20210
http://www.doleta.gov/programs/onet
http://www.onetcenter.org
o-net@dol.gov

Target Population: Adolescents, young adults, and adults. Individuals seeking to identify their work values and use them to explore careers; high school and postsecondary students as well as adults. Should be 16 years and older with a minimum of a sixth-grade reading level.

Statement of the Purpose of the Instrument: The O*NET Work Importance Profiler (WIP) is a computerized self-assessment career exploration tool that allows customers to focus on what is important to them in a job. It helps people identify occupations that they may find satisfying, based on the similarity between their work values (such as achievement, autonomy, and conditions of work) and the characteristics of the occupations.

The O*NET Work Importance Locator (WIL) was produced by the O*NET project of the U.S. Department of Labor, Employment and Training Administration under the direction of David Rivkin and Phil Lewis. The Human Resources Research Organization (HumRRO) was the primary contractor in developing the Instrument (McCloy et al., 1999a). Their team was led by Rodney McCloy. Trefoil Corporation and eGuidance Solutions developed the software for the instrument. Gary Carter, John Boyle, and Dan Connell initiated and participated in much of the research effort associated with developing the instrument (McCloy et al., 1999b).

Titles of Subtests, Scales, Scores Provided: There are six types of work values measured: Achievement, Independence, Recognition, Relationships, Support, and Work Conditions.

Forms and Levels Available, with Dates of Publication/Revision of Each: Version 3.0 is available, released in 2001.

Date of Most Recent Edition of Test Manual, User's Guide, Etc.: The O*NET Work Importance User's Guide, designed for workforce development professionals, was released in 2001. Other editions include the WIP Software (2002), WIL User Guide (2000), O*NET Occupation Master List (2000), WIL Card Sheet (2000), O*NET Occupations Combined List (2000), and WIL Instrument (2000).

Language in Which Available: English only.

Time:

    Actual Test Time: Approximately 15-30 minutes.

    Total Administration Time: Varies.

Norm Group(s) on Which Scores Are Based: These instruments are not norm-referenced. Extensive pilots and evaluations were conducted. See the User's Guide, development and technical reports at http://www.onetcenter.org for more information.

Manner in Which Results Are Reported for Individuals: Raw numerical scores associated with each work value label are presented. Six numerical scores are provided, one for each work value area; top work values are indicated. Client receives a 24-page preprinted score report. Counselees transfer their top two (highest scores) work values from the WIL to the score report. The score report walks the counselee through several phases that enable the client to use their top two work values to explore careers: (1) the score report defines the work values for the client, (2) the counselee selects a job zone-level of education, training, and work experience they have now or wish to pursue- which they will use to help select occupations to explore, (3) six steps are presented that enable the counselee to use their top work values and job zone to select occupations to explore, (4) if the counselee is not satisfied with their results, alternatives are presented to help the client

O*NET Work Importance Locator and Work Importance Profiler

continue his or her career exploration, and (5) lists of occupations sorted by work values area and job zone are presented. Counselees can explore occupations in these lists in the O*NET system. Additionally, they are directed towards expanded lists of occupations to explore.

For the WIP, the counselee is presented with several screens. In addition to reviewing these results, a counselee can print out top work values, a 21-need score profile, definitions of the work values and needs, and the definitions of the job zone they selected to use to help identify occupations to explore. Note, for ease of use, the score report focuses on the counselee's top two work values rather than the 21-need score profile. Counselees can print out the list of occupations that best match their score profile and selected job zone. These occupations can be found on the O*NET website. There are several other options within the WIP where counselees can select to print additional information. The client is also presented with several screens that explain the next steps in career exploration.

Report Format/Content for Group Summaries: Not available.

Machine Scoring: Not available.

Hand Scoring: Hand scored by counselee in fewer than 5 minutes.

Local Machine Scoring: Not available.

Computer Software Options Available: All materials can be downloaded free of charge at the website. WIP is the computerized version of instrument. The software can be downloaded to your computer from http://www.onetcenter.org.

Cost of Materials: All materials are free of charge from the O*NET center website.

>   **Specimen Set:** All materials (instrument print shop files, score report, demonstration version of the instrument, user's guide designed for counselors, technical development reports) are available for download free of charge at http://www.onetcenter.org/WIL.hmtl or for WIP it is http://www.onetcenter.org/WIP.hmtl.

>   **Counselee Materials:** All materials (instrument print shop files, score report, demonstration version of the instrument, user's guide designed for counselors, technical development reports) are available for download free of charge at http://www.onetcenter.org/WIL.hmtl or for WIP it is http://www.onetcenter.org/WIP.hmtl. O*NET Work Importance Locator Instrument (Instrument Booklet, Work Importance Locator Cards; Work Importance Locator Card Sorting Sheet) and O*NET Work Importance Locator Score Report.

Published Reviews of the Instrument in the Last 15 years:

Ciechalski, J. C. (2009). [O*NET Work Importance Locator and Work Importance Profiler.] In E. A. Whitfield, R. W. Feller, & C. Wood (Eds.), *A counselor's guide to career assessment instruments* (5th ed., pp. 286-296). Broken Arrow, OK: National Career Development Association.

Kelley, K. N., & Michael, W. B. (2005). [O*Net Work Importance Locator]. In R. A. Spies & B. S. Plake (Eds.), *The sixteenth mental measurements yearbook.* Lincoln, NE: Buros Center for Testing.

Spies, R. A., & Plake, B. S. (Eds.). (2005). [Work Importance Locator.] In R. A. Spies & B. S. Plake (Eds.), *The sixteenth mental measurements yearbook.* Lincoln, NE: Buros Center for Testing.

O*NET Work Importance Profiler and Work Importance Locator

Reviewed by:

Jennifer J. Del Corso

Department of Counseling and Human Services
Old Dominion University

Description

The O*NET Work Importance Profiler (WIP) and Work Importance Locator (WIL) are part of the Occupational Information Network (O*NET). O*NET is an online comprehensive resource developed by the U.S. Department of Labor's (USDOL's) Office of Policy and Research that educates, assesses, identifies, and organizes occupational information (U.S. Department of Labor, Employment and Training Administration, 2000, 2002a). Specifically, O*NET links specific career exploration tools (i.e., Interest Profiler, Work Importance Locator/Profiler, and Ability Profiler) to a comprehensive occupational database. This database replaced the *Dictionary of Occupational Titles* and is designed to collect, organize, describe, and disseminate data on occupational characteristics and worker attributes (U.S. Department of Labor, Employment and Training Administration, 2000, 2002b).

The WIP is similar to the WIL, with the exception that the questions are answered on a computer (U.S. Department of Labor Employment and Training Administration, 2000). The purpose of the WIL and WIP is to help individuals become aware of their work values, as well as which occupations are most likely to meet those needs. Based on the Theory of Work Adjustment, individuals have the highest degree of job satisfaction when they work in an environment congruent with their values (Dawis & Lofquist, 1984). The WIL Paper-and-Pencil and WIP help individuals identify and organize their work needs and values in order of importance. Both versions (WIL and WIP) were modeled on the Minnesota Importance Questionnaire (MIQ), which had individuals rate the importance of specific work characteristics on a five-point Likert scale (Rounds, Henley, Dawis, Lofquist, & Weiss, 1981). Unlike the MIQ, the WIL and WIP are self-administered and scored.

Both forms (WIL and WIP) can be found online at http://www.onetcenter.org/WIL.html and http://www.onetcenter.org/WIP.html, respectively. They are free and available to the public. O*NET requires a simple registration of one's name, email address, and title/position in order to download the forms, software, and user guides. Currently, the latest software for WIP is version 3.0 and takes approximately 20-30 minutes to complete (U.S. Department of Labor Employment and Training Administration, 2002a). Likewise, the WIL Paper-and-Pencil takes approximately 15-45 minutes to complete (U.S. Department of Labor, Employment and Training Administration, 2000).

The WIL consists of 20 work value cards. Each card corresponds with one of six work values: achievement, independence, recognition, relationships, support, and working conditions. Individuals are first asked to think about how important it would be to have an occupation corresponding with the value description on the card. Next, they are asked to sort the cards into one of five columns from 5 (*most important*) to 1 (*least important*). Four cards must be placed in each column. Each card is scored with the point value indicated on the column (e.g., column five = 5 points). The WIL provides a simple work value worksheet on page 5 of the WIL booklet for individuals to record their scores (U.S. Department of Labor, Employment and Training Administration, 2002a, p. 5). Individuals complete the worksheet to reveal the total score per work value. The individual then uses the Work Importance Locator Score Report to indicate their two highest work value scores. The report describes what these values mean and how to use them as they explore occupations.

Individuals must choose from one of five job zones. Zones are categorized by the degree of preparation: Job Zone 1 requires little-to-no preparation, Zone 2 some preparation, Zone 3 medium preparation, Zone 4 considerable preparation, and Zone 5 extensive preparation. After identifying a job zone and the two highest

O*NET Work Importance Locator and Work Importance Profiler

work values, individuals are instructed to explore the WIL O*NET Occupations Master List to identify occupations in their job zones that link with their highest work value (U.S. Department of Labor, Employment and Training Administration, 2002b).

The WIP is a computerized software program that directs individuals to rank and rate 21 work needs: ability utilization, achievement, activity, advancement, authority, autonomy, co-workers, company policies and practices, compensation, creativity, ethics, independence, recognition, responsibility, security, social service, social status, supervision–human relations, supervision-technical, variety, and work conditions. These needs are subcategories that fall under the six larger work values listed above for the WIL. Next, individuals are instructed to select a Job Zone. From there, an occupations report is generated. This report indicates occupations that correspond to the work values rated most important by the user in accordance with their preferred Job Zone.

The WIL and WIP are self-administered and can be used individually or in group settings such as training programs, classrooms, or job search programs (U.S. Department of Labor, Employment and Training Administration, 2000, 2002a). Individuals should have a minimum of an 8th-grade reading level so that they can adequately understand the test items. Developmentally, the WIL and WIP are appropriate for individuals age 16 years and older, such as high school and college students, unemployed workers, and individuals involved in a career transition (U.S. Department of Labor, Employment and Training Administration, 2000, 2002a). The assessments are best suited for individuals that have crystallized their identity and have some experience in the world of work (Kelly & Lee, 2002) as a majority of the questions require the user to rate their preferred work environment. As a result, younger users with limited or no work experience are asked to imagine what might be important to them and what they have heard about jobs from their school, parents, relatives, or friends (U.S. Department of Labor, Employment and Training Administration, 2000, 2002a).

Counselors can help individuals incorporate the results of the WIL and WIP by discussing the clients' highest work values and needs. These work values and needs then become a measure by which individuals can discern prospective job opportunities. Furthermore, if clients lack occupational information, the list of prospective occupations that correspond with their work values, may be quite useful in helping them specifically identify which positions potentially offer the greatest degree of job satisfaction. The WIL and WIP, allow individuals to grow in self and occupational awareness.

Technical Considerations

The development the WIP involved a pre-pilot, pilo,t and a main study. For the pre-pilot study, 10 employees were selected from Human Resources Research Organization and from the National Center for O*NET Development (McCloy et al., 1999a). During the pilot study, the WIP was administered to participants at 43 employment centers. Finally, the main study involved administration of the WIL, WIP, and MIQ to employment center clients and junior college students at 23 unspecified sites. It is not clear what sampling procedure (random, stratified, purposive) for pilot or main studies were used. Furthermore, it is unclear where these participants were geographically located.

The sample for the normative sample was 1,199 for the WIL, 941 for the WIP, and 550 for the MIQ (McCloy et al., 1999b). The sample consisted of a fairly even ratio of females to males: 606 females and 588 males for the WIP, 494 females and 440 males for the WIP, and 272 females and 277 males for the MIQ (McCloy et al., 1999b). The percentage of White, African American, and Latino respondents for the WIL Paper-and-Pencil were 45% , 38% and 13%, and the percentages for the WIP were 47%, 37%, and 12%, respectively (McCloy et al., 1999). The mean age of the sample for the first administration of the WIP and WIP was 35 years old, and 32 years old at the second administration (McCloy et al., 1999b). The average years of education were 13 (McCloy et al., 1999b). The time between Time 1 and Time 2 of the administration was approximately 4-8 weeks.

Test-retest reliability for the WIP were moderately high (0.63 correlation, with a range from .50 to .76) between Time 1 and 2 of the administration. Correlations for the values had a median of 0.62 (ranging .59 - .66), and 62% of respondents ranked the same value highest on both administrations. Furthermore, 52% ranked the same two highest values on both administrations of the test, and the top value on the first administration was ranked first or second on the second administration for 88% of respondents. Correlations of need profiles and work value profiles between the first and second administration were moderately high (r = .77 for needs and r = .72 for values). The results support the use of the top work values and needs (McCloy et al., 1999b).

With respect to internal consistency, value scales for the WIP were compared to the value scales of the MIQ: achievement, comfort, status, altruism, safety, and autonomy. Figures from the WIP ranged between .70 and .76 for 5 of the 6 value scales. The reliability for the Altruism scale was considerably lower, between .48 and .50. The internal consistency figures parallel the MIQ internal consistency reliabilities (McCloy et al., 1999b).

A comparison among instruments (WIP, WIL, and MIQ) was conducted to determine whether the WIP and WIL accurately measure work values (i.e., construct validity). The correlations for needs between the WIP and the WIL ranged from .61 to .73, and the correlations for values between these two measures ranged from .73 to .85. The correlations for needs between the WIP and MIQ ranged from .55 to .84, and the correlations for values between these two measures ranged from .67 to .84. Thus, the WIP, WIL, and MIQ measure similar constructs (McCloy et al., 1999a). Further evidence of the WIL's construct validity is indicated by a factor analysis to confirm whether the instruments accurately reflect the six hypothesized work values from the MIQ. Results indicate both instruments have similar factor structures (McCloy et al., 1999b). The data revealed moderate support for the present theoretical six factor work values model and was better supported theoretically by a seven-factor model which split the Comfort Value in two: Internal and External Comfort (McCloy et al., 1999b). As a result, the MIQ fit better in the seven-factor model than the theoretically developed six factor model on which the MIQ was based (McCloy et al., 1999b)

General Utility and Evaluation

The WIL and WIP overall are strong instruments for helping individuals identify, rate, and sort their work values and needs in accordance with the Theory of Work Adjustment (Dawis & Lofquist 1984). Furthermore, both assessments are tightly linked with a significant occupational database which enables individuals to explore possible career choices based on the results from the WIL and WIP. The user guides for the WIL, and WIP are easily found online at www.onetcenter.org and provide step-by-step instructions for self-administration. Although the assessments are self-administered and scored, this reviewer strongly recommends a counselor assists the client process the results as part of the career decision-making process. Both the WIL and WIP are useful for individuals from a wide range of ethnic, cultural, and socioeconomic backgrounds (Ciechalski, 2009). Results from the assessments help highlight what matters to individuals and offer a variety of occupations that may match those values. Individuals that lack self-knowledge and/or knowledge about what occupations tend to promote those values will find that both the WIL and WIP is an easy to use instrument for career exploration (Ciechalski, 2009).

Individuals with other career concerns (such as problems with career concern, control, or confidence), may not find the WIL and WIP as beneficial in addressing their specific career adaptability problem (Savickas, 2005). Furthermore, the occupational list that accompanies both assessments suggests that occupations are viewed as static, in that certain values/needs reside inherently within certain occupations. This is based on a trait-factor model approach, whereby individuals and occupations are perceived as possessing static traits or values. In line with the Theory of Work Adjustment, individuals experience job satisfaction by matching their values/traits with the values/traits within certain occupations. This is a traditional approach to career counseling. A postmodern approach would suggest that there is more fluidity within work environments than previous conceptualized by modern paradigms (Savickas et al., 2009). Not only do individuals develop, grow, and change over time, but occupations are not nearly as static as previously thought. For example, a teacher may be given a high score for autonomy, yet individuals, who rate low on autonomy on the WIL or WIP, should not rule out being a teacher. Instead, they can use their knowledge (that they prefer to work with others) by seeking out teaching positions and opportunities that collaborate with others (e.g., a teaching assistant, a resource teacher). In summary, the WIL and the WIP remain useful assessments to help increase self-knowledge and knowledge about the world of work.

References and Additional Resources

Ciechalski, J. C. (2009). [O*NET Work Importance Locator/Profiler.] In E. A. Whitfield, R. W. Feller, & C. Wood (Eds.), *A counselor's guide to career assessment instruments* (5th ed., pp. 296-295). Broken Arrow, OK: National Career Development Association.

Dawis, R. V. & Lofquist, L. H. (1984). *A psychological theory of work adjustment.* Minneapolis, MN: University of Minnesota Press.

Kelly, K. R., & Lee, W-C., (2002). Mapping the domain of career decision problems. *Journal of Vocational Behavior, 61*(2), 302-326. doi:10.1006/jvbe.2001.1858

Kelley, K. N., & Michael, W. B. (2005). [O*Net Work Importance Locator]. In R. A. Spies & B. S. Plake (Eds.), *The sixteenth mental measurements yearbook.* Lincoln, NE: Buros Center for Testing.

McCloy, R., Waugh, G., Medsker, G., Wall, J., Rivkin, D., & Lewis, P. (1999a). *Development of the O*NET Computerized Work Importance Profiler.* Raleigh, NC: National Center for O*NET Development- Employment Security Commission.

McCloy, R., Waugh, G., Medsker, G., Wall, J., Rivkin, D., & Lewis, P. (1999b). *Development of the O*NET Paper-and-Pencil Work Importance Locator.* Raleigh, NC: National Center for O*NET Development- Employment Security Commission.

Rounds, J. B., Henley, G. A., Dawis, R. V., Lofquist, L. H., & Weiss, D. J. (1981). *Manual for the Minnesota Importance Questionnaire.* Minneapolis, MN: University of Minnesota.

Savickas, M. L. (2005). The theory and practice of career construction. In S. D. Brown & R. W. Lent (Eds.), *Career development and counseling* (pp. 42-70). Hoboken, NJ: Wiley.

Savickas, M. L., Nota, L., Rossier, J., Dauwalder, J., Duarte, M., Guichard, J., Soresi, S., Van Esbroeck, R., and van Vianen, A. (2009). Life designing: A paradigm for career construction in the 21st century. *Journal of Vocational Behavior, 75,* 239-250. doi: 10.1016/j.jvb.2009.04.004

Spies, R. A., & Plake, B. S. (Eds.). (2005). [Work Importance Locator.] In R. A. Spies & B. S. Plake (Eds.), *The sixteenth mental measurements yearbook.* Lincoln, NE: Buros Center for Testing.

U.S. Department of Labor Employment and Training Administration. (2002a). *O*NET Work Importance Profiler User's Guide.* Washington DC: U.S. Government Printing Office.

U.S. Department of Labor Employment and Training Administration. (2002b). *O*NET Work Importance Locator Occupations Master List.* Washington DC: U.S. Government Printing Office.

U.S. Department of Labor Employment and Training Administration. (2000). *Work Importance Locator Score User's Guide.* Washington DC: U.S. Government Printing Office.

A Counselor's Guide To Career Assessments Instruments

Self-Directed Search, Fourth Edition, and Career Explorer
John L. Holland

Psychological Assessment Resources, Inc.

16204 N. Florida Avenue
Lutz, FL 33549
http://www.parinc.com/

Target Population: Adolescents, young adults, and adults.

Statement of the Purpose of the Instrument: The Self Directed Search, fourth edition (SDS-R) is a self-administered test that helps individuals identify the occupations that best suit their interests and skills.

Titles of Subtests, Scales, Scores Provided: Holland Code, numerical scores in six Holland (RIASEC) categories (Realistic, Investigative, Artistic, Social, Enterprising, Conventional), Aspirations code.

Forms and Levels Available, with Dates of Publication/Revision of Each: Professional User's Guide; Technical Manual; Form R Assessment Booklet; Form R Occupations Finder; Form R Occupations Finder; Dictionary of Holland Occupational Codes (DHOC), 3rd Edition; The Self-Directed Search and Related Holland Career Materials: A Practitioner's Guide. All Qualification Level A. Publication date for all: 1994, except DHOC (1996), Practitioner's Guide (1998), and Occupations Finder (2010).

Date of Most Recent Edition of Test Manual, User's Guide, Etc.: 1994 (except DHOC, 1996; Practitioner's Guide, 1998; and Occupations Finder, 2010).

Languages in Which Available: English, Canadian English, Canadian French, Spanish, also translated into more than 20 other languages.

Time:

Actual Test Time: 20-30 minutes.

Total Administration Time: 35-45 minutes.

Norm Group(s) on Which Scores Are Based: 2,602 students and working adults: 1,600 females and 1,002 males, ranging in age from 17 to 65 years, with 75% Whites, 8% African Americans, 7% Latinos, 4% Asian Americans, 1% Native Americans, and 5% from other ethnic backgrounds; data were collected in 10 high schools, 9 community colleges, 19 colleges or universities, and a variety of other sources throughout the United States.

Manner in Which Results Are Reported for Individuals: Raw scores and a summary code (Holland Code) are provided. Percentile ranks for high school students, college students, and adults are included. Form R Windows Internet Version/Form R Software Portfolio (SDS-SP) Interpretive Report (10-15 page report) includes careers and educational programs that match the person's Holland Code. Report also describes the RIASEC system and provides concrete suggestions for further exploration.

Report Format/Content for Group Summaries: Not available.

Machine Scoring: SDS-SP or Internet Version. Costs of software options: SDS-SP Form R Module CD-ROM or download $589.00, 25 administrations $115.00. Internet version options costs are as follows: $4.95 (U.S.) per report (1-99 uses) or $3.95 (U.S.) per report (100+ uses).

Cost of Materials: Due to possible price changes since publication date, be sure to check the publisher's website. Professional User's Guide $34.00, e-manual version $29.00; Technical Manual $34.00, e-manual version $29.00; Technical Manual & Professional User's Guide $64.00; Form R Assessment Booklets (pkg/25) $43.00; Form R Occupations Finder (pkg/25) $55.00; Form R You and Your Career Booklets (pkg/25) $34.00; Form R Educational Opportunities Finder Booklets (pkg/25) $55.00.

Specimen Set: SDS Form R Introductory Kit which includes SDS Professional User's Guide, Technical Manual, 25 Assessment Booklets, 25 Occupations Finder, and 25 You and Your Career Booklets $186.00.

Counselee Materials: Form R Assessment Booklet (not reusable): A booklet containing a self-guided section on personal ratings of SDS scales and additional sections on how to organize your answers, what your summary code means, some next steps, and some useful books.

Form R You and Your Career Booklet (reusable): A booklet that provides additional interpretive information on personality types, occupations, and making career decisions.

Educational Opportunities Finder (reusable): A booklet listing over 750 fields of study in universities, colleges, vocational schools, and community colleges that match Holland codes.

Leisure Activities Finder (reusable): A booklet listing over 700 leisure activities that match Holland codes.

Occupations Finder (reusable): A booklet with over 1,300 occupations listed by three-letter Holland codes. New edition is cross-referenced with the O*NET database.

Published Reviews of the Instrument in the Last 15 Years:

Ciechalski, J. C. (2001). [Self-Directed Search (4th ed.).] In J. T. Kapes & E. A. Whitfield, *A counselor's guide to career assessment instruments* (4th ed., pp. 276-287). Columbus, OH: National Career Development Association.

Ciechalski, J. C. (2009). [Self-Directed Search (4th ed.).] In E. A. Whitfield, R. W. Feller, & C. Wood (Eds.), *A counselor's guide to career assessment instruments* (5th ed., pp. 304–308). Broken Arrow, OK: National Career Development Association.

Osborn, D. (2002). [Self-Directed Search.] *Rehabilitation Counseling Bulletin, 46,* 57-59. doi: 10.1177/00343552020460010801

SELF-DIRECTED SEARCH, FOURTH EDITION, AND CAREER EXPLORER

Reviewed by

Caroline A. Baker

Department of Counseling and School Psychology
University of Wisconsin River Falls

Description

The Self-Directed Search (SDS) was developed by John Holland in the 1950s and has been empirically researched and revised to its current form and content (Krieshok, 1987; Nauta, 2010). Published by Psychological Assessment Resources, Inc. (PAR), there are four forms, each used with different populations, to assist with educational and career planning. The SDS Form R: 4th Edition includes an *Assessment Booklet* (1994), *The Occupations Finder—Revised Edition* (2010), *You and Your Career* (1994), *The Leisure Activities Finder* (1997), and *The Educational Opportunities Finder* (1997). This form is designed for use with clients from high school to adulthood. The SDS Form Easy (E): fourth edition is designed for high school students or adults with educational or reading challenges, and it consists of an *Assessment Booklet* (1996), *The Jobs Finder* (1996), and *You and Your Job* (1995).

Additionally, there are the SDS Form Career Planning (CP) and SDS Career Explorer (CE) versions of the assessment. The SDS Form CP is designed to assist adults transitioning in their career and consists of an *Assessment Booklet* (1990), *Career Options Finder* (2001), and *Exploring Career Options* (1990). Finally, the SDS Career Explorer is developmentally designed for adolescents in middle school or junior high school. The associated documents include a *Self-Assessment Booklet* (1994), a *Careers Booklet* (2000), *Exploring Your Future with the SDS* (1994), and a *Teacher's Guide* (1994). To assist the professional administering the assessment, a *Technical Manual* (1997) provides the theoretical background of the SDS as well as gives statistical analysis of validity and reliability of the assessment related to different populations. More important, perhaps, is the *Professional Users Guide* (1997), which guides the professional through the administration and interpretation of the SDS in group or individual settings. The SDS can be administered in paper-and-pencil format or on a computer through software or Internet access. There are several options for purchasing the hard copy version of the SDS.

A Counselor's Guide To Career Assessments Instruments

The SDS is a "self-administered, self-scored, and self-interpreted career counseling tool" that was developed "(a) to multiply the number of people a counselor can serve, and (b) to provide a career counseling experience for people who do not have, or who do not wish to have, access to a vocational counselor" (Holland, Powell, & Fritzsche, 1997, p. 1). The main composition of the SDS Forms R, E, CE, and CP involves the *Assessment Booklet, Occupations/Jobs Finder,* and interpretive booklets. The SDS Form R *Assessment Booklet* starts with the Occupational Daydreams section in which the client lists career goals and ideas and then determines the code from the Occupations Finder. Next, the client completes scales and ratings for activities, competencies, occupations, and self-estimates on abilities and interests. Items in this section require the client to respond with Like/Dislike, Yes/No, or scaling from 1 (low) to 7 (high). Once the scales and ratings have been completed, the client moves to the section, How to Organize Your Answers, where the client sums her or his scores and determines the three-letter summary code. The client then can use the What Your Summary Code Means and Some Next Steps sections to re-examine the *Occupations Finder* using her or his new summary code. The other forms of the SDS are nearly identical in format, but are adapted for specific population needs with simplified wording, two-letter summary codes, and elimination of the Occupational Daydreams for the Career Planning form.

The assessment, arranged in progression, guides the user with concise and clear instructions, and maintains simplicity in design. The timing to administer or complete the SDS is 35-45 minutes for the hard copy, or 20-30 minutes for the online version. The SDS Form R is written at an eighth-grade reading level, and is designed for use with high school and adult populations. The Form E is written at a fourth-grade reading level for clients with reading or other educational challenges.

The SDS may be used with individuals or in group settings, with the counselor providing minimal pre-instruction. However, experts recommend that score interpretation should occur in collaboration with the counselor so that clients thoroughly examine the meaning of their score using all permutations of the three-letter summary code (Krieshok, 1987; Osborn & Reardon, 2006). Scores can assist the client with self-awareness of interests and skills, and provide some direction in career development.

Technical Considerations

The Technical Manual provides detailed statistical analysis of the SDS in its many forms. Specifically, Form R was normed using a sample of 2,602 students and adults from around the United States, including 1,600 females and 1,002 males ranging in age from 17 to 65 years. The majority of the sample was White (75%), with African Americans (8%), Hispanics (7%), Asian Americans (4%), Native Americans (1%), and "other" ethnic backgrounds (5%) together made up the remaining 25% (Holland, Powell & Fritzche, 1997). Further discussion of gender, age, and ethnic background differences may be found in the manual.

The Technical Manual reports internal consistency coefficients (KR-20) ranging from .72 to .92 for the Activities, Competencies, and Occupations scales, while the summary scale coefficients ranged from .90 to .94. Further, test-retest reliability was measured using a sample of 73 adults representing the normative group, resulting in correlations ranging from .76 to .89 (Holland, Fritzsche, & Powell, 1997). The authors suggest the results "[imply] that summary scales have substantial stability" (p. 20). Validity was measured using the correlation of percentage of hits between the Occupational Daydreams code and the Summary code, resulting in a hit rate of 54.7%. The authors maintain that this falls within range of similar interest inventories. The Technical Manual provides an entire chapter on construct validity of the SDS, as well as similar overall statistics for the other versions.

General Utility and Evaluation

Both the *Professional User's Guide* and the *Technical Manual* contain detailed information to assist with understanding and administering the SDS. The *Professional User's Guide* targets the counselor or other practitioner who will help individuals or groups complete the assessment. A discussion of Holland's theory, an overview of the materials, and scoring and interpretive guidance is included. The *Technical Manual* provides the statistical evidence and support for the assessment, and compares earlier versions with the current form. Other reviews have been completed, exploring specifically the Holland constructs of differentiation, congruence,

Self-Directed Search, Fourth Edition, and Career Explorer

and/or consistency/internal coherence, or comparing the hard copy and online versions (Krieshok, 1987; Lumsden, Sampson, Reardon, & Lenz, 2002). These reviews indicate that the SDS is generally positively appraised when evaluated as a career counseling tool.

References and Additional Resources

Ciechalski, J. C. (2001). [Self-Directed Search (4th ed.).] In J. T. Kapes & E. A. Whitfield, *A counselor's guide to career assessment instruments* (4th ed., pp. 276-287). Columbus, OH: National Career Development Association.

Ciechalski, J. C. (2009). [Self-Directed Search (4th ed.).] In E. A. Whitfield, R. W. Feller, & C. Wood (Eds.), *A counselor's guide to career assessment instruments* (5th ed., pp. 304–308). Broken Arrow, OK: National Career Development Association.

Holland, J. L., Fritzsche, B. A., & Powell, A. B. (1997). *Technical manual.* Lutz, FL: Psychological Assessment Resources, Inc.

Holland, J. L., Powell, A. B., & Fritzsche, B. A. (1997). *Self-Directed Search: Professional user's guide.* Lutz, FL: Psychological Assessment Resources, Inc.

Krieshok, T. S. (1987). Testing the test: Review of the Self-Directed Search. *Journal of Counseling & Development, 65,* 512-514.

Lumsden, J. A., Sampson, J. D., Reardon, R. C., & Lenz, J. G. (2002). *A comparison study of the paper, personal computer (PC), and internet versions of Holland's Self-Directed Search.* (Technical Report No. 30). Tallahassee, FL: The Center for the Study of Technology in Counseling and Career Development, Florida State University.

Nauta, M. M. (2010). The development, evolution, and status of Holland's theory of vocational personalities: Reflections and future directions for counseling psychology. *Journal of Counseling Psychology, 57,* 11-22. doi: 10.1037/a0018213

Osborn, D. S., & Reardon, R. C. (2006). Using the Self-Directed Search: Career Explorer with high risk middle school students. *Career Development Quarterly, 54,* 269-273.

Osborn, D. (2002). [Self-Directed Search.] *Rehabilitation Counseling Bulletin, 46,* 57-59. doi: 10.1177/00343552020460010801

A COUNSELOR'S GUIDE TO CAREER ASSESSMENTS INSTRUMENTS

STRONG INTEREST INVENTORY AND SKILLS CONFIDENCE INVENTORY

E.K. Strong (SII)
Nancy E. Betz, Fred H. Borgen, and Lenore W. Harmon (SCI)

CPP, Inc., and Davies-Black® Publishing

1055 Joaquin Road, 2nd Floor
Mountain View, CA 94043
650.969.8901
800.624.1765
Fax: 650.969.8608
http://www.cpp.com

Target Population: Adolescents, young adults, and adults; age 14 and older Strong Interest Inventory or 15 or older Skills Confidence Inventory.

Statement of the Purpose of the Instrument: The Strong Interest Inventory (SII) assessment tool measures a client's interests in a broad range of occupations, work activities, leisure activities, and school subjects. The Skills Confidence Inventory (SCI) measures clients' perceived level of confidence in performing skills related to the six General Occupational Themes (GOTs). The report shows whether a client has very little, little, moderate, high, or very high confidence in skills related to the six GOTs. It is recommended that the instruments be used concurrently.

Titles of Subtests, Scales, Scores Provided: The SII provides scores for the six GOTs (Realistic, Artistic, Investigative, Social, Enterprising, Conventional), Occupational Scales (244), Basic Interest Scales (30), and Personal Style Scales (5). The SCI indicates scores for the six GOTs. Results are prioritized into the following categories: High Priority; High Confidence, High Interest; Possible Options If Interest Develops; High Confidence, Little Interest, Good Option If Confidence Increases; Little Confidence, High Interest, Low Priority; Little Confidence, Little Interest.

Forms and Levels Available, with Dates of Publication/revision of Each: SII: Profile (2004); Interpretive Report (2004); Career Report with the MBTI Instrument (2005); Strong and SCI Profile (2004). SCI: Level B (1996).

Date of Most Recent Edition of Test Manual, User's Guide, Etc.: 2005 (SII; manual supplement published in 2012) and 2005 (SCI).

Languages in Which Available: SII: English, Korean, Portuguese, Argentinian Spanish. SCI: English and Canadian French.

Time:

Actual Test Time: SII: 35-40 minutes; SCI: fewer than 30 minutes.

Total Administration Time: SII: 35-40 minutes; SCI: 40-50 minutes.

Norm Group(s) on Which Scores Are Based: The SII was normed for a national sample of more than 55,000 individuals stratified by age, gender, and ethnicity according to U.S. Census data. Percentiles for the SCI are based on 1,147 working adult participants and the return rate across gender/occupation combinations ranged from 50%. The normative sample of college students consisted of 706 enrolled in introductory psychology courses at the Ohio State University and Iowa State University.

Manner in Which Results Are Reported for Individuals: For the SII standard scores and verbal labels are provided in a profile; approximate percentile equivalents based from 1.0 to 5.0 are included for the SCI. The SII basic report includes the Strong Profile (Standard, High School, or College Editions). The basic SCI report includes Holland's Hexagon and the General Occupations and is included as a one-page report at the end of the six-page Strong Profile. The report shows whether a client has very little, moderate, high, or very high confidence in skills related to the six GOTs. The SCI is available only in combination with materials for the SII.

Report Format/Content for Group Summaries: Not available.

Machine Scoring: The SII includes mail-in software and a web administration site. For the SCI, the mail-in scoring has a five-day turnaround period. It is a one-page report that follows the six-page Strong Profile. The price of scoring is included in the original ordering price.

Hand Scoring: Not available.

Local Machine Scoring: Not available.

Computer Software Options Available: SII: Standard administration and CPP web administration. SCI: Computerized adaptive administration.

Cost of Materials: Please refer to the publisher's website.

Additional Comments of interest to Users: For the SCI, lack of experience may lead to lower skills confidence scores, rendering the scores somewhat less meaningful. Lower levels of confidence should be considered to indicate areas where new learning might be attempted.

Published Reviews of the Instruments in the Last 15 Years:

Ciechalski, J. C. (2010). [Skills Confidence Inventory, revised edition.] In R. A. Spies, J. F. Carlson, & K. F. Geisinger (Eds.), *The eighteenth mental measurements yearbook.* Lincoln, NE: Buros Center for Testing.

Denzine, G. M. (2010). [Skills Confidence Inventory, revised edition.] In R. A. Spies, J. F. Carlson, & K. F. Geisinger (Eds.), *The eighteenth mental measurements yearbook.* Lincoln, NE: Buros Center for Testing.

Jenkins, J. A. (2009). [Strong Interest Inventory and the Skills Confidence Inventory.] In E. Whitfield, R. W. Feller, & C. Wood (Eds.), *A counselor's guide to career assessment instruments* (5th ed., pp. 309-319). Broken Arrow, OK: National Career Development Association.

Kantamneni, N., & Scheel, M. J. (2010). [Strong Interest Inventory.] In R. A. Spies, J. F. Carlson, & K. F. Geisinger (Eds.), *The eighteenth mental measurements yearbook.* Lincoln, NE: Buros Center for Testing.

Kelly, K. R. (2010). [Strong Interest Inventory.] In R. A. Spies, J. F. Carlson, & K. F. Geisinger (Eds.), *The eighteenth mental measurements yearbook.* Lincoln, NE: Buros Center for Testing.

STRONG INTEREST INVENTORY
AND SKILLS CONFIDENCE INVENTORY

Reviewed by:

Jeffrey A. Jenkins

School of Justice Studies
Roger Williams University

Description

The Strong Interest Inventory (SII), first developed in 1927 by Edward K. Strong as the Strong Vocational Interest Blank, has undergone numerous revisions and been the subject of extensive research in a variety of fields over its 85-year history. Indeed, few psychological measures of any type can claim to have developed in tandem with the professions of education and psychology as has the SII. As a measure of career and vocational interests, the current revision of the instrument has both benefited and contributed to the expansion of the field of career development and the important life-changing issues it addresses.

As a well-known psychological measure, the SII continues to be studied extensively and used in professional practice to guide the career search. It measures career and vocational interests, that is, the preferences of individuals for those aspects of occupations that most appeal to them. Although the primary use of the SII is in career counseling, the revised manual notes that the SII may also be useful for other decisions, such as identifying "preferences for activities and situations that are not specifically work related—for example, interests in recreational activities or preferences for types of people that may guide decisions about leisure time or living arrangements." (Donnay, Morris, Schaubhut, & Thompson, 2005, p. 2).

The SII consists of 291 items presented as statements relating to the world of work or life activities. Respondents indicate the extent of their preference for each item on a five-point scale *(Strongly Like, Like, Indifference, Dislike, Strongly Dislike)*. In prior editions, a three-point scale was used. Examples include "Being your own boss," "Reading a book," and "Security guard." These reported preferences are compared to patterns of responses by people working in various occupations. Item responses are summarized as scores on six General Occupational Themes (GOTs; Realistic, Investigative, Artistic, Social, Enterprising, and Conventional) based largely on Holland's vocational classification system. In addition, scores are reported on 30 Basic Interest Scales (e.g., Computer Hardware and Electronics, Athletics, Social Sciences), 122 Occupational Scales (e.g., Accountant, Firefighter, Respiratory Therapist), and five Personal Style Scales (Work Style, Learning Environment, Leadership Style, Risk Taking, and Team Orientation).

The 2005 version of the SII, while unchanged in overall format and approach from earlier editions, is improved and updated from earlier versions in significant ways. The first of these involved the addition or revision of numerous items resulting in fewer items overall (291 items, down from 317 in the 1994 version). The fewer items resulted in six, rather than the former eight, sections of the SII. Item responses were also changed from a three-point Likert format to a five-point scale for all items, improving variability of response choice and making response choices consistent for the entire instrument. The GOTs remain unchanged, although some involve fewer items than previously while measuring the same construct.

The second improvement involves revisions of and additions to the Basic Interest Scales (BISs). These include renaming ten of the scales, eliminating four, and adding ten new scales. These changes better reflect career choices available today.

The third type of revision related to the Occupational Scales (OSs), which were increased from 211 to 244 in the 2005 revision, expanding the range of occupational interests available to users. The OSs were further revised in 2012 to more closely align scores on the SII with current occupations. This revision resulted in the removal of some older scales and the addition of new ones, resulting in a new total of 260 scales from the former 244. The Strong Interest Inventory Manual Supplement (Herk & Thompson, 2012) discusses the 2012 OSs revisions. SII interpretive reports also have been updated to reflect changes in the OSs.

The fourth type of revision includes the addition of a new Personality Style Scale (PSS): Team Orientation. This new PSS is intended to measure the extent to which respondents prefer to work independently or with others. Other changes in the PSSs were also made, the most important of which was revising the Risk Taking PSS to better measure a range of risk taking behavior. Finally, revisions of the Administrative Indexes in the report profile were made. The most important of these was the removal of the infrequent response index and replacing it with a "typicality" index that reveals inconsistent response patterns.

The SII may also be used with a companion instrument, the Skills Confidence Inventory (SCI), developed in 1996. The SCI compares respondents' interests and confidence in their abilities to the GOTs, allowing practitioners to hone the career decision-making process. Although a revised SCI Manual was published in 2005 (Betz, Borgen, & Harmon, 2005), the SCI itself has not been revised since its initial development. The revised SCI Manual updates research using the instrument, and further discusses its relationship and use with the revised SII.

The SII is intended to assist career counselors and their clients as they engage in an exploration of the client's interests. Understanding these interests may assist the client in decision making across the life span. In this regard, the SII is useful for a accomplishing a number of beneficial counseling activities, including identifying the client's specific interests, choosing a field of study in the college years, considering occupations in which those interests may best be pursued, changing careers, or remaining active in retirement. Along with the SCI, the SII offers the career counselor both a practical and a theoretical basis for issues explored in the counseling session.

As the SII Manual recommends, the SII is most useful when the client has been oriented toward its administration and interpretation. As with any psychological assessment, the purpose of the SII should be clarified prior to administration and the meaning of each of the specific scales found in the profile explained and discussed (see American Educational Research Association, American Psychological Association, & National Council on Measurement in Education, 1999). Perhaps most important is emphasizing the distinction between "interests" and "abilities," since, without guidance, clients may confuse what they "like" with what they "are good at." The SII Manual also recommends that clients be given an explanation of Holland's (1997) theory of vocational choice and the six general occupational interests.

Strong Interest Inventory and Skills Confidence Inventory

The SCI is used in conjunction with the SII by helping the client to understand how good they believe themselves to be at various activities. As noted above, the SCI Profile provides a comparison of the client's interests and perceived confidence in their abilities in each of the six GOTs. This is a useful tool for helping the client explore high interest/high confidence areas regarding vocational and occupational choices, as well as addressing areas of high interest where clients have low confidence in their abilities.

Technical Considerations

Norms for the SII consist of a sample of 2,250 working men and women. These were randomly selected from a pool of over 20,000 respondents to be generally representative of the United States workforce in terms of ethnicity and gender. The specific rates of inclusion in the sample are reported in the Manual, as are other demographic characteristics. Development of the norm sample for the 2004 SII marked a departure from prior norm group data gathering methods. For the first time, the majority of respondents included in the norm group responded to the web-based version of the SII. The norm group, previously referred to as the General Reference Sample, is now called the General Representative Sample (GRS) to reflect a greater attempt to achieve representativeness through proportional selection based on gender and ethnicity. Unless otherwise indicated, the GRS was also the sample used for the reliability and validity studies of the latest version of the SII. Reliability estimates for the SII are high for all scores reported. Cronbach's alpha for all six of the GOTs is .90 or greater, and test-retest reliabilities average .85 over the six scales. The BISs exhibit a similar degree of reliability. Coefficient alpha ranges from .80 to .92 across the 30 BISs. Test-retest reliabilities fall within the same range. For the newly revised 260 OSs (130 female, 130 male), test-retest reliability was reported in the SII Manual Supplement to range from .71 to .93. The PSSs are also highly reliable. Coefficient alpha ranges from .82 to .87, and test-retest reliabilities are similarly high. Finally, reliability of the SCI is reported in the SCI Manual to range from .84 to .88. Published studies have confirmed both the internal consistency (Betz & Gwilliam, 2002) and test-retest (Parsons & Betz, 1998) reliability of the SCI, reporting scale reliabilities in the .80 to .90 range. While the reliability estimates of the SII are based on adequate research samples of varying sizes, it is worth noting that the SII Manual also reports reliabilities separately for males and females. For most scales, these estimates do not differ greatly and thus allow a greater degree of confidence in the use of the SII with males and females.

A considerable number of studies have produced evidence of validity for the SII. For the 1994 version of the SII, the concurrent, predictive, and construct validity of the various SII scales has been shown (for the GOTs, see Donnay & Borgen, 1996; Savickas, Taber, & Spokane, 2002; for the BISs, see Borgen & Lindley, 2003; Donnay & Borgen, 1996; for the OSs, see Dik & Hansen, 2004; Strong, 1935; Zarrella & Schuerger, 1990; and for the PSSs, see Kahn, Nauta, Gailbreath, Tipps, & Chartrand, 2002; Lindley & Borgen, 2000). A growing number of studies have also examined the validity of the 2005 edition. Bailey, Larson, Borgen, and Gasser (2008) examined the equivalence of the 1994 and 2005 versions with male and female college students, finding significant correlations between the old and new versions for the SII scales. Armstrong, Fouad, Rounds, and Hubert (2010) used the GOT and BIS profiles to differentiate gender and employment status in students and employed adults. The GOTs and the BISs of the 2005 SII have been used to predict job satisfaction (Rottinghaus, Hees, & Conrath, Borges, & Hartwig, 2009). Moreover, vocational interests measured by the SII have been used to significantly predict medical students' work values (Duffy et al., 2009).

Several studies of the 2005 SII's ability to predict the college major choices of students have been conducted. For example, Pulver and Kelly (2008) used the GOTs to correctly predict over 45% of college students' choices of major after four semesters. In addition, the ability of the SII to discriminate among major family classifications chosen by college students has been shown. (Larson, Wu, Bailey, Borgen , & Gasser, 2010).

As noted above, the OSs underwent significant revisions in 2012. The SII Manual Supplement focuses primarily on the technical characteristics of the new OSs, with particular attention paid to the validity of the new scales. Discriminant validity was reported in terms of the intercorrelations among OSs within each SII Theme code. Within each of the six GOTs (Realistic, Investigative, Artistic, Social, Enterprising, and Conventional), the median correlation among the OSs was substantially higher than the median correlation among the OSs overall. This provides some evidence that the new OSs are able to discriminate among the themes based on the interests of people working in occupations reflective of those themes. Further, the relationship between

A COUNSELOR'S GUIDE TO CAREER ASSESSMENTS INSTRUMENTS

the 2012 OSs and the GOTs were examined. These correlations were largely in the expected directions. For example, in the new sample of females used in the development of the 2012 OSs, the correlation between the "Middle School Teacher" OS and the "Social" GOT was .81; the correlation between the Social GOT and the "Network Administrator" GOT was .10. This demonstrates the ability of the new OSs to differentiate among occupations based on GOT scores, their central purpose. Similarly, the correlations between the new OSs and the PSSs were in the expected directions.

For the SCI, Betz, Borgen, Kaplan, and Harmon (1998) examined concurrent validity by studying gender differences in skills confidence within occupations. Based on a national sample of adults, they found only minimal gender differences in confidence within occupations, consistent with the theoretical expectation that women and men in the same occupation should have the same degree of confidence in their skills. Predictive validity of the SCI has also been shown by Betz et al. (1998), who were able to predict Holland job family based on SCI scores, and Bonitz, Armstrong, and Larson (2010), who used cutoff scores from the SII and SCI in college students and adults to predict their levels of interests and confidence.

Administration of the SII and SCI on the publisher's website is available. This is a preferable way of administering the instruments since it allows the respondent to more quickly work sequentially through the items, records their responses, and provides immediate scoring and report generation.

General Utility and Evaluation

A strength of the SII over the years has been its ability to assist respondents in understanding their interests in terms of both their personal activities and the demands of the workplace. This is particularly true of the current version of the SII, which is more user-friendly and more clearly addresses its measurement goals than past versions. The SII integrates well with the SCI, and together they provide organized and well-formatted profiles and reports that provide insights about the client that are directly relevant to the counseling session. In addition, the resources available to counselors, including classroom training, website information, and test manuals are extensive.

If there is a weakness in the current version of the SSI, it is in the manner in which data in the GRS were gathered, affecting the norms. The GRS was largely made up of respondents identified by their web surfing for career information using online search engines. Only about 10% of those identified in this manner eventually became members of the norm group. This self-selected group may be a sufficient basis for score comparison, but it may not. Although Internet use is now ubiquitous, by only selecting respondents who surf the web for career information the sample is limited to those with potential greater interest and ability in computer technology and those who may limit their career choice research to such sources.

Nonetheless, the SII maintains its position as a premier inventory in the measurement of career interests. Its history, timely revisions, solid technical characteristics, and interpretive reports make it tool that every career counselor should understand and use.

References and Additional Resources

American Educational Research Association, American Psychological Association & National Council on Measurement in Education. (1999). *Standards for educational and psychological testing.* Washington, D.C.: American Educational Research Association.

Armstrong, P. I., Fouad, N. A., Rounds, J., & Hubert, L. (2010). Quantifying and interpreting group differences in interest profiles. *Journal of Career Assessment, 18*, 115-132.

Bailey, D. C., Larson, L. M., Borgen, F. H., & Gasser, C. E. (2008). Changing of the guard: Interpretive continuity of the 2005 Strong Interest Inventory. *Journal of Career Assessment, 16*, 135-155.

Betz, N. E., Borgen, F. H., & Harmon, L. W. (2005). *Skills confidence inventory manual* (revised ed.). Mountain View, CA: CPP, Inc.

Betz, N. E., Borgen, F. H., Kaplan, A., & Harmon, L. W. (1998). Gender and Holland type as moderators of the validity and interpretive utility of the Skills Confidence Inventory. *Journal of Vocational Behavior, 53*, 281-299.

Betz, N. E., & Gwilliam, L. (2002). The utility of measures of self-efficacy for the Holland themes in African American and European American college students. *Journal of Career Assessment, 10*, 283-300.

Bonitz, V. S., Armstrong, P. I., & Larson, L. M. (2010). RIASEC interest and confidence cutoff scores: Implications for career counseling. *Journal of Vocational Behavior, 76,* 265-276.

Borgen, F. H., & Lindley, L. D. (2003). Optimal functioning in interests, self-efficacy, and personality. In W. B. Walsh (Ed.), *Counseling psychology and optimal human functioning* (pp. 55-91). Hillsdale, NJ: Lawrence Erlbaum Press.

Dik, B. J. & Hansen, J. C. (2004). Development and validation of discriminant functions for the Strong Interest Inventory. *Journal of Vocational Behavior, 1,* 1-9.

Donnay, D. A. C., & Borgen, F. H. (1996). The incremental validity of vocational self-efficacy: An examination of interest, self-efficacy, and occupation. *Journal of Counseling Psychology, 46,* 432-447.

Donnay, D. A. C., Morris, M. L., Schaubhut, N. A., & Thompson, R. C. (2005). *Strong Interest Inventory manual* (revised ed.). Mountain View, CA: CPP, Inc.

Duffy, R. D., Borges, N. J., & Hartung, P. J. (2009). Personality, vocational interests, and work values of medical students. *Journal of Career Assessment, 17,* 189-200.

Herk, N. A., & Thompson, R. C. (2012). *Strong Interest Inventory manual supplement.* Mountain View, CA: CPP, Inc.

Holland, J. L. (1997). *Making vocational choices: A theory of vocational personalities and work environments* (3rd ed.). Odessa, FL: Psychological Assessment Resources.

Kahn, J. H., Nauta, M. M., Gailbreath, R. D., Tipps, J. & Chartrand, J. M. (2002). The utility of career and personality assessment in predicting academic progress. *Journal of Career Assessment, 10,* 3-23.

Larson, L. M., Wu, T. F., Bailey, D. C., Borgen, F. H., & Gasser, C. E. (2010). Male and female college students' college majors: The contribution of basic vocational confidence and interests. *Journal of Career Assessment, 18,* 16-33.

Lindley, L. D., & Borgen, F. H. (2000). Personal style scales of the Strong Interest Inventory: Linking personality and interests. *Journal of Vocational Behavior, 57,* 22-41.

Parsons, E., & Betz, N. E. (1998). Test-retest reliability studies of the Skills Confidence Inventory. *Journal of Career Assessment, 6,* 1-12.

Pulver, C. A., & Kelly, K. R. (2008). Incremental validity of the Myers-Briggs Type Indicator in predicting academic major selection of undecided university students. *Journal of Career Assessment, 16,* 441-455.

Rottinghaus, P. J., Hees, C. K., & Conrath, J. A. (2009). Enhancing job satisfaction perspectives: Combining Holland themes and basic interests. *Journal of Vocational Behavior, 75,* 139-151.

Savickas, M. L., Taber, B. J., & Spokane, A. R. (2002). Convergent and discriminant validity of five interest inventories. *Journal of Vocational Behavior, 61,* 139-184.

Strong, E. K. (1935). Predictive value of the Vocational Interest Test. *Journal of Educational Psychology, 26,* 332.

Zarrella, K. L., & Schuerger, J. M. (1990). Temporal stability of occupational interest inventories. *Psychological Reports, 66,* 1067-1074.

A COUNSELOR'S GUIDE TO CAREER ASSESSMENTS INSTRUMENTS

STUDY OF VALUES, FOURTH EDITION
Richard E. Kopelman, Janet L. Rovenpor, and Robert B. Allport

Richard E. Kopelman
Baruch College/CUNY
Zicklin School of Business
One Bernard Baruch Way
New York, NY 10010
646.312.3629
Richard.Kopelman@baruch.cuny.edu

Target Population: Adolescents, young adults, and adults.

Statement of the Purpose of the Instrument: The Study of Values (SOV) measures the relative strength of six values: Theoretical, Economic, Aesthetic, Social, Political, and Religious.

Titles of Subtests, Scales, Scores Provided: Scores are provided for each of the six value orientations, and scoring guidelines may be obtained by contacting the first author.

Forms and Levels Available, with Dates of Publication/Revision of Each: 2003.

Date of Most Recent Edition of Test Manual, User's Guide, Etc.: Fourth edition was published in the following article: Kopelman, R. E., Rovenpor, J. L., & Guan, M. (2003). The Study of Values: Construction of the fourth edition. *Journal of Vocational Behavior, 62,* 203-220. There is no manual.

Languages in Which Available: English only.

Time:

    Actual Test Time: Varies.

    Total Administration Time: 20-30 minutes.

Norm Group(s) on Which Scores Are Based: Both the third and fourth editions of the SOV were administered to 121 graduate students and 58 undergraduate students enrolled in business-related programs.

Manner in Which Results Are Reported for Individuals: A counselor reviews subscales with the client, with scores obtained by using a scoring grid with checked boxes on the SOV itself. A free copy of the scoring grid is available electronically upon request to the first author.

Report Format/Content for Group Summaries: Not available.

Machine Scoring: Not available.

Hand Scoring: Hand scored by counselor. A scoring grid is available on request from the first author.

Local Machine Scoring: Not available.

Computer Software Options Available: Not available. An online version is available via license from the authors.

Cost of Materials: No cost. The SOV is in the public domain.

    Specimen Set: Not available.

    Counselee Materials: Copies of the SOV.

Published Reviews of the Instrument in the Last 15 Years: Not available.

STUDY OF VALUES, FOURTH EDITION

Reviewed by:

W. Matthew Shurts

Department of Counseling and Educational Leadership
Montclair State University

Description

The Study of Values (SOV), Fourth Edition, is a non-projective personality measure based on the work of Eduard Spranger. It measures the relative strength of six values: Theoretical, Economic, Aesthetic, Social, Political, and Religious. It is intended for use with upper-level high school students, college students, and adults (Kopelman, Rovenpor, & Guan, 2003).

The SOV consists of 45 items presented in two parts. The 30 "controversial statements or questions" in Part I are forced-choice couplets where the respondent must distribute three points between two options. For example, a sample item from Part I is the following: "Assuming that you have sufficient leisure time, would you prefer to use it: (a) developing your mastery of a favorite skills; (b) doing volunteer social or public service work?". Based on the strength of preference, the respondent can either assign three points to one choice and zero points to the other (summing to three), or they can assign two points to one choice and one point to the other (also summing to three). The 15 "situations or questions" in Part II require straightforward rank ordering of four possible attitudes or answers. For example, one item is "At an evening discussion with close friends, are you more interested when the conversation concerns (a) the meaning of life; (b) developments in science; (c) literature; (d) poverty and social amelioration."

The SOV yields scores on six value orientations, with higher scores indicating greater identification with that specific orientation. The instrument's authors identify and define the value orientations as follows: Theoretical (the discovery of truth: empiricism, intellectualism): Economic (that which is useful: resourceful, practical affairs): Aesthetic (form and harmony: grace, artistry in life): Social (love of people: altruism, sympathy, caring): Political (power in all realms; influence; leadership): Religious (unity of life; comprehension of life's meaning, holiness) (Kopelman & Rovenpor, 2006). The individual answer options for each SOV item correspond with one of the six value orientations. The number of items related to the six values range from 17 to 22. Because all test takers will have the same total score over the six values (240), albeit distributed in different ways, the scores are ipsative and must be interpreted intra-individually (Radcliffe, 1965).

There is no test manual for the SOV. Instructions for how to complete the inventory are printed on the instrument itself; administrators should familiarize themselves with these directions in advance. Respondents typically complete the instrument in 20-30 minutes. The layout of the test is rather unique: respondents write their answers in boxes on the test itself, and these boxes are located in one of six columns. Each column corresponds to one of the six value orientations; however, the orientations are not identified by name on the test. A sample item and response is provided at the beginning of Part I and Part II to help the test taker understand the correct method for responding.

No scoring instructions are provided on the instrument. Counselors who wish to use the instrument can contact the first author by email to request a scoring grid (Richard.Kopelman@baruch.cuny.edu), as no other scoring guidelines appear to be available in any publication or online.

The SOV was designed to measure Spranger's six value orientations in an indirect fashion. In contrast to several notable value measures that require respondents to rank or rate broad values directly, which assume respondents can consciously access and accurately report relatively abstract concepts, the SOV uses realistic behavioral scenarios. This is notable, as several researchers have suggested that one's abstract values may shift in a realistic behavioral scenario (e.g., Peng, Nisbett, & Wong, 1997). Because of this difference, the SOV may be a good supplement or alternative to more popular values inventories used in vocational counseling (e.g., Rokeach Value Survey, Schwartz Value Scale, various values card sorts).

A Counselor's Guide To Career Assessments Instruments

The bulk of the literature on previous versions of the SOV focused on its use with high school, college, and graduate students. More recently, the updated SOV has shown utility in high school classroom guidance and post-secondary academic advisement (e.g., choosing a major or graduate area of study). For example, Kopelman, Prottas, and Tatum (2004) found that according to college deans, the SOV value categories yielded distinct "ideal" profiles in five of six disciplines they studied. Deans identified the following values as most appropriate and aligned with their respective disciplines: business administration: Economic; fine arts: Aesthetic; social work: Social; divinity: Religious; and chemistry/physics: Theoretical). This suggests that college academic or career counselors could use the SOV to determine potential goodness of fit for a student with a particular major and to explore discrepancies for students who may feel mismatched with her or his area of study. For example, if a sophomore Business major presenting with academic issues and unhappiness with his courses scores highest in the Social value orientation and much lower in the Economic value, the counselor might want to explore how the student chose the major, what his understanding of Business is (and his career goals), and other possible alternative paths that might better fit his high Social value. Similarly, high school counselors might use SOV results in a similar manner as they might a values card sort, having students explore why they value what they value and how certain careers may align more directly with their specific values.

The SOV also could be a helpful resource when working with individuals experiencing a career transition (e.g., considering quitting, loss of a job, retirement). Individuals facing change are open to reassessing their plans and examining what they want out of their career and/or life. Looking at results from the SOV might aid counselors working with individuals in transition by helping them identify where they are most likely to derive meaning from a job or other activity (for individuals moving into retirement). For example, if a musician who was struggling to make ends meet due to a lack of work completed the SOV and scored highest in Religious and Aesthetic, the counselor might explore careers in music ministry and/or the possibility of applying to graduate school for religious training.

Technical Considerations

The SOV was originally developed in 1931, and it was revised in 1951 with updated norms. Subsequent revisions in 1960 and 1970 only changed the User's Manual and scoring sheet. By the late 1980s, the SOV was no longer in print, due in part to its antiquated language and terminology and lack of current norms. Revisions to 15 of the 45 test items were made in 1997 resulting in the current (fourth) edition; however, this updated edition wasn't published until 2003. The new test items appeared in the *Journal of Vocational Behavior* (Kopelman et al., 2003), but with no scoring or interpretation instructions. The changes to the instrument included replacing dated pronouns, broadening examples of religiosity, and incorporating more current cultural referents and mores.

Both the third and fourth editions of the SOV were administered to 121 graduate students and 58 undergraduate students enrolled in business-related programs. Limited demographic data are provided: 54% of the sample was male and 73% of students had been employed within the previous 12 months. Means and standard deviations for those participants are available in the Kopelman et al. (2003) publication. This is the only reported norming for the current version of the instrument. The authors did complete a validation study comparing the updated and original versions, and demonstrated psychometric consistency. However, the 1951 norms are not recommended as a basis for comparison in the present day.

Cronbach's alphas were computed on the six value dimensions using the 1997 sample ($N = 179$) with the following results: Theoretical ($r = .59$), Economic ($r = .72$), Social ($r = .66$), Political ($r = .55$), Aesthetic ($r = .68$), and Religious ($r = .80$). The average value for the dimensions was .67, which is rather low. This appears to be the only reliability data gathered from this sample.

Kopelman et al. (2003) conducted a validation study comparing the students' dimension scores on the fourth edition to the previous iteration of the SOV. The mean scores across the six dimensions were not significantly different when comparing the versions. This appears to be the only validity data gathered from the small 1997 norm group.

Study of Values, Fourth Edition

General Utility and Evaluation

The fourth edition of the SOV is in the public domain and does not have a formal manual. There were manuals for previous editions; however, they are not available for sale, and they are based on items and norms from 1951. Counselors who wish to use the SOV are encouraged to review the Kopelman et al. (2003) article in which they discuss the updated fourth edition of the instrument, including the means and standard deviations from their sample. Counselors can also contact Dr. Richard Kopelman (Richard.Kopelman@baruch.cuny.edu) to obtain scoring instructions. The scoring grid provides sufficient information for scoring; however, it does not contain any definitions of the six value orientations, nor does it provide guidelines for interpretation, and no alternative interpretation guidelines are available.

In the 1960s and 1970s, the SOV was one of the most widely-used personality inventories (Kopelman et al., 2003). It received mixed reviews in *Mental Measurements Yearbook* (MMY) and in the literature in general during that period, with most reviewers endorsing it as a viable test despite limitations. In separate reviews, both Hogan (1972) and Radcliffe (1965) highlighted several problematic technical and practical elements, including interpretation challenges due to ipsative scoring, a restricted range of use (e.g., all the values are honorific in nature; seems suited for college students specifically), and lack of evidence regarding the unidimensionality of the scales. Yet Hogan (1972) summarized that "it provides dependable and pertinent information concerning individual cases" (para. 8), and Radcliffe (1965) stated, "it should continue to be widely used" (para. 17). In a non-MMY discussion of the SOV, Feldman and Newcomb (1969) argued that the instrument "provides the best single source of information about value changes during the college years (pp. 18-19).

Despite the belief that it would continue to be widely used (Hogan, 1972; Radcliffe, 1965), the SOV fell out of favor during the late 1970s and 1980s, primarily due to its outdated norms, vocabulary, and references (no significant test modifications after 1951). The instrument ceased publication in the mid-1980s. Kopelman et al. (2003) created a revised fourth edition of the SOV in 1997 (published in 2003). Although it is now in the public domain, there are limited psychometric data and supporting materials.

Even with the updated language and examples, there are still several items on the fourth version of the SOV that require specific historical knowledge and context in order to respond appropriately (e.g., "Ayn Rand" is a choice for one of the questions). Other revised items try to incorporate more "current" individuals (compared to the third edition), but even those are becoming outdated (e.g., "Colin Powell") and may not accurately reflect the anticipated value for all respondents. These observations may be particularly relevant to counselors interested in using the instrument with young adult populations.

Kopelman et al. (2003) conducted a validation study that confirmed the new SOV shared the same structure as its predecessor version. However, this positive information must be tempered by remembering that only 177 college and graduate students completed the study, and sharing similar structure matters little if current norms are not developed. In addition, it cannot be assumed that the current SOV version has similar psychometric properties to the third edition in general, especially across varying populations. The absence of a formal manual is understandable because the instrument is not commercially available; however, it makes obtaining, administering, scoring, and interpreting the test much more difficult and limits the scope and confidence regarding what a counselor will learn from SOV results.

Despite these limitations, the SOV offers a unique indirect approach toward values assessment in comparison to other notable values inventories. By asking respondents to provide preferences regarding realistic behavioral statements, the SOV reduces abstract, overly self-conscious responses to items. Given the lack of psychometric research done on the SOV, it can only be recommended as a supplement to more direct methods of values assessment. In its current iteration, the SOV should be interpreted cautiously and from an ipsative perspective, meaning counselors should look at each individual's pattern of the six scores and should not focus on norms. If used as a way to introduce the topic of how one's values impact decision making, the SOV would be appropriate in individual counseling, group counseling, vocational counseling, classroom guidance, and academic advising.

References and Additional Resources

Feldman, K. A., & Newcomb, T. M. (1969). *The impact of college on students.* San Francisco, CA: Jossey-Bass.

Hogan, R. (1972). [Study of Values.] In O. Buros (Ed.), *The seventh mental measurements yearbook.* Lincoln, NE: Buros Center for Testing. [Electronic Version]

Kopelman, R. E., Prottas, D. J., & Tatum, L. G. (2004). Comparison of four measures of values: Their relative usefulness in graduate education advisement. *North American Journal of Psychology, 6,* 205-218.

Kopelman, R. E., & Rovenpor, J. L. (2006). The Allpost-Vernon-Lindzey Study of Values. In J. H. Greenhaus, & G. A. Callanan (Eds.), *Encyclopedia of career development* (pp. 16-18). Thousand Oaks, CA: Sage.

Kopelman, R. E., Rovenpor, J. L., & Guan, M. (2003). The Study of Values: Construction of the fourth edition. *Journal of Vocational Behavior, 62,* 203-220.

Peng, K., Nisbett, R. E., & Wong, N. Y. C. (1997). Validity problems comparing values across cultures and possible solutions. *Psychological Methods, 2,* 329-344.

Radcliffe, J. A. (1965). [Study of Values.] In O. Buros (Ed.), *The sixth mental measurements yearbook.* Lincoln, NE: Buros Center for Testing. [Electronic Version]

290

A COUNSELOR'S GUIDE TO CAREER ASSESSMENTS INSTRUMENTS

VALUES PREFERENCE INDICATOR
Everett Robinson and Ken Keis

CRG Consulting Resource Group International, Inc.
P.O. Box 8000 PMB 386
Sumas, WA 98295-8000
http://www.crgleader.com
info@crgleader.com

Target Population: Adults, Grade 10 reading level.

Statement of the Purpose of the Instrument: The Values Preference Indicator (VPI) is intended to be a self-awareness and educational tool while helping users gain a deeper understanding of the values that are most important to them.

Titles of Subtests, Scales, Scores Provided: Because the VPI is an exploratory tool for personal growth, there are no subtests, ratings, or scores.

Forms and Levels Available, with Dates of Publication/Revision of Each: Print revised 2005; Online revised 2007.

Date of Most Recent Edition of Test Manual, User's Guide, Etc.: 2011.

Languages in Which Available: Print version: English only. Online version: Chinese (simplified) and English.

Time:

    Actual Test Time: 20+ minutes (depends on numeracy level for the print version).

    Total Administration Time: Approximately 20 minutes.

Manner in Which Results Are Reported for Individuals: Self-exploration tool to end with a ranked list of the 21 values.

Machine Scoring: Scored online, self-interpreted.

Hand Scoring: Hand scored by counselee.

Local Machine Scoring: Not available.

Computer Software Options Available: Not available.

Cost of Materials: Due to possible price changes since publication date, be sure to check the publisher's website.

    Specimen Set: Print version: $20.00; Online version: $25.00

    Counselee Materials: Online test only.

Published Reviews of the Instruments in the Last 15 years: Not available.

VALUES PREFERENCE INDICATOR
Reviewed by:

Donna S. Sheperis

Core Faculty, MS Counseling Programs
Walden University

Description

The Values Preference Indicator (VPI) is not a traditional career assessment instrument as its name might infer. The VPI is a self-administered exercise designed to serve as an exploration of values that may benefit the user during career or workplace planning. The developer, Everett Robinson, marketed the first iteration of the VPI in 1990. The VPI is a "self-administering, self-scoring, and self-interpreting value sort" (Robinson, 2010,

Values Preference Indicator

p. 4). It is intended to be used as a standalone product or for use in conjunction with other products from the publisher, Consulting Resource Group International (CRG). The VPI can be used with individuals or in groups with a paraprofessional leader.

The VPI mission statement reads "The VPI was developed to help individuals learn how to identify their strongest values, needs, and fears so that they might better understand how these internal influences direct their daily lives, and impact their personal and working relationship" (Robinson, 2010, p. 6). This instrument is not a traditional career inventory in that it does not help the user discern job types, skills, or preferences. Rather, the VPI is intended to help users with personal development and understanding of values to help them better understand choices and plan for the future.

Multiple key assumptions were critical in development of the VPI:

1. People value different things.

2. People can value the same things for different reasons.

3. When allowed only a few choices (under pressure), people choose what's most important to them first.

4. When forced to rank order, people rank their most important values highest.

5. When forced to rate, people rate their most important values the highest.

6. Time is our ultimate value because we have no guarantees about life.

7. Values are developed from internal and external influences.

8. External influences are often situational.

9. Internal influences include needs and fears.

10. Values are usually linked to strong personal needs.

11. Most people cannot clearly articulate what they value the most.

12. Many individuals are frustrated with life because their most important values are unsatisfied.

13. People can plan to build values into their lives (Robinson, 2010, p. 7).

It is important to note that the test developer indicates that these assumptions were based on his previous work and understanding of human nature but were not grounded in empirical research.

Much of the premise of the VPI seems to be predicated on the eleventh statement, that most people cannot clearly articulate their personal values. In theory, test takers employ the instrument to help their highest values become apparent as they continue to rate and rank them by importance. Once this snapshot of key values is created, they can then assess where they are, where they would like to be, and what they need to work on. Again, this can be accomplished with or without a facilitator.

The VPI is comprised of three sections. The first section (Part One) includes 21 values. The 21 values are listed in a simple checklist with short definitions provided. In addition, there are spaces for the test taker to list values that are not included but might be important to him or her. The test taker is instructed to review the list and select the 10 most important values. The user then must rank order the values from 1 to 10 indicating the priority of the value (with the most important value placed at number 1). Examples of the values listed include: Accomplishment – to complete tasks, get results; Expertise – to be an expert in a special subject or skill area; and Tranquility – to enjoy peace and quiet and a life with few personal conflicts. The test developer refers to part one of the VPI as "window shopping" for values (Robinson, 2010).

In Part One, there is potential for test takers to select values that they think others would find important or that are the "wishes" of the user more than the true values. To address this, Part Two of the VPI helps users further prioritize values. The test taker is presented with 21 boxes each containing 5 of the values listed in Part One. In this section, the test taker matches and prioritizes each of the 21 values against each other five different times. Within each group of five, he or she ranks the values listed from 1 to 5. The test developer claims that this process allows the true values to become clear as they rank above the others in a systemic fashion (Robinson, 2010). The test guidelines state that because only a few values are presented at a time, and because users rank them over and over, the true values of importance emerge.

A Counselor's Guide To Career Assessments Instruments

Finally, Part Three involves the test taker transferring those rankings to a scoring grid which results in a ranking of the values. The ultimate goal is to explore the test taker's understanding of values to determine what he or she truly values. Part Three begins with three columns. In the first column, the test taker transfers his or her top 10 values from Part One. In the second column, he or she transfers the top 10 values from Part Two. The test taker is then instructed to review both lists considering what differences exist and why the lists might be different. In the third column, he or she creates a master list of values based on insights gained from taking the VPI. After completing the three columns, the test taker is presented with a chart of Primary Needs and Related Fears which correspond with the values included in the VPI. He or she is then asked to determine whether or not each of the values from the master list is being currently met in the Time and Energy Exercise. The test taker transfers his or her top seven values to a worksheet and indicate whether or not the needs are being met. This is called the time and energy status of the value. A test taker can then reflect on what he or she needs to do to continue to keep a need met or to get it met. Upon completion of the three forms of rank ordering values and the Time and Energy Exercise, the test taker is supposed to be left with a better understanding of true values and efforts towards having them met (Consulting Resource Group International, 2011).

The VPI is available in paper and online format. The 11-page paper format costs $20 per administration and the online version is $25 per administration. Because the VPI is self-administered, self-scored, and self-interpreted, there are no education, training, or competency standards the purchaser must meet in order to buy the VPI. In addition, there are no specified time limits for the administration of the test, but CRG estimates that the assessment takes approximately 40 minutes. According to the developer, the VPI was written at a 10th-grade reading level and is intended for anyone age 15 or above (E. Parkinson, personal communication, May 22, 2012).

The paper-and-pencil format of the VPI includes room for the user to make notes about the comparisons and values that emerge. The online format culminates in a report generated for the user. Key values are identified and values are prioritized based on the user's responses. Essentially, the online format performs the simple mathematical calculations required of the user in the paper-and-pencil format. No additional interpretive information is provided in either format.

The VPI was created to be used with or without a facilitator as a self-exploration activity rather than a standardized assessment. There are multiple options for using the VPI before or during counseling. Prior to career counseling, clients may be interested in exploring what they value in order to better understand their needs. Alternately, counselors may find that they refer clients to the VPI to help them generate a better understanding of their core values. Because there is no empirical basis for the VPI, it should be used with caution and only for the intended purpose of self-exploration. The results of the instrument should not be used in isolation. However, the results could provide some direction for career planning and may allow a career counselor insight into where further exploration might be warranted. Materials from the test developer along with a review of proponents of the VPI indicate that it is frequently used in corporate trainings, retreats, and by life coaches.

Technical Considerations

Because the VPI is not a traditional career assessment with psychometric properties, the customary reliability and validity information does not exist. The head of CRG, Ken Keis, cautions that the VPI is not a predictive index, but is a "behavioral and educational tool" (K. Keis, personal communication, April 19, 2012). There is no normative data available for the VPI.

General Utility and Evaluation

As a tool of self-exploration and understanding, the VPI has a number of uses. Clients may find the tool on their own prior to entering any formal counseling services. Counselors may recommend the tool as a basis for beginning exploration of needs. Finally, consultants may use the VPI in group settings to increase task group cohesiveness and understanding. To date, there are no research studies which have used the VPI.

The developers of the VPI are clear that this is an ipsative measure that is not intended to serve as a standardized assessment tool. CRG literature provides general guidelines for reflection on and interpretation of the values that the test taker identifies through the exercises contained in the inventory booklet (CRG, 2011; Robinson, 2010). These values may be beneficial to counselors who wish to help clients better understand what is important in their personal and professional lives. Additionally, identified values may prove integral to making career decisions. However, because there are no validity studies, it cannot be determined if the instrument is measuring what it purports to measure. Additionally, because there are no reliability data, there is no determination of whether the results are consistent from one measurement to another. Because this is a self-exploration exercise, it crosses cultural boundaries provided reading levels are met. Without any normative data, no comparisons can be made to any particular cultural group.

Overall, the VPI is intended to be a self-administered and self-interpreted exercise that may provide some information for reflection during the career counseling process. The VPI should be used with caution because of the lack of psychometric properties available. The VPI is relatively inexpensive and available directly to users. The company staff are accessible and available to answer questions.

References and Additional Resources

Consulting Resource Group International. (2011). *The Values Preference Indicator.* Author: Sumas, WA.

Consulting Resource Group International website: http://www.crgleader.com/home.html

CRG Testimonials: http://www.youtube.com/watch?v=kLjggcGtHqg

Hope Coaching: http://www.hopecoaching.org/index.html

Robinson, E. T. (2010). *The Values Preference Indicator guidelines.* Author: Sumas, WA.

Wide Range Interest and Occupation Test, Second Edition
Joseph J. Glutting and Gary S. Wilkinson

PRO-ED Inc.

700 Shoal Creek Blvd.
Austin, TX 78757-6897
info@proedinc.com
www.proedinc.com

Target Population: Children, adolescents, young adults, and adults; ages 9 to 80. Individuals or groups, those with a wide range of literacy levels and languages, including individuals who are English dominant and have a college education, people with limited English proficiency or little formal education, and individuals with learning disabilities and/or reading problems.

Statement of the Purpose of the Instrument: The purpose of the Wide Range Interest and Occupation Test, Second Edition (WRIOT-2) is to help people choose a satisfying career. The WRIOT-2 is an important tool for career selection because it provides participants with a better understanding of themselves, the types of occupations they prefer, their pattern of likes and dislikes among work-related activities, and the intensity and consistency of their response pattern.

Titles of Subtests, Scales, Scores Provided: There are 39 scales and each is organized according to three broad clusters: the Occupational Cluster, the Interest Cluster, and the Holland Type Cluster. Scales in the Occupational Cluster show the extent to which participants like 17 types of careers. The Interest Cluster has 16 scales and evaluates the needs, motives, and values that influence a participant's occupational choice. (The Interest Cluster is further arranged according to whether the scale provides information about the Functional Duties of work, Chosen Skill Level, Social Rewards, Conditions of Work, and data about a participant's Response Pattern). The Holland Type Cluster (new to the WRIOT-2) offers scores at the most global level of analysis, and the scores are supplementary. The Holland Type Cluster describes performance according to six occupational themes: Realistic, Investigative, Artistic, Social, Enterprising, and Conventional.

Forms and Levels Available, with Dates of Publication/Revision of Each: WRIOT-2 Picture Book and Response Form (paper-and-pencil form) and WRIOT-2 software program, 2003.

Date of Most Recent Edition of Test Manual, User's Guide, Etc.: 2003.

Languages in Which Available: English only.

Time:

Actual Test Time: 30 minutes.

Total Administration Time: 40 minutes for individual administration, or 50 to 60 minutes for group administration.

Norm Group(s) on Which Scores Are Based: Norms for the WRIOT-2 are based on a nationally stratified sample and are representative of individuals across the United States ages 9 through 80 years. Unlike the 1979 edition of the WRIOT, norms for the WRIOT-2 are no longer gender based.

Manner in Which Results Are Reported for Individuals: Derived scores for the WRIOT-2 are expressed as percentiles that help participants make sense of their own performance. (The WRIOT-2 adds to the interpretive process by presenting descriptive labels for each range of percentiles). Percentiles may also be converted to standard scores using the manual. The WRIOT-2 software program also produces a score profile for the participant and test examiner. Results are presented in a graphic portrayal of the individual's strengths and weaknesses in each of the 17 Occupational, 16 Interest, and 6 Holland-type scales. Occupations range from unskilled labor to the highest levels of technical, managerial, and professional training.

The software package that comes with the WRIOT-2 provides the following features: Test administration on the computer; Data entry of responses when the WRIOT-2 is administered using the pencil-and-paper format, Test scoring, Report generation, Report writing assistance by providing narrative options to WRIOT-2 findings, Scored and unscored data storage, Information on purchase, and Installation of additional scoring uses.

Wide Range Interest and Occupation Test, Second Edition

Report Format/Content for Group Summaries: Not available.

Machine Scoring: Not available.

Hand Scoring: Not available.

Local Machine Scoring: Not available.

Computer Software Options Available: Computerized adaptive administration. For the WRIOT-2, the only option is to use computer software for scoring. The counselor may use the computer software for scoring after administering the paper-and-pencil test.

Cost of Materials: Due to possible price changes since publication date, be sure to check the publisher's website.

> **Specimen Set:** Complete Kit (includes Examiner's Manual, 25 response forms, 1 full-color Picture Book, 1 computer administration CD): $371.00. The publisher offers pricing for purchasing these individual components.

> **Counselee Materials:** Picture Book (reusable), CD (reusable), response form (non-reusable).

Additional Comments of Interest to Users: The WRIOT-2 is a pictorial interest test, which does not require reading or language understanding. It provides a level of self-projected ability, aspirations, and social conformity to help coordinate instruction/therapy plans with interest/attitude patterns. Ideal for use with educationally and culturally disadvantaged, learning disabled, and deaf individuals, and those with intellectual disabilities. Picture titles can also be read to the blind.

Published Reviews of the Instrument in the Last 15 Years:

Bugaj, A. M. (2009). [Wide-Range Interest Occupation Test, Second Edition.] In E. A. Whitfield, R. W. Feller, & C. Wood (Eds.), *A counselor's guide to career assessment instruments* (5th ed., pp. 320-325). Broken Arrow, OK: National Career Development Association.

WIDE-RANGE INTEREST OCCUPATION TEST, SECOND EDITION

Reviewed by:

Albert M. Bugaj

Department of Psychology
University of Wisconsin, Marinette

Description

A revision of the Wide Range Interest-Opinion Test of 1979, the Wide Range Interest and Occupation Test, second edition (WRIOT-2; Glutting & Wilkinson, 2003a) is a nonverbal test meant to assist people in choosing careers. It is intended for individuals ages 9 to 80 and can be administered via computer or by paper-and-pencil with an accompanying picture book. When administered as a paper-and-pencil test, the data must be entered into the WRIOT-2 software program for scoring.

The WRIOT-2 requires no reading and is entirely nonverbal. The administration manual (Glutting & Wilkinson, 2003b) notes the test is suitable for a variety of individuals: those who are English dominant and have college educations, those who have limited English proficiency or little formal education, as well as people with learning disabilities and/or reading problems, and individuals with mental retardation.

Consisting of 39 scales organized into three clusters, the WRIOT-2 administration manual (Glutting & Wilkinson, 2003b) involves individuals "indicat[ing] whether they like, dislike, or are undecided about work situations illustrated in 238 pictures" (p. 1). The Occupation Cluster shows the extent to which test takers like 17 career areas. The Interest Cluster consists of 16 scales evaluating needs, motives, and values that influence occupational choice. The final cluster (Holland-Type), based on Holland's (1966, 1997) theory of occupational choice, identifies a person as a Realistic (e.g., "fix cars"), Investigative (e.g., "use an electron microscope"), Artistic (e.g., "work in a museum"), Social (e.g., "work as a minister"), Enterprising (e.g., "sell real estate"), or Conventional (e.g., "serve food at lunch counter") type.

A Counselor's Guide To Career Assessments Instruments

The WRIOT-2 can be easily and quickly administered. Scores are rapidly provided in the computerized version. The pictures in the Picture Book (Glutting & Wilkinson, 2008) are clearly printed, colorful, and clear. The pictures are reproduced with the same quality on the computerized version of the test. Both the manual and Picture Book are spiral-bound, and the Picture Book is printed on fairly heavy stock paper. Both should prove durable and long-lasting with proper handling and care. The paper-and-pencil form is completed using a response form provided by the publisher. The pictures in the booklet are printed two to a page and are numbered consecutively. A description of each picture and the cluster to which it relates can be found by consulting the manual; no other descriptions are found in the Picture Book. The presentation of the pictures in the computerized version is similar to the paper-and-pencil version (two to a "screen" and consecutively numbered). Instructions for the two versions are parallel. For example, in both, the first picture is introduced to the test taker, and the test taker is informed to click on "Like," "Dislike," or "Undecided" for the computerized version to indicate the test-takers attitude toward the work depicted. In the paper-and-pencil version, the test taker fills in a corresponding "L," "D," or "U" bubble on the response sheet. Responses for the paper-and-pencil version must be entered into the WRIOT-2 software program for scoring. As with all aspects of the computerized version of the test, this is a user-friendly process and results in the same score report as the computerized version.

Glutting and Wilkinson (2003b) note that the WRIOT-2 may be used to study changes in a person's interests during growth, decline, and life crises. The Occupational and Holland Type clusters can be used in career planning. The manual suggests the test can be used by counselors in elementary school through college, employment counselors, rehabilitation counselors, and clinical psychologists, to name a few. According to the manual, the total number of scores can be overwhelming to the test taker, so it is suggested that examiners discern which scores are most relevant to interpret with the test taker (Glutting & Wilson, 2003b). In order to facilitate the interpretation of the scores, the manual provides "brief descriptions" of each scale, as well as "extended descriptions" of each scale in the occupational cluster. Similar descriptions are provided for each other scales. This is also available on the computerized version of the test, and can be printed-out as "handouts" to share with the test taker. The manual suggests using the "extended descriptions" for the occupational scales for which the test taker received the three highest scores.

Technical Considerations

WRIOT-2 scores are expressed as percentile ranks and reported in comparison to general norms, with no breakdown according to gender or group. The normative sample of the WRIOT-2 consisted of 1,286 participants. The sample closely matched the U.S. population on age, gender, race/ethnicity, education, and geographic distribution as reported by the 2000 U.S. Census. Minor weightings applied to various groups in the sample brought the sample into alignment with census figures. No norms exist for the specialized groups for whom the test is said to be suitable (e.g., individuals with intellectual disabilities).

Internal consistency of the WRIOT-2 was determined by calculating Cronbach's alpha for each scale for six age groups (N = 1,286), the youngest ranging from age 9 to 14, the oldest being age 50 and older. With the exception of the scale measuring inconsistent response patterns, Cronbach's alpha was above .82 for all scales. On the Inconsistency scale, the average alpha across age groups was .68.

Test-retest reliability was determined for two age groups: adolescents (n = 67) and adults (n = 49). Median time between administrations was 23 days. Test-retest reliability was lowest for the inconsistency scale (.68 for adolescents; .44 for adults). Other test-retest reliabilities generally ranged from .61 to .91, being somewhat higher for adults. These measures were not obtained on specific groups such as individuals with limited English proficiency.

The WRIOT-2 manual (Glutting & Wilkinson, 2003b) indicates evidence of content validity. A preliminary set of 300 pictures was developed by revising items from the test's previous edition. A panel of judges placed each picture for the Occupational and Interest clusters into what they felt were appropriate occupational categories. Seventeen occupational categories matching 12 occupational areas specified by the Division of Testing of the U.S. Employment Service (U.S. Department of Labor, 1965) and other publications including the Complete Guide for Occupational Exploration (JIST Works, 1993) were used. Items were retained only if interrater agreement yielded Kappa coefficients of reliability of .80 or higher, and only if their item-total point-biserial correlations were .30 or higher during pre-testing of the items and again following standardization.

Wide Range Interest and Occupation Test, Second Edition

A similar three-step process determined the content validity of the Interest and Holland-type clusters, resulting in the final 238 items. Comparison of the pictures in the Holland-type scales to similar listings in the Dictionary of Holland Occupational Codes (Gottfredson & Holland, 1996) resulted in a high rate of agreement as to each items appropriate category (K + .88).

The manual states that approximately 92% of the pictures in the WRIOT-2 were rated as clear and unambiguous by a panel of judges. Neither the nature of the scale used in the ratings, nor the number of judges (referred to as "experts and users") is provided. Although the ratings of the pictures for clarity are an improvement over the earlier edition, and the occupations illustrated might appear unambiguous to "experts and users," it cannot be ascertained if they are unambiguous to the range of individuals who are potential test takers.

Convergent validity was determined by computing the intercorrelations among each scale on the WRIOT-2. Most intercorrelations (ranging between .50 and .87) proved to be logically consistent. However, because the same pictures are used for all three "clusters" on the test, inflated correlations between scales could result.

Several methods were used to determine the criterion and construct validity of the WRIOT-2. First, using a contrasted-groups approach, 503 individuals from the standardization sample were placed into a Holland-type classification on the basis of their occupations. Analysis of variance indicated participants received significantly higher scores for their own type in comparison to highly incongruent types. In another study reported in the WRIOT-2 manual (Glutting & Wilkinson, 2003b), the WRIOT-2 and the Strong Interest Inventory (SII) was administered to 72 adults. The criterion validity of the Holland-type scales was strongest, with each scale on the WRIOT-2 correlating significantly only with its SII counterpart (correlations ranging from .56 to .68). Correlations for occupational scales ranged from .40 to .73. The occupational scales of the WRIOT-2 were also subjected to a discriminant function analysis, resulting in five functions that were logically related to Holland types, although item overlap may have affected the results.

General Utility and Evaluation

The manual is well written and informative. The computer program loads without difficulty and is easy to navigate. The instructions to the test taker are straightforward. Both the computerized or paper-and-pencil formats of the test are easy to administer. The computer-generated report provides a brief description of each scale, and extended paragraph-length descriptions of the three highest scores on the Occupational cluster. There are extended descriptions for additional scales in the Occupation Cluster, and the Interest and Holland career clusters assessed can also be printed. This information is also available in the test manual. A "travel disc" allows the administration of the test on computers on which the full program has not been installed. This disc allows the collection of responses to test items, but scoring must be performed on a computer on which the entire program has been installed.

The pictures produced for the WRIOT-2 may be non-biased. They show a strong gender balance and a very good mix of individuals of diverse ethnic/racial backgrounds. The test can easily be described as non-biased in that regard. While the WRIOT-2 can be recommended for use with the general population, its use with specific populations (e.g., those with learning disabilities or limited reading ability) must be called into question. The test's norms are appropriate for the general population, a group for whom rigorous methods were used in development. For more specific groups, no norms were developed, nor were validity and reliability data collected. Further, it cannot be ascertained if groups such as individuals with intellectual disabilities would perceive the stimulus materials as unambiguous.

Of the WRIOT-2 clusters, the Holland-Type Cluster seems to be the most robust, with scores correlating with their counterparts on the SII. Individuals already established in specific occupational areas also received appropriate scores on this cluster. The Occupational Cluster appears somewhat weaker. Although many of the scales correlate with their SII counterparts, no data using a known-groups procedure are provided (i.e., data that could document strong criterion validity). Measures of convergent and divergent validity analyzing the relationships between the scales on the WRIOT-2 may also have been affected by item overlap.

The WRIOT-2 does appear to have strong internal consistency, as measured by Cronbach's alpha. Test-retest reliability is high. However, additional testing of specific scales is needed. For example, the "Likes scale" is designed to measure social desirability by counting the number of times a test taker selects "Like" as an

A Counselor's Guide To Career Assessments Instruments

option. However, social desirability bias could best be assessed by instructing a group of research participants to attempt to "fake good" on the test, using their response pattern as a criterion, or by examining the relationship of this scale to other test measuring social desirability.

Despite a lack of research on non-English-speaking populations, or on exceptional individuals, the WRIOT-2 should prove a useful research tool for studying the career interest of such individuals. However, it cannot be recommended as a counseling tool for those groups, although it is highly suitable for the general population.

References and Additional Resources

Bugaj, A. M. (2009). [Wide-Range Interest Occupation Test, Second Edition.] In E. A. Whitfield, R. W. Feller, & C. Wood (Eds.), *A counselor's guide to career assessment instruments* (5th ed., pp. 320-325). Broken Arrow, OK: National Career Development Association.

Glutting, J. J., & Wilkinson, G. (2003a). *The Wide-Range Interest and Occupation Test.* Wilmington, DE: Wide-Range, Inc.

Glutting, J. J., & Wilkinson, G. (2003b). *The Wide-Range Interest and Occupation Test administration manual.* Wilmington, DE: Wide-Range, Inc.

Glutting, J. J., & Wilkinson, G. (2008). *The Wide-Range Interest and Occupation Test picture book.* Wilmington, DE: Wide-Range, Inc.

Gottfredson, G. D., & Holland, J. L. (1996). *Dictionary of Holland Occupational Codes—Third edition.* Odessa, FL: Psychological Assessment Resources.

Holland, J. L. (1996). *The psychology of vocational choice.* Waltham, MA: Blaisdell.

Holland, J. L. (1997). *Making vocational choices: A theory of vocational personalities and work environments* (3rd ed.). Odessa, FL: Psychological Assessment Resources.

JIST Works. (1993). *Complete guide for occupational exploration.* Indianapolis, IN: Author.

U.S. Department of Labor. (1965). *Dictionary of occupational titles.* (3rd ed.; Vol. II: Occupational Classification). Washington, DC: U.S. Government Printing Service.

300

CHAPTER 13

CAREER DEVELOPMENT / CAREER MATURITY MEASURES

- Adult Career Concerns Inventory

- Barriers to Employment Success Inventory, Fourth Edition

- Career Commitment Measure

- Career Decision Self-Efficacy Scale and
  Career Decision Self-Efficacy Scale— Short Form

- Career Development Inventory

- Career Factors Inventory

- Career Search Efficacy Scale

- Career Thoughts Inventory

- Career Transitions Inventory

- Childhood Career Development Scale

- Job Search Attitude Inventory, Fourth Edition

- Job Search Knowledge Scale

- Job Survival and Success Scale, Second Edition

- Quality of Life Inventory

- WorkLife Indicator

ADULT CAREER CONCERNS INVENTORY
Donald Super, Albert Thompson, and Richard Lindeman

Vocopher

Kevin Glavin

http://www.vocopher.com/

kglavin@vocopher.com

Target Population: Adults, age 24 and older.

Statement of the Purpose of the Instrument: The Adult Career Concerns Inventory (ACCI) operationally defines Donald Super's model of career adaptability in adulthood and identifies the career activity an individual is most concerned with.

Titles of Subtests, Scales, Scores Provided: The ACCI follows Super's model of career adaptability to highlight salient adult concerns. Exploration Stage; Crystallization; Specification; Implementation; Establishment Stage; Stabilizing; Consolidating; Advancing; Maintenance Stage; Holding; Updating; Innovating; Disengagement Stage; Deceleration; Retirement Planning; Retirement Living; and Career Change Status. Four career stages (with substages for each) are represented, with 15 items per stage.

Forms and Levels Available, with Dates of Publication/Revision of Each: 1988.

Date of Most Recent Edition of Test Manual, User's Guide, Etc.: 1988.

Languages in Which Available: English only.

Time:

Actual Test Time: Varies.

Total Administration Time: 15-30 minutes.

Manner in Which Results Are Reported for Individuals: The test taker self-reviews scores to identify career concerns; counselors may process results with the test taker.

Machine Scoring Service: Scored online.

Hand Scoring: Not available.

Computer Software Options Available: Only available online.

Cost of Materials: No cost.

Specimen Set: No cost, online form with results.

Counselee Materials: Online test (not reusable).

Published Reviews of the Instrument in the Last 15 Years:

Glavin, K. (2008). [Adult Career Concerns Inventory.] In F. T. L. Leong (Ed.) *Encyclopedia of counseling, Volume 3: Career counseling.* Thousand Oaks, CA: Sage.

Levinson, E., Ohler, D., Caswell, & Kiewra, K. (1998). Six approaches to the assessment of career maturity. *Journal of Counseling and Development, 76,* 475-482.

ADULT CAREER CONCERNS INVENTORY
Reviewed by:

Spencer R. Baker

Department of Counseling
Hampton University

Description

The Adult Career Concerns Inventory (ACCI) is an assessment tool that measures concerns across career stages for adults. It has been used in career counseling and planning, needs analyses in groups of employees and of adult applicants for counseling, and studies of relationships between adult career adaptability and previous, concurrent, and subsequent socioeconomic and psychological characteristics (Super, Thompson, & Linderman, 1988).

The ACCI is designed to be self-administered and self-scored or machine-scored. Written at an eighth-grade reading level, the ACCI contains 61 items with demographic data items. Test takers respond to 60 items using a 5-point Likert scale, with higher scores indicating greater career concern: (1) *no concern;* (2) *little concern,* (3) *some concern;* (4) *considerable concern;* and (5) *great concern.* Test takers respond to one additional item that evaluates current career change status. Item 61 is differently formatted because it is not a part of the scale and is unscored. Item 61 has five options using a 5-point Likert scale ranging from (1) *I am not considering making a career change* to (5) *I have recently made a change and am settling down in the new field.*

The ACCI is based on Super's life-span developmental theory and assesses concerns in four career stages (exploration, establishment, maintenance, and disengagement). Exploration (ages 15 to 25) consists of surveying the world of work; establishment (ages 25 to 45) consists of getting established in a career; maintenance (ages 45 to 60 or 65) consists of maintenance behavior or concerns; and disengagement (beginning around age 60) consists of deceleration of tasks (Super et al., 1988). Each stage has three substages. Exploration substages include Crystallization, Specification, and Implementation. Establishment substages include Stabilizing, Consolidating, and Advancing. Maintenance substages include Holding, Updating, and Innovative. Disengagement substages include Deceleration, Retirement Planning, and Retirement Living. Each substage contains five career concerns items yielding 15 items per stage.

The ACCI is available in electronic format and can be found online at http://www.vocopher.com. Scores are calculated automatically and interpretations should be conducted ipsatively (Glavin, 2008). Self-administration takes approximately 15 to 30 minutes. There is no total "career concerns" score but there are stage and substage scores. A thorough background in career developmental theory is recommended for interpreting the resulting profile (Super et al., 1988; Whiston, 1990).

The ACCI is intended for use with male and female adults under age 25 to over 45 years. It was developed on the planfulness dimension of career adaptability and is not the only indicator of career concerns. Counselors need to incorporate other information specific to the client's occupational area to assess career adaptability. Others (e.g., Niles, Anderson, Hartung, & Staton, 1999) suggest that non-career concerns (emotional, cognitive and other issues) of the clients are important and should be included when assessing career adaptability.

The ACCI provides assistance in determining where the client should focus, where the client is most currently concerned relating to the career stages and substages, which indicate the individual's planfulness concerning his or her work-related future (Whiston, 1990). The ACCI is intended for use with adults in the work world who are rethinking their own careers, but also with older adolescents who are about to leave their schooling and are considering entry into an occupation (Glavin, 2008; Super et al., 1988). As an educational tool, an overview of the stages may give clients an indication of future developmental tasks they may encounter. Counselors may develop interventions (exploring different occupational fields) or use additional assessment instruments (interest inventories) based upon concerns in a specific stage or substage.

Technical Considerations

Preliminary norms were established with a small normative sample of 373 adults (136 men) with 83 within the under age 24 group, 128 in the ages 25 to 34 group, 76 ages 35 to 44 group, and 74 in the 45 and over age group. The small normative sample was biased educationally with a disproportionate number of college and professionally educated men and women compared to the general population. The original manual provides means, standard deviations, and raw scores for the normative sample across sex and age groups. The original manual (Super et al., 1988) identifies these norms as provisional only due to the small normative sample and its lack of diversity (i.e., short and long term unemployed, and special groups, such as blue collar, white collar, and managerial). The manual does not provide information regarding ethnicity of the normative sample. The manual cites that the most useful norms may be local norms. The ACCI has also been investigated with an Australian sample (457 employed individuals with 219 men and ages ranging from 17 to 70 years) and found clear support for the ACCI factor structure (Smart, 1994).

In addition to the normative sample, internal consistency using alpha coefficients are reported for two independent samples (academic professionals, $N = 68$; corporate employees, $N = 331$). The academic professional sample had substage alpha coefficients ranging from .76 (Deceleration) to .95 (Retirement Living) and stage alpha coefficients ranging from .92 (Exploration and Establishment) to .93 (Maintenance and Disengagement). The corporate employee sample had substage alpha coefficients ranging from .81 (Deceleration) to .95 (Retirement Living) and stage alpha coefficients ranging from .95 (Establishment and Disengagement) to .96 (Exploration and Maintenance). In a study of 104 graduate nursing students, stage alpha coefficients were found for Exploration, Establishment, Maintenance, and Disengagement as .95, .95, .94, and .93, respectively (Halpin & Ralph, 1990).

The original manual (Super et al., 1988) provides data on one validation study of employees of a large international corporation ($N = 393$ with 142 males). The sample ranged in age from 18 to 65 years. Stage concerns for both stage and substage scores were analyzed as indicators of chronological age and identified for approximately 50% of the subjects (i.e., criterion-related validity). When analyses were conducted by job level, the predictive ability increased. Separate analyses were conducted to discriminate levels of career satisfaction. Although differences were in the hypothesized direction, the results were not statistically significant. In addition, job satisfaction was examined, and statistically significant differences were found with some concerns regarding practical differences due to large sample sizes which influence statistical significance. In another study using graduate nursing students (Halpin & Ralph, 1990), students were administered the ACCI and the Career Development Inventory. The authors found support for the construct validity of the ACCI and reported that the ACCI seems to measure what it was designed to measure. The ACCI manual and other data can be obtained through the publisher's website.

General Utility and Evaluation

The ACCI has limitations due to its normative sample and limited validity evidence. Limited published information regarding the ACCI is available. One study (Whiston, 1990) provided limited support for use of the ACCI and recommended the ACCI be used with other instruments. Whiston (1990) did not provide demographic data regarding the study's samples. More studies are required to assess the usefulness of the ACCI. Although limited studies were conducted using the ACCI, the ACCI has a strong foundation in Super's developmental stages and substages.

References and Additional Resources

Glavin, K. (2008). [Adult Career Concerns Inventory.] In F. T. L. Leong (Ed.) *Encyclopedia of counseling, Volume 3: Career counseling.* Thousand Oaks, CA: Sage.

Glavin, K., & Rehfuss, M. (2005, June). *The Adult Career Concerns Inventory.* Presentation presented at the meeting of National Career Development Association, Orlando, FL.

Halpin, G., & Ralph, J. (1990). The adult career concerns inventory: Validity and reliability. *Measurement & Evaluation in Counseling & Development, 22*(4), 196-203.

Niles, S. G., Anderson, W. P., Jr, Hartung, P. J., & Staton, A. R. (1999). Identifying client types from Adult Career Concerns Inventory scores. *Journal of Career Development, 25*(3), 173-185.

Smart, R. M. (1994). Super's stages and the four-factor structure of the adult career concerns inventory in an Australian sample. *Measurement & Evaluation in Counseling & Development, 26*(4), 243-257.

Super, D. E., Thompson, A. S., & Linderman, R. H. (1988). *Adult Career Concerns Inventory: Manual for research and exploratory use in counseling.* Palo Alto, CA: Consulting Psychologists Press.

Whiston, S. C. (1990). Evaluation of the Adult Career Concerns Inventory. *Journal of Counseling & Development, 69,* 78-80.

306

A Counselor's Guide To Career Assessments Instruments

Barriers to Employment
Success Inventory, Fourth Edition
John J. Liptak

JIST Publishing, Inc.
8902 Otis Avenue
Indianapolis, IN 46216
http://www.jist.com
educate@emcp.com

Target Population: Adolescents, young adults, and adults.

Statement of the Purpose of the Instrument: The Barriers to Employment Success Inventory (BESI) helps individuals identify the barriers that keep them from getting a good job or getting ahead in their career. It then offers strategies for overcoming those barriers.

Titles of Subtests, Scales, Scores Provided: Personal and Financial, Emotional and Physical, Career Decision-Making and Planning, Job-Seeking Knowledge, and Training Education. Ten items each, with higher scores indicating greater perceived barriers. Subscale and total scores are provided.

Forms and Levels Available, with Dates of Publication/Revision of Each: Print and online versions, 2011.

Date of Most Recent Edition of Test Manual, User's Guide, Etc.: 2011.

Languages in Which Available: English only.

Time:

    Actual Test Time: 20-30 minutes.

    Total Administration Time: Varies.

Norm Group(s) on Which Scores Are Based: The normative sample from previous editions included male and female adults that included college students, long-term unemployed, offenders and ex-offenders, and clients on public assistance (i.e., welfare to work program).

Manner in Which Results Are Reported for Individuals: Raw scores are calculated for each of the five subscales. Subscale scores are profiled in three score ranges from easy-to-understand interpretations for each subscale. Scores between 10-19 indicate fewer barriers, 20-30 shows similar barriers as most unemployed adults, and scores between 31-40 indicate the respondent has more barriers than most unemployed adults. The BESI is self-administered and self-interpreted, although it is encouraged that counselors review scores and recommended strategies with counselees.

Report Format/Content for Group Summaries: Not available.

Scoring:

    Machine scoring: Not available.

    Hand scoring: Hand-scored by counselee.

    Local machine scoring: Not available.

Computer Software Options Available: Computerized adaptive administration.

Ways in which computer/online version differs: Automated scoring and automated report generation.

Cost of Materials: Due to possible price changes since publication date, be sure to check the publisher's website. Packages of 25 are available for $48.95 to $53.95 depending on the quantity ordered. The Administrator's Guide is free for download.

    Specimen Set: JIST offers a Barriers to Employment Success Package, which contains 25 copies of the Barriers to Employment Success workbook, 1 Barriers to Employment Success video, and 1 package of the BESI ($467.25).

    Counselee Materials: Paper-and-pencil assessment or online access (computer required).

Barriers to Employment Success Inventory, Fourth Edition

Published Reviews of the Instrument in the Last 15 Years:

Camara, W. J. (2002). [Barriers to Employment Success Inventory (2nd ed)]. In R. A. Spies & B. S. Plake (Eds.), *Sixteenth mental measurements yearbook* (pp. 90-93). Lincoln, NE: Buros Center for Testing.

Cavan, D. E. (2001, May). [Barriers to Employment Success Inventory.] *Newsnotes.* Retrieved from http://theaa-ceonline.com

Green, K. E. (2009). [Barriers to Employment Success Inventory (2nd ed).] In E. A.Whitfield, R. W. Feller, & C. Wood (Eds.), *A counselor's guide to career assessment instruments* (5th ed., pp. 328-332). Broken Arrow, OK: National Career Development Association.

BARRIERS TO EMPLOYMENT SUCCESS INVENTORY, FOURTH EDITION

Reviewed by:

Kathy E. Green

Morgridge College of Education
University of Denver

Description

The Barriers to Employment Success Inventory (BESI, 4th ed.) "helps individuals identify their major barriers to obtaining a job or succeeding in their employment" (Liptak, 2011, p. 1). It is a self-administered, self-scored, and self-interpreted paper-and-pencil or online measure intended to assess individuals' perceived barriers to getting a job, keeping a job, or succeeding in a job. Results, obtained immediately, can be used to open a dialogue between the job seeker and a counselor about employment-related barriers.

The BESI comprises five subscales with 10 items for each subscale. Subscales include the following: (a) Personal and Financial, concerns resources for basic survival; (b) Emotional and Physical, self-esteem, insecurity, anger, depression, and physical issues; (c) Career Decision-Making and Planning, goal setting and identifying values; (d) Job-Seeking Knowledge, effective job search and communication skills; and (e) Training and Education, knowledge and skills related to education or training. A sample item per subscale is, respectively, "Finding government programs that can help me," "Keeping a positive attitude," "Making career decisions that will help my future," "Learning effective job search skills," and "Learning how to read or write."

There are 50 items rated along a four-point response scale (0 = *none,* 1 = *little,* 2 = *some,* 3 = *great concern*). Item responses are written directly on the three-page foldout booklet, then summed for each subscale. Items are short and easy to read (e.g., "Learning effective job skills"). Color coding is used to indicate which responses are to be added together and transferred to a profile and interpretation guide, also on the booklet, that categorizes scores as low, average, or high on subscales. Examples of barrier interpretation and strategies for overcoming barriers (e.g., "be assertive in asking for help," "improve your academic skills") are provided with references listed to free, online resources. Space is provided for writing short- and long-term goals to overcome barriers. Items in the 4th edition were revised to "reflect changes in society and the world of work ... to reduce the BESI's reading level and to reduce redundant items" (Liptak, 2011, p. 10).

The BESI is relatively inexpensive, attractively presented, convenient, and easy to use tool provided as a three-page fold-out sheet that is not reusable. Straightforward, explicit directions are provided for self-administration, which should take about 20 minutes. Specifically, test takers are instructed to circle the number that best describes how much of a concern the statement is to them, add the circled scores, put each total in a box to the right, place an X along dotted lines to show the total score in each section, and finally review and check some ways of those listed to overcome barriers.

The BESI can be used in counseling as a preliminary measure for career counselors to open discussions or to get initial ideas about clients' self-perceptions of what they think prevents them from gaining or keeping suit-

A COUNSELOR'S GUIDE TO CAREER ASSESSMENTS INSTRUMENTS

able employment. BESI categories are mirrored in needs identified by programs designed to assist unemployed people reconnect with the labor market (e.g., Borgen, 1999). The BESI is similar to many other self-administered assessments. It can potentially promote introspection on the part of the client with respect to employment. As Liptak (2011) states, the BESI can be used as a tool to facilitate discussion between client and counselor about employment barriers and how barriers could be addressed.

Technical Considerations

Norms are implied as the Inventory shows scores as "fewer barriers in this category than others completing the BESI," "about the same level of barriers", or "more barriers than others completing the BESI" (Step 3). No data representative of a defined population are provided to justify norms, which seem to be based on results from convenience samples.

Reliability estimates for prior editions of the BESI are reported in the administrator's guide for each of the five subscales and for the scale overall (Liptak, 2011). Internal consistency reliability estimates for subscales range from .87 to .95 based on a sample of 150 adults. Test-retest reliability (6 month interval) ranges from .79 to .90 for the subscales based on a sample of 95 adults. Split-half reliability was reported as .90. Total scale internal consistency reported by Webster, Rosen, McDonald, Staton-Tindall, Garrity, and Leukefeld (2007) for a sample of 500 drug court participants was .97. No new reliability information is provided for the BESI 4th Edition though means and standard deviations from two Inventory administrations subsequent to the original administration are provided with some discussion of changes in means.

The manual provides evidence of content validity included in previous manuals. Items were originally generated based on literature review, interviews with unemployed adults, focus groups, and input from employment and career counselors, with items screened to eliminate bias due to race, gender, culture, and ethnic origin. Face validity is supported by item review by professional counselors for appropriateness and category placement. The original item pool of 100 items was reduced to 75 items based on their review. Although concurrent validity is referenced incorrectly as correlations between subscales in the manual, Webster et al. (2007) found low ($r \approx .2$) but statistically significant correlations between BESI total scores and race (higher BESI scores for non-White), employment status (higher BESI scores for unemployed drug court participants), and mental health status as measured by the Brief Symptom Inventory. No new validity information is provided for this edition.

General Utility and Evaluation

The administrator's guide is minimally useful. Approximately half of the 16-page guide is devoted to a review of the background of the BESI and a summary of some research in the area of employment barriers. Technical information is provided (four pages), but consists of category means from administrations to different samples of older BESI editions. No information is provided regarding BESI use with diverse populations. Information for establishing norms is not provided, and there is no validity information aside from content/face validity support.

Earlier editions of the BESI were reviewed by Cavan (2001), Camara (2002), and Green (2009). These reviewers agreed that the BESI is easy to use with high internal consistency and little to no support for validity. Cavan pointed out that while the BESI can be self-administered, its use is as a tool to open a dialogue with a career counselor and so self-interpretation of results is unlikely, particularly by clients with minimal job search skills and with lower education levels, and the BESI would best be used in an interview. Face and content validity are supported, with some minimal support for construct validity from Webster et al. (2007). Lacking further validation, the BESI may best be used as a tool to open a discussion in individual or group counseling rather than as a self-interpreted measure or as a tool to predict employment or training outcomes.

References and Additional Resources

Borgen, W. A. (1999). Starting points implementation follow-up study. *Journal of Employment Counseling, 36,* 95-114.

Camara, W. J. (2002). [Barriers to Employment Success Inventory (2nd ed)]. In R. A. Spies & B. S. Plake (Eds.), *Sixteenth mental measurements yearbook* (pp. 90-93). Lincoln, NE: Buros Center for Testing.

Cavan, D. E. (2001). [Barriers to Employment Success Inventory.] *Newsnotes.* Retrieved from http://theaaceonline.com

Green, K. E. (2009). [Barriers to Employment Success Inventory (2nd ed).] In E. Whitfield, R. Feller, & C. Wood (Eds.), *A counselor's guide to career assessment instruments* (5th ed., pp. 328-332). Broken Arrow, OK: National Career Development Association.

Liptak, J. J. (2011). *Barriers to Employment Success Inventory—Administrator's guide.* Indianapolis, IN: JIST Works.

Webster, J. M., Rosen, P. J., McDonald, H. S., Staton-Tindall, M., Garrity, T. F., & Leukefeld, C. G. (2007). Mental health as a mediator of gender differences in employment barriers among drug abusers. *The American Journal of Drug and Alcohol Abuse, 33,* 259-265.

A Counselor's Guide To Career Assessments Instruments

CAREER COMMITMENT MEASURE
Kerry Carson and Arthur Bedeian

Kerry Carson

University of Louisiana at Lafayette
P.O. Box 41812
Lafayette LA 70504
kcarson@louisiana.edu

Target Population: Adults.

Statement of the Purpose of the Instrument: The Career Commitment Measure (CCM) was developed to measure career commitment across three dimensions: career identity, career planning, and career resilience.

Titles of Subtests, Scales, Scores Provided: The CCM provides scores for its subscales (career identity, career planning, career resilience), with a maximum score of 20. A total score is also provided, with a maximum score of 60.

Forms and Levels Available, with Dates of Publication/Revision of Each: 1994.

Date of Most Recent Edition of Test Manual, User's Guide, Etc.: Not applicable.

Languages in Which Available: English only.

Time:

> **Actual Test Time:** Approximately 5 minutes.

> **Total Administration Time:** Varies.

Manner in Which Results Are Reported for Individuals: A counselor or other administrator provides the total and subscale scores and can explore career commitment with the client.

Report Format/Content for Group Summaries: Not available.

Machine Scoring: Not available.

Hand Scoring: Scored by counselor.

Computer Software Options Available: Not available.

Cost of Materials: No cost. Contact the primary author for additional information.

> **Specimen Set:** Not available.

> **Counselee Materials:** Copies of the CCM.

Published Reviews in the Literature within the past 15 Years: Not available.

CAREER COMMITMENT MEASURE
Reviewed by:
Carrie Wachter Morris
Department of Educational Studies
Purdue University

Description

The Career Commitment Measure (CCM) was developed to provide a psychometrically sound instrument to measure career commitment, defined as "ones motivation to work in a chosen vocation" (Carson & Bedeian, 1994, p. 240). Career commitment is conceptualized as multidimensional, consisting of three dimensions: career identity, career planning, and career resilience (see London, 1985). Each of these dimensions is represented within the CCM, which presents a shift from previous assessments that were one-dimensional.

The CCM is a 12-item measure, where each item can be scored on a 5-point Likert-type scale anchored by *strongly disagree* (1) and *strongly agree* (5), resulting in a maximum score of 60. Each of the three dimensions or subscales—career identity, career planning, and career resilience—has four associated items, which each add to a maximum component score of 20. Sample items include "My line of work/career field is an important part of who I am" (career identity dimension), "I have created a plan for my development in this line of work/career field" (career planning dimension), and "Given the problems in this line of work/career field, I sometimes wonder if the personal burdens are worth it" (career resilience dimension).

Diemer and Blustein (2007) in a study involving urban youth used a modified version of the CCM (modified by replacing "my line of work/career field" with "my career in the future" to better suit an adolescent population) to operationalize urban adolescents' commitment to working in the future and connection to the career development process. Scores from the adolescent sample (M = 41.67, SD = 5.87) were similar to obtained means from the original development study. When Diemer and Blustein combined items from the CCM with other career development instruments in exploratory and confirmatory factor analyses, four items loaded on a factor they described as Future Career Identification and six items loaded on a factor they entitled Work Role Resilience. The authors used these factors to describe, assess, and build upon the construct they coined *vocational hope.* They found that "maintaining a connection to working in the future in a more general sense, [and] maintaining a connection to one's chosen career field in the future is also an aspect of vocational hope for urban adolescents" (see pp. 109-112).

No reading level is listed for the CCM. In addition to its use with adults (Carson & Bedeian, 1994) and adolescents (Diemer & Blustein, 2007), Coogle, Head, and Parham (2006) included the CCM along with the Minnesota Satisfaction Questionnaire to investigate trainees working in a gerontological setting.

The CCM is included as an appendix in Carson and Bedeian (1994), and counselors are required to re-format the instrument should they choose to use the CCM with clients or students. Thus, it is up to counselors or other test administrators to ensure that the format is legible and attractive to those taking the assessment. The instrument is available through the Carson and Bedeian article, and it is advisable to request permission from the author.

Although uses of this instrument in counseling were not described by Carson and Bedeian (1994), it has uses in career counseling. The primary benefit is that it provides information about the level of commitment individuals have to their current career field or position. Unlike previous career commitment assessments, the CCM measures career commitment as distinctive from purely an intention to remain in a current career for adults. Thus, it measures factors specific to the individual's career identity, career planning, and career resilience that create a commitment to the position, rather an individual's desire to stay just because there is not a better option.

Given this information, a career counselor could work with clients to understand their attachment to a position and how that might factor in to work satisfaction or dissatisfaction that they are experiencing. For example, a low score on the career resilience dimension and a high score on the career identity dimension could generate conversations about current demands or problems in a specific position or field that are detrimental and potentially causing conflict with a client's professional identity. In which case, time spent exploring whether a change in how a client defines her or his career identity would be a valuable part of helping determine whether a change of career field might be beneficial.

Beyond the traditional career counseling setting, there are other potential uses for the CCM. For example, school counselors or those working with youth could use the modified version (see Diemer & Blustein, 2007) to explore connection to specific fields or the career development process. Particularly with adolescents who are sorting through potential postsecondary options, this might be a way to operationalize differences in how those adolescents view their connection to different careers, a career in general, or (with minor modification) other postsecondary options. The CCM could also be useful to spur exploration with those nearing retirement to assess how integral their current career is to their identity and discuss ways that they can ease the transition into retirement if career commitment — and particularly the career identity dimension — is particularly high.

A Counselor's Guide To Career Assessments Instruments

Technical Considerations

Carson and Bedeian (1994) conducted two pilot studies to finalize the CCM items, with samples drawn from undergraduate and MBA students, as well as employees in a loan office, fast food restaurant, law firm, human resources department, public high school, chemical plant, and financial institution. These two pilot studies comprised of 567 individuals and served to help narrow potential questions from 36 career commitment measures to 12. A principal axis factor analysis with oblique rotation completed after the first pilot study narrowed the pool from 36 items to 20 by eliminating items that did not clearly load onto one factor or that had other psychometric issues. Another principal axis factor analysis with an oblique rotation completed after the second pilot study showed four initial factors, but the reliability of the fourth was below .70, so it was dropped. In addition, to have the same number of items on the remaining three factors, the top four items loading on each factor were retained, giving a final 12-item CCM. The final 12-question form of the CCM was distributed to an estimation sample of 1,292 individuals comprised of adults in professions varying in degrees of "technical training, advanced education, formal testing and control of admission, professional association, codes of conduct, and sense of calling" (p. 242). Of these individuals, 476 responded (36.8% response rate).

The CCM demonstrates adequate reliability in available published studies. Internal consistency ranged from .79 (for career identity and career resilience) to .85 (for career planning) for samples of adults (Carson & Bedeian, 1984). Diemer and Blustein (2007) found for its urban adolescent sample an internal consistency of .70 (Diemer & Blustein, 2006; 2007). There is no evidence to date of other forms of reliability evidence.

Content validity was established through the use of two distinct sets of judges to sort 87 initially developed items into the three desired dimensions of career commitment. The first set of judges consisted of two first-year Ph.D. students in management. The second set of judges was advanced Ph.D. students in organizational behavior/organization psychology. The second set was responsible for further refinement of the items into cognitive, behavioral, and affective dimensions as well. These two sets of expert judges culled the initial set of 87 items down to the 36 that were used for pilot testing.

With respect to construct validity, a principal-axes factor analysis with oblique rotation was performed that indicated a three-factor structure, including career identity, career resilience, and career planning (Carson & Bedeian, 1994). Further, convergent validity was demonstrated by a significant relationship between the CCM and a seven-item career commitment measure (Blau, 1985). Discriminant validity was indicated by exploring the relationship between the CCM and a three-item career withdrawal measure (Michaels & Spector, 1982). From this, the three career withdrawal items and the seven items from Blau's measure loaded on one factor, and the CCM items loaded on three additional factors by its previously determined three-factor structure. This demonstrated that the CCM is distinct both from the unidimensional Blau career commitment measure, but also from a career withdrawal measure. There is no criterion-related evidence available for the CCM.

General Utility and Evaluation

There is no manual available. There are significant technical details regarding the establishment and psychometric properties of the CCM in Carson and Bedeian (1994). There is limited discussion of special populations or diversity considerations in this article, but a slightly modified version of the CCM have been used by other researchers for urban youth. Additional research on the psychometric properties and norming on other age groups (e.g., youth, individuals who are anticipating retirement) or diverse populations would expand the utility of the CCM beyond the initial sample.

The primary criticism of the CCM is that the sample that it was validated with was a primarily professional, White, adult population. Although there was diversity in careers, age, and tenure within current professions represented, there was little exploration of how other aspects of diversity might impact responses to items on the CCM. A secondary criticism is that, despite the extensive testing to establish factor structure, etc., there are limited psychometric data available regarding population norms.

Additionally, youth were noticeably absent, perhaps by choice, since typically high school youth are not thought of as having a career in the same way as an adult might. Diemer and Blustein, in their adaptation of the CCM for urban youth, found that the measure of career identity loaded onto a different factor than Vocational

Identity scale (Holland, Johnston, & Asama, 1993), and indicated more of a commitment to having a career in the future, rather than a commitment to a specific career or vocation.

References and Additional Resources

Blau, G. J. (1985). The measurement and prediction of career commitment. *Journal of Occupational Psychology, 58,* 277-288.

Carson, K. D. (1991). *A multidimensional career commitment measure (MCCM) gauging motivation to work in one's career field.* (Doctoral Dissertation). Retrieved from ProQuest Dissertations and Theses. (Accession Order No. 9219524)

Carson, K. D., & Bedeian, A. G. (1994). Career commitment: Construction of a measure and examination of its psychometric properties. *Journal of Vocational Behavior, 44,* 237-262.

Coogle, C. L., Head, C. A., & Parham, I. A. (2006). The long-term care workforce crisis: Dementia-care training influences on job satisfaction and career commitment. *Educational Gerontology, 32,* 611-631. doi: 10.1080/03601270500494147

Diemer, M. A., & Blustein, D. L. (2006). Critical consciousness and career development among urban youth. *Journal of Vocational Behavior, 68,* 220–232.

Diemer, M. A., & Blustein, D. L. (2007). Vocational hope and vocational identity: Urban adolescents' career development. *Journal of Career Assessment, 15,* 98-118. doi: 10.1177/1069072706294528

Holland, J. L., Johnston, J. A., & Asama, N. F. (1993). The vocational identity scale: A diagnostic and treatment tool. *Journal of Career Assessment, 1,* 1–12.

London, M. (1985). *Developing managers: A guide to motivating and preparing people for successful managerial careers.* San Francisco, CA: Jossey-Boss.

Michaels, C., & Spector, P. (1982). Causes of employee turnover: A test of the Mobley, Griffeth, Hand & Meglino model. *Journal of Applied Psychology, 67,* 53-59.

CAREER DECISION SELF-EFFICACY SCALE AND CAREER DECISION SELF-EFFICAY SCALE — SHORT FORM

Nancy E. Betz and Karen M. Taylor

Mindgarden, Inc.
855 Oak Grove Ave., Suite 215
Menlo Park, CA 94025
(650) 322-6300
http://www.mindgarden.com

Target Population: Young adults and adults. Undergraduate students, especially undecided students and those representing racial ethnic minority groups or underprepared students. Also for adults experiencing work adjustment concerns and women.

Statement of the Purpose of the Instrument: The Career Decision Self-Efficacy Scale (CDSE) measures an individual's degree of belief that he or she can successfully complete tasks necessary to making career decisions.

Titles of Subtests, Scales, Scores Provided: The five subscales include accurate self-appraisal, gathering occupational information, goal selection, making plans for the future, and problem solving. Responses are obtained on a 10-point scale ranging from Complete Confidence (9) to No Confidence (0). The item score can range from 0 to 9, with larger numbers reflecting "easier" items. An alternative five-level confidence continuum (ranging from No Confidence at all, scored 1, to Complete Confidence, scored 5) is available and has been shown to be as reliable and valid as the 10-level continuum (see Betz, Hammond, & Multon, 2005).

A total score reflecting self-efficacy expectations with regard to all 50 career decision-making tasks is calculated by summing the confidence ratings for the 50 items. The maximum score on the CDSE is 250 (short form) or 450 (50-item form). Confidence scores for each of the five subscales are calculated from the sum of responses to the 10 scale items; the maximum subscale score is 90 when the 10-level response is used (Betz & Taylor, 2012).

Forms and Levels Available, with Dates of Publication/Revision of Each: CDSE-Short Form, 1996. Fouad, Smith, and Enochs (1997; also Fouad & Smith, 1996) adapted the CDSE for use with middle school students. A revision of the CDSE for high school students was also conducted (Carnes, Carnes, Wooten, Jones, Raffield, & Heitkamp, 1995).

Date of Most Recent Edition of Test Manual, User's Guide, Etc.: 2012.

Language in Which Available: English; Hebrew version, using 6-item subscales.

Time:

Actual Test Time: 15 minutes (50-item form) and 10 minutes (short form).

Total Administration Time: 15 minutes (50-item form) and 10 minutes (short form).

Norm Group(s) on Which Scores Are Based: The CDSE was initially validated in samples of 346 college students, 156 students (68 males and 88 females) attending a private liberal arts college and 193 students (60 males and 130 females) attending a large state university. Both schools were located in the Midwest (Betz & Taylor, 2012).

Manner in Which Results Are Reported for Individuals: Counselors present subscale scores and the total score to the test taker. Mindgarden, Inc. provides two options: online data collection and scoring or purchase license to reproduce and use local scoring (by hand or using computer-scored answer sheets).

Report Format/Content for Group Summaries: Not available.

Cost of Materials: Due to possible price changes since publication date, be sure to check the publisher's website. Rights to administer the scales increase with desired sample size. For example, the cost is $110.00 per 100 administrations via license or $132.00 to purchase 100 on-line administrations and scoring services. For 200 administrations the cost would be $160.00 (license) or $192.00 (data collection and scoring services).

Specimen Set: Manual, including non-reproducible tests forms and scoring keys (both CDSE and CDSE-Short Form): $40.00.

Counselee Materials: Test form or online access to instrument.

Published Reviews of the Instrument in the Last 15 years:

Benish, J. K. (2001). [Career Decision Self-Efficacy Scale.] In Plake, B. S., & Impara, J. C. (Eds.), *The fourteenth annual mental measurements yearbook*. Lincoln, NE: Buros Center for Testing.

Benish, J. K. (2009). [Career Decision Self-Efficacy Scale.] In E. A. Whitfield, R. W. Feller, & C. Wood (Eds.), *A counselor's guide to career assessment instruments* (5th ed., pp. 339-344). Broken Arrow, OK: National Career Development Association.

Johnson, R. W. (2001). [Career Decision Self-Efficacy Scale.] In Plake, B. S., & Impara, J. C. (Eds.), *The fourteenth annual mental measurements yearbook*. Lincoln, NE: Buros Center for Testing.

CAREER DECISION SELF-EFFICACY SCALE AND CAREER DECISION SELF-EFFICACY SCALE — SHORT FORM

Reviewed by:

Joshua C. Watson

Department of Counseling and Educational Psychology
Mississippi State University-Meridian

Description

The Career Decision Self-Efficacy Scale (CDSE) was developed to measure an individual's degree of belief that he or she can successfully complete tasks necessary to making career decisions (Taylor & Betz, 1983). The CDSE is comprised of 50 statements based on the five domains of career competence originally proposed by John Crites (1978) in his model of career maturity. The five domains include accurate self-appraisal, gathering occupational information, goal selection, planning, and problem solving. Respondents are asked to rate each statement using a 5-point Likert scale response set with values ranging from 1 = *no confidence at all* to 5 = *complete confidence.* The 5-point response set represents a recent addition to the CDSE. Previous versions of the CDSE utilized a 10-point response set; however, the authors note research supporting the strong psychometric properties of the new response set (see Betz, Hammond, & Multon, 2005) and advocate for the use of the 5-point response set due to its easier administration, high reliability, and valid score results (Betz & Taylor, 2012). A short form of the CDSE (CDSE-SF) is available and contains 25 statements based on the same five domains of career competence and uses the same 5-point response set.

In terms of its design, the CDSE is a straightforward instrument. The 5-point response set is presented at the beginning of the instrument followed by a sample question illustrating how responses should be indicated. The 50 test items are presented in list format under the general lead-in question *"how much confidence do you have that you could ..."* Item content includes the ability to list several majors, use the Internet for job searching, and developing goals.

Age norms are not provided in the test manual. Although the CDSE was initially examined using a sample of college students, it is possible that it also can be used effectively with a younger student population. Previous researchers (Fouad, Smith, & Enochs, 1997) have adapted the instrument for use with middle school and high school students. However, the wording of some of the original test items and their focus on traditional college-level career exploration activities suggest that it is probably best to use the CDSE with a college student population.

The CDSE can be used as a tool to assist in planning treatment for a student seeking career counseling. Betz and Taylor (2012) recommend using the CDSE as a counseling intervention to assess an individual's confidence in approaching a variety of behaviors related to his or her career decision-making process. Specifically, the instrument can be used as a pre-post dependent measure of the effectiveness of career development interventions implemented with the student.

The total score can be used to identify those students who might potentially be "at risk" in terms of overall decision-making efficacy. These students may struggle with making decisions for reasons unrelated to career choice. As such, treatment efforts could be directed at understanding the underlying reason for their low feelings of efficacy toward making decisions. The subscale scores can be used to determine the behavioral areas in which low scores are reported. Interventions can be designed and implemented for these areas to effectively increase an individual's self-efficacy in that particular behavioral domain.

Technical Considerations

The original norm group included 346 college students attending schools in the Midwest. Specifically, 156 students (68 males and 88 females) who attended a private liberal arts college and 190 students (60 males and 130 females) who attended a large public state university served as the normative sample. Information pertaining to the ethnic and cultural background of the original norm group participants is not provided. This same group of 346 students also was used to later validate the 25-item CDSE-SF.

Initial reliability estimates computed by the authors were reported to be strong. For the original sample used to norm the CDSE, Taylor and Betz (1983) found an internal consistency reliability coefficient of .97 with subscale scores ranging between .86 and .89. For the CDSE-SF, the internal consistency reliability coefficient for the 25-item full-scale score was .94 and the subscale alphas ranged between .73 and .83 (Betz, Harmon, & Borgen, 1996). However, these results were based on the instrument when it was constructed using a 10-point response set. Betz, Hammond, and Multon (2005) reported that the new version of the CDSE with a 5-point response set provided scores as reliable as those obtained with the original 10-point response set. Alpha coefficient values ranged between .78 and .85 among 400 students in one sample and between .80 and .84 in another sample of 603 predominantly White students. Using the 5-point response set CDSE-SF, Chaney, Hammond, Betz, and Multon (2007) reported alpha coefficient values ranging from .78 to .85 among a sample of 220 African American college students. These results indicate that the revised instruments with the shortened response sets are as reliable as the original measures. While the reliability coefficients obtained in these previous reliability studies indicate that both the CDSE and CDSE-SF are highly reliable instruments, the authors provide no additional sources of reliability estimation in their test manual.

The CDSE has been validated across multiple studies using multiple methodologies. Evidence of the instrument's content, concurrent, and construct validity is documented by an extensive list of past research included in the test manual. Assessing the factor structure of the CDSE, factor analytic studies (Lo Presti et al., 2013; Miller et al., 2009) provide support for the five-factor model based on Crites' (1978) theory of career maturity. In addition, convergent validity has been demonstrated in a number of studies in which strong relationships between the CDSE and CDSE-SF scales and a number of related constructs including career indecision (Betz, Klein, & Taylor, 1996; Taylor & Betz, 1983), vocational identity (Betz, Harmon, et al., 1996), and career exploration behaviors (Blustein, 1989; Peterson, 1993) have been found.

General Utility and Evaluation

The manual provides information on the development, administration, scoring, interpretation, and functionality of the CDSE and CDSE-SF instruments. The authors include a brief review of the self-efficacy and career maturity theories as they serve as the theoretical foundation for both instruments. The section on administration simply states that test users should adhere to all local and national ethical standards and best practices for use of standardized tests. No information is provided in terms of the amount of time in which students should be able to complete the instruments, nor whether they are better administered as individual or group assessments. Instructions on scoring the instruments and interpreting the scores are clear, and a sample of each instrument is included.

The CDSE is a well-developed instrument with sound psychometric properties. Almost 30 years of research studies are referenced in the manual and indicate that the constructs of career decision making included in the instrument are based on an evidence-based model. The instrument is easy to both administer and score and should take relatively little time for a student to complete. The total and subscale scores provide counselors with valuable information that can be used to design and evaluate career counseling interventions. Overall the

Career Decision Self-Efficacy Scale and Career Decision Self-Efficacy Scale — Short Form

CDSE appears to be a useful assessment tool. Previous researchers using the CDSE have found it to be applicable across gender (Betz, Klein, et al., 1996; Miller et al., 2009) and cultural groups (Betz & Borgen, 2010; Peterson, 1993), providing further support for its use in counseling practice.

References and Additional Resources

Benish, J. K. (2001). [Career Decision Self-Efficacy Scale.] In Plake, B. S., & Impara, J. C. (Eds.), *The fourteenth annual mental measurements yearbook.* Lincoln, NE: Buros Center for Testing.

Benish, J. K. (2009). [Career Decision Self-Efficacy Scale.] In E. A. Whitfield, R. W. Feller, & C. Wood (Eds.), *A counselor's guide to career assessment instruments* (5th ed., pp. 339-344). Broken Arrow, OK: National Career Development Association.

Betz, N. E., & Taylor, K. M. (2012). *Manual for the Career Decision Self-Efficacy Scale and CDSE-Short Form.* Menlo Park, CA: Mindgarden Inc.

Betz, N. E., Hammond, M., & Multon, K. (2005). Reliability and validity of response continua for the Career Decision Self-efficacy Scale. *Journal of Career Assessment, 13,* 131-149. doi:10.1177/1069072704273123

Betz, N. E., Harmon, L. W., & Borgen, F. H. (1996). The relationships of self-efficacy for the Holland themes to gender, occupational group membership, and vocational interests. *Journal of Counseling Psychology, 43,* 90-98. doi:10.1037/0022-0167.43.1.90

Betz, N. E., Klein, K., & Taylor, K. (1996). Evaluation of a short form of the Career Decision Self-Efficacy Scale. *Journal of Career Assessment, 4,* 47-57. doi:10.1177/10690727960040010

Betz, N. E., & Borgen, F. (2009). Comparative effectiveness of CAPA and Focus online career assessment systems with undecided college students. *Journal of Career Assessment, 17,* 351-366. doi:10.1177/1069072709334229

Blustein, D. L. (1989). The role of goal instability and career self-efficacy in the career exploration process. *Journal of Vocational Behavior, 35,* 194-203. doi:10.1016/0001-8791(89)90040-7

Carnes, A. W., Carnes, M. R., Wooten, H. R., Jones, L., Raffield, P., & Heitkamp, J. (1995). Extracurricular activities: Are they beneficial? TCA Journal. 23, 37-45.

Chaney, D., Hammond, M., Betz, N., & Multon, K. (2007). The reliability and factor structure of the Career Decision Self-efficacy Scale-SF with African Americans. *Journal of Career Assessment, 15,* 194-205. doi:10.1177/1069072706298020

Crites, J. O. (1978). *Career Maturity Inventory.* Monterey, CA: CTB/McGraw Hill.

Fouad, N. A., Smith, P. L., & Enochs, L. (1997). Reliability and validity evidence for the Middle School Self-Efficacy Scale. *Measurement and Evaluation in Counseling and Development, 30,* 17-31.

Fouad, N. A., Smith, P. L., (1996). A test of a social cognitive model for middle school students: Math and Science. *Journal of Counseling Psychology, 43,* 338-346.

Johnson, R. W. (2001). [Career Decision Self-Efficacy Scale.] In Plake, B. S., & Impara, J. C. (Eds.), *The fourteenth annual mental measurements yearbook.* Lincoln, NE: Buros Center for Testing. [Electronic Version]

Lo Presti, A., Pace, F., Mondo, M., Nota, L., Casarubia, P., Ferrari, L., & Betz, N. (2013). An examination of the structure of the Career Decision Self-Efficacy Scale among Italian high school students. *Journal of Career Assessment.* [Electronic Version]

Miller, M. J., Kerrin Sendrowitz, R., Brown, S. D., Thomas, J., & McDaniel, C. (2009). A confirmatory test of the factor structure of the short form of the Career Decision Self-Efficacy Scale. *Journal of Career Assessment, 17,* 507-519. doi:10.1177/1069072709340665

Peterson, S. L. (1993). Career decision-making self-efficacy and institutional integration of underprepared college students. *Research in Higher Education, 34,* 659-683. doi:10.1007/BF00992155

Taylor, K. M., & Betz, N. E. (1983). Applications of self-efficacy theory to the understanding and treatment of career indecision. *Journal of Vocational Behavior, 22,* 63-81. doi:10.1016/0001-8791(83)90006-4

CAREER DEVELOPMENT INVENTORY
Albert Thompson, Richard Lindeman, Donald Super, Jean Pierre Jordaan, and Roger Myers

Vocopher

Kevin Glavin

Reviews by publisher

http://www.vocopher.com/
kglavin@vocopher.com

Target Population: Adolescents, young adults, and adults; Forms available for Grades 8-12 and college students.

Statement of the Purpose of the Instrument: The Career Development Inventory (CDI) is designed to measure an individual's readiness to make vocational and educational decisions. It may be used as a supplement with an interest inventory to determine how best to interpret the interest inventory results.

Titles of Subtests, Scales, Scores Provided: Career Planning, Career Exploration, Decision Making, and Knowledge of the World of Work. A fifth scale, Knowledge of Preferred Occupation, should not be used with individuals below Grade 11. Composite scales available for the CDI include Career Decision Attitudes, Career Decision Knowledge, and Career Orientation. Three summary scores are available: Career Development—Attitudes scale (includes Career Planning and Career Exploration scales); The Career Development—Knowledge and Skills scale (includes Decision-Making and World-of-Work Information scales); and a Career Orientation Total that includes all scales.

Forms and Levels Available, with Dates of Publication/Revision of Each: School Form and College Form, 1984.

Date of Most Recent Edition of Test Manual, User's Guide, Etc.: 1984.

Languages in Which Available: English only.

Time:

    Actual Test Time: Varies.

    Total Administration Time: 60 minutes.

Manner in Which Results Are Reported for Individuals: Standard scores and percentiles.

Machine Scoring: Scored online. The test taker is able to review results online during administration.

Hand Scoring: Not available.

Computer Software Options Available: The CDI is only available online.

Cost of Materials: There is no cost associated with the CDI.

    Specimen Set: No cost, online form with results.

    Counselee Materials: Online test (not reusable).

Published Reviews of the Instrument in the Last 15 Years:

Sundre, D. L. (1998). [Career Development Inventory.] In J. C. Impara, & B. S. Plake (Eds.). *The thirteenth mental measurements yearbook* (p. 48). Lincoln, NE: Buros Center for Testing.

Glavin, K., & Savickas, M. L. (2006). Career Development Inventory. In Greenhaus, J. H., & Gerard, G. C. (Eds.) *Encyclopedia of career development.* Thousand Oaks, CA: Sage.

Glavin, K., & Savickas, M. L. (2007). Career Development Inventory. In N. J. Salkind (Ed.) *Encyclopedia of measurement and statistics.* Thousand Oaks, CA: Sage.

CAREER DEVELOPMENT INVENTORY

Reviewed by:

Dale Pietrzak

Director of Academic Evaluation and Assessment
University of South Dakota

Description

The Career Development Inventory (CDI) is intended to be used as a measure of readiness to enter into meaningful career decision making (career maturity). It is based to largely in the work of Donald Super (1957). Super's (1957) career development theory was based in the work of Havighurst (1953) and others (Thompson, Lindeman, Super, Jordaan, & Myers, 1981, 1984). While officially out of print, it has recently been made available online with the permission of the authors and prior publisher through "The Online Career Collaboratory" (http://www.vocopher.com). There are two versions of the inventory available: a School form for Grades 8-12 and a College form intended primarily for use with undergraduate populations. While research using the College form has been conducted with graduate students, its use appears to be atypical with this population (Savickas & Hartun, 1996; Thompson et al., 1981, 1984). A relatively extensive review of the psychometrics and research base of the CDI between 1984 and 1995 was published in 1996 (Savickas & Hartung, 1996). There are two primary manuals for the CDI (see Thompson et al., 1981, 1984).

The stated purpose of the CDI is to develop an objective measure of career maturity and is intended to help speed the understanding and working with career development issues. "Career development includes occupational awareness, planfulness, desire to explore the world of work, recognition of changes in tasks of vocational development that one faces with increased age and social responsibility, and knowledge of the world of work and appropriate occupations" (Thompson et al., 1981, p. 1). It is two-part assessment tool per form designed using Likert scale, multiple choice, and problem-solving simulations formats (although primarily multiple choice). Part 1 includes items addressing career decision making and Part 2 focuses on knowledge of preferred occupations. Either part can be independently administered, however part one would be the most commonly used module. yet is likely intended to be used with those having reached a greater level of career decision skill. Completion of each part averages about 60 minutes.

The School and College forms each includes eight scales that cover two broad categories and provide three summary scores. The Career Development—Attitudes (CDA) scale/score subsumes the two scales of Career Planning (CP) and Career Exploration (CE). The Career Development—Knowledge and Skills (CDK) scale/score subsumes the two scales of Decision-Making (DM) and World-of-Work Information (WW). The Career Orientation Total (COT) score/scale includes a total based on the CP, CE, DM, and WW scales.

The item content varies. An example of Part 1 item content with a Likert-type format is "Working with others on career issues with another is important". This item contains five response options: "A. I have not yet given any thought to this; B. I have given some thought to this, but haven't made any plans yet; C. I have some plans, but am still not sure of them; D. I have made definite plans, but don't know yet how to carry them out; and E. I have made definite plans, and know what to do to carry them out." Other sections in Part 1 ask the respondent to make a determination of the best option for someone based on a sample scenario (i.e., problem-solving simulation format). For example, an item might state something like Sally has good test scores in math but has made poor grades in high school. The school counselor had advised Sally not to go to college because of the chance of failure. Sally thinks that is not a problem, wants to go ahead with a two-year program, and has been admitted to a non-selective college. What should Sally do? These types of items offer four responses such as: "A. Forget about college and seek a satisfying job; B. Repeat basic Math courses in order to make a good start; C. Take the regular Math course if the program is not too demanding; and D. Get private tutoring in Math."

Part 2 has sections which ask for selections of occupational titles/types from lists. For example, a respondent may be asked to "Check the list of occupations in the area of art that you might be particularly interested in (mark all that apply): costume designer, graphic artist, ceramics, sculpture and painting."

A COUNSELOR'S GUIDE TO CAREER ASSESSMENTS INSTRUMENTS

The current form of administration is directly online with no downloaded software. The computer systems requirements are not listed on site, but it ran on three different Windows-based systems when tested. It appears to operate on systems that support Java and are able to operate a Windows browser. The presentation format showing on the computer screen was easy to view and easy to respond to overall. Anyone who is used to using a computer to point and click for responding should be able to navigate the site easily.

The results in the form of a standard score and percentile are provided at the end of each of the two parts. There is the ability for a counselor to group reports to be presented together. The administration allows for self-review of the data, though the materials at the end do not send a test taker to the CDI manual. These materials send the test taker to the Career Maturity Inventory (CMI) manual. It is not clear in these manuals what the relationship is between the CMI and CDI. Although they each follow the same theory, the normative and interpretative processes appear to be different. It would be improper to interpret the results using the CMI manual. The site appears to wish that people use the CMI rather than the CDI at this point.

The screen display uses a gray-based easily viewed contrasting presentation. This makes it easily readable, even for those who are color blind. The online system catches items that are not responded to and prompts the test taker to complete the missing items. It will not progress until respondents provide appropriate responses for all items.

The assessment of career maturity has utility not only for individual career counseling where career concerns regarding readiness to make a meaningful career decision may be an issue, but also as an outcome measure for undergraduate career-development programs. The utility of the tool requires some familiarity with the tool and theory to be best utilized. The site is not intended as a self-administration site for the general public. There are no interpretative reports, for example. An untrained user would have limited ability to make use of the information that is provided.

Technical Considerations

There are several technical considerations in examining the test. The normative basis of the School form appears to have been collected from the late 1970s to early 1980s. The College form norms appear to have been collected largely from the early 1980s. The manuals present data on these normative groups, and in both cases these were not as representative nationally as one might like. Further, there have been significant cultural changes since the time the tests were developed. Changes in career education in schools and colleges has shifted in many ways over that time, and, as the research in the manuals points out, there can be a significant impact of such education on CDI results. These considerations would suggest using the current normative data cautiously in a counseling setting. As a researcher, this may be less limiting in a pretest-posttest situation where change or group comparisons may be more important. Scores are reported using a percentile and standard score with a mean of 100 and a standard deviation of 20. The need for the manual to connect these scores to the interpretive ranges is needed, though in general the 70th percentile is considered significant.

The reliability data presented in the manuals for the School form are presented in a relatively straightforward manner. The reliability data from the College form is found in the manual but must be searched for in some cases.

The reliability of the DM, WW, and PO scales on the School form (and thus to some extent the CDK Scale) suggest caution in clinical use and may be problematic for statistical analysis for researchers. In assessing reliability it is assumed that a construct will be consistently responded to (internal consistently) and as stable over time as the underlying construct. In the case of a constructs like DM and CDK, which are intended to be related to cognitive measures (knowledge and skills), there is a relative lack of stability over time. Further, DM and PO on the School form shows both substandard internal consistency and stability. The lack of specifics on the internal consistency of the College form for these scales makes it difficult to judge the internal consistency; however, the cognitive scales appear to be generally lower than desirable in the same areas as the School form. As with the School form, the stability of the DM, WW, PO, and CDK scales are below expectations given the nature of the target construct. This makes the use of these scales questionable in clinical and research contexts.

Cronbach's alphas for the School form are provided in a Grade by Gender manner: The alpha ranges for the scales are the following: .85 to .90 (CP); .75 to .81 (CE); .58 to .70 with 7 of 8 below .70 (DM); .77 to .87 (WW);

Career Development Inventory

.53 to .71 with 7 of 8 below .70 (PO); .82 to .87 (CDA); .79 to .88 (CDK); and .82 to .87 (CDT). The stability ranges of the School form listed in the manual for three weeks (Grade by Gender) were the following: .65 to .86 with 1 of 10 under .70 (CP); .56 to .85 with 4 of 10 under .70 (CE); .54 to .78 with 7 of 10 under .70 (DM); .49 to .79 with 9 of 10 below .70 (WW); .53 to .71 with 11 of 12 below .70 (PO); .70 to .86 (CDA); .59 to .86 with 5 of 10 below .70 (CDK), and .73 to .90 (CDT). The manual (Thompson et al., 1984) provides the following for the College form: "... obtained coefficient alphas of .91 and .83 for the two affective scales, and of .61 for the cognitive scales (Scale C)" (p. 8). The manual also reports coefficients for the College form as "coefficients ranging from .73 (Scale C) to .97 (Scales A and B)." The stability of the College form was reported for two weeks by gender. These ranges were the following: .90 to .88 (CP); .79 to .89 (CE); .63 to .69 (DM); .43 to .42 (WW); .55 to .75 (PO); .87 to .89 (CDA); .54 to .64 (CDK); and .66 to .80 (CDT).

The content-related evidence of validity for the tools appears well considered. The convergent and discriminant validity appears to be well considered and, given the limitations of the reliability noted previously, solid. This is one of the relatively few tools that has a rather large cross-cultural research base and data supporting construct validity and other forms of validity (Savickas & Hartung, 1996; Thompson et al., 1981, 1984). The research into this set of tools cross-culturally is impressive and makes it certainly one of the better understood tools from a cross-cultural perspective.

General Utility and Evaluation

In summarizing the general utility of the CDI, the accessibility and usability of the online materials is well done. Some of the Likert item sections seem to be tedious and some screen formatting changes in those areas could potentially help with administration time as well. As previously noted, it is not clear why the results point to a different set of manuals than those for the CDI. The directions to find the CDI manuals are not clear either, which complicates this, but the CDI manuals can be found in the administrators section of the website. The link found with the results points the user to the CMI which appears to be a different tool than that of the CDI. Reading the CMI manual does not appear directly applicable to the CDI normative base or CDI interpretation. This makes the interpretation by those unfamiliar with the CDI more difficult. The scores are reported as standard scores and percentiles, but all interpretations and interpretive materials are based on percentiles. While interpretation is easily accomplished once the appropriate CDI manuals are located, the lack of a clear link to them and the need to manually search for them makes this somewhat difficult. The CDI normative base also seems to be in need of updating. Career education and focus on it at both the K-12 and higher education levels has changed substantially over the past 20-30 years. As several of the scales, especially the cognitive scales, are educationally related, this suggests that the need for updated the norms is well overdue. It is of note though that the owners of the http://www.vocopher.com website recommend using the CMI and CAAS which are more recently developed and intended to address essentially the same areas as the CDI.

The positive is that the core scales needed by many counselors found in Part 1 (CDA, CP, and CE) appear strong and well-developed. They have a relatively long research history with substantive cross-cultural research available. Further, in research contexts, or educational settings using these scales as an outcome measure (particularly pre-post testing) where the normative base is not as critical, these core scales provide a well-developed and researched measure. The weaker area of the tool appears to be the Knowledge and Skills scales and the PO scale. This weakness is alluded to in the manual, and the suggestion is that these be used in specialized way. However, given the limitations noted in the discussion of the reliability data, and weaker support of these scales cross-culturally, it would be suggested that any use of the cognitive scales be undertaken with caution.

References and Additional Resources

Glavin, K., & Savickas, M. L. (2006). Career Development Inventory. In Greenhaus, J. H., & Gerard, G. C. (Eds.) *Encyclopedia of career development.* Thousand Oaks, CA: Sage.

Glavin, K., & Savickas, M. L. (2007). Career Development Inventory. In N. J. Salkind (Ed.) *Encyclopedia of measurement and statistics.* Thousand Oaks, CA: Sage.

Havinighurst, R. J. (1953). *Human development and education.* New York, NY: Longmans Green.

Impara, J. C., & Plake, B. S. (Eds.). (1998). *The thirteenth mental measurements yearbook.* Lincoln, NE: Buros Center for Testing.

Savickas, M. L., & Hartung, P. (1996). The Career Development Inventory in review: Psychometric and research findings. *Journal of Career Assessment, 4*(2), 171-188. doi:10.1177/106907279600400204

Sundre, D. L. (1998). [Career Development Inventory.] In J. C. Impara, & B. S. Plake (Eds.). *The thirteenth mental measurements yearbook* (p. 48). Lincoln, NE: Buros Center for Testing.

Super, D. E. (1957). *The psychology of careers.* New York, NY: Harper.

The Online Career Collaboratory (n.d). Retrieved from http://www.vocopher.com

Thompson, A. S., Lindeman, R. H., Super, D. E., Jordaan, J. P., & Myers, R. A. (1981). *Career Development Inventory: Volume 1 user's manual.* Palo Alto, CA: Consulting Psychologist Press. Retrieved from http://www.vocopher.com

Thompson, A. S., Lindeman, R. H., Super, D. E., Jordaan, J. P., & Myers, R. A. (1984). *Career Development Inventory: Volume 2 technical manual.* Palo Alto, CA: Consulting Psychologist Press. Retrieved from http://www.vocopher.com

CAREER FACTORS INVENTORY
Judy M. Chartrand, Steven B. Robbins, and Weston H. Morrill

Consulting Psychologists Press, Inc. (CPP, Inc.) and Davies-Black Publishing

1055 Joaquin Road, 2nd Floor
Mountain View, CA 94043
650.969.8901
FAX: 650.969.8608
http://www.cpp-db.com

Target Population: Adolescents, young adults, and adults; primarily targeted for college students but may be used with high school students. Eighth-grade reading level.

Statement of the Purpose of the Instrument: The Career Factors Inventory (CFI) is designed to help people identify their own difficulties in the career-planning and decision-making process.

Titles of Subtests, Scales, Scores Provided: Need for Career Information, Need for Knowledge, Career Choice Anxiety, and Generalized Indecisiveness. Scores provided per scale.

Forms and Levels Available, with Dates of Publication/Revision of Each: 1997.

Date of Most Recent Edition of Test Manual, User's Guide, Etc.: 1997.

Languages in Which Available: English only.

Time:

    Actual Test Time: 5 to 10 minutes.

    Total Administration Time: Varies.

Norm Group(s) on Which Scores Are Based: Two samples: 409 college students from a large western university, 331 college students from a large southeastern university.

Manner in Which Results Are Reported for Individuals: Self-scoring booklet covering results for each of the scales. Internet accessible via http://www.skillsone.com. Narrative text is provided.

Report Format/Content for Group Summaries: Not available.

Machine Scoring: Scored via website; immediate results.

Hand scoring: Scored by counselee in approximately 5 minutes.

Local machine scoring: Not available.

Computer Software Options Available: Internet administration available via http://www.skillsone.com

Cost of Materials: Due to possible price changes since publication date, be sure to check the publisher's site. Technical Guide, $55.50.

    Specimen Set: Not available.

    Counselee Materials: Self-scorable booklets (package of 10): $55.50. Visit CPP online assessment website for pricing for online administration.

Published Reviews of the Instrument in the Last 15 Years:

D'Costa, A. (2001). [Career Factors Inventory.] In B. S. Plake & J. C. Impara (Eds.), *The fourteenth mental measurements yearbook* (pp. 219-221). Lincoln, NE: Buros Center for Testing.

D'Costa, A. (2009). [Career Factors Inventory.] In E. A. Whitfield, R. W. Feller, & C. Wood (Eds.), *A counselor's guide to career assessment instruments* (5th ed., pp. 345-349). Broken Arrow, OK: National Career Development Association.

Luzzo, D. A. (2001). [Career Factors Inventory.] In J. T. Kapes & E. A. Whitfield (Eds.), *A counselor's guide to career assessment instruments* (4th ed., pp. 331-335). Columbus, OH: National Career Development Association.

CAREER FACTORS INVENTORY

Reviewed by:

Ayres D'Costa

Emeritus Associate Professor of Education
The Ohio State University

Description

The Career Factors Inventory (CFI; Chartrand, Robbins, & Morrill, 1997) is "designed to help under-graduate students determine whether they are ready to engage in the career decision-making process" (Chartrand & Robbins, 1997, p. 1). The CFI consists of 21 items requiring a Likert-type response, using five rating levels. Most of the items use the categories *Strongly Disagree* (1) to *Strongly Agree* (5). The CFI provides scores on four scales (Need for Career Information, Need for Knowledge, Career Choice Anxiety, and Generalized Indecisiveness). A sample item provided in the technical guide (Chartrand & Robbins, 1997) is: "Before choosing or entering a career area, I need to gather more information about one or more occupations."

A good feature of the CFI is that it is self-scorable. There also is good assistance in the inventory itself for plotting an Individual Profile based on its four scores and for interpreting this Profile. Among the good features of this instrument are the several "Reproducible Masters" presented in the Appendix of the technical guide and are available to counselors to help clients fully utilize the CFI and its scores. A useful revision allows the CFI to be self-administered online, with the Report and Interpretation also provided online.

Career choice is a critical challenge in vocational counseling. Therefore, the CFI, which claims to address career indecision, therefore has the potential to be an important counseling tool. The CFI does well in addressing two important causes for career indecision, namely a lack of information about oneself or about careers, and poor decision-making approaches due to anxiety or general indecisiveness. However, it does not address counseling challenges related to diagnosing or following up bad career choices.

Technical Considerations

The norms presented in the technical guide for interpreting CFI scores are based on convenience samples of college students in general psychology courses at two universities. No justification is provided for extending the interpretation beyond these limited samples, other than "career decision making was deemed salient for these individuals" (Chartrand & Robbins, 1997, p. 7). To judge other more diverse clients, such as high school students and special adult groups, using the distribution of scores obtained by this select college group appears inappropriate. No attempts are apparent in the technical guide to pool data for more diverse norms given the wide variety of clients claimed to have been successfully tested using the CFI.

While the CFI's inherent simplicity makes it obvious and vulnerable to faking, it is a remarkable tool with respect to its construct definition effort that has implications for its validity. The technical guide (Chartrand & Robbins, 1997) indicates that 31 items were initially written, based on a review of the literature, to represent five constructs associated with career decision making. Principal components factor analyses, including confirmatory factor analysis, were used to decide on the current four constructs.

The goodness of fit results for the four constructs, as well as the other discriminant/convergent validity studies, appeared reasonably convincing. The validity of the four scales, based on correlations with similar scales from other instruments, appear to be supportive of the authors' claims, although there are some glaring exceptions. Several of the correlations are low (i.e., below .30), and a couple appear to be in a direction opposite to that ordinarily expected. One table that is noteworthy is the change in CFI scores following counseling intervention. In other words, assuming the intervention was indeed effective, CFI was able to document it, although one wishes statistical tests of significance were also conducted and made available.

Gender differences were noted only for General Indecisiveness, with females reporting greater indecisiveness. No ethnic group differences were noted. Again, no statistical tests of significance were conducted.

A Counselor's Guide To Career Assessments Instruments

In assessing the reliability indices presented in the technical guide for the online version, it should be noted that the individual item error variances reported are quite high, indicating a serious problem for this item style. The test-retest (two-week and three month administration intervals) and internal consistency reliability indexes range in the .60s and .80s, the higher values occurring for the only trait measure among the four scales, General Indecisiveness. The other reliability indexes are modest.

In order to enhance the utility and interpretation of the test, the authors recommend that, before taking the CFI, students be helped to understand its purpose and the four scales it measures. Although this clarifies CFI's intent, it also makes this self-report instrument extremely easy to fake.

A 2012 check of published research by this reviewer (d'Costa, 2001, 2009) indicates that the CFI has been widely utilized in professional counseling and has generated several new insights especially those related to career indecision theory. This suggests that the 1997 technical guide (Chartrand & Robbins, 1997) is in serious need of important revision and update. There is considerable new information that could be summarized and incorporated into the technical guide.

Some of the earlier comments by this reviewer still bear repetition and emphasis. The interpretation of scores identifies three regions using two arbitrary statistical cutoffs, "Mean" and the "Mean plus one Standard Deviation," and assumes a normal distribution of scores. No justification, theoretical or empirical, is provided for these assumptions or interpretations.

The technical guide recommends plotting the four scale scores and joining these points to obtain a polygon-like profile. This approach, while commonly used, can lead to over-interpretation. There is no rationale for the sequence of the four scales, other than they belong together in pairs to two major constructs, Lack of Information and Difficulty in Decision-Making.

Nevertheless, the very practical Interpretation Model and the clinical counseling approach presented in chapter 4 of the technical guide (Chartrand & Robbins, 1997) are impressive. The case studies presented with the relevant CFI profiles should be very helpful to counselors.

General Utility and Evaluation

The CFI is a counseling tool that assesses readiness for career decision making in terms of its four scales. A special feature is its ability to help undecided persons uncover the source of their indecision. Two sources of indecision obstacles, Information Needs and Decision Needs, are specifically addressed. The Applications and technical guide (Chartrand & Robbins, 1997) claims that the CFI "has been used successfully in a variety of educational, business, and counseling settings" (p. 15). Now that the CFI is available online, it is a very flexible tool that can be used by students both in and out of school/college environments. Counselors can direct students to the CFI, help them understand their assessment report, and most importantly, help them remedy their information/knowledge deficiencies. This last step could take the form of personal counseling and pointing out or providing access to critical career information.

The online version constitutes a definite improvement of the original CFI. Students can now administer the CFI to themselves at their own personal convenience, and in complete privacy. Scoring, while it has been a simple process, is now automatic, since it is handled completely by computer. This includes a detailed report, with some explanations, which can be printed and kept in one's personal records for future reference and follow-up.

An obvious critique of this instrument is its overarching and therefore somewhat presumptuous title. Nevertheless, the CFI must be recognized as a quick and simple tool designed to do a limited job, namely determine readiness for career decision making in terms of the four factors assumed to be the key problems. The term *Career Factors Inventory* used in the title may be misleading because it is too broad. The CFI is not a typical career decision-making tool in that clients are not enabled to make good career decisions. Nor is it an inventory of all factors related to careers or the choice thereof. It merely addresses readiness to make decisions, and that, too, in a very simplistic way. The reader is referred to related instruments such as the revised *Career Maturity Inventory* (Crites & Savickas, 1995); the *Career Decision Difficulties Questionnaire* (Lancaster, Rudolph, Perkins, & Patten, 1999), and the *Career Planning Inventory* (Westbrook & Sloan, 2006).

Career Factors Inventory

Another major problem in the CFI is an inherent weakness in the wording of several of the items, which, in the mind of this reviewer, poses a serious validity concern. The phrase, *"Before choosing or entering a particular career area, I need to . . ."* is intended by the authors to reflect a compelling feeling, which is then scored as a deficit or need. Students who agree are deemed to indicate a deficit; therefore, a lack of readiness for career decision making. Unfortunately, this choice of phrasing can also be understood as asking a student to reflect a belief about what is appropriate to do in the particular circumstance. It is quite reasonable to agree to the special "need" as an appropriate or wise step you believe you should first take. For example, it is wise to need to talk to, or recognize the importance of talking to engineers before choosing engineering as a career. Therefore, scoring this response as a deficit could add to the item error variance and also adversely impact the validity (interpretation) of the CFI scores. The high item error variance and low validity coefficients reported in the technical guide might be reflections of this problem.

Assuming that the confusing phrase mentioned above can be clarified in the CFI administration process, this reviewer believes that the CFI is a limited but reasonable counseling tool. A change in title would also be in order to more accurately reflect what this Inventory is designed to do. With these limitations recognized and corrected, this reviewer applauds the authors' efforts to meet psychometric standards appropriate to this potentially useful counseling instrument. Indeed, a 2012 search of the literature related to the CFI yielded more than 50 citations, most of which are in respectable journals. This speaks to the instrument's credibility and use. Significant efforts have been made to establish its construct and discriminant validity, so as also document the CFI's utility for special populations, such as in medical rehabilitation settings and groups other than those in the United States.

References and Additional Resources

Chartrand, J. W. & Robbins, S. B. (1997). *Career Factors Inventory: Applications and technical guide.* Palo Alto, CA: Consulting Psychologists Press.

Chartrand, J. W., Robbins, S. B. & Morrill, W. H. (1997). *Career Factors Inventory: Self-scorable booklet and interpretation.* Palo Alto, CA: Consulting Psychologists Press.

Crites, J. O., & Savickas, M. L. (1995). *Career Maturity Inventory.* Clayton, NY: Information Systems Management, Careerware.

D'Costa, A. (2001). [Career Factors Inventory.] In B. S. Plake & J. C. Impara (Eds.), *The fourteenth mental measurements yearbook* (pp. 219-221). Lincoln, NE: Buros Center for Testing.

D'Costa, A. (2009). [Career Factors Inventory.] In E. A. Whitfield, R. W. Feller, & C. Wood (Eds.), *A counselor's guide to career assessment instruments* (5th ed., pp. 345-349). Broken Arrow, OK: National Career Development Association.

Lancaster, B. P., Rudolph, C. E., Perkins, T. S., & Patten, T. G. (1999). The reliability and validity of the Career Decision Difficulties Questionnaire. *Journal of Career Assessment, 7,* 393-413.

Luzzo, D. A. (2001). [Career Factors Inventory.] In J. T. Kapes & E. A. Whitfield (Eds.), *A counselor's guide to career assessment instruments* (4th ed., pp. 331-335). Columbus, OH: National Career Development Association.

Westbrook, B., & Sloan, S. (2006). Construct validity and predictive validity of the Career Planning Inventory. *Journal of Career Assessment, 14,* 385-404.

A COUNSELOR'S GUIDE TO CAREER ASSESSMENTS INSTRUMENTS

CAREER SEARCH EFFICACY SCALE
V. Scott Solberg, Glenn Good, Dennis Nord, Cheryl Holm, Robin Hohner, Nicole Zima, Mary Heffernan, & Ann Malen

---

V. Scott Solberg

Boston University
School of Education
957 Commonwealth Avenue
Boston, MA 02215
ssolberg@bu.edu

Target Population: College students, individuals initially entering the workforce or reentering after being absent for a period of time, or individuals changing jobs or careers.

Statement of the Purpose of the Instrument: The Career Search Efficacy Scale (CSES) is designed to assess the degree of confidence a person has for performing a variety of career search tasks.

Titles of Subtests, Scales, Scores Provided: Job Search Efficacy, Interviewing Efficacy, Networking Efficacy, and Personal Exploration Efficacy. The CSES provides subscale scores with higher scores on each subscale indicating higher confidence.

Forms and Levels Available, with Dates of Publication/Revision of Each: 1994.

Date of Most Recent Edition of Test Manual, User's Guide, Etc.: Not available.

Languages in Which Available: English only.

Time:

Actual Test Time: Approximately 10 minutes.

Total Administration Time: Approximately 60 minutes.

Manner in Which Results Are Reported for Individuals: Counselors provide subscale scores to clients and explore degree of confidence related to the career search process.

Report Format/Content for Group Summaries: Not available.

Machine Scoring: Not available.

Hand Scoring: Scored by counselor.

Computer Software Options Available: Not available.

Cost of Materials: Open access; contact the primary author.

Specimen Set: Not available.

Counselee Materials: Copy of instrument.

Published Reviews of the Instrument in the Last 15 Years: Not available.

CAREER SEARCH EFFICACY SCALE

Reviewed by:

Pamela Doubrava-Smith and Richard S. Balkin

Department of Counseling and Educational Psychology
Texas A&M University-Corpus Christi

Description

The Career Search Efficacy Scale (CSES) was developed to measure the career search efficacy of individuals who are in the process of finding a job or career, reentering the job market, or changing jobs or careers (Ryan,

Solberg, & Brown, 1996). The scale is a self-report measure that identifies the confidence an individual has for performing four career search tasks: job search efficacy, interviewing efficacy, networking efficacy, and personal exploration efficacy. The scale can be used to evaluate an individual's perceived effectiveness of completing activities associated with selecting and searching for a career (Solberg, Good, & Nord, 1994; Solberg, Good, Nord, Holm, et al., 1994).

The CSES consists of 35 items: 14 items for job search efficacy, 8 items for interviewing efficacy, 8 items for networking efficacy, and 5 items for personal exploration efficacy. Each item begins with the phrase, "How confident are you in your ability to" followed by a description of a career search task. A 10-point scale ranging from 0 (*very little*) to 9 (*very much*) is used to identify the degree of confidence for each item (Solberg, Good, Nord, Holm, et al. 1994). Higher scores on each subscale indicate higher confidence in that area while lower scores indicate lower confidence (Solberg, Good, & Nord, 1994). Examples of individual items from each of the four career tasks measured by the scale include "How confident are you in your ability to evaluate a job during an interview", "How confident are you in your ability to conduct an information interview", "How confident are you in your ability to identify and evaluate your personal values", and "How confident are you in your ability to use your social network to identify job opportunities."

No scoring or user manual is provided for use with this measurement. Solberg, Good, Nord, Holm, et al. (1994) identified four subscales. Ryan et al. (1996) used the CSES as a unidimensional measure with a single total score for confidence in conducting a variety of career search activities, but no guidelines for scoring or use of the instrument in this way are evident. To determine what items on the scale should be scored together, the administrator must consult Solberg, Good, Nord, Holm, et al. (1994). Since the CSES is a self-report measure, the length of time for each individual completing the scale may vary. The CSES was constructed to be used with a variety of populations, including college students, individuals reentering the work force after being absent for a period of time, or individuals who are changing jobs or careers. General adolescent and adult populations can benefit from this scale (Solberg, Good, & Nord, 1994).

The assessment is useful for career counselors to explore areas of confidence with clients in the job search process with respect to job search efficacy, interviewing efficacy, networking efficacy, and personal exploration efficacy. Higher career search self-efficacy ratings on a particular subscale indicate that clients possess adequate information or skills in that area and will be likely to engage in the behaviors associated with that scale with ease. Lower career search self-efficacy ratings on a particular subscale indicate that a client may have difficulty in the area and could require assistance and encouragement from the career counselor for tasks related to that area (Solberg, Good, & Nord, 1994). For example, individuals who score high on items related to job search efficacy but low on items related to interviewing efficacy may benefit from career counseling that focuses on interviewing skills, mock interview sessions, and observation of effective interviews to enhance confidence in interviewing efficacy. Skills related to job search efficacy should be encouraged by the career counselor, but will not need to be the focus of counseling.

Technical Considerations

The normative sample consisted of 82 male and 110 female college students from two medium-sized university settings. Participants were randomly selected from a larger study of 427 participants and received course credit for their participation. The race/ethnicity of the participants was 168 White/Caucasian, 11 African American, 5 Asian American, 4 Latino/Hispanic (4 did not indicate race/ethnicity). Participants from the university on the West Coast consisted of 48 males and 27 females with the sample consisting of 5 sophomores, 20 juniors, and 51 seniors. Participants from the Midwest university consisted of 62 females and 55 males with 85 freshman, 18 sophomores, 7 juniors, and 6 seniors. The normative sample is small and is not an adequate representation of the diverse population.

Cronbach's alpha for the normative sample is .97 (total scale), meaning high internal reliability evidence is present for the CSES. The individual subscale coefficients for the normative sample are as follows: Job Search Efficacy (.95), Interviewing Efficacy (.91), Networking Efficacy (.92), and Personal Exploration Efficacy (.87; Solberg et al, 1994). This suggests high internal consistency for each of the subscales scores of the CSES.

Evidence of content validity was established by aligning item content with categories identified by Taylor and Betz (1983) and career self-help manuals. However, no formal evaluation of the item content was noted by Solberg, Good, Nord, Holm, et al. (1994). Evidence of internal structure was established through principal component analysis on the initial 72 items using 192 predominately White (87.5%), female (57%) college-aged participants. Four components were retained, accounting for approximately 68% of the variance in the model. Evidence of relationship to other variables was established by investigating the relationship between the subscales of the CSES to subscales of the Career Decision-Making Self-Efficacy Scale (Taylor & Betz, 1983, now referred to as the Career Decision Self-Efficacy Scale), the Personal Attributes Questionnaire (Spence & Helmreich, 1978), the Interpersonal Facility scale (Jones et al., 1986), and the Rathus Assertiveness Schedule (Rathus, 1973). Both convergent and discriminant evidence were noted in correlations of the CSES subscales and the aforementioned scales/subscales.

General Utility and Evaluation

The CSES is not a published instrument, so there are no formal reviews in publications such as *Mental Measurements Yearbook* or a published manual. Despite this limitation, a body of literature related to career search efficacy is evident with utilization of the CSES. Preliminary research on the CSES indicates a promising instrument, but limitations are evident.

A formal scoring protocol was not outlined. Scoring of the instrument as a unidimensional measure and with four subscale scores was evident in past research, but the utility and efficacy of such scores was not established. Evidence of internal structure is preliminary at best, with a limited sample size of 192 participants on an initial pool of 72 items and use of principal component analysis, rather than exploratory factor analysis, as the method for identifying initial evidence of internal structure (see Dimitrov, 2012). Use of a cross-cultural sample was limited, and cross-cultural samples may yield a different factor structure. Nota, Ferrari, Solberg, and Soresi (2007) indicated the CSES had three factors for 764 participants in Italy.

In summary, the CSES may be helpful in evaluating career search efficacy, but counselors should be cautious in using the results due to the preliminary nature of the existing research. Psychometric properties appear to be strong, but further analyses may be beneficial in addressing factor structure across diverse participants and developing scoring protocols based on best practices in career counseling.

References and Additional Resources

Dimitrov, D. M. (2012). *Statistical methods for validation of assessment scale data in counseling and related fields.* Alexandria, VA: American Counseling Association.

Nota, L., Ferrari, L., Solberg, V., & Soresi, S. (2007). Career search self-efficacy, family support, and career indecision with Italian youth. *Journal of Career Assessment, 15,* 181-193. doi:10.1177/1069072706298019

Rathus, S. A. (1973). A 30-item schedule for assessing assertive behavior. *Behavior Therapy 4,* 398-406

Ryan, N., Solberg, V., & Brown, S. (1996). Family dysfunction, parental attachment, and career search self-efficacy among community college students. *Journal of Counseling Psychology, 1,* 84-89. doi:10.1037/0022-0167.43.1.84

Solberg, V., Good, G. E., & Nord, D. (1994). Career search self-efficacy: Ripe for applications and intervention programming. *Journal of Career Development, 21,* 63-72. doi:10.1007/BF02107104

Solberg, V., Good, G., Nord, D., Holm, C., Hohner, R., Zima, N., Heffernan, M., & Malen, A. (1994). Assessing career search expectations: Development and validation of the career search efficacy scale. *Journal of Career Assessment, 2,* 111-123. doi:10.1177/106907279400200202

Spence, J. T., & Helmreich, R. L. (1978). *Masculinity & femininity: Their psychological decision, correlates, and antecedents.* Austin, TX: University of Texas Press.

Taylor, K. M., & Betz, N. E. (1983). Application of self-efficacy theory to the understanding and treatment of career indecision. *Journal of Vocational Behavior, 22,* 63-81, doi:10.1016/0001-8791 (83) 90006-4

CAREER THOUGHTS INVENTORY
James P. Sampson, Jr., Gary W. Peterson, Janet G. Lenz, Robert C. Reardon, and Denise E. Saunders

Psychological Assessments Resources, Inc.

16204 North Florida Avenue
Lutz, FL 33549
http://www4.parinc.com

Target Population: Adolescents (high school students), young adults, and adults.

Statement of the Purpose of the Instrument: The Career Thoughts Inventory (CTI) is a self-administered and objectively scored measure of negative career thinking designed to improve the quality of career decisions and the quality of career service delivery.

Titles of Subtests, Scales, Scores Provided: (1) Decision-making Confusion, (2) Commitment Anxiety, (3) External Conflict; and CTI Total Score as well as scores on the three construct scales.

Forms and Levels Available, with Dates of Publication/Revision of Each: Professional Manual; Workbook; Test Booklet. All qualification Level B. Publication date for all: 1996.

Date of Most Recent Edition of Test Manual, User's Guide, Etc.: 1996.

Language in Which Available: English only.

Time:

    Actual Test Time: Varies.

    Total Administration Time: 7 to 15 minutes.

Norm Group(s) on Which Scores Are Based: National sample of more than 1,650 adults, college students, and high school students.

Manner in Which Results Are Reported for Individuals: The CTI yields a CTI Total Score as well as scores on three construct scales. Exercises in the CTI Workbook help individual improve career thinking and develop an Individual Action Plan.

Report Format/Content for Group Summaries: Not available.

Machine Scoring: Not available.

Hand Scoring: Scored by counselor in approximately 5 minutes.

Computer Software Options Available: Not available.

Cost of Materials: Due to possible price changes since publication date, be sure to check the publisher's website.

    Specimen Set: CTI Introductory Kit (includes Manual, Five Workbooks, and 25 Test Booklets): $232.00.

    Counselee Materials: CTI Professional Manual: $52.00; CTI Workbook: $14.00; CTI Workbooks package of 10: $134.00; CTI Test Booklets package of 25: $65.00; and CTI E-Manual: $45.00.

Published Reviews of the Instrument in the Last 15 Years:

Hilbert, H. B. (1997, January). *Career Thoughts Inventory: A review and critique.* Paper presented at the annual meeting of the Southwest Educational Research Association, Austin, TX. (ERIC Document Reproduction Service No. ED 408 526).

Feller, R. W., & Daly, J. (2009). [Career Thoughts Inventory.] In E. A. Whitfield, R. W. Feller, & C. Wood (Eds.), *A counselor's guide to career assessment instruments.* Broken Arrow, OK: National Career Development Association.

CAREER THOUGHTS INVENTORY

Reviewed by:

Jacqueline J. Peila-Shuster
Rich Feller

School of Education
Colorado State University

Description

The Career Thoughts Inventory (CTI) assesses dysfunctional thinking in terms of career problem solving and career decision making for high school students, college students, and adults. Designed to integrate assessment with intervention in the delivery of career services, it is also useful in determining the level of career services needed. It may be used with its 36-page companion workbook *Career Thoughts Inventory: Improving Your Career Thoughts* (Sampson, Peterson, Lenz, Reardon, & Saunders, 1996a).

The CTI and its accompanying workbook are based on the Cognitive Information Processing (CIP) theoretical approach to career development and a cognitive therapy approach to mental health (Sampson, Peterson, Lenz, Reardon, & Saunders, 1996b). Sampson et al. (1996b) indicated that CIP was selected as a basis for developing the CTI and CTI Workbook because it addressed problem-solving and decision-making aspects of career development, explained the impact of metacognitions (both positive and negative) on career issues, and served as a conceptual basis to develop career problem solving and decision making skills. The assessment developers also used cognitive therapy approaches as the basis to explain relationships between cognitions, behaviors, and emotions, and to provide therapeutic approaches for addressing dysfunctional career thoughts. The professional manual that accompanies the assessment goes into greater depth regarding theory and provides information regarding key aspects of the CIP approach.

The CTI contains 48 statements describing individual thoughts while contemplating career decisions. All items are written as negative statements to reflect dysfunctional thinking (e.g., "no field of study or occupation interests me" and "I know so little about the world of work") (Sampson et al., 1996b). Individuals rate their level of agreement with these statements on a four-point scale from (0) *strongly disagree* to (3) *strongly agree*. The CTI total score includes all items and serves as an overall indicator of dysfunctional thoughts in career decision making and career problem-solving. Higher scores indicate greater dysfunctional career thinking. Additionally, the CTI provides three construct scale scores: (a) Decision Making Confusion (DMC; 14 items), which refers to dysfunctional career thoughts and consequent emotions that interfere with the career decision making process and/or lack of knowledge about the career decision making process; (b) Commitment Anxiety (CA; 10 items), which suggests a lack of ability to commit to a career choice and anxiety about career decision-making process outcomes; and (c) External Conflict (EC; 5 items), which refers to problems in balancing one's perceptions about their career with the involvement of significant others in career decision making (Sampson, et al., 1996b).

The CTI is easily administered, typically taking fewer than 15 minutes to complete. The four-page test booklet begins with a short introduction and instructions. The following two pages contain 48 statements in which clients circle answers automatically transposed to a carbonless bottom sheet that can be hand scored in 5 to 8 minutes. The final test booklet page consists of conversion scales from raw scores to *T*-scores and percentiles for various populations (adults, college students, and high school students).

In direct client service delivery, the CTI can be used as (a) a screening measure to identify individuals more likely to experience problems with career decision making and problem solving due to dysfunctional thinking, (b) a needs assessment to help specify the nature of dysfunctional thinking and determine appropriate career interventions, and (c) a learning resource to be integrated with counseling interventions to address specific dysfunctional thoughts (Sampson et al., 1996b). For example, as a screening measure, the CTI helps determine the level of career services needed. Those experiencing a higher score, and thus greater dysfunctional thinking, likely need more services. As a needs assessment, scores in specific subscales, or even individual questions, can assist in directing counseling intervention towards addressing those specific dysfunctional thoughts. Exercises

A Counselor's Guide To Career Assessments Instruments

in the CTI workbook can then be used within career counseling sessions, or to augment them, to facilitate cognitive restructuring and action planning.

The CTI has been used in research, evaluation, and theory development (Feller & Daly, 2009). It has been used to measure dysfunctional career thoughts as a dependent variable across a broad spectrum of research focusing on a variety of populations from individuals with differing abilities and disabilities (Lustig & Strauser, 2008; Painter, Prevatt, & Welles, 2008), to immigrants (van Ecke, 2007), to students at community colleges (Starling & Miller, 2011). It has also been used to better understand a broad range of concepts in relation to dysfunctional career thoughts including, but not limited to, career indecision (Kleiman et al., 2004), job satisfaction (Painter, Prevatt, & Welles, 2008), and factors such as rumination and maximizing as contributors to dysfunctional career thoughts (Paivandy, Bullock, Reardon, & Kelly, 2008).

Technical Considerations

Demographic data for the adult (n = 571), college student (n = 595), and high school student (n = 396) normative groups are provided in the *Professional Manual*. Geographic distribution included southern, midwestern, western, and northeastern areas for the adult sample, and southern, midwestern, and western regions for the college and high school age samples. Development of local client norms is recommended by the authors, especially to assist with the screening function of the CTI (Sampson et al., 1996b).

Although the adult group had a much greater representation of females (66%) compared to males (34%), the authors indicated that this was not inappropriate since females are more likely to seek counseling assistance (Sampson et al., 1996b). Ethnicity was generally representative of the national adult population. Most of the adults in the sample (80%) were not receiving career assistance and were employed full- or part-time (75%) or were not seeking employment (12%).

Representation of females to males in the college sample was 57.8% to 42.2%, and most students were undergraduates (88.4%). According to Sampson et al. (1996b), ethnicity was generally representative of U.S. college students. A little over half of the students were receiving career assistance, which included a broad spectrum of services from academic advising to cooperative education to career-related workshops.

Students in the high school sample were either in 11th or 12th grade and approximately 54% of the sample was female. Representation of ethnic groups was generally representative of U.S. high school students (Sampson et al., 1996b). It should be noted that in the high school sample, 18.7% did not supply ethnicity information.

In reliability studies reported in the *Professional Manual*, sound evidence for internal consistency and test-retest was provided. There were high internal consistency coefficients (Cronbach's alpha) of .93-.97 for the CTI Total score and .90-.94 for DMC across all groups. Internal consistency coefficients for adult and college student groups for CA (.91 and .88, respectively) were also high, and while lower for the high school student group (.79), they were adequate. The EC construct scales scores were lower for all three groups, but still adequate (.74-.81). The low EC scores could also be reflective of the small number of items in that scale (n = 5) (Sampson et al., 1996b). Studies mentioned previously (Kleiman et al., 2004; Lustig & Strauser, 2008; Paivandy et al., 2008) that involved college student groups found similar internal consistency results for the CTI Total and DMC scores, but slightly lower internal consistency coefficients for CA (.80-.82) and EC (.68-.75).

Test-retest correlations over a four-week period were reported for college and high school students, but not for an adult sample. College student test-retest correlations were .86 for CTI Total score and .82, .79, and .74, respectively, for the DMC, CA, and EC scales. For the high school sample, correlations were .69 for the CTI Total score; the DMC, CA, and EC scales were .72, .70, and .52, respectively. While one would not expect test-retest correlations to be as high as internal consistency measures given the nature of the constructs being measured, the high school sample's correlations were low, especially for the EC scale (Feller & Daly, 2009).

In terms of validity, sound evidence was found for content and construct (both convergent and criterion-related) validity. Evidence for content validity was based upon the use of the Cognitive Information Processing (CIP) theory of career development (Sampson et al., 1996b) as the theoretical basis for item and construct scale development. The eight content dimensions of CIP ensured "that a broad range of relevant aspects of career problem solving and decision making would be included in the instrument" (Sampson et al., 1996b, p. 52).

Analyses regarding construct validity suggested that a "single powerful confusion entity" was a pervasive factor in dysfunctional career thinking (Sampson et al., 1996b, p. 58). As evidence of convergent validity, the CTI Total and construct scale scores were negatively correlated with several instruments: My Vocational Situation (Holland, Daiger, & Power, 1980), Career Decision Scale (Osipow, Carney, Winer, Yanico, & Koschier, 1987), Career Decision Profile (Jones & Lohmann, 1998), and the Revised NEO Personality Inventory (Costa & McCrae, 1992). Furthermore, evidence for criterion-related validity indicated significant differences between individuals seeking career services and those not seeking career services in samples taken from two large universities with students seeking services receiving statistically significant higher scores on the CTI and its subscales.

Overall, the CTI is a technically sound instrument with good evidence for its reliability and validity. The exception to this is the EC scale which has low test-retest reliability, especially for high school students, as well as lower internal consistency coefficients, especially as compared to the other subscales.

General Utility and Evaluation

The CTI manual is very thorough and understandable. It provides information on the use of the CTI, and its development, standardization, and validation. In providing the theoretical basis for the CTI, the manual delivers succinct and helpful information on CIP theory and its application. Administration, scoring, interpretation, and use of the CTI are covered. In addressing diversity issues, Sampson et al. (1996b) acknowledged that individuals' career thoughts are products of their experiences and mediated by personal and cultural contexts. They go on to suggest that the CTI be used collaboratively with clients to help examine environmental factors influencing dysfunctional career thoughts, and that counselors use their multicultural knowledge to alter cognitive reframing statements in the workbook to better address diversity issues.

Assessments quickly gather useful information to help with client conceptualization, to deliver new insights and knowledge, and to provide helpful language to describe clients and organize thoughts. In addition to these functions, the CTI helps clients take action. "Tools that help clients learn what to do next offer positive advantages to the counseling process" (Feller & Daly, 2009, p. 352). By pinpointing areas of dysfunctional thoughts, action can be taken immediately to start addressing them. This can be done on an item-specific (question-by-question) level, as well as construct levels (DMC, CA, EC). Furthermore, the CTI workbook helps individuals interpret their scores and assists with "the cognitive restructuring, action planning, and learning necessary to effectively engage in exploratory, problem solving, and decision making behaviors" (Sampson, et al., 1996b, p. 15). The CTI can also be used as a tool for career counseling service delivery by helping establish levels of intervention needed, leading to more effective and efficient resource allocation and utilization.

Although the CTI reportedly can be self-administered and scored, Feller and Daly's (2009) review indicated that students had difficulties in scoring due to "limited test-taking support information on the test booklet" (p. 352). It is therefore recommend that a practitioner be present to administer and help score the assessment, either one-on-one with an individual or within a group session. Furthermore, individuals may also react to the negative phrasing of the questions (see Feller & Daly, 2009). Thus, it may be helpful to prepare the assessment taker as to what to expect.

Interpretation by a competent career practitioner is critical in helping a client receive the greatest benefit from the CTI. Sampson et al. (1996b) recommend that practitioners using the CTI have training in human behavior, helping skills, assessment, career development, career service delivery, and cognitive-behavior therapy, as well as be familiar with the CTI professional manual, have completed all parts of the assessment, and use supervision as appropriate. Furthermore, the counselor needs to understand the workbook as well as how to facilitate the client's use of the inventory and the workbook. The CTI is a well-constructed assessment and is soundly based on, and integrated with, CIP theory. While this cognitive approach may be resisted by some, the clarity of this assessment is manifest and valuable.

A Counselor's Guide To Career Assessments Instruments

References and Additional Resources

Costa, P. T., Jr., & McCrae, R. R. (1992). *Revised NEO Personality Inventory.* Lutz, FL: Psychological Assessment Resources.

Feller, R. W., & Daly, J. (2009). [Career Thoughts Inventory (CTI).] In E. A. Whitfield, R. W. Feller & C. Wood (Eds.), *A counselor's guide to career assessment instruments* (5th ed., pp. 350-355). Broken Arrow, OK: National Career Development Association.

Feller, R. W., & Daly, J. (2009). [Career Thoughts Inventory.] In E. A. Whitfield, R. W. Feller, & C. Wood (Eds.), *A counselor's guide to career assessment instruments.* Broken Arrow, OK: National Career Development Association.

Hilbert, H. B. (1997, January). *Career Thoughts Inventory: A review and critique.* Paper presented at the annual meeting of the Southwest Educational Research Association, Austin, TX. (ERIC Document Reproduction Service No. ED 408 526).

Holland, J. L., Daiger, D. C., & Power, G. (1980). *My Vocational Situation.* Palo Alto, CA: Consulting Psychologists Press.

Jones, L. K. (1989). Measuring a three-dimensional construct of career indecision among college students: A revision of the Vocational Decision Scale: The Career Decision Profile. *Journal of Counseling Psychology, 36*(4), 477-486. doi: 10.1037/0022-0167.36.4.477

Jones, L. K., & Lohmann, R. C. (1998). The career decision profile: Using a measure of career decision status in counseling. *Journal of Career Assessment, 6,* 209-230. doi: 10.1177/106907279800600207

Kleiman, T., Gati, I., Peterson, G., Sampson, J., Reardon, R., & Lenz, J. (2004). Dysfunctional thinking and difficulties in career decision-making. *Journal of Career Assessment, 12,* 312-331. doi: 10.1177/1069072704266673

Lustig, D. C., & Strauser, D. R. (2008). The impact of sense of coherence on career thoughts for individuals with disabilities. *Rehabilitation Counseling Bulletin, 51*(3), 139-147. doi: 10.1177/0034355207311313

Osipow, S. H., Carney, C. G., Winer, J., Yanico, B., & Koschier, M. (1987). *Career Decision Scale.* Lutz, FL: Psychological Assessment Resources.

Painter, C. A., Prevatt, F., & Welles, T. (2008). Career beliefs and job satisfaction in adults with symptoms of attention-deficit/hyperactivity disorder. *Journal of Employment Counseling, 45*(4), 178-188.

Paivandy, S., Bullock, E. E., Reardon, R. C., & Kelly, F. D. (2008). The effects of decision-making style and cognitive thought patterns on negative career thoughts. *Journal of Career Assessment, 16*(4), 474-488. doi: 10.1177/1069072708318904

Sampson, J. P., Peterson, G. W., Lenz, J. G., Reardon, R. C., & Saunders, D. E. (1996a). *Career Thoughts Inventory: Improving your career thoughts.* Lutz, FL: Psychological Assessment Resources.

Sampson, J. P., Peterson, G. W., Lenz, J. G., Reardon, R. C., & Saunders, D. E. (1996b). *Career Thoughts Inventory: Professional manual.* Lutz, FL: Psychological Assessment Resources.

Starling, P. V., & Miller, G. (2011). Negative thought patterns of undecided community college students: Implications for counselors and advisors. *Community College Journal of Research & Practice, 35*(10), 756-772. doi: 10.1080/10668920903381839

van Ecke, Y. (2007). Attachment style and dysfunctional career thoughts: How attachment style can affect the career counseling process. *Career Development Quarterly, 55*(4), 339-350.

CAREER TRANSITIONS INVENTORY
Mary J. Heppner

Mary J. Heppner

201 D Student Success Center
University of Missouri-Columbia
Columbia, MO 65211
heppnerm@missouri.edu
career@missouri.edu

Target Population: Adults in career transition.

Statement of the Purpose of the Instrument: The purpose of the Career Transitions Inventory (CTI) is to assess psychological strengths and barriers for adults in career transition.

Titles of Subtests, Scales, Scores Provided: Five factors: readiness, confidence, perceived support, control, and decision-making independence.

Forms and Levels Available, with Dates of Publication/Revision of Each: 1994.

Date of Most Recent Edition of Test Manual, User's Guide, Etc.: 1994.

Language in Which Available: English, Chinese, Japanese, and French.

Time:

    Actual Test Time: Varies.

    Total Administration Time: 15 minutes.

Norm Group(s) on Which Scores Are Based: Adults in career transition, potentially 350 adults who identified primarily as White and living in the Midwestern United States.

Manner in Which Results Are Reported for Individuals: High, medium, and low scores are based on adults in career transition norm group, with the highest and lowest 20% indicating the highs and lows and 60% in the middle. Self-scoring and interpretive materials about what a high, medium, and low score means are included.

Report Format/Content For Group Summaries: Not available.

Machine Scoring Services: Not available.

Hand Scoring: Hand scored by counselee, clerk, or counselor in approximately five minutes.

Computer Software Options Available: Not available.

Cost of Materials: Due to potential price changes since publication date, be sure to check with the instrument's author.

    Specimen Set: One examination copy with interpretative guide, $10.00 (includes shipping and handling).

    Counselee Materials: One packet of 25 instruments with interpretive booklet and Journal of Vocational Behavior article describing the CTI's development, $150.00 plus shipping fee of $5.00 for 1-2 packets and $6.00 for 3 or more packets; one packet of 10 instruments with interpretive booklet and article, $75.00 plus $5.00 shipping fee.

Published Reviews of the Instrument in the Last 15 Years:

Drummond, R. J. (2003). [Career Transitions Inventory.] In B. S. Plake, J. C. Impara, & R. A. Spies (Eds.), *The fifteenth mental measurements yearbook.* Lincoln, NE: Buros Center for Testing.

Kirnan, J. P. (2009). [Career Transitions Inventory.] In E. Whitfield, R. Feller, & C. Wood (Ed.), *A counselor's guide to career assessment instruments* (5th ed., pp. 356-360). Broken Arrow, OK: National Career Development Association.

CAREER TRANSITIONS INVENTORY

Reviewed by:

Jean Powell Kirnan
David J. Rothman

Psychology Department
The College of New Jersey

Description

The purpose of the Career Transitions Inventory (CTI) is to assess an adult's resources and barriers during career transition. A career transition is defined as a task change within the same job, a position change, or an occupation change. Unlike traditional career counseling tools, the CTI goes beyond a measure of interests and abilities and instead considers the psychological factors that impact the process of career change. In many cases, the identification of interests and abilities is insufficient if a client faces psychological barriers or lacks the resources for change. Items on the CTI address psychological processes such as locus of control, self-efficacy, and social support (Heppner, Multon, & Johnston, 1994) within the context of career transition, thus providing the counselor with a single tool with a common language and specific suggestions for intervention (Heppner, 1998).

The CTI has a single form consisting of 40 statements (half of which are reverse scored) to which the respondent indicates their level of agreement on a six-point Likert scale ranging from 1 *(strongly agree)* to 6 *(strongly disagree)*. Responses are compiled into raw scores to create five scales: Readiness (13 items), Confidence (11), Personal Control (6), Support (5), and Independence (5). Readiness is based largely on motivation and identifies the degree to which the respondent is willing to engage in the activities necessary for career change. Confidence reflects self-efficacy in that it measures belief in one's own ability to be successful in career planning activities. Personal Control determines the extent to which one feels in control as opposed to being controlled by external forces during career transition. Support reflects the aid the respondent has from others for this transition. Finally, Independence indicates the degree to which the career change decision is the respondent's own to make or if other people in their life exert influence.

Self-administration and self-scoring of the CTI take about 15 minutes and can be achieved individually or in a group. The CTI consists of three separate components: (1) the questionnaire, (2) a three-page carbon copy answer form composed of white, yellow, and pink sheets, and (3) a results page which provides interpretation of scores for each of the five scales

The CTI questionnaire presents the 40 statements in a single-spaced format, making it difficult to "keep one's place" as the respondent moves back and forth from the questionnaire to the separate answer sheet. Of greater concern, however, are the response options and general formatting of the answer sheet. A key appears at the top of the sheet listing the six possible response options of: 1 = strongly agree (SA), 2 = moderately agree (MA), 3 = slightly agree (SA), 4 = slightly disagree (SD), 5 = moderately disagree (MD), and 6 = strongly disagree (SD). Below this box, the abbreviations are listed across each of three columns as SA, MA, SA, SD, MD, and SD. This style is confusing as "S" represents both "strongly" and "slightly". However, in the section where respondents circle their answers, the response options are presented numerically, as 1 through 6, resulting in the need to refer back to the key at the top of the page. A simple solution is to differentiate "strongly" from "slightly" and provide the abbreviations, not numerals, for the respondent to circle. Also of concern is the placement of the questions on the answer sheet. Each row contains one question but that question may exist in any one of three columns. Thus, items often skip columns, making it easy for the respondent to lose their place, especially as they are attempting to simultaneously follow the separate, single-spaced questionnaire. Reformatting the questionnaire and answer sheet or converting to a computerized version should be considered.

Despite these concerns, the scoring process is straightforward and easy. Answers line up in columns on the carbon undersheets making it easy to derive scale scores by adding the corresponding numbers in each column. Scale scores are then transferred onto the results page. This score sheet provides an interpretation based on ranges of low, medium, and high scores along with a description of what each score typically means. For four of the scales (i.e., Readiness, Confidence, Personal Control, and Support), high scores are a positive indication for career change. The scale of Independence requires more careful interpretation as the author indicates that scoring high on this scale may be positive in some situations and negative in others.

It is recommended that the CTI be used in conjunction with traditional measures of interests, skills, and work values. A counselor can use the CTI scores to begin a dialog on common barriers to transition, ultimately focusing on the client's specific strengths and needs. This more holistic approach allows for a conversation that considers both the career and personal domains of the client (Gysbers, Heppner, & Johnston, 1998).

Technical Considerations

The materials provided for this review fail to offer information on the meaning of a score or the normative sample. However, a book chapter (Gysbers et al., 1998) reveals that the low, medium, and high score designations are based on the bottom 20%, middle 60%, and top 20% of the normative sample. While unclear who constituted this sample, it is reasonable to assume this to be one of the samples reported as a part of the validity studies. Heppner et al. (1994) noted that these samples are predominantly White and largely from the Midwestern United States.

Internal reliability estimates were obtained by calculating Cronbach's alphas on a sample of 300 individuals yielding coefficients for the five scales as follows: Readiness (.87), Confidence (.83), Personal Control (.69), Support (.66), and Independence (.67). Test-retest reliability was demonstrated with a sample of 43 graduate students over a three-week interval, producing the following estimates per scale: Readiness (.74), Confidence (.79), Personal Control (.55), Support (.77), and Independence (.83). These results suggest acceptable reliability in the longer scales of Readiness and Confidence, with mixed findings for Support and Independence. The consistently low reliability coefficients for Personal Control is troublesome. The authors note that "further examination of this factor is needed to determine the reasons for this lower stability" (Heppner et al., 1994, p. 65). However, there is no evidence that this has been addressed.

The validity of the CTI is established by a series of studies providing evidence of construct validity including factor analysis, divergent and convergent validity, and the relationship of CTI scores with relevant demographic variables. The original CTI consisted of 72 items, 12 for each of the proposed six factors derived from the counseling literature. A factor analysis on a sample of 300 adults in career transition identified the five factors used today and resulted in the elimination of many items due to either low factor loadings or loading on more than one factor. The same sample was further analyzed for a variety of relevant demographic factors with results largely supporting expectations. Married respondents had higher scores on support; younger respondents had higher scores on readiness, confidence, and support; and length of time in transition positively correlated with all CTI subscales except control (Heppner et al, 1994).

A sample of 104 adults who experienced involuntary layoffs completed the CTI, Holland's My Vocational Situation (MVS), and the Hope Scale as part of a career-planning workshop, providing divergent and convergent evidence for construct validity. The CTI correlated positively with Vocational Identity and Barriers subscales of the MVS and also performed as predicted with the Hope Scale, correlating positively with the Agency measure but not with the Pathways measure. The authors summarized these findings stating that individuals with more resources had clearer vocational identities and confidence in their ability to transition (Heppner, 1998).

General Utility and Evaluation

The major strength of the CTI continues to be its unique position as the only counseling tool that focuses on the barriers and resources involved in the process of adult career transition. The instrument has a strong development based on theory and counseling literature and supported by initial statistical analyses of reliability and validity. However, no additional research or support materials have been produced since the introduction of the CTI in 1994.

The most glaring deficiency of the CTI continues to be the lack of a comprehensive manual and the small normative sample. While individuals ordering the CTI are sent articles on the instrument's development, this is not adequate; a formal manual detailing test development, normative sample, score derivation, reliability, and

Career Transitions Inventory

validity is needed. One of the articles (Heppner, 1998) and a separate book chapter (Gysbers et al., 1998) present case studies as well as 10 procedures to guide counselors in discussing CTI results with clients, information that would be beneficial to a counselor and should also be included in a manual.

While socioeconomically diverse, the small normative sample is restricted ethnically and geographically. The authors themselves (Heppner et al., 1994) called for a broadening of normative data since the "role of ethnicity has not been studied in the career transition process" (p. 71). Critical questions remain as to whether the career transition process works similarly for select groups such as those who are economically/educationally disenfranchised or those with differing cultural norms.

Little has changed with the CTI, although much has changed with career transition. The high unemployment rate brought on by the recession of 2008 has resulted in many unplanned career changes. In addition to the recession, there is less job stability and more transitions over the course of one's employment. As recently as the 1970s, workers held an average of 3 to 4 jobs during their careers, a figure that is now estimated at 7 to 10 jobs (Cascio & Aguinis, 2011). The need for counseling tools to aid in career transition has never been greater.

It is disappointing that the recommendations made in earlier reviews, and those of the authors themselves, have gone unheeded. The CTI is a psychometrically sound instrument, especially useful as a tool in a broader counseling context. The creation of a comprehensive manual, expansion of norms, and research on subgroups could result in a great instrument.

References and Additional Resources

Cascio, W. F., & Aguinis, H. (2011). *Applied psychology in human resource management.* New York, NY: Prentice Hall.

Drummond, R. J. (2003). [Career Transitions Inventory.] In B. S. Plake, J. C. Impara, & R. A. Spies (Eds.), *The fifteenth mental measurements yearbook.* Lincoln, NE: Buros Center for Testing.

Gysbers, N. C., Heppner, M. J., & Johnston, J. A. (1998). *Career counseling: Process, issues, and techniques.* Boston, MA: Allyn & Bacon.

Heppner, M. J. (1998). The Career Transitions Inventory: Measuring internal resources in adulthood. *Journal of Career Assessment, 6*(2), 135-145.

Heppner, M. J., Multon, K. D., & Johnston, J. A. (1994). Assessing psychological resources during career change: Development of the Career Transitions Inventory. *Journal of Vocational Behavior, 44,* 55-74.

Kirnan, J. P. (2009). [The Career Transitions Inventory.] In E. Whitfield, R. Feller, & C. Wood (Eds.), *A counselor's guide to career assessment instruments* (5th ed., pp. 356-360). Broken Arrow, OK: National Career Development Association.

Kirnan, J. P. (2009). [Career Transitions Inventory.] In E. Whitfield, R. Feller, & C. Wood (Ed.), *A counselor's guide to career assessment instruments* (5th ed., pp. 356-360). Broken Arrow, OK: National Career Development Association.

CHILDHOOD CAREER DEVELOPMENT SCALE
Donna E. Schultheiss and Graham B. Stead

Donna E. Schultheiss and Graham B. Stead

Cleveland State University
2121 Euclid Avenue
Cleveland, OH 44115
216.687.5063
216.687.5378
d.schutheiss@csuohio.edu

Target Population: Children and adolescents. The U.S. form is designed for children in Grades 4 through 6 and the South African form is designed for children in Grades 4 through 7.

Statement of the Purpose of the Instrument: The purpose of the Childhood Career Development Scale (CCDS) is to measure childhood career progress. The CCDS is based on Super's (1990) theoretical model of childhood career development.

Titles of Subtests, Scales, Scores Provided: Planning, Self-Concept, Information, Interests, Locus of Control, Curiosity/Exploration, Key Figures, Time Perspective. Raw scores per subscale are provided.

Forms and Levels Available, with Dates of Publication/Revision of Each: The South African form was published in 2003 (Stead & Schultheiss, 2003). The U.S. form was published in 2004 (Schultheiss & Stead, 2004).

Date of Most Recent Edition of Test Manual, User's Guide, Etc.: Not applicable.

Languages in Which Available: English only.

Time:

Actual Test Time: 20 minutes.

Total Administration Time: 25 minutes.

Norm Group(s) on Which Scores Are Based: Students in Grades 4 through 6, primarily African American and White.

Manner in Which Results Are Reported for Individuals: Percentiles and T scores are provided.

Report Format/Content for Group Summaries: Not available.

Machine Scoring: Not available.

Hand Scoring: Hand scored by counselor in approximately 10 minutes.

Local Machine Scoring: Not available.

Computer Software Options Available: Not available.

Cost of Materials: Due to possible price changes since publication date, be sure to check with the authors. The instruments are available by contacting the authors.

Specimen Set: Not available.

Counselee Materials: Paper-and-pencil version of the CCDS.

Published Reviews of the Instrument in the Last 15 Years:

Dykeman, C. (2009). [Childhood Career Development Scale.] In E. A. Whitfield, R. W. Feller, & C. Wood (Eds.), *A counselor's guide to career assessment instruments* (5th ed., pp. 361-365). Broken Arrow, OK: National Career Development Association.

Childhood Career Development Scale

Reviewed by:

Cass Dykeman

Department of Educational Studies
Oregon State University

Description

The Childhood Career Development Scale (CCDS; Schultheiss & Stead, 2004) is a measure of Donald Super's (1990) nine theorized components of childhood career development (i.e., Curiosity, Exploration, Information, Interests, Key Figures, Locus Of Control, Planning, Self-Concept and Time Perspective). The purpose of the CCDS is twofold: (1) to provide a measure for assessing career programming effectiveness, and (2) to provide a tool for researching childhood career development. Both CCDS forms contain eight subscales reflecting Super's theorized components. With the U.S. form, *Curiosity* and *Exploration* are combined into one subscale. With the South African (S.A.) form, *Curiosity* and *Exploration* are separate subscales and there is no *Interests* subscale. The U.S. form is 52 items in length and the S.A. form is 48.

Table 1 contains a sample item from each subscale of the U.S. form. For all items children are asked to respond to items using the five-point Likert-type scale: *SA — STRONGLY AGREE (I AGREE A LOT), A — AGREE, U — UNCERTAIN (I AM NOT SURE), D — DISAGREE,* and *SD — STRONGLY DISAGREE (I DO NOT AGREE AT ALL).*

Table 1

CCDS U.S. Form Subscales

Subscale	Number of Items	Example Items
Curiosity/Exploration	7	I wonder about things I learned in school
Information	6	I wonder about different jobs
Interests	6	I know what games I like to play
Key Figures	5	I want to do the same job as someone I look up to
Locus Of Control	7	I have control over the things I do
Planning	11	It is important to plan for the future
Self-Concept	6	I know what kind of friend I am
Time Perspective	4	I think about where I will work when I'm grown up

Scoring both CCDS forms is straightforward. For each subscale, the scores from the items of a subscale (score range: 1-5) are added together for a total subscale raw score. The total subscale raw score ranges differ from subscale to subscale and form to form. The CCDS is a pencil-and-paper test. The scoring key contains the information needed to score the instrument accurately (Schultheiss & Stead, (2005a).

Schultheiss and Stead (2004) ran a gender by grade multivariate analysis of variance for the U.S. form, and 5th and 6th graders scored significantly higher on the *Information* subscale and females scored significantly higher on the *Curiosity/Exploration* subscale. No gender by grade interaction was uncovered. Stead and Schultheiss (2010) used the S.A. form to conduct a gender by grade by language (English, Afrikaans, Xhosa) multivariate analysis of variance study. No main effect for gender, grade, or language was encountered. Also, no interaction of the three was observed.

The CCDS was designed to measure career programming effectiveness, and provide a vehicle to research childhood career development. With respect to measuring career programming effectiveness, K-12 educators

A Counselor's Guide To Career Assessments Instruments

and school counselors are held more accountable for the effectiveness of their professional work today, and the CCDS represents a rigorous instrument that may be useful in assessing career programming effectiveness. However, for psychometric reasons that are addressed in the next section, the CCDS is not recommended as a summative program evaluation tool. High stake decisions (e.g., position funding) are made with summative evaluations, and the present psychometric unknowns outweigh the potential benefits of CCDS use. The CCDS is useful for formative program evaluation. For example, a school counselor could administer the CCDS to his or her 5th graders. If that school counselor found that the mean total subscale score for *Key Figures* was much lower in its range compared to the other subscales, the school counselor could focus career development activities on implementing a mentorship program. Thus, identifying specific career needs of students can enhance a school counselor's efficiency. CCDS results, however, should not be used to make clinical decisions about career interventions for that individual.

For its second purpose of researching childhood career development, the CCDS can be useful for examining the effectiveness of the myriad of career interventions that a school counselor can employ. Also, counselors can analyze what intensity of an intervention is needed to make a positive impact on a child's career development.

Technical Considerations

The U.S. form of the CCDS was normed with 893 urban elementary school students from one Midwestern city. The norming group was roughly even between males and females, and the sample included African Americans (58%), Whites (37%), and those identifying as another race/ethnicity (5%). The norming group contained 4th graders (10%), 5th graders (48%), and 6th graders (42%). The CCDS Norm Table-U.S. Form contains percentile and T scores for the raw scores on each of the eight subscales (Schultheiss & Stead, 2005b). Standard Error of Measurement (SEM) information is not presented in this table.

Subscale internal consistency estimates (i.e., Cronbach's α) for the U.S. form sample ranged from .66 to 84. Table 2 contains the complete information on subscale internal consistency. Test-retest reliability for the CCDS is unknown at present. As noted by Schultheiss and Stead (2004), research on CCDS test-retest reliability is needed.

Table 2

CCDS Subscale Internal Consistency (74-item version)

Subscale	Cronbach's α
Curiosity/Exploration	.66
Information	.72
Interests	.68
Key Figures	.68
Locus Of Control	.79
Planning	.84
Self-Concept	.84
Time Perspective	.69

Schultheiss and Stead (2004) followed the recommended practices in measurement research in establishing the CCDS's content (via expert panel), convergent (via correlational methods), and construct (via factor analysis) validity. Research on the predictive and discriminant validity of the CCDS is needed (Schultheiss & Stead, 2004; Stead & Schultheiss, 2003). Finally, the issue of the different factor structures of the U.S. and S.A. forms needs to be addressed.

General Utility and Evaluation

The CCDS represents an important advancement in the measurement of childhood career development. The few instruments that previously have attempted to measure this aspect of child development lacked theoretical and/or psychometric soundness (Schultheiss, & Stead, 2004). This reviewer recommends the use of the CCDS for formative program evaluation and career development research. In order for the CCDS to reach its full potential as a clinical, evaluation, and research tool, the following must be generated: (1) standardized national norms, (2) test-retest reliability information, (3) discriminate validity information, (4) predictive validity information, (5) explanation for the different factor structure of the two forms, (6) delineation of scores that represent a problematic level of career development, and (7) a test manual.

References and Additional Resources

Dykeman, C. (2009). [Childhood Career Development Scale.] In E. A. Whitfield, R. W. Feller, & C. Wood (Eds.), *A counselor's guide to career assessment instruments* (5th ed., pp. 361-365). Broken Arrow, OK: National Career Development Association.

Schultheiss, D. E. P., & Stead, G. B. (2004). Childhood Career Development Scale: Scale construction and psychometric properties *Journal of Career Assessment, 12,* 113-134.

Schultheiss, D. E. P., & Stead, G. B. (2005a). *Childhood Career Development Scale and Scoring Key* (52-item U.S. Version). Cleveland, OH: Authors.

Schultheiss, D. E. P., & Stead, G. B. (2005b). *Norm table for Childhood Career Development Scale-U.S. Form.* Cleveland, OH: Authors.

Stead, G. B., & Schultheiss, D. E. P. (2003). Construction and psychometric properties of the Childhood Career Development Scale. *South African Journal of Psychology, 33,* 227-235.

Stead, G. B., & Schultheiss, D. E. P. (2010). Validity of Childhood Career Development Scale scores in South Africa. *International Journal for Educational and Vocational Guidance, 10,* 73-88. doi: 10.1007/s10775-010-9175-y

Super, D. E. (1990). A life-span, life-space approach to career development. In D. Brown. & L. Brooks (Eds.), *Career choice and development* (2nd ed., pp. 197-261). San Francisco, CA: Jossey-Bass.

A Counselor's Guide To Career Assessments Instruments

JOB SEARCH ATTITUDE INVENTORY, FOURTH EDITION
John J. Liptak

JIST Publishing, Inc.

8902 Otis Avenue
Indianapolis, IN 46216
http://www.jist.com

Target Population: Adolescents, young adults, and adults.

Statement of the Purpose of the Instrument: The Job Search Attitude Inventory (JSAI) helps individuals identify their key attitudes about looking for a job and consider suggestions for improvement and for becoming more self-directed in the job search.

Titles of Subtests, Scales, Scores Provided: Scores in four categories representing key attitudes, beliefs, and approaches regarding the job search process: Luck vs. Planning, Uninvolved vs. Involved, Help from Others vs. Self-Help, Passive vs. Active, and Pessimistic vs. Optimistic.

Forms and Levels Available, with Dates of Publication/Revision of Each: 2010.

Date of Most Recent Edition of Test Manual, User's Guide, Etc.: 2010.

Languages in Which Available: English only.

Time:

Actual Test Time: 15-25 minutes.

Total Administration Time: 15-25 minutes.

Norm Group(s) on Which Scores Are Based: For the JSAI, four groups were used to develop norms that are included in the administrator's guide: youth between the ages of 12 and 18, college and community college students, welfare-to-work clients, and offenders.

Manner in Which Results Are Reported for Individuals: Raw scale scores are profiled into three score ranges (scores between 8 and 16 indicate that the respondent is other-directed, scores between 17 and 23 are average, and scores between 24 and 32 indicate that the respondent is self-directed in searching for and finding employment). The JSAI includes easy-to-understand interpretations for each scale. Five raw scale scores (Luck vs. Planning, Uninvolved vs. Involved, Help from Others vs. Self-Help, Passive vs. Active, Pessimistic vs. Optimistic) are included on the JSAI.

Assessment is self-scoring and self-interpreting. Interpretation Guide and Improvement Plan are included with each assessment. Respondents follow a series of five steps to complete the JSAI.

Report Format/Content for Group Summaries: Not available.

Machine Scoring: Not available.

Hand Scoring: Hand scored by counselee in fewer than 5 minutes.

Local Machine Scoring: Not available.

Computer Software Options Available: Computerized adaptive administration; standard administration online.

Ways in which computer/on-line version differs: Automated scoring and automated report generation.

Cost of Materials: Due to possible price changes since publication date be sure to check the publisher's website. The administrator's guide can be downloaded for free from the JIST website.

Specimen Set: Free.

Counselee Materials: Test booklets (package of 25): $51.95 with discounts available for large-volume orders. Each package includes a free Administrator's Guide.

---
title: *Job Search Attitude Inventory, Fourth Edition*

> **Published Reviews of the Instrument in the Last 15 Years:**
>
> Fleenor, J. W. (2005). [Job Search Attitude Inventory (second edition).] In R. A. Spies & B. S. Plake (Eds.), *The sixteenth mental measurements yearbook* (pp. 503-505). Lincoln, NE: Buros Center for Testing.
>
> Fleenor, J. W. (2009). [Job Search Attitude Inventory (third edition).] In E. A. Whitfield, R. W. Feller, & C. Wood (Eds.), *A counselor's guide to career assessment instruments* (5th ed., pp. 366-370). Broken Arrow, OK: National Career Development Association.
>
> O'Neill, T. R. (2005). [Job Search Attitude Inventory (second edition).] In R. A. Spies & B. S. Plake (Eds.), *The sixteenth mental measurements yearbook* (pp. 505-506). Lincoln, NE: Buros Center for Testing.

JOB SEARCH ATTITUDE INVENTORY, FOURTH EDITION

Reviewed by:

John W. Fleenor

Center for Creative Leadership
Greensboro, NC

Description

The Job Search Attitude Inventory, Fourth Edition (JSAI), is a self-administered inventory that provides a brief assessment of the motivation level of individuals who are involved in the job search process. The purpose of the JSAI is to provide job seekers with a profile of their attitudes towards the job search process, and to provide feedback on how they can become more motivated to find employment. Published by JIST Works, the JSAI includes a self-scored test booklet and an administrator's guide (Liptak, 2010). The JSAI is also available online at the JIST website.

The JSAI can be administered individually or in groups. There is no time limit for the administration, although the average completion time is 20 minutes, depending on factors such as age and reading ability. During the administration, counselors should inform test takers of the purpose of the assessment. The items are written at or below the eighth-grade reading level. Respondents indicate their level of agreement on 40 items using a four-point Likert scale, ranging from *strongly agree* to *strongly disagree.* Test takers respond to each item directly in the test booklet. Then, they self-score their responses and transfer the scores to a graphic profile, which plots their scores on the five JSAI dimensions: (a) Luck vs. Planning, (b) Uninvolved vs. Involved, (c) Help from Others vs. Self-Help, (d) Passive vs. Active, and (e) Pessimistic vs. Optimistic. Possible scale scores range from 8 to 32. Step-by-step scoring instructions are included in test booklet.

According to Liptak (2010), there are two types of job seekers—those who are self-directed and those who are other-directed. Self-directed job seekers are more aware of their strengths and weaknesses than are those who are other-directed. Self-directed job seekers believe they can find a job largely on their own. Other-directed job seekers believe that they need to rely on others for help in finding a job. On the JSAI scales, scores between 8 and 16 indicate attitudes that are other-directed; scores between 17 and 23 indicate that the respondent is not completely dependent on others, but, he or she could take more control of the job search process; scores between 24 and 32 indicate attitudes that are self-directed.

The current version of the JSAI represents the fourth edition of the instrument. In this revision, the following enhancements were made to the JSAI: (a) a new scale (Pessimistic vs. Optimistic) was added, (b) the wording of some items were changed to make them more relevant to the world of work of today, and, (c) interpretation materials were revised to reflect recent changes in the job search landscape.

The JSAI is designed to make job seekers more aware of their attitudes toward the job search process. The author suggests that the instrument will be useful for (a) predicting who will be more likely to find a job, (b) determining who will better benefit from job search services, and (c) for use as a pre- and post-test to measure

A Counselor's Guide To Career Assessments Instruments

the effectiveness of job-search training programs. Because self-directed individuals can benefit from relatively inexpensive services (e.g., job search assistance), the JSAI is touted as a cost-effective method for determining the services that a job seeker should receive.

The JSAI is based on the premise that increasing individuals' self-esteem can enhance their self-directed motivation to search for a job. Helwig (1987) indicated that the individual's attitudes towards unemployment and the job search process itself is the most important factor in finding a job. According to Helwig, personal motivation to find a job can be more important than job search skills themselves. Individuals who fail to display self-directed motivation in the job search often exhibit tendencies of learned helplessness—the belief that they are not in control of their own fate (Wood, 1989).

Possible uses of the JSAI include outplacement counseling, employment counseling, job search assistance, career counseling, rehabilitation counseling, and correctional counseling. For example, the JSAI can be used as a pre-test to ascertain attitudes that may be a hindrance to the job-search process. By identifying these attitudes in advance, counselors can better direct their energies in the counseling process. The JSAI can be used as the first step in assessing an individual's job search needs. Additionally, it can be used as a motivational tool for encouraging individuals to become more self-directed by providing feedback on how to do so.

Technical Considerations

The manual presents the means and standard deviations for four of the five scales for a sample of 135 adults (70 males and 65 females). No statistics for the new JSAI scale (Pessimistic vs. Optimistic) are presented in the manual. Descriptive statistics for the JSAI scales are presented for 554 convicted offenders, 296 welfare-to-work clients, 535 college students, and 308 youths (ages 12 to 18).

A rational-empirical method (Crites, 1978) was used to develop the instrument. The author conducted a review of the literature, case studies, and interviews with unemployed adults to develop the item content for the scales. The resulting pool of 50 items was reviewed by professional counselors, who assigned the items to one of the five scales. Intercorrelations among the scales were calculated using the sample of 135 adults described above. These intercorrelations were in the acceptable range. The highest correlation among the scales was .58, indicating the independence of the scales.

The author reports the estimates of reliability for the scales, including split-half, coefficient alpha, and test retest reliabilities. These reliabilities were calculated using the scores of the sample of 135 adults described above. The reliabilities were generally in the acceptable range; however, the split-half reliability of the Uninvolved vs. Involved scale was somewhat low (.53). Typically, the minimum acceptable reliability for scales used for decision-making purposes is .70. The instrument was validated using content validation strategy—no evidence of criterion-related validity is presented in the manual.

General Utility and Evaluation

The JSAI appears to have utility as a measure of the attitudes of job seekers. The test is a short, self-scored instrument for which the interpretation is relatively straightforward. A strength of the instrument is that test takers receive immediate feedback that is presented graphically. With the exception of the split-half reliability of the Uninvolved vs. Involved scale, the reported reliabilities of the JSAI are acceptable. No reliability information, however, is presented for the Pessimistic vs. Optimistic scale, which was added in the fourth edition of the JSAI.

The instrument was validated using a content validation procedure; no evidence of criterion-related validity is provided in the manual. A criterion-related validity study would require a study of the relationship between the test scores and success in finding a job. Without evidence of validity, it is not known if the instrument accurately predicts how well an individual will actually do in the job search process. The test results, therefore, should be interpreted with caution.

Norms for comparison purposes are available for convicted offenders, welfare-to-work clients, college students, and youths (ages 12-18). Before the instrument can be recommended to counselors without reservation (a) some evidence of criterion-related validity is necessary, (b) estimates of reliability should be based on larger

Job Search Attitude Inventory, Fourth Edition

sample sizes, (c) the psychometric properties of the Pessimistic vs. Optimistic scale should be reported in the manual, and (d) norms are needed for additional groups that may be taking the instrument (e.g., unemployed adults).

References and Additional Resources

Crites, J. (1978). _Theory and research handbook for the Career Maturity Inventory,_ 2nd edition. Monterey, CA: CB/McGraw-Hill.

Fleenor, J. W. (2005). [Job Search Attitude Inventory (second edition).] In R. A. Spies & B. S. Plake (Eds.), _The sixteenth mental measurements yearbook_ (pp. 503-505). Lincoln, NE: Buros Center for Testing.

Fleenor, J. W. (2009). [Job Search Attitude Inventory (third edition).] In E. A. Whitfield, R. W. Feller, & C. Wood (Eds.), _A counselor's guide to career assessment instruments_ (5th ed., pp. 366-370). Broken Arrow, OK: National Career Development Association.

Helwig, A. (1987). Information required for job hunting: 1,121 counselors respond. _Journal of Employment Counseling, 24,_ 184-190.

Liptak, J. J. (2010). _Job Search Attitude Inventory (fourth edition): Administrator's guide._ Indianapolis, IN: JIST Works.

O'Neill, T. R. (2005). [Job Search Attitude Inventory (second edition).] In R. A. Spies & B. S. Plake (Eds.), _The sixteenth mental measurements yearbook_ (pp. 505-506). Lincoln, NE: Buros Center for Testing.

Wood, C. J. (1989). Learned helplessness: A factor in counseling displaced homemakers. _Journal of Employment Counseling, 26,_ 4-10.

Author Note: Portions of this review are based on reviews of the second edition of the JSAI that were previously published in the _Sixteenth Mental Measurements Yearbook_ (Fleenor, 2005; O'Neil, 2005).

A Counselor's Guide To Career Assessments Instruments

Job Search Knowledge Scale
John Liptak

JIST Publishing, Inc.
875 Montreal Way
St. Paul, MN 55102
http://www.jist.com
educate@emcp.com

Target Population: Adolescents (high school students), young adults, and adults.

Statement of the Purpose of the Instrument: The Job Search Knowledge Scale (JSKS) is designed to assess how much an individual knows about looking for work or the job search process.

Titles of Subtests, Scales, Scores Provided: Identifying Job Leads, Direct Application to Employers, Resumes/ Cover Letters, Employment Interviews, Following Up. There are 12 items per scale, with higher scores indicating greater knowledge of the respective aspect of the job search process.

Forms and Levels Available, with Dates of Publication/Revision of Each: Paper-and-pencil form and online form available, 2009.

Date of Most Recent Edition of Test Manual, User's Guide, Etc.: 2009.

Languages in Which Available: English only.

Time:

Actual Test Time: Varies.

Total Administration Time: 20-30 minutes.

Manner in Which Results Are Reported for Individuals: Standard scores.

Report Format/Content for Group Summaries: Not available.

Machine Scoring: Available for online form.

Hand Scoring: Hand scored by counselee.

Computer Software Options Available: Not available.

Cost of Materials: Due to possible price changes since publication date, be sure to check the publisher's website.

Specimen Set: $46.95 (package of 25), and administrator's guide.

Counselee Materials: 25 hand-scorable (not reusable) combined test and answer sheets. Online forms available for $12.50 each for 1-5000 tests and $10.00 each for 5001+ tests.

Published Reviews of the Instrument in the Last 15 Years:

Dean, G. J. (2007). [Job Search Knowledge Scale.] In R. A. Spies, B. S. Plake, K. Geisinger, & J. Carlson (Eds.), *The seventeenth mental measurements yearbook.* Lincoln, NE: Buros Center for Testing.

Hattrup, K. (2007). [Job Search Knowledge Scale.] In R. A. Spies, B. S. Plake, K. Geisinger, & J. Carlson (Eds.), *The seventeenth mental measurements yearbook.* Lincoln, NE: Buros Center for Testing.

JOB SEARCH KNOWLEDGE SCALE

Reviewed by:

Dixie Meyer

Department of Counseling and Family Therapy
Saint Louis University

Description

The Job Search Knowledge Scale (JSKS) is "designed to meet the need for a brief assessment instrument to measure a person's knowledge about finding a job" (Liptak, 2009a, p. 4). The JSKS is designed to assess career obtainment knowledge. It may also be known as an abilities test with a specific focus on job search comprehension. The JSKS (2009) is currently in its second edition (2009). The original scale was published in 2005.

The JSKS is a self-administered 60-item test that includes five subscales representing aspects of the job search process (12 items per subscale): Identifying Job Leads, Direct Application to Employers, Resumes and Cover Letters, Employment Interviews, and Following Up. The JSKS has a dichotomous answer response format requiring the test taker to answer true or false to each statement. Correct answers are assigned one point. Score ranges for each of the five subscales are 0-12. Scores from 0-3 represent little knowledge on that subscale, scores from 4-8 represent some knowledge, but an area of growth; and scores from 9-12 indicate the test taker has a "great deal of knowledge" of that particular subscale (Liptak, 2009b).

Self-administration and scoring of the JSKS involves five steps: (1) completing the 60 items, (2) scoring the items by counting the number of correct responses per subscale, (3) interpreting subscale scores, (4) reviewing information for improving knowledge about the job search process, and (5) providing the test taker space to create long-term and short-term goals based on the five assessed areas. There is an allotted 20 to 30 minutes to complete each of these steps. For the average test taker, this should be enough time to complete. Although 20-30 minutes seems an appropriate amount of time allotted, this test has the potential for a great amount of variability to complete this test. For example, if the test taker scored in the 0-3 range on each subscale, he or she may need to read the information provided for each subscale at Step 4. Each of the sections (subscales) in Step 4 has quite a bit of information and provides additional resources to increase learning. For a test taker to fully comprehend this section alone may take 20 minutes. Furthermore, Step 5 requires the test taker to generate both long- and short-term goals for each section. This step may be time consuming for individuals carefully integrating all that they have learned from Steps 1-4.

The test format is user-friendly and is available in paper-and-pencil and online versions. The five steps for the paper-and-pencil version are found on one large sheet of paper that is folded down to an 8.5" × 11" sheet of paper. The test taker follows the arrows to unfold the test to the step he or she is currently completing. The arrows as well as the colors printed on the test, the font size, and the layout make the unfolding and steps easy to follow. The instrument is written at an eighth-grade reading comprehension level and is intended for individuals at the middle school level and beyond (Liptak, 2009a). The online version may be retrieved at the publisher website (http://jist.emcpublishingllc.com/page-jist/resources/online-assessments/).

The quality of the JSKS makes it applicable in multiple manners in a counseling setting. It could be used with school-aged individuals and those in higher education in courses or in career centers to address knowledge of the job search and obtainment process. It could be used as a class exercise. For example, educators could assess how students scored and attend to subscales with lower scores to provide additional knowledge about the job search process. This test could also be used in career counseling or at any career centers. The focus on learning and creating goals may help individuals develop a tangible plan for job obtainment. It would be beneficial to use this instrument in early counseling sessions to guide learning throughout the course of counseling and set goals for counseling. Not only could this test be used at the beginning of career counseling or in an educational setting, but also it could be used at a final counseling session or career counseling program. This instrument may be used to evaluate effectiveness of a vocational program (Joutras, 2011). For example, this instrument could be used to as a post-test to measure learning outcomes.

Technical Considerations

In the administrative guide, Liptak (2009a) indicates that the normative sample is adults affiliated with various settings (e.g., prisons, career counseling services, and government funded programs). However, it is not clear how the individuals were affiliated with these settings. The sample (N = 530) was composed of men (n = 290) and women (n = 240) with an age range from 18-65. No other information is provided about the normative sample.

Adequate reliability was found for the JSKS (Liptak, 2009a). Internal consistency alphas ranged from .75 to .91 across subscales: Identifying Job Leads subscale (.75), Direct Application to Employers (.82), Resumes and Cover Letters (.90), Employment Interviews (.84), Following Up (.91). Test-retest reliability was measured with 100 adults over a one-month period. Correlations ranged from .79 to .90: Identifying Job Leads subscale (.82), Direct Application to Employers (.79), Resumes and Cover Letters subscale. (87), Employment Interviews (.85), and Following Up (.90). Liptak (2009a) indicated concurrent validity was determined by calculating interscale correlations, which ranged from .19 to .47. The available evidence for concurrent validity is inadequate, and the JSKS requires additional validity studies. Further, the manual provided shows differences between males and females on each subscale; however, it is unclear if differences between the means by sex are significant. Nonetheless, the manual indicated females' mean highest scores were on the Identifying Job Leads, Direct Application to Employers, and Resumes and Cover Letters subscales. Subscales with males scoring highest on average are the Direct Application to Employers and Resumes and Cover Letters subscales. Liptak (2009a) suggested that lower scores on the Employment Interviews and Following Up subscales indicated that both sexes are the least educated about these topics. Similar to concurrent validity, more information on construct validity is needed.

General Utility and Evaluation

The administrative guide provides a broad range of information that will be helpful to test administrators. It presents a strong case for the need for this type of instrument, such as the transient nature of the workplace and frequency of job changes throughout the lifespan. The test and the subscales are thoroughly described in the guide with more information about each of the five steps provided for clarity. A case illustration is provided as an example and may be used to help a career counselor work with a client.

The administrative guide also provides information about the test construction process including the use of research and how items were reviewed for multicultural sensitivity. For example, items that referenced gender, ethnicity, and other cultural factors were eliminated during test construction. Changes between the first and second editions are noted for comparison.

Despite the informative nature of the administrative guide, more information could be provided about the normative sample (e.g., means and standard deviations for age, ethnic composition, and profession). Furthermore, clarification could be made in the validity description due to the incorrect usage of the term concurrent validity. An area of potential research for this instrument could examine reliability and validity with individuals from a variety of settings to support its use across industries (e.g., service and administrative) and diverse populations.

This test has multiple qualities that make it a useful test. It can be self-administered and self-scored. This may be especially useful in school settings when a teacher or counselor may not have the time to score each test. The use of self-initiative may also be reflective of the important skills of agency needed for job obtainment. For example, it is the responsibility of the job seeker to singularly interview for positions, to decide what positions and offers to accept, and to perform the tasks required for the position. The test may be administered individually or in groups, which may make it easier for agencies or schools to use the test. Further, the JSKS is comprehensive in that one component of the test is to create an action plan and develop goals to achieve based on the test taker's current understanding of job search knowledge. Because test takers develop their own goals, the goals are personal and thus more likely to be appropriate for the test taker. Goals may also be used in the counseling treatment plan with the counselor. The goals may provide a starting part for counseling, and goals could be evaluated for achievability.

Despite the strengths of the test, there are some concerns. The test is written at an 8th-grade reading level, yet one recommended population is middle school. This test may be difficult for students in lower grade levels. Thus, it may be more appropriately applicable for those in 8th grade and beyond. The reading level may also prove difficult for adults with diminished reading ability (e.g., individuals recovering from a brain injury, illiterate adults). Further, many of the questions are more geared towards "white collar" or professional/administrative type positions, which may leave out a great number of the recommended populations.

The JSKS is an assessment of knowledge, yet, on the same page where test takers respond to items, correct responses are provided (i.e., Steps 1 and 2). Even if individuals did not look ahead to Step 2 for the correct responses, there is a pattern in the items to the correct answers that respondents could detect early in the administration process. When using self-scoring on an abilities test, individuals may be tempted to falsify information or change their responses to the correct responses. School-age individuals may be particularly interested in performing well since test performance may be rewarded. Therefore, falsifying information or providing socially desirable responses to get a higher score may be done more frequently in these settings. Although the argument could be made that in those instances they are still learning the correct answer, it does not take into account that individuals may only seek out responding in the correct manner without ever reading the items.

Despite these concerns or reservations with this test, the JSKS a unique test that may be used in a variety of settings such as schools, rehabilitation centers, and career centers. The test is comprehensive and test takers provide their own direction for where to go after the test is taken. Finally, few career development tests are currently available with a step-by-step process that leads to goal development. Based upon the review of this test, this test is recommended as a test to measure job search knowledge.

References and Additional Resources

Dean, G. J. (2007). [Job Search Knowledge Scale.] In R. A. Spies, B. S. Plake, K. Geisinger, & J. Carlson (Eds.), *The seventeenth mental measurements yearbook.* Lincoln, NE: Buros Center for Testing.

Hattrup, K. (2007). [Job Search Knowledge Scale.] In R. A. Spies, B. S. Plake, K. Geisinger, & J. Carlson (Eds.), *The seventeenth mental measurements yearbook.* Lincoln, NE: Buros Center for Testing.

Joutras, D. (2011). *The job search knowledge scale: Assessing consumers of a CARF exemplary-rated comprehensive vocational evaluation program.* Unpublished master's thesis. Southern Illinois University Carbondale, Carbondale, IL.

Liptak, J. (2009a). *Job search knowledge scale: Administrator's guide.* Indianapolis, IN: JIST Works.

Liptak, J. (2009b). *Job search knowledge scale.* Indianapolis, IN: JIST Works.

JOB SURVIVAL AND SUCCESS SCALE, SECOND EDITION
John J. Liptak

JIST Works, Inc.

7321 Shadeland Station, Suite 200
Indianapolis, IN 46256-3923
800.648.JIST
877.454.7839
http://www.jist.com
info@jist.com

Target Population: Adolescents, young adults, and adults.

Statement of the Purpose of the Instrument: The Job Survival and Success Scale (JSSS) is designed to help individuals identify their most and least effective job survival and success skills, including the key "soft skills" that employers desire most. It then guides them to create a "Success Plan" for improving those skills.

Titles of Subtests, Scales, Scores Provided: Scores in five categories representing the most desirable skills and traits for the world of work: Dependability, Responsibility, Human Relations, Ethical Behavior, and Getting Ahead.

Forms and Levels Available, with Dates of Publication/Revision of Each: 2009.

Date of Most Recent Edition of Test Manual, User's Guide, Etc.: 2009.

Languages in Which Available: English only.

Time:

Actual Test Time: 20-30 minutes.

Total Administration Time: 20-30 minutes.

Norm Group(s) on Which Scores Are Based: The administrator's guide contains norms tables (based on very small samples) for adults, college students, and high school students. The instrument was constructed for use with persons age 16 and older. Specifically, the JSSS was developed using three norms groups: high school students from ages 16 to 18; college students from ages 17 to 23; and adult, non-college students from ages 20 to 67.

Manner in Which Results Are Reported for Individuals: Raw scores for each of the scales are profiled into three score ranges (High, Average, and Low) with easy-to-understand interpretations for each scale. Self-scoring and self-interpreting. Five raw scale scores (Dependability, Responsibility, Human Relations, Ethical Behavior, and Getting Ahead.) can be compared to the norms developed for the population taking the JSSS. Profile Interpretation and Success Plan are included with each assessment. Respondents follow a series of five steps to complete the JSSS.

Report Format/Content for Group Summaries: Not available.

Machine Scoring: Not available.

Hand Scoring: Hand scored by counselee in fewer than 5 minutes.

Local Machine Scoring: Not available.

Computer Software Options Available: Not available.

Cost of Materials: Due to possible price changes since publication date be sure to check the publisher's website. Administrator's guide also available for free download from http://www.jist.com.

Specimen Set: Free.

Counselee Materials: Test booklets (package of 25): $46.95 with discounts available for large-volume purchases. Each package includes a free administrator's guide.

Job Survival and Success Scale, Second Edition

Additional Comments of Interest to Users:

The JSSS is the only work-related assessment to measure Emotional Intelligence skills used in the workplace. The JSSS has been used in recent research studies to identify the Emotional Intelligence of today's workforce. The JSSS can be used to improve job retention rates of employees. The JSSS can be used in conjunction with the Job Search Attitude Inventory (JIST Publishing) and Barriers to Employment Success Inventory (JIST Publishing) in a comprehensive employment counseling approach.

Published Reviews of the Instrument in the Last 15 Years:

Austin, J. T., & Tischendorf, S. D. (2007). [Job Survival and Success Scale.] In K. F. Geisinger, R. A. Spies, & B. S. Plake (Eds.), *The seventeenth mental measurements yearbook* (pp. 447-449). Lincoln, NE: Buros Center for Testing.

Johnson, S. B. (2007). [Job Survival and Success Scale.] In K. F. Geisinger, R. A. Spies, & B. S. Plake (Eds.), *The seventeenth mental measurements yearbook* (pp. 449-451). Lincoln, NE: Buros Center for Testing.

Sauser, W. I., Jr. (2009). [Job Survival and Success Scale.] In E. A. Whitfield, R. W. Feller, & C. Wood (Eds.), *A counselor's guide to career assessment instruments* (5th ed., pp. 372-375). Broken Arrow, OK: National Career Development Association.

JOB SURVIVAL AND SUCCESS SCALE, SECOND EDITION

Reviewed by:

William I. Sauser, Jr.

College of Business
Auburn University

Description

According to the administrator's guide (Liptak, 2009), the Job Survival and Success Scale, second edition (JSSS) "is designed to meet the need for a brief assessment instrument to identify a person's attitudes and knowledge about keeping a job and getting ahead in the workplace.... [It] is intended for use in comprehensive career guidance programs, middle and high schools, employment counseling programs, college counseling centers, college career and placement offices, or any agency that works with clients or students looking for employment" (p. 6). As indicated on the JSSS cover, it "is not a test." Rather, it is a self-administered, self-scoring inventory designed to help the person completing it "identify your most effective and least effective job survival and success skills, also known as soft skills." Skill sets considered include dependability, responsibility, human relations, ethical behavior, and getting ahead.

In my opinion, this instrument is best used as a guidance tool for counselors working with individuals who are seeking first-time employment or trying to determine why they have had difficulty retaining jobs. Most of my comments about the first edition of the JSSS apply equally to the second edition. Key changes from the first edition to the second are a revision of some of the items to update terminology, revised directions, and streamlined interpretive materials, all intended "to make the assessment more user-friendly" (Liptak, 2009, p. 11).

Like its predecessor edition, the JSSS second edition consists of 60 items grouped into five categories (12 items each): Dependability, Responsibility, Human Relations, Ethical Behavior, and Getting Ahead. Each item is rated on a four-point scale: 4—*A lot like me*, 3—*Somewhat like me*, 2—*A little like me*, and 1—*Not like me* (with occasional reverse-scored items interspersed throughout the instrument). An example item, provided in the directions for completing the form, is "On the job, I would follow the dress code." Scores for the five categories are calculated simply by summing the scores for the 12 items within each category. The individual is then asked to "profile your scores" by plotting them on a colorful graph, and interpretations are then supplied for low, average, and high scores as indicated by plots on the graph. The individual is then instructed to work through a series of checklists (one for each of the five dimensions) to identify ways to improve job survival and success skills. In a too brief final step, the individual is invited to create a success plan by listing "ways that you can become a more successful employee."

The JSSS is attractive, colorful, and engaging. It is easy to complete, can be administered to groups or individuals, is self-scoring (with easy-to-follow instructions), and contains interpretive information directly on the instrument itself. It is well designed for use within a one-hour counseling session.

The JSSS can be best used as a device to guide job seekers and their counselors in a fruitful mutual exploration of "soft" skills, their importance for success in the workplace, the job seeker's current self-reported level of those skills, and a focused discussion of how to enhance those skills to better prepare the individual for success in the workplace. The real value of the instrument, in my opinion, is dependent on the degree to which the job seeker engages in this exercise and the counselor provides insight and guidance. The instrument is not designed for fine levels of measurement and can easily be faked in order for the job seeker to "look good" or "look bad." As a self-report device, the accuracy of the JSSS is dependent on the individual's depth of self-perception. The device possesses some utility for the counseling setting, but is—in my opinion—too simplistic to provide deep insight into the individual's readiness to succeed in the work environment.

Technical Considerations

As was its predecessor form, the JSSS second edition is technically very weak. Norms (actually, means and standard deviations) presented in the administrator's guide (Liptak, 2009) are based on what appear to be small samples of convenience—52 college students, 98 high school students, and 51 adults, respectively (the same numbers reported for the first edition, suggesting the instrument was not carefully re-normed after revision). An omnibus table is included based on scores of 484 males and 610 females to whom the instrument was given in "subsequent administrations" (p. 15) "with a variety of populations, including unemployed adults, ex-offenders, college students, and welfare-to-work clients" (p. 11). It is unclear whether these subsequent administrations used the original or revised edition of the JSSS.

Evidence for internal consistency and stability is also based on small samples (110 adults and 75 adults, respectively), but is encouraging, with coefficient alphas ranging from .87 to .92 and test-retest correlations from .79 to .89 across the five dimensions. These statistics are based, however, on the first edition of the JSSS. There is no additional information on the reliability of the JSSS, second edition.

Validity evidence is clearly a major weakness of both editions of the JSSS. The first edition was apparently devised (according to the administrator's guide) based on the theoretical work of Goleman (1995, 1998) and others on *emotional intelligence,* plus a smattering of ideas about other "soft skills" and career and job-search skills. Although the JSSS is convincingly face-valid, there is no real evidence presented in the administrator's guide (Liptak, 2009) to support any claims of psychometric validity. Interestingly, no additional work on validity appears to have been attempted when the second edition of the JSSS was produced.

General Utility and Evaluation

The administrator's guide provides little useful information beyond what has been presented above. The brief sections on "understanding your scores" (pp. 7-8) and "understanding the job success profile" (pp. 8-9) are largely repetitive of the information printed on the form itself, as are the instructions for administration. Reviewers of the original version of the JSSS (Austin & Tischendorf, 2007; Johnson, 2007; Sauser, 2009) were unanimous in their concern about the JSSS's lack of psychometric quality and their call for additional research on the instrument. The latter two reviewers did, however, see some utility for the JSSS in an employment counseling context. Since there is little evidence of substantive change between the first and second editions of the JSSS, these earlier comments still apply.

Helping their clients obtain (and retain) employment is clearly an important focus for counselors, and instruments such as the JSSS, second edition, *when used by a skilled counselor to guide an individual to hone job-seeking skills,* have some merit. I encourage additional research on the effectiveness of the JSSS, second edition. Counselors may also want to investigate the wealth of resources found on the JIST website.

Finally, there is only one form of the JSSS, second edition. According to the administrator's guide, this single form is designed for use with "individuals at any age at or above the junior high school level" (p. 6). I agree that the JSSS is appropriate for use with high school and college students as well as adults who can read and com-

Job Survival and Success Scale, Second Edition

prehend in English at approximately the tenth-grade level. Bilingual counselors may be able to administer the instrument orally to those whose native language is not English, but there is no discussion in the administrator's guide about the usefulness or interpretation of the JSSS with non-English-speaking persons.

References and Additional Resources

Austin, J. T., & Tischendorf, S. D. (2007). [Job Survival and Success Scale.] In K. F. Geisinger, R. A. Spies, & B. S. Plake (Eds.), *The seventeenth mental measurements yearbook* (pp. 447-449). Lincoln, NE: Buros Center for Testing.

Goleman, D. (1995). *Emotional intelligence.* New York, NY: Bantam Books.

Goleman, D. (1998). *Working with emotional intelligence.* New York, NY: Bantam Books.

Johnson, S. B. (2007). [Job Survival and Success Scale.] In K. F. Geisinger, R. A. Spies, & B. S. Plake (Eds.), *The seventeenth mental measurements yearbook* (pp. 449-451). Lincoln, NE: Buros Center for Testing.

Liptak, J. (2009). *Job Survival and Success Scale, Second Edition, Administrator's guide.* Retrieved from http://jistemcp.com/productattachments/index/download?id=553

Sauser, W. I., Jr. (2009). [Job Survival and Success Scale.] In E. A. Whitfield, R. W. Feller, & C. Wood (Eds.), *A counselor's guide to career assessment instruments* (5th ed., pp. 372-375). Broken Arrow, OK: National Career Development Association.

QUALITY OF LIFE INVENTORY
Michael B. Frisch

Pearson Assessments

Clinical Assessment
19500 Bulverde Road
San Antonio, TX 78259
www.pearsonassessments.com

Target Population: Adolescents, young adults, and adults; age 17 and older, sixth-grade reading level.

Statement of the Purpose of the Instrument: The Quality of Life Inventory (QOLI) is a measure of positive psychology and mental health, providing an overall score and a profile of problems and strengths in 16 areas of life such as love, work, and play.

Titles of Subtests, Scales, Scores Provided: The 16 areas addressed in the QOLI assessment are Health, Self-Esteem, Goals and Values, Money, Work, Play, Learning, Creativity, Helping, Love, Friends, Children, Relatives, Home, Neighborhood, and Community.

Forms and Levels Available, with Dates of Publication/Revision of Each: 1994.

Date of Most Recent Edition of Test Manual, User's Guide, Etc.: 1994.

Language in Which Available: English only.

Time:

> **Actual Test Time:** Varies.

> **Total Administration Time:** 5 minutes.

Norm Group(s) on Which Scores Are Based: Normative data are based on 798 nonclinical adults sampled from 12 states from the Northeast, the South, the Midwest, and the West. An attempt was made to match the 1990 U.S. Census data as closely as possible.

Manner in Which Results Are Reported for Individuals/Groups: The QOLI profile report graphically presents an overall quality of life score and a weighted satisfaction profile for the 16 areas assessed. It also provides a brief narrative description of the person's overall classification and lists areas of dissatisfaction that may need further exploration.

Machine Scoring: The QOLI test can be administered locally on Q Local Software. The assessment is scored via Q Local Software as well. Each profile report is approximately $2.80 per report. The Q Local Software has an annual license fee of $89.00. Time required for scoring and returning is 5 minutes.

Hand Scoring: Hand scored by counselee in approximately 10 minutes. Answer sheets for paper-and-pencil version are $21.50 per 5-24 sheets.

Computer Software Options Available: Q Local Software.

Cost of Materials: Due to possible price changes since publication date, be sure to check the publisher's website. Starter kits to be used with the Q Local software (not included) or the hand-scoring format are available at the Pearson website. Prices range from $23.60 to $113.30.

Published Reviews of the Instrument in the Last 15 Years:

Barnes, L. L. B. (2001). [Quality of Life Inventory.] From B. S. Plake & J. C. Impara (Eds.), *The fourteenth mental measurements yearbook.* Lincoln, NE: Buros Center for Testing.

Johnson, R. W. (2001). [The Quality of Life Inventory.] From B. S. Plake & J. C. Impara (Eds.), *The fourteenth mental measurements yearbook.* Lincoln, NE: Buros Center for Testing.

QUALITY OF LIFE INVENTORY

Reviewed by:

Laurie A. Carlson

Department of Counseling and Career Development
Colorado State University

Description

The Quality of Life Inventory (QOLI) is an easily used assessment tool based upon Quality of Life Theory (Frisch, 1994), a blending of cognitive therapy and positive psychology. The basic premise behind the theory and QOLI is that an individual's quality of life is equated with life satisfaction. Frisch (1994) defined life satisfaction as an objective and subjective determination of the gap between the importance of life areas and perceived attainment of those life goals. The QOLI examines 16 constructs posited to be unique contributors to life satisfaction: "Health, Self-Esteem, Goals-and-Values, Money, Work, Play, Learning, Creativity, Helping, Love, Friends, Children, Relatives, Home, Neighborhood, and Community" (Frisch, 1994, p. 6). It is interesting to note that factor analytic procedures with results from a clinical sample of 217 indicated that the 16 scales loaded into a two-factor solution: self-oriented and other-oriented (McAlinden & Oei, 2006). The results of the factor analytic procedure adds statistical support to what is generally known about a person's quality of life, that it is influenced by both internal and external factors. Internal (self) factors included the subscales of health, self-esteem, goals-and-values, learning, work, play, creativity, and helping. The external (other) factors included the subscales of neighborhood, home, community, children, love, money and relatives. The friends subscale loaded into both self and other factors (McAlinden & Oei, 2006).

Each of the 16 constructs are measured with two items (32 items total), the first requiring the individual to indicate importance of the construct on a three-point scale (0 = *not important* to 2 = *extremely important*), and the second asking the individual to indicate level of current satisfaction on a six-point scale (−3 = *very dissatisfied* to +3 = *very satisfied*). The satisfaction scores are then multiplied by the importance scores yielding a "weighted satisfaction score" (ranging from −6 to +6) for each area. These weighted scores are then added together and divided by the number of areas that were rated important or extremely important to yield a total raw score. The manual provides tables for converting the total raw score to *T*-scores or percentiles (Frisch, 1994).

Items include a general description of the construct to aid in understanding, and the entire instrument is written at the sixth-grade reading level. The layout of the instrument is intuitive and friendly. The QOLI is appropriate for individuals 17 years of age or older and may be administered individually or in groups (Frisch, 1994). The instrument takes about five minutes to complete and is available for either paper-and-pencil or computer administration. Hand scoring of the paper-and-pencil version is clearly outlined in the test manual using step-by-step instructions and should generally take no longer than several minutes to score (Johnson, 2001). The QOLI is available from Pearson Assessments in an electronic version (Q-local). The advantage, however, to using the hand-scored version is that the instrument includes an opportunity for the client to add narrative reflection regarding the nature of concerns or problems in each of the 16 areas. Specifically, the hand-scored version includes a section that allows the client to provide a narrative explanation of their responses to each of the 16 quality of life indicators.

The QOLI is grounded in positive psychology and adheres to the precept that life satisfaction and subjective well-being are inextricably intertwined with psychological and physical health. Frisch (1994) identified a broad range of literature that supports the premise that reduced quality of life leads to a greater degree of psychological distress and disease. The QOLI has been successfully used in measuring treatment outcomes, treatment planning, and screening individuals who are at risk for health problems. Specifically, Frisch (1994) indicated the instrument can be used to (a) gain a more complete view of the client's mental status, (b) gain a more complete view of the client's physical health status, (c) predict future health problems, (d) aid in measuring medical health outcomes, (e) aid in developing new treatments, and (f) provide a integrative construct for understanding and treating mental disorders.

The QOLI has been used successfully with geriatric clients (Bourland et al., 2000) and more recently with inpatient psychiatric patients (Angstman, Schuldberg, Harris, Cochran, & Peterson, 2009). No literature emerged related to the use of the QOLI with culturally or ethnically diverse clients, and this is an area that calls for more exploration. Since the narrative response area of the hand-scored version serves to strengthen the applicability of the instrument and provides material for discussion with the client, the hand-scored version may be more useful with populations that might not be clearly represented in the standardization sample.

Technical Considerations

The standardization sample of 798 individuals from 12 states across the country roughly matches the 1992 Census data with respect to racial/ethnic characteristics and gender (Frisch, 1994), but the demographic data included in the manual do not clearly describe the sample with regards to other pertinent demographic characteristics (Barnes, 2001). The manual indicates that the standardization sample was non-clinical and that the instrument was primarily administered in groups (Frisch, 1994). Barnes (2001) pointed out that the sampling procedure is not clearly articulated in the manual and that some of the participants were paid.

Reliability for the QOLI was measured using both a two-week test-retest and computing a coefficient alpha. The test-retest study included a subgroup of the normative sample numbering only 55 participants and yielded a rather weak reliability coefficient of .73 (Frisch, 1994). Although statistically significant at $p < .01$, this coefficient is markedly smaller than those reported in the earlier version of the QOLI ($r = .91$ over 33 days and $r = .80$ over 18 days; Johnson, 2001). Internal consistency analyses yielded a coefficient alpha of .79 using the sum of the weighted satisfaction ratings instead of the raw score. Frisch (1994) indicated that using the weighted score is appropriate as the process for computing the raw score is not the same for all individuals; and in correlation analysis, the correlation between the sum of the weighted scales and the QOLI raw score was .99.

The manual for the QOLI outlines the process used for examining convergent and discriminant validity as well as sensitivity to clinical treatment. Validity coefficients for QOLI T-scores with scores from the Satisfaction With Life Scale and the Quality of Life Index are .56 and .75, respectively. The QOLI yielded a statistically significant, yet small, coefficient of .25 with the Marlowe-Crowne Social Desirability Scale. Frisch (1994) presented data supporting sensitivity to clinical treatment through a rather small ($N = 13$) study of bibliotherapy with a sample of clinically depressed individuals. Predictive and treatment validity has been supported in work with college students (Frisch et al., 2005), older adults with generalized anxiety disorder (Bourland et al., 2000), patients with anxiety and depression (McAlinden & Oei, 2006), and most recently with inpatient psychiatric patients (Angstman et. al, 2009).

General Utility and Evaluation

QOLI presents a theoretically sound instrument that aids in working with a multitude of clients through the positive psychology approach, although one must be aware that this instrument has not been revised or re-standardized since 1994. The instrument is comprehensive, yet concise enough to be highly useful for practitioners in multiple settings. The time of administration and scoring is minimal (generally 10-20 minutes for both), and generates not only a "score," but also material for further work with the client. The "Hand-Scoring Starter Kit" includes the manual as well as 50 administrations, making the instrument rather economical for the practitioner.

The manual is intuitive, easy to use, and generally comprehensive. The manual sections are well-written regarding test interpretation and treatment guidance, which constitute separate sections in the manual and provides strong guidance for the test user. In addition to these resources provided within the manual itself, sample reports and sample progress reports for the QOLI are provided at the publisher's website. The nature of the construct, quality of life, indicates that the instrument is appropriate for a multitude of settings, including clinical, school, and career settings.

The true strength of the instrument lies in the way that the practitioner uses the information gathered. Certainly, the narrative comment portion of the hand-scored version provides further insight into the client's quality of life and material for discussion in treatment planning and implementation. This feature also lends to a more culturally sensitive application of the instrument. One can certainly use the instrument for the purpose

Quality of Life Inventory

of quantifying client perception of quality of life or treatment outcomes, yet it seems that one would then not be fully using all that the instrument has to offer.

References and Additional Resources

Angstman, S., Schuldberg, D., Harris, K. J., Cochran, B., & Peterson, P. (2009). Use of the quality of life inventory for measuring quality of life changes in an inpatient psychiatric population. *Psychological Reports, 104*(3), 1007-1014. doi: 10.2466/PR0.104.3.1007-1014

Barnes, L. L. B. (2001). [Quality of Life Inventory]. From B. S. Plake & J. C. Impara (Eds.), *The fourteenth mental measurements yearbook.* Lincoln, NE: Buros Center for Testing.

Bourland, S. L., Stanley, M. A., Snyder, A. G., Novy, D. M., Bech, J. G., Averill, P. M., & Swann, A. C. (2000). Quality of life in older adults with generalized anxiety disorder. *Aging & Mental Health, 4,* 315-323.

Frisch, M. B., Clark, M. P., Rouse, S. V., Rudd, M. D., Paweleck, J. K., Greenstone, A., & Kopplin, D. A. (2005). Predictive and treatment validity of life satisfaction and the quality of life inventory. *Assessment, 12,* 66-78. doi: 10.1177/073191104268006

Frisch, M. B. (1994). *Quality of life inventory: Manual and treatment guide.* Minneapolis, MN: NCS Pearson Assessments.

Johnson, R. W. (2001). [Quality of Life Inventory]. From B. S. Plake & J. C. Impara (Eds.), *The fourteenth mental measurements yearbook.* Lincoln, NE: Buros Center for Testing.

McAlinden, N. M., & Oei, T. P. S. (2006). Validation of the quality of life inventory for patients with anxiety and depression. *Comprehensive Psychiatry, 47,* 307-314. doi: 10.1016/j.comppsych.2005.09.003

Pearson Assessments. (2012). *Quality of life inventory (QOLI).* Retrieved from http://psychcorp.pearsonassessments.com/HAIWEB/Cultures/en-us/Productdetail.htm?Pid=PAg511.

Varni, J. W., Burwinkle, T. M., & Seid, M. (2006). The PedsQL4.0 as a school population health measure: Feasibility, reliability, and validity. *Quality of Life Research, 15,* 203-215. doi: 10.1007/s11136-005-1388-z

A Counselor's Guide To Career Assessments Instruments

WorkLife Indicator
Center for Creative Leadership in conjunction with Ellen Ernst Kossek

---

Center for Creative Leadership
One Leadership Place
P.O. Box 26300
Greensboro, NC 27438
www.ccl.org/leadership/index.aspx
info@ccl.org

Target Population: Working adults.

Statement of the Purpose of the Instrument: The WorkLife Indicator (WLI) is designed to assess an individual's approach for managing the boundaries between work and family.

Titles of Subtests, Scales, Scores Provided: Behaviors, Identity, Control.

Forms and Levels Available, with Dates of Publication/Revision of Each: Online form published in 2011.

Date of Most Recent Edition of Test Manual, User's Guide, Etc.: Technical Manual, Facilitator's Guide, and Feedback Report and Development Planning Guide published in 2011.

Languages in Which Available: English only.

Time:

    Actual Test Time: 10 minutes.

    Total Administration Time: 10 minutes.

Manner in Which Results Are Reported for Individuals: Graphic representation of standard scores and descriptions of profiles.

Machine Scoring: Online scoring.

Hand Scoring: Not available.

Computer Software Options Available: Not available.

Cost of Materials: Due to possible price changes since publication date, be sure to check the publisher's website.

    Specimen Set: Survey, scoring, and feedback report and development planning guide are $30.00 for 1-50 assessments, $28.00 for 51-100 assessments, $26.00 for 101-150 assessments, $24.00 for 151-200 assessments, $20.00 for 201+ assessments. For facilitators, access to support materials, including Technical Manual, Facilitator's Guide and slide show debrief template. Group profile report is $100.00.

    Counselee Materials: Online administration, requiring computer and Internet access.

Published Reviews in the Last 15 Years: Not available.

WorkLife Indicator

Reviewed by:

Rebecca A. Newgent

Department of Counselor Education
Western Illinois University – Quad Cities

Description

The WorkLife Indicator (WLI) was developed by the Center for Creative Leadership in partnership with Ellen E. Kossek. The WLI is a self-report assessment that is currently only available in English and was designed to help a working adult "understand his or her approach to managing work-life boundaries" (Hannum, Braddy,

WorkLife Indicator

Leslie, Ruderman, & Kossek, 2011, p. 4). It can be used as part of a training program or as part of coaching or development initiatives to help increase effectiveness on and off the job. This career-related assessment focuses on behaviors, identity, and control in relation to work-life boundaries (Hannum, Kossek, & Rudderman, 2011). The assessment is currently administered online, though a paper-based, self-score version is in development.

A pilot version of the WLI was developed based on the work of Kossek and Lautsch (2007). The online assessment was published in 2009 and the Technical Manual, Facilitator's Guide, and Feedback Report and Development Planning Guide were published in 2011 by the Center for Creative Leadership. A Debrief Session Slideshow Template and Sample Invitation and Reminder Emails are available from the Center for Creative Leadership. The WLI costs $30.00 per participant (discounts available for quantity), which includes administration of one online self-survey, scoring of the assessment, and an integrated feedback report and development planning guide. Group reports of aggregated individual data are also available. Organizations interested in taking the WLI can place their order by calling the Center for Creative Leadership's Client Services Group or at http://www.ccl.org.

The purpose of the WLI is the measure how individuals manage "the boundaries between work and family (their Behaviors), the degree to which an individual identifies with and invests in work and family roles (Identity), and the degree to which an individual feels in control of how he or she manages the boundaries between work and family (Control)" (Hannum, Braddy, et al., 2011, p. 5). Note that the term "family" refers to family unit, extended family, and friends. Together, the factors of Behaviors, Identity, and Control form an individual's profile. The WLI perspective related to work-life integration "holds that perceptions of control over work-life boundaries and whether work-life relationships are congruent with one's preferences for segmentation or integration are more important than whether you integrate or separate work and family" (Hannum, Braddy, et al., 2011, p. 5).

The WLI consists of five scales or dimensions. The Family Interrupts Work scale consists of six items that measure the extent that family life interrupts work life. The Work Interrupts Family scale consists of seven items that measure the extent that work life interrupts family life. These two scales make up the Behaviors factor. The Work Focused scale consists of three items that measure the extent to which an individual's identity interconnects with work. The Family Focused scale consists of three items that measure the extent to which an individual's identity interconnects with family. These two scales make up the Identity factor. The final factor, Control, consists of one scale, Boundary Control. This scale consists of three items that measure the extent to which individuals feel in control of the boundaries between work and family (Hannum, Braddy, et al., 2011; Hannum, Kossek, et al., 2011).

The WLI consists of 22 scored items on a five-point Likert-type scale ranging from 1 (Strongly Disagree) to 5 (Strongly Agree). Sample items include the following: "I take care of personal or family needs during work," "I control whether I have clear boundaries between my work and personal life," and "I allow work to interrupt me when I spend time with family or friends" (Center for Creative Leadership, 2009, p. 1). The scores for each of the five scales are categorized into Low, Middle-range, and High categories for interpretation. For example, a Low categorization on the Family Interrupts Work scale on the Behaviors factor indicates, "Your family life does not interrupt your working hours" (Hannum, Kossek, et al., 2011, p. 10). A High categorization on the Family Focused scale of the Identity factor indicates, "You strongly identify with and invest yourself in your family" (Hannum, Kossek, et al., 2011, p. 11). Another example is a Mid-range categorization on the Boundary Control scale of the Control factor indicates a moderate sense of control between work and family life.

The combination of the five scales forms the WLI Profile. There are 60 different profile configurations depending on the scale categorizations (Low, Middle-range, or High). For the Behaviors factor, there are five categorizations: Integrators, Separators, Work Firsters, Family Firsters, and Cyclers. For example, a Separator would be an individual who scores Low on Family Interrupts Work and Low on Work Interrupts Family, whereas an Integrator would be an individual who scores High on Family Interrupts Work and High on Work Interrupts Family. For the Identity factor, there are four categorizations: Work Focused, Family Focused, Dual Focused, and Other Focused. An individual would be Dual Focused who scores Middle-range on Work Focused and Middle-range on Family Focused. For the Control factor, there are three categorizations: High Boundary Control, Midlevel Boundary Control, and Low Boundary Control (Kossek, Ruderman, Hannum, & Braddy, 2011). The combination of each of the three categorizations forms the WLI Profile. For example, an individual who is

A Counselor's Guide To Career Assessments Instruments

an Integrator, Dual Focused, with Low Boundary Control would have the profile as a Dual Focused Integrator with Low Boundary Control. This profile indicates:

> You may experience blending as negative and stressful. You may not feel in control over shifting your attention and energy between work and family or nonwork activities. Work and personal-life demands habitually feel at odds. You may feel that you are constantly putting out a fire or reacting to an external cue. You may feel pulled in different directions and constantly needed by others. The difficulty you experience adapting your boundaries makes it stressful meeting the needs of both work and family. You may feel like you are not very successful at managing either work or personal roles and take on some depressive symptoms. (Hannum, Braddy, et al., 2011, p. 26)

WLI profiles for all 60 configurations are available in the Technical Manual (Hannum, Braddy, et al., 2011).

The WLI instructions state that "For each statement, decide which of the answers best applies to you" (Center for Creative Leadership, 2009, p. 1). Demographic and additional items for research purposes are also included, which take approximately five minutes to complete. This review of the WLI estimated the Flesh Reading Ease as 62.9 and the Flesh-Kincaid Grade Level as 6.3. Each of the 22 items is numbered and every other item presented on alternate green shades. While the alternating shades is helpful, the discrimination is minimal, which may make for a difficult read for some. The Sample Report (Kossek et al., 2011) is a very thorough document that contains an introduction to the WLI, an individual's profile comparison and detailed profile, and a development planning guide. The Sample Report is well presented and easy to read. Additional resources are also included.

The WLI specifically measures how individuals manage the balance between work and life (family). Counselors can use this assessment to help individuals find "the best way to manage their energy and time" (Kossek et al., 2011, p. 5). Assessment results can be used to help individuals better understand their priorities and behaviors related to managing the balance between work and life. Counselors can assist individuals with a debriefing of the report and develop a plan for how best to make changes to improve overall effectiveness of their work and family lives. Counselors can help "ensure that data are interpreted in a way that optimizes receptivity and impact" (Center for Creative Leadership, 2012, Self Assessment Tools) and help to "develop a plan to increase effectiveness on and off the job" (Center for Creative Leadership, 2012, WorkLife Indicator Overview).

Technical Considerations

The normative sample included 595 practicing leaders (males = 53%, females = 47%) with an average age of 44.58 years (SD = 7.73) representing a variety of industries and different management levels (41% upper-middle managers, 32% top-level managers/executives, 23% first-level managers, and 4% other). Ethnicity of the sample was primarily White/Caucasian (79%) with 6% Asian, 4% Hispanic, 3% Black, 1% Native American, and 7% other. Note that the data presented in this section are from the pilot study of the WLI. Based on the pilot data, two items were added to the WLI, one on the Work Focused scale and one on the Family Focused scale.

A mean for each of the five scales is computed and scores on each of the scales are categorized as high, medium, or low. Cutoff scores for each of the categories were determined based upon the pilot study. Means, standard deviations, and Cronbach's alpha were used in norming the WLI scales and includes Family Interrupts Work (M = 3.35, SD = .64, α = .73), Work Interrupts Family (M = 3.38, SD = .78, α = .84), Work Focused (M = 4.23, SD = .57, α = .76), Family Focused (M = 3.55, SD = .84, α = .82), and Boundary Control (M = 3.83, SD = .76, α = .84). Participants also completed 13 measures for use in establishing the validity of the WLI. Detailed information on the additional measures and scale development is available in the Technical Manual (Hannum, Braddy, et al., 2011).

Work Interrupts Family was positively correlated with Work-Family Conflict (r = .40, p < .01) and Work-Family Integration (r = .58, p < .01). Work Focused was correlated with Self-Engagement (r = .54, p < .01) and Boundary Control was positively correlated with Psychological Job Control (r = .48, p < .01) and Work Schedule Fit (r = .50, p < .01). Family Interrupts Work and Family Focused were correlated with each other (r = .30, p < .01). Discriminant validity evidence was limited. Criterion validity was established by correlating the five scales of the WLI with outcomes (intention to turnover, psychological distress, work withdrawal, health, and time adequacy). "The multiple regression analyses revealed that WorkLife Indictor measures accounted for a statistically significant amount of variance in each of the five outcomes" (Hannum, Braddy, et al., 2011, p. 12). Time Adequacy accounted for 30% of the variance with Work Withdrawal accounting for 16% of the variance. Psychological Distress accounted for 13% followed by Health at 9% and Turnover at 8% of the variance.

General Utility and Evaluation

Both the Technical Manual (Hannum, Braddy, et al., 2011) and the Facilitator's Guide (Hannum, Kossek, et al., 2011) provide detailed information about the WLI. The Technical Manual is a useful resource for test organizers who want information related to the development and psychometrics of the original WLI used in the pilot study. The Facilitator's Guide is a helpful resource for professionals who use and administer the WLI. The Facilitator's Guide provides exercises for counselors and facilitators to help individuals with understanding their results and to develop a plan to make changes when necessary. The WLI is normed on English speaking adults who are primarily White. Neither the Technical Manual nor the Facilitator's Guide addresses special populations or diversity considerations.

The WLI has not been reviewed by *Test Critiques, Tests in Print,* or *Buros Mental Measurements Yearbook.* Searches for research on and studies using the WLI in academic research databases indicate a *Journal of Vocational Behavior* monograph as the only peer-reviewed publication using WLI. The Center for Creative Leadership provides some resources on the research behind the WLI. At present, the main source of information about the WLI is from the publisher and available on the Center for Creative Leadership's website, and the supporting psychometric information is associated with the piloted version of the WLI.

The WLI has its roots in the work of Kossek and Lautsch (2007). These authors developed a schema for developing a better relationship between the roles of work and family. The WLI appears to be a useful tool in understanding individuals' preferences for how they interact with their families, their work style, and how they manage the relationship and balance between family and work. Additional supporting materials are available at http://www.ccl.org/leadership/assessments/WLIOverview.aspx?campaign=WLI.

References and Additional Resources

Center for Creative Leadership. (2009). *The WorkLife Indicator.* Greensboro, NC: Author.

Center for Creative Leadership. (2012). *CCL website.* Retrieved from http://www.ccl.org/leadership/index.aspx

Hannum, K. M., Braddy, P. W., Leslie, J. B., Ruderman, M. N., & Kossek, E. E. (2011). *WorkLife Indicator: Increasing your effectiveness on and off the job technical manual.* Greensboro, NC: Center for Creative Leadership.

Hannum, K. M., Kossek, E. E., & Ruderman, M. N. (2011). *WorkLife Indicator: Increasing your effectiveness on and off the job facilitator's guide.* Greensboro, NC: Center for Creative Leadership.

Kossek, E. E., & Lautsch, B. A. (2007). *CEO of me: Creating a life that works in the flexible job age.* Upper Saddle River, NJ: Wharton School Publishing.

Kossek, E. E., Ruderman, M. N., Braddy, P. W., & Hannum, K. M. (2012). Work-nonwork boundary management profiles: A person-centered approach. *Journal of Vocational Behavior, 81*(1), 112–128.

Kossek, E. E., Ruderman, M., N., Hannum, K., M., & Braddy, P. W. (2011). *WorkLife Indicator: Increasing your effectiveness on and off the job feedback report and development planning guide.* Greensboro, NC: Center for Creative Leadership.

CHAPTER 14

PERSONALITY MEASURES

- California Psychological Inventory, Third Edition

- Career Key

- Clifton StrengthsFinder or StrengthsFinder 2.0

- Jackson Personality Inventory – Revised

- Myers–Briggs Type Indicator

- NEO Personality Inventory – 3

- Personal Style Indicator

- Sixteen Personality Factor Questionnaire and Career Development Report

- Student Styles Questionnaire

California Psychological Inventory, Third Edition
Harrison Gough

Consulting Psychologists Press (CPP, Inc.)

CPP, Inc., and Davies-Black Publishing
1055 Joaquin Road, 2nd Floor
Mountain View, CA 94043
650.969.8901
800.624.1765
Fax: 650.969.8608
http://www.cpp.com

Target Population: Adolescents, young adults, and adults; age 13 and older, with at least a fourth-grade reading level.

Statement of the Purpose of the Instrument: The California Psychological Inventory (CPI 434) is designed to evaluate interpersonal behavior and social interactions within normal individuals.

Titles of Subtests, Scales, Scores Provided: The inventory contains 462 items which can be scored to yield 20 scales. The 20 scales are the following: Dominance, Capacity for Status, Sociability, Social Presence, Self-Acceptance, Independence, Empathy, Responsibility, Socialization, Self-Control, Good Impression, Communality, Well-Being, Tolerance, Achievement via Conformance, Achievement via Independence, Intellectual Efficiency, Psychological-Mindedness, Flexibility, and Femininity/Masculinity.

Forms and Levels Available, with Dates of Publication/Revision of Each: CPI 434: Revised 3rd edition 1996; CPI 260 (short form), 2002. The CPI 260 assesses normal adult personality characteristics. It differs from the CPI 434 in that it was developed specifically for the workplace and other organizational settings. It was updated with newer language, revised scales, and new interpretive material. The CPI 260 has been used in leadership development and as a selection tool.

Date of Most Recent Edition of Test Manual, User's Guide, Etc.: 1996.

Languages in Which Available: English and multiple languages; consult manual.

Time:

Actual Test Time: 45 minutes.

Total Administration Time: CPI 434: 45 to 60 minutes; CPI 260: 25 to 30 minutes.

Norm Group(s) on Which Scores Are Based: Norms are available for males only, females only, and male/female data combined. The CPI was developed and normed on non-psychiatric or non-clinical populations. The normative sample includes 6,000 men and women.

Manner in Which Results Are Reported for Individuals: Standard scores are presented. Profile, narrative, and configural supplements are available. (Comparative profiles are based on both gender-specific and combined male/female norms.)

Report Format/Content for Group Summaries: Available by request.

Machine Scoring: Scoring centers in Minneapolis, Washington, D.C., Palo Alto; scoring turn-around time is 24 hours (excluding mailing time).

Hand Scoring: Scored by clerk in approximately 60 minutes.

Local Machine Scoring: Available. Provisions/conditions/equipment required: 640 K memory, 80 column printer, DOS 2.0 or greater, IBM PC /IBM-XT/IBM PC-AT or IBM PC compatible, half-sized expansion card slot.

Computer Software Options Available: 5- or 10-year leases range from $600.00 to $800.00.

Cost of Materials: Due to possible price changes since publication date, be sure to check the publisher's website.

Specimen Set: Assessment (434 and 260 versions) reports and support materials with either 5 or 10 booklets and mail-in answer sheets for profile, narrative, and configural analysis reports; one manual; practical guide.

A COUNSELOR'S GUIDE TO CAREER ASSESSMENTS INSTRUMENTS

Prices increase with complexity of reports desired: CPI 434 Profile: $20.95 each (online administration); CPI 434 Narrative Report: $41.95 each (online administration); CPI 434 Configural Analysis Report: $51.95 each (online administration); CPI 260 Client Feedback Report: $26.95 each online administration; CPI 260 Coaching Report for Leaders: $40.95 each (online administration).

Counselee Materials: CPI Manual; Reusable $99.50; A Practical Guide to CPI Interpretation; Reusable $91.50; CPI 260 Manual: Reusable $93.50; CPI 260 Client Feedback Report Guide for Interpretation; Reusable $41.50; CPI 260 Coaching Report for Leaders User's Guide; Reusable $41.50; CPI 260 Coaching Report for Leaders Advanced Guide for Interpretation (Reusable) $51.50.

Published Reviews of the Instrument in the Last 15 Years:

Atkinson, M. J. (2003). [California Psychological Inventory, Third Edition.] In B. S. Plake, J. C Impara, and R. A. Spies (Eds.), *The fifteenth mental measurements yearbook* (pp. 159-161). Lincoln, NE: Buros Center for Testing.

Hattrup, K. (2003). [California Psychological Inventory, Third Edition.] In B. S. Plake, J.C . Impara, and R. A. Spies (Eds.), *The fifteenth mental measurements yearbook* (pp. 161-163). Lincoln, NE: Buros Center for Testing.

CALIFORNIA PSYCHOLOGICAL INVENTORY, THIRD EDITION
Reviewed By:
Robert C. Chope
Department of Counseling
San Francisco State University

Description

The California Psychological Inventory (CPI 434) is a self-report inventory created to assess everyday folk concepts that people use to describe themselves and the individuals and groups that surround them. The shorter CPI 260, derived from the CPI 434, also provides a self-assessment but additionally offers a coaching report for leaders who have access to the respondent's data. The coaching report presents information on leadership style, leadership strength, and areas where improvements in leadership can be suggested.

The items yield standard scores on three vector scales, the original 20 folk concept scales (everyday common dimensions of personality), and seven special purpose scales (six on the CPI 260). Six of the original 13 special purpose scales have been dropped from all of the protocols, although they can be handscored with scoring keys available in an appendix (see Gough & Bradley, 2005). Interestingly, 171 items of the CPI 434 were taken from the Minnesota Multiphasic Personality Inventory (MMPI; Hathaway & McKinley, 1943) and 158 items are concurrently in use on the MMPI-2 (Butcher, Dahlstrom, Graham, Tellegen, & Kaemmer, 1989).

The profile report offers the vector scales scores, folk scales scores with gender specific and combined gender norms, and the seven special purpose scales scores, all of which are given greater articulation below. The broader narrative report enlarges on the scales scores that are presented graphically in the profile report and in addition, includes 100 California Q-sort items based on Block's (1961) California Q-set. These are offered in nine categories which move from "extremely characteristic or salient" to "extremely uncharacteristic or negatively salient." The configural analysis report contains the five components of the narrative report but adds an interpretation based upon combinations of two or more scales originally conceived by McAllister (1996). There are two types of interpretations, one empirically based and the other more speculative.

The three vector scales, derived from factor analysis, form a cuboid typology reflecting how an individual scores on three dimensions. Vector one is reminiscent of the aged introversion, extroversion orientation (internality/externality), reflecting an orientation toward the interpersonal world, while vector two focuses upon an orientation to authority and social values (norm questioning/norm favoring). Together these two vectors structure four lifestyle quadrants or types, titled Alpha, Beta, Gamma, and Delta. Alphas are productive joiners and good leaders, Betas tend to be more ancillary followers and preservationists, Gammas are social skeptics and social change advocates, while Deltas are self-reflecting innovators. Vector three (self-realization) speaks to an individual's orientation toward self, including self-actualization, ego integration, and potential.

California Psychological Inventory, Third Edition

These dimensional scales are presented first on the different reports as a "classification for type and level" and help to guide further interpretation of the original 20 folk concept scales (i.e., Dominance, Capacity for Status, Sociability, Social Presence, Self-Acceptance, Independence, Empathy, Responsibility, Socialization, Self-Control, Good Impression, Communality, Well-Being, Tolerance, Achievement via Conformance, Achievement via Independence, Intellectual Efficiency, Psychological-Mindedness, Flexibility, Femininity/Masculinity). The 20 folk concept scales are presented in four different classes. The scales have common, easily understood, everyday names and descriptors. Four of the CPI 434 scales were given new names in the CPI 260: Socialization became Social Conformity, Intellectual Efficiency became Conceptual Fluency, Psychological Mindedness became Insightfulness, and Femininity/Masculinity became Sensitivity.

The seven special purpose scales are related to occupational issues (Managerial Potential, Work Orientation, Law Enforcement Orientation) and personal characteristics (Creative Temperament, Leadership Potential, Amicability, and Tough-Mindedness [which was left off the CPI 260]). All appear to be useful in coaching or counseling people with work related issues. The six scales that have been eliminated from the protocols (Baucom Scales for Masculinity and Femininity, Anxiety, Narcissism, Dicken Social Desirability, and Dicken Acquiescence) can be scored with keys made available in the appendix of the manual (Gough & Bradley, 1996/2002).

The test is available online and through paper-and-pencil administrations with mail-in scoring. The CPI 434 is long, but the True/False nature of the items allows for reasonably fast responses to the queries. The reports are well designed, attractive, and easy to understand for any counselor who has training in assessment and descriptive statistics.

Each protocol is reviewed electronically for evidence of invalidity. However, the counselor should look for consistency and the possibility of faking by noting extreme scores on the Good Impression, Communality, and Well-Being scales. Thereafter the protocol can be classified via the cuboidal model and then considerations can be made for the highest and lowest elevations on the 20 folk scales along with the special purpose scales.

Counselors can be well served by following the protocol interpretation with a clinically focused discussion. This may include exploring whether or not the client has realized his or her potential and has a life that is congruent with former expectations, current circumstances, and the data presented in the protocol.

The CPI 434 is not designed for the assessment of psychopathology, although early on research demonstrated that very low scores on the folk scales can demonstrate poor personal adjustment (Higgens-Lee, 1990). The CPI 434 can be a standalone instrument, but it is quite useful in consort with other measures. Both the CPI 434 and 260 have been brought into team building exercises and are effective, practical tools for exploring career and managerial alternatives. The mostly positive, unassuming scale names allow clients to understand themselves while they also look at their lifestyle, relationships, and career choices. Counselors have been known to use the instrument to assist people in fostering better communication.

To aid with interpretation, there are eight illustrative cases in the CPI 434 manual that can guide users. A skilled counselor should be able to integrate the protocol data with clinical information to develop a potent profile of a client. A CPI Practitioners Group for LinkedIn and a comprehensive bibliography of the instrument covering the years 1948-2002 are on the publisher's website.

Technical Considerations

The normative samples are large (3,000 for each gender) but are heavily weighted toward young and well-educated individuals. While there are some data for special populations (e.g., Irish entrepreneurs), there is a lack of data for any multicultural populations.

Reliability and validity data are comparable to other measures of personality. Retest reliability data are presented in 1, 5, and 25-year intervals, useful for demonstrating long-term stability in scale traits but not necessarily useful in demonstrating shorter term changes (Atkinson, 2003). Internal consistency estimates for the vector scales and most of the folk and special scales are above .70.

Extensive criterion-related and construct validity are also presented in the manual supporting the strong validity of empirical scales even when they may be factorially complex. Speaking to the practical orientation of the instrument, there is a robust focus on predictive validity. Construct validity evidence is on the order of .40 to .80 for the folk and vector scales (Atkinson, 2003).

General Utility and Evaluation

The CPI 434 manual provides extensive reference tables for comparative purposes but users may be more pleased with the practical guide to the CPI (McAllister, 1996). However, there are criticisms regarding the lack of construct validity for the instrument and the justifications for the criteria used in developing the folk scales (Hattrup, 2003).

The CPI 434 has been available in one form or another for more than 55 years. It has a well-established track record among clinicians, even with criticisms from researchers concerned about the lack of purity and complexity of some of the scales. Items appear to have an unfortunate middle class bias regarding education and lifestyle and may not feel relevant to a more "wired" generation. The CPI 260 manual does present evidence for the use of that instrument with African Americans and other people of color, although the ethnic samples are comparatively small.

Nevertheless, the inventory has strong representation in the career counseling and coaching arena. It can assist in recruitment, team building, assessing leadership, exploring appropriate employment alternatives, and motivation. The newer CPI 260 was developed to capitalize on the needs of career counselors, coaches, and trainers focusing on strengths and areas for needed improvement and may prove to be more relevant and efficient for training purposes than the CPI 434. A new CPI 260 Configural Report is forthcoming according to the publisher.

References and Additional Resources

Atkinson, M. J. (2003). [California Psychological Inventory, third edition.] In B. S. Plake, J. C Impara, and R. A. Spies (Eds.), *The fifteenth mental measurements yearbook* (pp. 159-161). Lincoln, NE: Buros Center for Testing.

Block, J. (1961). *The Q-sort method in personality assessment and psychiatric research.* Springfield, IL: Charles C. Thomas.

Butcher, J. N., Dahlstrom, W. G., Graham, J. R., Tellegen, A., & Kaemmer, B. (1989). *Manual for the restandardized Minnesota Multiphasic Personality Inventory: MMPI-2. An administrative and interpretative guide.* Minneapolis: University of Minnesota Press.

Gough, H. G., & Bradley, P. B. (1996/2002). *CPI manual* (3rd edition). Mountain View, CA: CPP, Inc.

Gough, H. G., & Bradley, P. B. (2005). *CPI 260 manual.* Mountain View, CA: CPP, Inc.

Hathaway, S. R., & McKinley, J. C. (1943). *Minnesota Multiphasic Personality Inventory.* Minneapolis, MN: University of Minnesota Press.

Hattrup, K. (2003). [California Psychological Inventory, Third Edition.] In B. S. Plake, J. C . Impara, and R. A. Spies (Eds.), *The fifteenth mental measurements yearbook* (pp. 161-163). Lincoln, NE: Buros Center for Testing.

Higgens-Lee, C. (1990). Low scores on the California Psychological Inventory as predictors of psychopathology in alcoholic patients. *Psychological Reports, 67,* 227-232.

McAllister, L. W. (1996). *A practical guide to CPI interpretation* (3rd ed.). Mountain View, CA: CPP, Inc.

CAREER KEY
Lawrence K. Jones

Career Key, Inc.

http://www.careerkey.org
productsupport@careerkey.biz

Target Population: Adolescents, young adults, and adults. The Career Key was written at the sixth-grade reading level and is intended for use with middle school, high school, and two- and four-year college students and adults in the United States and Canada.

Statement of the Purpose of the Instrument: The Career Key is a self-administered test designed to measure the six Holland personality types and link the results to matching career clusters/pathways, careers, college majors, or training programs. It provides information about each option — to assist individuals make good career and educational decisions.

Titles of Subtests, Scales, Scores Provided: Enterprising, Social, Artistic, Realistic, Investigative, and Conventional. Raw scores have a potential range of 0 to 22.

Forms and Levels Available, with Dates of Publication/Revision of Each: Paper-and-pencil and online versions available. Paper-and-pencil version was initially published in 1987 and was most recently revised in 2012 (available in PDF format). The online version was launched in 1997. The occupations used in matching, and their links to the U.S. Department of Labor's Occupational Outlook Handbook (OOH) are continually updated, as are the occupations for the Self-Employment Key (http://www.self-employmentkey.org), and The CareerKey Canada (http://www.careerkey-ca.org) (2012) that are linked to Canadian sources (Working in Canada and the National Occupational Classification service). eBooks: 5 Steps to Choosing the Right Career Cluster, Field or Pathway (2012); Match Up! Your Personality to College Majors (2012); The Career Key Manual (2012); White Papers: Choose a College Major Based on Your Personality (2012); Personality-College Major Match and Student Success: A Guide for Professionals Helping Youth and Adults Who are in College or are College-Bound (2012).

Date of Most Recent Edition of Test Manual, User's Guide, Etc.: The manual is continually updated.

Languages in Which Available: English, Arabic, Chinese, Spanish, Romanian, Korean, Vietnamese, Turkish, and Urdu.

Time:

Actual Test Time: Varies.

Total Administration Time: 10-15 minutes.

Manner in Which Results Are Reported for Individuals: Raw scores.

Machine Scoring: Scored online.

Hand Scoring: Hand scored by counselee for the paper-and-pencil version.

Computer Software Options Available: Mobile phone users are redirected to a mobile version.

Cost of Materials: Due to potential price change since publication date, be sure to check the publisher's website.

Specimen Set: Not available.

Counselee Materials: Paper-and-pencil version: $9.95 each, or 25 for $12.50. The online version can be accessed for $9.95, or for $1.00 each when purchasing 30+ assessments.

Published Reviews of Instrument in the Last 15 Years:

Levinson, E. M., Zeman, H. L., & Ohler, D. L. (2002). A critical evaluation of the web-based version of the Career Key. *The Career Development Quarterly, 51*, 26-35. doi: 10.1002/j.2161-0045.2002.tb00589.x

CAREER KEY

Margaret M. Nauta

Department of Psychology
Illinois State University

Description

The purpose of the Career Key is to assess individuals' resemblance to the Holland (1997) vocational personality types (Realistic, Investigative, Artistic, Social, Enterprising, Conventional [RIASEC]), relate their type(s) to matching occupations/majors, and encourage career exploration. Each RIASEC type is assessed by seven occupations for which respondents rate their interest and four items on which they rate their preferences for activities, perceived competencies, values, and self-perceptions using three-point scales. Raw scores with a potential range from 0 to 22 are generated, with higher scores reflecting a greater resemblance to the type. Scores are strictly ipsative.

All materials for the online version are accessible from its ad-free website, which contains information about career decision making and resources for career exploration. The website is up-to-date and all links were functional. The paper-and-pencil format of the Career Key has clear instructions and is printed with an easily legible font.

Although the scoring for the paper-and-pencil version is straightforward, it may tax those with limited attention skills because in one section of the manual the item responses that need to be summed are interspersed rather than grouped together. The manual summarizes research showing that scoring error rates among high school and college students were low, but supervision of scoring is recommended. A nice feature of the paper version, and one not present with the online version, is that users graph their raw scores on a provided chart, which makes it easy to identify the highest scores and relative differences in strength among them. (Note, however, that guidelines for determining which RIASEC type scores are significantly higher than others based on the standard error of difference are not provided).

Scoring errors are not an issue with the online version because RIASEC raw scores are computer generated. Although users should have no difficulty identifying their highest scores, the RIASEC scores are organized alphabetically rather than graphically or in rank order; the latter would have been preferable.

After completing either the paper-and-pencil or online version, respondents are encouraged to explore occupations (grouped by Holland type and "work group") based on their highest-ranked RIASEC types. Other Career Key materials assist users in identifying majors or training programs that correspond to their personality type(s). The online Career Key is particularly convenient because the occupations users mark as being of interest link directly to resources with career information.

The Career Key's most obvious use is to help those in early stages of career exploration identify training programs or occupations that are congruent with their dominant personality type(s). It is suitable for use with individual clients or for group administrations. It could be used with adults who are contemplating a career change, although its identification of congruent careers based on single-point Holland types may be of limited value. For such adults, tools that use multiple-point codes to narrow users' focus by homing in on occupations that match both their dominant and secondary personality types may be preferable. The Career Key's RIASEC scores could be used to facilitate clients' exploration of materials that use three-point Holland code classifications for environments, but it is not clear from the available psychometric data whether the precision of measurement offered by the Career Key would warrant such a nuanced interpretation. The RIASEC scores can also be used to identify and explore Career Clusters/Pathways, college majors, and postsecondary training programs.

Technical Considerations

The Career Key yields RIASEC type raw scores with no normative comparisons. Norms do not appear in any published literature. The manual describes studies in which the original Career Key used with students at varying grade levels produced RIASEC scores with internal consistency scores ranging from .69 to .92. Internal

A COUNSELOR'S GUIDE TO CAREER ASSESSMENTS INSTRUMENTS

consistency estimates for the most recent version (in either format) are not reported. Among fairly small college-student samples the one- and two-week test-retest reliability coefficients of scores from the current version ranged from .68 to .91 and did not differ significantly for the online vs. paper versions (Buchan, DeAngelis, & Levinson, 2005; Levinson, Zeman, & Ohler, 2002). Reliability estimates for the current version with younger students and adults are not available.

When three-point Holland codes from the original Career Key were compared with those from the Self-Directed Search (SDS) and the Vocational Preference Inventory (VPI), the agreement was in a range described by Holland (1985, p. 85) as "reasonably close matches." The original Career Key's scores also reasonably fit the pattern of relationships expected for Holland's hexagonal model. Limited data are available regarding the validity of scores from the current Career Key, but Levinson et al. (2002) found that correlations between like-named scales on the Career Key and the SDS were .65 or higher, with the exception of Conventional, which was .47. The Career Key and SDS had the same letter in the first position in 72% of cases and the same letter in the second position in 37% of cases.

General Utility and Evaluation

The manual is easy to read and efficiently summarizes available research on the Career Key. Users should note, however, that most of the data were obtained using the longer, original version of the Career Key. Little attention to diversity is given in the manual and materials. This may be of less concern than if scores were norm-referenced, but more information about the Career Key's development samples would be ideal.

Arguably, the most well-developed part of the Career Key is its website and ancillary materials. Both effectively place interest/personality type assessment in context and link to a wealth of information about careers and college majors. Some interpretive materials are tailored to particular client groups (e.g., students interested in using their scores to explore green or military careers).

The primary appeal of the Career Key for many users will be its brevity and convenience, particularly that of the online version. When bulk purchases are made, the low cost also holds appeal. Finally, the assessment tool is embedded within materials that explain the scores in user-friendly language and offer recommendations for next steps in career exploration.

Until more data regarding the current Career Key's psychometric properties are available, counselors may want to use caution when using the Career Key for any purpose other than to make recommendations for additional exploration. Buchan et al. (2005) and Levinson et al. (2002), however, noted the available data suggest the scores are stable over short time periods and, with the possible exception of the Conventional subscale, may have adequate validity for other purposes. Additional psychometric data derived from broader samples would help counselors make better-informed decisions about the Career Key's utility with diverse client groups.

Overall the Career Key lacks the visual sophistication and degree of empirical scrutiny of some competitors. However, if additional evidence for its reliability and validity with diverse groups become available, the Career Key's brevity, cost, and ancillary materials make it appealing as a tool for stimulating exploration among groups of users who are in early stages of career decision-making.

The Career Key is innovative in that it was among the first online career-interest inventories and was, initially, free of charge. Although it is no longer a no-cost assessment tool, a portion of sales are donated by the publisher to charitable organizations.

References and Additional Resources

Buchan, B. D., DeAngelis, D. L., & Levinson, E. M. (2005). A comparison of the web-based and paper-and-pencil versions of the Career Key interest inventory with a sample of university women. *Journal of Employment Counseling, 42,* 39-46. doi: 10.1002/j.2161-1920.2005.tb00897.x

Career Key Inc. (n.d.). *Career Key manual.* Retrieved from http://www.careerkey.org

Holland, J. L. (1985). *Making vocational choices: A theory of vocational personalities and work environments.* Englewood Cliffs, NJ: Prentice Hall.

Holland, J. L. (1997). *Making vocational choices: A theory of vocational personalities and work environments* (3rd ed.). Odessa, FL: Psychological Assessment Resources.

Jones, L. K. (2012). *The Career Key.* Retrieved from http://www.careerkey.org/

Levinson, E. M., Zeman, H. L., & Ohler, D. L. (2002). A critical evaluation of the web-based version of the Career Key. *The Career Development Quarterly, 51,* 26-35. doi: 10.1002/j.2161-0045.2002.tb00589.x

A Counselor's Guide To Career Assessments Instruments

Clifton StrengthsFinder or StrengthsFinder 2.0
Tom Rath

Gallup Organization
1001 Gallup Drive
Omaha, NE 68102
http://www.strengthsfinder.com

Target Population: Adolescents, young adults, and adults. Grade 10 reading level. The instrument is modifiable for individuals with disabilities, including those with visual impairments. The StrengthsExplorer, available for those ages 10-14, is not included in this review.

Statement of the Purpose of the Instrument: Since the development of the Clifton StrengthsFinder (CSF), the tool has been used primarily by consultants in the workplace to promote employee development and associated productivity. In the last few years, with the development of StrengthsQuest (Clifton & Anderson, 2002; Clifton, Anderson, & Schreiner, 2006), a set of guidance tools designed to help college students use their strengths to pursue their academic and social goals, the CSF has been administered on more than 200 campuses. The web-based talent assessment tool measures a person's talent within 34 themes that are indicative of success.

Titles of Subtests, Scales, Scores Provided: The 34 talent themes are the following: Achiever, Activator, Adaptability, Analytical, Arranger, Belief, Command, Communication, Competition, Connectedness, Consistency, Context, Deliberative, Developer, Discipline, Empathy, Focus, Futuristic, Harmony, Ideation, Includer, Individualization, Input, Intellection, Learner, Maximizer, Positivity, Relator, Responsibility, Restorative, Self-Assurance, Significance, Strategic, and Woo. Top five talent themes are identified without raw or normative data.

Forms and Levels Available, with Dates of Publication/Revision of Each: 2007.

Date of Most Recent Edition of Test Manual, User's Guide, Etc.: 2007.

Languages in Which Available: 24 languages including Dutch, German, Arabic, Swedish, Thai, Japanese, Korean, Italian, Portuguese, Bulgarian, English, Spanish (Latin American), Spanish (Spain), French, Hebrew, Polish, Romanian, etc.

Time:

    Actual Test Time: 30-45 minutes.

    Total Administration Time: 30-45 minutes.

Norm Group(s) on Which Scores Are Based: Score report is based on the relative intensity ratings and a proprietary scoring formula.

Manner in Which Results Are Reported for Individuals: Summary scores are not given. Instead a report listing the individual's top five talent ("signature") themes based on intensity are provided along with "action items" for each theme. The individual may request a full list of all 34 themes, but this must be done through a personal feedback session with a Gallup consultant.

Report Format/Content for Group Summaries: Not available.

Machine Scoring: Not available.

Hand Scoring: Not available.

Local Machine Scoring: Not available.

Computer Software Options Available: Standard administration online.

377

Cost of Materials: Due to possible price changes since publication date, be sure to check the publisher's website. The CSF is only available in an online version requiring the participant to purchase the book (Rath, 2007) to obtain an access code. The book costs approximately $15.00. (Note: used versions of the book may lack a usable access code, negating the usefulness of the purchase). Use of the access code to take the test provides access to the assessment and establishes a personal account which stores results and provides access to other website-based resources.

Specimen Set: Not available.

Counselee Materials: Book (Rath, 2007) and access code. StrengthsQuest: Discover and Develop Your Strengths in Academics, Career, and Beyond (Clifton, Anderson, & Schrein, 2006).

Published Reviews of the Instrument in the Last 15 Years:

Clifton, D. O., Anderson, C. E. & Schreiner, L. A. (2006). *Strengths Quest: Discover and develop your strengths in academics, career, and beyond (2nd ed.). NY, NY:* Gallup Press.

Lopez, S. J., Hodges, T., & Harter, J. (2005). *Clifton StrengthsFinder technical report: Development and Validation.* Omaha, NE: Gallup Press.

Lopez, S. J., & Tree, H. A. (2009). [Clifton StrengthsFinder or StrengthsFinder 2.0.] In E. A. Whitfield, R. W. Feller, & C. Wood (Eds.), *A counselor's guide to career assessment instruments* (5th ed., pp. 388-394). Broken Arrow, OK: National Career Development Association.

Clifton StrengthsFinder or StrengthsFinder 2.0

Reviewed by:

Mike Hauser

Private Practice
Chattanooga, Tennessee

Katie Hillis

School of Education
University of Tennessee at Chattanooga

Description

The Clifton Strengthsfinder or StrengthsFinder 2.0 (CSF) purports to identify innate talents ("signature strengths" is used interchangeably with "talents") the individual can then use to initiate a strengths-based personal growth process. This approach is conceptually based on positive psychology principles (Lopez, 2009; Seligman & Csikszentmihalyi, 2000). The assessment and related materials are primarily used in occupational and academic settings. It is not designed or intended to be used for employment decisions, clinical assessments, or the formation of any mental health diagnoses.

The assessment is comprised of 177 paired descriptors. Each question presents a pair of self-descriptive phrases configured in a scale that represents the poles of a continuum. The participant chooses the phrase that he or she thinks best describes him- or herself, and then indicates the magnitude of that representation. Upon completion the participant is directed to the publisher's website. On the website, each participant is provided their personal results, with links to reports and related resources. The participant's top five signature strengths are presented in rank order. Clifton hypothesized that these talents were "naturally recurring patterns of thought, feeling, or behavior that can be productively applied" (Hodges & Clifton, 2004).

Descriptions of all 34 talents can be found in the book and the website. The online reports consist of one-page summaries of strengths, quotes from people who share those strengths, and some broad suggestions for what to do next. The Resources section provides worksheets for comparing strengths as well as a link to Strengths Consulting.

The Strengths Insight and Action-Planning Guide is the document that presents results. Although strengths are ranked, there is no information concerning the magnitude of the rankings, nor is there any explanation of how your strengths interact with one another. In an assessment that chooses five strengths out of 34 possibilities, it would be valuable to know how strongly each strength was endorsed. Gallup suggests that participants use a standardized checklist to begin capitalizing on signature strengths. For more personalized information, a private consultation with a Gallup consultant can be scheduled ($550.00 per hour).

The format of questions, although straightforward, can make it difficult to choose an answer. Descriptors are not necessarily opposites, so it is possible to believe strongly in each extreme of the continuum. A participant cannot indicate strong agreement with both poles as the test formats central choice is "neutral." The test moves quickly considering the number of items and the limited response time. Each access code can only be used once; a counselor who wants to assess multiple participants would have to purchase one book per client.

The CSF can be used in counseling to identify a client's personal strengths for career counseling purposes. Discussion of strengths may help clients gain insight and clarify their career goals and values. Results provide insight into current levels of job satisfaction and pathways for improvement. The CSF may also be used to understand and improve group dynamics in an organization. Discussion questions are provided for use in both organizations and families, while a matrix allows team members to share their strengths. These resources provide management with information useful for personnel decisions and enhancing team effectiveness.

Technical Considerations

Revision of the original CSF was based on more than one million cases that completed the original tool. Gallup (Asplund, Lopez, Hodges, & Harter, 2009) reports that more than 3.9 million, worldwide, have completed the original CSF. There is no demographic information provided for this sample.

The Technical Report describing the development and validation of the latest CSF lacks clear or concise information regarding reliability and validity. A large portion of the cited information was authored by individuals who are employees of the Gallup Organization. The preponderance of information used in the report to describe the validity and reliability of the instrument (Asplund et al., 2009) pertain to the first instrument.

There is no manual for this instrument per se; however, the Technical Report (Asplund et al., 2009) was used for the purpose of this review. The reliability information seems to support the claim of consistent reliability performance. Table 1 provides the internal consistency reliability information.

Table 1.

Internal Consistency Reliability Statistics of the 34 CSF 2.0 Themes

	Min.	Max.	Mean	Std. Dev.
Alpha (n = 46,902)	.52	.79	.68	.07
Alpha-Retest (n = 2,219)	.55	.78	.68	.06

Data taken from Asplund et al., 2009.

Sheperis, Young, and Daniels (2010) stated that, "Correlation values higher than .80 are considered as satisfactory or good" (p. 219). The one-month retest interval reveals that four of the 34 themes reached .80; at three months, three themes reached .80; and at six months only one of the test-retest values reached .80; with the mean score of all 34 themes reaching .70 at one month, .70 at three months, and .67 at the six months test-retest interval. Test-retest reliability data are presented in Table 2.

Table 2.

Test-retest Reliability Statistics of the 34 CSF 2.0 Themes

	Min.	Max.	Mean	Std. Dev.
Retest at 1-month	.53	.81	.70	.07
Retest at 3-months	.50	.82	.70	.07
Retest at 6-months	.48	.80	.67	.08

Data taken from Asplund et al., 2009.

The authors of the Technical Report (Asplund et al., 2009) stated that, "from a validity standpoint, the CSF looks very strong" and "Studies have produced evidence of congruence with the Big Five (Harter & Hodges, 2003), 16PF (Schreiner, 2006), and CPITM (Schreiner, 2006)" (p. 14). All supporting references refer to the original version of the instrument. Although there is a strong resemblance to the first version, version two has been modified such that it cannot be assumed that the validity and reliability data are identical. With that said, there is a paucity of information offered with which to make a conclusion regarding the validity of the CSF.

General Utility and Evaluation

The Technical Report, serving as the only manual available for the CSF, is lacking in many ways. The report is also lacking in administrative and interpretive information. The participant who has taken the online test is offered no further guidance on how to use the results. The participant can return to the book (Rath, 2007) and read the "Ideas for Action" associated with each theme. The "Ideas for Action" are brief bulleted comments offering some suggestions for maximizing the participant's talents. The Technical Report is lacking in details regarding validity and reliability information, especially in regards to the newest edition of the instrument. It would be difficult to defend the value of this instrument from the information available in the Technical Report.

The assumption of the CSF is that learning your strengths can be used to create lasting change. While clients do learn their strengths, they may walk away with questions about how to capitalize on them. The affordability of the assessment may be misleading to clients who want to implement their results, since this may require the assistance of either a Gallup specialist or a career counselor.

The publisher's website offers supporting resources. Nearly half of these documents present verbatim information from the book. Unique resources include a Certificate Generator, a Strengths Screensaver, and Guides for Strengths-Based Discussions in Organizations and at Home.

References and Additional Resources

Asplund, J., Lopez, S. J., Hodges, T., & Harter, J. (2009). *The Clifton StrengthsFinder 2.0 technical report: Development and validation.* Omaha, NE: Gallup Press.

Clifton, D. O., Anderson, C. E. & Schreiner, L. A. (2006). *Strengths Quest: Discover and develop your strengths in academics, career, and beyond (2nd ed.).* New York, NY: Gallup Press.

Hodges, T. D., & Clifton, D. O. (2004). Strengths-based development in practice. In P. A. Linley & S. Joseph (Eds.), *Positive psychology in practice* (pp. 256-268). Hoboken, NJ: Wiley & Sons.

Lopez, S. J. (2009). *Encyclopedia of positive psychology.* Malden, MA: Wiley-Blackwell.

Lopez, S. J., & Tree, H. A. (2009). [Clifton StrengthsFinder or StrengthsFinder 2.0.] In E. A. Whitfield, R. W. Feller, & C. Wood (Eds.), *A counselor's guide to career assessment instruments* (5th ed., pp. 388-394). Broken Arrow, OK: National Career Development Association.

Rath, T. (2007). *StrengthsFinder 2.0.* New York, NY: Gallup Press.

Seligman, M. E. P., & Csikszentmihalyi, M. (2000). Positive psychology: An introduction. *American Psychologist, 55,* 5-14. doi: 10.1037/0003-066X.55.1.5

Sheperis, C., Young, J. S., & Daniels, M. H. (2010). *Counseling research: Quantitative, qualitative, and mixed methods.* Boston, MA: Pearson.

Harter, J. K., & Hodges, T. D. (2003) *Construct validity study: StrengthsFinder and the Five Factor Model* [technical report]. Omaha, NE: Gallup Press.

Schreiner, L. A. (2006). *A technical report on the Clifton StrengthsFinder with college students.* Retrieved from https://www.strengthsquest.com/Content/?CI=25195

A Counselor's Guide To Career Assessments Instruments

Jackson Personality Inventory–Revised
Douglas N. Jackson

SIGMA Assessment Systems, Inc.

P.O. Box 610984
Port Huron, MI 48061-0984
http://www.sigmaassessmentsystems.com

Target Population: Adolescents, young adults, and adults; age 16 and older. Useful in schools, colleges, university counseling services, employment offices and agencies, business and industry, vocational rehabilitation, and adult counseling centers.

Statement of the Purpose of the Instrument: The Jackson Personality Inventory–Revised (JPI-R) is the second edition of a test designed to measure personality functioning for use in schools, universities, and industry.

Titles of Subtests, Scales, Scores Provided: The instrument measures 15 bipolar scales that are organized into five conceptually integrated clusters termed Analytical (A), Emotional (E), Extroverted (Ex), Opportunistic (O), and Dependable (D). The 15 scales are as follows: Complexity (A), Breadth of Interest (A), Innovation (A), Tolerance (A), Empathy (E), Anxiety (E), Cooperativeness (E), Sociability (Ex), Social Confidence (Ex), Energy Level (Ex), Social Astuteness (O), Risk Taking (O), Organization (D), Traditional Values (D), and Responsibility (D). Scores are provided for individual scales as well as the five clusters.

Forms and Levels Available, with Dates of Publication/Revision of Each: 1994. Original instrument was developed in 1975.

Date of Most Recent Edition of Test Manual, User's Guide, Etc.: 1994.

Languages in Which Available: English and French.

Time:

Actual Test Time: 35-45 minutes.

Total Administration Time: 45 minutes.

Norm Group(s) on Which Scores Are Based: Norms include the responses of 1,107 individuals (367 males and 740 females) drawn from educational institutions in North America. A second set of norms is based on the responses of 893 (629 male and 264 female) blue-collar workers. A third set of norms is derived from the responses of 555 senior executives. These sets of norms are representative of scale scores from three relatively large and unique segments of the population.

Manner in Which Results Are Reported for Individuals: Raw scores, percentiles. The JPI-R Basic Report consists of a profile of the 15 JPI-R scale scores, description of high and low scores for each scale, a profile of the five JPI-R cluster scores, administrative indices and a table of raw responses. The JPI-R is also available for administration online at http://www.sigmatesting.com, through hand scoring, mail-in service, and software scoring.

Report Format/Content for Group Summaries: Not available.

Machine Scoring: Mail-in scoring service costs are as follows for basic reports: 1 report: $13.00; 1-3 packages (10 reports per package): $75.00; 4+ packages (10 reports per package): $65.00. Time required for scoring and returning is 48 hours, excluding mail time. Internet scoring per administration are priced as follows: 1-9: $20.00; 10-24: $15.00; 25-99: $14.00; and 100+: $12.00.

Hand Scoring: Hand scored by counselor or clerk in approximately 10 minutes.

Local Machine Scoring: Not available.

Computer Software Options Available: Computerized administration; standardized administration online. SigmaSoft JPI-R for Windows software allows the counselor to administer and score the JPI-R directly on his or her computer. This software also makes it easy to input answers or scale scores from paper-and-pencil administrations and can import data scanned from special forms using an optical mark reader. The JPI-R

381

for Windows software produces the Basic Report and a Data Report. The Data Report contains the scores found in the Basic Report in a format designed for use by other programs. Coupons are required to be able to produce each report: 4 and 2 coupons, respectively.

Ways in Which Computer/Online Version Differs: Computer administration must be done on the computer containing the software; the online version can be completed on any computer with Internet access.

Cost of Materials: Due to possible price changes since publication date, be sure to check the publisher's site.

Specimen Set: Kit includes manual (CD-ROM only), five reusable test booklets, five Quick Score Answer Sheets, five Profile Sheets, one machine scorable answer sheet for a JPI-R Basic Report, and one online password: $95.00. Test manual (CD-ROM only) is available for $24.00.

Counselee Materials: JPI-R reusable test booklets for hand scoring or mail-in service (package of 25): $63.00; JPI-R Quick Score Answer Sheets (package of 25): $77.00; JPI-R Profile Sheets (package of 25): $52.00. SigmaSoft JPI-R for Windows (includes 10 coupons): $150.00. Scoring prices for coupons (software version) are $2.30 each for 1-99 coupons, $2.00 for 100-499 coupons, and $1.75 for 500+ coupons.

Published Reviews of the Instrument in the Last 15 Years:

Pittenger, D. J. (1998). [Jackson Personality Inventory-Revised.] In J.C. Impara & B. S. Plake (Eds.), *Thirteenth mental measurements yearbook.* Lincoln, NE: Buros Center for Testing.

Zachar, P. (1998). [Jackson Personality Inventory-Revised.] In J.C. Impara & B. S. Plake (Eds.), *Thirteenth mental measurements yearbook.* Lincoln, NE: Buros Center for Testing.

Zachar, P. (2009). [Jackson Personality Inventory-Revised.] In E. A. Whitfield, R. W. Feller, & C. Wood (Eds.), *A counselor's guide to career assessment instruments* (5th ed., pp. 395-399). Broken Arrow, OK: National Career Development Association.

JACKSON PERSONALITY INVENTORY–REVISED

Reviewed by:

Peter Zachar

Department of Psychology
Auburn University at Montgomery

Description

The Jackson Personality Inventory–Revised (JPI-R) is the second edition of a test designed to measure personality functioning for use in schools, universities, and industry. The instrument measures 15 bipolar scales that are organized into five conceptually integrated clusters termed Analytical (A), Emotional (E), Extroverted (Ex), Opportunistic (O), and Dependable (D). The 15 scales are as follows: Complexity (A), Breadth of Interest (A), Innovation (A), Tolerance (A), Empathy (E), Anxiety (E), Cooperativeness (E), Sociability (Ex), Social Confidence (Ex), Energy Level (Ex), Social Astuteness (O), Risk Taking (O), Organization (D), Traditional Values (D), and Responsibility (D). Created by Douglas Jackson 1994, a prominent developer of psychological tests, the constructs measured were derived from research in personality and social psychology plus Jackson's professional experience.

The items are readily comprehensible sentences to which an examinee answers *True* or *False*. The scales have 20 items each. Scores on a scale can range from 0 to 20. On each scale, an examinee can earn one point on 10 of the items by answering *True*. On the other 10 items for that scale they have to answer *False* to earn a point. Because of this, an examinee cannot earn a high score because she has a bias to answer *True*, or earn a low score because she has a bias to answer *False*.

The JPI-R is intended for use in counseling and industry, particularly career counseling and team building. The manual specifically discourages drawing inferences about psychiatrically relevant personality traits based on test results. Although an examinee's fit for a wide range of careers might be usefully explored with this test, careers in the business world would be particularly appropriate. Because it is also designed for use by industry

A Counselor's Guide To Career Assessments Instruments

as a selection instrument, the JPI-R lends itself to discussion of personal and career maturity for college-age students. For example, a student low on organization and responsibility may be encouraged to further explore her plans for a managerial career. A student scoring low on extroversion and social astuteness who plans to enter sales may also benefit from a discussion of typical behaviors and criteria for success in his intended field. A test such as this can serve as an impetus for exploration, and is probably more useful in counseling when there is a mismatch between reported dispositions and intended occupation and/or vocational interests. Evidence linking the scales with particular occupations or management styles, however, is lacking.

Administration is easy. Both English and French versions of the test are available. The automated scoring versions are cheaper and less subject to error, but if hand scoring is preferred, the layout of the carbonless forms makes the process simple. The Sigma Assessment Systems website states that the test is appropriate for ages 16 and older, but younger examines would have to be assessed using the college norms.

Technical Considerations

The strengths of Jackson's approach to scale development include high internal consistency, scales that do not overlap with each other, minimization of socially desirable response biases, and efficiency. These features, as expected, can be attributed to the JPI-R. The manual is written for experts in measurement, although some useful administration guidelines are provided early on to make it more user-friendly. One helpful addition is a listing of items by scale in Appendix A. For example, all the items on the complexity scale are presented together. Studying these lists is important for understanding what a scale measures because scale names can be misleading. Users should also study what a scale is correlated with to further understand what it measures. Correlates of the various scales with other instruments are also presented in the manual, although they would be interpretable only to someone who is already familiar with the other instruments.

Gender-specific norms are available for college students, blue collar workers, and business executives. The manual reports Cronbach's alphas for the 15 basic scales. They appear to be reasonably adequate (i.e., most alphas are in the .70s and .80s, but a few were in the .60s). One of the unusual aspects to this test is that it bucks the current trend toward dimensionally pure constructs in favor of more heterogeneous constructs. To assess these broader constructs, the manual reports Bentler's theta coefficient, based on the claim that coefficient alpha underestimates internal consistency when the constructs are not unidimensional. The theta coefficients for all scales were between .75 and .95.

Internal consistency indices are not presented for the five clusters. Given that they were derived from a factor analysis of the basic scales and that they have a larger number of items, these reliability coefficients should be high and their absence is a curious omission. Nor have the cluster been adequately replicated. Their inclusion may be trading on the dubious but popular assumption that a five factor personality structure represents a final carving of nature at its joints. No test-retest correlations were presented in the manual research. Doster et al. (2000) suggested that the 13-week temporal stability of the 15 scales are minimally adequate (r_{xx} = .74 to .89) for all but the responsibility scale (r_{xx} = .63).

Reflecting its emphasis on careers in business, this revised edition of the test eliminates the kinds of questions placed on clinical validity scales that are often experienced by test takers as irrelevant during personnel selection. One of the advantages of the computer-based and web-based version of this test is that they calculate an infrequency score and a response consistency index. Despite the reasons given for eliminating the original JPR infrequency scale (e.g., it shortened the test), assessing profile validity may still be important in career and personnel settings. Unfortunately, these two scales were not validated in a systematic way, and cutoffs for rejecting profiles were not appropriately evaluated.

The manual includes a lengthy discussion of *modal profile* analysis, which is an attempt to derive a typology based on measuring personality dimensions. Ten male personality types and 10 female personality types are presented. Unfortunately, not enough information to actually use a modal profile analysis is provided, nor is its application demonstrated in any meaningful way.

General Utility and Evaluation

Jackson has an excellent reputation among those in the counseling profession. Students should find the test attractive for theses and dissertations. Counselors will be attracted to the non-psychiatric focus, and examinees will find the test easy to take. Its psychometric properties are adequate, but the whole test package is at best partially developed. Although the manual is not written for career counselors, the test is potentially relevant to career counseling and personnel selection. More information about use in specific industries is needed. In relation to the current dominance of tests derived from factor analysis that offer coherent structural models of personality, the constructs in the JPI-R seem to be coddled together in an idiosyncratic way. It would be useful for the publisher to demonstrate what kind of incremental validity this test has relative to the more unidimensional tests related to the five factor model and its various siblings. At present, the claim that this test measures something additional is argued for but not actually demonstrated.

References and Additional Resources

Doster, J. A., Wilcox, S. E., Lambert, P. L., Rubino-Watkins, M. F., Goven, A. J., Moorefield, R., & Kofman, F. (2000). Stability and factor structure of the Jackson Personality Inventory-Revised. *Psychological Reports, 86,* 421-428.

Jackson, D. N. (1994). *Jackson Personality Inventory – Revised Manual.* Sigma Assessment Systems: London, Ontario.

Pittenger, D. J. (1998). [Jackson Personality Inventory-Revised.] In J. C. Impara & B. S. Plake (Eds.), *Thirteenth mental measurements yearbook.* Lincoln, NE: Buros Center for Testing.

Sigma Assessment Systems. (n.d.). *Jackson Personality Inventory-Revised.* Retrieved from http://www.sigmaassessment-systems.com/assessments/jpir.asp

Sigma Assessment Systems. (n.d.) *JPI-R sample report.* Retrieved from http://www.sigmaassessmentsystems.com/samplereports/jpirreport.pdf

Zachar, P. (1998). [Jackson Personality Inventory-Revised.] In J. C. Impara & B. S. Plake (Eds.), *Thirteenth mental measurements yearbook.* Lincoln, NE: Buros Center for Testing.

Zachar, P. (2009). [Jackson Personality Inventory-Revised.] In E. A. Whitfield, R. W. Feller, & C. Wood (Eds.), *A counselor's guide to career assessment instruments* (5th ed., pp. 395-399). Broken Arrow, OK: National Career Development Association.

A COUNSELOR'S GUIDE TO CAREER ASSESSMENTS INSTRUMENTS

MYERS-BRIGGS TYPE INDICATOR
Isabel Briggs Myers and Katharine Cook Briggs

Consulting Psychologists Press (CPP), Inc.
1055 Joaquin Road, 2nd Floor
Mountain View, CA 94043
http://www.cpp.com

Target Population: Adolescents, young adults, and adults; ages 14 and older; seventh-grade reading level.

Statement of the Purpose of the Instrument: The Myers-Briggs Type Indicator (MBTI) instrument is a questionnaire designed to make Jung's ideas about psychological type useful in everyday life. It identifies a person's four basic type preferences that combine into one of 16 different personality types. These results help you understand normal differences in the way people think, communicate, and interact—differences that can be the source of much misunderstanding. The MBTI has been used for more than 70 years to establish greater understanding between individuals, and has been translated into more than 21 different languages for use around the world.

Titles of Four Pairs of Opposite Preferences Known as Dichotomies: Extraversion (E) and Introversion (I), Sensing (S) and Intuition (N), Thinking (T) and Feeling (F), Judging (J) and Perceiving (P). Additional "Facets" are provided via Form Q of the assessment (5 facets for each dichotomy, 20 facets in total).

Forms and Levels Available, with Dates of Publication/Revision of Each: 1998.

MBTI Complete: based on Form M and includes an interactive interpretive session online that provides verified type.

Form M: Profile, Interpretive Report, Interpretive Report for Organizations, Team Report, Career Report, Work Styles Report.

Form Q: Profile, Interpretive Report.

Combined: Newly revised Strong and MBTI Career Report, Leadership Report Using Firo-B & MBTI, Strong and MBTI Career Report.

Forms F, G, J, and K are out of print.

Date of Most Recent Edition of Assessment Manual, User's Guide, Etc.: 2011.

Languages in Which Available: The MBTI assessment is available in a many languages including English, Spanish, German, French, Dutch, Italian, Arabic, Korean, Portuguese, Danish, Norwegian, Chinese, Swedish, Russian, and more. To see the most current list, visit the publisher's website.

Time:

Actual Test Time: Varies.

Total Administration Time: 25-90 minutes depending on MBTI Form and delivery mechanism and pace of test taker.

Norm Group(s) on Which Results Are Based: The MBTI is normed on 3,009 adults 18 years and older, comprising diversity in age, gender, and racial/ethnic group. Demographics match the 1990 U.S. Census percentages.

Manner in Which Results Are Delivered: MBTI assessment results are delivered in a variety of ways including the utilization of the online, software and paper formats. A wide array of reports is available as well. To view the latest selection of samples, visit the publisher's website.

Cost of Materials: Check the publisher's website or call 800.624.1765 (CPP Customer Service).

Published Reviews of the Instrument in the Last 15 Years:

Mastrangelo, P. M. (2001). [Myers-Briggs Type Indicator, Form M]. In B. S. Plake & J. C. Impara (Eds.), *The fourteenth mental measurements yearbook.* Lincoln, NE: Buros Center for Testing.

Mastrangelo, P. M. (2009). [Myers-Briggs Type Indicator]. In E. A. Whitfield, R. W. Feller, & C. Wood (Ed.), *A counselor's guide to career assessment instruments* (5th ed., pp. 400-406). Broken Arrow, OK: National Career Development Association.

MYERS-BRIGGS TYPE INDICATOR

Reviewed by:

Amanda C. La Guardia

Department of Educational Leadership and Counseling
Sam Houston State University

Description

The Myers-Briggs Type Indicator (MBTI) was first published in 1962 after being developed during World War II (Form A copyrighted in 1943) by Isabel Briggs Myers and her mother Katharine Briggs. The construct of the instrument was developed utilizing the published works of C. G. Jung following its translation into English in 1923, in which his theory of psychological types was described. Myers and Briggs were fascinated by the typologies and thought they might be useful in assisting people searching for jobs to find areas of work congruent with their interests and attitudes. During the 1950s, the norming population for the original version included medical students and high school students to assist in determining the predictive value of the inventory for specialty selection and, for the high school students, aptitude and grades (McCaulley, 1990).

Since its original release, several forms and revisions have taken place reflective of the continuous research conducted on its efficacy. Between 1988 and 1997, four forms of the inventory were available, and currently it is one of the most frequently used personality inventories in the world. Form M, which reflects a revision released in 1998, consists of 93 items and is available in three report versions (complete, profile, and self-scored) and typically takes approximately 45 minutes to complete. Form Q, released in 2001, is designed to build on results from the Step I Form M by exploring 20 facets associated with the four-letter type results; consisting of an additional 51-items (Briggs Myers, McCaulley, Quenk, & Hammer, 2009). The MBTI evaluates four pairs of opposite personality typologies, referred to as *dichotomies,* resulting in a four-letter personality profile. Personality preferences include *introversion* or *extraversion, sensing* or *intuition, thinking* or *feeling,* and finally *judging* or *perceiving* yielding 16 possible types. Further, Form Q evaluates five facets within each dichotomy to provide more specific results regarding personality preferences and individual behavior. The items presented to the counselee are worded simplistically, are brief, and easily understood with dichotomous agreement/disagreement response choices (Mastrangelo, 2009).

As the MBTI is used by organizations, individuals, and counselors to help determine career and business decisions, a revision of the scale was completed in 1998 to update item wording and scoring to improve the accuracy of results (Briggs Myers et al., 2009). The goal of the assessment is to provide people with an accessible way to utilize and apply Jungian type theory so that individuals and groups can better understand how each of us relates to the world and how our way of relating affects career choice and performance. By providing respondents with a forced-choice question related to one of the four dichotomous categories, the MBTI reveals preference in relation to the specified index being assessed rather than evaluating a deficit of a personality trait (i.e., having less *extraversion* and more *introversion*). According to Briggs Myers et al. (2009), each of the four categories assessed by the MBTI are theorized to interact with one another in unique ways leading to the character descriptions possible once the assessment is complete. In essence, the inventory assesses the way people perceive the world around them and how those perceptions lead to decisions and conclusions regarding behavior, ideas, and attitude (Myers, 1980).

The most recent versions of the MBTI use item response theory (IRT) as the scoring methodology. Due to the computational demands of this method, it has only come into recent use since the advent of computer scoring (Harvey & Hammer, n.d.). The hand-scored version of the assessment does not use IRT to determine dichotomous personality trait placement since computer evaluation is not available; rather it employs unit weighting of items to achieve results. A complete version of the form is available that includes questions to assist respondents in better understanding their personality traits. This version takes 60-90 minutes to complete and is intended for those who wish to obtain additional descriptive information regarding their best-fit typology.

When scoring, one will notice that the Form M item breakdown includes 21 items for the Extraversion-Introversion scale, 26 items for the Sensing-Intuition scale, 24 items for the Thinking-Feeling scale, and 22 items for the Judging-Perceiving scale for a total of 93 scale items. Item preference is described in neutral or positive terms so each dichotomy is portrayed as equally acceptable to respondents. Each preference category includes a clarity score interpretation based on raw points, including levels of slight, moderate, clear, and very clear. The reasoning for providing these levels is to help those interpreting scores with clients to emphasize the direction of the preference rather than competence, maturity, or preference proficiency (Briggs Myers et al., 2009). Scoring for the MBTI typically takes approximately 10 minutes for the administrator. Analysis and review of the results may take longer depending on the needs of the client; however, the simplistic format of the results (i.e., a four letter score) allows for ease in understanding and memorability.

The Form Q was developed using the same item theory base as the Form M; however, due to the decreased number of items associated with each of the 20 facets available, determining a scoring mid-point is more problematic. Therefore, according to Quenk, Hammer, and Majors (2001), the intention of the Step II assessment is to "give insight into an individual's distinctive ways of expressing type" and "patterns of facet scores within dichotomies may reflect the ways in which less preferred aspects of personality are expressed" (p. 7). The goal of both forms is to provide both a nomothetic and ideothetic approach to understanding personality. This approach means that the inventories seek to predict behavior using a general knowledge base related to the larger population regarding typologies (nomothetic) as well as evaluating individual differences in relation to the general typologies (ideothetic) to assist in situational behavior prediction. In addition to the Step I and Step II assessments, there is a third step that includes an additional seven comfort-discomfort scales.

With regard to counseling, the underlying premise that all types are equally valued lends itself to the strengths-based approach inherent to the counseling philosophy. All items are framed as neutral or positive in order to promote this perspective through the instrument, therefore, the language used is affirming of client typology and individuality. When using the instrument, a counselor can empower clients by focusing on the strengths inherent to their unique four-letter typology in order to assist in motivating clients toward achieving their stated goals while facilitating self-awareness. Further, to assist counselors in the conceptualization of client issues, the MBTI manual provides information regarding typical behaviors associated with each of the eight preference areas in an attempt to assist practitioners to encourage clients based on client preferences for interacting with the world around them. The MBTI may be useful for individual, career-oriented, family, and even couples counseling for the purposes of increasing personal insight, decision making, and improving relational communication. In working with younger clients, it is important to note that typologies can change over the lifespan and younger clients may not be as clear about their preferences; therefore, MBTI characteristics should not be thought of as stagnant or permanent. However, with older clients, the four-letter typologies can be somewhat stable depending on the degree to which a person identifies with a particular preference area.

As with all assessment instruments, the environment in which the client took the inventory as well as her or his mental state at the time should be considered when making interpretations. The inventory may not be useful for all clients, so counselors should use their clinical judgment when making decisions regarding the possible utility of the MBTI. It is recommended that counselors administer the inventory on site when the option is available to provide a somewhat controlled and common setting for test taking; i.e., an environment in which the counselor is familiar so as to make more appropriate interpretations. Timing is also a factor, as clients with shortened attention spans may have difficulty completing the inventory and may need breaks – especially if Form Q is used. Counselors should take their clients attention span into consideration when deciding which form of the MBTI would be of most use to their clients.

Technical Considerations

In developing Form M, a national sample of adults over the age of 18 was pooled with the goal of achieving a sample that matched 1990 U.S. Census data on gender and ethnicity. There were about 3,000 respondents with White females being over-represented and Black males being under-represented. Although the category of "Hispanic" was included in the ethnic identity demographics, those responding positively to this category were equally distributed among the categories of "White" and "Black". Breakdown of gender and ethnicity closely matched census data in the final national representative sample used for Form M item analysis.

With regard to reliability as reported in the MBTI manual (Briggs, Myers et al., 2009), Form M shows improvement over previously constructed forms. Split half reliabilities range from .89-.94 using a Spearman-Brown formula with logical and consecutive procedures. Internal consistency ranged from .89-.94 for all age groups, with alphas consistently at .90 or above for ages ranging from 22 to 70. For African-Americans from the national sample, alphas ranged from .84 to .91 for the four dichotomous areas and .87 to .91 for those identifying as Latino(a)/Hispanic. From the national sample, internal consistency ranged from .88 to.92 for females and .90 to .93 for males. Test-retest reliabilities for Form M are generally higher than the previous Form G. Form M was tested at a four-week interval, with coefficients ranging from .83 to .97 for the four dichotomous typologies from three independent samples.

As reported in the manual, a confirmatory factor analysis using the national sample for Form M revealed the adjusted goodness of fit to be .949 and the non-normed fit index to be .967 with median fitted residuals at 0.008 "indicating an excellent fit to the four-factor model" (p. 173). Correlations exist between the MBTI preference scales and a variety of other similar scales serve to support the convergent validity of the four preference scale areas (for instance, the "Big Five" personality domains—Extraversion with E/I). With regard to the Form M "evidence has been accumulated to address the question of the validity of whole types and of type dynamics theory" in that "there are characteristics of whole types that are not predictable from knowledge of the individual preferences alone or from simple additive models of the preferences" (p. 219).

As the items presented tend to be vaguely worded to allow for a simplistic understanding of the concept being described, it is possible that individuals with differing personality characteristics could find themselves agreeing highly with similar items due to the positive description of the item. This common agreement issue could influence the predictive validity of the instrument as a whole. Therefore, it has been suggested that the MBTI be used as a processing tool to help create insight about preferences with regard to work and relationship building. It should not be used as a tool to predict what type of job or environment would be best suited for the client based on the typological result.

General Utility and Evaluation

The MBTI assessment is a widely used and popular assessment tool in a variety of counseling settings, specifically with regard to career exploration, choice, and development. According to the MBTI Career Report, occupational lists associated with the assessment were derived from more than 92,000 adults who were employed at the time of development who also reported as being satisfied with their job. The database used to assess possible career placement included more than 22 job families and 282 specific professions. While the MBTI may be useful in helping individuals find work that is meaningful to them, it is not intended to delineate concrete career areas for clients. Rather, the instrument is intended to provide information regarding areas that might be most congruent with client characteristic preferences with the knowledge that individuals have access to all eight preference areas. An improved career report has been developed for Form M to assist in use with a broader range of clients and to improve the ease of interpretation for practitioners. Modification to this effect can be found in the MBTI Career Report User's Guide. While the MBTI is a useful assessment tool, it should not be used in isolation and the inclusion of at least one additional assessment tool, especially with regard to career counseling, has been recommended by critiques of the instrument. As with any assessment process, a variety of formal and informal methods are important when assisting clients in making decisions regarding future goals, career or otherwise.

The manual has a chapter specifically developed for career assessment, and includes some general evaluations and analyses related to how each typology may perform in different work settings. As "occupational trends do not seem to vary across all 16 types" and only vary with regard to the J-P subscale, the holistic use of the

MBTI for career counseling is questionable (Mastrangelo, 1990, p. 403). While the MBTI has been translated into a variety of other languages, its cultural versatility has not been extensively researched. Little information exists as to whether it is useful with regard to considerations of multiculturalism and diversity of experience. The manual presents information related to common results for males and females and individuals from different ethnic backgrounds within the United States and internationally.

References and Additional Resources

Briggs Myers, I., McCaulley, M. H., Quenk, N. L., & Hammer, A. L. (2009). *MBTI manual: A guide to the development and use of the Myers-Briggs type indicator instrument* (3rd ed.). Mountain View, CA: CPP, Inc.

Hammer, A. L. (2005). *MBTI career report: User's guide.* Mountain View, CA: CPP, Inc.

Harvey, R. J., & Hammer, A. L. (n.d.). *Item response theory.* Retrieved from http://harvey.psyc.vt.edu/Documents/TCP_IRT98.pdf

Mastrangelo, P. M. (2009). [Myers-Briggs Type Indicator-Form M] In E.A. Whitfield, R.W. Feller, & C. Wood, *A counselor's guide to career assessment instruments* (5th ed., pp. 400-406). Broken Arrow, OK: National Career Development Association.

Mastrangelo, P. M. (2001). [Myers-Briggs Type Indicator, Form M]. In B. S. Plake & J. C. Impara (Eds.), *The fourteenth mental measurements yearbook.* Lincoln, NE: Buros Center for Testing.

Mastrangelo, P. M. (2009). [Myers-Briggs Type Indicator]. In E. A. Whitfield, R. W. Feller, & C. Wood (Ed.), *A counselor's guide to career assessment instruments* (5th ed., pp. 400-406). Broken Arrow, OK: National Career Development Association.

McCaulley, M. H. (1990). The Myers-Briggs type indicator: A measure for individuals and groups. *Measurement & Evaluation in Counseling & Development, 22*(4), 181-191.

Myers, I. B. (1980). *Gifts differing.* Palo Alto, CA: CPP, Inc.

Schaubhut, N. A., & Thompson, R. C. (2011). *MBTI step II: Manual supplement.* Retrieved from https://www.cpp.com/Pdfs/MBTI_StepII_Man_Supp.pdf

Quenk, N. L., Hammer, A. L., & Majors, M. S. (2001). *MBTI step II manual: Exploring the next level of the type within the Myers-Briggs type indicator form Q.* Mountain View, CA: CPP, Inc.

NEO PERSONALITY INVENTORY-3
Paul T. Costa and Robert R. McCrae

Psychological Assessment Resources, Inc.

16204 N. Florida Avenue
Lutz, FL 33549
http://www.parinc.com
http://www.sigmatesting.com

Target Population: Adolescents, young adults, and adults; ages 12 and older. The NEO Personality Inventory-3 (NEO PI-3) can be administered in individual or group settings.

Statement of the Purpose of the Instrument: According to the NEO-PI-3 manual, "The inventories are concise measures of the five major dimensions, or domains, of personality and the most important traits or facets that define each domain. Together, the five broad domain scales and the 30 specific facet scales allow a comprehensive assessment of adolescent and adult personality" (McCrae & Costa, 2010, p. 1).

A new feature that might be of interest to career development professionals is the NEO Job Profiler, a tool that identifies personality traits that clients can use to explore an occupation or career interest area.

Titles of Subtests, Scales, Scores Provided: Neuroticism, Anxiety, Angry Hostility, Depression, Self-Consciousness, Impulsiveness, Vulnerability, Extraversion, Warmth, Gregariousness, Assertiveness, Activity, Excitement-Seeking, Positive Emotions, Openness; Fantasy, Aesthetics; Feelings, Actions, Ideas, Values, Agreeableness, Trust, Straightforwardness, Altruism, Compliance, Modesty, Tender-Mindedness, Conscientiousness, Competence, Order, Dutifulness, Achievement Striving, Self-Discipline, and Deliberation. The response options are organized on a five-point Likert scale ranging from *strongly disagree* to *strongly agree*.

Forms and Levels Available, with Dates of Publication/Revision of Each: Form M

There are two forms of the NEO PI-3. Form S is a self-report, hand-scorable, and scannable booklet containing 240 items. Form R contains the same questions, but it is presented in the third person and can be used for observer reports for peers, spouses/partners, or expert ratings.

The NEO-PI-R is still available in print and computer versions.

Date of Most Recent Edition of Test Manual, User's Guide, Etc.: 2010.

Languages in Which Available: English only. The NEO PI-3 is currently being translated into Greek. The previous version of the NEO (NEO PI-R) is available in 34 languages.

Time:

    Actual Test Time: 35 to 45 minutes.

    Total Administration Time: 35 to 45 minutes.

Norm Group(s) on Which Scores Are Based: Norms for the new edition were based on responses from the Phase 1 adolescent sample and the Phase 2 adult sample.

Manner in Which Results Are Reported for Individuals: *T*-scores and percentiles, using adolescent and adult norms, are presented in a profile format. Scores are available by gender.

Report Format/Content for Group Summaries: Profiles based on *T*-scores and Summary.

Machine Scoring: Answer sheets may be sent to Psychological Assessment Resources, Inc. (PAR) for scoring and interpretation.

Hand Scoring: Hand scored by counselee, clerk, or counselor.

Local Machine Scoring:

    Provisions/Conditions/Equipment Required: Requires OpScan pencil reading scanner and NEO On-Site Scanning Software.

Computer Software Options Available: Completed scannable answer sheets can also be scored and interpreted with the On-Site Scanning Module of the NEO Software System. The NEO-PI-3 also can be scored and/or administered electronically using the NEO Software System. The NEO Software System is an online modular system that allows participants to complete the tool on-screen via counter serial numbers. The NEO Software System allows for online administration and is compatible with NEO-3 inventories.

Cost of Materials: Due to possible price changes since publication date, be sure to check the publisher's site.

Specimen Set: The NEO PI-3 is available as comprehensive adult and adolescent kits, both $330.00. The kits contain the following: the NEO Inventories Professional Manual, 10 Reusable Form S Item Booklets, 10 Reusable Form R Item Booklets [5 Male and 5 Female], 25 Hand-Scorable Answer Sheets, 25 Form S Adult/Adolescent Profile Forms, 25 Form R Adult/Adolescent Profile Forms, 25 Adult/Adolescent Combined-Gender Profile Forms [Form S/Form R], and 25 Your NEO Summary Feedback Sheets in a soft-sided attaché case.

Counselee Materials: NEO Inventories Professional Manual: $61.00; NEO Inventories Professional e-Manual: $56.00; NEO Reusable Form S Item Booklet (10 per package): $41.00; NEO Reusable Form R Item Booklet (10 per package): $41.00; NEO PI-3 Hand-Scorable Answer Sheets (package of 25): $45.00; NEO PI-3 Form S and Form R Adult/Adolescent Profile Forms (package of 25): $45.00 each; Your NEO Summary Feedback Sheets (package of 25): $35.00; NEO Job Profiler Book (package of 25): $40.00; see website for additional products.

Published Reviews of the Instrument in the Last 15 Years:

Stebleton, M. (2009). [NEO Personality Inventory-Revised.] In E. A. Whitfield, R. W. Feller, & C. Wood (Eds.), *A counselor's guide to career assessment instruments* (5th ed., pp. 407-412). Broken Arrow, OK: National Career Development Association.

NEO PERSONALITY INVENTORY-3

Reviewed by:

Michael J. Stebleton

Department of Postsecondary Teaching and Learning
University of Minnesota-Twin Cities

Description

The NEO Personality Inventory (NEO-PI-3; Costa & McCrae, 2010) is the most current version of Paul Costa and Robert McCrae's personality instrument. It replaces the second edition, the NEO-PI-R, which was published in 1992; the original edition was published in 1985. The NEO-PI-3 has been revised to be suitable for assessing personality traits in middle school students and adolescents. The authors of the manual state that 37 of the 240 items have been replaced from the previous NEO PI-R, and the new items are easier to comprehend and have better psychometric qualities.

The instrument and corresponding materials are based on the extensively researched five-factor model (FFM) of personality. The NEO PI-3 measures five major areas or domains of personality according to the FFM: Neuroticism (N), Extraversion (E), Openness to Experience (O), Agreeableness (A), and Conscientiousness (C). There are 30 lower level facets for these five domains: (1) Neuroticism facets: Anxiety, Angry Hostility, Depression, Self-Consciousness, Impulsiveness, and Vulnerability; (2) Extraversion facets: Warmth, Gregariousness, Assertiveness, Activity, Excitement-Seeking, and Positive Emotions; (3) Openness to Experience facets: Fantasy, Aesthetics, Feelings, Actions, Ideas, and Values; (4) Agreeableness facets: Trust, Straightforwardness, Altruism, Compliance, Modesty, and Tender-Mindedness; (5) Conscientiousness facets: Competence, Order, Dutifulness, Achievement Striving, Self-Discipline, and Deliberation.

The NEO-PI-3 has a variety of uses and applications including counseling, clinical psychology, and psychiatry. Other applications could include behavioral medicine (e.g., HIV/AIDS research), health psychology, educational research, and career counseling and industrial/organizational psychology. It is not designed to measure psychopathology or assess psychiatric disorders.

A Counselor's Guide To Career Assessments Instruments

The NEO-PI-3 can be used as a complement to other vocational interest assessments, such as the Strong Interest Inventory (SII), the Self-Directed Search (SDS), and the Campbell Interest and Skill Survey (CISS). The NEO-PI-3 should not take the place of these other well-validated instruments specifically designed to assess career interests (McCrae & Costa, 2010). The instrument may be useful for screening and placement, especially because the NEO-PI-3 does help to point towards individuals' strengths through the Conscientiousness (C) domain. The manual also lists key limitations including the possibility of evaluative bias.

Career development practitioners who work with undecided clients will likely find the NEO-PI-3 to be useful. Many career development practitioners use the Myers-Briggs Type Indicator (MBTI) in individual appointments and life-career planning courses. The NEO-PI-3 may be used as a complement to the MBTI or as an alternative to assess personality preferences (McCrae & Costa, 1989). Additionally, the NEO inventories have been used in a range of more recent studies, including the relationship between personality traits and work values (Duffy, Borges, & Hartung, 2009). Betz and Borgen (2010) used the NEO to explore healthy personalities and its application to positive psychology concepts. Interested readers may opt to explore additional research studies on the NEO that are published in the *Journal of Career Assessment*.

The manual and other practical features are well-written and organized. Overall, the format of the instruments meets the requirements for legibility, attractiveness, convenience, and durability; there was a potential concern regarding item content (see limitations). It includes a comprehensive overview of practical, user-friendly information plus scholarly sections on directions for future research, development and validation, and an extensive reference section.

Technical Considerations

The technical aspects of the NEO-PI-3 (based on the NEO PI-R) are especially strong and impressive—including norms, reliability, and validity. The norms for the new edition were based on responses from the Phase 1 adolescent sample and the Phase 2 adult sample. Adult and adolescent norms based on gender are provided. The differences in profile outcomes between NEO-PI-3 and the previous edition are modest. College norms profile forms were added in 1991.

There are limited new reliability measures for the updated version at this time. Based on the previous NEO PI-R, the reliability and stability measures are solid. Domain level reliabilities range from .86 to .95 for both self-reports and observer ratings. Facet reliabilities range from .56 to .81 in self-reports and from .60 to .90 in observer ratings according to the manual. Test-retest reliability ranged from .66 to .92. The authors of the instrument emphasized that the NEO PI-3 is one of the few instruments that measures enduring traits over time assessed by both self-report and by the ratings of others.

Validity measures are equally as impressive based on measures from the previous edition (i.e., the NEO PI-3 was recently released but validity will likely be maintained). The NEO PI-R manual included a comprehensive overview of studies conducted on validity, including consensual, convergent, divergent, and construct. Consensual validity between self and peer/spouse rating correlations are from .35 to .54. Convergent, divergent, and construct validity correlates were all relatively high. Studies conducted on NEO-PI facet scales found relationships between constructs on a variety of career assessments, including Holland's Self-Directed Search (SDS) and the Myers-Briggs Type Indicator (MBTI) Jungian types. For example, Holland's Investigative Types were most closely connected to Openness to Ideas (O5), and Artistic Interests were most highly correlated to Aesthetics (O2) (Costa, McCrae, & Holland, 1984).

Finally, the NEO PI-R has extensive cross-cultural application. For example, the NEO has demonstrated cross-cultural replicability of the FFM, including data from French and Filipino translations.

General Utility and Evaluation

The NEO PI-3 is a well-researched instrument that can be used to complement other vocational interest inventories. There are several potential strengths and weaknesses of the instrument. Potential strengths include the following:

393

- Validity and reliability: As indicated, the NEO PI-R is a solid tool that has been validated against other personality measures. Additionally, the reliability including the retest reliability is an advantage; these measures should remain consistent with the new edition.

- Ease of use: It takes less than an hour to complete and self-score; it can be completed online. Clients can complete in one session and get immediate results with interpretive assistance from a career practitioner. The directions are well-written and easy to follow. Plus, the new edition allows users as young as 12 years old and adults with lower reading abilities to complete the tool, due to improvements in the wording of some items.

- Supported by comprehensive and cross-cultural research: There is extensive research done on the Big Five personality measures and the NEO. Career counselors can easily access additional literature about the assessment, plus it can be applied to a diverse clientele.

Potential limitations include the following:

- Item format and content criteria: According to one review in the twelfth *Mental Measurements Yearbook* (Juni, 1995), the item format and content criteria are not well-developed. This version seemed to address this concern, yet several questions included double negative statements and proved to be difficult to interpret. Despite the instrument's cross-cultural applicability, the wording of certain items may present a challenge to clients where English is not the first language (although this has been improved with the new edition). I work frequently with recent immigrant college students at a large four-year research university, and many of these students would have trouble interpreting some of the items (e.g., item #239: I would rather be known as "merciful" than as "just").

- Potential lack of supplemental interpretative materials for participants: Two colleagues who completed the inventory expressed a need for a more comprehensive explanation of the domains and facets. The document Your NEO Summary is brief and concise, but does not thoroughly explain the meaning of the domains and facets. Furthermore, one colleague stated a need for more applied suggestions, including areas for individual development, based on his individual scores. In the new edition, this critique was addressed by adding several new features, including the NEO Style Graph Booklet, NEO Problems in Living Checklist, and others.

- Possible limited clinical utility: Butcher and Rouse (1996) contended that the NEO-PI-R may have limited clinical use due to variation with facet scores within the domain. They argued that a personality assessment should provide more useful information about a person's psychological functioning (p. 94). The authors (McCrae and Costa) countered this critique by arguing that personality at the domain level is a beginning point, and the NEO-PI-3 serves this function.

In summary, career development practitioners will want to use the tool as a complement but not as a substitute for other career assessments. I would recommend the NEO-PI-3 in conjunction with other developed career tools (e.g., Strong Interest Inventory). Likewise, career counselors in academic settings may find the NEO-PI-3 to be useful when working with undecided students who are engaged in the career decision-making process.

References and Additional Resources

Betz, N. E., & Borgen, F. H. (2010). Relationships of the Big Five personality domains and facets to dimensions of the healthy personality. *Journal of Career Assessment, 18,* 147-160.

Butcher, J. N., & Rouse, S. V. (1996). Personality: Individual differences and clinical assessment. *Annual Review Psychology, 47,* 87-111.

Costa, P. T., Jr., McCrae, R. R., & Holland, J. L. (1984). Personality and vocational samples in an adult sample. *Journal of Applied Psychology, 69,* 390-400.

Costa, P. T., Jr., McCrae, R. R., (2010). *NEO Inventories: NEO Personality Inventory-3 (NEO-Pl-3)* Lutz, FL: Psychological Assessment Resources.

Duffy, R. D., Borges, N. J., & Hartung, P. J. (2009). Personality, vocational interests, and work values of medical students. *Journal of Career Assessment, 17,* 189-200.

Juni, S. (1995). [Revised NEO Personality Inventory.] In J. C. Conoley & J. C. Impara (Eds.), *The twelfth mental measurements yearbook* (pp. 863-868). Lincoln, NE: Buros Center for Testing.

McCrae, R. R., & Costa, P. T., Jr. (1989). Reinterpreting the Myers-Briggs Type Indicator from the perspective of the five-factor model of personality. *Journal of Personality, 57,* 17-40.

McCrae, R. R., & Costa, P. T., Jr. (2010). *NEO inventories for the NEO Personality Inventory-3 (NEO-PI3): Professional manual.* Lutz, FL: Psychological Assessment Resources.

Stebleton, M. (2009). [NEO Personality Inventory-Revised.] In E. A. Whitfield, R. W. Feller, & C. Wood (Eds.), *A counselor's guide to career assessment instruments* (5th ed., pp. 407-412). Broken Arrow, OK: National Career Development Association.

PERSONAL STYLE INDICATOR
Ken Keis, Terry Anderson, and Everett Robinson

CRG Consulting Resource Group International, Inc.

P.O. Box 8000 PMB 386
Sumas, WA 98295-8000
http://www.crgleader.com
info@crgleader.com

Target Population: Adolescents, young adults, and adults; age 15 or older.

Statement of the Purpose of the Instrument: The Personal Style Indicator (PSI) is designed to increase mutual understanding, acceptance, and communication among people and to increase self-awareness.

Titles of Subtests, Scales, Scores Provided: Behavioral/Action; Cognitive/Analysis; Interpersonal/Harmony; Affective/Expression.

Forms and Levels Available, with Dates of Publication/Revision of Each: 2006.

Date of Most Recent Edition of Test Manual, User's Guide, Etc.: 2006.

Languages in Which Available:

Print version: Arabic, Dutch, English, French, Japanese, Spanish, Swedish, Vietnamese. Online version: Chinese (simplified), English, German, Indonesian, Spanish, Swedish.

Time:

Actual Test Time: Varies.

Total Administration Time: Approximately 90 minutes.

Manner in Which Results Are Reported for Individuals: Standard scores.

Report Format/Content for Group Summaries: Not available.

Machine Scoring: Scored online.

Hand Scoring: Hand scored by counselee (print version only).

Computer Software Options Available: Not available.

Cost of Materials: Due to possible price changes since publication date, be sure to check the publisher's website.

Specimen Set: The cost for the PSI is $20.00 for each test booklet, which contains the PSI instrument and brief explanation of the results. An additional 48 page, In-Depth Interpretations booklet costs $20.00 and contains interpretative information related to each of the various combinations of Personal Style scores. The online version costs $45.00, while the Trainer's guide and Professional's Guide costs $40.00 and $75.00, respectively. Finally, a CRG Models Master Handouts binder and CD for the PSI costs $175.00, and a PSI PowerPoint CD and binder costs $175.00.

Counselee Materials: Test booklet/test access, Print: $40.00, Online: $45.00.

Published Reviews of the Instrument in the Last 15 Years:

Austen, J. T. & Singh, K. (1998). [Personal Style Indicator.] In J. C. Impara & B. S. Plake (Eds.), *The thirteenth mental measurements yearbook* (pp. 153-156). Lincoln, NE: Buros Center for Testing.

Denzine (2007). [Personal Style Indicator.] In K. F. Geisinger, R. A. Spies, J. F. Carlson, & B. S. Plake (Eds.), *The seventeenth mental measurements yearbook.* Lincoln, NE: Buros Center for Testing.

PERSONAL STYLE INDICATOR

Reviewed by:

Paul R. Peluso

Department of Counselor Education
Florida Atlantic University

Description

The Personal Style Indicator (PSI) was developed by Terry D. Anderson, Everett Robinson, and Ken Keis. The PSI was originally published in 1986 and was most recently revised in 2005. The purpose of the PSI is to assess *personal* style, an aspect of personality that contains "a complex set of behaviors and attitudes that strongly affect the way you present yourself to others" (Consulting Research Group [CRG], 2011a, p. 5).

The PSI scales were created to measure personal styles rather than personality per se. This was a deliberate choice by the authors to move away from a fixed view of personality constructs. Instead, the PSI is designed to provide information on how a person interacts with his or her environments. They assert that understanding one's personal style can help a person identify preferred responses to elements like time, people, tasks, or situations. This understanding can be beneficial for individuals in their workplace or any other group tasks (CRG, 2011a).

The authors state the PSI was developed using the theoretical assumptions underlying the work of Bandura (1978), Jung (1928), Lewin (1936), Horney (1942), and Fromm (1964). The authors of the PSI break down personal style into four dimensions: (1) Behavioral—energy to behave or take action; (2) Cognitive—to think about or analyze; (3) Interpersonal—to be concerned with harmony toward others; and (4) Affective—to be expressive in an intuitive, creative manner. The authors make the assumption that an individual has a finite amount of resources to devote to each of these dimensions and that different individuals will devote disproportionate energy to different dimensions, thus creating their own "personal style." Some individuals will have greater intensity in one dimension and weaker intensity in other areas, which will characterize their approach to the world. According to Denzine (2007), there are biological factors that can determine which of the dimensions are utilized more, including hemispheric brain-side dominance (left/right), sensitivity of the reticular activating system in the brain, and intensity of arousal level. However, I found no studies to date that corroborate these assertions.

There are 16 test items for the Personal Style Indicator with four descriptor words per item. Each descriptor word has three subdescriptor words for clarification as well (e.g., "self-reliant" has the following subdescriptor words: "confident", "secure", "independent"). Individuals are required to rank order each of the four descriptor words by putting a 4 by the word that best describes them, followed by a 3 for the next best-fitting word, and so on. So, for example, one item may have the words: "bold", "calculating", "trustworthy", and "outgoing" that must be rank ordered according to a person's perception of "fit." Adding down the columns of each of the four words across all 16 items scores the test. This will yield four scores each ranging from a minimum of 16 and a maximum of 64. A check of the math can be done by summing all four categories, which should equal 160. Each of the four column scores is then transferred to a scoring sheet, which reveals the category names for the columns: Behavioral, Cognitive, Interpersonal, and Affective. The scores are then measured against a graph ranging from 20 to 60.

According to the manual, every individual has all four dimensions in varying strengths, but the higher scores in some dimensions indicates the relative "influence" that the particular dimension has on an individual's personal style. Conversely, the lowest scores reflect a weaker influence of that particular dimension on one's personal style. The majority of test takers will have two scores over 40, and two below 40. The combination of category scores, particularly the two scores over 40, represents an individual's personal style. Further interpretations of each combination (21 different combinations in all), are provided in both the test booklet and in the *In-depth Interpretations* booklet (CRG, 2011b).

Although not specified in the test manual, total time of administration, scoring, and interpretation of PSI can take between 30 and 40 minutes. Basic reading skills appear to be necessary to complete and interpret the test (Austen & Singh, 1998; Denzine, 2007). The authors note the PSI is appropriate for individuals 14 or 15 years of age and older, and test takers should be able to read at the ninth- to tenth-grade level. There is no information regarding the effectiveness of reading the test aloud to individuals who are unable to read.

There are six steps involved in fully understanding and interpreting an individual's scores on the PSI (CRG, 2011a). First is "understanding your personal style," which are the scores on the four personal style dimensions (i.e., behavioral, cognitive, interpersonal, and affective). The second step is graphing each of these scores on a standard graph. This allows for the participant to see which of the four dimensions is dominant. The third step is learning about the general style tendencies, or in which of the dimensions an individual is stronger or weaker. The fourth step is "determining your interpretive summary for your style." Here, individuals are guided in creating their own interpretative summary based on their primary and secondary patterns based on their previous scores. Individuals are advised to incorporate elements that "fit" with their assessment of themselves. The fifth step is developing style flexibility and improving credibility. This includes information on knowing where a person's style might clash with another, as well as how to interact with styles that clash with one's own. Finally, the sixth step is designing a plan to increase effectiveness. This includes reflection questions about one's style, its relative merits and drawbacks, as well as alternative strategies that could be developed to create more flexible responses.

While not overtly stated in the technical manual, this scale appears to be a tool most appropriate for non-clinical adult populations. According to the authors, it is appropriate to use the PSI as a communication tool during personal, marriage, and family counseling sessions, as well as for career and life-coaching situations (CRG, 2011b). However, there is not a lot of clinical information that is presented in the interpretive manual. At best, the instrument might generate some discussion on general style or approach to situations, or may be a useful tool for ascertaining individual strengths or preference. The profile reports provide specific action steps for understanding team dynamics and relations in the workplace, but there is not much else for clinicians to use (Austen & Singh, 1998).

Technical Considerations

One of the greatest limitations of the PSI is the lack of psychometric information concerning the norming of the scale, reliability, or validity analysis. Specifically, there is no information about the sample used to develop the scales. In addition, there is no information about the application of the inventory to different genders or cultural/ethnic groups (Austen & Singh, 1998; Denzine, 2007). Denzine (2007) found a reported internal consistency by the test authors of greater than .85; it is unclear what type of internal consistency this represents. However, there are no reported test-retest reliability studies conducted. Instead, the test authors claim that the PSI was not designed to be a standardized test, but to encourage researchers to perform larger scale testing. Similar to Denzine, I could not find any studies to date that have done so.

Perhaps more limiting than the absence of reliability data is the absence of validity data. In their original review of the PSI, Austen and Singh (1998) noted that the PSI authors argued that the instrument is a developmental learning tool, and therefore chose not to use commonly accepted psychometric standards that are valid for all measurement instruments. Further, Austen and Singh lamented that instead of seizing the opportunity to conduct validity research, the authors chose to develop workshops for using the PSI in various non-clinical capacities. In the current version of the PSI, validity is discussed in vague general terms, but is absent of any evidence of predictive or construct validity. Lastly, there is no evidence of concurrent validity tests with other measures of interpersonal behavior, communication style, and personality (Denzine, 2007). At the bare minimum, the PSI has face validity, which is the lowest level of validity for any measure.

General Utility and Evaluation

The PSI could be a useful tool for generating insight to an individual's preferred method of behaving in a given situation. In addition, it appears that the PSI has some use in discussing potential group interactions with individuals that endorse the same styles, or different styles. The test and interpretive guides are appropriately written, and contain thorough discussions of each of the styles, different style combinations, and how the different style combinations may interact (across individuals). However, it is not clear that this inventory is superior to other related inventories that have better psychometrics, or have been more widely researched

Personal Style Indicator

(e.g., Myers-Briggs Type Indicator). In fact, without more information about the validity of the instrument, it is really difficult to recommend this for use with either a clinical population or as a research instrument. As Denzine (2007) noted, there is little empirical evidence supporting the underlying theoretical structure for the PSI (in fact, it is hard to reconcile disparate theoretical approaches of Jung, Bandura, and Horney), and there are no published studies that have used this scale. Indeed, Austen and Singh (1998) noted this in their original review of the PSI, but it was seemingly not taken into consideration for the revision of the scale. Given all of this, I must concur with her findings: "Although the PSI is easy to administer and score, and the reports are interesting and easy to interpret, there are several elements missing in the demonstration of a psychometrically sound measure of personal style. Given these limitations, there is a need for more sophisticated and ongoing research on the PSI before its use can be recommended" (p. 3).

References and Additional Resources

Austen, J. T. & Singh, K. (1998). [Personal Style Indicator.] In J. C. Impara & B. S. Plake (Eds.), *The thirteenth mental measurements yearbook* (pp. 153-156). Lincoln, NE: Buros Center for Testing.

Bandura, A. (1978). The self-system in reciprocal determinism. *American Psychologist, 33,* 344-358.

Consulting Resource Group. (2011a). *Personal Style Indicator.* Sumas, WA: Author.

Consulting Resource Group. (2011b). *Personal Style Indicator in-depth interpretations.* Sumas, WA: Author.

Denzine (2007). [Personal Style Indicator.] In K. F. Geisinger, R. A. Spies, J. F. Carlson, & B. S. Plake (Eds.), *The seventeenth mental measurements yearbook.* Lincoln, NE: Buros Center for Testing.

Fromm, E. (1964). *The heart of man: Its genius for good and evil.* New York, NY: Harper & Row.

Horney, K. (1942). *Self-analysis.* New York, NY: Norton.

Jung, C. G. (1928). *Contributions to analytical psychology.* New York, NY: Harcourt Brace.

Lewin, K. (1936). *Principles of topological psychology.* New York, NY: McGraw-Hill.

Personal Style Indicator. Retrieved from: http://www.crgleader.com

SIXTEEN PERSONALITY FACTOR QUESTIONNAIRE AND CAREER DEVELOPMENT REPORT

Raymond B. Cattell, A. Karen Cattell, and Heather E.P. Cattell

Institute for Personality and Ability Testing, Inc.

P.O. Box 1188
Champaign, IL 61824-1188
217-352-4739
FAX: 217-352-9674
http://www.ipat.com
custserv@ipat.com

Target Population: Adolescents, young adults, and adults; age 16 and older. Fifth-grade reading level required.

Statement of the Purpose of the Instrument: The Sixteen Personality Factor (16PF) Questionnaire is designed to measure normal personality dimensions that are useful in a variety of settings to predict a wide range of life behaviors. Popular uses include career counseling, employee selection and development, leadership development, individual and couples counseling, and executive coaching. The 16PF Career Development Report is reviewed alongside the 16PF Questionnaire.

Titles of Subtests, Scales, Scores Provided: Five Global Factors (Extraversion, Anxiety, Tough-Mindedness, Independence, Self-Control); 16 Primary Factors (Warmth, Reasoning, Emotional Stability, Dominance, Liveliness, Rule-Consciousness, Social Boldness, Sensitivity, Vigilance, Abstractedness, Privateness, Apprehension, Openness to Change, Self-Reliance, Perfectionism, Tension). Institute for Personality and Ability Testing, Inc. (IPAT) reports provide additional scores. The number and type of additional projected scores vary by report.

Forms and Levels Available, with Dates of Publication/Revision of Each: 1993.

Date of Most Recent Edition of Test Manual, User's Guide, Etc.: 16PF Fifth Edition Manual, 2009. Manual for the 16PF Career Development Report, 2008.

Languages in Which Available: The 16PF is available in 20 languages, including English and American Spanish.

Time:

    Actual Test Time: Approximately 35-50 minutes to complete in the paper-and-pencil format and 25-35 minutes by computer.

    Total Administration Time: Varies.

Norm Group(s) on Which Scores Are Based: A sample of more than 10,000 individuals was selected based upon a stratified random sampling procedure using sex, race, age, and education level to match the 2000 U.S. census figures. It was normed for test takers between the ages of 16 to 82.

Manner in Which Results Are Reported for Individuals: Scores are provided per scale; three validity scales are also included. A wide variety of reports can be generated for the 16PF Questionnaire. Reports vary in complexity ranging from basic reports that provide scores only, to more complex reports containing narrative and predicted scores based upon empirical research. The 16PF Career Development Report is one of the many report options available. The 16PF Career Success Report is a new report option that is designed to help college students identify suitable career options and increase self-awareness to facilitate personal development.

Report Format/Content for Group Summaries: Not available.

Machine Scoring: Answer sheets are processed the day they are received and returned via U.S. mail unless expedited options are specified. Cost varies based on the type of report that is chosen.

Hand Scoring: Although hand-scoring options are available, neither the 16PF Career Development Report nor the 16PF Career Success Report can be produced when hand scoring is chosen.

Local Machine Scoring: IPAT's OnSite system software allows users to administer and score questionnaires on a computer and generate interpretive reports. Users can also hand enter or scan pencil-marked answer sheets.

Sixteen Personality Factor Questionnaire and Career Development Report

---

Online Options Available: The 16PF Questionnaire can be administered and scored online via the NetAssess testing platform. Test takers complete the assessment via IPAT's secure website, and the report is emailed back to the qualified user. Numerous report options, including the 16PF Career Development Report and 16PF Career Success Report, are available.

Cost of Materials: Please contact the publisher for pricing information at custserv@ipat.com or 800.225.4728. Publisher's website: http://www.ipat.com

Counselee Materials: Test booklet and answer sheet or computer, depending upon the administration method.

Published Reviews of the Instrument in the Last 15 Years:

McLellan, M. J. (2002). [Sixteen Personality Factor Questionnaire, Fifth Edition.] In J. C. Conoley & J. C. Impara (Eds.), *Twelfth annual mental measurements yearbook.* Lincoln, NE: Buros Center for Testing. [Electronic Version]

Rotto, P. C. (2002). [Sixteen Personality Factor Questionnaire, Fifth Edition.] In J. C. Conoley & J. C. Impara (Eds.), *Twelfth annual mental measurements yearbook.* Lincoln, NE: Buros Center for Testing. [Electronic Version]

SIXTEEN PERSONALITY FACTOR QUESTIONAIRE AND CAREER DEVELOPMENT REPORT

Reviewed by:

Michelle Perepiczka

Department of School Counseling
New York Institute of Technology

Description

The Sixteen Personality Factor Questionnaire (16PF) was originally published in 1949; the current fifth edition was published in 1994. The 16PF is a 185-item tool that measures personality of the average American adult along 16 Primary Factors related to personality, 5 Global Factors (second-order factors), and 3 Response Style Indices that assess social desirability. The 16PF can be used in a variety of settings including clinical, organizational, university, research, and high school settings. It can be administered in six-month intervals or after major life transitions that impact the test taker. The content in the 16PF was written at the fifth-grade level based on the Flesch-Kincaid formula.

The Career Development Report (CDR) uses the scales from the assessment to understand a test taker's personality, and then generates personal and career lifestyle information. The report offers insight into personal and career strengths that a test taker can use as a "reality check" to review how the test taker perceives himself or herself. The CDR can be used for a variety of purposes including but not limited to the following: personnel development in an organization, personnel sections/hiring, personnel placement, on-the-job performance effectiveness reviews and planning, leadership development, executive coaching, career transitions or outplacement counseling, career exploration, and personal counseling.

Each Primary Factor contains 10 to 15 items, the Response Style Indices contain 12 items, and the Global Factors contain 5 items. The 16 Primary Factors, which are the higher order factors, and matching letter codes are, Warmth (A), Reasoning (B), Emotional Stability (C), Dominance (E), Liveliness (F), Rule-Consciousness (G), Social Boldness (H), Sensitivity (I), Vigilance (L), Abstractedness (M), Privateness (N), Apprehensive (O), Openness to Change (Q1), Self-Reliance (Q2), Perfectionism (Q3), and Tension (Q4). The matching dichotomous Primary Factor scores are, Warm vs. Reserved (A), Abstract-Reasoning vs. Concrete-Reasoning (B), Emotionally Stable vs. Reactive (C), Dominant vs. Deferential (E), Lively vs. Serious (F), Rule-Conscious vs. Expedient (G), Socially Bold vs. Shy (H), Sensitive vs. Utilitarian (I), Vigilant vs. Trusting (L), Abstracted vs. Grounded (M), Private vs. Forthright (N), Apprehensive vs. Self-Assured (O), Open to Change vs. Traditional (Q1), Self-Reliant vs. Group-Oriented (Q2), Perfectionistic vs. Tolerates Disorder (Q3), and Tense vs. Relaxed (Q4).

A Counselor's Guide To Career Assessments Instruments

The Global Factors, which are the second-order factors developed from intercorrelations of the Primary factors, are Extraversion, Anxiety, Tough Mindedness, Independence, and Self-Control. The matching dichotomous Global Factor scores are Extraversion vs. Introversion, Independence vs. Accommodating, Tough-Mindedness vs. Receptive, Self-Control vs. Unrestrained, Anxiety vs. Low Anxiety. The three Response Style Indices are Impression Management (IM), Infrequency (INF; measuring non-purposeful, random responding), and Acquiescence (ACQ; measuring agreeing-to-agree responding).

The CDR report was created from the original work of Verne Walter on the Personal Career Development Profile (PCDP). In the course of 30 years of consulting work with executive leaders and their personnel, Walter identified a need for an extensive computer-generated interpretative report that would help his clients effectively make personal and work-related lifestyle choices. Walter noted the new report (i.e., what is now the CDR) would need to be user friendly, lack technical language, and be framed in a strengths-based perspective.

The CDR report is designed to help test takers increase their awareness of strengths and unique differences from others in order to maximize their full work potential, move forward in their careers, and increase personal satisfaction while following their natural tendencies. The CDR produces three vocationally focused sections including Broad Patterns, Leadership/Subordinate Role Patterns, and Career and Occupational Interests.

The 10 Broad Patterns assessed are Emotional Adjustment, Creative Potential, Effective Leadership, Elected Leadership, Leadership Preference, Structured Situation Pattern, Formal Academic Interest, Work Pattern Preference, Learning Situation Preference, and Risk-Taking/Adventure Interest. The Leadership/Subordinate Role Patterns include three separate categories with related subscales. First is Leadership Roles, which is comprised of Authoritarian, Participative, and Permissive. Second is Subordinate Roles, which consists of Ingratiator, Cooperative, and Free Thinking. The final is Leadership/Subordinate Interaction Roles, which includes Confrontive, Controlling, Objective, and Supportive. The third section of the CDR includes the Career/Avocational Activity Interest and Career Field Interest scores. The Career/Avocational Activity Interests lists particular activities or situations within seven categories (Influencing, Organizing, Helping, Creating, Analyzing, Producing, Adventuring/Venturing) the test taker may enjoy engaging based on how his or her lifestyle patterns predict identified career-interest patterns. The Career Field and Occupational Interest is a list of occupations (selected from a limited set of 27 careers and 98 occupations) that correlate with high significance, high-average significance, and average significance to the Career/Avocational Activity Interest.

The CDR narrative report organizes the above mentioned data into 10 specific areas for the test administrator to interpret for the test taker. The narrative report illustrates the connection between the personality factors and various areas of vocation that are calculated. The 10 categories found in the report are (1) Introduction section, which provides general information about the report itself to the test taker; (2) Problem-Solving Resources, which identifies how a test taker learns and attempts to solve work-related problems; (3) Patterns for Coping with Stressful Conditions, which analyzes a test taker's methods of coping with stress; (4) Interpersonal Interaction Styles, which outlines how a test taker relates to, interacts with, and communicates with others as well as how he or she works independently; (5) Organizational Roles and Work-Setting Preferences, which classifies how a test taker functions in leadership or subordinate roles as well as the type of work setting best suited for the individual; (6) Career Activity Interests, which lists identified activities or situations the test taker may enjoy, and the Career Field and Occupational Interest lists the occupations the test taker may find as a good fit based on the Career Activity Interest; (7) Personal Career Lifestyle Effectiveness Considerations, which addresses significant lifestyle patterns and behaviors to consciously guard against using or to avoid in order to be perceived positively, appreciated, and supported by others; (8) Self-Review and Planning Exercises, which offers a set of reflection activities to help the test taker process the information provided in the report, reflect on his or her strengths, interests, and areas for further development, as well as create a plan for future steps; (9) Score Summary Pages, which lists the raw scores for each of the scales for the administrator's use; and (10) Summary of Items Responses and Summary Statistics.

The 185 test items have a three-choice format with two choices commonly being dichotomous (endorse or do not endorse) and the middle choice is a question mark (?). Examples of dichotomous responses used are *True* and *False* or *Hardly Ever* and *Often*. The question mark is available for test takers to choose in the event neither option captures his or her intended response or the test taker cannot decide.

Sixteen Personality Factor Questionnaire and Career Development Report

The exception to the dichotomous format are the Reasoning scale items (B), which are separated in the back of the test booklet and have separate instructions for the test taker. The Reasoning items are formatted as problem-solving questions. For instance, test takers are asked to identify the next number in a series of numbers or are challenged to complete an analogy.

The 16PF can be administered to individuals or groups. Test takers use either a reusable test booklet with an answer form or self-administer using a computer that is equipped with the IPAT OnSite System software or access to the online site. The paper-and-pencil format can be hand or computer scored. The counselor can hand score the answer sheet by using a set of scoring keys, General Population Norms Table, and 16PF Fifth Edition Questionnaire Scoring and Feedback Guide. With this format, the counselor reviews the answer keys to ensure no more than 12 items are left blank because the assessment cannot be scored if 13 or more items are incomplete. Response Style Indices are converted into percentiles. Extreme scores on the three scales (as defined by at or above 95th percentile or below 5th percentile) may suggest the accuracy of the test taker's response set may be jeopardized. The counselor initially reviews these indices to assess the validity of the test taker's responses overall. Then, the Global Factors are calculated and the Primary Factor scales follow. To calculate the Global Factors and Primary Factors, raw scores are initially converted to z-scores and linear transformation is applied to obtain the sten scores ranging from 1 to 10 with a mean of 5.5 and standard deviation of 2. The sten scores are charted for interpretation.

Computer scoring of the 16PF, with administration in either format, can be done by the IPAT OnSite service, online service, or mail and fax service at IPAT. The benefits to using the online or IPAT OnSite services are immediate scoring and processing of reports as well as reduction in scoring error. The CDR report is only computer-generated. Information is not available to manually create the CDR score summaries and construct the corresponding narrative.

Researchers made various updates to the 16PF from the prior edition. For instance, the content of the test items was revised to be more modern, test items and response choices were shortened to be more concise, items were reworded to avoid social desirability, difficult to translate items were revised, and language was updated to remove bias in gender, race, and culture. The Impression Management (IM) index replaced the previous Faking Good and Faking Bad scales. The Acquiescence (ACQ) and Infrequency (INF) scales were also added. Empathy and Self-Esteem scales were newly developed. Finally, reliability and validity were re-evaluated.

The 16PF can be incorporated into career services targeted to industrial and organizational, clinical and counseling, educational, and research settings. The assessment can fulfill various purposes within these settings including predicting educational achievement, creativity, and leadership. Interpersonal skills, marital adjustment, and psychology adjustment can also be measured. The assessment can also be used to outline occupational profiles to be used for candidate selection, candidate placement, career development, out-placement, and career transition exploration.

The CDR can be used in conjunction with other vocational tools to enhance the counseling or consultation process with the test taker. Suggested tools include, but are not limited to, the *Occupational Outlook Handbook* (U.S. Department of Labor, 1991a), *Guide for Occupational Exploration* (Farr, 1993), the *Dictionary of Occupational Titles* (U.S. Department of Labor, 1991b). Other compatible online resources to also consider using with test takers are O*NET, CareerOneStop, and Career Cluster.

Thoroughly processing the report with the test taker is required to ensure full and accurate understanding of the information and encourage self-exploration of strengths, individual uniqueness, interest, and abilities. Short- and long-term goals as well as an action plan can be developed with the test taker. The Self-Review and planning exercises in the CDR report can be integrated into this process.

Technical Considerations

The 16PF norms are based on a large sample size (N = 10,261) reflecting the general population characteristics in the 2000 U.S. Census. It was normed for test takers between the ages of 16 to 82. Counselors may choose to administer the assessment to younger test takers based on the individual's maturity level. The sample was obtained by using stratified random sampling focused on sex, race, age, and education level.

A COUNSELOR'S GUIDE TO CAREER ASSESSMENTS INSTRUMENTS

Researchers used effect size to assess the need for demographic specific norms. Gender-specific norms were created as effect sizes greater than $d = .50$ were found for Warmth (A), Sensitivity (I), and Apprehension (O) scales, with females scoring higher than males. Both gender-specific norms and combined-gender norms are available for the needs of the testing situation. Race, age, and education effect sizes were also assessed. For race, Reasoning (B) had a medium effect size. Education had a medium effect and positive correlation with Reasoning (B) and a small to moderate effect with negative relationship with Vigilance (L). Even though these differences were found, the researchers determined no need for race, age, or education specific norms.

The researchers assessed three forms of reliability for the 16PF including internal consistency, test-retest reliability (two week and two month), and equivalency between the fifth and fourth editions (Form A). The normative sample ($N = 10,261$) was used to assess for internal consistency. Internal consistency values for the Primary Scales ranged from .68 to .87 (Warmth, Reasoning, Emotional Stability, Dominance, Liveliness, Rule-Consciousness, Social Boldness, Sensitivity, Vigilance, Abstractedness, Privateness, Apprehensive, Openness to Change, Self-Reliance, Perfectionism, and Tension), and Global Factor ranged from .90 to .81 (Extraversion, Anxiety, Tough Mindedness, Independence, and Self-Control). Test-retest reliability was also assessed at two-week and two-month review periods. The sample for the two-week interval comprised of undergraduate and graduate students ($N = 204$) in Texas and Wisconsin. Primary Factors values ranged from .56 to .79 (Warmth, Reasoning, Emotional Stability, Dominance, Liveliness, Rule-Consciousness, Social Boldness, Sensitivity, Vigilance, Abstractedness, Privateness, Apprehensive, Openness to Change, Self-Reliance, Perfectionism, and Tension), and Global Factor values ranged from .84 to .91 (Extraversion, Anxiety, Tough Mindedness, Independence, and Self-Control). The sample for the two month interval consisted of undergraduate students from the Midwest ($N = 159$). Primary Factor values ranged from .56 to .79 (Warmth, Reasoning, Emotional Stability, Dominance, Liveliness, Rule-Consciousness, Social Boldness, Sensitivity, Vigilance, Abstractedness, Privateness, Apprehensive, Openness to Change, Self-Reliance, Perfectionism, and Tension), and Global Factor values ranged from .70 to .82 (Extraversion, Anxiety, Tough Mindedness, Independence, and Self-Control). Equivalency between the 16PF Fifth Edition and 16PF Fourth Edition (Form A) was assessed via component, correlational, and regression analyses with a general population sample ($N = 462$) who took both versions of the assessment during the same administration session. Researchers reported most of the 16PF Fifth Edition Primary scales and their matching scales on the Fourth Edition had high loadings from the component analysis. A correlational analysis was completed to assess the difference in the index of reliability and product moment correlations. Researchers reported a high degree of correspondence for each scale (z-transformed values ranging from .14 to .45). Regression analyses were done to examine the shared domain coverage and predictability of each Primary Factor. Researchers reported the fifth edition accounted for virtually every personality domain in the fourth edition. Any differences in the forms were attributed to revision of content items and addition of new items.

To externally assess construct validity of the 16PF, researchers compared the Global Factor and Primary Factor scales of the 16PF to four current and comprehensive measures of normal personality: The Personality Research Form-Form E (PRF; Jackson, 1984), the California Psychological Inventory (CPI; Gough, 1987), The NEO Personality Inventory-Revised (NEO PI-R; Costa & McCrae, 1992), and the Myers-Briggs Type Indicator (MBTI; Myers & McCaulley, 1985). The 16PF Fifth Edition was compared to each personality instrument separately and included independent samples of college students for the related analysis. Three validity analyses were conducted for each comparison: (a) correlations between the 16PF Fifth Edition Global Scales and the scales of the comparison assessment, (b) the 16PF Fifth Edition Global scales were regressed on the comparison assessment scales, and (c) the 16PF Fifth Edition five Global Scales were combined with the scales of the comparison assessment and subjected to a principle component analysis. Researchers reported the 16PF scales captures the same constructs of the comparison instruments and is equal to the 16PF Fourth Edition. Predictive validity for the 16PF is limited based on the research reports currently available. However, literature supports the 16PF to accurately predict behaviors in the workplace, assess employee stress and burnout, and assist with candidate selection.

Researchers specifically assessed the validity of the CDR measures by using the Motivational Systems Analysis (MSA; Sweeney, 1985), Response to Power Measure (RPM, Sweeney, 1972), Campbell Interest and Skills Survey (CISS; Campbell, Hyne, & Nilsen, 1992), and Strong Interest Inventory (SII; Harmon, Hansen, Borgen, & Hammer, 1994). The Primary Factor Scales were analyzed to determine if they predict the constructs

405

of the four assessments. Researchers indicated the Primary Factors effectively predicted the dimensions in the comparison scales, which supports the validity of the Broad Patterns, Leadership/Subordinate Roles Patterns, Career, and Occupational Interest dimensions in the CDR.

General Utility and Evaluation

The manual for the 16PF was reviewed by McLellan (1995) and Rotto (1995) and expresses similar perspectives of this review. Specially, the manual is quite user friendly. The chapters are organized well and information is easy to find. The tables are clearly labeled and comprehensive. Each of the analyses is presented separately and summaries are also provided for a general overview.

It should be noted that the information specific to the CDR is only found the in CDR manual and not in the 16PF Manual. There is only brief mention of the available reports, such as the CDR, in the 16PF Manual. There is also no mention of the 16PF Career Success Report, which focuses on college students to assist this group with career planning, personal development, and future planning. Thus, various resources and related forms are overlooked in the 16PF Manual.

In the CDR manual, there is only a general overview of the Personality Factors and Global Factors; however, detailed information about the instrument itself is not available. Test administrators are referred to the respective manuals for the information needed. There is a bit of back and forth between the two resources to find all of the information one might need.

Walter (2008) provided words of caution throughout the CDR manual which for test administrators should note. These seem to be very helpful for interpreting the CDR for the test taker. For instance, the authors explain the career and avocational interest patterns should be carefully interpreted as any emotional distress the test taker was experiencing at the time of administration may impact the predictor equations. Counselors are encouraged to thoroughly interview test takers to ensure they capture comprehensive information about the individual. Additional tips are included in the respective sections. The CDR authors also provide step-by-step instructions on how to interpret the report and prepare for sharing information with the test taker. Answers to frequently asked questions are included as well. An example case study is also available in the manual. Counselors can also review example CDR narrative reports, case studies, testimonials, and general information about the assessment on the publisher's website. The website also announces opportunities to attend 16PF workshops.

The authors of the 16PF and CDR also encourage a strengths-based approach to interpreting scores. For instance, the narratives in the CDR report focus on unique differences and strengths instead of weaknesses. Judgmental and critical language is avoided in the narrative and suggested for test administrators to avoid as well. Focus is on self-awareness and capitalizing on who the test taker naturally is instead of trying to stretch or mold the test taker into a different version of his or her self.

Even though the manual is rather thorough, some helpful information is missing in a few sections. For instance, the standard error of measurement for the Primary Factor and Global Factor scales is missing from the reliability reports. In the CDR predictive validity in organizations section, there is mention of resources that support the predictive validity; however, the citations for these reports or mention of the specific constructs are missing. Also, the extended details about the sample groups for the validity assessments for the CDR are missing.

General limitations in validity for the 16PF is the application of the scales is limited to the definition of the Primary and Global Scales, which is true for all assessments. A qualitative interview would be helpful in collecting additional data from the test taker in order to present a more comprehensive assessment. Other limitations of the CDR report is the narrative does not take into account a test taker's training, education, goals, or expressed desires in a career. Thus, some information in the report may not be fitting to the test taker. The test administrator would need to account for this additional information.

The 16PF also has limited predictive ability because the instrument only accounts for current behaviors such as creativity, social skills, and problem solving. Future behaviors such as motivation and dedication are not predicted. Test administrators should keep this in mind and use the data cautiously especially when using the information for candidate selection, placement, or development. The researchers recommend the 16PF be incorporated into an assessment battery that also includes an interview for qualitative data.

References and Additional Resources

Campbell, D., Hyne, S. A., & Nilsen, D. L. (1992). *Campbell Interest and Skills Survey.* Minneapolis, MN: National Computer Systems.

Cattell, H. (2004). *16PF fifth edition technical manual.* Champaign, IL: IPAT.

Conn, S. R., & Rieke, M. L. (1994). *16PF fifth edition technical manual.* Champaign, IL: IPAT.

Conn, S. R., & Rieke, M. L. (2002). *16PF fifth edition administrator's manual.* Champaign, IL: IPAT.

Costa, P. T., Jr., & McCrae, R. R. (1992). *Professional manual for the revised NEO Personality Inventory.* Odessa, FL: Psychological Assessment Resources.

Farr, J. M. (Ed.). (1993). *Guide for occupational exploration.* Indianapolis, IN: JIST Works, Inc.

Gough, H. G. (1987). *The California Psychological Inventory administrator's guide.* Mountain View, CA: CPP, Inc.

Harmon, L. W., Hansen, J. C., Borgen, F. H., & Hammer, A. L. (1994). *Strong Interest Inventory applications and technical manual.* Palo Alto, CA: CPP, Inc.

IPAT. (n.d.). *16PF Questionnaire.* Retrieved from http://www.ipat.com/assessment_tools/tests_and_reports/Pages/16PFF ifthEditionQuestionnaire.aspx

Jackson, D. N. (1984). *Personality Research Form, Form E.* Port Huron, MI: Sigma Assessment Systems.

McLellan, M. J. & Rotto, P. C. (1995). [Sixteen Personality Factor Questionnaire (5th ed.)]. In B. S. Plake & J. C. Impara (Eds.), *The twelfth mental measurements yearbook.* Lincoln, NE: Buros Center for Testing.

Myers, I. B., & McCaulley, M. H. (1985). *Manual: A guide to the development and use of the Myers-Briggs Type Indicator.* Mountain View, CA: CPP, Inc.

Russell, M. & Karol, D. (1994). *16PF fifth edition administrator's manual.* Champaign, IL:IPAT.

Sweeney, A. B. (1972). *Handbook: Response to power measure.* Wichita, KS: Test Systems, Inc.

Sweeney, A. B. (1985). *Handbooks: Motivational systems analysis.* Wichita, KS: Test Systems, Inc.

U.S. Department of Labor. (1991a). *Occupational outlook handbook.* Washington, DC: US Government Printing Office.

Walter, V. (2008). *Manual for the 16PF career development report.* Champaign, IL: IPAT.

U.S. Department of Labor. (1991b). *Dictionary of occupational titles* (4th ed.). Washington, DC: US Government Printing Office.

408

STUDENT STYLES QUESTIONNAIRE
Thomas Oakland, Joseph Glutting, and Connie Horton

The Psychological Corporation

19500 Bulverde Road
San Antonio, Texas 78259
800.872.1726
http://www.pearsonassessments.com

Target Population: Children and adolescents; ages 8 to 17. Grades 3-12.

Statement of the Purpose of the Instrument: The Student Styles Questionnaire (SSQ) measures learning, relating, and working styles of students.

Titles of Subtests, Scales, Scores Provided: Extroverted/Introverted, Thinking/Feeling, Practical/Imaginative, Organized/Flexible. Scores are provided for each scale, and interpretations are provided for various combinations of styles.

Forms and Levels Available, with Dates of Publication/Revision of Each: 1996.

Date of Most Recent Edition of Test Manual, User's Guide, Etc.: Manual and Classroom Applications Booklet, 1996.

Languages in Which Available: English only.

Time:

   Actual Test Time: Untimed.

   Total Administration Time: Can be completed in fewer than 30 minutes.

Norm Group(s) on Which Scores Are Based: Approximately 8,000 students in standardization sample; stratified by age, sex, race/ethnicity, geographic region, and school type.

Manner in Which Results Are Reported for Individuals: Prevalence-based *T*-scores are provided. The professional report sections include: General Description; Personal Styles—Imported Beliefs, Social Factors, Family Factors; Educational Styles—Attitudes Toward School, Relationships with Teachers, Relationships with Classmates, Learning Styles, Instructional Styles, Curriculum Content; Occupational Styles; Room for Growth; Summary.

Report Format/Content for Group Summaries: Not available.

Machine Scoring Service: Not available.

Hand Scoring: Hand scored by clerk or counselor.

Local Machine Scoring: Available, requires Record Forms, Windows Kit.

Computer Software Options Available: Not available.

Cost of Materials: Due to possible price changes since publication date, be sure to check the publisher's website.

   Specimen Set: Manual, Classroom Applications Booklet, package of 5 Ready Score Answer Documents, and Question Booklet: $78.65.

   Counselee Materials: Question Booklets (reusable), package of 25: $92.50; Ready Score Answer Documents, package of 25: $49.60; Manual: $108.20; Record Forms (local machine scoring), package of 25: $25.50; Classroom Applications Booklet (reusable): $32.80.

Published Reviews of the Instrument in the Last 15 Years:

Bruno, M. (2009). [Student Styles Questionnaire.] In E. A. Whitfield, R. W. Feller, & C. Wood (Eds.), *A counselor's guide to career assessment instruments* (5th ed., pp. 413-419). Broken Arrow, OK: National Career Development Association.

Schraw, G. (2001). [Student Styles Questionnaire.] In B. S. Plake & J. Impara (Eds.), *The fourteenth annual mental measurements yearbook*. Lincoln, NE: Buros Center for Testing.

Stewart, J. R. (2001). [Student Styles Questionnaire.] In B. S. Plake & J. Impara (Eds.), *The fourteenth annual mental measurements yearbook*. Lincoln, NE: Buros Center for Testing.

STUDENT STYLES QUESTIONNAIRE

Reviewed by:

Michelle L. Bruno

Department of Counseling
Indiana University of Pennsylvania

Description

The Student Styles Questionnaire (SSQ) is designed to detect individual differences among children in regards to their preferences, personal styles, and temperaments (Oakland, Glutting, & Horton, 1996). This instrument analyzes student preferences along four scales or paired styles (Extroversion/Introversion, Practical/Imaginative, Thinking/Feeling, and Organized/Flexible) by having students consider realistic scenarios and choose their preferred style. The SSQ is modeled after the Jungian concepts that are evident in instruments such as the Myers-Briggs Type Indicator (MBTI). The SSQ uses a forced-choice format for the 69 test items. Each question contains a real-life scenario with 20% of items reflecting each of the following categories: activities with friends and within groups, school-related activities, recreation and entertainment, family and work-related activities, and general personal qualities.

The SSQ is scored using a six-point weighting scheme for each test item. Each item is weighted in terms of the strength of the preference ranging from 1 (*mild*) to 3 (*strong*). The manual includes an appendix that provides scores assigned to each pair on the 69 test items, and these are listed on the carbon scoring sheet for ease in calculating scores. The first step is to calculate the raw scores using the perforated, self-carbon form. Inside, the carbon sheet reveals the preferences linked with that item and the strength of the preference. Some test items fall into more than one of the four dichotomies; when this occurs, the carbon sheet lists which score should be entered for each of the preferences. The SSQ uses prevalence-based *T*-scores because evidence reports that preferences are not distributed along the bell curve; thus, SSQ scores that fall between 50 and 54 are considered indicative of mild preference, 55 and 64 moderate preference, 65 and 74 strong preference, and scores above 74 indicative of a very strong preference.

In addition to this scoring index, the SSQ authors posit that there are three options for interpretation of results. Method one, the recommended starting point for interpretation, involves examining the eight basic styles grouped by the four pairs (Extroverted or Introverted, Practical or Imaginative, Thinking or Feeling, and Organized or Flexible). The second method, the Keirseian Combinations, emphasizes interpreting combinations of styles across two scales (e.g., Imaginative-Thinking). The third method emphasizes the four-style combination across all the scales (e.g., Extroverted-Imaginative-Thinking-Organized)

The SSQ is standardized for students ages 8 to 17 years. It is an untimed instrument, but is reportedly completed in less than 30 minutes by most students. It can be administered either individually or in groups, with groups over 30 requiring a second proctor be present. For use with younger and less developmentally mature students, the SSQ should be administered in groups of 15 students or fewer, and for use with older and more developmentally mature students, groups of 70 or more are acceptable. To accommodate students with disabilities, the SSQ can be read (or signed) to students and responses can be recorded by the proctor.

The instrument's directions are written at a third-grade reading level in a large font, and the test questions are printed in a smaller blue font and could be improved by using better spacing and/or a different font. The forced-choice design of the instrument makes administration convenient and easy. The manual contains a convenient checklist for before, during, and after administration.

The manual provides information on how scores can be used to note typical patterns in social interactions as well as career information (potential occupations and potential barriers to success; see Chapters 4-6 of Oakland et al., 1996, for complete information). The SSQ has utility as a tool in consultation with school staff in regards to classroom placement, identification of potential causes of disruptive or problematic classroom behavior/performance, group formation, and to assist new and transfer students adjusting to a new environment.

A Counselor's Guide To Career Assessments Instruments

Counselors can collaborate with teachers to use the SSQ to help improve the environment for all students, as supported by third edition of the American School Counselor Association (ASCA) National Model (2012), which emphasizes academic, personal/social, and career development as key areas for every student. Academic and personal development could be focused on by conducting classroom guidance that helps students learn more about their preferences as learners and gain insight into patterns of interacting and decision-making styles. These skills can carry over into other areas such as gaining interpersonal skills and identifying unique assets. Further, emphasizing individual differences can contribute to a positive climate that embraces diversity among students. The SSQ could contribute to enhancing career development of students by helping them identify subject areas and fields that are congruent with temperament and interest. Through collaboration with teachers, school counselors can use results from the SSQ to create guidance lessons that address all three areas emphasized by the ASCA model. Additionally, the SSQ can be used in school counseling to select the modality (individual versus group counseling) and interventions that are congruent with student preferences.

Technical Considerations

The SSQ used a standardization sample of more than 14,000 students in the United States and Puerto Rico. A stratified sample was gathered based on age, sex, race/ethnicity, geographic region, and school type (public, parochial, private). The SSQ sample closely approximates the 1990 U.S. Census in all of these categories. The sample used more than 180 students at each age level (spanning ages 8 to17), which reportedly exceeds industry standards. The sample was balanced in regards to sex, with the largest discrepancy being 2%. The manual contains a chart depicting the racial/ethnic composition of the sample, which was within three points of desired percentages in each racial/ethnic group. Regarding school type, the normative sample was within 1.5% of the desired range. Updates are recommended as the census data are now more than 20 years old.

Reliability scores for the SSQ were achieved using internal consistency indices and test-retest strategies. Cronbach's alphas for the standardization sample were .79 (Practical-Imaginative), .80 (Thinking-Feeling), and .87 (Organized-Flexible and Extroversion-Introversion). Given that the SSQ is designed with the developmental level of youth in mind, the instrument is intended to be as concise as possible; however, this likely produces a lower estimate of internal consistency (Oakland et al., 1996). To augment these figures, test-retest reliabilities were conducted with a seven-month interval and resulted in reliability coefficients ranging from .67 to .80, with an average of .74 for the four scales ($n = 137$ youth). The authors failed to report statistical power for these findings. Al-Balhan (2008) provided additional evidence of internal consistency reliability for a sample of middle school students ($\alpha = 0.76$).

The support for internal validity is offered through item analysis, expert consensus, and factor analysis. Initially, the authors used theoretical considerations to place each item within a scale, and those items subsequently were reviewed by a panel of experts. Oakland and colleagues (1996) noted that the dichotomous nature of items resulted in use of factor analysis, including parcel analysis. Detailed tables of item and parcel scores are provided in the manual and support a four-factor structure (Rounds & McKenna, 2001). Intercorrelations between the four scales range from −.03 (Practical-Imaginative and Extroverted-Introverted) to .24 (Organized-Flexible and Practical-Imaginative). As none of the four dimensions were highly correlated, independence among the scales is likely (Oakland et al., 1996; Rounds & McKenna, 2001).

In establishing external validity, the authors provide comprehensive information. Using several research studies, the SSQ scores were compared concurrently to other variables. For example, students' activity preferences were examined in relation to answers on the SSQ. Correlations between activity preferences (e.g., parties, quiet time alone, reading, school) and SSQ styles indicate significant correlations for 10 of the 16 pairs. Using convenience samples, Oakland and colleagues (1996) conducted two additional studies to examine concurrent validity by comparing students' scores on the SSQ (predictors) with responses on the Values Inventory (VI; Oakland, 1990) and the MBTI (criterion). In study one, multivariate correlations were significant for the relationships between SSQ scores and both the helpfulness domain (.54) and the loyalty domain (.38). In study two, multivariate correlations indicated significant relationships between scores on the SSQ and three of the four MBTI scales in the expected direction.

Student Styles Questionnaire

Further evidence of external validity is offered through four studies that examine divergent validity by comparing the SSQ to each of the following instruments: Weschler Intelligence Scale for Children-Third Edition (WISC-III; Weschler, 1981), California Achievement Test (CAT; CTB/McGraw-Hill, 1985), and the Metropolitan Achievement Test-Sixth Edition (MAT6; Prescott, Balow, Hogan, & Farr 1985). Overall, results from these studies indicate that style preferences as measured by the SSQ are independent of achievement and ability scores (Schraw, 2001).

General Utility and Evaluation

Overall, the manual is user-friendly. Strengths include detailed descriptions and case examples of interpretation using the 8 basic styles method (chapters 4, 5, & 7). The authors recommend that interpretation begin using the eight basic styles as opposed to the four Keirseian combinations or 16 style combinations. It should be noted that explanations on validity for the three methods are lacking (Schraw, 2001). A second strength is the inclusion of comparisons of strengths and pitfalls that students may display based on their style preference, and suggestions for minimizing these issues in the classroom. Major limitations of the manual include overly general information on Kierseian and 16-style combinations; these are mostly descriptive in nature and may lack utility with diverse cultures. As Schraw noted (2001), there is a paucity of information on whether the three interpretation methods provide similar information. There are several items that assess preference for time alone versus with family, and responses may be more indicative of cultural upbringing than preference. Further, it is unclear if young children can discern the difference between a preference and a behavior, as many are concrete thinkers. Finally, although the questions are designed to be appropriate at a third-grade reading level, some questions seem inappropriate for some children. Designing developmentally congruent questions may be useful.

The instrument is easy to use and affords school personnel an opportunity to gather information quickly. This information has relevance for academic performance, teaching methodologies, counseling modalities and techniques, and potential use for clarity between parents/guardians and children regarding learning styles and temperament. Al-Balhan (2008) reported an impact on science grades when teachers adjusted teaching methods based on learning style. An additional strength is the convergent validity with the MBTI instrument (Schraw, 2001) Additional empirical support could be useful.

References and Additional Resources

Al-Balhan, A. M. (2008). The student style questionnaire in relation to improved academic scores in Kuwaiti middle-school science classes. *Social Behavior & Personality, 36*, 217-228.

American School Counselor Association. (2012). *The ASCA National Model: A framework for school counseling programs, third edition.* Alexandria, VA: Author.

Bruno, M. (2009). [Student Styles Questionnaire.] In E. A. Whitfield, R. W. Feller, & C. Wood (Eds.), *A counselor's guide to career assessment instruments* (5th ed., pp. 413-419). Broken Arrow, OK: National Career Development Association.

CTB/McGraw-Hill. (1985). *California Achievement Test.* Monterey, CA : Author.

Joyce, D., & Oakland, T. (2005). Temperament differences among children with conduct disorder and oppositional defiant disorder. *The California School Psychologist, 10,* 125-136.

Jung, C. G. (1971). *Psychological types.* (translated by R. F. C. Hull, rev. of Trans, by H. G. Baynes). Princeton, NJ: Princeton University Press. (Original work published 1921).

Myers, I. B., & McCaulley, M. H. (1985). *Manual: A guide to the development and use of the Myers-Briggs Type Indicator.* Palo Alto, CA: Consulting Psychologists Press.

Myers, I. B., & Myers, P. B. (1980). *Gifts differing.* Palo Alto, CA: Consulting Psychologists Press.

Oakland, T. (1990). *The Values Inventory.* Austin, TX: Author.

Oakland, T., Glutting, J., & Horton, C. (1996). *Student Styles Questionnaire.* San Antonio, TX: The Psychological Corporation.

Prescott, G. A., Balow, I. H., Hogan, T. P., & Farr, R. C. (1985). *Metropolitan Achievement Tests, sixth edition.* San Antonio, TX: The Psychological Corporation.

A Counselor's Guide To Career Assessments Instruments

Rounds, J., & McKenna, M. C. (2001). Student Styles Questionnaire (SSQ). In J. T. Kapes, & Whitfield, E. A. (Eds.). *A counselor's guide to career assessment instruments* (4th ed., pp. 413-419). Columbus, OH: National Career Development Association.

Stafford, M. E. (1994). Validity of the STAR: Student Styles Questionnaire: Racial-ethnic comparisons. *Dissertation Abstracts International, 55,* (10A). (UMI No. 95-06097).

Schraw, G. (2001). [Student Styles Questionnaire]. In B. S. Plake & J. C. Impara (Eds.), *The fourteenth mental measurements yearbook* (pp.1197-1198)). Lincoln, NE: Buros Center for Testing.

Stafford, M. E., & Oakland, T. D. (1996a). Racial-ethnic comparisons of temperament constructs for three age groups using the Student Styles Questionnaire. *Measurement & Evaluation in Counseling & Development, 29,* 100-110.

Stafford, M. E., & Oakland, T. D. (1996b). Validity of the temperament constructs using the student styles questionnaire: Comparison for three racial-ethnic groups. *Journal of Psychoeducational Assessment, 14,* 109-120.

Stewart, J. R. (2004). [Student Styles Questionnaire]. In B. S. Plake & J. C. Impara (Eds.), *The fourteenth mental measurements yearbook* (pp. 1198-1199). Lincoln, NE: Buros Center for Testing.

Weschler, D. (1981). *Weschler Intelligence Scale for Children – Revised.* San Antonio, TX: The Psychological Corporation.

414

CHAPTER 15

INSTRUMENTS FOR SPECIAL POPULATIONS

- Ashland Interest Assessment

- Becker Work Adjustment Profile, Second Edition

- BRIGANCE Transition Skills Inventory

- Geist Picture Interest Inventory, Revised Eighth Printing

- Life Centered Career Education Complentency Assessment: Knowledge and Performance Batteries

- Picture Interest Career Survey, Second Edition

- Reading–Free Vocational Interest Inventory, Second Edition

- Workplace Sexual Identity Management Measure

ASHLAND INTEREST ASSESSMENT
Douglas N. Jackson and Connie W. Marshall

SIGMA Assessments Systems, Inc.
P.O. Box 610757
Port Huron, Michigan
USA 48061-0757
800.265.1285
800.361.9411
http://www.SigmaAssessmentsSystems.com

Target Population: Adolescents and adults, age 15 and older. Although it can be used by the general population, it was specifically designed to accommodate individuals with restricted abilities due directly or indirectly to any one or a combination of educational, physical, emotional, cognitive, or psychiatric conditions.

Statement of the Purpose of the Instrument: The Ashland Interest Assessment (AIA) is an inventory of career interests especially designed to be appropriate and easily understood by persons faced with variety of barriers to employment. Accordingly, the language level, content, and potential career options of the AIA were carefully chosen to address conditions that restrict a person's ability to make use of other widely used inventories. The AIA may be employed for educational and career exploration counseling, and decision making, and for conducting research concerning vocational interest, job satisfaction, and personnel classification.

Titles of Subtests, Scales, Scores Provided: Arts and Crafts, Sales, Clerical, Protective Service, Food Service, Personal Service, Health Care, General Service, Plant or Animal Care, Construction, Transportation, and Mechanical.

Forms and Levels Available, with Dates of Publication/Revision of Each: 1997.

Date of Most Recent Edition of Test Manual, User's Guide, Etc.: 1997.

Languages in Which Available: English and French.

Time:

    Actual Test Time: 35 minutes.

    Total Administration Time: 45 minutes.

Norm Group(s) on Which Scores Are Based: Norms were collected from employment agencies, schools, learning centers, psychiatric hospitals, and mental health associations. The AIA was normed on 725 females and 725 males.

Manner in Which Results Are Reported for Individuals: Raw Scores, Percentiles. The AIA Extended Report consists of a profile of the scores on the 12 Basic Interest scales, as well as a description of these scales. A profile of Similarity to 12 Occupational Groups and a narrative summary of the three highest-ranked Occupational Groups with links to the O*NET codes are also included. A summary report is provided for the counselor.

Report Format/Content for Group Summaries: Not available.

Mail-in Scoring Service: Available, can be processed within 48 hours.

Hand Scoring: Scored by counselor in approximately 15 minutes.

Computer Software Options Available: Computerized administration, reports are generated immediately. Online Testing Platform: Available 24 hours a day, 7 days a week; reports are scored and generated immediately.

Cost of Materials: Due to possible price changes since publication date, be sure to check the publisher's website. Test manual: $24.00.

    Specimen Set: $90.00 (includes a test manual on CD-ROM, five question and answer booklets, five profile sheets, five scoring sheets, one set of scoring templates, and one machine scorable question and answer booklet).

    Counselee Materials: A set of 25 question and answer booklets and a set of 25 response sheets (profile and scoring sheets) are $63.00 and $71.00, respectively. A set of templates costs $37.00. For mail-in machine scoring, question and answer booklets are $75.00-$85.00 for a set of 10 (price discounts are provided for

A COUNSELOR'S GUIDE TO CAREER ASSESSMENTS INSTRUMENTS

higher volumes ordered). A software installation package that includes 10 scoring coupons costs $150.00. To take the test and receive a report online costs $8.00 per administration with a SigmaTesting.com account. Additional pricing options are available on the publisher's website.

Published Reviews of the Instrument in the Last 15 Years:

Herrmann, A., & Shaff, C. (2009). [Ashland Interest Assessment.] In E. A.Whitfield, R. W. Feller, & C. Wood (Eds.), *A Counselor's guide to career assessment instruments* (5th ed., pp. 422-427). Broken Arrow, OK: National Career Development Association.

McCowan, R. J., & McCowan, S. C. (2001). [Ashland Interest Assessment.] In B.S. Plake & J. C. Impara (Eds.), *The fourteenth mental measurements yearbook.* Lincoln. NE: Buros Center for Testing.

ASHLAND INTEREST ASSESSMENT
Reviewed by:

Lori Ellison

Department of Counseling
Marshall University

Description

The Ashland Interest Assessment (AIA) is an instrument designed for individuals age 15 and older to assess vocational interests and match potential jobs with those interests. It encourages career exploration with those who have employment challenges such as "educational, physical, emotional, cognitive, or psychiatric conditions" (Sigma Assessment Systems Inc., 2012a). Such conditions may include a developmental delay, traumatic brain injury, learning disability, or chronic psychiatric disorder.

Items on the AIA are descriptions of activities, written at a third-grade level, and associated with jobs in one of 12 categories called "Basic Interest Scales" (Jackson & Marshall, 1997, p. 1). These scales are Arts & Crafts, Sales, Clerical, Protective Service, Food Service, Personal Service, Health Care, General Service, Plant or Animal Care, Construction, Transportation, and Mechanical. Items are presented in 144 forced-choice dyads, each dyad representing two different scales and 24 items per interest scale. Respondents are to select which of the two activities listed would be most enjoyable for them and fill in the corresponding circle (Jackson & Marshall, 1997).

Scores are presented to the respondent in a results profile bearing a percentile score based on comparison to the norm scores for the respondents' gender. Counselors are to explain the percentile scores so that respondents can understand what they represent. Scores are also compared to occupational groups who are working in jobs that corresponded to each of the 12 Basic Interest Scales. Respondents for the AIA are then compared to these workers' responses to see where respondents' scores are most similar in their interests (Jackson & Marshall, 1997). The profile report will give respondents their top three occupation groups along with a description that includes the group name, examples of tasks these workers might perform in their jobs, and a listing of sample jobs from the O*NET system that are associated with these occupational groups. The report also explains what information can be provided by O*NET about the jobs and where to go to access additional information on the Internet. A sample report may be found at the publisher's website (Sigma Assessment Systems, Inc., 2012b).

The AIA can be taken in a paper-and-pencil format or online. Administration involves a script found in the manual to clearly explain the procedures for marking the answer sheets for group or individual administration (Jackson & Marshall, 1997). Respondents take an average of 35 minutes to complete the AIA, but can take between 20 and 90 minutes (McCowan & McCowan, 2001). The online version is designed to keep the administration simple (single dyads on the screen at a time) and user-friendly (e.g., "Next" and "Back" buttons prompt to move between items).

Gainful employment drives individuals to seek not only compensation for their labor, but a sense of accomplishment, achievement, and self-worth (Lindstrom, Doren, & Miesch, 2011). For the differently abled, this requires extra support, training, and appropriate employment transitions (Lindstrom et al., 2011). Counselors need tools to help these adults find their way into a job that not only provides income, but also is a good match to their interests and abilities (Lorenz, 2011). The AIA is designed to "provide information that is useful for discovering the types of careers that coincide with a person's vocational interests" (Jackson & Marshall, 1997, p. 3). However, it should be stressed that this is not an assessment of the respondent's ability to perform a task (Jackson & Marshall, 1997).

Finding a career path that is not only functional but enjoyable helps the worker find fulfillment and increases the chances they will stay with that career (Jackson & Marshall, 1997; Turner, Unkefer, Cichy, Peper, & Juang, 2011). Those "misemployed" in jobs that do not match their interests are more prone to either leave the job or be terminated for poor work habits (e.g., absenteeism, behavior issues) than those who were employed in jobs matching their personal interests (Turner et al., 2011). The AIA provides a means for counselors to help these individuals find fulfilling careers.

Technical Considerations

The normative sample for the AIA was gathered by administering the assessment to 1,450 Canadian adults ages 15 to 64 years old. The sample represents 1 out of every 250 adults who fit the target population (Jackson & Marshall, 1997). There are no published studies to date that provide additional AIA psychometric data.

The reliability for the normative sample has much to do with why a forced choice format was chosen. In the early stages of formulating this assessment, an individual item form of the test yielded a high reliability coefficient; however, the likelihood of response bias weakened the impact. The forced choice version for the 12 Basic Interest Scales yields a range of Cronbach's alphas between .58 and .86, which remains fairly strong (Jackson & Marshall, 1997). Due to issues with response bias, one final administration of the inventory was conducted with a demographically similar, but smaller sample and compared to the larger sample. Three groups of Cronbach's alpha scores were calculated for three groups: males, females, and all participants by each of the 12 scales. Cronbach's alphas for these three groups ranged between .72 (General Service) and .90 (Construction) for all participants, between .69 (General Service) and .88 (Construction) for males, and between .73 (General Service) and .87 (Health Care) for females (Jackson & Marshall, 1997).

Jackson and Marshall (1997) conducted four phases of instrument construction to determine the most appropriate items for this assessment. In Phase I, both the interest scales and appropriate items for each were generated. The scales for this inventory were gleaned by use of the Canadian Classification and Dictionary of Occupations, The National Occupational Classification, structured interviews with members of the target population, and the Career Directions Inventory (CDI) and the Jackson Vocational Interest Survey (JVIS). Test items were devised differently from the CDI and JVIS to assure suitability for the target population. The normative sample for this phase was a total of 201 adults, 115 males and 86 females chosen from rehabilitation and remedial education programs. Phase II involved refining the format of the instrument from an individual item assessment to a forced choice format due to response bias. The sample for this phase came from the same agencies as those in Phase I. It included 55 males and 43 females.

In Phase III, they tested the final version of the AIA with a new, smaller sample ($N = 88$) of individuals from comparable backgrounds to the samples for Phases I and II, but none of these respondents were in the original samples. This administration of the inventory yielded higher reliability coefficients from previous administrations. Phase IV sought to standardize the AIA using a national sample of 1,450 individuals evenly matched by sex and all of whom met the criteria of at least one identifiable "hindering factor" to their employability (Jackson & Marshall, 1997, p. 50). In addition, there are two validity indices that measure responses not answered and consistency across responses to ensure that the respondent answers are not random or contrived, which would render results unusable.

Jackson and Marshall's (1997) factor analysis of the Basic Interest Scales show the scales loaded on four factors. One factor identified outdoor activities (i.e., Plant/Animal Care, Construction, and Transportation). Another factor identified activities that emphasize attention to detail and abiding by rules (i.e., Clerical, Protective Service, and Health Care). A third identified a single factor with an independent spirit (i.e., Arts and Crafts). The fourth and final factor identified with maintaining a clean/orderly environment (i.e., Health Care and General Service). Loadings on these factors indicated a broader interest for females than males, and males tended to show more preference for "blue collar" jobs. Further validity studies beyond face and construct validity and factor analysis of the Basic Interest Scales are not found in the descriptions of this assessment's development.

General Utility and Evaluation

The manual is well-written and organized. It includes information needed to understand, administer, score, and interpret the AIA as well as information describing its development and parameters. The appendices include scoring key, a listing of items by scale, a listing of the agencies from whom the normative sample were taken, sample profiles for the different scales, and a listing of possible jobs associated with each of the scales that would be appropriate for the target population. The instructions for administering, scoring, and interpreting the AIA are easy to understand and use. The explanation of the process of development and testing the AIA for reliability and construct validity were sufficiently detailed and a strong case for both was presented. McCowan and McCowan (2001) noted the AIA is a well-written, well-designed, well-tested, and a useful tool. They found the manual user-friendly and the ease of administration and scoring is clear.

Limitations of the AIA would likely include the paucity of validity studies other than construct validity reported in the manual and just how useful this instrument might be outside the target population. More study on the validity of the instrument would strengthen its usefulness. Perhaps comparing this to another measure of job satisfaction would give more evidence of its ability to measure how happy a respondent would be with a job that came out of their profile. The authors stated that this instrument could be useful for a broad range of respondents, but that it is so focused on accessibility for those with these disabilities may make it difficult to find use in the general population (Jackson & Marshall, 1997). The focus toward satisfaction with this particular range of employment opportunities would still be limiting to those who could achieve a higher level of employment and/or education.

The Sigma Assessment Systems website has a number of excellent resources available. The site has links for career counselors to help identify other possible inventories that might be of use as well as the information for computer scoring, hand scoring, and mail-in scoring of these assessment instruments. There are a number of links to professional organizations that could be of assistance to career counselors and their clients. Software downloads, online ordering, and online qualification for the assessment administrators is available for ease of use of these published assessment tools. This site can be accessed at the publisher's website.

References and Additional Resources

Herrmann, A., & Schaff, C. (2009). [Ashland Interest Assessment.] In E.A. Whitfield, R.W. Feller, & C. Wood (Eds.), *A counselor's guide to career assessment instruments* (5th ed., pp. 422-427). Broken Arrow, OK: National Career Development Association.

Jackson, D. N., & Marshall, C. W. (1997). *Ashland Interest Assessment manual.* Port Huron, MI: Sigma Assessment Systems, Inc.

Lindstrom, L., Doren, B., & Miesch, J. (2011). Waging a living: Career development and long term employment outcomes for young adults with disabilities. *Exceptional Children, 77,* 423-434.

Lorenz, D. C. (2011). A proposed integrative model for enhanced career development for young adults with disabilities. *Adultspan: Theory Research & Practice. 10,* 24-33.

McCowan, R. J., & McCowan, S. C. (2001). [Ashland Interest Assessment.] In B.S. Plake & J. C. Impara (Eds.), *The fourteenth mental measurements yearbook.* Lincoln. NE: Buros Center for Testing.

Sigma Assessment Systems, Inc. (2012a) *Ashland Interest Assessment.* Retrieved from http://www.sigmaassessmentsystems. com/assessments/aia.asp

Sigma Assessment Systems, Inc. (2012b) *Ashland Interest Assessment sample report.* Retrieved from http://www.sigmaassessmentsystems.com/samplereports/aiareport.pdf

Turner, S., Unkefer, L. C., Cichy, B. E., Peper, C., & Juang, J. (2011). Career interests and self-estimated abilities of young adults with disabilities. *Journal of Career Assessment, 19,* 183-196.

420

BECKER WORK ADJUSTMENT PROFILE, SECOND EDITION
Ralph L. Becker

Elbern Publications
P.O. Box 9497
Columbus, OH 43209
ebecker@insight.rr.com

Target Population: Individuals who are school-age to adult (ages 13-69) with special needs such as mental retardation/intellectual disability, learning disability, physical disability, emotionally disturbed, economically disadvantaged, or developmentally disabled (e.g., has autism, cerebral palsy, epilepsy).

Statement of the Purpose of the Instrument: The Becker Work Adjustment Profile, second edition (BWAP:2) is designed to assess the vocational competency and needed work supports of individuals who are classified with special needs to be successful in the workplace or related areas of work. The instrument assesses the vocational competence of individuals for work placement or training in five levels: Day Care, Work Activity, Extended Workshop, Transitional, and Community-competitive. Work supports are listed/assessed from least to most supports for an individual as Limited, Low, Moderate, High, and Extensive.

Titles of Subtests, Scales, Scores Provided: The subtests are listed as Work Habits & Attitudes, Interpersonal Relations, Cognitive Skills, Work Performance and Skills, and a composite score called Broad Work Adjustment. Raw scores are converted to standard scores, percentiles, and levels of vocational competency and supports.

Forms and Levels Available, with Dates of Publication/Revision of Each: 2005.

Date of Most Recent Edition of Test Manual, User's Guide, Etc.: 2005.

Languages in Which Available: English only.

Time:

Actual Test Time: 10 minutes or fewer.

Total Administration Time: 15 minutes or fewer.

Norm Group(s) on Which Scores Are Based: Norm groups included individuals characterized with mental retardation or an intellectual disability, learning disability, physical disability, emotional disturbance, and economic disadvantage. Separate norms for special populations are being considered at this time to strengthen the BWAP:2.

Manner in Which Results Are Reported for Individuals Standard scores, Percentiles, and levels of vocational competency and supports as descriptive ratings are provided. A two-page report of client performance completed by the examiner includes a graphic profile of performance for each examinee.

Report Format/Content for Group Summaries: Not available.

Machine Scoring: Not available.

Hand Scoring: Scored by counselor within approximately 15 minutes.

Local Machine Scoring: Not available.

Computer Software Options Available: Not available.

Cost of Materials: Due to possible price changes since publication date be sure to check with publisher.

Specimen Set: Two test booklets and one manual: $41.00.

Counselee Materials: Manual: $40.00 (reusable), Package of 25 test booklets $33.75 (non-reusable), package of 50 test booklets $31.75 per set of 25 (non-reusable), and Value Kit: 25 test booklets and one manual: $70.75 (only manual is reusable).

Published Reviews of the Instrument in the Last 15 Years:

Austin, J. T., & Tischendorf, S. D. (2007). [Becker Work Adjustment Profile: 2.] In R. A. Spies & B. S. Plake (Eds.), *The seventeenth mental measurements yearbook.* Lincoln, NE: Buros Center for Testing.

Becker Work Adjustment Profile, Second Edition

Reviewed by:

James T. Austin

Center on Education and Training for Employment
The Ohio State University

Description

Counselor work increasingly addresses and includes diverse populations; among the largest populations are individuals with special needs. Individuals may be diagnosed with issues of a cognitive, behavioral, or emotional nature. Traditionally referred to as MR/DD for mental retardation/developmental delay, individuals with cognitive delays are typically classified on the basis of general mental ability scores. As part of services that are often outlined in treatment plans, it is often useful to focus on occupational and vocational themes. Researchers have begun to address perceptions by employers of applicants or incumbents with disabilities (Graffam, Shinkfield, Smith, & Polzin, 2002). Such a vocational focus may include levels of supported-sheltered and non-supported work for individuals in the MR/DD and similar populations, representing a construct of employability, which establishes a need to create measurement tools for practitioners and for researchers. This review focuses on the Becker Work Adjustment Profile 2 (BWAP:2; Becker, 2005).

The BWAP:2 is completed by a rater-observer to measure vocational competency in special needs populations in competitive or sheltered work situations. It can best be described as a re-standardization of the 1989 Work Adjustment Profile (the items did not change as noted in the Becher 2005, User's Manual on p. 40). In particular, individuals from categories of mental retardation, learning disabled, physically disabled, emotionally disturbed, and economically disadvantaged were included in the revision standardization sample which yields normative scores.

The BWAP:2 used by a rater-observer is laid out as a Questionnaire Booklet. Page 1 provides a section for documenting background information about the examinee and the evaluator (name, sex, date, grade, date of birth, age in years/months, IQ, school/facility, primary disability, secondary disability, name of evaluator, title of evaluator). Precise instructions to the rater-observer are provided at the bottom of the first page. Pages 2 through 12 present 63 ratings in four domains: Work Habits/Attitudes (HA) with 10 items, Interpersonal Relations (IR) with 12 items, Cognitive Skills (CO) with 19 items, and Work Performance Skills (WP) with 22 items. For each item there are anchor statements ranging from levels 0 to 4, from the lowest level to the highest level of vocational competence. A rater-observer completes the BWAP:2, totals the points, and enters the totals at the end of each domain. The rater-observer can then complete an Individual Profile Form (page 13) in four sections including (1) background information (repeated from page 1), (2) Score Summary featuring entries for the raw score, T-score ($M = 50$, $SD = 10$), Percentile, Work Placement, and Work Support needs together with specific Norm Used and Broad Work Adjustment (BWA) and (3) Vocational Competency Profile with T-scores and a set of work/training placements. The profile is followed by a page entitled *Interpretation of Results* to permit a narrative component. This tool is available only in paper form.

The spiral-bound user's manual (Becker, 2005) contains six chapters, references, and two annexes (Appendix A in the manual provides Normative Tables and Placements/Supports Guidelines; appendix B provides three case studies). In chapter 1, Becker (2005) articulated four methods of client work evaluation: work samples, job analysis, standardized tests, and situational assessment. The BWAP:2 is a situational assessment (associated with advantages and disadvantages; for example, knowledge of and opportunity to observe rated individuals). Secondly, the nature of vocational competence as being closely related to work adjustment is discussed. In addition, it is noted that vocational competence is considered to be typical rather than maximal performance. In the remainder of the first chapter, the profile in its entirety is discussed, the Questionnaire Booklet is briefly described including a Level B requirement for rater-observers (American Educational Research Association [AERA], American Psychological Association [APA], & National Council on Measurement in Education [NCME], 1999), and six research topics are offered as examples of BWAP:2 usage.

A Counselor's Guide To Career Assessments Instruments

Chapters 2 through 4 present the basics of administration, scoring, and use, while the last two chapters provide evidence of reliability and validity. Chapter 2 presents a discussion of the administration and scoring of the BWAP:2. The instrument should be completed by a rater-observer who has, according to the user's manual and Questionnaire Booklet, "... closely observed the daily work behavior of the client and has knowledge of the individual's work adjustment" (Becker, 2005, p. 1). The estimated time to complete the instrument is 15 minutes, although it is unclear whether the interpretation of results is included. The completed item page in Figure 2.1 (Work Habits/Attitudes) in the User's Manual is useful, and it is clear how interventions might be structured from a review of the items (that is, eating habits at work would be a pinpoint target for this hypothetical individual). Chapter 3 presents material concerning completion of the individual profile form and then moves to the interpretation of raw and normative scores. A sample Individual Profile Form (Figure 3.2) is helpful in that it provides quantitative and qualitative information, in addition to a visual representation of a sample profile. Chapter 4 presents material on normative procedures (discussed below).

Extensive information is available regarding the re-standardization of the BWAP:2 between 2002 and 2005. The approach is norm-referenced, and the test theory is classical. Procedures are described in different parts of the user's manual, with chapters 5 and 6 concentrating on reliability and validity support for use of the BWAP:2. Because the profile items are unchanged, my review is concentrated within the technical section below. For this review, I examined the Questionnaire Booklet and a 69-page user's manual (Becker, 2005). No other technical documents were provided for review by the publisher. I examined, in addition, reviews of the first edition of the BWAP by Bolton (1992) and by Gory (1992) to identify and verify changes suggested for the BWAP:2. Bolton and Parker (2008) provided extensive coverage of measurement related to various aspects of rehabilitation practice.

Becker (2005) provided information regarding the re-standardization of the revised Work Adjustment Profile. In the User's Manual, Table 4.1 categorizes the standardization sample by diagnostic category and gender, and presents norms, means, and standard deviations for chronological age and IQ, and IQ range. No information is given about the method of IQ assessment, which makes it hard to evaluate the procedure. The sample was geographically diverse as shown in Table 4.2, but may not be nationally representative (further detail is required). Sites in 20 states were included in the norm sample, with random samples drawn by the administrator of each site. Table 4.3 contains a breakdown of the standardization sample into four levels of mental retardation: mild, moderate, several, and profound. The normative data are found in Appendix A, collapsed across age levels, in Tables A.1 to A.5 with T-scores (73 to 27 top to bottom) presented in the left most column, raw scores for each of the domains and Broad Work Adjustment in the middle five columns, and percentiles (99 to 1) presented in the rightmost column.

Technical Considerations

Chapter 5 of the user's manual pertains to reliability, with estimates of reliability for the BWAP:2 derived from subsamples based on diagnostic category (N's ranging from 76 to 105). The estimates presented in Tables 5.1–5.6 and discussed include internal consistency (Cronbach alpha) for domain and for BWA total score (range .80 to .93), test-retest estimates over a two-week interval (range .82 to .96 across domains), standard errors of measurement (range 0.91 to 5.84), and interrater reliability estimated by pairs of rater-observers for a sample of 117 adults in three sheltered workshops (range .82 to .89 across domains, .87 for Broad Work Adjustment). These values, representing multiple estimates of reliability, demonstrate appropriate obtained levels. The importance of taking into consideration the standard error of measurement and using measures other than the BWAP:2 scores in making decisions regarding vocational competence is acknowledged. The standard error of measurement for the BWAP:2 is summarized in Table 5.7 as a matrix (domain X category) with three levels of confidence (95, 90, 68). This section also includes a brief case on interpreting an individual's scores using standard error of measurement. Helpful and detailed information is one hallmark of this tool.

Validity is regarded as the quintessence of test or scale quality (Bolton & Parker, 2008; Power, 2006). This primacy will be maintained in the forthcoming revision of the 1999 *Standards for Educational and Psychological Tests* (AERA, APA, & NCME, 1999). Chapter 6 of the user's manual pertains to validity, which is presented within traditional categories of content, criterion, and construct evidence. This tripartite view represents pre-1999 *Standards* interpretations, which have moved toward the primacy of construct validity.

Evidence of content validity is asserted in two ways: rationales for the four domains and statistical item analysis. The former rationale is based on research conducted in the mid-1960s and may require revisiting at some point in time to incorporate recent advances (Bolton & Parker, 2008). The scale analysis ($N = 1,194$ from the standardization sample) is a combination of test item analysis (depending heavily on the point biserial correlation) and exploratory principal factors analysis (using common variance as the starting point). The item analysis resulted in median point–biserial coefficients that seem large relative to commonly reported values in technical reports (.67, .61, .79, and .65 for the domains and .70 for BWA). The factor analysis resulted in a four-factor solution accounting for nearly identical proportions of variance compared to the first edition scale (same items, different standardization sample), which should support potential user confidence through replication. A suggestion involves applying the confirmatory approach to factor analysis to provide a stronger test of the items as assigned to the domain structure, and to facilitate a comparison between a general factor model (Broad Work Adjustment only) and a four factor solution, or a hierarchical solution with first level and a second level BWA factors.

Criterion-related validity is discussed, although the description seems to portray convergent validity, which is the notion that separate instruments that measure the same characteristics or traits are highly correlated. Criterion-related validity typically is regarded as how well one instrument predicts success in some defined outcome, here the vocational work adjustment domain. Becker (2005) described correlation of the BWAP:2 scores with the American Association on Mental Retardation (AAMR) Adaptive Behavior Scale, which also, in part, measures vocational competence. (The AAMR is now known as the American Association for Intellectual and Developmental Disabilities.) These data are used to address a recommendation not to use the placements provided with the first edition. Development of supports, to the credit of the developer, is also discussed in light of Bolton's (1992) critique that the work placement levels and work supports should be disregarded because of lack of supporting evidence.

Construct validity is addressed explicitly in chapter 6 on page 44. The treatment consists of a definition and proposal of six testable hypotheses. Additional issues suggested for investigation include consequential validity associated with use of the instrument, as well as the categories of evidence.

General Utility and Evaluation

The re-standardization is based on an instrument that was revised and reviewed in *The Eleventh Mental Measurements Yearbook* by Bolton (1992) and subsequently by Austin and Tischendorf (2007). This tool is recommended for those interested in vocational placements from sheltered up to competitive. Still, several issues require clarification and would be helpful in future documentation and revision of the BWAP:2:

1. The economically disadvantaged subgroup is included with various mentally and psychologically diagnosed subgroups. A more detailed rationale for inclusion of this particular group, including research to support it, would be beneficial (for example, the "generational poverty" stream of research and intervention). Further, the learning disabled group is a wide-ranging category; additional detail would be helpful.

2. The largest emphasis is provided on mental retardation, and the theoretical model, although never clearly stated, may be dated when compared with recent approaches to concepts such as learning disability.

3. Item response theory might be helpful in analyzing data and conceptualizing the constructs; confirmatory factor analysis might be helpful in evaluating the construct validity of the four domains and the BWA composite score. A Rasch faceted approach is an appropriate method of estimation, with the capability to conduct "Item Mapping" of rated individuals against rating dimensions. This could be tied into the findings of Graffam et al. (2002) that employers report focusing on personal appearance and work performance when making personnel decisions.

4. Comparing systematically ordered levels of "opportunity to observe" or familiarity across rater-observers might establish the validity of observational data. It is important that the familiarity of vocational competence is standardized across all raters.

5. Another consideration would be to examine the effects of increasing the length of the retest period (more than two weeks). It would be possible to compare such results to the results of the two-week retest period. A combination of longer retest period and high obtained values would strengthen the already-impressive reliability evidence.

A Counselor's Guide To Career Assessments Instruments

6. It would be interesting to have the results of the standardization sample (N = 4,019) further broken down by age (instead of mean age by disadvantage), ethnicity, and sex. It would also be beneficial to have the data provided that would include any statistically significant differences in regard to age, ethnicity, and sex. This could be accomplished with access to the dataset maintained by the publisher.

7. The influence of technology is permeating education and work, from social media to cloud computing and storage. It is legitimate to inquire about how technology could affect the BWAP:2 in terms of technical quality; e.g., storing scores in a data warehouse in order to update norms over time.

8. Lastly, the forthcoming revision of the 1999 *Standards* is expected to be approved during 2012-2013, and publication and application will follow. There will be changes — testing fairness seems to be collapsed into a single chapter—but the primacy of validity will remain. It will be important to re-align the BWAP:2 with the new standards when they are released. Indeed, this should be accomplished across testing and assessment practice within counseling and rehabilitation.

Shifts in practice and policy occur in the fields of mental retardation and vocational rehabilitation across a range of disabilities (cf. Drebing et al. 2012). This means that reliable, valid, and unbiased client evaluation is crucial for a range of counseling purposes. These purposes range from individual intervention planning to program evaluation and from basic research to policy evaluation. The BWAP:2 was re-standardized to improve the rating of vocational competency by observers of individuals from five special populations. Four domains and a total composite score (Broad Work Adjustment) are used in developing a profile and work placement that can be related to work support needs. The BWAP:2 instrument is easily administered and scored by rater-observers with ample opportunity to observe the focal individual. The evidence provided concerning the revision and standardization supports the use of scores from the instrument. Consider that a large sample of 4,019 was used to develop the norms, although it is unbalanced in favor of mental retardation diagnosis (1,621/4,019 = 40%). Several improvements have been made to this instrument, including a revised version of the score summary (IPF), expanded normative tables, updated normative standardization data, example case studies, and attention to previous reviewer suggestions. A Chinese language version is available (Li & Tsang, 2002), but should be updated to the second edition before usage. Any issues that remain in no way preclude use of the BWAP:2 but are suggestions to continue development of the knowledge base to support evidence-based practice. In conclusion, this is an excellent and recommended tool that would benefit from technology infusion and continued research into validity of score interpretations.

References and Additional Resources

American Educational Research Association, American Psychological Association, & National Council on Measurement in Education (1999). *Standards for educational and psychological testing.* Washington, DC: Authors

Austin, J. T., & Tischendorf, S. D. (2007). [Becker Work Adjustment Profile: 2.] In R. A. Spies & B. S. Plake (Eds.), *The seventeenth mental measurements yearbook.* Lincoln, NE: Buros Center for Testing.

Becker, R. L. (2005). *Becker Work Adjustment Profile, second edition user's manual.* Columbus, OH: Elbern Publications.

Bolton, B. (1992). [Becker Work Adjustment Profile.] In J. J. Kramer & J. C. Conoley (Eds.), *The eleventh mental measurements yearbook* (pp. 83-84). Lincoln, NE: Buros Center for Testing.

Bolton, B., & Parker, M. (Eds.). (2008). *Handbook of measurement and evaluation in rehabilitation* (4th ed.). Gaithersburg, MD: Aspen Publishers.

Drebing, C. E., Bell, M., Campinell, E. A., Fraser, R., Malec, J., Penk, W., & Pruitt-Stevens, L. (2012). Vocational services research: Recommendations for next stage of work. *Journal of Rehabilitation Research & Development, 49,* 101-120.

Gory, E. L. (1992). [Becker Work Adjustment Profile. In J. J. Kramer & J. C. Conoley (Eds.), *The eleventh mental measurements yearbook.* (pp. 84-86). Lincoln, NE: Buros Center for Testing.

Graffam, J., Shinkfield, A., & Smith, K., & Polzin, U. (2002). Factors that influence employer decisions in hiring and retaining an employee with a disability. *Journal of Vocational Rehabilitation, 17,* 175-181.

Li, R. S. Y., & Tsang, H. W. (2002). The Chinese version of the Becker Work Adjustment Profile for use by people with developmental disabilities – BWAP-CV – Becker Work Adjustment Profile. *Journal of Rehabilitation, 68,* 52-58.

Power, P. W. (2006). *A guide to vocational assessment* (4th ed.). Odessa, FL: Pro-Ed.

426

A COUNSELOR'S GUIDE TO CAREER ASSESSMENTS INSTRUMENTS

BRIGANCE TRANSITION SKILLS INVENTORY
Albert H. Brigance

Curriculum Associates
153 Rangeway Road
North Billerica, MA 01862
http://www.curriculumassociates.com

Target Population: Adolescents; middle and high school students.

Statement of the Purpose of the Instrument: The BRIGANCE Transition Skills Inventory (TSI) helps educators easily assess independent living, employment, and additional post-secondary skills to support transition planning for middle and high school students.

Titles of Subtests, Scales, Scores Provided: The tool provides criterion-referenced scores for four areas: Academic Skills (e.g., speaking, writing, math), Post-Secondary Opportunities (e.g., interests, communication, technology), Independent Living (e.g., food, clothing, money, housing), and Community Participation (e.g., resources, citizenship, signs). There are hundreds of subtests that all fall within these categories.

Forms and Levels Available, with Dates of Publication/Revision of Each: Not available.

Date of Most Recent Edition of Test Manual, User's Guide, Etc.: 2010.

Languages in Which Available: English only.

Time:

    Actual Test Time: Varies.

    Total Administration Time: Varies.

Norm Group(s) on Which Scores Are Based: Not available.

Manner in Which Results Are Reported for Individuals: Results are reported to assessment administrator through the TSI Record Book. Each 81-page TSI Record Book is pre-printed and is used to manually record the result of each assessment question for each individual. By using pens or pencils of different colors to record assessment data, a color-coded record is developed that is ongoing, graphic, and easily interpreted.

Report Format/Content for Group Summaries: The BRIGANCE Online Management System offers individual and group reports.

Machine Scoring: Not available.

Hand scoring: Scored by counselor.

Computer Software Options Available: Browser-based Online Management System provides an online Record Book, exportable goals and objectives, and progress reporting feature (i.e., teacher, administrator, and family reports).

Cost of Materials: Due to possible price changes since publication date, be sure to check the publisher's website.

    Specimen Set: The Complete Transitions Kit: $599.00 (TSI and Transition Skills Activities).

    Counselee Materials: The BRIGANCE TSI items are priced as follows: Kit, $259.00; TSI, $199.00; TSI Record Books 10-pack, $39.00; TSI Record Books 100-pack, $359.99. The BRIGANCE Online Management System service provides one- or three-year student licenses (10 license minimum for new customers) ranging from $6.00 to $8.00 and $15.00 to $20.00 each, respectively, depending on the number of licenses.

Published Reviews of the Instrument in the Last 15 Years: Not available.

BRIGANCE Transition Skills Inventory

BRIGANCE Transition Skills Inventory

Reviewed by:

Jonna L. Bobzien

Department of Communication Disorders and Special Education
Old Dominion University

Description

The BRIGANCE Transition Skills Inventory (TSI) is one of the assessment tools within the BRIGANCE family of assessment instruments. The TSI is a compilation of two previously published assessments, the Employability Skills Inventory and the Life Skills Inventory, and involves significant content additions and updates. The TSI consists of a series of more than 100 criterion-referenced assessments targeting skills necessary for students with special needs as they begin post-secondary transition preparations (Curriculum Associates, 2010). The TSI measures skills and transition service needs in four key areas: Academic Skills (e.g., speaking, writing, math), Post-Secondary Opportunities (e.g., interests, communication, technology), Independent Living (e.g., food, clothing, money, housing), and Community Participation (e.g., resources, citizenship, signs). The required assessment materials include the TSI assessment manual and accompanying TSI student Record Book which is used to track individual student progress over time in each of the four key areas. Because classroom teachers are the targeted assessors, no specific training in the administration of the assessment or interpretation of results is required. Furthermore, the publisher advertises the assessment as having "easy-to-follow directions that can be adapted for students at different skill levels" (Curriculum Associates, 2010, p.1). Despite the apparent ease of administration, no total administration time was stated. Due to variation in the number of skills to be assessed per session and the heterogeneous nature of the targeted population, the assessment period differs for each student. Further, assessment can take place over multiple days and include a single or multiple assessments during that period.

The TSI is intended to serve as a tool that provides assistance to school personnel as they establish appropriate transition goals for middle and high school students with special needs. The publisher states the TSI "can help special education programs to meet the requirements for transition planning and effectively support the success of students with special needs as they prepare to transition out of high school" (Curriculum Associates, 2010, p. 10). Specifically, the TSI targets assessment in four major relevant skill areas. The first series of assessments focus upon academic skills: students are required to participate successfully in real-life situations (e.g., writing personal data, ordering food, following a schedule, purchasing products). The next series of assessments concentrate on the students post-secondary interests and choices (e.g., educational interests, career interests, work ethics) as well as their level of knowledge and skill related to post-secondary opportunities (e.g., resume writing, employment forms, computer skills). The independent living series of assessments center on skills students need to function self-sufficiently (e.g., following recipes, purchasing food, laundering clothes, riding a bus). The final series of assessment focus upon the understanding of community resources available (e.g., post office, library, recreation facilities), as well as skills related to citizenship (e.g., reading a ballot, casting a vote, going to a polling center).

In addition to the four main assessment areas, there is a final section of the TSI which serves as a tool for student self-assessment. The purpose of the self-assessment is to assist the student become more aware of traits, behaviors, attitudes, and skills needed for success in post-secondary settings (e.g., work, life, education, and community). The results of all assessments are chronicled in the corresponding TSI Record Book. The Record Book is intended for use with one student and provides ongoing, graphic, and easily interpreted data. In addition to tracking student progress, the Record Book can be used to communicate data on the student's development to both parents and transition team members.

Each relevant skill area section is comprised of a several age-appropriate, criterion-referenced assessments. The academic skills section is comprised of 29 assessments targeting reading grade placement, listening and speaking skills, functional writing skills, and math skills. A few specific assessment topics in the academic skills section include reading vocabulary grade-placement, general speaking skills, writing skills, and math

A COUNSELOR'S GUIDE TO CAREER ASSESSMENTS INSTRUMENTS

skills. Sample items within each assessment topic include pronunciation of words (grade placement), speaking/language skills used in daily situations such as answering "why" questions and giving directions (general speaking skills), written responses to personal data questions such as color of hair, birthday, and address (writing skills), and math direction words, calendar usage, and weight measurements (math skills). The premise behind this assessment section is to determine the level of student's academic skills needed to perform independently in real-life situations.

The post-secondary opportunities portion contains 30 individual assessments focusing upon interests and choices, job-related writing skills, job-related knowledge and skills, and communication/technology skills. A sample of assessment topics in this section include career interests, simple employment application information, abbreviations, parts of manual basic telephone skills, and everyday technology skills. The series of assessments in this section are meant to assist students to develop educational and career awareness, as well as to develop vocational and technical skills that foster success in post-secondary settings.

The independent living portion of the TSI is the largest section, containing 46 assessments that target skills related to food, clothing, housing, money and finance, health, and travel/transportation. Sample items within each assessment topic include food vocabulary, reading menus, and following basic recipes (food); personal clothing sizes and reading clothing labels (clothing); tenant agreements and understanding housing ads (housing); understanding price signs, making change, and balancing a checkbook (money and finance); medical vocabulary, medicine labels, and effects of drugs (health); and traffic signs/symbols, driver's license application, and reading road maps (travel/transportation).The goal of this section of the TSI is to establish a basic level of knowledge in skill areas related to independent living.

The fourth section, community participation, consists of 19 individual assessments in the areas of community resources, community signs, and citizenship. These assessments are meant to measure a student's comprehension of resources available in the community. A sample of assessment topics in this section include warning signs, seeking community assistance, voting, and using a post office.

The final section of the TSI is the self-assessment and rating scales portion of the tool. This section allows the student to rate themselves on personal traits, behaviors, attitudes, and skills needed to be successful in work, education, the community, and life. The self-assessment section is comprised of 12 individual assessments pertaining to topics such as speaking skills (talks *with* person rather than *at* person, speaks in complete sentences, forms clear questions), listening skills (tunes out noises and distractions, doesn't talk and listen at same time, avoids getting angry), self-concept (makes good decisions, happy with self, can be depended upon), job requirements (follows directions, checks quality of work, stays focused), health practices (gets enough rest, eats a balanced meal, seeks medical attention when necessary), and driving (remains calm, shows courtesy and consideration, uses seat belt).

Once administration is complete, the results from each individual assessment targeted within the four relevant skill areas are examined. The premise of the TSI is to yield assessment data referenced to a prescribed standard for performing a skill, basically identifying specific skills that have and have not been mastered by the student. Assessment results are recorded using multiple methods, unique to each skill area examined. For example, results for academic skills and community resources are typically based on the performance of the student, on specific skills, whereas results for independent living and post-secondary are often presented in a rating-scale format (e.g., much improvement needed, could be improved, acceptable, or very good). Although the overall goal of the individual assessments is not to provide a quantitative score, the results provide a "basis for comparison against a prescribed standard for performing a skill" (Curriculum Associates, 2010, p. 10). Consequently, appropriate educational goals and objectives addressing transition skills can be created using the individual assessment results. Although the TSI contains more than 100 individual assessments, administration is not meant to target every skill described in the manual. Practical use of the tool requires the administrator to select priority skills based upon a student's individual needs, thus limiting the number of assessments actually completed with the student. The actual administration of these assessments is intended to occur across several settings, allowing for flexibility in the assessment method. Furthermore, the assumption is that the TSI is a tool that will be used for ongoing monitoring of progress. The same protocol and Record Book can be used multiple times for an individual student by dating assessment results and using colored pencils and/or pens to record results and progress.

BRIGANCE Transition Skills Inventory

The primary function of the TSI is to provide a basic understanding of the current transition skills demonstrated by middle school and high school students with special needs. As established by Public Law 94-142 (IDEA, 1990), all students over the age of 16 with disabilities are required to have an Individualized Transition Plan (ITP) created by a multidisciplinary team. Whereby the BRIGANCE assessment tools were originally created by a school psychologist (Brigance, 1995), ITP members such as educators, counselors, and psychologists may find the results of the TSI beneficial when assisting an adolescent in developing realistic long-term transition goals and objectives. Such a tool is beneficial given the unfortunate disregard and involvement of crucial school personnel (e.g., school counselors, therapists) in current transition plan creation, specifically multi-year plans that explore academics, career interests, and self-advocacy (Hitchings et al., 2001; Milsom, 2007). For example, school counselors may be able to utilize the TSI results when advising students with disabilities regarding vocational options and enrollment in institutions of higher education. The creation of effective transition goals will assist the student and family with post-secondary planning while providing information regarding the student's strengths and weaknesses with regards to vocational planning. Furthermore, the self-assessment portion of the TSI promotes self-awareness which can assist in the development of realistic life-long goals.

Technical Considerations

Within the TSI assessment, the specific criteria targeted align with the four transition requirements outlined by IDEA: (1) Administration of age-appropriate, non-discriminatory transition assessments; (2) Identification of student's strengths and transition service needs; (3) Development of an Individualized Education Plan (IEP) that includes a student's present level of performance, measurable post-secondary goals, and recommendations on how to meet the goals; and (4) Regular consultation with parent or guardian. Regrettably, there is a lack of technical data provided for the TSI. The publisher indicates a lack of need for reliability and/or validity data since the assessment tool is criterion-referenced rather than norm-referenced. Interested readers, however, can review field testing information on predecessor assessment tools (i.e., Employability and Life Skills Inventories; see Carlson, 2009). Nevertheless, the paucity of technical data is a concern given that this tool is intended to drive academic and vocational planning for students with special needs. Specifically, a lack of content validity (i.e., are items on assessment considered important?) and construct validity (i.e., to what extent does TSI measure development and readiness skills?) is unfortunate. Additionally, since the TSI a relatively new BRIGANCE assessment, this author could find no evidence of field test locations or professional recommendations for this particular tool.

General Utility and Evaluation

Despite the absence of empirical support, the TSI appears to be a positive new organization of two previous instruments in the BRIGANCE family of assessments. The information and instructions provided in the TSI manual are easy to interpret and allow for modification of assessment methods as deemed necessary. This flexibility increases the overall utility of the tool by providing access to a wider range of students with special needs (e.g., moderate or severe intellectual disabilities, autism, limited English proficiency, speech-language impairments). Despite the large amount of material introduced, the information presented in the TSI manual and the TSI Record Book is thorough, concise, and well-organized. Also, a free, online introductory training regarding the use of the TSI is available at the publisher's website.

The TSI manual provides clear and precise directions for each assessment, as well as suggestions that outline acceptable modifications to the testing method for each assessment. For example, students may respond to questions using oral, written, or gestural responses, and some assessments may be completed in group settings rather than one-on-one. An additional benefit of the TSI is that all assessment materials in the manual are reproducible as needed. Furthermore, for an additional cost, educators may purchase the BRIGANCE Transition Skills Activities manual. This complementing manual provides lesson plans, and classroom-based and community-based activities that target skills assessed by the TSI. Finally, to assist assessment administrators with data collection, an Online Management System that works seamlessly with the TSI is available. This online system supports management of assessment data for up to 30 students per single license by providing guidance for writing transition goals/objectives, as well as generating individual and group progress reports for

A Counselor's Guide To Career Assessments Instruments

distribution to administrators and families (Curriculum Associates, 2010). Overall, due to its comprehensiveness, convenience and flexibility, the new BRIGANCE TSI should emerge as an appealing post-secondary planning instrument for use in both educational and clinical settings.

References and Additional Resources

Brigance, A. H. (1995). BRIGANCE Diagnostic Life Skills Inventory. *Intervention in School & Clinic, 30*(5), 313-315. doi: 10.1172/105345129503000512

BRIGANCE Special Education System (n.d.). *The online management system.* Retrieved from http://www.BRIGANCE.com

Carlson, J. V. (2009). [BRIGANCE Diagnostic Life Skills Inventory and BRIGANCE Diagnostic Employability Skills Inventory.] In E. A. Whitfield, R. W. Feller, & C. Wood (Eds.), *A Counselor's Guide to Career Assessment Instruments* (5th ed.). Broken Arrow, OK: National Career Development Association.

Curriculum Associates. (2010). *BRIGANCE Transition Skills Inventory.* North Billerica, MA: Author.

Hitchings, W. E., Luzzo, D. A., Ristow, R., Harvath, M., Retish, P., & Tanners, A. (2001). The career development needs of college students with learning disabilities: In their own words. *Learning Disabilities Research & Practice, 16*(1), 8-17.

Individuals with Disabilities Education Act of 1990 (IDEA), 20 U.S.C. §1400 et seq. (1990).

Milsom, A. (2007). School counselor involvement in postsecondary transition planning for students with disabilities. *Journal of School Counseling, 5*(23), 1-22.

A COUNSELOR'S GUIDE TO CAREER ASSESSMENTS INSTRUMENTS

GEIST PICTURE INTEREST INVENTORY, REVISED EIGHTH PRINTING
Harold Geist

Western Psychological Services

12031 Wilshire Blvd.
Los Angeles, CA 90025-1251
http://www.wpspublish.com

Target Population: Children, adolescents, young adults, and adults. Specific population uses include the following: students with disabilities, students of low reading ability or non-readers, educationally deprived students, eighth grade through adult populations, individual and group administrations, adults with developmental disabilities, deaf individuals, youth involved in the juvenile justice system, and young children who lack verbal and reading abilities.

Statement of the Purpose of the Instrument: The purposes of this inventory are as follows: (1) assess quantitatively 11 male and 12 female general interest areas, (2) identify motivating forces behind occupational choice, (3) provide an interest inventory for working with those having limited verbal abilities, (4) provide possible additional information through projective uses, and (5) expand research.

Titles of Subtests, Scales, Scores Provided: Subtests: Picture Triad booklet (for male and female) and Motivation Questionnaire (for male and female).

Scales include seven motivational areas (Could Not Say, Family, Prestige, Financial, Intrinsic and Personality, Environmental, and Past Experience) and interest areas (Persuasive, Clerical, Mechanical, Musical, Scientific, Outdoor, Literary, Computational, Artistic, Social Service, Dramatic, and Personal Service; Personal Service only for females).

Two basic groups of scores are obtained from the Geist Picture Interest Inventory (GPII):
1. Interest: 11 for males, 12 for females
2. Motivation: 7 for males, 7 for females

Forms and Levels Available, with Dates of Publication/Revision of Each: Eighth printing, 1988.

Date of Most Recent Edition of Test Manual, User's Guide, Etc.: The most current version of the GPII was updated in 1971 and consists of 27 items for female examinees and 44 items for male examinees. The GPII is in its eighth printing, September 1988.

Languages in Which Available: English only.

Time:

Actual Test Time: 10 to 20 minutes (untimed but examinees are encouraged to work rapidly).

Total Administration Time: 30-50 minutes.

Norm Group(s) on Which Scores Are Based: Geist's initial instrument was piloted on 1,500 boys in Grades 4-12 from four different communities in California. A female form was developed for the 1964 revision. Norms are provided for an extensive array of groups for both men and women, including U.S. mainland in Grades 8-12, trade school, and university; social workers, artists, librarians, and physical education instructors; vocational rehabilitation clients; and those diagnosed with schizophrenia.

Manner in Which Results Are Reported for Individuals: Scores are collected as raw scores and converted into *T*-scores in order to be able to make standard comparisons. The *T*-score which corresponds to the raw score in each interest area is entered in the "*T*-score" column. If the Counselor wishes, the T scores can be plotted to form the *GPII Interest Profile*. In general, a *T*-score over 70 indicates the examinee has a high interest in an area, while a *T*-score under 30 indicates he or she does not like or enjoy activities in the interest area as compared with other interest areas.

The GPII is a self-administering paper-and-pencil instrument. Males are provided with Form M, females with Form F, and told to complete the Picture Triad Booklet according to directions. When there is a severe reading disability, directions and questions under the triads are read aloud to the examinee, who circles the drawings

433

of his or her choice. A sample triad of drawings is part of the instructions. After the examinee reads the cover page, he or she can respond to GPII items properly.

Report Format/Content for Group Summaries: The group administration procedure is the same as individual administration except that the examiner asks if directions are clear and if not, he or she clarifies and illustrates responses to items by reading the directions and discussing the sample item (GPII manual).

Machine Scoring: Not available.

Hand Scoring: Hand scored by counselor.

Local Machine Scoring: Not available.

Computer Software Options Available: Not available.

Cost of Materials: Due to possible price changes since publication date be sure to check the publisher's website. The initial kit costs around $100.00, and includes the manual and 10 test booklets each for male and female. Male and female test booklets can be purchased separately in packets of 20, averaging $2.00 per test booklet.

Specimen Set: $100.00 (includes 10 test booklets each for males and females, and manual).

Counselee Materials: Picture Triad booklet: Male (Form M) contains 44 triads of drawings, representing major vocations and avocations. Also included is the GPII interest profile (not reusable); Picture Triad booklet: Female (Form F) contains 27 triads of drawings based on the rationale operating in Form M. Also included is the GPII interest profile, initial directions, and information concerning the counselee (not reusable); Motivation Questionnaire: Male (Form M) contains the *GPII Motivating Forces Profile* (not reusable, optional for counselee to complete) and Motivation Questionnaire: Female (Form F) used with the female test booklet (not reusable, optional for counselee to complete).

Published Reviews of the Instrument in the Last 15 Years:

Vacha-Haase, T., & Enke, S. (2009). [Geist Picture Interest Inventory.] In E. A. Whitfield, R. W. Feller, & C. Wood (Eds.), *A counselor's guide to career assessment instruments* (5th ed., pp. 440-445). Broken Arrow, OK: National Career Development Association.

GEIST PICTURE INTEREST INVENTORY, REVISED EIGHTH PRINTING

Reviewed by:

Tammi Vacha-Haase

Serena Enke

Psychology Department
Colorado State University

Description

The Geist Picture Interest Inventory (GPII) is a pictorial interest inventory best known for its use with populations having limited verbal ability. The first version of the Geist Picture Interest Inventory (GPII) was developed in the 1950s by Harold Geist with the goal of creating a measure of vocational interest that was less dependent on verbal ability than the existing or more traditional interest measures (Geist, 1959). Geist's initial instrument was piloted on 1,500 boys in Grades 4-12 from four different communities in California. A female form was developed for the 1964 revision. Now in its eighth printing, the most current version of the GPII was updated in 1975 and consists of 27 items for female examinees and 44 items for male examinees.

The GPII is a self-administering paper-and-pencil instrument, generally requiring 10-25 minutes to complete, with an additional 20-40 minutes needed to complete the optional checklist. This instrument is appropriate for a variety of populations and can be administered individually or in groups.

A COUNSELOR'S GUIDE TO CAREER ASSESSMENTS INSTRUMENTS

Instead of answering a verbal question, examinees completing the GPII choose one of three pictures portraying either a person (men on the male form and women on the female form) in an occupation or activity, or a tool associated with an occupation. For example, female examinees choose between a waitress, a physical therapist, and an elevator operator. Male examinees choose from picture triads such as potter, cellist, and medical doctor. Sets of pictures are accompanied by a question such as "Which would you rather do?" or "Which are you most interested in doing?" After administration, the pictures can be used to gather additional projective information from the examinee.

Each picture is associated with at least one of 11 interest areas: Persuasive, Clerical, Mechanical, Musical, Scientific, Outdoor, Literary, Computational, Artistic, Social Service, and Dramatic (the first 10 match those suggested by G. F. Kuder in 1956). The test is scored by adding the number of marks in each interest area column. An examinee's profile displays the *T*-scores for each area. Rather than using gender specific norms in different occupations, norms representing how similar an examinee's scores are to a typical or satisfied person in a particular occupation may be more useful during interpretation to decrease possible gender stereotyping.

For a more in-depth understanding of examinee interests, the GPII includes an optional measure that explores the motivations behind each of the examinee's answers. After completing the primary instrument, examinees choose one of 35 reasons for each selected career choice on a grid checklist. The motivators combine to form seven categories: *Could Not Say, Family, Prestige, Financial, Intrinsic and Personality, Environmental,* and *Past Experience.* Little guidance is offered regarding the scoring or interpretation of this optional measure, and no norms are provided. However, Geist recommended that motivations which the examinee chooses over 60% of the time should be "considered carefully" in interpretation, as the examinee was "influenced" by this category in occupational choices (Geist, 1959).

The pictorial nature of the GPII makes it ideal for use with young children who may not have the verbal ability to complete other types of interest inventories. This instrument is also appropriate for populations with a decreased verbal ability and/or those whose first language is not English. The GPII is often used for specialized populations, such as deaf individuals whose primary language is signed, with separate norms available for deaf individuals (Geist, 1962a) as well as other groups. Other potential uses include the learning disabled or populations with higher percentages of learning disabilities, such as juvenile delinquents (Kronenberger & Quatman, 1968). The GPII can be used with the developmentally disabled, although Burg and Barrett (1965) found it necessary to both show the picture and give an oral description, in addition to reading the questions out loud.

Technical Considerations

Norms are provided for an extensive array of groups for both men and women, including U.S. mainland in Grades 8-12, trade school, and university; social workers, artists, librarians, and physical education instructors; vocational rehabilitation clients, and those diagnosed with schizophrenia.

The reliability and validity of results from the GPII tend to be acceptable, but are not without criticism (Tiedeman, 1960). Research suggests that test-retest reliability of GPII scores over a six-month interval varies considerably depending on the sample used (e.g., .62 for eighth graders in Puerto Rico; .87 for the U.S. mainland sample.) Correlations with the Kuder scales are generally statistically significant, and Geist (1959) suggested "that the GPII scores may be more valid than the Kuder scores for examinees with reading handicaps" (p. 422.) A five-year follow-up on the norming samples used in the original GPII indicated that most examinees were employed in professions that matched the interests they indicated on the GPII (Geist, 1962b).

General Utility and Evaluation

The GPII is a short, simple approach to gathering information about vocational interests, easily scored, and relatively simple to interpret, especially for those familiar with the Kuder scales. Because it requires minimal verbal ability, it offers practitioners the opportunity to provide vocational information to populations that might otherwise be overlooked.

A long-standing question exists regarding the accuracy of Geist's basic premise that pictures better represent an occupation in comparison to verbal descriptions or job titles (Geist, 1959). As each drawing represents only a small portion of the job, whereas a job title may bring to mind a more complete picture, it remains unclear

Geist Picture Interest Inventory, Revised Eighth Printing

whether the intention of the GPII is for the examinee to choose *activities* or *occupations* that are of interest. Additional concern exists regarding the ambiguity or confusing nature of the pictures, as a number of drawings are not easily recognizable, allowing for varying interpretations.

The most salient criticism of the GPII is the test's clear lack of modern-day representation, having last been revised in the 1970s. Clothing and instruments are clearly outdated (e.g., nurses wearing pointed paper caps and people using typewriters), with a notable absence of diversity (e.g., ethnic-racial, physical ability). Although the publisher describes the test as being widely used "especially with culturally different and educationally deprived individuals," there is little to no recognition of cultural differences in the pictures included on the test. The GPII also appears to perpetuate gender stereotypes. For example, the medical pictures on the female form overwhelmingly depict nurses, rather than physicians. It should be noted that several pictures represent vocations that may no longer be viable (e.g., switchboard operator or television repairman) and many of the more recent or fastest growing occupations available today are not represented (e.g., athletic trainer, biomedical engineer, network systems and data communications analyst, translator, or hazardous materials removal worker.) The GPII simply is not reflective of the 21st century.

References and Additional Resources

Burg, B. W., & Barrett, A. M. (1965). Interest testing with the mentally retarded: A bi-sensory approach. *American Journal of Mental Deficiency, 69*(4), 548-552.

Geist, H. (1959). The Geist Picture Interest Inventory: General form: Male. *Psychological Reports, 5*, 413-438.

Geist, H. (1962a). Occupational interest profiles of the deaf. *Personnel and Guidance Journal, 51*(1), 50-55.

Geist, H. (1962b). A five year follow-up of The Geist Picture Interest Inventory. *California Journal of Educational Research, 13*(5), 195-208.

Kronenberger, E. J., & Quatman, G. L. (1968). Performance of institutionalized juvenile delinquents on the Geist Picture Interest Inventory. *Psychological Reports, 22*, 185-186.

Tiedeman, D. V. (1960). Geist Picture Interest Inventory. *Personnel and Guidance Journal, 38*, 506-507.

LIFE CENTERED CAREER EDUCATION COMPETENCY ASSESSMENT: KNOWLEDGE AND PERFORMANCE BATTERIES

Donn E. Brolin

The Council for Exceptional Children (CEC)

1920 Association Drive
Reston, VA 20191-1589
http://www.cec.sped.org

Target Population: Students in Grades 9-12 with mild mental retardation (i.e., intellectual disability) and specific learning disabilities. It can also be used (with caution) with lower grades and other populations such as at-risk students, adults, and students with emotional and behavioral disorders.

Statement of the Purpose of the Instrument: The purpose of the Life Centered Career Education Competency Assessment: Knowledge and Performance Batteries (LCCE) is to identify areas of strengths and weaknesses in 20 of the 22 competencies comprising the Life Centered Career Education curriculum and to gauge effectiveness of the instructional program. It can provide a comprehensive career/life skills assessment.

Titles of Subtests, Scales, Scores Provided: Subtests: Daily Living Skills Questions; Personal Social Skills Questions; Occupational and Guidance Questions. Scores are recorded by administrator on a form called the Student Competency Assessment Record (SCAR).

Forms and Levels Available, with Dates of Publication/Revision of Each: The Knowledge Battery (KB) comes in two forms, A and B. The original publication date is 1992. Minor revisions were made in 1997, and the LCCE was updated for 2012. The KB is written at a fourth-grade reading level. It is presented in a multiple choice format.

Date of Most Recent Edition of Test Manual, User's Guide, Etc.: 2012.

Languages in Which Available: English only.

Time:

Actual Test Time: 2-4 hours, depending on abilities of students taking the test.

Total Administration Time: 2-4 hours.

Norm Group(s) on Which Scores Are Based: The test is not norm referenced. Standardized on students in Grades 9-12 who have mild mental retardation or specific learning disabilities.

Manner in Which Results Are Reported for Individuals: Scores are provided at both the competency and domain level. The scores are reported as a total number correct out of a total of 10 questions. There are 10 questions for each of the first 20 competencies. A score of 8 is considered "competent," i.e., passing.

The Student Competency Assessment Record (SCAR) is used to record student's knowledge scores.

Report Format/Content for Group Summaries: Not available.

Machine Scoring: Not available.

Hand Scoring: Hand scored by counselor or clerk in 5-10 minutes.

Local Machine Scoring: Provisions/conditions/equipment Required: If a scoring machine is available and students are able to successfully use Scantron-type answer sheets, a 200-item sheet can be used. The test administrator will need to create an answer sheet for the machine available.

Computer Software Options Available: Not available.

Cost of Materials: Due to possible price changes since publication date be sure to check the publisher's website.

Specimen Set: Complete set (included three CD-ROMs, a teacher's copy of each of the three accompanying student workbooks, performance batteries, knowledge batteries, a copy of LCCE teacher's guide) $1,424.95

Counselee Materials: Test booklets: $20.00 (package of 10). If separate answer sheets are used, the booklets are reusable. It is illegal to photocopy the test booklets.

Life Centered Career Education Competency Assessment: Knowledge and Performance Batteries

Additional Comments of Interest to Users: The Knowledge Battery is part of the complete curriculum package and can also be purchased separately. A Pictorial Knowledge Battery for the Modified Curriculum is under development.

There is also an LCCE Performance Battery. The Performance Batteries (PB) were designed to go a step beyond ascertaining students' knowledge of the LCCE competencies, and to actually assess students' ability to apply the LCCE competencies in their lives. Like the Knowledge Battery the Performance Battery is curriculum-based.

The PB consists of two alternate forms for each of the 21 competency units. The majority of the items are performance-based. It is composed of open-ended questions, role-playing scenarios, card-sorting, and other hands-on activities.

Published Reviews of the Instrument in the Last 15 Years:

Sligar, S. R., & Burke, R. (2009). [Life Centered Career Education Competency Assessment: Knowledge and Performance Batteries.] In E. A. Whitfield, R. W. Feller, & C. Wood (Eds.), *A counselor's guide to career assessment instruments* (5th ed., pp. 446-451). Broken Arrow, OK: National Career Development Association.

LIFE CENTERED CAREER EDUCATION COMPETENCY ASSESSMENT: KNOWLEDGE AND PERFORMANCE BATTERIES

Reviewed by:

Steven R. Sligar

Matthew Putts

Department of Addictions and Rehabilitation Studies
East Carolina University

Description

The Council for Exceptional Children (CEC) has completed an 18-month revision of the Life Centered Career Education: A Competency Based Approach (LCCE), first published in 1978. The new curriculum, Life Centered Education: A Competency Based Approach (LCE), omits career to reflect a broader scope and the more holistic focus found in contemporary transition services (American Foundation for the Blind, 2012; CEC, 2011). The LCE contains three independent, though interrelated, screening instruments: the LCE Competency Rating Scale (CRS), the LCE Knowledge Battery (KB), and LCE Performance Battery (PB; CEC, 2013). All three are designed to collect baseline data for interventions included in the LCE curriculum. The primary target group remains as Grade 7 through 12 students in special education, though the Teachers Manual (CEC, 2013) states that some of the lesson plans may be useful for elementary age children. The target audience is students with mild to moderate disabilities. The complete LCE includes online screening instruments and the curriculum, which is divided into three domains: Daily Living Skills (DLS); Self Determination and Interpersonal Skills (SDIS); and Employment Skills (ES). The LCE curriculum is comprised of 20 competencies (DLS-9, SDIS-7 and ES-4; see Table 1) with 94 subcompetencies (DLS-41, SDIS-29, and ES-24).

The Teacher's Guide (CEC, 2013) addresses cultural concerns and accommodations. First is that inter-agency collaboration should include cultural considerations (p. 8) and the LCE materials were reviewed to insure the removal of any cultural or other stereotypes. The example cited is that the term "marriage" in the DLS domain has been changed to relationship, thereby reflecting current social mores (p. 24). Accommodations are discussed in the section Alternative Strategies and Tools for Differentiating Instruction. The focus is on providing accommodations or modifications that meet the student's needs but "are not be so extreme as to violate the validity of those assessment tools" (the KB, p. 24; PB; p. 24).

The current revision preserves the underlying philosophy of its creator, Donn Brolin, which may be broadly described as helping students learn knowledge and skills necessary to be a successful adult. Brolin's (1997) original notion was to infuse career education into the curriculum, and the CEC revision committee was able to pull from more than 30 years of experience with the LCCE as well as incorporate educational, legal, and other societal changes to produce the LCE.

Table 1

LCE Competencies by Curriculum Area*

Daily Living Skills	Self-Determination and Interpersonal Skills	Employment Skills
1. Managing personal finances	10. *Understanding self-determination*	17. *Knowing and exploring employment possibilities*
2. Selecting and managing a household	11. *Being self-aware*	18. *Exploring employment choices*
3. Caring for personal needs	12. *Developing interpersonal skills*	19. Seeking, securing, and maintaining employment
4. Demonstrating relationship responsibilities	13. Communicating with others	20. *Exhibiting appropriate employment skills*
5. Buying, preparing, and consuming food	14. *Good decision making*	
6. Buying and caring for clothing	15. *Developing social awareness*	
7. Exhibiting responsible citizenship	16. *Understanding disability rights and responsibilities*	
8. Utilizing recreational facilities and engaging in leisure		
9. *Choosing and accessing transportation*		

*Note. Italics indicate curriculum or competency areas that have changed in the recent online version. Two competency areas were deleted from the Employment Skills curriculum, leaving 20 competency areas in this version of the LCE.

The redesigned Competency Rating Scale (CRS) provides a way to standardize and organize student assessment using the 20 competencies and 94 sub-competencies from the LCE. The assessment consists of observations of student behaviors with the 94 sub-competencies serving as the items for rating.

The CRS Manual is divided into four sections. Section I—Rating Student Performance contains the rating key: 0 = *Not Competent* (unable to perform any of the criteria), 1 = *Partially Competent* (performs at least one of the criteria), 2 = *Competent* (performs all of the criteria), and NR = *Not Rated*. The manual suggests conducting these ratings when the student enters middle or high school and continuing at the end of each school year until graduation. One rater is preferred, but provisions are made for multiple raters. Section II—Using the CRS Record Form includes identifying information and instructions on how to complete the form. The form contains a yes/no check box to indicate if the graduating student can perform any 0 or 1 rated subcompetencies with assistance from individuals normally in the student's environment. The rater may also add information about any specific occupational skill training by using Competency 22 Occupational Guidance and Preparation Domain. Scoring instructions are also included. Section III (explanations of and behavioral criteria for the subcompetencies) and Section IV (CRS results interpretation) were not available for this review.

The LCE Knowledge Battery (KB) is a standardized, criterion-referenced instrument with 453 multiple-choice items (I) divided into the DLS (I = 246), SDIS (I = 199), and ES (I = 88) domains. The DLS items contain five with pictures of coins and bills of different denominations, two items with the same shirt and sales tag, and one figure showing a row of houses. Neither the SDIS nor the ES contained any pictures or diagrams. The items are presented continuously with a black sans-serif font on a white background, and a faint blue line separates each question. The test taker indicates a selected answer by clicking on a button.

Life Centered Career Education Competency Assessment: Knowledge and Performance Batteries

The questions are linked to each of the LCE objectives. Administration time is approximately 1-3 hours per domain because the counselor selects questions to build the test based on curriculum objectives. For example, to build an assessment, the counselor logs in to the website, selects Build a Knowledge Battery, then selects the Domain (e.g., DLS), followed by a competency (e.g., Managing Personal Finances), and creates the assessment. Example test content includes identify the correct value of color pictures of actual coins (DLS), identify plans for the future and how that makes one feel (SDIS), and identify consequences at work for actions (ES). Questions have been updated to include topics such as the ADA, Internet, online banking, and entitlement. There are questions that include all of the above or none of the above as possible answers, which limit responses in the test taker's favor (Jacobs, 2004).

No standardization information was available for this review. The Teacher's Guide (CEC, 2013) states that small group (6-8 students) administration is acceptable. However, larger groups with proctors may yield inaccurate results, especially for students with mild intellectual disabilities. Administration instructions that include voice-enabled delivery of questions for non-readers are provided in the KB links (p. 159).

The Performance Battery (PB) is a non-standardized, criterion-referenced instrument comprised of two alternative forms for each of the 20 competency units. The CEC website describes the PB as items that are "performance-based with open-ended questions, role-playing scenarios, card-sorting exercises and other hands-on activities." The PB was not available for this review.

The LCE website provides a user-friendly report for each student. The counselor selects the Reports tab, creates a report name, and applies filters by curriculum (DLS, SDIS, and/or ES) and results (i.e., student, school year, grade level, location, teacher, and start/end dates). The report lists each of the assessed areas with percent correct and number correct/total questions, for example, Buying and Caring for Clothing 11.11% (2/18) and, if prior year scores are available, lists those as well.

Technical Considerations

The revised LCE became available in 2012. The revision included two primary aspects. First was a conversion from a paper-and-pencil instrument to an online format. There was no information provided about the test website's compatibility with assistive technology (e.g., screen-reading software or peripherals) or other accessibility issues like legibility (e.g., availability of changing font size or color). We conducted a manual check and found the test site easy to navigate with an intuitive design. Second was a review and update of the items. Given the change in medium and the additions and deletions of response items, information needs to be made available about test-retest reliability. The Teachers Guide (2013) notes "the use of specific behavioral criteria and precise definition of rating values is intended to enhance the reliability and validity of the ratings" (p. 158). Education experts reviewed and ranked the items that were linked to subcompetencies. No additional psychometric information was provided. We copied the questions from the website and pasted the text into a Word document. We then ran readability statistics of two commonly used programs (Sligar & Zeng, 2011) and obtained the following scores: Flesch Reading Ease of 71.8 (fairly easy) and Flesch-Kincaid Grade Level of 6.3. No technical manual was available for review.

General Utility and Evaluation

The reviewers received a spreadsheet with 465 questions for the KB (note: the CEC website reports 468 items, but our count of the online battery yielded 453 items) and guest access to the test portal. The KB may serve as a standalone instrument, but is designed to be used as a screening for the LCE. There are direct links to the curriculum built into the assessment. The reviewers did not have sufficient information to comment on the CB or CRS. Users may receive training from the CEC.

For counselors, the results provide a functional description of the student and may be used to determine placement and progress within the LCE. The information may be used to develop goals and objectives for Individual Education Plans (IEP) or Individualized Transition Plans (ITP). In addition, the LCE conceptual framework combines three developmental stages (readiness, career exploration, and career preparation) with four career roles (work done at home, volunteer work, work as an employee, and other productive avocational activities;

Brolin & Gysbers, 1989). This framework may serve as a useful heuristic for counseling. However, we caution against solely using the LCE results to determine vocational and life skills knowledge; other information must be incorporated in the interpretation of the results.

References and Additional Resources

American Foundation for the Blind. (2012). Transition curriculum and assessment tool. *Journal of Visual Impairment & Blindness, 106*(9), 574.

Brolin, D. E. (1997). *Life center career education* (5th ed.). Arlington, VA: Council for Exceptional Children.

Brolin, D. E., & Gysbers, N. C. (1989). Career education for students with disabilities. *Journal of Counseling and Development, 68,* 155-159.

Council for Exceptional Children. (2011). *Life centered education (LCE) transition curriculum.* Retrieved from http://www. cec.sped.org/Content/NavigationMenu/Publications2/LCETransitionCurriculum/default.htm

Council for Exceptional Children. (2013). Life centered education: Skills for the 21st century (the teacher's guide). Arlington, VA. Retrieved from https://lce.cec.sped.org/assets/pdf/lce_teacher_guide.pdf

Jacobs, L. C. (2004). *How to write better tests: A handbook for improving test construction skills.* Bloomington, IN: Indiana University. Retrieved from http://www.indiana.edu/~best/write_better_tests.shtml

Sligar, S. R., & Zeng, X. (2011). Website accessibility and readability evaluation of community rehabilitation programs. *Vocational Evaluation and Career Assessment Professionals Journal, 7*(2), 10-26.

A Counselor's Guide To Career Assessments Instruments

Picture Interest Career Survey, Second Edition
Robert Brady

Jist Publishing, Inc.

875 Montreal Way
St. Paul, MN 55102
http://jist.emcpublishingllc.com/page-jist/
educate@emcp.com

Target Population: Children, adolescents, young adults, and adults; ages 10-65.

Statement of the Purpose of the Instrument: The Picture Interest Career Survey, second edition (PICS-2) provides an accessible way for people with limited reading ability or special needs to explore their career interests and find a job that fits.

Titles of Subtests, Scales, Scores Provided: Realistic, Investigative, Artistic, Social, Enterprising, and Conventional.

Forms and Levels Available, with Dates of Publication/Revision of Each: 2011.

Date of Most Recent Edition of Test Manual, User's Guide, Etc.: 2011.

Languages in Which Available: English, but picture-based.

Time:

    Actual Test Time: Varies.

    Total Administration Time: 15 minutes.

Manner in Which Results Are Reported for Individuals: Standard scores.

Machine Scoring: Not available.

Hand Scoring: Hand scored by counselee.

Computer Software Options Available: Not available.

Cost of Materials: Due to possible price changes since publication date, be sure to check the publisher's website. Administrator's guide is available for download at no cost.

    Specimen Set: Sample instrument available at no charge (limit 1); 12-page booklets (package of 25; not reusable): $48.95.

    Counselee Materials: 12-page booklet (not reusable). Career Locator and Career Planning Worksheet available for download at no cost.

Published Reviews of Instrument in Last 15 Years:

Porter, J. Y. (2010). [Picture Interest Career Survey.] In R. A. Spies, J. F. Carlson, & K. F. Geisinger (Eds.), *The eighteenth mental measurements yearbook* (pp. 426-428). Lincoln, NE: Buros Center for Testing.

Picture Interest Career Survey, Second Edition

Reviewed by:

Julia Y. Porter
Division of Education
Mississippi State University, Meridian

Description

The Picture Interest Career Survey, Second Edition (PICS-2; Brady, 2011a) is a 36-item picture interest inventory based on John Holland's RIASEC occupational coding system (Holland, 1992) and Prediger's (1982)

Picture Interest Career Survey, Second Edition

interest categories and work tasks. The current version of PICS-2 contains 18 pictures for each of the six vocational personality types in RIASEC (Realistic, Investigative, Artistic, Social, Enterprising, Conventional) and 27 pictures for each of the four areas of Prediger's interest categories and work tasks (people, data, things, ideas). For each of the 36 items, test takers are presented with three drawings that represent different work activities for a total of 108 pictures. For each item, the test taker selects the drawing that is the most interesting to him or her by circling that picture. Counselors may view sample items on the publisher's website.

PICS-2 may be administered individually or in group settings. Scoring options include self- scoring or administrator scoring, with an estimated scoring time of five minutes. Scoring results in a three letter code (tied scores will result in more than one code) called the Occupational PICS Code which is based on scores from six vocational personality areas: Realistic, Investigative, Artistic, Social, Enterprising, and Conventional. Maximum score on each of the six vocational personality areas in the code is 18. This code can be explored in more depth using the Career Locator, which lists more than 600 jobs from the O*NET Dictionary of Occupational Titles. Education and training requirement information is provided for each of the jobs listed. After helping the test taker narrow his or her job interests, the Career Planning Worksheet guides the test taker through realistic job exploration and building a job profile. The Career Locator, Career Planning Worksheet, and Administrator's Guide may be found on the publisher's website.

PICS-2 can be used to help clients of different age groups and ability levels identify and explore career interests. The format is language free, which makes it useful in working with individuals who do not read well or for whom English is their second language. Survey responses result in a PICS Occupational Code that can be used with other RIASEC system materials such as the O*NET Dictionary of Occupational Titles, Enhanced Occupational Outlook Handbook, and the Dictionary of Holland Occupational Codes to help clients explore career options.

Technical Considerations

A series of 12 research studies begun in 2003 that ranged from $n = 8$ to $n = 70$ resulted in a standardization sample of $N = 313$. A table that summarizes the research results is available on Page 6 of the online Administrator's Guide.

Brady (2011b) computed the reliability for the PICS-2 for a sample of 34 working adults aged 22 to 80 ($M = 50.6$ years) using the alternate-form method, which compares the consistency of scores for two alternate but equivalent forms of the same instrument. Data from the Spearman rho rank order correlations used to compare the two sets of scores resulted in a significant Spearman (rs) median correlation coefficient of .94 ($p < .001$). In addition, Brady (2011b) computed alternative-form reliability for the PICS-2 for a sample of 92 students aged 16 to 19 ($M = 17.2$ years). Data from the Spearman rho rank order correlations used to compare the two sets of scores in this study resulted in a significant Spearman (rs) median correlation coefficient of .92 ($p < .001$). No other reliability evidence is available.

Concurrent validity studies were conducted in 2007 ($N = 60$), 2008 ($N = 73$), 2009 ($N = 77$), and 2010 ($N = 34$) on the PICS-1 (Brady, 2011b), which is the foundation for the PICS-2. Combined results from the studies resulted in $N = 244$ with an age range of 18 to 65 years with 36% being female and 64% male. Ethnicity of participants included White (77.8%), African American (16%), Mexican American (5%), Native American (0.8%), and Asian American (0.4%). As reported in the Administrator's Guide (Brady, 2011b), the "C index of 14.50 ($SD = 2.07$, range 10 to 18, 95% $CI = 14.24$, 14.76) fell significantly higher ($t = 41.45$, $p < .0001$) than the theoretical population mean of 9. These results continued to confirm the strength of the PICS as a valid measure of career interest." (p. 8). Concurrent validity studies were conducted on the PICS-2 in January 2011 ($N = 35$) and February 2011 ($N = 92$) (Brady, 2011b), which resulted in C Indexes of 15.69 and 14.73, respectively; these indexes were found to be significantly higher than the theoretical population mean of 9 ($p < .0001$). Based on content validity data collected since 2007 on the PICS-1, five item illustrations were "updated or have undergone minor changes or refinements in order to address ... concerns" (Brady, 2011b, p. 9) before being included in the PICS-2.

444

General Utility and Evaluation

The PICS Adminstrator's Guide (Brady, 2011b) includes a brief primer on RIASEC vocational personality types (Holland, 1992). The guide also includes a diagram of the hexagonal circumplex model showing the relationship between Holland's vocational personality types and Prediger's interest categories and work tasks (p. 13), which is a good review for test administrators and can also be used in explaining the test purpose and results depending on the age and ability level of the test taker.

The PICS-2 addresses a need to provide alternative instruments for individuals who may not do well on traditional paper-and-pencil interest inventories because of challenges such as language or ability levels. Strengths of PICS-2 include the ease of administering and scoring and its compatibility with the RIASEC system. Another strength is the PICS Career Planning Worksheet, which is an easy to read and use career exploration worksheet which is provided free to PICS-2 users.

While preliminary findings indicate that PICS-2 is a valid and reliable instrument, additional research studies are needed with larger sample sizes to be able to generalize research findings. PICS-2 should be used with caution and in conjunction with other researched instruments because reliability and validity data are limited and additional standardization tests are needed to verify the appropriateness of PICS-2 with diverse populations (Porter, 2010).

References and Additional Resources

American Educational Research Association, American Psychological Association, & National Council on Measurement in Education. (1999). *Standards for Educational and Psychological Testing.* Washington, DC: American Educational Research Association.

Brady, R. P. (2011a). *Picture Interest Career Survey, second edition* (PICS-2). St. Paul, MN: JIST Works.

Brady, R. P. (2011b). *Picture Interest Career Survey, second edition administrator's guide.* Retrieved from http://jist.emcp.com/productattachments/index/download?id=674

Holland, J. L. (1992). *Making vocational choices: A theory of vocational personalities and work environments.* Odessa, FL: Psychological Assessment Resources, Inc.

Prediger, D. J. (1982). Dimensions underlying Holland's hexagon: Missing link between interest and occupations? *Journal of Vocational Behavior, 21,* 259-287.

Porter, J. Y. (2010). [Picture Interest Career Survey.] In R. A. Spies, J. F. Carlson, & K. F. Geisinger (Eds.), *The eighteenth mental measurements yearbook* (pp. 426-428). Lincoln, NE: Buros Center for Testing.

446

READING-FREE VOCATIONAL INTEREST INVENTORY, SECOND EDITION
Ralph L. Becker

Elbern Publications

P.O. Box 9497
Columbus, OH 43209
ebecker@insight.rr.com

Target Population: Adolescents, young adults, and adults; ages 12 and older. Used with individuals with intellectual disabilities or learning disabilities, other special-needs students, and adults with disadvantages.

Statement of the Purpose of the Instrument: The Reading-Free Vocational Interest Inventory (R-FVII:2) is a non-reading inventory to realistically measure the vocational interests of special-needs students and adults; people who are mentally retarded, learning disabled, or educationally disadvantaged I as well as students in regular classrooms.

Titles of Subtests, Scales, Scores Provided: The 11 scales include the following: Animal Care, Automotive, Building Trades, Clerical, Food Service, Horticulture, Housekeeping, Laundry Service, Materials Handling, Patient Care, and Personal Service. Scores are provided for 11 scales and 5 clusters (Mechanical Interest, Outdoor Interest, Mechanical-Outdoor Interests, Food Service–Handling Operations Interest, and Clerical–Social Service Interest).

Forms and Levels Available, with Dates of Publication/Revision of Each: One form is available for males and females. Separate norms are available by gender and type of disability.

Date of Most Recent Edition of Test Manual, User's Guide, Etc.: 2000. Previous editions were published in 1975 and 1981.

Languages in Which Available: English only.

Time:

Actual test time: 20 minutes or fewer.

Total administration time: Approximately 20 minutes and can be easily administered in a 45-minute class session.

Norm Group(s) on Which Scores Are Based: Individuals with intellectual disabilities or learning disabilities, those economically disadvantaged, and those in regular classrooms.

Manner in Which Results Are Reported for Individuals: Standard Scores, Percentiles, and Descriptive Ratings (i.e., High Average) for scales and cluster scores are provided. A "Record of Interest and Cluster Scores" Format reports on an individual's scores in 11 areas and 5 clusters. A graphic profile of interests is produced that visually represents the range of vocational interest for each area as "High, Above Average" to "Low" interest in the measured scales.

Report Format/Content for Group Summaries: Not available.

Machine Scoring: Not available.

Hand Scoring: Hand scored by clerk or counselor in approximately 10 minutes.

Local Machine Scoring: Not available.

Computer Software Options Available: Not available.

Cost of Materials: Due to possible price changes since publication date, be sure to check with the publisher. The R-FVII:2 is distributed by multiple publishers, and prices vary.

Specimen Set: Manual: $44.00-$62.00. A specimen kit includes a manual and test booklet.

Counselee Materials: Test booklets (package of 20): $42.00-$75.00; Book of Occupational Titles: $35.00-$54.00. The Occupational Titles List (OTL:2, 2001) is a supplement to the R-FVII:2. It includes more than 900 realistic job titles for people who have mental or physical disabilities.

Reading-Free Vocational Interest Inventory, Second Edition

Published Reviews of the Instrument in the Last 15 Years:

Gratz, Z. (2003). [Reading-Free Vocational Interest Inventory: 2.] In B. S. Plake, J. C. Impara, & R. A. Spies (Eds.), *The fifteenth mental measurements yearbook* (pp. 718-719). Lincoln, NE: Buros Center for Testing.

Gratz, Z. (2009). [Reading-Free Vocational Interest Inventory: 2.] In E. A. Whitfield, R. W. Feller, & C. Wood (Eds.), *A counselor's guide to career assessment instruments* (5th ed., pp. 452-457). Broken Arrow, OK: National Career Development Association.

Pope, M. (2003). [Reading-Free Vocational Interest Inventory: 2.] In B. S. Plake, J. C. Impara, & R. A. Spies (Eds.), *The fifteenth mental measurements yearbook* (pp. 719-722). Lincoln, NE: Buros Center for Testing.

READING-FREE VOCATIONAL INTEREST INVENTORY, SECOND EDITION

Zandra S. Gratz

School of Psychology
Kean University

Description

The Reading-Free Vocational Interest Inventory: 2 (R–FVII:2) is a 55-item measure of vocational interest. Each item is a triad of three line drawings; each drawing presents a person engaged in a work activity. Forced choice, test takers are asked to select the picture they would like to do the best. Pictures are simple line drawings with no shading. The nature of the line drawings is such that they appear to be ethnically uniform. Also many of the drawings appear to portray gender stereotypes (e.g., female nursing assistant). Also other reviewers (e.g., Pope, 2003) as well as I have found difficulty in determining exactly what some pictures were depicting.

Scoring is relatively clear. Raw scores are recorded on a matrix comprised of item number by interest area. Interest area raw scores are translated into standard scores (*T*-scores) via tables in the manual; scores may be further reduced into one of five cluster scores. Raw cluster scores may be translated into cluster coefficients through the use of tables provided in the manual. The final stage involves generating a graphic profile as to where the test takers' 11 interest area standard scores and five cluster coefficients fell. This sheet is likely to provide the most interpretive information and make the ratings column on the record sheet obsolete.

The R–FVII:2 is designed for those diagnosed with an intellectual or learning disability, those disadvantaged, and participants in sheltered workshops. The R–FVII-2 author also indicates the measure can be used to assess interests of students in regular classroom. The R–FVII-2 may have limited use in today's counseling environment. The nature of vocations has changed considerably since the advent of the measure. As noted in earlier reviews (Gratz, 2003, 2009), the extent to which the measure adequately represents the occupations currently available is questionable. Also, as noted by Pope (2003), although reading is not a necessary prerequisite for taking the test, the test taker must be able to understand the picture. This accentuates the concerns noted earlier regarding the extent to which some pictures adequately depict a job task.

Technical Considerations

Over 15,000 participated in the norm sample. Interest area norms are stratified by age and gender within classification. Classifications include Mental Retardation (mental retardation is now referred to as intellectual disability), Learning Disabled, Adult Disadvantaged, Regular Classroom, and Adult Work Sheltered. Age by classification (other than Adult Work Sheltered) is divided into two categories; approximately 12 to 15.9 and 16 to 18.9 (some variation by classification). Adult Sheltered Workshop norm participants were age 19 to 59.9.

A Counselor's Guide To Career Assessments Instruments

The manner in which norm data were obtained was extensive and included participants selected at random from a variety of states and settings (public and private schools, vocational rehabilitation centers, community training centers) for all groups except Adult Disadvantaged which were sampled from only one region ("distressed Appalachian counties," Becker, 2001, p. 25). Although the limitation in sampling of Adult Disadvantaged is noted, the numbers and percents of persons sampled by region are not presented. Also, although adult age categories are broad (e.g., ranging from approximately 18 to 59), the mean ages are approximately 25; thus, most participants in Adult Disadvantaged and Adult Sheltered Work norm sample are relatively young and do not represent the full age range reported. This may be a limitation for the counselor working with an older client.

Internal consistency estimates of reliability by interest area, stratified by age (younger and older) and gender, ranged from .74 to .95; 82% of the coefficients were above .80. Internal consistency estimates for cluster scores, based on a larger number of items, were all .80 or above. Although substantial sample sizes were evident, internal consistency estimates of reliability were based only on those categorized as having an intellectual disability.

A series of test-retest reliability estimates are presented in the manual (Becker, 2000). Test-retest reliability estimates for interest areas are broken down by classification, gender, and age. Studies used a two-week interval, and most results were .80 or higher. The exception to this was the Materials Handling score; for this interest area 75% of the coefficients reported were below .80. Although specifics were not presented as discussed in the manual, cluster score test reliability estimates were all above .80. Overall, the R–FVII:2 presents sufficient evidence of reliability.

With regard to validity, the list jobs/interests used in the R–FVII:2 were based on a jobs guide (Peterson & Jones, 1964) for persons with an intellectual disability. The first version of the instrument had separate booklets and different job categories by gender. The current version includes one booklet for males and females. Reasonable discrimination indexes are reported between interest areas as well as between cluster scores.

Criterion related validity was generated by comparing individual's R–FVII-2 scores to that of the Geist Picture Interest Inventory (Geist, 1988). Across most comparisons, with the exception of Materials Handling, correlations across measures were statistically significant. The theory behind the manner in which scales were matched across measures is neither known nor evident; also, the Laundry Service interest area of the R–FVII-2 is not included in the analyses.

Studies were conducted which examined R–FVII:2 score profiles of those already working in jobs within each interest area. Results suggest that respondents scored highest on the R–FVII:2 interest area in which they were employed, as compared to the other Interest Areas. However data by interest area are based on relatively few participants and significance levels are not reported.

General Utility and Evaluation

The manual (Becker, 2000) is relatively cogent and laid out in a logical manner. Although relatively little training would be necessary to administer the R–FVII-2, training is necessary to generate scores. While the detachable scoring and interpretation sheets help the scoring process, the need to access specific tables in the manuals requires training on the part of the person doing the scoring. Normative data are available by gender, age category, and disability. As noted, all pictures are ethnically uniform but may also portray gender stereotypes (Pope, 2003). I agree with many of the comments made in earlier reviews (e.g., Pope, 2003; Gratz, 2003, 2009). The measure sports considerable psychometric evidence. However, concerns remain with regard to the clarity of the pictures as well as issues of gender and ethnic diversity among the characters portrayed in the pictures. Beyond this, the age of the R–FVII-2 may make it inappropriate for today's job environment. In particular, there is a paucity of technical/computer-related tasks depicted. Also, the few depicted (e.g., item 31e) do not look like the technology of today. Not only might the addition of a technology interest area be appropriate, but the pictures need to reflect the current technology (e.g., laptop or tablet, as compared to a desktop with CRT).

Reading-Free Vocational Interest Inventory, Second Edition

References and Additional Resources

Becker, R. L. (2000). *Reading-Free Vocational Interest Inventory: 2 manual.* Columbus, OH: Elbern Publications.

Geist, H. (1988). *Geist Picture Interest Inventory.* Los Angeles, CA: Western Psychological Services.

Gratz, Z. (2003). [Reading-Free Vocational Interest Inventory: 2.] In B. S. Plake, J. C. Impara, & R. A. Spies (Eds.), *The fifteenth mental measurements yearbook* (pp. 718-719). Lincoln, NE: Buros Center for Testing.

Gratz, Z. (2009). [Reading-Free Vocational Interest Inventory: 2.] In E.A. Whitfield, R. W. Feller, & C. Wood (Eds.), *A counselor's guide to career assessment instruments* (5th ed., pp. 452-457). Broken Arrow, OK: National Career Development Association.

Peterson, R. O., & Jones, E. M. (1964). *Guide to jobs for the mentally retarded.* Pittsburgh, PA: American Institute for Research.

Pope, M. (2003). [Reading-Free Vocational Interest Inventory: 2.] In B. S. Plake, J. C. Impara, & R. A. Spies (Eds.), *The fifteenth mental measurements yearbook* (pp. 719-722). Lincoln, NE: Buros Center for Testing.

A Counselor's Guide To Career Assessments Instruments

Workplace Sexual Identity Management Measure

Mary Z. Anderson, James Croteau, Y. Chung, and Teresa DiStefano

Mary Z. Anderson

3110 Sangren Hall
Western Michigan University
Kalamazoo, Michigan 49008
mary.anderson@wmich.edu

Target Population: Lesbian and gay adults.

Statement of the Purpose of the Instrument: The Workplace Sexual Identity Management Measure (WSIMM) is designed to assess sexual identity management for lesbian women and gay men.

Titles of Subtests, Scales, Scores Provided: Passing, Covering, Implicitly Out, and Explicitly Out. Items are scored on a four-point Likert scale.

Forms and Levels Available, with Dates of Publication/Revision of Each: 2010.

Date of Most Recent Edition of Test Manual, User's Guide, Etc.: 2010.

Languages in Which Available: English only.

Time:

    Actual Test Time: Varies.

    Total Administration Time: Varies.

Manner in Which Results Are Reported for Individuals: Standard scores.

Machine Scoring: Not available.

Hand Scoring: Scored by counselor.

Computer Software Options Available: Not available.

Cost of Materials: No cost; contact the primary author.

    Specimen Set: Not available.

    Counselee Materials: Copies of the instrument.

Published Reviews of the Instrument in the Last 15 Years: Not available.

Workplace Sexual Identity Management Measure

Reviewed By:

Cirleen DeBlaere
Department of Counseling and Psychological Services
Georgia State University

Bethany L. Perkins
Department of Education and Human Services
Lehigh University

Description

The Workplace Sexual Identity Management Measure (WSIMM) consists of 31 items to assess the workplace sexual identity management strategies employed by lesbian and gay individuals (Anderson, Croteau, Chung, &

Workplace Sexual Identity Management Measure

DiStefano, 2001). Since its initial development, modified versions of the WSIMM have been created to address recommendations made by Anderson et al. in the original article (cf. WSIMM-R; Lance, Anderson, & Croteau, 2010) and to assess the identity management strategies of transgender individuals (cf. WSIMM-TF; Brewster, Velez, DeBlaere, & Moradi, 2012). The WSIMM takes approximately 5-10 minutes for the average test taker to complete.

Lance et al. (2010) defined workplace sexual identity management as the "actions lesbian, gay, and bisexual (LGB) workers take to manage information concerning their sexual orientation" (p. 19). The authors of the measure (Anderson et al., 2001) noted that prior conceptualizations and assessments of sexual identity management strategies had been limited in scope and level of sophistication. More specifically, the typical mode of measurement for sexual identity management had been to ask workers to report in one or two items the number of individuals in their workplace who were aware of their sexual minority status. Responses could be recorded as the actual number of individuals who were aware of their sexual minority identity or along a range (e.g., no one knows, only close friends know, some know, everyone knows; Anderson et al., 2001).

In an effort to develop an assessment based on a more comprehensive conceptualization of workplace sexual identity management and on the reported experiences of lesbian and gay workers, Anderson and colleagues (2001) used existing qualitative studies to guide their measure's development. In particular, the authors based their conceptualization of sexual identity management strategies on the work of Griffin (1992). Griffin (1992) articulated four strategies on a continuum from greatest level of concealment (i.e., *Passing*) to openly revealing one's sexual orientation (i.e., *Explicitly Out*). Thus, the items of the WSIMM are intended to assess *Passing* (i.e., manufacturing information to be perceived as heterosexual), *Covering* (i.e., omitting information to avoid being identified as a sexual minority person), *Implicitly Out* (i.e., being truthful about aspects of one's life, but not explicitly identifying oneself as lesbian or gay), and *Explicitly Out* (i.e., explicitly identifying as lesbian or gay to others in the workplace) strategies. Griffin and the authors acknowledge that workers may use multiple identity management strategies. However, these strategies are likely to coalesce around a specific point on the continuum. Consequently, an individual who uses Passing strategies is unlikely to also use strategies that represent an Explicitly Out form of identity management.

The WSIMM presents a series of short statements that correspond to Passing, Covering, Implicitly Out, and Explicitly Out strategies. Workers are asked to report the frequency with which they use each strategy from a scale of 1 (*never/seldom*) to 4 (*almost always/always*). Scores are obtained by averaging the item scores for each respective strategy. Higher scores indicate greater use of that strategy type; workers may obtain a score of 1 to 4 for each strategy. Mean scores for each subscale were 1.11 (*SD* = .18) for Passing, 1.28 (*SD* = .35) for Covering, 2.52 (*SD* = .55) for Implicitly Out, and 2.59 (*SD* = .92) for Explicitly Out with the scale development sample of lesbian women and gay men (Anderson et al., 2001). An example of a Passing item is, "Use names or pronouns of the other sex to refer to the same-sex person with whom I am dating or living." An example of a Covering item is, "Omit names or pronouns when talking about someone I am dating or living with so that my sexual orientation is unclear." An example of an Implicitly Out item is, "Openly associate with coworkers known to be gay or lesbian, and let others think that I am gay or lesbian too, if they want to." An example of an Explicitly Out item is, "Correct others when they make comments that imply that I am heterosexual (e.g., they ask if I have been in a relationship with someone of the other sex) by explaining that I am lesbian or gay."

Given that sexual identity disclosure impacts work satisfaction, work relationships, and commitment to work of sexual minority individuals (Mock, Sedlovskaya, & Purdie-Vaughns, 2010), the frequency and type of sexual identity management strategies used by clients can be important to assess in counseling. As Anderson et al. (2001) highlighted, two factors are likely important in the complex decision-making process of strategy selection for sexual minority workers: "the worker's sense of self related to their sexual orientation" and "the work environment in relation to sexual orientation" (p. 246). Thus, learning the strategies currently being used by a client can provide important diagnostic information about a client's sexual identity development as well as their perception of their work environment. For instance, Anderson and colleagues discussed that protection from discrimination and workplace hostility can be one motivation for using Passing or Covering strategies. Accordingly, if a client reports using such strategies, a counselor may want to assess the level of acceptance of sexual minority persons in the individual's workplace as well as specific incidents of discrimination that may have taken place.

A COUNSELOR'S GUIDE TO CAREER ASSESSMENTS INSTRUMENTS

Similarly, counselors may also want to examine not only total scores for each sexual identity management strategy, but also the item-level data. Client responses to individual items can provide insight into the specific ways in which, or areas in which, the individual is concealing or revealing their sexual minority identity. Moreover, such information could be the foundation for the exploration of alternative strategies that the client may use in the workplace to meet their needs. In this way, counselors are helping clients to furnish their "toolbox" of concordant strategies.

The WSIMM could also be used as a measure of client change. As discussed previously, although workers may make use of different strategies, the strategies are likely to cluster around a specific place on the Passing to Explicitly Out continuum. Anderson et al. (2001) asserted that a move along the continuum will only occur if there is a change within the individual regarding their sexual orientation or within the workplace with regard to sexual orientation issues. Consequently, it may be useful to administer the WSIMM at multiple time points over the course of counseling to assess client change. For example, a move from predominately Passing/Covering strategies to primarily Implicitly Out/Explicitly Out strategies could be an indication of a more affirming personal sense of sexual minority identity, a change in work environment (including relationships with colleagues), or some combination of the two.

Finally, the WSIMM could be used by a counselor to assist clients with selecting jobs, companies, and careers that align with their indicated or wished for strategies (i.e., person-environment fit). For instance, if a client reports that strategies that reflect more revelation of sexual identity in the workplace is an important personal variable, a counselor could assist the client in exploring vocational options (e.g., sexual minority identity affirming companies) that will provide a good fit with those strategies. The Human Right's Campaign's (http://www. hrc.org) annual "Best Places to Work" list can be one helpful resource.

Technical Considerations

The WSIMM was developed with a normative sample of 172 lesbian and gay student affairs professionals who were members of the Network for Gay, Lesbian, and Bisexual Concerns within the National Association of Student Personnel Administrators (Anderson et al., 2001). Participants ranged in age from 23 to 63 years, with the majority (55.6%) reporting Explicitly Out strategies as their predominant sexual identity management strategy (Implicitly Out [38%], Covering [6.4%]) and no participants reporting used of Passing techniques as their primary strategy. The sample was predominately White ([87.1%]; African American [5.3%], Latina(o) [5.3%], Asian/Pacific Islander (1.8%]) and held advanced degrees ([89.6%]. Participants resided in a variety of U.S. geographic regions and represented small town/rural, mid-size city, large city suburb, and large city locations. Additional studies that have used the WSIMM or modified forms of the WSIMM (e.g., WSIMM-R, WSIMM-TF) have obtained meaningful results with other samples of predominately White sexual minority K-12 schoolteachers (Lance et al., 2010), military veterans (Moradi, 2009), and transgender individuals (Brewster et al., 2012).

The adequacy of the reliability of the WSIMM subscales varies by strategy. Covering (α= .73) and Explicitly Out (α = .91) strategies have evidenced good reliability (Ponterotto & Ruckdeschel, 2007) with the normative sample, while the Passing (α = .37) and Implicitly Out (α = .53) strategies have exhibited less internal consistency. Reliability of the Passing and Implicitly Out subscales has been found to be greater with the WSIMM-R (Passing, α = .59; Covering, α = .79; Implicitly Out, α = .75; Explicitly Out, α = .95) version of the measure. Reliability of the WSIMM-TF (Covering, α = .66; Implicitly Out, α = .80; Explicitly Out, α = .86) has also been supported.

Anderson et al. (2001) argued that identity management strategies are likely to remain fairly consistent over short intervals because considerable shifts in either an individual's sense of self or work environment in relation to sexual orientation are necessary for change in primary strategies to occur. In partial support of their contention, test-retest reliability over a two-week period was .77 and .87 for the Covering and Explicitly Out subscales, respectively. Similar to the internal consistency reliability estimates previously reported, values were lower for the Passing (r = .62) and Implicitly Out (r = .59) management strategies (Anderson et al., 2001). Taken together, the Covering and Explicitly Out strategies of the WSIMM appear to demonstrate the most consistent reliability with lesbian and gay workers.

Workplace Sexual Identity Management Measure

Item-total correlations were examined for the Passing, Covering, Implicitly Out, and Explicitly Out subscales. Covering and Explicitly Out items were generally correlated greater than .30 with their subscale total scores. Conversely, the majority of Passing items were correlated less than .30 with the total subscale score and Implicitly Out items appeared to represent two distinct subsets of items. Anderson et al. (2001) noted that the item-total correlations obtained with the Passing and Implicitly Out items could be due to limited variability of item responses for Passing strategies and ambiguous wording of certain Implicitly Out items.

In addition to item-total correlations, Anderson et al. (2001) conducted several analyses to investigate the construct validity of the WSIMM. First, an exploratory factor analysis was conducted to examine the extent to which the four hypothesized strategies of Passing, Covering, Implicitly Out, and Explicitly Out were represented by the measure items. A three-factor model was found to provide the best fit to the data representing a factor comprised of Passing and Covering items, an Implicitly Out factor, and an Explicitly Out factor. The authors noted that Griffin's (1992) conceptualization was generally supported, but also suggested that the items be reexamined with a sample that was more inclusive of individuals using Passing strategies. Furthermore, the authors noted the need to potentially modify some of the ambiguously worded Implicitly Out items.

Bivariate correlations between the hypothesized subscales indicated that, as anticipated, the Passing subscale was significantly and positively associated with the Covering ($r = .36$) and negatively related to the Explicitly Out ($r = -.22$) subscales. The Covering and Explicitly Out subscales were significantly and negatively related to one another ($r = -.66$). The Implicitly Out subscale was not found to be related significantly to any other strategy subscale, potentially reiterating the need to further clarify the Implicitly Out subscale.

Anderson et al. (2001) also examined the relationship between the four subscale scores and several indicators of disclosure. The authors found that both Passing and Covering strategies were significantly and negatively related to degree of disclosure and satisfaction with degree of disclosure at work. Explicitly Out scores were significantly and positively related to these indicators. Implicitly Out strategies were not correlated significantly with any disclosure measures. Lastly, as hypothesized by the authors, WSIMM subscale scores were not significantly related to a measure of job satisfaction. The authors explained that the enhanced integrity and leadership associated with more open identity strategies in the workplace may offset the potential costs of outness, resulting in a null relationship between disclosure and job satisfaction.

As a final indicator of validity, the authors compared workers' self-reported rank ordering of identity management strategies used in the workplace and their mean scores on the Passing, Covering, Implicitly Out, and Explicitly Out subscales. Individuals who reported Covering to be their predominate identity management strategy indicated using Covering and Implicitly Out strategies with equal frequency, but more often than either Passing or Explicitly Out strategies. As expected, workers who reported that Implicitly Out and Explicitly Out strategies were most self-descriptive also endorsed Implicitly Out and Explicitly Out subscales, correspondingly, with greater frequency than any other subscale. No workers indicated Passing as their predominant identity management strategy. Thus, the workers' self-described identity management strategy and subscale scores generally corresponded.

Derivative forms of the WSIMM have also evidenced good validity. For instance, the subscale scores of the WSIMM-R, including the revised Implicitly Out items, were found to be correlated significantly and in the expected directions with each other and another measure of identity management. Similarly, the WSIMM-TF Covering, Implicitly Out, and Explicitly Out subscale scores were generally found to be related significantly to one another and additional measures of workplace climate, discrimination experiences, and several aspects of job satisfaction.

General Utility and Evaluation

The WSIMM is easily administered via paper-and-pencil or electronic formats. Also, as the measure includes clear directions for workers that introduce the assessment, minimal guidance is needed from the counselor. Based on prior studies using the WSIMM and its derivatives, this assessment appears appropriate for use with individuals 18 year of age and older.

Despite being developed over a decade ago, psychometric data with the WSIMM remains limited. Additional studies are needed to examine the reliability and validity of this measure with sexual and gender minority samples that represent greater diversity with regard to other key social variables (e.g., race, ethnicity, socioeconomic status). It is also important to note that bisexual individuals have not been included in substantial numbers in prior studies investigating the WSIMM and that this measure may not be appropriate for use with bisexual individuals. Indeed, in one study, bisexual participants reported that it was difficult to respond to WSIMM items when not in a same-sex relationship even when the language of the measure had been amended to be inclusive of bisexual individuals (Lance et al., 2010).

To date, the Passing subscale of the WSIMM has received limited empirical support. However, as the normative sample and subsequent samples have had few, if any, individuals who identify using Passing strategies as their predominate form of sexual identity management in the workplace, it is unclear at this time whether the lack of support for this subscale reflects methodological concerns (e.g., sample characteristics) or a need to reevaluate the conceptualization of sexual identity management as possessing four distinct dimensions. Conversely, the Covering and Explicitly Out subscales have performed consistently well across lesbian and gay samples, supporting the use of these scales as indicators of a continuum of sexual identity management strategies from concealment of sexual orientation to actively disclosing sexual minority identity in the workplace.

In the case of the Implicitly Out subscale, both Anderson et al. (2001) and Lance et al. (2010) recommend the use of modified items aimed at reducing ambiguous language. These revised items are included in the WSIMM-R and demonstrated an improved internal consistency reliability estimate (i.e., $\alpha = .75$) compared to the original version. Some authors have also suggested that select Implicitly Out items may represent a sexual and gender minority advocacy construct (Brewster et al., 2012). Given the consistent support for the Covering and Explicitly Out subscales and the developing support of Implicitly Out items with lesbian, gay, and transgender workers, the WSIMM and its derivatives show promise as assessments of identity management strategies with sexual and gender minority individuals. Furthermore, as accumulating research supports the links between identity management strategies and important vocational variables (e.g., job satisfaction and perceived workplace climate), the WSIMM could provide counselors with valuable diagnostic information.

References and Additional Resources

Anderson, M. Z., Croteau, J. M., Chung, Y. B., & DiStefano, T. M. (2001). Developing an assessment of sexual identity management for lesbian and gay workers. *Journal of Career Assessment, 9*(3), 243-260. doi:10.1177/106907270100900303

Brewster, M. E., Velez, B., DeBlaere, C., & Moradi, B. (2012). Transgender individuals' workplace experiences: The applicability of sexual minority measures and models. *Journal of Counseling Psychology, 59*(1), 60-70. doi:10.1037/a0025206

Griffin, P. (1992). From hiding out to coming out: Empowering gay and lesbian educators. In K. M. Harbeck (Ed.), *Coming out of the classroom closet* (pp. 167-196). Binghamton, NY: Harrington Park Press.

Lance, T. S., Anderson, M. Z., & Croteau, J. M. (2010). Improving measurement of workplace sexual identity management. *The Career Development Quarterly, 59*(1), 19-26. doi:10.1002/j.2161-0045.2010.tb00127.x

Mock, S. E., Sedlovskaya, A., & Purdie-Vaughns, V. (2010). Gay and bisexual men's disclosure of sexual orientation in the workplace: Associations with retirement planning. *Journal of Applied Gerontology, 30*(1), 123-132. doi:10.1177/0733464809358081

Moradi, B. (2009). Sexual orientation disclosure, concealment, harassment, and military cohesion: Perceptions of LGBT military veterans. *Military Psychology, 21*(4), 513-533. doi:10.1080/08995600903206453

Ponterotto, J. G. & Ruckdeschel, D. E. (2007). An overview of coefficient alpha and a reliability matrix for estimating adequacy of internal consistency coefficients with psychological research measures. *Perceptual and Motor Skills, 105,* 997-1014. doi:10.2466/pms.105.3.997-1014

CHAPTER 16

QUALITATIVE AND ALTERNATIVE APPROACHES TO STANDARDIZED ASSESSMENTS

- Career Genogram
- Career Style Interview
- Future Career Autobiography
- Intelligent Career Card Sort
- Knowdell Card Sorts
- Life Role Analysis
- My Career Chapter
- My System of Career Influences
- Possible Selves Mapping

458

CAREER GENOGRAM

Rae Wiemers Okiishi

Private Practice
2940 Monroe Drive
Ames, IA 50010

Target Population: Children, adolescents, young adults, and adults.

Statement of the Purpose of the Instrument: The career genogram, a paper-and-pencil assessment, is used to explore career decision making in accordance with the client's worldview, identified influential individuals, and perceptions of work success.

Forms and Levels Available, with Dates of Publication/Revision of Each: 1987.

Date of Most Recent Edition of Test Manual, User's Guide, Etc.: Not applicable.

Time:

Actual Test Time: Development of a genogram may take 50-90 minutes. Exploratory discussion may continue for more sessions.

Total Administration Time: Varies, at least one session.

Sample(s) in which assessment was developed: The career genogram is developed based the genogram activity used in family therapy.

Manner in Which Results are Reported for Individuals/Groups: In-session discussion and interpretation with a counselor. No scoring key available or applicable.

Cost of Materials: No cost.

Specimen Set: Not available.

Counselee Materials: Paper and pencils.

Published Reviews of the Instrument in the Last 15 Years:

Gibson, D. M. (2005). The use of genograms in career counseling with elementary, middle, and high school students. *The Career Development Quarterly, 53*(4), 353-361.

Malott, K. M., & Magnuson, S. (2004). Using genograms to facilitate undergraduate students' career development: A group model. *The Career Development Quarterly, 53*(2), 178-186.

McGoldrick, M., Gerson, R., & Petry, S. (2008). *Genograms in family assessment* (3rd ed.). New York, NY: Norton.

McMahon, M., Patton, W., & Watson, M. (2003). Developing qualitative career assessment processes. *The Career Development Quarterly, 51*(3), 194-202.

Moon, S. M., Coleman, V. D., McCollum, E. E., Nelson, T. S., & Jensen-Scott, R. L. (1993). Using the genogram to facilitate career decisions: A case study. *Journal of Family Psychotherapy, 4*, 45-56.

Okocha, A. A. G. (1998). Using qualitative appraisal strategies in career counseling. *Journal of Employment Counseling, 35*(3), 151-159.

CAREER GENOGRAM
Reviewed by:
Elizabeth A. Prosek
Department of Counseling and Higher Education
University of North Texas

Description

The genogram is a visual representation of a client's family of origin traditionally used in family therapy. Okiishi (1987) introduced the genogram as an effective tool in career counseling. This paper-and-pencil qualitative assessment graphically represents three family generations and is used to explore career decision making in accordance with the client's worldview, identified influential individuals, and perceptions of work success (Malott & Magnuson, 2004; Okiishi, 1987). Similar to its purpose in family therapy, the career genogram serves as a catalyst for discussion with a client, as well as a concrete visual aid used as a reference in future counseling sessions. Consistent with the career development literature, "discussions and reflections of family influence assist individuals in achieving insight and clarity regarding their career decisions" (Malott & Magnuson, p. 178). Therefore a genogram, reflective of family members and their chosen careers, can be easily incorporated into a holistic approach in career counseling.

Constructing a career genogram is a collaborative process between the counselor and client. The counselor guides the process and completes the diagram as the client describes family members. Developing a genogram may take 50-90 minutes, depending on the resulting exploratory discussion. It may be that the career genogram is developed in one session, while the exploration of career decision making and perception of work success occurs throughout the remaining sessions.

Okiishi (1987) outlined a three-step approach to the utilization of a genogram in career counseling: (1) construction of the genogram, (2) identification of occupations, and (3) exploration of the client. In Step 1, construction of the career genogram, the counselor creates the career genogram using paper and pencil as the client describes three family generations. For example, in Figure 1 the counselor asked the client, Elizabeth, to begin her family diagram with her paternal grandparents, then worked on the right side of the diagram to add maternal grandparents. The discussion began more concretely as Elizabeth listed names of family members. The counselor inquired if any family members were deceased and cross-hatched patterns were added to all four grandparents. In Step 2, identification of occupations, the counselor labels the work experiences of each family member based on client report. Figure 1 page 463 displays the identified occupations of each family member to the right of his or her name. Elizabeth struggled with her mother's occupational label, as Cathy's long-term job did not reflect her college degree in teaching. The counselor recognized both occupations were important to Elizabeth's story and therefore included both. The conversations in Step 2 lead naturally into Step 3, exploration of the client, in which the counselor facilitates discussion of career choices, values, and success. It is during this final step that clients articulate their career decision-making process, gaining further insight in career exploration. For example, because Elizabeth's mother's college degree choices were limited to teaching or nursing, Elizabeth was discouraged from those occupational areas. Elizabeth discussed her career decision-making process had to adapt because her original plan was to become a special education teacher. There are various career considerations to discuss with clients including, but not limited to, financial expectations, familial career patterns, age and work, job satisfaction, and disadvantages of family work experience (Malott & Magnuson, 2004; Okocha, 1998). Using Figure 1 as an example, Elizabeth identified the familial influence of a flexible work schedule. This value stemmed from the first generation's time-consuming work schedules and multiple jobs that kept them away from home. The importance of flexibility was evident among Elizabeth and her siblings.

Using this assessment tool within career counseling requires counselor familiarity with the construction of genograms (Okiishi, 1987). Family counseling literature provides many resources for interpreting genograms in counseling (see Bowen, 1980; McGoldrick, Gerson, & Petry, 2008). When used appropriately by a trained professional, genograms promote many benefits to the counseling process, including flexibility, holistic interpretation, debriefing, and promotion of a collaborative environment between the counselor and client (Okiishi, 1987; Okocha, 1998).

Career counseling literature supports the use of genograms across the lifespan. Gibson (2005) outlined how the concept can be formatted for use in the school setting with elementary, middle, and high school students. Gibson proposed that at the elementary level, career family trees provide an initial simple guide to work experiences of the family, but also opens communication about careers between children and influential adults. For middle school students, career genograms focused on what and how career decisions were made by family members. At the high school level, the focal point becomes the students' motivational factors within the career decision-making process (Gibson, 2005).

The genogram continues to be valued at the collegiate level of career development. Malott and Magnuson (2004) proposed a five-week curriculum based on genogram activities for career exploration with undergraduate students that used a group format with supporting individual discussion sessions. The program evaluation indicated positive feedback from students, who reported the exploration of personal and professional development within the genogram format was beneficial to their career decision-making process (Malott & Magnuson, 2004). In adulthood, research literature asserts the use of the genogram as an effective tool when exploring potential change of careers (Moon, Coleman, McCollum, Nelson, & Jensen-Scott, 1993). Career changes may be a result of unemployment or underemployment. There is also potential for career counseling when transitioning from military to civilian employment. Moon et al. (1993) specifically highlighted the influence of life span development on desire to change careers. Values related to occupational choices may be affected by other lifestyle choices such as having children or financing education.

Technical Considerations

The genogram is based in Bowen's (1980) family systems therapy work. Bowen's theory asserts that individuals are influenced by their context, specifically the family system. The genogram allows for clients to recognize patterns among multiple generations of the family. The insight gained may increase client understanding of current belief systems and/or choices. The family diagram protocols and symbols were further categorized by McGoldrick and Gerson and updated in textbooks over the last 30 years (see McGoldrick et al., 2008). Career counselors implementing the genogram as a tool in career exploration may find the text as a helpful reference in constructing the graphic representations.

Qualitative assessment in career counseling incorporates the meaning made from context or systems that may be overlooked in standard quantitative assessments of individual traits and abilities (McMahon, Patton, & Watson, 2003). The collaborative nature of qualitative assessments, such as the genogram, empowers the client to be an active participant in career exploration, rather than being advised to appropriate careers based on assessed traits (Okocha, 1998). McMahon et al. (2003) outlined parameters to establish rigor in qualitative career assessments: ground in theory, test the process, assess time frame, foster holism, write readable instructions, create simple steps, allow for flexibility, encourage collaboration, and debrief the experience. The career genogram, as described in this review, meets the proposed qualifications of rigor. It is grounded in Bowen Family Systems theory, adaptable to the clinical hour, and incorporated into a holistic approach. The outlined three-step instructions are simple, flexible, and allow for discussion or debriefing. Furthermore, use of the career genogram is documented to be appropriate across the lifespan (Gibson, 2005; Malott & Magnuson, 2004; Moon et al., 1993). The flexible nature of the genogram also allows for use among diverse populations (Okocha, 1998). For example, clients may add influential individuals to their genograms who are not blood relatives, such as step-parents or godparents. Discussion of the genogram may elicit family-of-origin cultural considerations and/or influences to the career decision-making process.

General Utility and Evaluation

The genogram is a qualitative assessment adapted for use in career counseling. It is simple in nature, while allowing for in-depth insight into familial influences of a client's worldview and perceptions of work success (Malott & Magnuson, 2004; Okiishi, 1987). The genogram can be constructed within a 50-minute clinical session, but referred to throughout the remaining counseling relationship. This qualitative assessment adapts well to culturally diverse populations and is established as age-appropriate across the developmental lifespan (Gibson, 2005; Malott & Magnuson, 2004; Moon et al., 1993; Okocha, 1998). The genogram provides an opportunity for clients to actively participate in and explore their career decision-making process.

References and Additional Resources

Bowen, M. (1980). *Key to the genogram.* Washington, DC: Georgetown University Hospital.

Gibson, D. M. (2005). The use of genograms in career counseling with elementary, middle, and high school students. *Career Development Quarterly, 53*(4), 353-361.

Malott, K. M., & Magnuson, S. (2004). Using genograms to facilitate undergraduate students' career development: A group model. *The Career Development Quarterly, 53*(2), 178-186.

McGoldrick, M., Gerson, R., & Petry, S. (2008). *Genograms in family assessment* (3rd ed.). New York, NY: Norton.

McMahon, M., Patton, W., & Watson, M. (2003). Developing qualitative career assessment processes. *Career Development Quarterly, 51*(3), 194-202.

Moon, S. M., Coleman, V. D., McCollum, E. E., Nelson, T. S., & Jensen-Scott, R. L. (1993). Using the genogram to facilitate career decisions: A case study. *Journal of Family Psychotherapy, 4,* 45-56.

Okiishi R. W. (1987). The genogram as a tool in career counseling. *Journal of Counseling and Development, 66,* 139-143.

Okocha, A. A. G. (1998). Using qualitative appraisal strategies in career counseling. *Journal of Employment Counseling, 35*(3), 151-159.

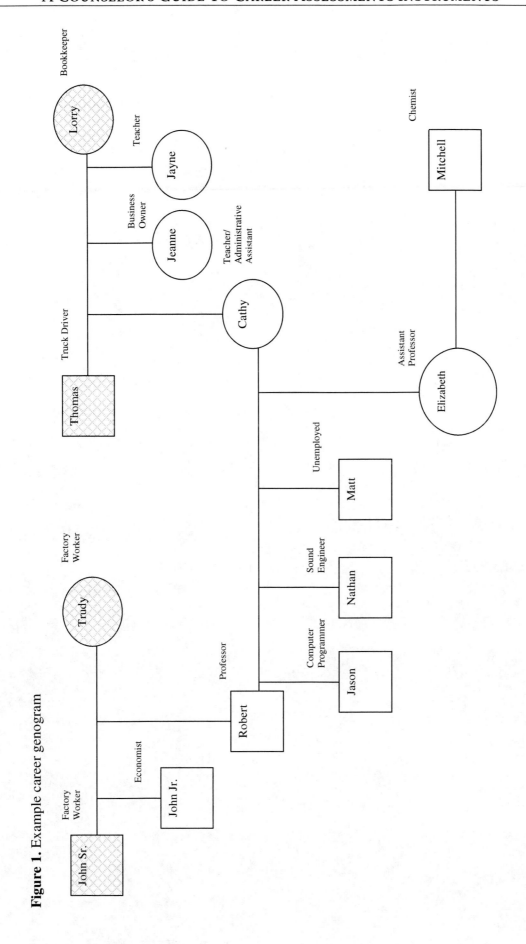

Figure 1. Example career genogram

464

CAREER STYLE INTERVIEW

Mark Savickas

Kevin Glavin
Vocopher
kglavin@vocopher.com
http://www.vocopher.com

[handwritten: Super's theory]

Target Population: Adolescents, young adults, and adults.

Statement of the Purpose of the Instrument: The Career Style Interview (CSI) is designed to enable individuals to tell, hear, and author their life story for use in school and work in a way that is personally meaningful and matters to others.

Forms and Levels Available, with Dates of Publication/Revision of Each: 1989. Available as the Career Construction Interview (2012) and as the *My Career Story: An Autobiographical Workbook for Life-Career Success* (2012).

Date of Most Recent Edition of Test Manual, User's Guide, Etc.: 2012.

Time:

Actual Test Time: Varies dependent upon time needed to process responses with individuals or complete the workbook.

Total Administration Time: Usually 1 to 2 hours.

Sample(s) in Which Assessment was Developed: Individual case studies, young adults ages 18-30.

Manner in Which Results Are Reported for Individuals/Groups: Reported in narrative, co-constructed with individuals highlighting their life story, or in written form in completed workbook.

Computer Software Options Available: All forms and workbook are downloadable for free from http://www.vocopher.com.

Cost of Materials: Free to qualified professionals, available for download at http://www.vocopher.com.

Specimen Set: Not available.

Counselee Materials: Directions in various articles, videos, and at http://www.vocopher.com in the My Career Story workbook.

Published Reviews of the Instrument in the Last 15 Years:

Rehfuss, M., Cosio, S., & Del Corso, J. (2011a). Counselors' perspectives on using the Career Style Interview with clients. *Career Development Quarterly. 59,* 208-218.

Taber, B., & Briddick, W., (2011). Adlerian-based career counseling in an age of protean careers. *Journal of Individual Psychology, 67,* 107-121.

Taber, B., Hartung, P., Briddick, W., Briddick, H., & Rehfuss, M. (2011). Career Style Interview: A contextualized approach to career counseling. *Career Development Quarterly, 59,* 274-287.

*[handwritten: * narrative approach to assessment]*

Career Style Interview

CAREER STYLE INTERVIEW
Reviewed by:

Mark Rehfuss

Department of Counseling and Human Services
Old Dominion University

Description

The Career Style Interview (CSI) assessment was developed by Mark L. Savickas and is primarily a qualitative collaborative interview. The assessment is used in Career Style Counseling (Savickas, 2009), is consistent with the counseling for Life Design paradigm (Savickas, 2012a), and is the foundational assessment for the theory of Career Construction (Savickas, 2005, 2012b). The assessment, as an Adlerian-based method of career counseling, has only been slightly modified since its first publication by Savickas in 1989. The measure consists of seven core questions focused upon drawing out life themes and facilitating greater self-knowledge (Taber et al., 2011). The assessment is an interview that can take from one to two hours to administer and review or, with the recent publication of the My Career Story (MCS) workbook, it can be given as a take-home exercise (Savickas & Hartung, 2012). The assessment is best administered in two sessions, with the questions being explored during a first counseling session and discussed after counselor review with the individual during the second session (Savickas, 2005, 2009).

The client and counselor collaborate throughout the administration of the CSI to identify, interpret, and construct what the person prefers, how the person copes, and why the person pursues what they do through work (Savickas, 2005, 2009). The CSI provides a means of determining and then linking an individual's vocational personality, career adaptability, and life theme into an organized whole. This understanding allows the individual to see the unity of their motivations and the consistencies of their past, present, and future career paths. Overall, the CSI is a tool designed to enable individuals by clarifying how their work can enhance personal meaning and matter to others.

The CSI was initially developed by Savickas in 1989 as a measure to clarify life stories in relation to career decisions. The instrument draws from several historical models of assessment including the Adlerian focus on revealing the work task and the constructivist focus on telling, hearing, and clarifying the life story (Savickas, 2009; Taber & Briddick, 2011). The model values and uses narrative or self-stories to reveal individual meaning-making for past, present, and future career decisions. It seeks to unify the subjective and objective influences upon individuals' career trajectories and facilitate a link between their life passions and motivations and their career choices and desires. Although the CSI was initially used with individuals undecided on their career choice, its ability to address a broad spectrum of career concerns has encouraged its use with a variety of career counseling issues and diverse clients ranging from adolescents to mature adults.

The CSI measure consists of seven basic questions related to identified need, interests, family, role models, and early recollections (Savickas, 2005, 2009; Taber & Briddick, 2011). They include the following:

- Whom did you admire when you were growing up? Tell me about him or her.

- What magazines do you read regularly? What do you like about them? What TV shows do you really enjoy? Why?

- Tell me about your favorite book/movie.

- What do you like to do with your free time? What are your hobbies? What do you enjoy about these hobbies?

- Do you have a favorite saying or motto? Tell me a saying you remember hearing.

- What were your favorite subjects in junior high and high school? Why? What subjects did you hate? Why?

- What are your earliest recollections? I am interested in hearing three stories about things you recall happening to you when you were between three and six years old.

A Counselor's Guide To Career Assessments Instruments

The questions explore the purpose for career counseling, role models, favorite television shows and books, favorite mottos, hobbies, favorite school subjects, and recollection of several early memories. Responses to these questions are captured in the client's own words and transcribed by the counselor. Upon completion of the questions, the counselor uses written notes to highlight client themes. The client's repeated words, phrases, verbs, and concepts are used in this identification process. The transcribed notes serve as a starting point of reference as the client and counselor engage in reflection and discussion about the content of the interview. The CSI process is a collaborative event whereby the counselor and client validate, construct, and refine the themes noted in the interview.

The process of theme validation often begins with reflection upon the interest preferences or vocational personality of the individual (Savickas, 2005, 2009, 2012a, 2012b). Vocational personality relates to what an individual prefers to do and where those preferences fit with the world of work. John Holland's differential theory of vocational personality is a typical framework used for this task. Using the Holland RIASEC model as a framework to view the client's answers related to school subjects, hobbies, and role models, the counselor can often identify their primary codes and discuss what these preferences may mean for the person related to work. This coding can also be used to develop a basic statement of success using the success formula rubric. This statement identifies what it takes for the individual to feel successful and can then be used by the individual in modifying current work roles/tasks or in making decisions about work that would foster self-actualization. How individuals go about making career decisions, however, is related to their career adaptability.

An individual's CSI narrative responses often reveal how the person interacts with or adapts to career developmental tasks, transitions, and setbacks (Savickas, 2005, 2009). This career adaptability consists of four career-related dimensions: concern, control, curiosity and confidence. Though adaptive individuals continually develop their attitudes, beliefs and competencies in each of these four areas, the CSI can highlight when they struggle to grow in one or more of these dimensions and allow it to be addressed within the counseling process.

The CSI uses several questions that are reflective as well as projective in nature. The first identifies the individual's early role models (Savickas, 2005, 2009; Taber & Briddick, 2011). Early role models are often an encapsulation of solutions to problems or challenges individuals faced in their early life. They can serve as a personal prototype for how to successfully make career and life decisions and are often conceptualized as an attempt of the individual to enact a self-concept. Similarities and differences between the individual and the role models are explored with the counselor clarifying some of the reasons for their selection and how they may relate to work. The second are questions related to earliest recollections or memories (Savickas, 2005, 2009; Taber & Briddick, 2011). This question is not looking for accurate truth, but exploring and highlighting repeated themes that permeate the individual's life and are expressed through their recollection stories. The individual often selects and shares recollections that provide a solution to their current career problem or exhibit the strength needed to successfully manage it. These stories frequently reveal fright, uncertainty, or rejection, but can also include excitement, support, and security. The counselor notes the description and clarifies the emotions in the recollection, clarifying any relationship to the client's present career context. In addition to recounting several recollections, the person is asked to give each one an active title. These role models, stories, and narratives are combined to identify themes that cut across the individual's interview and life.

Individual's life themes succinctly organizes their behavior and demonstrates the consistency of their personhoods over time (Savickas, 2005, 2009; Taber & Briddick, 2011). It answers the why question behind their life and career actions while also highlighting their motivations and beliefs. Life themes often include a meta-narrative of turning a lifelong preoccupation into an occupation or past personal pain into other's gain. The counselor looks for the life theme by focusing upon the glue that seems to hold all of an individual's narrative facts together and clarifies the individual's life passion. The life theme discussion, construction, and validation are a process of illumination that can be facilitated by a focused review of the verbs, words, phrases, and themes repeated throughout the CSI. The CSI and the resultant narrative interpretation seek to clarify refine the theme that fills the individual's life with meaning and mattering.

Technical Considerations

The CSI as a whole, but especially in its new versions, appears to be more rigorous and consistent with qualitative career assessment reliability (McMahon, Patton, & Watson, 2003). It is clearly grounded in and reflective of the processes described in the theory of career construction (Savickas, 2009). The assessment has been used since 1989 and has been found to be useful for those that apply it and to those that have been the recipients of its application (Rehfuss, Cosio, & Del Corso, 2011a; Rehfuss, Del Corso, Glavin, & Wykes, 2011b). The assessment appears to foster a holistic understanding of the individual by actively seeking to co-construct the individual's life story with regards to work. The assessment is much easier to understand and apply with the recent development of the My Career Story (MCS) workbook (Savickas & Hartung, 2012) that includes explanatory directions coupled with the demonstration videos of its application. The new MCS version of the assessment is more time efficient and fosters increased flexibility of application as most of the components along with explanations of their purpose are contained within a single workbook. The new MCS version also helps to clarify the application using small logical steps that facilitates exploration, review, and integration for the individual and provides them with a resource they can use overtime. Overall, the assessment in its newer forms has become more rigorous and helpful as a qualitative career assessment.

General Utility and Evaluation

The assessment itself in addition to the original single page of questions has recently been adapted into a new form for counselors (i.e., Career Construction Interview [CCI]) and expanded into a self-guided assessment workbook (i.e., MCS). Both versions of the assessment are available free for download at http://www.vocopher.com. The CCI is helpful in that it provides structured space for recording responses to each question as well as several structured pages to help the counselor organize and process the responses. The MCS is helpful in that it allows an individual to go through the assessment on their own, providing specific directions and reflective questions that walk the individual through the process of completing and processing their story. This written form may facilitate more reflective thinking in individuals and could be helpful with individuals that are less verbally expressive. The MCS form is designed to be used by the individual alone or in a group or class setting, while the new CCI form is designed for use by a counselor with an individual in session.

The assessment has been used with a variety of individuals at differing points in the career process. However, few studies of its effectiveness with any populations have been published. Most publications are example case studies. The qualitative nature of the instrument has limited its application in research studies as larger samples of individuals having received the measure are difficult to secure. The few studies that do exist on the CSI indicate its usefulness to both the therapist and the client; however, more research is needed to validate the assessment fully (Rehfuss et al., 2011a; Rehfuss et al., 2011b). The assessment overall appears to meet the described goals; however, interpretation of the results and discussion with the client is often dependent upon the therapist's skill and experience. Savickas has several videos available through the American Psychological Association that demonstrate the use of the assessment and are helpful in training counselors to use the instrument. These video demonstrations in addition to the MCS manual provide guidance on how to apply the assessment.

References and Additional Resources

McMahon, M., Patton, W., & Watson, M. (2003). Developing qualitative career assessment processes. *Career Development Quarterly. 51*, 194-202.

Rehfuss, M., Cosio, S. & Del Corso, J. (2011a). Counselors' perspectives on using the Career Style Interview with clients. *Career Development Quarterly. 59*, 208-218.

Rehfuss, M., Del Corso, J., Glavin, K., & Wykes, S. (2011b). Impact of the Career Style Interview on individuals with career concerns. *Journal of Career Assessment, 19*, 405-419. doi:10.1177/1069072711409711

Savickas, M. L. (1989). Career style assessment and counseling. In T. Sweeney (Ed.), *Adlerian counseling: A practical approach* (3rd ed., pp. 289-320). Muncie, IN: Accelerated Development Press.

Savickas, M. L. (2005). The theory and practice of career construction. In S. D. Brown & R. W. Lent (Eds.), *Career development and counseling: Putting theory and research to work* (pp. 42-70). Hoboken, NJ: John Wiley & Sons.

A Counselor's Guide To Career Assessments Instruments

Savickas, M. L. (2009). Career style counseling. In T. Sweeney (Ed.), *Adlerian counseling: A practitioner's approach* (5th ed.; pp. 183-207). New York, NY: Routledge.

Savickas, M. L. (2012a). Life design: A paradigm for career intervention in the 21st century. *Journal of Counseling & Development, 90,* 13-19.

Savickas, M. L. (2012b). *Career Construction Interview.* Retrieved from http://www.vocopher.com.

Savickas, M. L., & Hartung, P. J. (2012). *My career story: An autobiographical workbook for life-career success.* Retrieved from www.vocopher.com.

Taber, B., & Briddick, W., (2011). Adlerian-based career counseling in an age of protean careers. *Journal of Individual Psychology, 67,* 107-121.

Taber, B., Hartung, P., Briddick, W., Briddick, H., & Rehfuss, M. (2011). Career Style Interview: A contextualized approach to career counseling. *Career Development Quarterly, 59*(3), 274-287.

470

A COUNSELOR'S GUIDE TO CAREER ASSESSMENTS INSTRUMENTS

FUTURE CAREER AUTOBIOGRAPHY

Mark Rehfuss

Old Dominion University
Norfolk VA 23529
mrehfuss@odu.edu

Target Population: Adolescents, young adults, and adults.

Statement of the Purpose of the Instrument: The Future Career Autobiography is an assessment tool used to measure change in an individual's occupational narrative over time or after a career intervention.

Forms and Levels Available, with Dates of Publication/Revision of Each: 2009.

Date of Most Recent Edition of Test Manual, User's Guide, Etc.: Not applicable.

Time:

Actual Test Time: Varies based on time needed for reviewers to compare occupational themes.

Total Administration Time: 10 minutes.

Sample(s) in Which Assessment was Developed: Undergraduate college students ages 18 to 23 (30 women, 18 men; 7 self-identified as racial/ethnic minorities).

Manner in Which Results Are Reported for Individuals/Groups: Results are reported by charting occupational/ life themes and highlighting changes in pre/post themes from unclear to formalized. No scoring key available or applicable.

Cost of Materials: No cost.

Specimen Set: Not available.

Counselee Materials: Directions included in the original article (Rehfuss, 2009).

Published Reviews of the Instrument in the Last 15 Years: Not available.

FUTURE CAREER AUTOBIOGRAPHY

Reviewed by:

Kaprea F. Johnson

Department of Counseling and Human Services
Old Dominion University

Description

The Future Career Autobiography (Rehfuss, 2009) is an assessment tool based in narrative theory and is used to measure change in an individual's occupational narrative over time or after a career intervention. Narrative theory has many strong supporters for its use in counseling and specifically for its use in career counseling (e.g., Bujold, 2004; Cochran, 1997; Reid, 2005). This theoretical approach is appropriate for its focus on helping the client construct alternate stories, being flexible, and attending to restorying client narratives over the course of the therapeutic relationship (Androutsopoulou, Thanopoulou, Economou, & Bafiti, 2004; Cochran, 1997). In career counseling, narrative approaches have been supported because of its holistic nature and use as a measurement of change (Cochran, 1997).

The Future Career Autobiography is used as a measurement of career intervention effectiveness. This brief measure is used to gain information on a client's "personal and career motives, values, and direction" before and after a career intervention (Rehfuss, 2009, p. 83). Clients are provided a piece of paper and a pencil. The paper is entitled, "Future Career Autobiography", and counselors provide the following instructions: "Please use this page

Future Career Autobiography

to write a brief paragraph about where you hope to be in life and what you hope to be doing occupationally five years after graduating from college" (p. 83). (The "five years after graduation from college" stem was revised to "five years from now" to be more applicable to diverse populations.) After approximately 10 minutes of writing, counselors collect the paper and begin the review process. Reviewing involves several steps: (1) transcription by assistants directly on the document, highlighting verbs, phrases, and occupational themes, (2) a review by counselors, and (3) additional outside reviewers for triangulation purposes. This process is completed again after eight weeks or at the end of the career intervention, and the additional step of comparing the pre- and post-responses is employed. Clients are not included during the review or transcription process. Counselors and outside reviewers look for similarities and changes, specifically dealing with occupational themes.

Rehfuss (2009) provided an example of how the Future Career Autobiography can be used as a measure of career intervention effectiveness. Rehfuss administered the Future Career Autobiography to 48 undecided undergraduate students ages 18 to 23 years old in an eight-week career exploration course at the beginning and end of the course. After the eight weeks, participant responses were paired together and reviewed for changes in occupational themes. Outside reviewers noted several occupational themes across both administrations: achievement, relationships, security, and occupational desires. Rehfuss highlighted that after a career exploration course for undecided majors, there were changes in participant narratives about career and life, more specifically occupational goals became more crystallized and clear for 38 of the 48 participants.

Although Rehfuss (2009) conducted his study before and after a career exploration course, this measure is versatile and can be used with a variety of populations. The narrative therapy approach to the measure, simple instructions, short administration time, and free cost make it feasible for use by many counselors in a variety of settings including schools, traditional counselor offices, and non-traditional counselor settings. For instance, narrative approaches in career counseling have been shown to be effective with a range of clients from international students (Arthur & Popadiuk, 2010) to adolescents of divorce (Thomas & Gibbons, 2009). Therefore, a measure such as the Future Career Autobiography could be ideal in assessing whether career counseling and interventions are helping clients change their narrative about their career.

Technical Considerations

The Future Career Autobiography is a qualitative assessment of career intervention effectiveness based on narrative theory. With many qualitative approaches, there are no derived numerical scores created from the analysis. Rather, counselors using this career measure determine change based on written responses from the participants before and after a career intervention (e.g., career exploration course, individual or group career counseling, workshops, seminars).

Although there is minimal research available, two studies to date (i.e., Rehfuss, 2009; Rehfuss & DiFabio, 2012) employed multiple researchers during the analysis, which is important in triangulating and validating findings (Mays & Pope, 2000). Rehfuss and DiFabio (2012) sought to add support for the use of the Future Career Autobiography as a qualitative measure of change. Their study included, in two conditions, 82 Italian professional women who were between the ages of 22 and 58 (40 in an experimental group, 42 in a control group). Results showed that the FCA was able to detect change in occupational themes for those that received a career intervention.

General Utility and Evaluation

The Future Career Autobiography is very user-friendly. It has simple instructions for participants, requires a relatively short time to administer (i.e., 10 minutes), and involves simple analysis. It is a measure that most counselors will be able to use to analyze the effectiveness of a career intervention. The Future Career Autobiography seems appropriate for all ages and can be adapted for work with diverse and special populations. As an example, the Future Career Autobiography can be used as a measure of career intervention effectiveness with high school students after a school counselor conducts a career classroom guidance lesson or a series of guidance lessons focused on career exploration. Another example is a college counselor or career counselor administering the Future Career Autobiography to college students before and after a career fair to see if career fairs are effective in helping students crystalize occupational plans.

References and Additional Resources

Androutsopoulou, A., Thanopoulou, K., Economou, E., & Bafiti, T. (2004). Forming criteria for assessing the coherence of clients' life stories: a narrative study. *Journal of Family Therapy, 26,* 384-406.

Arthur, N., & Popadiuk, N. (2010). A cultural formation approach to career counseling with international students. *Journal of Career Development, 37,* 423-440.

Bujold, C. (2004). Constructing career through narrative. *Journal of Vocational Behavior, 64,* 470-484.

Cochran, L. (1997). *Career counseling: A narrative approach.* Thousand Oaks, CA: Sage.

Mays, N., & Pope, C. (2000). Assessing quality in qualitative research. *British Medical Journal, 320,* 50-52.

Rehfuss, M. C. (2009). The future career autobiography: A narrative measure of career intervention effectiveness. *Career Development Quarterly, 58,* 82-90.

Rehfuss, M. C., & DiFabio, A. (2012). Validating the future career autobiography as a measure of narrative change. *Journal of Career Assessment, 20,* 1-11.

Reid, H. L. (2005). Narrative and career guidance: Beyond small talk and towards useful dialogue for the 21st century. *International Journal for Educational and Vocational Guidance, 5,* 125-136.

Thomas, D. A., & Gibbons, M. M. (2009). Narrative theory: A career counseling approach for adolescents of divorce. *Professional School Counseling, 12,* 223-229.

INTELLIGENT CAREER CARD SORT
Michael Arthur, Polly Parker, and Norman Amundson

Intelligent Career Card Sort
52 Harold Parker Road
Andover, MA 01810
http://www.intelligentcareer.net
info@intelligentcareer.net

Target Population: Young adults and adults.

Statement of the Purpose of the Instrument: The Intelligent Career Card Sort (ICCS) is a multidimensional card sort exercise that aims to assist clients claim ownership of their career decision-making process by increasing competencies for three dynamic and interdependent ways of knowing. These are (a) knowing-why, (b) knowing-how, and (c) knowing-whom. The ICCS demands clients' active participation and requires counselors/consultants to actively engage in the clients' life and career development process. The ultimate goal is for the client to formulate an action plan that is meaningful, informed and realistic. The ICCS is a career exploration exercise that can be experienced either face-to-face, over the web, or in training workshops and group modalities.

Forms and Levels Available, with Dates of Publication/Revision of Each: Not applicable.

Date of Most Recent Edition of Test Manual, User's Guide, Etc.: General information is available on the ICCS website and is continually updated. A counselor's guide is available upon completion of training.

Time:

Actual Test Time: Approximately 45 minutes.

Total Administration Time: From five hours upward for individual and group clients.

Sample(s) in Which Assessment was Developed: Not applicable.

Manner in Which Results Are Reported for Individuals/Groups: Online summaries, completion of worksheets, and records of exchanges between counselors and clients.

Computer Software Options Available: Computerized adaptive administration, standard administration online. The card sort exercise is online only. Follow-up with clients can be either face-to-face or online, or a combination of the two. The ICCS provides a comprehensive system for one-on-one counseling or workshop activities to be delivered online.

Cost of Materials: Due to possible price changes since publication date, be sure to check the publisher's website. Fees for online training are $600.00 per person for six one-hour sessions, with six free uses for clients. Homework is assigned between the sessions. A discounted fee for two people of $1100.00 is also available. With two people, the approach is for them to act as peer coaches to one another under an ICCS supervisor. Training is done over Skype video, using a set of training slides that are for the counselor/consultant to keep when the training is over.

Specimen Set: Not available.

Counselee Materials: All website services are reusable. Fees are per individual client and vary across for-profit or not-for-profit use and across individual and group administrations. Substantial discounts are applied for group use in educational settings. Contact the administrators at info@intelligentcareer.net for more information.

Published Reviews of the Instrument in the Last 15 Years: Not available.

THE INTELLIGENT CAREER CARD SORT

Reviewed by:

Ana C. Berríos-Allison

Career Connection
The Ohio State University

Description

In the ever changing world of work, career interventions are being developed to respond to a paradigm shift toward boundaryless careers, where sequences of job opportunities go beyond single employment settings (DeFillippi & Arthur, 1996; Parker, 2006). Different work roles and responsibilities continue to evolve in a job market facing the most rapid transformative moment in economic history (Parker, 2008). Fast changes in information and communication technology, increasing globalization, and greater competition are all contributing to these changes in the workplace.

The more traditional approach toward a career embraces decision making in a linear progression of related jobs, each with more responsibility and prestige. In contrast, new frameworks will need to emphasize the creation of resilient career strategies that respond not only to the personal quest of meaning making, but also to the increasing realities of social and global demands. Taking greater personal and social responsibility and being less dependent on employers' outcomes will become progressively more the norm, given the emerging social, cross-cultural, political, and economic realities of involuntary job losses, lateral job movements, and career interruptions (Eby, Butts, & Lockwood, 2003). Likewise, changes in the workplace will require individuals to manage their choices more proactively by being adaptable, self-initiating, and collaborative. With the use of the Intelligent Career Card Sort (ICCS), clients are invited to similarly manage the integration of these complex decision-making processes through self-reflection and discussion of life experiences and career planning.

The ICCS was developed in 1995 by an international team led by Michael Arthur, Polly Parker, and Norm Admunson to bring the whole person into the process of career development. Based on the Intelligent Career Model (Arthur, Claman, & DeFillippi, 1995), this approach is grounded in three subjective ways of learning and supports the development of the ICCS as a multi-dimensional career exploratory exercise. ICCS clients can claim ownership of their career decision-making process by increasing competencies in three dynamic and interdependent ways of knowing. These are (a) *knowing-why,* (b) *knowing-how,* and (c) *knowing-whom* (Parker, 2002).

Knowing-why involves the understanding of personal motivations, interests, values, aptitudes, and the personal meanings attributed to work experiences over time. It includes not only attitudes toward family and community, but also addresses one's readiness, curiosity, and flexibility to changing circumstances (Parker, 2008). This way of knowing becomes a means to interpret and reconstruct vocational and personal identities throughout the life span. It acknowledges individuals' work motivation and personal values to support career decisions, adaptability and commitment to personal growth (Amundson, Parker, & Arthur, 2002). Knowing-how refers to work- or professional-related skills and levels of expertise required to perform a job. Diversifying one's skill set and adapting to a variety of work contexts require individuals to learn life/career management skills that include both content (i.e., self-knowledge, occupational, and environmental factors) and process (i.e., decision making and career planning) (Parker, 2008). Finally, knowing-whom entails one's personal and work-related relationships that facilitate the creation of social and occupational networks as well as personal support systems. Interpersonal connections are needed to transition into the job market and overcome personal, social, economic, and occupational barriers. These relationships allow for formal and informal interactions that can provide relevant information needed to enhance employment opportunities, skill-learning possibilities, and overall career development (Parker, 2008). Moreover, this kind of support can bring career communities together to encourage skill building and vocational identity, meeting an important social/global need in the fast-paced world of work (Amundson et al., 2002).

A Counselor's Guide To Career Assessments Instruments

Grounded in the previously described "three ways of knowing," the ICCS is a career exploration exercise that can be experienced either face-to-face or over the web and in training workshops and group modalities. The ICCS is offered in a variety of languages including English, Portuguese, Danish, French, German, and Italian. The estimated time of completion is around 45 minutes, during which clients are invited to sort 115 cards on the basis of whether the statements reflect a current career behavior or belief. The cards are subdivided into three color-coded sections (i.e., blue, yellow, and green) of 40 cards representing the knowing-why (blue color-coded), 38 cards for knowing-how (yellow color coded), and 37 cards for knowing-whom (green color-coded) (Amundson et al., 2002). Sample statements for each of the three ways of knowing are listed in Table 1.

Table 1
ICCS Sample Card Statements

Knowing-Why	Knowing-How	Knowing-Whom
I want stability in my present location. I like to gain a sense of achievement from my work. I like to make a contribution to society. I want employment to support my lifestyle. I enjoy working in a supportive atmosphere.	I seek to learn from the projects in which I participate. I seek training and development for a future job. I pursue skills and knowledge specific to my occupation. I seek to become a more strategic thinker. I learn through being open to fresh ideas.	I work to sustain my relationships with school or college friends. I maintain or develop relationships with people outside my workplace. I try to develop new friendships. I build relationships with people inside my occupation. I work with people who can learn from me.

Note. Written permission obtained from Michael Authur to reproduce these items.

Clients at different life and career stages can use the ICCS, from college students ready to transition to the workplace to any worker looking at more effective ways of understanding and learning the why, how, and with whom they work (Parker, 2008; Wnuk & Amundson, 2003). The process begins with one color-coded set of cards. Clients are asked to sort the cards into "Yes," "Maybe," or "No" piles according to their subjective appeal. The selected cards are then further refined until clients select what they see as the seven most important card statements and place them in rank order. This process is repeated for all three ways of knowing. The next step is to print or display clients' selections for each of the three ways of knowing and to clarify meanings and provide examples supporting their card selections. Clients are invited to do this by either working directly with an ICCS licensed counselor/consultant, or with an ICCS peer coach under supervision. A further option is for clients to work at their own pace making notes over the web while consulting online with a licensed counselor/consultant.

As opposed to self-administered card sorts that do not require counselor intervention, the ICCS provides a unique holistic view for effective career counseling. Used in an open-ended manner, the ICCS is an opportunity for clients and career practitioners to exchange notes and engage in dynamic constructive dialogues to attend clients' unique life and work experiences (Amundson et al., 2002). Through active listening and subjective interpretation, clients discuss how past experiences have led them to their choice of cards, and also to identify links between cards representing different ways of knowing. Clients are then invited to identify the most important life themes (usually around 10) that have emerged from these interactions and reflections, and finally to develop action plans in response to each theme.

Clients can also use metaphors and creative means to identify any surprises and/or oversights in the identification of themes and determination of next action steps (Amundson et al., 2002). It is recommended to follow up with a licensed counselor/consultant, either face-to-face and/or through online confidential interactions, for at least four sessions, one for each way of knowing and one to integrate all results for future direction.

One of the advantages of the ICCS is that it can be used broadly with other career interventions to facilitate the career development process. For example, results from the Strong Interest Inventory, Skills Confidence Inventory, and Myers-Briggs Type Indicator, among others, can also be used to predict the knowing-why of interests and personality type in situations where clients may be facing changing career circumstances (Amundson et al., 2002). Additionally, the ICCS can also be integrated with constructivist frameworks (Savickas, 2005) and/or chaos theory (Bright & Pryor, 2005) given that clients' interpretation of the same card statements will not be the same and will reveal unique life experiences. Counselors can use the ICCS results to assist clients understand their personal narratives or unpredictable life circumstances to accommodate and thrive in the world of career transitions (Parker, 2006). More broadly, the ICCS can also be used in organizational settings in combination with performance evaluations to discuss, for example, workers' job skills (knowing-how), levels of motivation (knowing-why), and means of career support (knowing-whom) (Amundson et al., 2002).

Counselors can assist clients to integrate feedback from both occupational and organizational sources to identify strengths and areas of growth (Amundson et al., 2002). The role of the counselor is to actively engage with clients creating a supportive environment that can provide for transformative experiences. Ultimately, the goal is to formulate an action plan that is informed and realistic and facilitates the dynamic interconnections of the three ways of knowing for future implementation (Parker, 2008). This process may involve action plans such as accepting a job offer a client is attracted to (knowing-why to knowing-how) to enjoying the experience of the job (knowing-how to knowing- why), to making new connections through the job (knowing-how to knowing-whom), and/or finding support from others to change careers or giving back to one's community (knowing-whom to knowing-why), among others (Parker, Khapova, & Arthur, 2009). The result can be an empowered worker who has explored the meaning within and/or across the three ways of knowing in their personal and employment realities and feels confident to sustain employability and personal and social growth, as well as maintenance of new and past productive relationships (Parker, 2008).

Technical Considerations

Two empirical studies support the use of the ICCS. Parker (2000) reported that participants favored the experience of the card sort process to develop personal narratives as opposed to writing in journals under a series of imposed set of directions. Eby et al. (2003) examined perceived career satisfaction, perceived internal marketability, and perceived external marketability in a sample of 458 alumni from a large southern university. Results indicated support for the ICCS's validity. Specifically, results of partial correlations and dominance analysis showed that within the knowing-why category, career success was more likely predicted among participants who hold a strong sense of career identity and have realistic career goals based on self-knowledge of strengths and weaknesses. Outcomes also showed that knowing-how predicted career success through the importance of skill building. The significance was linked to the importance of acquiring transferable skills that will make employers and employees more marketable across organizational and international boundaries. Lastly, the role of mentoring and formation of career communities provided evidence of the connection between the knowing-whom and career success.

General Utility and Evaluation

The ICCS emerges as a multidimensional card sort exercise that meets clients wherever they are in their career development process while being sensitive to the three ways of knowing and changes in the world of work. The ICCS gives clients the freedom to choose from a number of different options within an organizing framework. It differs from most other card sorts in that it recognizes that the meanings associated with selected cards must come from clients. No assumptions are made until clients describe what the card statements mean to them and provide one or more relevant examples to support their choices. The ICCS also demands active clients' participation and requires counselors/consultants to actively engage in the clients' career development process. The success of this process may be more likely to occur among individuals who have insight, hold realistic expectations, and are open to explore and act on their choices. Nonetheless, career practitioners can assist introverted clients to explore the three ways of knowing as they relate to their underlying values and beliefs about their occupational choices (Parker et al., 2009).

Career practitioners interested in becoming a licensed ICCS counselor/consultant can request an ICCS training workshop at http://www.intelligentcareer.net. The license allows using the ICCS in individual and group modalities and provides access to the ICCS website and its full range of services. Additionally, licensed ICCS counselors /consultants can participate in the global ICCS community and have access to newsletters, bulletin boards, and other licensed consultants creating their own comprehensive support system of professionals.

References and Additional Resources

Amundson, N., Parker, P., & Arthur, M. (2002). Merging two worlds: linking occupational and organizational career counseling. *Australian Journal of Career Development, 11*(3), 26-35.

Arthur, M. B., Claman, P. H., & DeFillippi, R. H. (1995). Intelligent enterprise, intelligent career. *Academy of Management Executive, 9,* 1-15.

Bright, J. E. H., & Pryor, R. G. L. (2005). The chaos theory of careers: A user's guide. *Career Development Quarterly, 53,* 291-305. doi: 10.1002/j.2161-0045.2005.tb00660.x.

Eby, L. T., Butts, M., & Lockwood, A. (2003). Predictors of success in the era of the boundaryless career. *Journal of Organizational Behavior, 24,* 689–708. doi: 10.1002/job.214

DeFillippi, R. J., & Arthur, M. B. (1996). Boundaryless contexts and careers: A competency-based perspective. In M. B. Arthur & D. M. Rousseau (Eds.), *The boundaryless career* (pp. 116-131). New York, NY: Oxford University Press. doi: 10.1002/job.4030150403

Intelligent Career Card Sort. (n.d). Retrieved from http://www.intelligentcareer.net

Parker, P. (2000). *Career communities.* Unpublished doctoral dissertation, University of Auckland, New Zealand.

Parker, P. (2002). Working with the Intelligent Career Model. *Journal of Employment Counseling, 39*(2), 83-96. doi: 10.1002/j.2161-1920.2002.tb00840.x

Parker, P. (2006). Card sorts: Constructivist assessment tools. In M. McMahon & W. Patton (Eds.), *Career counselling: Constructivist approaches* (pp. 176–186). Abingdon, Oxford: Routledge.

Parker, P. (2008). Promoting employability in a "flat" world. *Journal of Employment Counseling, 45,* 1-13.

Parker, P., Khapova, S.N., & Arthur, M.B. (2009).The intelligent career framework as a basis for interdisciplinary inquiry. *Journal of Vocational Behavior, 75*(3) 291-302. doi:10.1016/j.jvb.2009.04.001

Savickas, M. L. (2005). The theory and practice of career construction. In S. D. Brown & R. W. Lent (Eds.), *Career development and counseling: Putting research and theory to work* (pp. 42-70). Hoboken, NJ: Wiley.

Wnuk, S. M. & Amundson, N. E. (2003). Using the intelligent careers card sort with university students — Effective techniques. *Career Development Quarterly, 51*(3), 274-284.

480

KNOWDELL CARD SORTS:
CAREER VALUES CARD SORT,
MOTIVATED SKILLS CARD SORT,
AND OCCUPATIONAL INTERESTS CARD SORT
Richard L. Knowdell

Career Research & Testing, Inc.
P.O. Box 611930
San Jose, CA 95161
Career Trainer & Training Systems
http://www.careertrainer.com/
careertrainer@trainingsys.com

Target Population: There are no specified ages, grades, or groups for these assessments, but it is best suited for those seeking employment or exploring careers.

Statement of the Purpose of the Instrument: The Career Values Card Sort (CVCS) helps clients to identify personal values that impact career satisfaction, the degree to which these values impact satisfaction, and any related issues these values could have with their current or future career plans (Knowdell, 2006). The Motivated Skills Card Sort (MSCS) assists clients to identify valuable employability skills, determine their motivation to use employability skills, identify which skills need to be enhanced, and identify which skills they would rather not use in a job. Through these objectives, clients can articulate an attractive work scenario that they would like to pursue in their current life or in the future and effectively market them for that job (Knowdell, 2006, 2013a, 2013b). The Occupational Interests Card Sort (OICS) is a tool that clients can use to identify examples of attractive jobs and career clusters (Knowdell, 2005c).

Forms and Levels Available, with Dates of Publication/Revision of Each: Only one form and level are available for each card deck, workbook, and worksheet.

Date of Most Recent Edition of Test Manual, User's Guide, Etc.: CVCS: Card deck (2005), Workbook (2006), and Worksheet (2011); MSCS: Card deck (2005), Workbook (2013), and Worksheet (2011); and OICS: Card deck (2010), Workbook (2013), and Worksheet (2010).

Time:

Actual Test Time: 5-20 minutes depending on the client's speed. Clients are encouraged to move quickly, trusting their initial reactions to information on the cards. The time required to process the results will vary depending on which questions and activities are used.

Total Administration Time: Administration time is minimal for this assessment. Since it is a card sort, there is no need to score the assessment. Clients should be encouraged to copy their card sort results on to a worksheet for future reference and discussion, which could take 10-20 minutes.

Sample(s) in Which Assessment was Developed: Not applicable.

Manner in Which Results Are Reported for Individuals/Groups: Results of the card sorts are known to the client as they complete the assessment. This process is the same when the assessment is administered to individuals and groups.

Computer Software Options Available: The MSCS and CVCS are available online.

Cost of Materials: Due to possible price changes since publication date, be sure to check publisher's website. The CVCS, MSCS, and OICS card decks range in price from $9.00-$14.00. Reduced prices for card decks are available depending on the quantity ordered. Workbooks (or Manuals) range in price from $9.00-$11.00. A set of 25 worksheets for each assessment cost $24.00.

Specimen Set: All Knowdell card sort kits have similar materials and formats. A Planning Kit, which contains 1 card deck, 1 workbook, and 1 worksheet, ranges in price from $15.20 to $19.20 depending on the assessment. Kit components can be purchased separately. Expanded resources for purchase include transparencies, PowerPoint DVDs for large group presentations, and an administrative instruction DVD (CareerTrainer,

2012).Workbooks for each sort provide general background information on the card sort topic, instructions to complete the card sort, forms to record results, discussion questions, and a variety of process activities. Worksheets for each sort also provide abbreviated instructions, a sheet to record results, and a small set of probing questions.

Counselee Materials: The counselee will need the card deck and either a worksheet or a manual in order to complete the assessment. The card deck may be retained by the counselor. The counselee may keep the worksheet or manual; however, it may not be reused.

Published Reviews of the Instrument in the Last 15 Years:

Diamond, E. E. (1998). [Career Values Card Sort.] In J. C. Impara & B. S. Plake (Eds.), *The thirteenth mental measurements yearbook.* Lincoln, NE: Buros Center for Testing. [Electronic Version]

Kinnier, R. T. (1998). [Career Values Card Sort.] In J. C. Impara & B. S. Plake (Eds.), *The thirteenth mental measurements yearbook.* Lincoln, NE: Buros Center for Testing. [Electronic Version]

Kinnier, R. T., & Kernes, J. L. (2002). Career Values Card Sort Kit (CVCS). In J. T. Kapes & E.A. Whitfield (Eds.), *A counselor's guide to career assessment instruments* (4th ed., pp. 218-221). Columbus, OH: National Career Development Association.

Slaney, R. B., Moran, W. J., & Wade, J. C. (1994). [Vocational Card Sorts.] In J. T. Kapes, M. M. Mastie, & E. A. Whitfield (Eds.), *A counselor's guide to career assessment instruments* (3rd ed., pp. 347-360). Alexandria, VA: National Career Development Association.

Knowdell Card Sorts:
Career Values Card Sort,
Motivated Skills Card Sort,
and Occupational Interests Card Sort

Reviewed by:

Justin R. Fields

Central Crossing High School and
Department of Counselor Education
The Ohio State University

Description

Richard Knowdell created several card sorts including the Career Values Card Sort (CVCS; Knowdell, 2005a, 2006), Motivational Skills Card Sort (MSCS; Knowdell, 2005b, 2013a), and the Occupational Interests Card Sort (OICS; Knowdell, 2013b), which were designed to be a part of an organized individual or group career development program particularly in a work setting. The CVCS is based on the belief that a client's understanding of how his or her personal values can manifest in a job setting, and how those personal values match a specific job, is an essential process in finding job satisfaction. The CVCS serves as a values clarification tool to allow a client to define what he or she needs to thrive in a job placement. Specifically, the CVCS helps clients identify personal values that impact career satisfaction, the degree to which these values impact satisfaction, and any related issues these values could have with their current or future career plans (Knowdell, 2006). The client is intended to experience the CVCS like a game of solitaire. The CVCS has 54 cards, each labeled with a career value and a one-sentence description of that value. Clients are asked to sort each card into one of five categories, which represent the degree of importance the client places on a particular value (i.e., *Always, Often, Sometimes, Seldom,* and *Never*). Clients are encouraged to act quickly and on initial feelings as they sort. Upon completion of the sort, a series of process questions and activities encourage the client to develop a deeper understanding of how his or her career values impact current and future career aspirations. For example, the career values that a client identifies as "Always Important" can be compared for congruence with a client's life and career events. Other activities, like a memory scan, encourage clients to identify exceptional career circumstances where they experienced high levels of conflict or congruence between jobs and career values. Depending on which activities are chosen, additional writing and discussion will add additional time.

The MSCS assists clients to identify valuable employability skills. Furthermore, the MSCS helps clients to determine their motivation to use employability skills, to identify which skills need to be enhanced, and to identify which skills they would rather not use in a job. Through these objectives, clients can articulate an attractive work scenario that they would like to pursue in their current life or future and effectively market them for that job (Knowdell, 2013a). Knowdell (2013a) stated that one's ability to understand their skills is especially helpful during uncertain times in the workforce where jobs can be scarce and people may be forced to change jobs. Understanding one's skills can allow clients to reframe their qualifications for jobs outside of their formal training and find new satisfying fields of work (Knowdell, 2013a).

The MSCS consists of two stages. First, clients identify what skills they like and dislike to use. Next, clients clarify the level of proficiency with which they do each skill. To facilitate these stages, clients use a deck of 48 cards, each labeled with a specific skill and a brief description of that skill. Clients are directed to sort each card into one of five categories which distinguish the degree to which they enjoy using the skill *(Totally Delight in Using, Enjoy Using Very Much, Like Using, Prefer Not to Use, and Strongly Dislike Using)*. After completing this first step, clients sort each card again within each level of preference into one of three additional categories. These new categories identify the degree of proficiency with which they perform each skill. For example, the client will take all of the cards in the *Totally Delight in Using* category and sort each card into one of three levels of proficiency: *Highly Proficient, Competent,* or *Lack Desired Skill Level.* When this second sorting process is completed, a client should be able to see both what skills they enjoy using the most and the degree to which they feel proficient in using each skill. In this fashion, clients can view the skills they are most motivated about (totally delight in using/highly proficient), skills they enjoy but need to increase their level of confidence in (totally delight in using/lack desired skill level) and their potential "burnout" skills (prefer not to use/highly proficient). After recording their answers, clients can process the results of the sort with probing questions provided in the workbook or worksheet. In addition, supplemental activities are available in the workbook to expand this process. For example, supplemental activities include positive feedback inventories, brainstorming exceptional instances/skills, and creating collages.

The OICS is a tool that clients can use to identify examples of attractive jobs. The nature of work and life often means that a career can be a large part of an individual's identity. Knowdell (2013b) suggested that the process by which people approach career exploration is critical. In developing this tool, Knowdell referenced the concept of "career clusters" to help develop insight into occupational interests. The OICS workbook also references the work of Richard Bolles and John Holland, who grouped jobs into clusters to help organize thoughts around careers.

To complete the OICS, clients sort 110 cards, each listing an occupation, into one of five categories. These categories articulate the level of interest the client has toward that specific occupation: *Definitely Interested, Probably Interested, Indifferent, Probably Not Interested,* and *Definitely Not Interested.* Clients then record these five lists on provided worksheets for future reference and analysis. For example, clients are asked to take the occupations listed in the categories "Definitely Interested" and "Probably Interested" and group them into similarly themed clusters. Clusters that emerge from these categories can become important themes for consideration in a job search. Similar to the other card sorts, supplemental activities are available in accompanying workbooks. Examples of these supplemental activities for the OICS include interest worksheets and fantasy role plays.

These card sorts have a degree of utility individually and in concert with each other. For example, both the CVCS and the MSCS could be used to help clients clarify the qualities they are looking for in a new career or the types of skills they possess that can be used to market themas they seek new employment. Clients may also repeat these sorts at different stages of life or after receiving training to see if responses have changed at all. These card sorts could also be used together to try and develop a more thorough picture of a potential career profile for a client. Each test could be completed independently, and the client and counselor can collectively analyze results for common themes, offering reassurance or validation of similar responses.

Knowdell Card Sorts

Knowdell initially designed these instruments to be used with people already working, often in places where jobs were changing within an organization. However, in a current era of restructuring, downsizing, and generally unpredictable employment, counselors could use these sorts as they work with clients who have been the victim of job cuts or reassignments. If these card sorts are used with adolescents or people with limited work experience, they can provide a useful intervention to begin to understand how they can identify attractive career fields, to identify marketable skills for a resume, or to develop an understanding of how personal values and lifestyles can interact and complement work life.

Technical Considerations

Each of the reviewed Knowdell cards sorts shares similar theoretical foundations in test structure. The card sorts are an adapted format of q-sort techniques that allow individuals to distinguish between different categories they assess. Through categories clients are able to group, rank, and sort items, ideas and topics in a visual format that can help to clarify feelings and thoughts. This process helps clients to create a reference of measure with their thoughts (Knowdell, 2006). The card sort format is viewed as an effective, involving, and innovative career counseling technique (Slaney & MacKinnon-Slaney, 1990). Card sorts are designed to create a different experience than what a client may typically expect from an assessment. At their best, card sorts can help clients organize new information about a phenomenon in a meaningful way (Williams, 1978). Specifically, clients are aware of the results or outcome of the assessment as they complete the card sort activity. The card sort experience brings information to the surface that will allow clients to understand, compare, and process new knowledge of self (Slaney, Moran, & Wade, 1994).

The CVCS was developed to be more user-friendly than other assessments that were available when the sorts were first developed (Knowdell, 2006). Because of the gamelike structure of the assessment, clients may feel more at ease than with other more formal inventories. Furthermore, processing the results of the card sort may feel much less threatening to clients as they discuss what they see on the cards in front of them.

Another unique feature of the Knowdell card sorts is the particular insight that clients take away from the assessment. Specifically, the CVCS and the MSCS are intended to assist clients to achieve job satisfaction and/or a successful job change by looking at values, skills, and/or interests as opposed to other card sorts that identify characteristics of occupations that are important to an individual when making a career choice (Slaney et al., 1994).

A review of the literature for each of the Knowdell card sorts yielded no empirical testing or evidence of methodological rigor. Casual references to informal tests for traits like user-friendliness and clarity are found in the description of the tests development in the CVCS workbook (Knowdell, 2006). However, no such references or details about test development are made of the MSCS (Knowdell, 2013a) or OICS (Knowdell, 2013b) workbooks. Furthermore, no references to formal norming procedures are evident in the test materials or literature. A previous edition of *A Counselor's Guide to Career Assessment Instruments* noted a similar lack of empirical testing regarding the validity and reliability of Knowdell card sorts (see Kinnier & Kernes, 2002). This is noted as the primary weakness of these instruments.

General Utility and Evaluation

The CVCS, MSCS, and OICS can be useful counseling tools for a range of clients with different levels of career experience. By targeting a unique aspect of career exploration, clients may feel comfortable completing the sorts and have an opportunity to develop insight into different components of their values, skills, and interests as they relate to the world of careers. Depending on the age level and the work experience of a client, varying levels of success may be achieved. For example, clients who are of school age may have difficulty understanding some terms or they may have limited knowledge of some careers without further definition or assistance from a counselor. This could also limit the speed at which the sort is completed. Despite the test materials indicating that these sorts can be completed by clients of different ages and stages, this reviewer believes it will be more successful with clients with more work and/or life history.

Test packages are easy to manage, are presented in a clean and attractive format, and require little time to understand and complete. Clients can complete sorts in as little as five minutes with varying amounts of additional time needed to complete supplemental processing activities. The cards are packaged just like many household games, which creates a playful, relaxed atmosphere for clients. Furthermore, many of the activities involve creative scenarios that encourage imagination.

The nature of these assessments draw strength from the card sort format; however, the results may require additional knowledge or resources to connect clients to next steps in the exploration process. One supplemental activity for the MSCS, for example, requires clients to take the motivated skills they have identified through the sort and brainstorm careers that involve those specific skills. For optimum success, this activity requires either a sound knowledge of the various skills related for a wide range of careers or a collection of resources that can be a bridge between the awareness of preferred skills and the understanding of different components of jobs. Furthermore, there is no formal system or tool that can be used to connect results from one card sort to the next. For example, if a client wanted to connect results between the CVCS, MSCS, or the OICS, there is no way within the assessments to know if the identified values, skills, and occupations have any congruence with each other or existing jobs.

The supplemental activities in the workbooks offer good variations for clients and counselors to consider. Specifically, these can be helpful for clients who are not as able or comfortable to simply process through standard interviewing. However, some clients may not find some of the supplemental activities to be as engaging or helpful for a variety of reasons. For example, one supplemental activity in the MSCS workbook asks clients to make an artistic collage highlighting their skills identified in the test. Athough this may satisfy the interest of an artistic client, the ability for a client to develop a deeper insight into their motivated skills may not be likely through this activity. Another supplemental activity in the OICS workbook asks clients to write a script of a conversation between themselves and work personified. The intent is to help clients clarify their relationship with work; however, many clients may see this as a cumbersome way of developing more insight. Overall, the CVCS, MSCS, and OICS are options that counselors can use to assist clients in their growth toward career development goals.

References and Additional Resources

Career Trainer. (2012). *Knowdell assessment supplies.* Retrieved from http://www.careertrainer.com/trainingsys/knowdell-assessment-supplies-ff80818123928a0901241785cf9d5150-c.html

Diamond, E. E. (1998). [Career Values Card Sort.] In J. C. Impara & B. S. Plake (Eds.), *The thirteenth mental measurements yearbook.* Lincoln, NE: Buros Center for Testing. [Electronic Version]

Kinnier, R. T., & Kernes, J. L. (2002). Career Values Card Sort Kit (CVCS). In J. T. Kapes & E. A. Whitfield (Eds.), *A counselor's guide to career assessment instruments* (4th ed., pp. 218-221). Columbus, OH: National Career Development Association.

Kinnier, R. T. (1998). [Career Values Card Sort.] In J. C. Impara & B. S. Plake (Eds.), *The thirteenth mental measurements yearbook.* Lincoln, NE: Buros Center for Testing. [Electronic Version]

Kinnier, R. T., & Kernes, J. L. (2002). Career Values Card Sort Kit (CVCS). In J. T. Kapes & E.A. Whitfield (Eds.), *A counselor's guide to career assessment instruments* (4th ed., pp. 218-221). Columbus, OH: National Career Development Association.

Knowdell, R. (2005a). *Career values: Card sort card deck.* San Jose, CA: Career Research & Testing Inc.

Knowdell, R. (2005b). *Motivated skills: Card sort card deck.* San Jose, CA: Career Research & Testing, Inc.

Knowdell, R. (2005c). *Occupational interest: Card sort career planning kit.* San Jose, CA: Career Research & Testing, Inc.

Knowdell, R. (2006). *Exploring your career values workbook.* San Jose, CA: Career Research & Testing, Inc.

Knowdell, R. (2013a). *Motivated skills: Card sort career planning kit.* San Jose, CA: Career Research & Testing, Inc.

Knowdell, R. (2013b). *Occupational interests: Card sort career planning kit.* San Jose, CA: Career Research & Testing, Inc.

Slaney, R. B., & MacKinnon-Slaney, F. (1990). The use of vocational card sorts in career counseling. In C. E. Watkins & V. L. Campbell (Eds.), *Testing in counseling practice* (pp. 317-371). Hillsdale, NJ: Lawrence Erlbaum Associates.

Slaney, R. B., Moran, W. J., & Wade, J. C. (1994). [Vocational card sorts.] In J. T. Kapes, M. M. Mastie, & E. A. Whitfield (Eds.), *A counselor's guide to career assessment instruments* (3rd ed., pp. 347-360). Alexandria, VA: National Career Development Association.

Slaney, R. B., Moran, W. J., & Wade, J. C. (1994). [Vocational Card Sorts.] In J. T. Kapes, M. M. Mastie, & E. A. Whitfield (Eds.), *A counselor's guide to career assessment instruments* (3rd ed., pp. 347-360). Alexandria, VA: National Career Development Association.

Williams, S. K. (1978). The Vocational Card Sort: a tool for vocational exploration. *The Vocational Guidance Quarterly*, *26*(3), 237-243.

LIFE ROLE ANALYSIS

Norman C. Gysbers

Department of Educational, School, and Counseling Psychology
University of Missouri–Columbia
201 Student Success Center
Columbia, Missouri 65211-6060
Gysbersn@missouri.edu

Target Population: Adolescents, young adults, and adults.

Statement of the Purpose of the Instrument: The Life Role Analysis is a qualitative career assessment for exploring clients' life roles, the impact of messages from their family and culture, and the relationship to their career transitions.

Forms and Levels Available, with Dates of Publication/Revision of Each: The Life Role Analysis has been presented in publications in 1992, 2003, and 2006 (Gysbers, 2006; Gysbers, Heppner, & Johnston, 2003; McDaniels & Gysbers, 1992).

Time:

Total Test Time: 20-60 minutes.

Total Administration Time: Varies.

Sample(s) in Which Assessment was Developed: Not applicable.

Manner in Which Results Are Reported for Individuals/Groups: In-session discussion and interpretation with a counselor. No scoring key available or applicable.

Cost of Materials: No cost.

Specimen Set: Not available.

Counselee Materials: Not applicable.

Published Reviews of the Instrument in the Last 15 Years:

Brott, P. E. (2005). A constructivist look at life roles. *Career Development Quarterly, 54,* 138-149. doi:10.1002/j.2161-0045.2005.tb00146.x

LIFE ROLE ANALYSIS

Reviewed by:

Sonya Lorelle

Department of Pshychology and Counseling
Governors State University

Description

The Life Role Analysis is a qualitative career assessment for exploring clients' expectations regarding their life roles. It provides a structure to understand clients' career transitions and related dynamics in terms of the experiential and situational contexts in which they have developed (Gysbers, 2006; Gysbers, Heppner, & Johnston, 2003; McDaniels & Gysbers, 1992). Counselors ask clients to analyze the costs and benefits of messages they received from their family, community, culture, and media and encourage them to reflect on whether they are satisfied with how they have defined their roles based on these expectations or whether they would like to make any changes (Brott, 2005). The counselor facilitates a collaborative conversation, in which the clients are "active participants in becoming aware of and exploring the variety of life roles" (Brott, 2005, p. 138). This active process is guided by constructivist and feminist tenets of allowing clients to construct their own reality and exploring the social impact of that narrative.

Life Role Analysis

To begin the exploration, counselors discuss the clients' life roles such as parent, spouse, and worker, as well as the settings and life events that have impacted those roles and their current concerns (Gysbers, 2006). Counselors can ask clients to organize these roles on paper with three circles labeled in terms of how their roles were five years ago, where they are currently, and what their expectations are for five years in the future. In each of the circles clients are asked to arrange smaller circles that represent these life roles and their placements correspond to the relative importance and relationship among those roles.

For example, a 40-year-old woman comes to counseling to address feelings of conflict regarding returning to work after being a stay-at-home mom for 10 years. Gysbers (2006) suggested leads such as "tell me about how the roles—parent, spouse, learner, worker—overlap for you" (p. 106). When arranging her roles, she may place her mother role as overlapping all other roles in the circle labeled five years ago. Though in her present day circle, she may arrange her mother role as a priority but not overlapping her other roles as much. The counselor could then ask "tell me about how this representation helps explain the problems with which you are dealing" (Gysbers, 2006, p. 106). A discussion about the shift in the arrangement of her roles could be a valuable place to explore as she may make the connection to her inner conflict to feelings of loss related to the diminishing role she had prided herself in for so long, the feeling of guilt for not investing as much in that role as she had in the past, and how this is impacting her decision to return to complete a master's degree as she had considered doing before having children.

The cultural and family messages regarding her expectations about female roles could also be explored to help clarify what she most values, what she wants her roles to look like in five years, and what decisions she may make based on those values (Brott, 2005). Brott (2005) also suggested questions to facilitate the analysis by asking "What continually motivates you in your worker role? In your family role? In your leisure role? If you could do one thing differently in your life, what would it be?" (p. 144).

Because the assessment is a collaborative and flexible process, the format and the time to administer the assessment can vary widely from counselor to counselor and from client to client depending on style and depth of exploration. For example, an in-depth exploration of all the roles and each of the time periods could take an entire session. The Life Role Analysis would be most helpful alongside other assessment tools. Brott (2005) referred to six other assessment tools that could be used in conjunction and would remain consistent with a constructivist approach: life space map, life line, life-space genogram, life roles circles, life roles assessment, and goal map. By integrating assessments, counselors can guide their clients through a process of building rapport; encourage clients to be the expert on their own life story; assess, analyze and challenge current values, and explore the cultural impact on those values; and develop an action plan to create a life based on those desired values (Brott, 2005).

Counselors may also find it helpful to integrate this tool with quantitative assessments as well. Standardized assessments such as the Values Scale or the Life Roles Inventory can introduce the concepts of life roles and values and increase awareness of the roles and values. As a qualitative tool, the Life Role Analysis can then be used to explore the meaning of these roles to the client in a more in-depth and culturally sensitive way as the clients become the expert on their analysis.

Given that the Life Role Analysis requires the client to be at a developmental stage that allows awareness and insight, this assessment would be practical and applicable for counselors who work with adolescents and university students, who are in the process of deciding on career directions, as well as adults who are considering a career transition. This process can help to clarify goals and consider educational and occupational options. This assessment also provides an opportunity to consider career transitions in the context of other life concerns given that "it is sometimes difficult to identify, sort out, and understand the dynamics (life career themes) involved" (Gysbers, 2006, p. 105). School counselors could also use the assessment in classroom guidance and during group or individual counseling when addressing career development (Brott, 2005). By introducing the concepts of life roles and inviting students to examine the various roles they have in their lives and the impact their life events, culture and media, students can build self-awareness while being challenged to critically think about their own values. This process could not only model valuable skills that they can draw on throughout their life transitions, but could be a developmentally appropriate task for students who are in the process of identity formation.

Technical Considerations

Gysbers (2006) stated that "Qualitative career assessments are particularly useful in helping adult clients understand the origins and contexts of their concerns because these assessments focus directly on the experiences, situations, and conditions in which these concerns are embedded" (p. 96). McMahon, Patton, and Watson (2003) proposed several criteria for developing and critiquing qualitative career assessments. There are several areas in which the Life Role Analysis meets those standards.

First, McMahon et al. (2003) suggested the assessment should be grounded in theory. The Life Role Analysis is guided by several theoretical orientations: constructivism, Adlerian theory, Super's *life rainbow* model, and feminist theory. The process for which the assessment is conducted is grounded in constructivism and postmodern thought, which posits that individuals construct their reality and narratives about their worlds (Brott, 2005). According to Singer (2004), "individuals craft narratives from experiences, tell these stories internally and to others, and ultimately apply these stories to knowledge of self, others, and the world in general" (p. 437). Therefore, following these post-modern and constructivist principles, counselors should be a collaborator in helping clients to reconstruct these internal stories and create new meaning, so that they can apply these new understandings for future decisions and relationships (Brott, 2005). The Life Role Analysis integrates with this constructive counseling style in which the counselor seeks to understand the clients' narrative through the context of their development and their life roles, and helps to co-create meaning.

The concept of including life roles in career counseling exploration is rooted in Adlerian theory and Super's *life rainbow* model. Adler emphasized lifestyles and considered the social impact on an individual's development to be significant. According to Adler, life tasks such as work, friendship, and love are interconnected, and how people behave and make meaning of the world is a process of integrating personal beliefs and values with feedback from their social worlds (Carlson, Watts, & Maniacci, 2006). Donald Super was one of several career theorists that considered these concepts of life roles when conceptualizing career development. Super's model of the *life rainbow* and the Archway "called attention to the relationships of job roles with other life roles (e.g., family, leisure, learner, citizen) and the concept of role salience, which is the importance of each role to the person" (Brott, 2005, p. 140). The Life Role Analysis applies these concepts by specifically attending to this interconnection of the roles, the meaning individuals make regarding those roles, and the impact of the social context.

It is also critical to consider the impact of specific factors such as gender, race and ethnicity, spirituality, social class, and sexual orientation have on influencing the development of life roles (Gysbers, 2006). The Life Role Analysis also integrates feminist theory by considering the impact of gender and other cultural factors on career development. While women can benefit from the examination of gender socialization, men may discover the impact of their own gender-role conditioning through the assessment. For example, men may desire to expand their family or leisure roles to balance their worker role. Brott (2005) suggested that this exploration can "help both women and men differentiate between what they have been taught is socially acceptable or desirable and what is actually healthy for them" (p. 144).

With respect to other criteria for sound qualitative career assessment, McMahon et al. (2003) suggested the process should foster holism, encourage cooperative participation between the counselor and client, and be a focused and flexible process. This technique is specifically focused on life roles and is extremely flexible as it is a collaborative exploration of the client's unique narrative. Given the emphasis on messages from the family, culture, media and the context for their internal beliefs about individuals' life roles, the assessment has a strength in its holistic nature.

The Life Role Analysis technique has not been validated or compared to other valid measures. Future research could involve comparing the Life Role Analysis to other career assessments, evaluating the client's experience with the assessment, and exploring specific career outcomes such as change in the career narrative, retention, and engagement in exploratory career behaviors, as Rehfuss, Del Corso, Glavin, and Wykes (2011) suggested for another qualitative career assessment, the Career Style Interview.

The Life Role Analysis also currently relies solely on one source for gathering information, which is the verbal interview with the client. Other creative methods, such as drawings or sandtray, could potentially be used in addition to an interview in order to add to the rich data collected about life roles. Counselors could also conduct the assessment alongside other techniques such as a life-space genogram or goal map to increase the usefulness of the technique (Brott, 2005).

General Utility and Evaluation

Given the emphasis on clients as experts, and the exploration of their personal narrative and the personal evaluations of their life roles rather than evaluating them based on a predetermined construct, one benefit of the Life Role Analysis is that it is applicable to use with diverse populations. Messages received and motivations about careers can vary widely for men and women, for different generations, and for various cultural groups. For example, consider an Asian high school student who presents as anxious about post-graduation life as he speaks about his expected role in his country of taking care of his mother financially after graduation. This message varies widely from the message middle-class high school students in the United States receive about "following your dreams" and "anything is possible." Instead of predefining how to plan a career path that is based on Western ideals of individualism, achievement, and success, the Life Role Analysis places the counselor in the position of seeking to learn about this unique person, his or her roles and values, and how these have impacted the client's career decisions (Brott, 2005).

Given that the Life Role Analysis examines three time periods, there is an implied understanding that life roles are dynamic rather than static. By considering life roles and career development as a lifelong process, the assessment would be applicable with young individuals at the beginning of their career development process, as well as older individuals who may be transitioning to post-retirement life.

When clients seek career counseling, the complexity of situations and social and emotional contexts that contribute to their concerns can create confusion given that the career concern is rarely isolated from the other dynamics in the clients' lives. The Life Role Analysis helps to provide a structure for beginning to clarify the layers of complexity in order to increase understanding and elucidate goals (Gysbers, 2006). One way the technique assists in this clarification process is by providing a common language and framework for comprehending the various tensions and internal and external conflicts they face. While the assessment does provide a structure, it is still flexible enough to allow the clients to attend to what is most important for their unique concern.

There are some potential limitations of the assessment. For example, McMahon et al. (2003) suggested qualitative career assessments should be easy to read, have easily understood instructions with a sequence that is logical and simple with achievable steps, and have instructions written for the client. One potential limitation of the assessment is that the description provides a general outline of steps to take and ideas about communication leads to use with clients. As mentioned, this flexibility is a strength as it can be tailored to meet the needs of the client; however, with this flexibility it is probable that the effectiveness of the assessment will depend primarily on counselor competence. A semi-structured interview could give counselors who are not trained in Adlerian, constructivism, or feminist theories more guidance on how to effectively implement with clients. Finally, McMahon et al. suggested an assessment should include a debriefing process. Although Brott (2005) discussed how it is important to debrief with the client after they have analyzed their life roles, there is no specific debriefing process for this assessment.

Overall, for counselors who are interested in integrating aforementioned theories and taking a holistic approach during the career counseling process, this assessment may be a useful tool to incorporate with their clients. The flexibility and emphasis on cultural and social factors impacting life roles adds to the appeal of using the tool with diverse populations. Further development and research is recommended in order to evaluate the assessment's effectiveness and impact on the career development process.

References and Additional Resources

Brott, P. E. (2005). A constructivist look at life roles. *The Career Development Quarterly, 54,* 138-149. doi:10.1002/j.2161-0045.2005.tb00146.x

Carlson, J., Watts, R. E., & Maniacci, M. (2006). *Adlerian therapy: Theory and practice.* Washington, DC: American Psychological Association.

Gysbers, N. C. (2006). Using qualitative career assessments in career counselling with adults. *Journal for Educational and Vocational Guidance, 6,* 95-108. doi:10.1007/s10775-006-9102-4

Gysbers, N. C., Heppner, M. J., & Johnston, J. A. (2003). *Career counseling: Process, issues, and techniques,* (2nd ed.). Boston, MA: Allyn & Bacon.

McDaniels, C., & Gysbers, N. C. (1992). *Counseling for career development: Theories, resources, and practice.* San Francisco, CA: Jossey-Bass.

McMahon, M., Patton, W., & Watson, M. (2003). Developing qualitative career assessment processes. *Career Development Quarterly, 51,* 194-202. doi:10.1002/j.2161-0045.2003.tb00601.x

Singer, J. A. (2004). Narrative identity and meaning-making across the adult lifespan: An introduction. *Journal of Personality, 72,* 437–460. doi:10.1111/j.0022-3506.2004.00268.x

Rehfuss, M. C., DelCorso, J., Glavin, K., & Wykes, S. (2011). Impact of the career style interview on individuals with career concerns. *Journal of Career Assessment, 19,* 405-419. doi: 10.1177/1069072711409711

492

A COUNSELOR'S GUIDE TO CAREER ASSESSMENTS INSTRUMENTS

MY CAREER CHAPTER

Peter McIlveen

University of Southern Queensland- Toowoomba Campus
West Street
Toowoomba QLD 4350
Australia
peter.mcilveen@usq.edu.au

Target Population: Children (with revision), adolescents (with revision), young adults, and adults.

Statement of the Purpose of the Instrument: My Career Chapter provides a structured, theory-driven qualitative assessment of career development. It guides clients through a series of written exercises that provide a comprehensive examination of various factors influencing career, including how career paths may fit within other life roles and future goals.

Forms and Levels Available, with Dates of Publication/Revision of Each: 2008. McIlveen, Patton, and Hoare (2007) provided suggestions for adapting it for use with children and adolescents.

Time:

    Actual Test Time: Approximately 2 hours.

    Total Administration Time: Varies.

Sample(s) in Which Assessment was Developed: Adult, college students, and career counselors.

Manner in Which Results Are Reported for Individuals/Groups: In-session discussion and interpretation with a counselor. No scoring key is available or applicable.

Cost of Materials: No cost.

    Specimen Set: Not available.

    Counselee Materials: Printed copy of the assessment.

Published Reviews of the Instrument in the Last 15 Years: Not available.

MY CAREER CHAPTER

Reviewed by:

Hannah B. Bayne

Department of Counselor Education
Virginia Polytechnic Institute and State University – Northern Virginia Center

Description

My Career Chapter was created to provide a structured, theory-driven qualitative assessment of career development. Founded in constructivist, narrative, and systems theory, My Career Chapter aims to provide clients with a comprehensive examination of various factors influencing their careers, as well as how their career paths may fit within other life roles and future goals. Created by Peter McIlveen (2008), this assessment guides individuals through several written exercises aimed at encouraging self-reflection to view careers through a holistic lens.

My Career Chapter addresses a need within career counseling for assessment tools that can be incorporated within the counseling interview and that can acknowledge the complexity of career influences on an individual (McIlveen, Ford, & Dun, 2005; McMahon, 2005). Based on the systems theory framework of career (McIlveen & Patton, 2010), the focus of the assessment is on how clients tell the story of the various components of their lives and how this story may impact career decision making. By considering career through a narrative framework,

493

My Career Chapter

clients can step back and more objectively see how different factors interact on a larger scale. From that vantage point, clients may be better able to work with a counselor to determine the ideal balance of internal and external factors. The systems theory framework presents career as a complex interplay between internal (e.g., values) and external (e.g., environmental) influences, as well as recursiveness (i.e., the tendency to repeat patterns over time), temporal influences (i.e., past, present, future), and change (McMahon, 2005). Because these elements all continuously interact in various ways, career is never a static process. Instead, the act of exploring career through a systems-theory lens enables clients to learn how to think about career and increase awareness of changing forces that may impact decision making. Clients thus begin to see the interconnectedness of their life roles, which can help them understand career as a complex and variable entity.

My Career Chapter uses the categories of systems theory to structure the assessment and provide credibility for the items used. A constructivist paradigm also informs the content of the instrument by acknowledging that through career counseling the client and counselor work together to co-create knowledge and meaning. The assessment thus uses the counseling interview as a key component for processing the exercise and arriving at new understandings of the client's experience. As is true with most constructivist frameworks, this instrument is epistemologically post-positivist, in that the purpose is not to arrive at an objective "truth," but rather a subjective understanding of career forces based on the client's and counselor's interpretations. Narrative theory provides an additional theoretical foundation in that clients are guided through several written exercises that result in an autobiographical "story," which can then be read back in its entirety to help clients achieve new meanings.

The My Career Chapter assessment consists of seven steps, all requiring self-reflection and written responses to various prompts. As such, completion time varies for each individual. McIlveen (2007) stated that previous administrations of the assessment show the average time of completion to be around two hours, though it will likely vary with a client's level of literacy, attention to the task, and depth of responses. For the first step of the assessment, clients are given some warm-up questions to facilitate the self-reflection that will be needed for the remaining stages. In this first stage, clients are encouraged to take notes but need not write an answer to each question. Questions in this stage include items such as "how does the current employment market affect your career plan?" and "what work have you done and how has it influenced your direction?" (McIlveen, 2008). After reflecting on these questions, clients are presented with a figure depicting the systems-theory of career counseling (Step 2). This model contains internal and external influences, as well as symbols indicating change and the influences of past, present, and future orientations (McMahon, 2005). Through the written directions, clients are told to consider each influence and take notes on any reactions they may have towards the model.

In the third step of the assessment, clients are provided with a matrix based on the systems-theory model they just viewed. The matrix consists of personal influences (e.g., interests, values, education) on one side and societal or environmental influences (e.g., the nature of the job market, location, media, family) along the top. Clients are asked to consider each combination of personal vs. environmental influences as they work their way through the matrix, rating each pair based on its compatibility. For example, a client may determine that industry trends (environmental) are incompatible with his or her skills and abilities (personal). The client would then rate that category as incompatible, according to the scale provided. The purpose of this stage is to help clients see how their personal influences fit within the larger sphere of societal and environmental trends and influences. Similarly, the fourth step requires clients to complete an additional matrix, this time comparing and contrasting personal influences. An identical list of personal influences runs along the vertical and horizontal axes of the matrix and clients are again asked to rate the compatibility of each combination. For example, a client might determine that his or her health is incompatible with career dreams and aspirations, or that a career is very much compatible with his or her morals. Clients are then asked to make note of anything significant within the matrix ratings.

In step five, clients begin the process of writing the manuscript. Detailed initial instructions provide a rationale for the task the client is about to complete, indicating that the process of writing will help him or her engage in career planning processes by becoming more aware of overt and covert influences. To add structure to the task, the manuscript consists of client responses to sentence stem completions. The sentences are based once again upon the systems-theory model and are grouped by personal and environmental factors. For each of the career influences (15 personality influences and eight environmental influences), clients are asked to complete five sentences. The first three sentences in each category ask the client to view each influence through a past, present, and future lens. Therefore, when asked about career (a personal influence), clients must complete the sentences: "in the past, my career ...," "the main issue for me and my career at the moment is ...," and "I hope that in the future ..." The fourth sentence involves the client indicating how he or she feels emotionally about each influence on a five-point scale ranging from very positive to very negative. In considering personal skills, for example, a client is prompted to circle a reaction to the statement "I mostly feel very positive/positive/ indifferent/negative/very negative in relation to my skills and abilities because ..." Finally, in the fifth sentence, the client using the same rating scale indicates the degree to which each influence impacts his or her career at the moment. If family has a high degree of influence on a client's career choice, he or she would select a descriptor of whether this influence is more positive or negative, responding to the question "family has a very positive/ positive/ neutral/ negative/ very negative impact on my career life because ..." Upon completing the question stems for each category of career influences clients will have 120 responses that make up their manuscript.

In the sixth step of the assessment, clients are instructed to read the manuscript through the perspective of a younger self. Channeling a "self" five years younger, clients act as an editor and observer of the manuscript, viewing it with a critical eye and providing feedback and suggested changes. Once these changes are made clients can engage in the final step of the process. This seventh step involves the client responding to the "editor's" comments. Sentence stems for responses are included to assist the client with creating concluding thoughts based on the process. Statements are grouped into strengths, obstacles, and statements about the future. In this section clients respond to items such as "my current career strengths are ...," "I am confident that I can overcome ...," and "I want the next chapter of my career story to begin with ..." Clients can then complete final notes about the process, including anything that was not captured within the concluding statements.

When the final process is completed, clients can return for a career counseling appointment to talk through some of the more relevant themes that emerged. Counselors are encouraged to read the manuscript aloud during the session so that the client can once again hear his or her words, this time through the voice of another. Beyond the structured assessment itself, there are few guidelines for how to facilitate exploration of themes within the counseling setting. This is likely due to the constructivist paradigm that encourages the co-creation of knowledge between counselor and client. Through this lens, processing the assessment will be unique for each counselor/ client dyad, and items that were important to one client may be irrelevant to others. Career counselors seeking more structure may wish to employ additional constructivist and narrative strategies in conjunction with this assessment (Brott, 2004; McIlveen et al., 2005).

Technical Considerations

In order to lend credibility and structure to the creation of the My Career Chapter assessment, McIlveen (2007) used the guidelines for qualitative assessments outlined by McMahon, Patton, and Watson (2003). Among these recommendations are grounding assessments in theory, testing the process, ensuring that the process is user-friendly and easy to understand, and incorporating the role of the counselor and the counseling interview. To aid in credibility and ensure transferability of the process to various settings, McIlveen used these recommendations when forming the assessment (McIlveen et al., 2005). My Career Chapter was firmly grounded in systems theory, which informed the content for each of the steps of the process as well as the specific items within each section. Constructivist and narrative theories contributed to the design of the assessment as a storied, autobiographical approach to career exploration.

This assessment has been minimally tested, although qualitative and quantitative explorations have returned positive results. The assessment has been tested through ethnographic research as a tool for self-supervision (McIlveen, 2011), phenomenological research of counselors' self-administration and reflections on its utility in career counseling (McIlveen, 2007; McIlveen, Patton, & Hoare, 2007, 2008), and a quantitative study of clients in a college career counseling center (McIlveen et al., 2005). In using My Career Chapter as a tool for self-supervision, McIlveen (2011) noted that the process itself may seem cumbersome for many clients, though he adds that his own process of engaging in each category resulted in both a deeper understanding of the influences on his own career as well as a better grasp of how clients might experience the assessment process. In another study, career counselors completed the assessment as part of a workshop and were later interviewed about their experiences (McIlveen et al., 2005). These interviews revealed that, though the assessment could be a valuable tool in career counseling, it might not be suitable for every client. Counselors in this study noted that the duration of the assessment itself may discourage clients, and many perceived the assessment would only be suitable for adult populations with certain levels of literacy and insight. Another study of school counselors echoed this concern, though participants indicated that adjustments could be made to the assessment to facilitate its use for younger populations (McIlveen et al., 2007).

Across previous studies participants have emphasized that the assessment's key strengths lay in the fact that it is firmly grounded in theory, takes a holistic approach to career, and can be a powerful tool to incorporate into the counseling interview. A study of college-aged students revealed that reactions to completing My Career Chapter were generally positive and did not result in negative feelings, though after taking the assessment they did not immediately perceive progress in their career exploration (McIlveen et al., 2005). The authors noted that further exploration within a counseling interview would likely contribute to perceived progress.

These studies all contribute to trustworthiness of the assessment, demonstrating its utility in different settings and through various perspectives. As a qualitative assessment based on a constructivist-interpretivist paradigm, My Career Chapter does not assume that there is one true way to implement the assessment, nor does it assume that the experience can be standardized in every setting. Instead, it lends itself to interpretation by the user, providing structure in the form of tasks and instructions, but leaving the act of meaning making to the client and counselor. The role of the counselor is thus seen as a critical component of this assessment process. In fact, hearing their stories read aloud back to the students was one of the more powerful components of the exercise, according to career counselors (McIlveen, 2007). Therefore, although this assessment is designed to be completed alone as homework, processing the major themes and categories within the counseling session is critical to the process.

General Utility and Evaluation

As noted by participants in previous studies, this assessment can appear cumbersome and will likely take an individual at least two hours to complete. For clients who are engaged in career exploration and who appreciate the chance to be self-reflective, this assessment would likely be an enjoyable and rewarding task. As a measure of career influences, it is comprehensive and holistic, allowing clients to explore all facets of personal and environmental influence. It also provides career counselors operating from systems, narrative, and constructivist career counseling theories with a structured assessment for use in the counseling relationship. However, some participants in previous evaluations of the model felt overwhelmed by the breadth and scope of the assessment, with one participant comparing it to a scholarly task that was more laborious than enjoyable (McIlveen, 2007). Others acknowledged that the length of time required may at first be discouraging, but several career counselors noted that the length itself may be beneficial in that clients must stay engaged and delve deeper than would be possible with a shorter assessment.

It may be safe to assume, then, that My Career Chapter may not be advisable for all clients. Clients seeking very brief career counseling services, clients with low verbal and literacy levels, and clients with low insight or sustained attention may not be appropriate for the assessment in its current form. Counselors may be able to divide the assessment into shorter more manageable sections rather than asking that it be completed all at once, though this format has not yet been created or tested to determine its utility (McIlveen et al., 2007). It is also unclear whether this assessment would be effective for children and adolescents. In previous studies, participants indicated that My Career Chapter was suitable for most adults, but that it would not be appropriate with younger populations (McIlveen, 2007). Another study utilized guidance counselors to evaluate the suitability of the assessment for students and found that many saw great potential in using My Career Chapter as a guidance tool. They did, however, indicate that the assessment may need to be broken down into more manageable tasks, and suggested allowing students to talk through each activity in pairs rather than writing out responses to every statement. The counselors also expressed concern that students may lack the levels of reflection for career influences needed to complete all parts of the model.

Although extensive research on the assessment's suitability for diverse populations has not been conducted, it seems likely that most groups could benefit due to the narrative and constructivist principles inherent in the assessment. Clients are provided with the opportunity to elicit their own examples of personal and environmental influences, making the assessment flexible and sensitive to unique life experiences. Future research is needed to determine the limitations of this assessment across demographic groups.

A COUNSELOR'S GUIDE TO CAREER ASSESSMENTS INSTRUMENTS

In terms of its utility, instructions for completing the assessment are clear and provide an explanation of why each exercise is beneficial for career exploration. Because the instructions are so comprehensive, most clients should be able to self-administer the assessment outside of the career counseling setting. Space is provided for writing responses, though some individuals may choose to write longer responses on a separate sheet of paper. Clients do not need any additional materials to complete the assessment. Given the heavy emphasis on systems theory it seems advisable for career counselors to have a firm understanding of this theory prior to administering and processing My Career Chapter with a client.

Overall this assessment is an excellent option as a qualitative career measure, especially for clients who are committed to a lengthier and more thorough counseling process. The process of writing out responses across many dimensions of career influences may help clients identify core issues. This can be very helpful for clients who seem overwhelmed and unsure of career direction, particularly if they are struggling to manage conflicting life roles or influences. Assigning this assessment as homework could help to focus subsequent career counseling sessions. As with any assessment, counselors should be intentional about ensuring that it is appropriate for each client. Future research of this assessment with various populations and within different counseling settings is needed and may result in new considerations.

References and Additional Resources

Brott, P. (2004). Constructivist assessment in career counseling. *Journal of Career Development, 30*, 189-200.

McIlveen, P. (2007). Counsellors' personal experience and appraisal of My Career Chapter. *Australian Journal of Career Development, 10*, 12-19.

McIlveen, P. (2008). *My Career Chapter: A dialogical autobiography* (Doctoral dissertation). University of Southern Queensland, Toowoomba, Australia.

McIlveen, P. (2011). Life themes in career counselling. In M. McMahon & M. B. Watson (Eds.), *Career counseling and constructivism: Elaboration of constructs* (pp. 73-85). New York, NY: Nova Science Publishers.

McIlveen, P., Ford, T., & Dun, K. (2005). A narrative sentence-completion process for systems career assessment. *Australian Journal of Career Development, 14*, 30-39. doi: 10.2255/1038-4162.14.3.0016

McIlveen, P., & Patton, W. (2010). My Career Chapter as a tool for reflective practice. *International Journal for Educational and Vocational Guidance, 10*, 147-160. doi: 10.1007/s10775-010-9181-0

McIlveen, P., Patton, W., & Hoare, P. (2007). My Career Chapter: Guidance counsellors' appraisal of its suitability for adolescents. *Australian Journal of Guidance and Counselling, 17*, 148-159.

McIlveen, P., Patton, W., & Hoare, P. (2008). An interpretative phenomenological analysis of adult clients' experience of My Career Chapter. *Australian Journal of Career Development, 17*, 51-62.

McMahon, M. (2005). Career counseling: Applying the systems theory framework of career development. *Journal of Employment Counseling, 42*, 29-42.

McMahon, M., Patton, W., & Watson, M. (2003). Developing qualitative career assessment processes. *Career Development Quarterly, 51*, 194-202.

A COUNSELOR'S GUIDE TO CAREER ASSESSMENTS INSTRUMENTS

MY SYSTEM OF CAREER INFLUENCES
Mary McMahon, Wendy Patton, and Mark Watson
Australian Council for Education Research (ACER)
Press19 Prospect Hill Rd, Camberwell, VIC 3124, Australia
ABN: 19 004 398 145 1800 338 402, +61 3 9277 5447
Fax: +61 3 9277 5499
https://shop.acer.edu.au/acer-shop/app
sales@acer.edu.au

Target Population: Adults, young adults, and adults.

Statement of the Purpose of the Instrument: My System of Career Influences (MSCI) allows clients to reflect on past, present, and future factors that influence their career development through story development. It is a brief workbook to assess clients' current career plans through developing and interpreting narratives.

Forms and Levels Available, with Dates of Publication/Revision of Each: 2005.

Time:

    Actual Test Time: 30-40 minutes.

    Total Administration Time: 30-40 minutes.

Sample(s) in Which Assessment was Developed: Adolescents and young adults.

Manner in Which Results Are Reported for Individuals/Groups: In-session discussion and interpretation with a counselor. No scoring key is available or applicable.

Computer Software Options Available: Not available.

Cost of Materials: Due to possible price changes since publication date, be sure to check the publisher's website.

    Specimen Set: Guide and booklet: $38.95.

    Counselee Materials: Facilitator's Guide: $36.95; Ten (10) Test Booklets: $20.95.

Published Reviews of the Instrument in the Last 15 Years: Not available.

MY SYSTEM OF CAREER INFLUENCES
Reviewed by:

Malik S. Henfield

Department of Rehabilitation and Counselor Education
University of Iowa

Description

My System of Career Influences (MSCI; McMahon, Patton, & Watson, 2005) is a qualitative career assessment that takes into account that individuals have the ability to exercise human agency in developing career goals and expectations. Qualitative career assessment, generally speaking, is designed to be flexible and interactive, with a great deal of importance placed on the connection between counselor and client. When using this assessment, the role of the counselor is to create a collaborative client-counselor relationship, with the client assuming a more active role as opposed to being a passive recipient of knowledge. Informed by the worldview of constructivism, MCSI is grounded in the systems theory framework (STF) of career development (McMahon & Patton, 1995; Patton & McMahon, 1999, 2006) and takes an array of life circumstances and backgrounds into consideration in the career development process.

The STF is a "holistic metatheoretical framework" (McMahon & Watson, 2008, p. 281) that considers client's content influences and process influences in the career development process. Content influences are comprised of

My System of Career Influences

an individual's personal characteristics, as well as the environment in which her or she interacts with others such as schools, families, and communities. These influences are thought to be open yet interconnecting individual, social, and environmental-societal systems that are constantly changing and interacting with one another in such a way that shapes career development. According to McMahon and Watson (2008), the individual system is of utmost importance and central to the STF due to its range of intrapersonal influencers such as race, social class, gender, personality, ability, and other factors. Individuals, though, are thought of as both systems and subsystems as they do not live in isolation from others and are part of a much larger environmental-social system, which is comprised of public policies and other elements that impact individuals' lives and subsequent career decisions. The process influences consist of interactions between influences *(recursiveness)*, changes over time, and chance, and are indicative of the dynamic interconnected nature within and between systems. According to the framework, due to interdependent interactions among systems, careers cannot always be planned in a predictable, linear fashion as unexpected events (e.g., illness, accidents, natural disasters) have the potential to influence the direction of one's career. MSCI is a qualitative career assessment designed to, essentially, have clients develop a personalized STF. More specifically, MSCI allows clients to reflect on past, present, and future factors that influence their career development. MSCI provides a framework to be used as a guide in helping clients to create career stories that detail the reality of their career development. With the emphasis placed on the client to create their own stories, counselors are then allowed to gain a strong understanding of how clients perceive factors influencing their careers. MSCI is a brief workbook created to help adolescents and adults assess their current career plans by articulating stories related to their lives and the meaning they make of those stories. More specifically, by completing worksheets, clients are expected to reflect on their system of careers influences within the context of their past, present, and future. The workbook is intended to be an exercise in developing in-depth understanding of the individual meanings clients ascribe to their personal career choices.

Each page moves the client through a different point in the career development process with each page consisting of common elements: (a) general information, (b) instructions, (c) examples, and (d) an area to write responses. The assessment is designed to be self-guided but counselors and other educators are advised to work closely with clients to answer any questions and provide clarification when necessary. It can be used when working with clients in individual and group settings. Given the informal nature of qualitative career assessment (Okocha, 1998), administrative time limits are loosely defined. For example, the authors suggest the entire workbook be administered in 30 to 40 minutes; however, they also strongly recommend that counselors grant additional time to debrief and respond to any questions.

The cover page of MSCI offers an introduction to the assessment and provides space for clients to fill out identifying information (name, gender, date, school or organization, and year level). Page 2 titled, "My Present Career Situation," requires clients to respond to open-ended questions related to past, present, and future career-related options, roles, and decisions such as "What strategies or approaches have you used in your previous decision making" and "List any jobs you have considered for your future" to provide a baseline for a reflection process. Pages 3, 4, 5, and 6 contain questions and diagrams that are direct extensions of the STF designed to aid in creating an individualized system of influences. Page 3, titled "Thinking About Who I Am," focuses on the individual system of influences by asking clients to indicate intrapersonal factors that may influence their next career decision, such as age, gender, and culture. Page 4, titled "Thinking about the People Around Me" is based on the social system of the STF and requires clients to reflect on interpersonal factors such as family, friends, co-workers, and mass media. Page 5, titled "Thinking about Society and the Environment" is grounded in the STF's environmental-societal system of influences. On this page, clients are expected to explore aspects of their lives such as financial support, location of resources, access to public transportation, and job availability that may influence their career decisions. Page 6, titled "Thinking about my Past, Present and Future" focuses on content influences as defined in the STF. On this page, clients are asked to reflect on critical incidents in their past and present, as well as future goals that may have an impact on their career decision-making.

The next three pages are designed to allow clients to make sense of the career influences they summarized on pages 3 through 6. Specifically, page 7, titled "Representing My System of Career Influences," offers instructions on how to complete a MSCI diagram; an example is also included for increased understanding. Once the instructions have been read and understood, clients skip page 8 briefly and proceed to page 9, titled "My System of Career Influences," which is a tear-off sheet that provides an opportunity for clients to create their personal

MSCI diagram using information gleaned from pages 3-6. Page 8, titled "Reflecting on My System of Career Influences" consists of 10 questions designed to give clients the opportunity to tear off the MSCI diagram they constructed on page 9 and explore their perceptions in relation to the visual representation of their career influencers. These discussions can be held individually or in groups with a counselor or other educators.

Technical Considerations

Compared to quantitative assessments, relatively little has been written about the qualities indicative of an adequate qualitative assessment. It is, however, understood that qualitative assessments should not be judged according to the same standards as quantitative assessments, given each tradition's epistemological differences. In response, McMahon, Patton, and Watson (2005) offered guidelines for constructing rigorous qualitative instruments: (a) ground the assessment process in theory, (b) test the career assessment process, (c) ensure that the process can be completed in a reasonable time frame, (d) design a process that fosters holism, (e) write the instructions for the client, (f) write readable and easily understood instructions, (g) sequence logical, simple, small, achievable steps; and provide a focused and flexible process, (h) encourage cooperative involvement of counselor and client, and (i) include a debriefing process. MSCI seems to adequately meet these criteria. For instance, given that it is firmly grounded in the fundamentals of constructivist theory—the STF of career development, specifically—it seems to have passed the first guideline requirement, which is to ground the assessment process in theory. Regarding testing the career assessment process, McMahon et al. (2005) noted they completed two stages of a testing and refinement process with one more stage underway. The results of the first two stages suggest the need for adjustments in wording and language, a more professional layout, and the development of a facilitator's manual. Regarding reasonable time to complete the assessment, although 30 minutes is suggested for completing MSCI, the authors contend that clients can complete different phases of MSCI over time, if necessary.

In terms of MSCI being a holistic process, since it is grounded in the STF, which emphasizes past, present, and future, as well as content and process influences, clients' perceptions of themselves are easily captured. Each page of MSCI has instructions that use personalized language such as "your next career decision" and "influence on you," which satisfies the guideline requiring instructions for the client. In relation, due to the personalized nature of the instructions, as well as the collaborative counselor-client nature of the assessment, MSCI also seems to satisfy the guideline requiring readable and understandable instructions. In terms of the instrument's steps, each page focuses on a particular aspect of the STF, which allows clients to focus on one distinct, yet interrelated part of their life before proceeding to another. The requirement for a focused and flexible process has been met by allowing clients to take the assessment at different times. Further, given the open-ended nature of the questions, MSCI allows clients to craft individualized responses that focus specifically on their own lives. As has been mentioned, given the qualitative nature of the assessment, a collaborative relationship between the counselor and client is critical, which meets the demands for a counselor/client involvement. Finally, a debriefing process is a fundamental aspect of MSCI in which open-ended questions are asked and diagrams are created with the goal being reflection on these products as part of a debriefing period.

General Utility and Evaluation

Based on what is currently documented in the literature, MSCI has the potential to assist students and adults in developing valuable insights regarding factors associated with their career development that they may not have considered beforehand. Such understanding cannot be understated. Further, according to qualitative assessment standards, it appears to have been constructed in a rigorous manner that makes sense according to qualitative epistemologies. However, MSCI does not appear to have rich documentation of its utility in the field of counseling over time and with different populations; as such, it is very difficult to gauge its effectiveness in comparison with other assessments. Additionally, there does not appear to be documentation of specific changes that were made from the first installment of the assessment to its current form. In addition, one could critique the utility of MSCI in helping students to develop concrete career plans; however, the same critique can probably be made of many qualitative career assessments. In general, the purpose of MSCI is to help individuals learn more about themselves and how multiple factors—sometimes outside of their control—influence career decisions; the assessment seems to do quite well in this regard. If more specific direction is needed for individuals to make a career decision, the onus seems to be on the facilitator as MSCI is intended to be a tool used to foster the relationship between counselor and client, which is in line with the qualitative tradition. Further, the instrument seems to have the potential to be effective with diverse populations due to its emphasis on salient aspects of clients' lives as stated in their own words.

References and Additional Resources

McMahon, M., & Patton, W. (1995). Development of a systems theory of career development. *Australian Journal of Career Development, 4,* 15-20.

McMahon, M., Patton, W., & Watson, M. (2003). Developing qualitative assessment processes. *Career Development Quarterly, 51*(3), 194-202.

McMahon, M., Patton, W., & Watson, M. (2005). *My System of Career Influences (MSCI): Facilitators guide.* Camberwell, Victoria, Australia: Australian Council for Educational Research Press.

McMahon, M. L., & Watson, M. B. (2008). Systemic influences on career development: assisting clients to tell their career stories. *Career Development Quarterly, 56,* 280-288.

McMahon, M. L., Watson, M. B., & Patton, W. (2005). Qualitative career assessment: Developing the My System of Career Influences relational activity. *Journal of Career Assessment, 13,* 476-490.

Okacha, A. A. G. (1998). Using qualitative appraisal strategies in career counseling. *Journal of Employment Counseling, 35,* 151-159.

Patton, W., & McMahon, M. (1999). *Career development and systems theory: A new relationship.* Pacific Grove, CA: Brooks/ Cole.

Patton, W., & McMahon, M. (2006). *Career development and systems theory: Connecting theory and practice* (2nd ed.). Rotterdam, Netherlands: Sense.

POSSIBLE SELVES MAPPING
Blythe Shepard and Anne Marshall

University of Lethbridge
4401 University Drive
Lethbridge, Alberta T1K 3M4, Canada
Blythe.shepard@uleth.ca
http://pathstothefuture.com/

Target Population: Children and adolescents in Grades 5 and up, young adults and adults.

Statement of the Purpose of the Instrument: The purpose of Possible Selves Mapping is to identify potential occupations to pursue or avoid as well as to determine the steps required to reach one's career goals.

Forms and Levels Available, with Dates of Publication/Revision of Each:

1999—Shepard and Marshall created and tested the assessment with children and adolescents in Grades 5-7.

2010—Shepard developed a Facilitator's Manual for rural youth (Future Bound: A Lifeworks Expedition Workshop for Rural Youth) with descriptions of Possible Selves Mapping.

Date of Most Recent Edition of Test Manual, User's Guide, Etc.: 2010.

Time:

Actual Test Time: 20-30 minutes.

Total Administration Time: 20-30 minutes.

Sample(s) in Which Assessment was Developed: 22 female and 20 male students (ages 11-13) in rural British Columbia, Canada. Although the students represented a variety of socioeconomic backgrounds, no additional demographic information is available about the sample.

Manner in Which Results Are Reported for Individuals/Groups: Students discuss their results with an interviewer and record the information on a Possible Selves Map. No scoring key is available.

Computer Software Options Available: Not available.

Cost of Materials: Materials include yellow and green index cards, a writing utensil, and a Possible Selves Map. The total cost is minimal.

Specimen Set: Not available.

Counselee Materials: No additional materials are needed.

Published Reviews of the Instrument in the Last 15 Years:

Marshall, A., & Wolsak, V. (2003). *Focusing on the journey: Life-career resources for youth in transition*. Retrieved from http://www.contactpoint.ca/natcon-conat/2003/pdf/pdf-03-13.pdf

Oyserman, D., & James, L. (2009). Possible selves: From content to process. In K. D. Markman, W. M. P. Klien, & J. A. Suhr (Eds.), *Handbook of imagination and mental simulation* (pp. 373-394). New York, NY: Psychology Press.

Wood, C., & Kaszubowski, Y. (2008). The career development needs of rural elementary school students. *The Elementary School Journal, 108,* 431-444.

POSSIBLE SELVES MAPPING

Reviewed by:

Rebecca E. Michel

Department of Psychology and Counseling
Governors State University

Description

Possible Selves Mapping (Shepard & Marshall, 1999) is an assessment tool designed to encourage career and life exploration. Rooted in self-concept theory, this qualitative assessment asks individuals to consider who they might "become" in the future. Through self-reflection and imagination, clients construct, rank, and evaluate hoped-for and feared possible selves (Markus & Nurius, 1986; Shepard & Marshall, 1999). Intentional exploration through Possible Selves Mapping is designed to help one consider career goals, fears, and self-concepts in order to engage in meaningful career planning (Wood & Kaszubowski, 2008).

The purpose of Possible Selves Mapping within career counseling is to identify potential occupations to pursue or avoid, as well as to determine the steps required to reach one's career goals. The assessment tool was originally designed for use with adolescents in Grades 5 to 7 (Shepard & Marshall, 1999) but may also be used with adults (Shepard & Quressette, 2010). The assessment takes approximately 20 to 30 minutes to complete, depending on the number of possible selves an individual constructs. Completion of the assessment provides the client with a Possible Selves Map for possible use in career and personal counseling. Possible Selves Mapping (Shepard, 2010; Shepard & Marshall, 1999) was adapted from Cross and Markus' (1991) written survey instrument to serve as a guide to assist clients in conceptualizing career aspirations. During the introduction, a counselor explains the concept of possible selves and provides developmentally appropriate examples (e.g., imagine yourself as a teacher, musician, or chef). The client is invited to relax and think about "what you hope to become" (positive projections) and "what you fear, dread, or don't want for yourself" (negative projections) in the future (Shepard & Marshall, 1999, p. 41).

The exercise itself includes five directions, which are recorded on a Possible Selves Map. During the first direction, the client is encouraged to list numerous positive and negative projections of possible selves on green and yellow cards, respectively. In the second direction, the client ranks the list of possible selves in order of importance. During the third direction, the client places a star on the card with the possible self he or she perceives most able to achieve. Using the chosen card, the client rates his or her capability to become that possible self on a seven-point Likert-type scale (1 = *not at all capable* to 7 = *completely capable*). In the fourth direction, the client evaluates his or her ability to achieve or prevent each possible self. The client is then asked, "How likely do you think it is that this possible self will happen?" and rate that likelihood using the same seven-point Likert-type scale (Shepard & Marshall, 1999, p. 42). In the final direction, the client reflects on actions that could bring about (or prevent) the possible selves from emerging. Following completion of the exercise, the client and interviewer debrief the experience by summarizing the Possible Selves Map. See Figure 1 for an example of a Possible Selves Map.

The Possible Selves Map can be used in individual and group settings. Individually, counselors can encourage clients to articulate their interests and values, develop short and long-term goals, and evaluate their progress. Individual administration is typically preferred for clients who may restrict self-reflection in front of peers (Shepard & Marshall, 1999). Upon completion, clients may deepen their awareness by sharing possible selves, hopes, aspirations, and fears with one another in a group setting.

Technical Considerations

The rigor of qualitative career measurements, such as Possible Selves Mapping, can be evaluated through guidelines provided by McMahon, Patton, and Watson (2003). The authors suggested qualitative assessments be (a) grounded in theory, (b) tested, (c) completed within a reasonable timeframe, (d) holistic, (e) written with readable instructions for the client, (f) created with achievable steps, (g) focused and flexible, (h) collaborative, and (i) debriefed. Possible Selves Mapping was developed to meet the majority of these standards.

A Counselor's Guide To Career Assessments Instruments

The assessment is based on the work of Markus and Nurius (1986), who expanded self-concept theory to include the construct of possible selves. According to these authors, possible selves are a person's thoughts about what they could become, hope to become, or fear they might become. Possible selves function as incentives for behavior, as a person will take actions to become or avoid becoming a certain way. For example, an individual who hopes to become an attorney would engage in behaviors to increase the likelihood of achieving that goal, such as studying for exams, participating in civic engagement, and abiding by the law. As such, development is seen as a process of "acquiring and then achieving or resisting certain possible selves" (Markus & Nurius, 1986, p. 955). Researchers have investigated the concept of possible selves using various interview protocols (Meara, Day, Chalk & Phelps, 1995; Perry & Vance, 2010). Shepard and Marshall (1999) created the assessment to serve as a specific procedure to investigate the connection among self-concept, identity, and future behaviors.

Possible Selves Mapping has been empirically tested with a sample of 42 adolescents (22 females, 20 males) living in a rural area (Shepard & Marshall, 1999). The participants, ages 11 to 13, reported heightened awareness of career ambitions, career obstacles, and actions required to achieve their goals. Students reported no difficulty imagining multiple variations of their selves in the future. In approximately 30 minutes, the participants constructed an average of 5.36 (SD = 1.81) hoped-for selves and 3.83 (SD = 1.29) feared selves. They also brainstormed several actions they could take to obtain hoped-for selves (M = 3.76, SD = 2.26) or prevent feared selves (M = 3.12, SD = 1.52) from emerging. The young adolescents described the process as a "kind of a neat way to think about the future" (Shepard & Marshall, 1999, p. 6). Although anecdotal evidence suggests the use of this assessment with adolescents, additional research is warranted to comprehensively explore the impact of Possible Selves Mapping with diverse populations (e.g., at-risk youth, individuals living in an urban setting).

Possible Selves Mapping invites participant involvement and fosters holism. Similar to other constructivist qualitative career assessments, counselors serve as curious questioners with an expert client, who shares stories about his or her abilities, values, and interests (McMahon & Patton, 2002). Possible Selves Mapping encourages clients to engage in career planning through assessment of desires, apprehensions, expectations, and priorities in a focused, yet flexible, dialogue. The instructions include simple, logical steps written in easily understood language. For example, during the debriefing section participants are asked to summarize the Possible Selves Map as if they "were talking with someone who knew nothing about them" (Shepard & Marshall, 1999, p. 42). Through collaborative exploration with counselors, clients develop insights about hopes and fears while uncovering a meaningful career story.

General Utility and Evaluation

Career counselors and researchers have explored possible selves with individuals in various cultures (Meara et al., 1995; Perry & Vance, 2010); however, few document the use of Possible Selves Mapping as a tool to guide their inquiry. Although the assessment has been beneficial for female adolescents and adults in rural communities (Shepard, 2005; Shepard & Quressette, 2010), the utility of Possible Selves Mapping with other populations is unknown. Vocational exploration will likely vary across cultures, and constructivist assessments such as Possible Selves Mapping, may provide a window by which to explore personal experiences and values to create a meaningful vocational experience (Neimeyer, 1992). Possible Selves Mapping can be a useful assessment for clients to construct and consider during career counseling. Knowledge of possible selves provides insight about how individuals might change from the person they are today. With this tool, clients are helped to explore numerous facets of possible selves, including hoped-for and feared careers, lifestyles, and relationships. Possible Selves Mapping can also be used to visualize various aspects of a career, such as the work environment, the job tasks/skills, and the training/education required. This concrete visual career depiction can serve as a guide for individuals and provide motivation to make progress toward their career goals. Through this process, clients can create meaningful and realistic action plans to reach their career goals.

References and Additional Resources

Cross, S., & Markus, H. (1991). Possible selves across the life span. *Human Development, 34,* 230-255.

Guenette, F., Marshall, A., & Morley, T. (2007). Career experiences and choice processes for secondary science students. In T. Pelton, G. Reis, & K. Moore (Eds.), *Connections '07* (pp. 77-84). Victoria, BC, Canada: University of Victoria.

Leondari, A., & Gonida, E. N. (2008). Adolescents' possible selves, achievement, goal orientations, and academic achievements. *Hellenic Journal of Psychology, 5,* 179-198.

Markus, H., & Nurius, P. (1986). Possible Selves. *American Psychologist, 41*(9), 954-969.

Marshall, A., & Wolsak, V. (2003). *Focusing on the journey: Life-career resources for youth in transition.* Retrieved from http://www.contactpoint.ca/natcon-conat/2003/pdf/pdf-03-13.pdf

McMahon, M., & Patton, W. (2002). Using qualitative assessment in career counseling. *International Journal of Vocational and Educational Guidance, 51,* 51-60.

McMahon, M., Patton, W., & Watson, M. (2003). Developing qualitative career assessment processes. *Career Development Quarterly, 51,* 194-202.

Meara, N. M., Day, J. D., Chalk, L. M., & Phelps, R. E. (1995). Possible selves: Applications for career counseling. *Journal of Career Assessment, 3,* 259-277.

Neimeyer, G. J. (1992). Personal constructs in career counseling and development. *Journal of Career Development, 18,* 163-173.

Oyserman, D., & James, L. (2009). Possible selves: From content to process. In K. D. Markman, W. M. P. Klien, & J. A. Suhr (Eds.), *Handbook of imagination and mental simulation* (pp. 373-394). New York, NY: Psychology Press.

Perry, J. C., & Vance, K. S. (2010). Possible selves among urban youths of color: An exploration of peer beliefs and gender differences. *The Career Development Quarterly, 58,* 257-269.

Shepard, B. (2003). Creating selves in a rural community. In R. M. Roth (Ed.), *Connections '03* (pp. 111-120). Victoria, BC, Canada: University of Victoria. Retrieved from http://education2.uvic.ca/Research/conferences/connections2003/07Shepard102.pdf

Shepard, B. (2004). In search of self: A qualitative study of the life-career development of rural young women. *Canadian Journal of Counselling, 38,* 75-90.

Shepard, B. (2005). Embedded selves: Co-constructing a relationally based career workshop for rural girls. *Canadian Journal of Counselling, 39,* 231-244.

Shepard, B. (2010). *Future bound: A lifeworks expedition workshop for rural youth.* Retrieved from pathstothefuture.com/pdf/Future_Bound-Blythe_Shepard.pdf

Shepard, B. (2011). *Mapping: A resource-oriented approach for adolescent clients.* Retrieved from http://counseling outfitters.com/vistas/ vistas11/Article_92.pdf

Shepard, B., & Hudson Breen, R. (2004). *Future bound: A life-career expedition workshop.* NATCON Papers 2004. Toronto, ON: National Consultation on Career Development. Retrieved from http://natcon.org/archive/natcon/papers/natcon_papers_2004_Shepard_Breen.pdf

Shepard, B., & Marshall, A. (1999). Possible selves mapping: Life-career exploration with young adolescents. *Canadian Journal of Counselling, 33,* 37-54.

Shepard, B., & Quressette, S. (2010). *Possible selves mapping intervention: Rural women and beyond.* Retrieved from http://counselingoutfitters.com/vistas/vistas10/Article_51.pdf

Wood, C., & Kaszubowski, Y. (2008). The career development needs of rural elementary school students. *The Elementary School Journal, 108,* 431-444.

Figure 1. *Possible Selves Map Example*

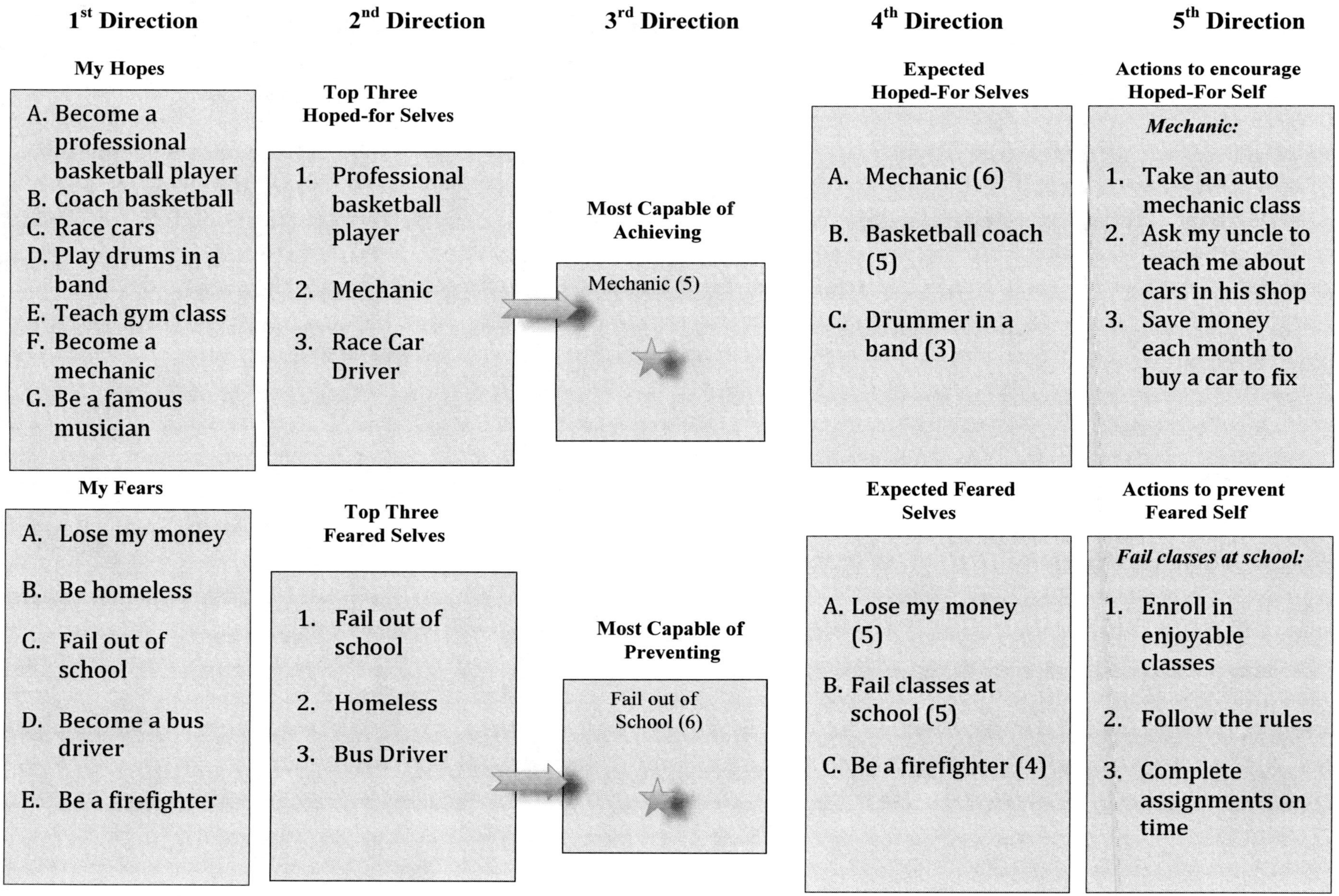

1st Direction

My Hopes

A. Become a professional basketball player
B. Coach basketball
C. Race cars
D. Play drums in a band
E. Teach gym class
F. Become a mechanic
G. Be a famous musician

My Fears

A. Lose my money
B. Be homeless
C. Fail out of school
D. Become a bus driver
E. Be a firefighter

2nd Direction

Top Three Hoped-for Selves

1. Professional basketball player
2. Mechanic
3. Race Car Driver

Top Three Feared Selves

1. Fail out of school
2. Homeless
3. Bus Driver

3rd Direction

Most Capable of Achieving

Mechanic (5)

Most Capable of Preventing

Fail out of School (6)

4th Direction

Expected Hoped-For Selves

A. Mechanic (6)
B. Basketball coach (5)
C. Drummer in a band (3)

Expected Feared Selves

A. Lose my money (5)
B. Fail classes at school (5)
C. Be a firefighter (4)

5th Direction

Actions to encourage Hoped-For Self

Mechanic:

1. Take an auto mechanic class
2. Ask my uncle to teach me about cars in his shop
3. Save money each month to buy a car to fix

Actions to prevent Feared Self

Fail classes at school:

1. Enroll in enjoyable classes
2. Follow the rules
3. Complete assignments on time

CHAPTER 17

ADDITIONAL CAREER ASSESSMENT INSTRUMENTS

Chris Wood
Danica G. Hays

Department of Counseling and Human Services
Old Dominion University

Introduction

In previous chapters of this book, 73 major career assessment instruments are described and reviewed. In this chapter, an additional 232 instruments are briefly described and essential information such as publisher, date of publication, intended populations, and published reviews is provided. These additional instruments may be useful for some career assessment applications. For example, types of instruments usually not included are those which primarily assess educational achievement, general intelligence, specific aptitude measures without broad applications, and abnormal personality and adjustment. The entries for each instrument are grouped into logical categories that are parallel, but are not identical to, those used to organize the major instrument reviews. Although each instrument is included under only one category, in many cases it can be argued that it could also fit into one or more other categories. The *User's Matrix,* provided in Appendix A, attempts to reflect this overlap of categories.

To facilitate the use of this chapter, the following key to the categories of information presented is provided:

- **Type of Instrument.** The categories used to organize the instruments in the order presented are

    a. Multiple Aptitude, Achievement, and Comprehensive Measures

    b. Specific Aptitude and Achievement Measures

    c. Interest Instruments

    d. Measures of Work Values, Satisfaction, and Environments

    e. Card Sorts

    f. Career Development/Maturity Measures

    g. Personality Measures

    h. Instruments for Special Populations

- **Name.** The name of the instrument is listed first in boldface. Common acronyms, when used, are provided in parentheses immediately following the name.

- **Publisher.** The name and limited contact information for the publisher are provided. Additional information is provided on the National Career Development Association (NCDA) webpage (http://www.ncda.org). Additional information about the instruments can also be obtained by contacting the publisher.

- **Date.** The date given refers to the initial date the instrument was published and/or when it was last revised. A range of dates, (e.g., 1960-1993) signifies ongoing development and revision of the instrument during that time span. No date indicates that the date of publication was unavailable.

- **Population.** The population refers to the group or groups of individuals for whom the publisher indicates the instrument is appropriate.

- **References.** Several of the major sources of instrument reviews are cited in an abbreviated form. Links to many of these sources are located in Appendix B. The key to the abbreviations is as follows.

    a. CG refers to *A Counselor's Guide to Career Assessment Instruments.* The number immediately following indicates the edition number.

509

Additional Career Assessment Instruments

b. MY refers to the *Mental Measurements Yearbook*. The number immediately following denotes the volume number.

c. TC is the abbreviation for *Test Critiques*. The number immediately following denotes the volume number.

d. TP is the abbreviation for *Tests in Print* and the number following indicates the edition.

e. T3 or T4 is the abbreviation for *Tests*—Third or Fourth Edition.

f. AT:98 refers to *Assessment for Transitions Planning: A Guide for Special Education Teachers and Related Service Personnel* (Clark, 1998).

g. MG and MD refer to *Measurement and Evaluation in Guidance* and *Measurement and Evaluation in Counseling and Development,* respectively. The number following the colon refers to the month and year of the issue in which the review is found (e.g., 10/92 denotes October, 1992).

h. B:93 refers to *Vocational Evaluation Systems and Software: A Consumer's Guide* (Brown et al., 1993).

- **Brief Description.** This section provides an overview of what is measured and includes the titles of some of the scales associated with each instrument. Additional comments are included for some instruments (e.g., to indicate a major use, special reports or support materials available, or training required for administration).

A COUNSELOR'S GUIDE TO CAREER ASSESSMENTS INSTRUMENTS

A. MULTIPLE APTITUDE, ACHIEVEMENT AND COMPREHENSIVE MEASURES

Name of Test/Publisher/Date/Population	Reference(s)	Brief Description
ACCU Vision – Workplace Success Skills Learning Resources http://www.learning-resources.com/index.cfm 1990 - 1999 High School to Adults		Designed to identify & measure workplace skills. Consists of 5 video modules divided into the following sections: Interpersonal Skills, Listening, Structuring Work Activities, Trainability, & Graphs & Charts. "Keyed to the SCANS foundational skills for entry level positions." Individual or group administration.
Activity Vector Analysis (AVA) Bizet Human Asset Management http://www.bizet.com/ 1948 - 1994 Prospective Employees		Designed to determine if an individual is a match for the job. Consists of 5 separate parts: Activity Vector Analysis, Job Rating Scale, Job Expectations, Behaviorally Based Interview Questions, & Job Model. Paper/pencil or computer administered; must be interpreted by a certified person.
Adult Measure of Essential Skills (AMES) Steck-Vaughn http://steckvaughn.hmhco.com/en/steckvaughn.htm 800.531.5015 1997 Adults		Standardized test of silent reading comprehension, communication (written), and mathematics.
Ball Aptitude Battery (BAB) The Ball Foundation 526 North Main Street Glen Ellyn, IL 60137 630.469.6270 info@ballfoundation.org 1995 High School Students to Adults	MY12	Instrument of 12 aptitudes for job placement and selection for high school students and adults.
Basic Skills Locator Test (BSLT) Piney Mountain Press http://www.pineymountain.com/ 1998 Age 15 to Adults	TP5	Designed to assess math & language skill levels of individuals functioning at the 12th grade level or below. Results provided in terms of GED & grade levels. Results correlated to DOL job classifications, OOH, DOT, & GOE. Computer scored, machine scored, or publisher scored. Computer version available.
Career and Vocational Form of the SOI-LA Basic Test SOI Systems http://www.soisystems.com/ 1975 Adolescents to Adults	T3	Measures 24 cognitive abilities which predict career & vocational options. Consists of subtests taken from the SOI-LA Basic Test. Paper/pencil tests. Suitable for groups. Instructions for self-administration. Computer analysis available.
Career IQ and Interest Test (CIQIT) Advantage Learning Solutions http://advantagelearningsolutions.com/ 1997 Age 13 to Adults		Assists individuals in identifying possible job choices. Consists of a CD-ROM that includes: vocational aptitude test, interest measure, & recent OOH information. Aptitude survey measures 6 factors such as: general ability & manual dexterity. Interest schedule measures 12 factors such as: artistic & nature.
Career Planning Survey ACT, Inc. http://www.act.org 2201 N. Dodge Street P.O. Box 168 Iowa City, IA 52243-0168 319.337.1000 1997 Grades 8-10	MY15	Intended to help students in Grades 8-10 identify and explore personally relevant occupations and high school courses; provide students with a general sense of direction for career exploration; and show students how occupations relate to each other, thus giving students a context in which to explore their career options.
Career Profile Assessment LIFECORP http://www.life-corp.com/ 1998 Junior High and High School Students		Assesses 10 aptitudes & 12 interests using a computer-based system. Aptitudes include: reasoning, mathematics, language, learning, numerical, spatial, & color discrimination. Interest assessment covers the 12 GOE categories. Output tied to DOT Worker Qualification Profile & New Concepts career information.
Career Programs Assessment Test (CPAT) ACT, Inc. http://www.act.org/ 1981 - 1994 Adults	T4	Measures both the entry-level & academic skills important to success in education programs offered by career schools, colleges & other post-secondary institutions. Basic skills test include: Language, Reading, & Numerical.
Career Technical Assistance Program (C-Tap) WestEd http://www.wested.org/cs/we/print/docs/we/home.htm 1998 Grade 9 to Adults		Designed to assist students in learning/refining career-technical skills & to assess readiness for entry-level jobs and/or post-secondary training. Consists of 3 parts: portfolio, project, & written scenario. Referenced to standards in career areas, such as: agriculture, business, & health careers.

Additional Career Assessment Instruments

Name of Test/Publisher/Date/Population	Reference(s)	Brief Description
COIN Basic Skills and Career Interest Survey COIN Educational Products http://www.coinedu.com/ 1996 High School to Adults		Provides aptitude and interest information for career planning. Basic skills component uses Wonderlic Basic Skills Test to assess math & language skills used in the workplace. Survey assesses activities in 7 areas of interest. Scores are combined & linked to matching occupations & reported in GED levels.
Comprehensive Ability Battery (CAB) Institute for Personality and Ability Testing (IPAT) http://www.ipat.com/ 1975 - 1982 Grade 10 to Adults	MY9 MY8 TP7 TP5 T4	Consists of 4 test booklets containing 20 subtests, each designed to measure a primary ability factor related to performance in industrial settings. Examples of scores reported are: verbal & numerical ability, clerical speed & accuracy, memory span, etc.
Employee Aptitude Survey (EAS) Psychological Services PSI http://corporate.psionline.com/ 1952 - 1995 Adults	CG3 TP7 MY14 MY6 MY5 TP5 T4	Designed as a diagnostic tool for employee selection & vocational guidance. Consists of 10 ability tests such as: Verbal Comprehension, Numerical Ability, Space Visualization, Visual Speed & Accuracy, Manual Speed & Accuracy, & Symbolic Reasoning. Machine or hand scored.
Employee Effectiveness Profile Jossey-Bass/Wiley 989 Market Street San Francisco, CA 94103 http://www.josseybass.com 1986 Adults	MY12	Designed to assist managers in identifying the overall effectiveness of individual employees.
Flanagan Aptitude Classification Test (FACT) Vangent, Inc. http://www.vangent.com/ 1951 - 1994 High School to Adults, Prospective Employees	MY7 TP7 TP5 T4	Designed to predict success in various occupational fields via composite occupational scores. Consists of 16 subtests such as: inspection, coding, memory, precision, assembly, scales, coordination, judgment & comprehension, arithmetic, patterns, components, tables, etc.
Flanagan Industrial Tests (FIT) Vangent, Inc. http://www.vangent.com/ 1960 - 1996 Adults	MY8 TC2 TP7 TP5 T4	Measures 18 aptitudes or job tasks involved in supervisory, technical, office, skilled, & entry-level job demands. Designed for selection, placement, reassignment, or reclassification of employees.
Hay Aptitude Test Battery Wonderlic, Inc. http://www.wonderlic.com/ 1947 - 1997 Adults	MY9 MY12 TP5 TP7 T4	Assesses clerical & numerical aptitude through 4 paper/pencil tests. Tests include: warm-up (which is not scored), number perception, name finding, & number series completion. Designed to aid in the selection of clerical workers. Hand scored.
Industrial Reading Test (IRT) Pearson Assessments http://www.pearsonassessments.com 1976 – 1978 Grade 10 to Adults	MY9 TP5 TP7 T4	Contains 9 readings passages & 38 test items on work-relevant topics to assess reading comprehension. Some passages depict sections of technical manual; others are written in the form of company memoranda. All passages are at the secondary reading level.
IPI Aptitude-Intelligence Test Series Industrial Psychology International (IPI) http://www.metritech.com/IPI/ipi_home.htm 1982 - 1986 Adults	TC2 TP5 T4	Consists of various aptitude & personality tests such as: dexterity, blocks, parts, numbers, tools, judgement, fluency, sales, etc. Aids in employee selection in 28 job fields such as: computer programmer, dental technician, sales, clerk, etc.
Job Seeking Skills Assessment The National Center for Disability Education & Training 3200 Marshall Ave, Suite 201 Norman, Oklahoma 73072-8032 405.325.0158 http://www.ncdet.org 1988 Adults	MY12	For assessing clients' ability to complete a job application form and participate in the employment interview, and to serve as a guide for integrating the results into program planning.
Job Skills Tests (See also **Basic Skills Tests**) Ramsay Corporation http://www.ramsaycorp.com/ 1981 - 1991 Job Applicants and Industrial Workers	MY9 TP5	Designed to measure abilities expected of all job applicants, such as reading, arithmetic, measurement, inspection, process monitoring, problem solving, and checking accuracy.

A COUNSELOR'S GUIDE TO CAREER ASSESSMENTS INSTRUMENTS

Name of Test/Publisher/Date/Population	Reference(s)	Brief Description
Learning Skills Profile Hay Group/Hay Resources Direct 116 Huntington Avenue Boston, MA 02116-5712 800.729.8074 Haytrg@haygroup.com http://www.hayresourcesdirect.haygroup.com 1993 Junior High to Adults	MY13	Assesses the gap between personal aptitudes and critical skills required by a job.
Leisure to Occupation Connection Search (LOCS) Super Solution Consultancy 1002-3045 Queen Frederica Dr. L4Y 3A2 Mississauga, ON, Canada +1.289.800.1870 http://www.drsafdarrehman.ca 1999 Adults		Measures transferable skills that have been developed in leisure pursuits.
Making a Terrific Career Happen (MATCH) EdITS http://www.edits.net Middle to High School		MATCH is a self-evaluation questionnaire that uses student's interests, abilities, and values to find careers. Scores help to find sample jobs, lists of classes and college majors, related skills and abilities, and activities useful for experience in those jobs.
Motivational Appraisal of Personal Potential (MAPP) ZH Computer 7400 Metro Blvd, Suite 350 Edina, MN 55439 2007 Adolescents to Adults		Identifies one's true motivations toward work and allows one to match oneself to job categories to see where one best fits.
Multidimensional Aptitude Battery (MAB) Sigma Assessment Systems http://www.sigmaassessmentsystems.com/ 1982 - 1999 Grade 10 to Adults	MY10 TC2 TP5 TP7 T4	Assesses aptitudes & intelligence through 5 verbal & 5 performance subtests. Yields a profile of scores. Can be individually or group administered using paper/pencil or IBM-compatible disk. Mail-in scoring generates narrative report.
NOCTI Occupational Competency Tests National Occupational Competency Testing Institute http://www.nocti.org/ 1986 Students in Vocational and Technical Programs	TP5	Multitude of competency tests in 3 categories: Experienced Workers, Industrial Assessments, Job Ready Assessments. Occupations include: Accounting, Appliance Repair, Carpentry, Commercial Art, Die Making, Electronics Technology, Mechanical, Medical Assistant, Pipefitter, Retail Trades, & many more.
Professional Employment Test Psychological Service PSI http://corporate.psionline.com/ 1986 - 1988 Potential Employees	MY12 TP7 TP5 T4	Assesses reading comprehension, reasoning, quantitative problem solving, & data interpretation. Consists of 40 items and yields one total score. Provides a sample item for each area with an explanation of the correct response. Individual or group administration.
PSI Basic Skills Test (BST) Psychological Services, Inc. http://corporate.psionline.com/ 1982-1986 Potential Employees	CG4 MY9 T5	Assesses abilities and skills that are important for successful performance in clerical, administrative, and customer service jobs.
Revised Beta Examination-Third Edition (BETA-III) Pearson Assessments http://www.pearsonassessments.com 1931 - 1999 Adults	MY9 TP5 T4	Assesses mental abilities in individuals having limited or no reading skills. Consists of 6 tests: mazes, coding, paper form boards, picture completion, clerical checking, & picture absurdities. Can be group administered. Available in Spanish.
Scholastic Level Exam (SLE) Wonderlic, Inc. http://www.wonderlic.com/ 1937 - 1988 Age 15 to Adults	MY14	A 50-question, 12-minute timed test of cognitive ability or aptitude for learning. Measures students' ability to understand instructions, keep up with classroom pace, solve problems & use occupational training on the job.
Schubert General Ability Battery (GAB) Slosson Educational Publications, Inc. http://www.slosson.com/ 1986 Grade 10 to Adults	MY7 TC3 TP7 TP5 T4	Assesses intellectual abilities including verbal, arithmetic, & syllogistic measures of reasoning ability. The 4 subtests are designed to indicate individual's levels of success and/or placement in school, college, & business.
Success Skills 2000 Employment Technologies http://www.etc-easy.com/ 1991 - 1997 High School to Adults		A video-based, computer-scored test for corporate recruiting & development of entry-level professionals in 4 major categories: engineering, professional/finance, supervision, & sales & marketing. Measures critical skills in 3 broad categories: applied problem solving, interpersonal effectiveness, & accountability.

Additional Career Assessment Instruments

Name of Test/Publisher/Date/Population	Reference(s)	Brief Description
Technical Test Battery (TTB) SHLAmericas http://www.shl.com/shl/americas 1992 Adults	T4 TP7	Consists of 4 separate instruments: Mechanical Comprehension designed to assess understanding of basic mechanical principles, Numerical Computation designed to assess numerical ability in a technical setting, Spatial Recognition to measure spatial ability, & Visual Estimation of spatial perception.
Tests for Everyday Living (TEL) Janet T. Landman 1980 High School		Series of tests which assess adolescents' knowledge and performance in daily living and prevocational skill areas.
Training House Assessment Kit The Richardson Co. Training Media http://www.rctm.com/ 2000 Supervisors and Managers		Designed to offer smaller organizations a wide range of reproducible assessments for managers to use to identify & target development needs. Consists of 25 instruments such as: Proficiency Assessment Report, Self-Awareness Profile, Dealing with Groups, The Apt Inventory, & Analytical Thinking Test.
USES General Test Aptitude Battery U.S. Employment Service 1979 Adults		Measures nine different aptitudes and can be used to help assess the likelihood that you will be successful in specific careers or training programs.
Valpar Aviator Valpar International http://www.valparint.com/ 1998 Age 15 to Adults		Computerized instrument that measures GED Reasoning, Math, & Language. Tests 7 aptitude factors such as: general learning ability, verbal, numerical, & spatial perception. Includes 2 pictorial interest surveys. Matches the interest & aptitude results with its internal occupational database. Computer administered.
Valpar Pro 3000 Valpar International http://www.valparint.com/ 1999 Age 15 to Adults		Windows-based version of Valpar's System 2000 modular software package. Consists of a required system manager & optional modules, such as: Career Planner, Compass (computerized assessment), Compass Lite (without work samples), DOT, OOH, & Spatial/Nonverbal assessment.
Valpar Test of Essential Skills (VTES) **Valpar International** http://www.valparint.com/ 1999 Age 15 to Adults		Provides both an academic grade-level score and Department of Labor work-related GED Language and Math scores. VTES English and Math are criterion-referenced, time-limited power tests of the basic language and math skills essential to success in the workplace.
Vocational Assessment and Curriculum Guide (VACG) Exceptional Education P.O. Box 15308 Seattle, WA 98155 206.262.9538 Adults	MY13	Designed to assess and identify skill deficits in terms of competitive employment expectations; to prescribe training goals designed to reduce identified deficits; to evaluate program effectiveness by reassessing the worker after training.
Vocational Evaluation System (See Career Profile Assessment) LIFECORP http://www.life-corp.com/ 1971 - 1997 Middle School to Adults		Audiovisual programs that assess individual's interest & ability for performing routine tasks. Activities encompass a number of job titles such as: Air Conditioning & Refrigeration, Cook & Baker, Diesel Engine Repair, Machine Trades, Drafting, & Masonry. Formerly known as the Singer Evaluation System.
VOC-TECH Quick Screener (VTQS) CFKR Career Materials http://www.cfkr.com/ 1984 - 1990 Grade 10 to Adults	MY12 TP5	A screening tool that assesses career aptitudes, interest, & training plans. Aids in matching career goals with jobs, & identifies job options & training. Designed for non-college bound persons. Computer version available.
V-TECS Assessments Vocational-Technical Education Consortium of States http://www.v-tecs.org/ 1986 - 1999 High School to Adults		V-TECS is a consortium of agencies that provide occupational skills training in business/industry, education, & the military. Criterion-referenced item banks for 31 occupations are available, consisting of 3 types of items: written, performance, & scenario. Tests tied to curriculum materials.
Watson-Glaser Critical Thinking Appraisal (WGCTA) Pearson Assessments http://www.pearsonassessments.com 1942 - 1994 Adults	MY13 T4 TC3 TP5 TP7	Measures 5 aspects of critical thinking: drawing sound inferences, recognizing assumptions, deductive reasoning, drawing conclusions, & evaluating arguments. The 80 items contain content that may be controversial, thereby providing a measure of the extent of bias effect on the ability to think critically.
Wesman Personnel Classification Test (PCT) Pearson Assessments http://www.pearsonassessments.com 1946 - 1965 Adults	MY7 TC3 TP5 TP7 T4	Measures 2 major aspects of mental ability: verbal reasoning & numerical ability. Verbal items are analogies, & numerical items include basic math skills & understanding of quantitative relationships. Aids in the selection of sales people & middle management personnel.

A COUNSELOR'S GUIDE TO CAREER ASSESSMENTS INSTRUMENTS

B. SPECIFIC APTITUDE AND ACHIEVEMENT MEASURES

Name of Test/Publisher/Date/Population	Reference(s)	Brief Description
Armed Services-Civilian Vocational Interest Survey (ASCVIS) CFKR Career Materials P.O. Box 99 Meadow Vista, CA 05722-0099 800.525.5626	MY10	Assesses interest in careers in the armed-services and related civilian jobs.
Bennett Hand Tool Dexterity Test (BHTDT) Pearson Assessments http://www.pearsonassessments.com 1981 High School to Adults		Measures manual dexterity & gross motor coordination. Subject removes 12 bolts from one vertical board & places them on another. Task requires the use of four tools: two open-end wrenches, one adjustable wrench, & one screwdriver.
Bennett Mechanical Comprehension Test (BMCT) Pearson Assessments http://www.pearsonassessments.com 1940 - 1994 Adults	MY11 MY16 TC8 TP5 TP7 T4	Assesses ability to understand physical & mechanical principles. The 68 test items can be group administered by company personnel or by optional tape recordings. Two equivalent forms available. Correlates score with DOT job categories.
Career and Life Explorer, Second Edition JIST Works, Inc. http://www.jist.com 2007 Grades 6-10		Helps students explore interests, hobbies, talents, and values. Students review over 250 occupations from the *Occupational Outlook Handbook* job titles arranged in six categories. The interest inventory portion is based on the RIASEC occupational coding system.
Clerical Abilities Battery (CAB) Pearson Assessments http://www.pearsonassessments.com 1985 - 1987 Adults	MY11 TP5 TP7 T4	Measures filing, proofreading, & mathematical skills. Tests ability to copy & compare information, use tables, & reason with numbers. The 7 tests can be administered separately or as a total battery. Available in 2 forms: A—industry, B—schools.
Clerical Skills Test Series Walden Personnel Testing and Training http://www.waldentesting.com 1990 Adults	MY16 TP7 T4	Measures clerical skills. A series of tests that measures proficiency in 20 areas such as: attention to detail, problem solving, spelling, alphabetizing & filing, PC graphics, bookkeeping, electronic knowledge, & mechanical comprehension. Hand scored.
Computer Operator Aptitude Battery (COAB) Vangent, Inc. http://www.vangent-hcm.com 1973 - 1974 Computer Operator Applicants and Trainees	TP7 TP5 T4	Consists of 3 subtests: sequence recognition, format checking, & logical thinking. Scores from subtests combine to predict job performance of computer operators & to identify those applicants with the potential to succeed as a computer operator.
Computer Programmer Aptitude Battery (CPAB) Vangent, Inc. http://www.vangent-hcm.com 1964 - 1993 Computer Programmer Trainees	TP7 MY11 TP5 T4	Assesses an individual's potential to succeed as a computer programmer. Consists of 5 aptitude subtests: verbal meaning, reasoning, letter series, number ability, & diagramming. Oriented for both computer-experienced & inexperienced students.
Crawford Small Parts Dexterity Test (CSPDT) Pearson Assessments http://www.pearsonassessments.com 1946 - 1981 High School to Adults	MY5 TP5 TP7 T4	Measures eye-hand coordination & fine finger dexterity in two parts. Part I—Subject uses tweezers to insert pins in close-fitting holes, & then places collars on the pins. Part II—Subject places small screws in holes by hand, & then uses a screwdriver to screw them down.
Customer Service Skills Assessment Program Employment Technologies http://www.etc-easy.com/ 1989 - 1997 High School to Adults		A video-based, computer scored diagnostic system that focuses on the key functions of the customer service job. Includes a series of multiple choice questions that are job-relevant & that provide a standardized assessment of a candidate's ability to do the job.
Dvorine Color Vision Test Pearson Assessments http://www.pearsonassessments.com 1944 - 1958 General Population	TP5 TP7 MY6 T4	Identifies defective color vision. Consists of 2 parts that determine type & degree of vision defect. Each plate features a design of colored dots against a background of contrasting dots which appear shapeless to the colorblind.
General Clerical Test (GCT) Pearson Assessments http://www.pearsonassessments.com 1944 - 1988 Adults	MY12 TC3 TP5 TP7 T4	Assesses abilities needed for many higher level administrative & paraprofessional positions. Consists of 9 tests which yield 3 ability scores: clerical speed & accuracy, numerical ability, & verbal ability.

Additional Career Assessment Instruments

Name of Test/Publisher/Date/Population	Reference(s)	Brief Description
Group Test of Musical Ability NFER-Nelson Publishing Co., Ltd (England) http://www.assessmentcentre.com 1988 Ages 7 – 14	MY12 TP7	Measures musical ability. Consists of 2 tests: a 24-item Pitch Test requiring the respondent to identify the higher of 2 notes & a 10-item Pulse Test requiring the respondent to compute number of pulses in a series of tempos. All test items and directions are in audio format.
Intuitive Mechanics Vangent, Inc. http://www.vangent-hcm.com 1956 - 1984 Adults	MY9 T4 TP5 TP7	Paper-and-pencil test that measures the ability to understand mechanical relationships or to visualize internal movement in a mechanical system. Used in vocational counseling or personnel selection to identify individuals with high mechanical interest & ability.
Job Skills PESCO, Inc. http://www.pesco.org 1998 Prospective Employees		Measures individual's proficiency with various software applications. Consists of 50 tests such as: Word, Access, Medical Secretary, Excel, Word Perfect, & Internet Basics. Three levels of testing in every standard test: basic, intermediate, & advanced skills. Companion to PESCO 2001 System.
Mechanical Aptitudes Vangent, Inc. http://www.vangent-hcm.com 1947 - 1996 Grade 12 to Adults	T4	Measures ability to learn mechanical skills in 3 areas: mechanical knowledge, space relations, & shop arithmetic. Designed for assistance in selection of entry-level applicants & trainees.
Mechanical Movements Vangent, Inc. http://www.vangent-hcm.com 1984 Adults	T3 TP7 TP5	Measures finger dexterity, eye-hand coordination, & visualization abilities required in office & factory tasks. May also be used by special educators to evaluate motor skills. Contains 7 subtests which can be used separately or in combination.
Minnesota Clerical Test (MCT) Pearson Assessments http://www.pearsonassessments.com 1933 - 1979 Clerical Applicants	MY9 MY6 TP5 TP7 T4	Measures clerical aptitude. Focus is on perceptual speed & accuracy in 2 tasks: name comparison & number comparison. Each part consists of 100 pairs that the subject must identify as identical or dissimilar. Screens entry-level positions such as typists, clerks, etc.
Minnesota Paper Form Board-Revised PsychCorp/Pearson Assessments http://www.pearsonassessments.com 1970 - 1995 Adults	MY9 TP5 T4	Consists of 64 two-dimensional diagrams which assess spatial perception & mechanical-spatial ability as they relate to artistic & mechanical aptitudes. Aids in employee selection for occupations such as drafting, engineering, & electrical work.
Minnesota Rate of Manipulation Test (MRMT) American Guidance Service/Pearson http://ags.pearsonassessments.com 1931 - 1969 Grade 7 to Adults	MY6 MY7 TP5 T4	Measures arm-hand dexterity using a form board with 60 round holes & 60 cylinders that fit into the holes. Consists of 5 different manipulative activities: placing, turning, displacing, one-hand turning, & two-hand turning. Also provides norms & instructions for the blind.
Minnesota Spatial Relations Test (MSRT) American Guidance Service/Pearson http://ags.pearsonassessments.com 1930 - 1979 Grade 10 to Adults	MY9 TP5 T4	Assesses spatial visualization ability & the ability to manipulate three-dimensional objects. This timed test consists of the transfer of blocks from one board to their proper place in the connected board as quickly as possible.
Musical Aptitude Profile The Riverside Publishing Co. http://www.riverpub.com 1965 - 1995 Grades 4 - 12	MY12 MY16 TP7 TP5	Measures an individual's musical aptitude. Assesses 3 basic factors: tonal, rhythmic, & expressive/aesthetic. Yields 11 scores such as: melody, harmony, tempo, meter, balance, & style. Directions & testing items are administered orally.
O'Conner Finger Dexterity Test Lafayette Instrument Company http://www.lafayetteinstrument.com 1920 - 1926 Age 14 to Adults	MY6 T3	Measures motor coordination, & finger & manual dexterity. Consists of plate containing 100 holes arranged in 10 rows. Subject's task is to insert small metal pins, in groups of three, as rapidly as possible.
O'Conner Tweezer Dexterity Test Lafayette Instrument Company http://www.lafayetteinstrument.com 1920 - 1928 Age 14 to Adults	MY6 T3	Measures motor coordination, & finger & manual dexterity. Consists of plate containing 100 holes arranged in 10 rows. Subject's task is to insert small metal pins, one by one, into each of the holes, using metal tweezers.
Office Skills Test Vangent, Inc. http://www.vangent-hcm.com 1977 - 1984 Entry Level Applicants in the Business Field	MY9 TP7 TP5 T4	Measures clerical ability of entry level job applicants via 12 subtests: checking, coding, filing, form completion, grammar, numerical, oral directional, punctuation, reading comprehension, spelling, typing, & vocabulary.

A Counselor's Guide To Career Assessments Instruments

Name of Test/Publisher/Date/Population	Reference(s)	Brief Description
Pennsylvania Bi-Manual Worksample American Guidance Service http://ags.pearsonassessments.com 1943 - 1945 Age 16 to 39	T4	Measures manual dexterity & eye-hand coordination in two parts: Assembly— requires manually assembling bolts & nuts, & then placing them in a hole in the board. Disassembly— requires removing the assemblies from the hole, taking them apart, & returning the parts to their bins.
Perceptual Speed Vangent, Inc. http://www.vangent-hcm.com 1987 Adults	T4 TP7 MY15	Measures the ability to quickly identify similarities & differences in visual configuration. This 5-minute timed test can be used to aid in selecting personnel for occupations requiring rapid perception of inaccuracies in written material, numbers, or diagrams.
Pictorial Reasoning Test (PRT) Vangent, Inc. http://www.vangent-hcm.com 1967 - 1973 Age 14 to Adults	T4	Provides a general measure of the learning potential of individuals from diverse backgrounds with reading difficulties. Helpful in identifying an individual's potential for training & employment.
Purdue Pegboard Vangent, Inc. http://www.vangent-hcm.com 1941 - 1992 Grade 9 to Adults	TP5 TP7 T4	Measures gross movement of hands, fingers, & arms, & tip of finger dexterity. Consists of pegboard containing 2 rows of 25 holes into which pins are inserted individually with the right hand, left hand, & both hands.
Short Employment Tests (SET) PsychCorp/Pearson Assessments http://www.pearsonassessments.com 1972 - 1993 Adults	MY13 T4 TP5 TP7	Measures verbal, numerical, & clerical aptitudes via 3 tasks: recognize synonyms, perform arithmetic computations, & locate proper names in an alphabetical list & assign codes to the amount associated with each name.
Short Tests of Clerical Ability (STCA) Vangent, Inc. http://www.vangent-hcm.com 1959 - 1997 Applicants for Office Positions	MY8 MY13 TP5 TP7 T4	Measures 7 clerical aptitudes & abilities: arithmetic, business vocabulary, checking, coding, directions- oral & written, filing, & language. Useful for selection & placement in various office jobs such as: secretary, stenographer, office clerk, etc.
Space Relations (Paper Puzzles) Vangent, Inc. http://www.vangent-hcm.com 1984 Adults	MY15 TP7 T4	Identifies individuals with mechanical ability & experience. Consists of 30 items that measure an individual's ability to visually select a combination of flat pieces which fit together to cover a given two-dimensional space.
Space Thinking (Flags) Vangent, Inc. http://www.vangent-hcm.com 1959 - 1984 Adults	TP5 TP7 T4	Measures the ability to visualize a rigid configuration when it is moved into different positions. This 5-minute timed test may be used to aid in identifying individuals with mechanical interest & ability.
Stromberg Dexterity Test (SDT) Pearson Assessments http://www.pearsonassessments.com 1945 - 1981 Adults	MY4 TP5 TP7 T4	Aids in choosing workers for jobs requiring speed & accuracy of arm & hand movement. Test consists of 54 red, blue, & yellow discs & a durable board containing 54 holes on one side. Subject is timed sorting discs by color, & placing them in the holes.
Technology and Internet Assessment H & H Publishing Company http://www.hhpublishing.com 1999 Middle School to Adult	TP7	Assesses an individuals strengths & weaknesses in basic computer knowledge, the Internet, & information technology skills. Scores yielded in 8 areas such as: use of computer, specific computer skills, basic Internet knowledge, & ethics of technology. Administered & scored via the Internet.
Test of Mechanical Concepts Vangent, Inc. http://www.vangent-hcm.com 1976 - 1986 Grade 8 to Adults	MY8 T4	Measures an individual's ability to visualize & comprehend basic mechanical & spatial interrelationships. Reports 4 scores: mechanical interrelationships, mechanical tools & devices, spatial relations, & total.
Valpar 300 Series Dexterity Modules (VDM) Valpar International http://www.valparint.com 1995 Age 15 to Adults		Measures motor coordination, & manual & finger dexterity. Five modules are currently available: Small Parts Assembly, Asymmetric Pin Placement, Tool Manipulation, Bi-Manual Coordination, & Angled Pin Placement. Modules are criterion referenced to DOL standards.
Wiesen Test of Mechanical Aptitude (WTMA) Psychological Assessment Resources http://www3.parinc.com 1999 Age 18 to Adult	MY14 TP7	Assesses mechanical aptitude. Consists of simple drawings that cover broad mechanical/physical concepts such as: basic machines, movement, gravity/center of gravity, basic electricity/electronics, transfer of heat, & basic physical properties. Individual or group administration.

Additional Career Assessment Instruments

C. INTEREST INSTRUMENTS

Name of Test/Publisher/Date/Population	Reference(s)	Brief Description
Business Career Interest Inventory Peregrine Partners 1330 Beacon Street, Suite 265 Brookline, MA 02446 1998-2010 Adults	CG5	Assesses the user's interests, abilities, and motivations, and then recommends specific business careers.
Career Assessment Battery Piney Mountain Press http://www.pineymountain.com 2005 High School to Adults		40-minute live-action video and multimedia format. The participants see and hear live-action occupational situations and make choices based on the Department of Labor's worker trait groups. Scoring can be by computer, batch, or publisher.
Career Assessment Inventory (CAI) Pearson Assessments http://www.pearsonassessments.com 1986 High School to Adults	CG4 MY8 MY10 T3	Measures one's occupational interests for use in career exploration and career decision making. The Enhanced Version provides a mixture of occupations that require various amounts of postsecondary education. The Vocational Version focuses on occupations requiring 0-2 years of postsecondary education.
Career Compass http://www.careervoyages.gov/careercompass-main.cfm 1988 - 1996 Junior High School to High School		Covers general career clusters, major work groups, & specific occupations based on student responses to 70 work activity questions. Program printouts provide a career interest profile, additional information, & a listing of related sample occupations for top 3 interest clusters.
Career Exploration Inventory JIST Publishing 8902 Otis Avenue Indianapolis, IN 46216 http://www.jist.com 2006 Junior High School to Adults	CG5 MY13	Helps individuals explore and plan three major areas of their lives- work, leisure activities, and learning. It asks users to reflect on 128 activities and consider their past, present, and future interest in them.
Career Exploration Series CFKR Career Materials P.O. Box 99 Meadow Vista, CA 05722-0099 800.525.5626 Adolescents to Adults	MY9 MY11 MY13	Designed for career guidance using a series of six job interest inventories that focus on specific occupational fields.
Career Guidance Inventory Wintergreen/Orchard House, Inc. 2 LAN Drive, Suite 100 Westford, MA 01886 1998-2010 Junior High School to Adults	MY8 MY9 MY11	Provides measures of relative interest in postsecondary instructional programs.
Chronicle Career Quest Chronicle Guidance Publications, Inc. http://www.chronicleguidance.com 1991-1993 Middle School to Adult	CG4	A group-administered career guidance instrument that includes three components: an *Interest Inventory,* a self-scoring *Interpretation Guide,* and a *Career Paths* occupational profile. For the interest inventory, Form S (short form) totals 108 items, while Form L (long form) includes 144 items both are scored across 12 interest areas based on U.S. Employment Service *Guide for Occupational Exploration.*
COIN Career Targets COIN Educational Products http://www.coinedu.com 1990 - 1993 Middle School to High School		Provides assessment, career exploration, & individual career plans. Includes: a self-scored, self-administered inventory linking students' interests to 14 career clusters, an exploration of the world of work, & activities that emphasize the importance of education & the development of a high school plan.
COIN Educational Inventory COIN Educational Products http://www.coinedu.com 1994 Grades 11 and 12		Provides an interest assessment to be used in post-secondary educational planning. Consists of 4 parts: Assessing Interests, Exploring Personal Interests & Post-Secondary Education & Training, Selecting Post-Secondary Training, and Choosing a Post-Secondary School.

A Counselor's Guide To Career Assessments Instruments

Name of Test/Publisher/Date/Population	Reference(s)	Brief Description
College Major Interest Inventory Consulting Psychologists Press, Inc. 3803 East Bayshore Road Palo Alto, CA 94303 800.624.1765 knw@cpp-db.com http://www.cpp-db.com High School and College Students	MY12	Identifies the academic majors that best match a student's pattern of interests.
Curtis Interest Scale York University Psychology Resource Center http://psycentre.apps01.yorku.ca/drpl/ High School to Adults	MY6	Provides a series of tasks, identified with various major occupational fields, to be rated or ranked in order of interest or preference, as a means of providing insight into the vocational interest pattern of individuals.
Education Interest Inventory-Revised (EII) Statistics Solutions 2627 McCormick Drive Suite 102 Clearwater, FL 33759 877.437.8622 http://www.statisticssolutions.com High School and College Students		Identifies an individual's preferences for college educational programs.
Explore the World of Work (E-WOW) CFKR Career Materials, Inc. http://www.cfkr.com 1989 - 1991 Adults	TP5 TP7 T3	Designed as a quick assessment using 36 graphics: 24 work activities & 12 work values. Developed for adult retraining & reentry programs. This instrument is a pictorial form of JOB-O to accommodate low reading levels. Available in Spanish.
Gordon Occupational Checklist II PsychCorp/Pearson Assessments 800.627.7271 http://www.pearsonassessments.com 1980 Adults		Designed for use with nonprofessionally oriented individuals that helps the counselor and client gain insight to careers matching the client's interest.
Guide for Occupational Exploration Inventory II (GOE) JIST Works, Inc. http://www.jist.com 1996 Grade 6 to Adults	T4 TP7	Explores career, education, & lifestyle options. Yields a graphic interest profile with 7 factors such as: leisure, home, & education/school. Eighth grade reading level. Cross-referenced to standard occupational information sources. Map with GOE information provided. Group or individually administered.
Guilford-Zimmerman Interest Inventory Consulting Psychologists Press, Inc. 1055 Joaquin Road 2nd Floor Mountain View, CA 94043 800.624.1765 custserve@cpp.com http://www.cpp.com High School to Adults	MY12	150-item measure of interests corresponding with Holland codes; nonprojective test.
High School Career-Course Planner CFKR Career Materials, Inc. http://www.cfkr.com 1983 - 1990 Adolescents	MY12 TP5 TP7 T3	Used to evaluate career interest & develop a course plan that is consistent with self-assessed career goals. Measures interests in 6 occupational areas: working with tools, working with people, creating new things, solving problems, & doing physical work.
Interest Explorer Riverside Publishing http://www.riverpub.com 1998 Middle School to Adults	CG4	Helps students and adults make educational and career-planning decisions about their futures. It provides information about students' interests in 14 career areas that are linked to publications of the Department of Labor.
Interest Determination, Exploration and Assessment System (IDEAS) Pearson Assessments http://www.pearsonassessments.com 1977-2000 Middle School to Adults	CG4 MY9	Designed as an introduction to career planning. It provides scores on 16 basic interest scales that help students and adults identify and explore occupational areas of interest.
Judgment of Occupational Behavior-Orientation 2000 + (JOB-O 2000) CFKR Career Materials http://www.cfkr.com 1978 - 1999 Grade 4 to Adults	CG1 MY9 MY10 MY12 TP5	Uses a 9-item questionnaire to yield 9 scores: education, interest, inclusion, control, affection, physical activity, hands/tool/machinery, problem solving, and creating ideas. Scores are compared to 120 job titles. Designed to emphasize job awareness and promote job exploration. Three versions: grades 4-6, 7-10, and 10-adult.

519

Additional Career Assessment Instruments

Name of Test/Publisher/Date/Population	Reference(s)	Brief Description
Leisure/Work Search Inventory JIST Publishing 875 Montreal Way St. Paul, MN 55102 800.328.1452 http://jist.emcp.com/ educate@emcp.com 1994 Adults	MY13	Links an individual's leisure activities to work and employment opportunities. Using 5 point scales, test takers rate their degree of interest in 96 leisure activity statements.
Occupational Interest Profile (OIP) Beilby http://www.beilby.com.au/ 2006 Adults		Assesses an individual's personal preferences for varying types of work based on the following categories; artistic, practical, scientific, administrative, caring, logical, and persuasive.
Pictorial Inventory of Careers (PIC) Talent Assessment, INC http://www.talentassessment.com/ 2006 Middle to High School		Students respond to live-action video segments of real work situations. By rating each segment, students determine what career/vocational area they like best. Assessment results identify areas of strong interest, dislikes, and areas which they have little or no knowledge.
School-to-Work Career Survey Piney Mountain Press http://www.pineymountain.com/ 2005 Middle to High School		Assists students in identifying career options in 5 career pathways: Art & Humanities, Agricultural & Environmental, Business & Marketing, Health & Human Services, & Engineering & Industrial. Consists of a 75-item survey delivered via a video, worksheets, or on a computer.
UNIACT IV ACT, Inc 2201 N. Dodge Street P.O. Box 168 Iowa City, IA 52243-0168 319.337.1000 http://www.act.org 1973 - 1984 High School to Young Adults	MY9 TC:1	A unisex interest inventory designed to eliminate sex-role stereotyping. A component of the ACT Career Planning Program & the Discover computer-based guidance system. Students respond to 90 activities grouped into 6 areas: science, creative arts, social service, business contact, business detail, & technical.
USES Interest Inventory U.S. Dept. of Labor, Employment and Training Administration http://www.doleta.gov 1981		Identifies client interests in relation to the Guide to Occupational Exploration (GOE) interest areas.
Values Scale (VS) Consulting Psychologists Press, Inc. http://www.cpp.com/ 1986 8th grade reading level and higher	CG4 MY10 T4	Helps people achieve career goals by identifying important extrinsic and intrinsic values. A self-report inventory of 106 scored items yielding 21 separate scales for the individual assessment of upper elementary school and middle school students as well as adult members of semi-skilled, skilled, clerical, managerial, and professional occupations.
Vocational Interest Exploration System (VIE) McCarron-Dial Systems http://mccarrondial.com 1991 Age 14 to Adults	T4	Computer-assisted interest assessment program designed to assess an individual's preferences for type of work & working conditions. Yields scores in 3 areas: selection of jobs based on work preferences, occupational exploration, & job review comparison. Individual administration.
Vocational Interest Inventory and Exploration Survey (VOC-TIES) Piney Mountain Press http://www.pineymountain.com 1994 Age 13 to Adults	MY12 T5	Designed for 3 major purposes: "to enable students to discover what vocational training entails; to determine student's vocational preferences; and to promote the concept of career equity by showing students in nontraditional roles." A non-reading test that presents 15 training programs by video. A selection of short-term career objectives is provided.
Work Exploration Checklist Finney Company http://www.finney-hobar.com 1993 - 2000 Grade 7 to Adult		Assesses an individual's interests in past, present, & future activities. Consists of a 4-page checklist yielding results in GOE codes & RIASEC themes. An electronic version is also available as part of the Occupational Guidance CD-Rom.

A COUNSELOR'S GUIDE TO CAREER ASSESSMENTS INSTRUMENTS

D. MEASURES OF WORK VALUES, SATISFACTION, AND ENVIRONMENTS

Name of Test/Publisher/Date/Population	Reference(s)	Brief Description
Campbell Organizational Survey (COS) Vangent http://www.vangent-hcm.com 1988 - 1994 Adults	MY12 TP5 T4	Assesses individual's attitudes about aspects of work. Provides scores on 17 scales such as: supervision, benefits, job security, and an index of overall satisfaction within the organization. Scores provided in individual profile report with charts and graphs. May be taken online via the Internet.
Career Anchors: Discovering Your Real Values Jossey-Bass Pfeiffer and Company, International http://www.pfeiffer.com 1990 Adults	MY13 TP5 T4	Identifies career anchors, uncovers real values to help make better career choices. Yields 8 scores, such as: technical/functional competence, general managerial competence, service/dedication to a cause, pure challenge, & lifestyle. Includes orientation & career anchor interviews. Group administered.
Career Values Scale Psychometrics Canada Ltd. 7125 77 Avenue Edmonton AB T6B 0B5 Canada 800.661.5158 info@psychometrics.com 1987-2002 Adults		Measures the values that influence career choice. It identifies ten core values that are helpful for career planning and development. It is useful for career development, individual coaching, and evaluating the fit between values and organizational culture
Fleishman Job Analysis Survey (F-JAS) Management Research Institute, Inc. http://www.managementresearchinstitute.com 1992 - 1996 Adults	TP5	A 74-item questionnaire used to determine ability requirements of jobs. Users respond to statements on a 7-point Likert-scale. Covers the full range of human abilities such as: cognitive, psychomotor, etc. Self-scored.
Individual Style Survey (ISS) Psychometrics Canada Ltd. http://www.psychometrics.com 1989 - 1990 Grade 9 to Adults	MY13 TP5	Provides a structured activity for self & interpersonal development, with an emphasis on the unique way in which individuals respond to events & people in the environment. Includes a self-perception form & 3 forms to give to others to assess the user's style.
Job Descriptive Index (JDI) Bowling Green State University http://showcase.bgsu.edu/IOPsych/jdi/index.html 1969 - 1997 Adults	MY12 TC9 TP5 T4	Provides an assessment of job satisfaction in any occupational field. Measures the following 5 components of satisfaction: work on present job, present pay, opportunities for promotion, supervision on present job, & people on present job.
Minnesota Importance Questionnaire (MIQ) Vocational Psychology Research http://www.psych.umn.edu/psylabs/vpr 1967 - 1981 Age 16 to Adults	CG1,2,3 MY11 TC2 TP5	Measures 20 psychological needs (and their 21 underlying values) found relevant to work satisfaction. Scores yielded include: ability utilization, achievement, recognition, supervision-technical, variety, altruism, & autonomy. Can be used with the MSQ. Part of Minnesota Work Adjustment Project.
Job Style Indicator (JSI) Consulting Resource Group International http://www.crgleader.com 1988 - 1993 Adults	MY13 TP5 T4	Contains 16 items which compare perceptions of a particular job with an individual's personal style. Reveals the preferred work style of a specific job & is useful in exploring the person-job match. Designed to complement the Personal Style Indicator.
Minnesota Satisfaction Questionnaire (MSQ) Vocational Psychology Research http://www.psych.umn.edu/psylabs/vpr 1963 - 1977 Age 16 to Adults	CG3 MY9 TC5	Measures an employee's satisfaction with his/her job. Long form consists of 100 items; short form consists of 20 items. Scores yielded on 20 scales such as: authority, company policy, social service, & human relations. Can be used with the MIQ. Part of Minnesota Work Adjustment Project.
Minnesota Job Description Questionnaire (MJDQ) Vocational Psychology Research http://www.psych.umn.edu/psylabs/vpr 1967 - 1968 Adults	MY8 TC6 TP5 T3	Measures the working environment in terms of a profile of need-satisfaction characteristics. Aids in the person-job match of jobs along 21 reinforcer dimensions such as variety, creativity, security, recognition, authority, independence, etc.
Position Analysis Questionnaire (PAQ) PAQ Services http://www.paq.com 1969 - 1992 Adults	MY12 TC5 TP5 T4	Contains 189 job elements sampling what employees do to get their jobs done. Focus is on 6 behavioral areas: information input, mediation processes, work output, interpersonal activities, work situation & job context, & miscellaneous aspects.
Position Classification Inventory (PCI) Psychological Assessment Resource http://www3.parinc.com 1991 Adults	T4	Uses Holland Codes to classify positions/occupations to assess person-job fit. Employees & supervisors complete an inventory which describes demands & skills required in a job by rating items on a 3-point scale. Both scores are compared to aid in determination of job fit.

Additional Career Assessment Instruments

Name of Test/Publisher/Date/Population	Reference(s)	Brief Description
Salience Inventory (SI) Vocopher: The Online Career Collaboratory http://www.vocopher.com 1985 - 1987 Grade 6 to Adults	CG3 MY11 TP5	Designed "to assess the relative importance of the work role in the context of other life roles." Consists of 170 items divided into 3 scales: commitment, partipation, & value expectation. Five major life roles are assessed under each of the 3 scales: homemaker, worker, student, citizen, & leisurite.
Rokeach Value Survey Consulting Psychologists Press (CPP) http://www.cpp.com/ 1967 - 1983 Age 11 to Adults	MY12 TP5 TC1 T3	A self-scoring survey which contains items related to life-style & behavioral values. Uses a list of 18 terminal values & 18 instrumental values to aid in the determination of value priorities & assist in making life choices. A value's score is its rank.
Survey of Interpersonal Values (SIV) Vangent http://www.vangent-hcm.com 1960 - 1993 Adolescents to Adults	TC2 TP5 T4	Measures 6 values involving relationships between people: support, conformity, recognition, independence, benevolence, & leadership. The 90 items are arranged in sets of 3, with each item ranked from "most" to "least" important.
Survey of Work Values Bowling Green State University http://showcase.bgsu.edu/IOPsych/jdi/measures.html 1975 - 1976 Employees	MY12 TP5 T4	Identifies individual's attitudes towards work. Consists of 54 items yielding scores in 6 areas: social status, activity preference, upward striving, attitude toward earnings, pride in work, & job involvement. Individual or group administration.
Values Preference Indicator (VPI) Consulting Resource Group International http://www.crgleader.com 1990 Adults	TP5 T4	Assesses personal value preferences. Consists of 3 parts: Identifying Key Values, Prioritizing Your Values, & Time Test. Yields 21 scores in areas, such as: accomplishment, acknowledgement, challenge, friendship, organization, expertise, & tranquility. Individual or group administration.
Work Environment Scale (WES) Consulting Psychologist Press (CPP) http://www.cpp.com 1974 - 1989 Employees and Supervisors	MY12 TP5 T4	Assesses the social climate of various work settings. Consists of 90 items yielding scores on 10 scales including: involvement, supervisor support, peer cohesion, autonomy, task orientation, work pressure, clarity, control, physical comfort, & innovation. Individual or group administration.
Workmate Piney Mountain Press http://www.pineymountain.com 1998 6th Grade to Adults		Designed to identify & examine work-related values, attitudes, and temperaments. Graphical printouts generated for 15 job-related areas such as: risking, competing, helping, persuading, receiving recognition, working with others, physical, & routine. Group or individual administration.
Survey of Personal Values (SPV) Vangent http://www.vangent-hcm.com 1964 - 1997 Grade 10 to Adults	MY10 TC2 TP5 T4	Measures 6 values: practical mindedness, achievement, variety, decisiveness, orderliness, & goal orientation. This self-report consists of 90 items. Each item contains 3 of the 6 values which are ranked by selecting "most" or "least" important.
Work Motivation Inventory (WMI) Teleometrics International http://www.teleometrics.com 1967 - 1973 Adults	MY8 TP5 T4	Yields 5 work maturation scores: basic creature comfort, safety & order, belonging & affiliation, ego-status, actualization, & self-expression. Separate measures are designed for managers & employees. Self or group administered.

E. CARD SORTS

Name of Test/Publisher/Date/Population	Reference(s)	Brief Description
Deal-Me-In http://www.careersystemsintl.com/dealmin.htm Career Systems 1985 - 1992 High School to Adults	CG3	A deck of 52 color-coded playing cards divided into suits that correspond to 4 interest categories: people, data, things, ideas. Can be used with a companion guide *(It's in the Cards)* that covers 22 job situations in 4 work areas: job search, job orientation, performance & reputation, & enrichment & enhancement.
Knowdell Leisure & Retirement Activities Card Sort CareerTrainer http://www.careertrainer.com/ 1992 - 1994 Retired Adults or Adults Planning to Retire	MY13 TP5 TP7	Assesses adults in planning retirement & understanding the process of change. Consists of 48 common pastimes such as: meditation, cultural events, group leadership, & entertaining. Cards are organized & classified to help individuals determine personal criteria related to retirement.
Kolb Learning Skills Profile (LSP) Hay Group – Hay Resources Direct http://www.haygroup.com/ 1993 Junior High to Adults	MY13 TP7 TP5	Measures skills critical to job performance. Assesses the following skill groups: interpersonal, information, analytical, & behavioral. The participant uses one or both decks of cards to rate his/her skills or the skill demands of his/her job. Self-administered. Learning Agenda worksheet is provided.

A COUNSELOR'S GUIDE TO CAREER ASSESSMENTS INSTRUMENTS

Name of Test/Publisher/Date/Population	Reference(s)	Brief Description
Missouri Occupational Card Sort (MOCS) University of Missouri Career Center http://career.missouri.edu/generalinfo/ 1982 Grade 11 to Adults	CG3 MG:10/81	An interest card sort designed to broaden knowledge of self & of specific occupations. Encourages further self & career exploration by increasing the number of occupations under consideration. Contains 90 occupations divided equally into the six Holland types.

F. CAREER DEVELOPMENT/MATURITY MEASURES

Name of Test/Publisher/Date/Population	Reference(s)	Brief Description
Career Action Inventory Career Systems http://www.careersystemsintl.com 1988 Adults		A 75-question self-assessment inventory to determine what an individual is doing now about career planning & professional development. Includes a comprehensive discussion of inventory results & offers specific ideas for taking action to improve chances for success.
Career Attitudes and Strategies Inventory (CASI) Psychological Assessment Resources 16204 N. Florida Avenue Lutz, FL 33549 custserv@parinc.com http://www3.parinc.com 1994 Adults	CG5 MY13	Helps to identify and clarify career problems and stimulates constructive discussion of these areas.
Career Beliefs Inventory (CBI) Consulting Psychologists Press, Inc. http://www.cpp.com 1991 8th Grade Reading Level and Older	CG4 MY12	Helps people identify career beliefs that may be preventing them from achieving their career goals. The BCI can help counselors initiate explorations of the career assumptions on which their clients operate.
Career Decision Scale (CDS) Psychological Assessment Resources http://www3.parinc.com 1976 - 1987 High School to Adults	CG2 CG3 MY9 TP5 TP7 T4	Provides estimates about students status in the career-decision making process; also used to judge the effectiveness of career development interventions. Consists of 19 items, yielding percentile scores on certainty & indecision scales. Hand scored.
Career Decision Profile Lawrence K. Jones CareerKey eBookStore http://www.careerkey.org Adults		16-item inventory designed to measure "career decision status." It assesses how decided individuals are about their career choice; how comfortable they are about it; and their reasons for being undecided.
Career Leverage Inventory Career Systems http://www.careersystemsintl.com 1983 - 1994 Adults		A 35-question survey designed to help employees identify & assess their realistic career options. Provides new ways to think about career growth, how to prioritize & set career goals, & how to build back-up plans so individuals always have options.
Career Maturity Inventory (CMI) http://www.vocopher.com 1995 Middle School to Adult	CG4	Career readiness assessment that measures attitudes and competencies necessary for youth and adults to make effective career decisions.
COIN Clue COIN Educational Products http://www.coinedu.com/ 1996 Grades 5 and 6		Provides activities in career exploration, assessment, and planning. Content includes activities to answer questions, such as: What is work?, Why is work important?, and How do I get the work I want? Jobs are grouped into 7 categories, including: Designers & Builders, Helpers & Healers, and Transportation.
Dole Vocational Sentence Completion Blank Arthur A. Dole	MY9	Semi-projective instrument which consists of 21 incomplete sentence stems. Responses are scored by assigning them to one or more of 29 standard categories. The category into which the most frequent number of responses is assigned is considered to be a reflection of the topic of most concern to the subject.
Employability Maturity Interview (EMI) National Center on Employment & Disability P.O. Box 1358 Hot Springs, AR 71902 http://www.ncdet.org	MY11	Assesses readiness for the vocational rehabilitation planning process.

Additional Career Assessment Instruments

G. PERSONALITY MEASURES

Name of Test/Publisher/Date/Population	Reference(s)	Brief Description
Adult Personality Inventory (API) Institute for Personality and Ability Testing (IPAT) http://www.IPAT.com 1982 - 1996 Age 16 to Adults	MY12 MY14 TC6 TP5 TP7 T4	Assesses individual differences in personality, interpersonal style, & career/life-style preferences. Consists of 324 items that measures 21 scales. The self-report inventory is computer scored. Designed for employee selection, counseling, & personal development programs.
Applicant Review IntegriView, LLC http://www.integriview.com 1983 - 1996 Job Applicants		Measures honesty & emotional stability. Consists of 102 items with 7 subscales, such as: personal honesty, honesty of others, punishment, past behavior, & moral reasoning. Scores are combined to form an honesty score. There are built in controls for faking & social-desirability response bias.
Comprehensive Personality Profile (CPP) Wonderlic, Inc. http://www.wonderlic.com 1996 Employers and human resource personnel	CG4 T4	Helps organizations effectively match candidates whose personality characteristics are most compatible with the demands of the job.
Edward Personal Preference Schedule (EPPS) PsychCorp/Pearson Assessments 800.627.7271 http://www.pearsonassessments.com clinicalcustomersupport@pearson.com 1970 Adults		Forced choice, objective, non-projective personality inventory, derived from the theory of H. A. Murray, which measures the rating of individuals in 15 normal needs or motives.
Employee Reliability Inventory (ERI) Bay State Psychological Associates, Inc. http://www.eri.com 1986 - 1998 Adults and Job Applicants	MY12 TP5 TP7 T4	Assesses various dimensions of pre-employment reliability and work behavior. Consists of 81 true-false items assessing behavior in 7 areas such as: freedom from disruptive alcohol & substance abuse, emotional maturity, long term job commitment, & safe job performance. Available in Braille and 5 languages.
Forer Vocational Survey Western Psychological Services 625 Alaska Ave. Torrance, CA 90503-5124 800.648.8857 http://www.wpspublish.com customerservice@wpspublish.com 1957 Adults		Incomplete sentences approach to the evaluation of personality as revealed by vocational pressures.
Fundamental Interpersonal Relations Orientation-Behavior (Firo-B) Consulting Psychologists Press (CPP) http://www.cpp.com/ 1967 - 1996 High School to Adults	MY9 MY15 T4	Measures interpersonal dynamics for building productive professional relationships & enhancing productivity & career potential. Based on a model that identifies 3 interpersonal expressed & wanted needs: inclusion, control, & affection.
Gordon Personal Profile-Inventory (GPP-I) Harcourt Assessment http://harcourtassessment.com 1951 - 1998 Grade 10 to Adults	MY13 TP7 TC2 TP5 T4	Combines 2 measures to assess 8 aspects of personality. The profile examines ascendancy, responsibility, emotional stability & sociability to yield a measure of self-esteem. Assesses cautiousness, original thinking, personal relations, & vigor.
Guilford-Zimmerman Temperament Survey (GZTS) (GZTS) Pearson Assessments http://www.pearsonassessments.com 1949 - 1978 Age 16 to Adults	MY9 TC8 TP5 T4	Identifies strengths & weaknesses associated with personality & temperament. The 10 traits measured are: activity, restraint, ascendancy, sociability, emotional stability, objectivity, friendliness, thoughtfulness, personal relations, & masculinity/femininity. A computer-generated report is also available.
Insight Inventory Insight Institute http://www.insightinstitute.com/insight-inventory.html 1990 - 1995 Ages 16 to Adults	MY13 MY14 TP5 TP7	Measures the ways a person uses his/her individual personality. Measures 4 personality styles: getting one's way (direct or indirect), responding to people (outgoing or reserved), pacing activity (urgent or steady), & dealing with details (unstructured or precise). Describes behavior at home & at work.

A COUNSELOR'S GUIDE TO CAREER ASSESSMENTS INSTRUMENTS

Name of Test/Publisher/Date/Population	Reference(s)	Brief Description
Job Choice Decision-Making Exercise Assessment Enterprises 925 Hayslope Drive Knoxville, TN 37919 865.690.4498 MSTAHL@UTK.EDU Adults	MY11	Serves as a behavioral decision-theory measurement approach to need for affiliation, need for power, and need for achievement.
Keirsey Character Sorter Prometheus Nemesis Book Company 1978 – 1997 Adults	TP7	Assesses temperaments. Consists of 36 items yielding scores as 2 letter MBTI type codes: Guardian (SJ), Artisan (SP), Idealist (NF) & Rational (NT). Each code is described & examples are given. Used with the book, *Please Understand Me*. Only available online.
Keirsey Temperament Sorter II Prometheus Nemesis Book Company 1978 – 1997 Adults		Assesses temperaments. Consists of 70 items similar to the MBTI form of questions (more indirect) & yields 16 four letter codes such as: ESTI, ENFJ, & ENTP. Used with the book, *Please Understand Me*. Available in 5 languages. Can be completed on line.
Learning Style Profile National Association of Secondary School Principals 1904 Association Drive Reston, VA 20191-1537 703.860.0200 nassp@nassp.org http://www.nassp.org Junior High and High School Students	MY12	Evaluates student learning style as the basis for student advisement and placement, instructional strategy, and the evaluation of learning.
Meyer-Kendall Assessment Survey Western Psychological Services 12031 Wilshire Blvd. Los Angeles, CA 90025-1251 310.478.2061 http://www.wpspublish.com. 1986-1991 Adults	MY12	Constructed to assess work-related personality style.
Occupational Personality Questionnaire (OPQ32) Saville & Holdsworth, Ltd http://www.shl.com/shl/en-int 1984 - 1990 Adults	MY11 TP5 TP7	Measures personality & motivational characteristics relevant to the world of work. OPQ32 explores 32 personality characteristics in multiple dimensions. Available in 28 languages.
Occupational Stress Inventory – Revised (OSI-R) Sigma Assessment Systems http://www.sigmaassessmentsystems.com Adults	CG3 MY11 MY14 TP5 TP7 T4	Measures occupational adjustment. Consists of 3 questionnaires: Oc-cupational Roles, Personal Strain, & Personal Resources. Raw scores & standard scores are provided for 14 scales. Administration available online.
Personal Audit Pearson Performance Solutions One North Dearborn, Suite 1600 Chicago, IL 60602 1941-1992 Adults	MY3 MY4	Assess individual personality characteristics of Seriousness, Firmness, Frankness, Tranquility, Stability, Tolerance, Steadiness, Persistence, and Contentment.
Personality Research Form (PRF) Sigma Assessment Systems http://www.sigmaassessmentsystems.com 1965 - 1996 Age 11 to Adults	CG3 TP5 TP7 MY10 T4	Measures personality within a normal range. Forms AA & BB consist of 440 items yielding scores on 22 scales; Forms A & B consist of 300 items yielding scores on 15 scales. Scores reported as standard *(T)* scores. Also available in French & Spanish. Hand or machine scored.
Personal Skills Map Chronicle Guidance Publications, Inc. 66 Aurora Street Moravia, NY 13118-3569 800.622.7284 CustomerService@ChronicleGuidance.com http://www.ChronicleGuidance.com Adolescents to Adults	MY13	Offers a means for the self-assessment of personal skills.
Sales Attitude Checklist Vangent, Inc. Creative Organizational Design http://www.creativeorgdesign.com/ 1960 - 1992 Individuals Interested in Sales Positions	MY9 TP5 TP7 T4	Assesses sales attitudes & habits via 31 self-descriptive forced-choice items. Specifically intended for use in identifying potentially successful salespeople.

Additional Career Assessment Instruments

Name of Test/Publisher/Date/Population	Reference(s)	Brief Description
Self-Motivated Career Planning Verne Walter and Melvin Wallace Institute for Personality and Ability Testing 1801 Woodfield Drive Savoy, IL 61874 800.225.4728 http://www.ipat.com 1984 High School Students to Adults		Group administered workbook designed to assist individuals to develop vocational objectives through self-administered exercises.
Singer-Loomis Inventory of Personality (SLIP) Moving Boundaries http://www.movingboundaries.com 1984 - 1996 Grade 9 to Adults	MY9 MY10 TP5 T3	Contains 15 situations, each followed by 8 items which the individual responds to using a 5-point Likert scale. Describes the user's personality from a Jungian perspective by providing the individual with a description of thought patterns & how situations or problems are approached.
Sixteen Personality Factor Questionnaire (16PF) Institute for Personality and Ability Testing, Inc. http://www.IPAT.com 1967-1969 Ages 16 and Older	CG4 MY8 MY9 T4	Measures 5 global factors (extraversion, stability, receptivity, accommodating, and self-control) and 16 personality factors (warmth, reasoning, emotional stability, dominance, liveliness, rule-consciousness, social boldness, sensitivity, vigilance, abstractedness, privateness, apprehension, openness to change, self-reliance, perfectionism, and tension).
Strategic Assessment of Readiness for Training (START) H & H Publishing Co. http://www.hhpublishing.com 1994 Adults	T4 MY14	Diagnoses learning strengths & weaknesses in work settings. Consists of 56 multiple-choice items measuring: anxiety, attitude, motivation, concentration, identifying important information, knowledge acquisition strategies, monitoring learning, & time management. Computer version available.
Strength Deployment Inventory Personal Strengths Publishing http://www.personalstrengths.com 1973 - 1996 Adults	MY14 TP5 TP7	Assesses individual's ability to relate to others under two conditions: when things are going well & when there is a conflict. Scores are yielded on 7 motivational value systems such as: altruistic-nurturing, assertive-directing, & flexible-cohering. Also, yields 13 scores relating to stages of conflict.
Styles of Teamwork Inventory (STI) Teleometrics International http://www.teleometrics.com 1963 - 1995 Adults	MY8 MY11 TP5 TP7 T4	Assesses individual's attitudes & behaviors concerning work-team situations. Consists of 80 items, yielding scores in 5 areas: synergistic, compromise, win-lose, yield-lose, & lose-leave. Inventory results in an overall preferred style. Individual or group administration.
SureHire Harcourt Assessment http://harcourtassessment.com 1998 Job Applicants		Assesses the competencies necessary for individuals seeking employment in convenience stores. Yields a graphical representation of percentile scores in 4 areas: problem solving, work orientation, customer service orientation, & a composite total. Individual or group administration.
Survey of Work Styles (SWS) Sigma Assessment Systems http://www.sigmaassessmentsystems.com 1987 - 1993 Adults	MY13 TP5 TP7	A computerized personality assessment which gathers information on 4 factors (self-awareness, centeredness, perceptions, & decision making). Identifies individuals as having 1 of 8 work styles, such as: forecaster, enthusiast, organizer, precisionist, caretaker, purist, etc.
Thurstone Temperament Schedule Vangent http://www.vangent-hcm.com/Home/ 1949 - 1991 Grade 9 to Adults	MY6 TP5 TP7 TC2 T4	Consists of 120 short questions that yield temperament profile scores for 6 personality traits: active, impulsive, dominant, stable, sociable, & reflective. Hand-scored carbon insert (answers transfer to scoring key on inside of test booklet). Appraisal/selection of applicants.
Viewpoint Psychological Services Inc. (PSI) http://www.psionline.com 1997 Job Applicants	MY16 TP7	Available in 5 different instruments or combinations of instruments: Workview-4 measures conscientiousness, trustworthiness, managing work pressure & getting along with others Workview-6 measures the above plus drug & alcohol avoidance & safety orientation; Serviceview measures people-related attitudes.
Vocational Implications of Personality (VIP) Talent Assessment http://www.talentassessment.com/ 1986 Grade 7 to Adults		A computerized personality based on jung's work with personality types to help individuals distinguish between vocational and avocational interest.
Vocational Preference Inventory (VPI) Psychological Assessment Resources http://www3.parinc.com 1953 - 1985 Grade 10 to Adults	MY10 TP5 TP7 T4	Assesses an individual's personality in areas, such as: interpersonal re-lations, values, self-concept, & coping behaviors. Consists of 160 occupational titles yielding scores on 11 scales including 6 Holland types & additional scales such as: acquiescence, masculinity-femininity, status, & self-control.

A COUNSELOR'S GUIDE TO CAREER ASSESSMENTS INSTRUMENTS

H. INSTRUMENTS FOR SPECIAL POPULATIONS

Name of Test/Publisher/Date/Population	Reference(s)	Brief Description
ARC Self-Determination Scale (ARC-SDS) The Beach Center on Disability http://www.beachcenter.org/ 1995 Adolescents	CG4	A 72 item self-reporting, paper-and-pencil instrument measuring four areas: autonomy, self-regulation, psychological empowerment, and self-realization.
Barsch Learning Styles Inventory – Revised Psychtest/ M.D. Angus & Associates Limited http://www.psychtest.com 1980 - 1996 Grade 9 to Adults	MY9 TP5 TP7	Measures learning through sensory channels. Self-report instrument consisting of 24 items yielding raw scores in 4 areas: auditory, visual, tactile, & kinesthetic. Completed in 5-10 minutes. Study tips component is provided to maximize individual's learning style.
C.I.T.E. Learning Styles Inventory Piney Mountain Press http://www.pineymountain.com/ 1988-98 Age 7 to Adults	MY12 TP5 T3	Assesses 9 areas: auditory language, visual language, auditory numerical, visual numerical, auditory-visual-kinesthetic, group learner, social learner, oral expressive, & written expressive. Vocational version considers environmental & working conditions. Audiovisual presentation available.
Enderle-Seversen Transition Rating Scales (ESTRS) ESTR Publications http://www.estr.net/publications.cfm 1991 Ages 14 to 21 with a Disability	AT:98	Provides information concerning transition for individuals with disabilities. Form J for students with mild disabilities consists of 84 items. Form R for students with moderate to severe disabilities consists of 136 items. Both forms have 5 subscales such as: jobs & job training, & home living.
Learning Styles Inventory Price Systems http://www.pricesystems.com/ 1976-96 Grades 3 to 12 – Special Populations	T4	Assesses individual learning preferences in the following areas: sociological needs, immediate environment, emotionality, & physical needs. Computerized summary of results is provided with suggested strategies for instructional and environmental alternatives to individual learning situations.
Learning/Working Styles Inventory (LWSI) Piney Mountain Press, Inc. http://www.pineymountain.com/ 1994 Grade 8 to Adult, Special Populations	CG4	For teachers and students to better understand the physical, social, environmental and working conditions under which an individual prefers to learn and work. The presentations are available in video and multimedia formats in order to meet the needs of special learners.
McCarron-Dial System McCarron Dial System http://www.mccarrondial.com/ 1973 - 1986 Special Populations	CG2 CG3 MY11 TP5 TP7 T4	Provides a comprehensive assessment to be used in educational & vocational planning. Assesses 5 factors: verbal-spatial-cognitive, sensory, motor, emotional, & integration coping. Includes 7 tests such as: Peabody Picture Vocational Test-R, Behavior Rating Scale, & Emotional Behavior Checklist.
Microcomputer Evaluation of Career Areas (MECA) The Conover Company, Ltd. http://www.conovercompany.com/Index.html 1986 - 1992 Grade 7 to 12, Disadvantaged & Disabled	B:93	Designed for vocational exploration via 15 work samples containing 3 tasks each, such as: automotive, building maintenance, cosmetology, graphic design, custodial housekeeping, electronics, small engines, food service, health care, business & office, manufacturing, distribution, & computers.
Personnel Tests for Industry—Oral Directions Test (PTI-ODT) Pearson Assessments http://www.pearsonassessments.com/ 1946 - 1974 Bilingual Persons with English as a Second Language	TP5 TP7 T4	A wide-range assessment of general mental abilities & an individual's comprehension of verbal, numerical, & oral directions. English test requires 15 minutes & is hand scored. Used as a screening device for vocational trainees & industrial personnel.. May be used with persons of limited English proficiency.
Pictorial Inventory of Careers (PIC) Talent Assessment http://www.talentassessment.com/ 1992 Middle School to Adults - Special Populations	CG2 CG3	Reading free instrument designed to measure vocational interests. Consists of 119 real-life pictorials depicting vocational technical careers from 17 vocational clusters & 11 career cluster definitions. Each cluster is represented by 7 scenes emphasizing the work environment, not the individual. Hand or machine scored.
Practical Assessment Exploration System (PAES) Talent Assessment http://www.talentassessment.com/ 1991 Special Populations		A Curriculum Based Vocational Assessment Program that provides hands-on evaluation. Evaluation & transition data includes job skill, quality of performance, work rate, interests, & behavioral barriers to employment & training.
Preliminary Diagnostic Questionnaire (PDQ) West Virginia Rehabilitation Research and Training Center Barron Drive, P.O. Box 1004 Institute, WV 25112-1004 1981 Adults	MY11	Assesses the functional capacities of persons with disabilities in relation to employability.

Additional Career Assessment Instruments

Name of Test/Publisher/Date/Population	Reference(s)	Brief Description
Prevocational Assessment Screen (PAS) Piney Mountain Press http://www.pineymountain.com/ 1985 - 1994 Grades 9 to 12 - Special Populations	CG3 MY12 TP5 TP7	Assesses motor & perceptual abilities for requirements of local vocational training programs. Yields 16 time & error scores in 8 areas: alphabetizing, etch-a-sketch maze, calculating, small parts, pipe assembly, o rings, block design, & color sort. Individual administration.
Responsibility and Independence Scale for Adolescents (RISA) Riverside Publishing http://www.riverpub.com/ 1990 - 1992 Ages 12 to 20 - Special Populations	MY12 TP5 TP7 T4 AT:98	Norm-referenced instrument that measures adolescents' adaptive behavior in the areas of responsibility and independence. Consists of 9 subscales in functional areas such as: self management, social maturity, social communication, domestic skills, money management, citizenship, personal organization, transportation skills, & career skills.
Skills Assessment Module (SAM) Piney Mountain Press http://www.pineymountain.com/ 1981 - 1994 Age 13 to 18 - Special Populations	MY11 TP5 T4 B:93	Assesses general aptitude, specific work behavior, & learning styles via 3 paper/pencil tests & 12 work samples such as: mail sort, payroll, computation, patient information memo, pipe assembly, block design, small parts, color sort, circuit board, etc.
Social and Prevocational Information Battery CTB/McGraw Hill 800.538.9547 http://www.ctb.com Customer_Service_Ind@ctb.com 1975 Students with Intellectual Disabilities	MY8 MY9 MY11	Series of nine tests designed to assess knowledge of skills and competencies widely regarded as important for the ultimate community adjustment of educable mentally retarded students. The nine areas are purchasing, budgeting, banking, job-related behavior, job search skills, home management, health care, hygiene, and functional signs.
Street Survival Skills Questionnaire (SSSQ) Harcourt Assessment http://harcourtassessment.com 1979-1993 Age 9 to Adult –Special Populations	CG4	Assesses community-relevant adaptive skills in a comprehensive fashion. Specifically, it provides an objective and reliable method of assessing various aspects of adaptive behavior, a baseline behavioral measure to gauge the effects of training, and a prediction of the individual's potential for success in adapting to community living conditions and vocational placement.
Talent Assessment Program (TAP) Talent Assessment, Inc. http://www.talentassessment.com/ 1988 Middle School to Adult - Vocationally Disabled	CG3	Reading-free assessment of functional aptitudes. Consists of 10 hands-on tests, such as: Form Perception, Ability to Follow Patterns, Color Discrimination, & Tactile Discrimination. Results are compiled into a profile that can be compared with job requirements in the DOT and OOH.
Transition Behavior Scale, 2nd edition (TBS-2) Hawthorne Educational Services, Inc. http://www.hes-inc.com/hes.cgi 1991 - 1999 High School - Special Populations	MY16 TP5 TP7 T4	Assesses the readiness of an individual to enter the world of employment & independent living. Consists of 62 items, yielding scores in 3 areas: work related behavior, interpersonal relations, & social/community expectations. Manual includes IEP goals, objectives, & interventions.
Transition Planning Inventory-Updated Version (TPI-UV) PRO-ED Inc. 700 Shoal Creek Blvd Austin, TX 78757-6897 info@proedinc.com http://www.proedinc.com 2006 Age 14 to Adults	CG5 MY17	Identifies and plan for the comprehensive transitional needs of students in areas mandated by the Individuals with Disabilities Education Act of 2004.
Transition to Work Inventory Harcourt Assessment http://harcourtassessment.com 1996 Middle School to Adult	MY14	Designed to ascertain the precise job-related challenges imposed by an individual's disability, assess worker-job fit for individuals with disabilities across a diverse set of jobs, and serve as a means of determining accommodation/job redesign needs for individuals with disabilities.
Valpar Component Work Sample Series Valpar International http://www.valparint.com/ 1974 - 1993 General Population & Industrially Injured Persons	CG1	Consists of 22 work samples designed to measure broad worker traits, such as: use of small tools, vocational readiness, upper extremity range of motion, simulated assembly, etc. Yields scores & clinical observations that can be used for job training & placement & for constructing programs.
Vocational Adaptation Rating Scales (VARS) Stoelting Co. http://www.stoeltingco.com/ 1980 Mentally Retarded Persons Age 13 to Adults	MY9 TP5 T4	Uses parents', teachers', & professionals' ratings to measure maladaptive behaviors likely to hinder vocational adjustment. Provides frequency & severity scores in 17 areas such as: verbal manners, communication skill, respect for property, rules & regulations, etc.
Vocational Decision Making Interview JIST Works, Inc http://www.jist.com/shop/web 1993 Special Populations	TP5 TP7 MY14	Assesses the vocational decision-making capacities of individuals with disabilities. Consists of 54 items, yielding scores in 4 areas: decision making, readiness, employment readiness, self-appraisal, & a total. Uses an interview format that is orally administered to individuals.

A COUNSELOR'S GUIDE TO CAREER ASSESSMENTS INSTRUMENTS

Name of Test/Publisher/Date/Population	Reference(s)	Brief Description
Vocational Interest Temperament and Aptitude System (VITAS) Vocational Research Institute http://www.vri.org/ 1979 Educationally Disadvantaged	CG1 T3 B:93	Contains 21 independent work samples based on 16 Work Groups. Samples include: laboratory, engineering & craft technology, production work, quality control, financial detail, oral communications, etc. Requires training to administer.
Vocational Training Inventory and Exploration Survey (VOC-TIES) Piney Mountain http://www.pineymountain.com/ 1986 - 1991 Disadvantaged & Mildly Handicapped Youth	T3	A multi media kit used to identify vocational interests, enhance vocational awareness, & promote sex equity by showing persons in non-traditional rolls. Includes a video for 15 commonly available vocational programs. Apple/IBM program provides printout of interests.
Wide Range Achievement Test (WRAT4) PAR Inc http://www3.parinc.com/ 1940 - 2006 Age 5 to Adult - Special Populations	MY12 TP5 TP7 T4	Assesses the skills necessary to learn how to read, spell, & perform basic arithmetic operations. Provides absolute, standard, & grade scores on each of the 3 subtests: Reading, Spelling, & Arithmetic. Individual administration. Two equivalent forms are available.
Work Adjustment Inventory (WAI) Psychological and Educational Publications http://www.psych-edpublications.com/ 1994 Adolescents and Young Adults - Special Populations	MY13 TP5 TP7 T4	A norm-referenced assessment of 6 work-related temperaments: activity, empathy, sociability, assertiveness, adaptability, & emotionality. Provides age- & gender- based scores that can be displayed graphically. Third grade reading level. Useful for transition planning for students with disabilities & at-risk youth.
Work Performance Assessment (WPA) National Clearinghouse of Rehabilitation Training Materials (NCRTM) http://www.ncrtm.org/ 1987 - 1988 Job Trainees - Special Populations	MY13 TP5 TP7	Assesses work-related social/interpersonal skills. Consists of 19 assessment situations involving supervisors, workers, & co-workers. Yields scores on 19 supervisory demands, such as: greet each trainee, explain supervisory error, provide detailed instructions, & socialize with each trainee.
Work Personality Profile (WPP) National Clearinghouse of Rehabilitation Training Materials (NCRTM) http://www.ncrtm.org/ 1986 Vocational Rehabilitation Clients	MY11 TP5 TP7	Assesses fundamental work role requirements that are essential to achievement and maintenance of suitable employment. Consists of ratings on 58 items, yielding 16 scores such as: acceptance of work role, ability to profit from instruction or correction, & ability to socialize with co-workers.
Work Readiness Cognitive Screen (WCS) HeadMinder, Inc. http://www.headminder.com/site/home.html 2001 Adults		Designed for professionals who assess vocational potential in clients with known or suspected cognitive problems, it tests memory, attention, and other key functions and integrates the results with pertinent information about the client's vocational experience, interests, and aptitudes.
Work Temperament Inventory (WTI) National Clearinghouse of Rehabilitation Training Materials (NCRTM) http://www.ncrtm.org/ 1993 Workers - Special Populations	MY13 TP5 TP7	Identifies an individual's traits & match those traits to occupations. Yields scores on 12 scales including: directive, repetitive, influencing, variety, expressing, judgments, alone, stress, tolerances, people, & measurable. Individual or group administration.

530

ABOUT THE AUTHORS

Chris Wood, PhD, NCC, NCSC, is an associate professor in Old Dominion University's Counseling and Human Services department and the graduate program director for the distance learning program. He has been an associate professor at Seattle University, a faculty member at the Ohio State University and the University of Arizona, a high school counselor, a counseling/guidance department chair, a counselor/group leader at a residential youth facility for adjudicated youth/troubled teens, and a career counselor at an alternative school serving grades 7-12. Dr. Wood has been Principal Investigator, Faculty Research Associate, or Research Methodologist on more than $3 million in grants, including more than a dozen research projects investigating the efficacy of career development interventions in K-12 settings. He was a career assessment coordinator and research assistant on a $1.3 million dollar Community Employment Education Center grant from the Office of Adult and Vocational Education and a Faculty Research Associate on a grant from the National Research Center for Career and Technical Education. Dr. Wood has more than 30 conference presentations and 30 publications, including articles in *Professional School Counseling, Journal of Counseling & Development, Journal of College Counseling, Counselor Education & Supervision, Career Planning and Adult Development Journal,* and *The Elementary School Journal.* He is currently the Head Editor for the *Professional School Counseling* journal, the flagship research journal for the American School Counseling Association (ASCA).

Danica G. Hays, PhD, LPC, NCC, is an associate professor of Counseling and Chair of the Department of Counseling and Human Services at Old Dominion University. She is a recipient of the Outstanding Research Award, Outstanding Counselor Educator Advocacy Award, and the Glen E. Hubele National Graduate Student Award from the American Counseling Association (ACA) as well as the Patricia B. Elmore Excellence in Measurement and Evaluation Award and President's Special Merit Award from the Association of Assessment and Research in Counseling (AARC). Dr. Hays served as Founding Editor of *Counseling Outcome Research and Evaluation,* a national peer-refereed journal of the AARC, and is Editor of *Counselor Education and Supervision,* a national peer-refereed journal of the Association for Counselor Education and Supervision. She served as President of the AARC in 2011-2012. Her research interests include qualitative methodology, assessment and diagnosis, trauma and gender issues, and multicultural and social justice concerns in counselor preparation and community mental health. She has published more than 75 articles and book chapters in these areas. In addition to this text, she has authored, coauthored or coedited five books to date: *Assessment in Counseling: A Guide to Psychological Assessment Procedures* (ACA), *Developing Multicultural Counseling Competence: A Systems Approach* (Pearson), *Qualitative Inquiry in Clinical and Educational Settings* (Guilford), *Mastering the National Counselor Exam and the Counselor Preparation Comprehensive Exam* (Pearson), and the *ACA Encyclopedia of Counseling* (ACA).

ABOUT THE AUTHORS

James T. Austin, PhD, is Senior Research Specialist and Director of Assessment Services at the Center on Education and Training for Employment in the College of Education and Human Ecology at The Ohio State University. He earned a PhD in Industrial-Organizational Psychology at Virginia Tech in 1987. His work involves managing projects to develop tests of occupational knowledge and skill used in career-technical education as well as conducting program evaluations. His research interests include measurement of educational and occupational outcomes, statistical-psychometric topics, and goal constructs.

Caroline Baker, PhD, NCC, is an assistant professor in the Counseling and School Psychology Department at the University of Wisconsin River Falls. Among other courses, she teaches Career Counseling to school counseling graduate students and has worked as a school counselor. Her experience with teaching Career Counseling has generated a strong research interest in teaching and learning of career theory and assessment.

Spencer R. Baker, PhD, NCC, CCFC, is an associate professor and coordinator of the graduate programs in Counseling of the Department of Counseling and a Research Scientist with the Behavioral Science Research Center at Hampton University. His current clinical experiences involve working with incarcerated fathers seeking to transition into better parents for their children and their re-entry into the workforce. His primary research interests include child development, cognitive development, the antecedents of adult personality, and psychometric properties of instruments used to assess individuals.

Richard S. Balkin, PhD, is an associate professor and program coordinator of the Addictions Program in the Department of Counseling and Educational Psychology at Texas A&M University–Corpus Christi. He has practiced in psychiatric hospitals, outpatient clinics, and community mental health centers since 1993. Dr. Balkin holds a professional license in Texas and has a specialization in supervision. Dr. Balkin is a past-president of the Association for Assessment and Research in Counseling, a division of American Counseling Association. His primary research interests include counseling outcomes, program evaluation, counseling adolescents, and gender and ethnic differences in counseling.

Hannah B. Bayne, PhD, NCC, is a visiting assistant professor of counseling at Virginia Tech–Northern Virginia Campus. She has had a variety of clinical experiences, including work in community mental health and college/university settings. She has also worked as a career counselor and student advisor at the college level. Her research interests include empathy conceptualization and development, counselor training, incorporating spirituality in counseling, counselor collaboration with medical professionals, and career and identity development.

Ana C. Berríos-Allison, PhD, LPC, is the Associate Director of Career Connection at The Ohio State University. Her expertise includes career counseling, individual and group counseling, academic advising, and adjunct teaching in the Counselor Education programs for The Ohio State University and University of Dayton. Her main areas of interest relate to the influence of family dynamics in career decision making, career and wellness, career transitions, and career and social justice issues.

Jonna L. Bobzien, PhD, is an assistant professor in the Department of Communication Disorders and Special Education at Old Dominion University. She has worked as a special educator for children with severe disabilities and autism, both in public schools and in residential facilities. Her research interests include academic instruction for students with severe disabilities, development of assistive technology for students with autism entering institutions of higher education, and training of personnel working with students with severe disabilities and autism.

Christine D. Bremer, PhD, was formerly a research associate at the Institute on Community Integration (ICI). She is now coordinator of faculty awards in the Provost's office at the University of Minnesota. Her work at ICI included co-authoring major documents on assessment, dropout, and graduation; she also worked with the National Center on Educational Outcomes to review and analyze dropout and graduation data concerning students with disabilities.

Michelle L. Bruno, PhD, LPC, is an associate professor in the Department of Counseling at Indiana University of Pennsylvania. She has worked with individuals and groups in settings including a university counseling center, outpatient mental health agency, and psychiatric hospitals. Her scholarship and research interests include empowerment for adolescent girls, relational aggression, cyberbullying, wellness and balance in life, mental health literacy in adolescents, and depression and suicide among college students. She is currently working in the schools to help girls examine traditional gender expectations regarding academic achievement and career choice.

Albert M. Bugaj, PhD, is a professor and former department chair of the Department of Psychology at the University of Wisconsin—Marinette. His research interests include psychological assessment, and the effectiveness of online pedagogy. In 2008, he received a Distinguished Reviewer Award from the Buros Center for Testing.

Andrew M. Burck, PhD, LPC (CO), LPCC (OH), is an assistant professor in the Counseling Department at Marshall University. He has worked in a variety of settings with individuals, groups, couples, and families while working in a community mental health setting, a community crisis center, a substance abuse center, a juvenile prison, and a university counseling center. His research interests include research methodology, assessment and diagnosis, addictions, and wellness.

Erika Raissa Nash Cameron, PhD, LMHC, NCC, ACS, is an assistant professor in the Department of School, Family, and Mental Health Professions at the University of San Diego. She has worked as a school counselor, career counselor, and clinical supervisor in a variety of settings including a primary, middle, and secondary school, university, mental health center, residential facility, and community agency. Her research interests include qualitative research methods, multicultural issues in counselor preparation, school counselor professional development, individual psychology, and issues surround military families.

Vicki L. Campbell, PhD, LP, is an associate professor and department chair in the Psychology Department at the University of North Texas. Her clinical experience includes work in university counseling centers and clinics. Her clinical and research interests include family influences on career and psychosocial development of adolescents and emerging adults, cultural differences in family influences, and career and psychological assessment.

Laurie A. Carlson, PhD, is an associate professor and chair of the Counseling/Career Development Program at Colorado State University (CSU) in the School of Education. Dr. Carlson's teaching duties include school counseling, counseling internship, and psychological and educational assessment. Her research interests include school counseling/climate, counseling children and adolescents, STEM-centric school counseling, and LGBT issues in school counseling. Dr. Carlson has been a faculty member at CSU since 2000.

Darrin L. Carr, PhD, is the former director of Counseling, Advising, and Programming at the Florida State University Career Center. Now an adjunct faculty member at Tallahassee Community College, his research interests include the use of technology to improve counselor training and the delivery of mental health services.

Sibyl Camille Cato, PhD, is an assistant professor in the Department of Counseling at Indiana University of Pennsylvania. She has worked as a middle school counselor focusing on personal and social, career, as well as academic development of individuals. Her research interests include school counselor advocacy, multicultural and international issues in school counseling, and counseling supervision and training.

Aaron H. Carlstrom, PhD, is a clinical assistant professor in the Psychology Department at the University of Wisconsin—Parkside, where he is a coordinator of the mental health certificate program. Previously, he was an associate professor in the Department of Special Education, Counseling and Student Affairs, and a psychologist in Counseling Services, both at Kansas State University. He has provided career counseling and education and taught assessment and career counseling courses. His research interests involve career education interventions, a STEM summer camp for middle and high school students, and work value priorities.

About the Authors

Robert C. Chope, PhD, is professor emeritus and former Chair of the Counseling Department at San Francisco State University where he founded the Career Counseling Program. He is also the founder of the Career and Personal Development Institute in San Francisco, a practice that he has had for more than 33 years. Dr. Chope is a licensed psychologist and a licensed marriage and family therapist. He is the author of four books, 85 refereed papers and he has been heard on more than 150 radio and television shows around the country. He is a fellow of the National Career Development Association (NCDA) and American Counseling Association, a recipient of the Robert Swan Lifetime Achievement in Career Counseling Award, a recipient of the 2004 NCDA Outstanding Career Practitioner of the Year Award and the 2007 Merit Award. In 2012, he was honored with the Eminent Career Award from NCDA.

Stephanie A. Crockett, PhD, NCC, is an assistant professor in the Counseling Department and the director of the Adult Career Counseling Center at Oakland University. She has provided career counseling to adolescents and adults in a variety of settings, including university career-counseling centers, public schools, and private practice. Her research interests include career-counseling outcome research, research and assessment in counseling, and multicultural issues in counselor preparation.

Nichole Sharee Comito is an undergraduate student at California University of Pennsylvania with a dual major in Philosophy and Creative Writing and dual minor in Psychology and Women's Studies. Her research interests include epistemology, metaphysics, abnormal psychology, personality and career testing, and fiction writing.

Ayres G. D'Costa, PhD, is an emeritus associate professor in the Department of Educational Policy and Leadership at The Ohio State University (OSU). He is the first author of the Ohio Vocational Interest Survey and served as an academic advisor to approximately 40 PhD and MA students during his 35-year career at OSU. Prior to OSU he worked as an associate director for the Association of American Medical Colleges, responsible for developing programs to improve medical school admissions. His research interests include the development of licensing/certification tests for mental health professions.

Cirleen DeBlaere, PhD, is an assistant professor of Counseling Psychology in the Department of Counseling and Psychological Services at Georgia State University. She has worked with individuals, couples, and groups in community mental health and university counseling centers. Dr. DeBlaere's research examines the experiences of individuals with multiple and intersecting marginalized identities. To date, her research has focused on the links of multiple discrimination experiences to mental health. She also investigates potential moderating and mediating variables in the discrimination–mental health relation to identify points of intervention and inform the development of mental health–promoting strategies for multiply marginalized individuals.

Jennifer J. Del Corso, PhD, LPC, is an adjunct assistant professor in the Department of Counseling and Human Services at Old Dominion University. She has published and presented extensively on career construction theory and the theory of career adaptability. Her publications have been included in *Journal of Individual Psychology, Journal of Career Assessment, Journal of Vocational Behavior,* and *Career Development Quarterly.* In addition to providing career counseling in private practice, she currently designs and consults with several national companies that provide career development for college athletes.

Bryan J. Dik, PhD, is an associate professor of Psychology at Colorado State University in Fort Collins. His research is primarily in the area of career development, especially perceptions of work as a calling; meaning, purpose, religion and spirituality in career decision making and planning; measurement of vocational interests; and career development interventions. He serves on the editorial boards of six research journals and is author or coeditor of three books.

Pamela Doubrava-Smith is a doctoral student in the Department of Counseling and Educational Psychology at Texas A&M University–Corpus Christi. She has worked with a variety of clients in multiple settings, including at-risk youth, couples counseling, individual counseling for adults and adolescents, and family counseling. She served as an editorial assistant for *Counseling and Values* and worked as a teaching assistant. Her primary research interests include spirituality/religion in counseling, counseling adolescents and high-risk youth, and pedagogy.

V. Casey Dozier, EdS, MS, is a psychology intern in the Counseling Psychology and School Psychology combined doctoral program at Florida State University. Her clinical experiences include interventions in a variety of settings, with an emphasis on personal and career counseling to assist college students of all ages. Some of her research and professional passions include supervision and training, underserved populations, anxiety disorders, and work and life balance.

Cass Dykeman, PhD, NCC, NCSC, MAC, WSCSC, is an associate professor of Counseling at Oregon State University where he serves as Lead for the PhD program. He received his master's in Counseling from the University of Washington and his doctorate in Counseling from the University of Virginia. Prior to his work in higher education, he worked as both an elementary school and high school counselor in Seattle. Dr. Dykeman has published two books and is in double digits in peer-reviewed articles and book chapters. In addition, he has received more than $1.2 million in federally sponsored external funding in the area of career counseling.

Lori Ellison, PhD, is an assistant professor in the Counseling Department at Marshall University. Dr. Ellison has nearly 21 years of experience in the field of counseling, including five years in a community mental health agency and almost 13 years as a college counselor before completing her PhD and becoming a counselor educator. During many of those years in both community and college settings, she was given the opportunity to work with clients on developing career goals and devising plans to work toward those goals. Her current research/clinical interests include supervision, assessment and remediation of at-risk counselors-in-training; trauma and grief work; resilience and strengths-based trauma counseling; disaster mental health; and counselor educators' experiences in academia.

Serena Enke, PhD, is a staff psychologist at the Jerry L. Pettis Memorial Veteran's Medical Center in Loma Linda, California, in addition to running a private practice serving community members. She provides psychotherapy to groups and individuals in both English and Spanish and specializes in empirically supported treatment for PTSD and insomnia. She also provides pre-surgical health psychology assessments for a variety of medical procedures. Her research interests include making vocational assessment more accessible to individuals whose first language is not English, especially native-signing deaf individuals.

Kathy M. Evans, PhD, NCC, is an associate professor and program coordinator of Counselor Education at the University of South Carolina. She has worked with individuals and groups in secondary schools, community colleges, and university counseling centers. She spent many years as a career counselor for a non-profit organization. Her research interests include multicultural, career, and feminist counseling as well as supervision of counselors and counselors-in-training.

Rich Feller, PhD, LPC, NCC, is a professor of Counseling and Career Development and University Distinguished Teaching Scholar at Colorado State University. President of the National Career Development Association (2012-2013), NCDA Fellow, and recipient of NCDA's Eminent Career Award, he is co-author of the Harrington-O'Shea Career Decision Making System, the Tour of Your Tomorrow video series, and developer of http://www.stemcareer.com.

Justin R. Fields, PhD, is a lecturer in the Counselor Education Program at The Ohio State University and is also a professional school counselor at Central Crossing High School. He works in an urban high school setting partnering with students, parents, administrators, and community members to address issues related to academic achievement, personal/social wellness, and college and career readiness. His research interests include school counselor training programs and college and career readiness.

About the Authors

John W. Fleenor, PhD, is senior research faculty in the product development group of the Center for Creative Leadership. He is responsible for the research and development of leadership assessments such as multi-rater feedback instruments. His work helps to provide leadership development tools for organizations around the world. His research interests include psychological measurement, instrument development, and research methodology.

Kurt F. Geisinger is Director of the Buros Center for Testing and Meierhenry Distinguished University Professor at the University of Nebraska. He served two terms as Council Representative for the Division of Measurement, Evaluation and Statistics in the American Psychological Association. He also represented the American Educational Research Association, the American Psychological Association, and the National Council on Measurement in Education on the ISO's International Test Standards committee. He was elected to the American Psychological Association's Board of Directors for 2011-2013. His primary interests lie in validity theory, admissions testing, proper test use, test use with individuals with disabilities and language minorities and the adaptation of tests from one language and culture to another.

Joanna Gorin, PhD, is an associate professor in the Measurement, Statistics, and Methodological Studies program at Arizona State University. Her main research and teaching interests are in cognitive-psychometric analysis of standardized test data and basic measurement and statistical training for non-quantitative educators and students.

Melinda M. Gibbons, PhD, NCC, is an associate professor and school counseling program coordinator in the Department of Educational Psychology and Counseling at the University of Tennessee. She has worked in school and mental health settings with children and adolescents. Her research interests include career development across the lifespan, career counseling for underserved populations, school counseling best practices, and cultural influences on career development.

Zandra S. Gratz, PhD, is a professor in the School of Psychology at Kean University. Her areas of expertise are research methodology, measurement, and evaluation. She has a long history as a program evaluation consultant. Her research interests include program evaluation, instruction, and assessment.

Kathy E. Green, PhD, is a professor in the Department of School and Counseling Psychology, Research Methods, and Information Science at the University of Denver. She has worked in test development and assessment for populations of children through the elderly. Her research interests include survey research, psychometric measurement models, and data quality.

Christi L. Gross, MEd, MA, is a doctoral student in the Department of Sociology at Kent State University. She received a MEd in School Counseling in 2008 from California University of Pennsylvania and a MA in Sociology from Kent State University in 2011. Her research interests include community mental health, social psychology, postpartum distress, and welfare-to-work/TANF programs.

Norman C. Gysbers, PhD, is a Curators' Professor in the Department of Educational, School, and Counseling Psychology at the University of Missouri–Columbia. He received his BA degree (1954) from Hope College and his MA (1959) and PhD (1963) degrees from the University of Michigan. His research and teaching interests are in career development, career counseling, and school guidance and counseling program development, management, and evaluation. He is author of 93 articles, 38 chapters in published books, 15 monographs, and 22 books. He has received many awards, most notably the National Career Development Association's Eminent Career Award and the American School Counselor Association's Mary Gehrke Lifetime Achievement Award in 2004. Gysbers was Editor of the *Career Development Quarterly,* 1962-1970; President of the National Career Development Association, 1972-1973; President of the American Counseling Association, 1977-1978; and Vice President of the Association of Career and Technical Education, 1979-1982. He was the Editor of *The Journal of Career Development* from 1978 until 2006.

Michael A. Hauser, PhD, LPC, NCC, is in private practice in northwest Georgia. He has worked with adolescents and adults, families, and couples in a variety of clinical settings, including an inpatient psychiatric hospital ward, state-contracted mental health agencies, and military career and performance counseling center. His research interests include spirituality and religion in counseling.

Malik S. Henfield, PhD, is an associate professor in the Rehabilitation and Counselor Education Department at the University of Iowa. His research interests include urban education, gifted education, as well as counselor education and school-based mental health and wellness services.

Katie Coggin Hillis, MEd, is a school counselor for a public school district in northwest Georgia. She has worked with students of all ages in both residential facilities and public schools. Her research interests include social justice, inequalities, gang involvement, and underachievement.

Edwin L. Herr, EdD, is a Distinguished Professor Emeritus of Education and Emeritus Associate Dean of the College of Education at The Pennsylvania State University. He served as the first director of the Bureau of Guidance Services in the Pennsylvania Department of Education and has provided career counseling to adolescents and adults for more than five decades. He has served as President of the American Counseling Association (ACA), National Career Development Association (NCDA), Association for Counselor Education and Supervision, and Chi Sigma Iota. Herr is a Fellow of ACA, NCDA, and the American Psychological Association.

Tara Hill, PhD, LPCC-S, is an assistant professor in the Department of Counseling and Human Services at Old Dominion University. She has worked clinically with adolescents and adults in community mental health agencies, schools, private practice, and correctional settings. Her research interests include assessment and measurement, clinical supervision, and offender treatment.

Kenneth F. Hughey, PhD, is a professor and department chair in the Department of Special Education, Counseling, and Student Affairs at Kansas State University. He has been a faculty member at Kansas State for more than 20 years and has taught courses in graduate programs in counseling, college student development, and academic advising. His research interests include school counseling, career counseling, and career advising.

Jeffrey A. Jenkins, EdD, JD, is a professor in the School of Justice Studies at Roger Williams University. He has practiced law in the areas of professional errors and omissions, employment, and insurance defense litigation, and taught research methods, statistics, psychological measurement, and a variety of law-related classes. His current research interests include the reliability and validity of survey instruments, gender differences, and public perceptions of the criminal law.

Kaprea F. Johnson, PhD, NCC, is an assistant professor in the Department of Counseling and Human Services at Old Dominion University. She has worked in a variety of settings including schools, mental health centers, and in a university career center as a career counselor. Her research and clinical interests include violence and problem-behavior prevention interventions, pro-social behavior and norms in school aged children, and university-community partnerships.

Karl N. Kelley, PhD, is a professor in the Department of Psychology at North Central College in Naperville, Illinois. His research focuses on issues related to organizational justice, perceptions of success in the workplace, and work-family integration. He teaches classes in Industrial Psychology, Statistics, and Psychological Assessment. He also consults with several organizations specifically with employee selection and motivation.

Richard Kinnier, PhD, is a professor in the Counseling and Counseling Psychology program at Arizona State University. His major research interests are in the areas of values and issues related to meaning in life.

Jean P. Kirnan, PhD, received her PhD in Psychometrics from Fordham University in 1986. She is currently a professor at The College of New Jersey, where she has taught in the Psychology Department since

About the Authors

1986, serving as department chair from 2005 to 2009. She is currently the chair of the Psychology Department's Assessment Committee as well as the chair of the Learning Outcomes Assessment Committee for the School of Humanities and Social Sciences. Dr. Kirnan recently established the TAPLab (Testing and Assessment in Psychology) to provide an opportunity for undergraduate students to explore advanced topics and projects in measurement. Current lab projects include the creation of the PASS (Predictors of Academic Success of Students) a measure of non-cognitive factors related to first-year college success, development of assessment tools for the department, and assisting community partners with their measurement and assessment needs. Dr. Kirnan has completed more than 20 invited test reviews and was recognized by the Buros Center for Testing as a Distinguished Reviewer.

Maria I. Kuznetsova, PhD, is an assistant academic professional lecturer in the Department of Psychology at the University of Wyoming. She teaches a variety of upper-division classes, such as Psychology of Adulthood, Adolescent Development, Introduction to Clinical Psychology, and Cognitive Development. Her research interests include adjustment of adopted individuals, multicultural issues, and general resilience aspects of children coming from adverse backgrounds and circumstances.

Amanda C. La Guardia, PhD, LPC, NCC, is an assistant professor of Counselor Education in the Department of Educational Leadership and Counseling at Sam Houston State University. Prior to receiving her doctorate from Old Dominion University, she worked as a family counselor with children in foster care for several years post-master's, administering assessments to assist families as they sought education, work, and relational improvement in addition to other typical in-home clinical work. Her research includes work on professional identity development, adolescent non-suicidal self injury, and applications of Adlerian and feminist counseling philosophies. Her specialty practice areas include work with children, families, and groups.

Richard Lapan, PhD, has had extensive experience providing counseling services (career, family, individual, group, and residential) to children, adolescents, and adults. Dr. Lapan serves as the Research and Evaluation Member to the Governing Board of the Massachusetts School Counselor Association. For the past 3 years, Dr. Lapan has developed a successful and sustainable partnership focusing on college and career readiness for middle school students in two urban school districts. In 2012, the Commissioner of Education in Massachusetts nominated Dr. Lapan to serve on the statewide Integrating Career and College Readiness Taskforce. The recommendations from this committee were accepted by the Massachusetts Board of Education and are now providing policy and practice direction to school districts.

A. Stephen Lenz, PhD, LPC, is an assistant professor in the Department of Counseling, Educational Psychology, and Research at The University of Memphis. He has worked with children, adolescents, adults, and families in community-based and university counseling settings. His research interests include career development with adolescents, holistic approaches to counseling, counselor education, and supervision, community-based program evaluation, counseling outcome research, single-case research, and instrument development.

Gabriel I. Lomas, PhD, LPC, NCC, RPT-S, is an associate professor of counseling in the Department of Education and Educational Psychology at Western Connecticut State University. He has worked with individuals from a variety of settings, including private practice, forensic, and academic settings. Lomas has extensive experience in assessment and treatment of individuals with disabilities, especially those who are deaf or hard-of-hearing. He currently maintains a small private practice which focuses on rehabilitation assessment and counseling.

Sonya Lorelle, PhD, LPC, NCC, is an assistant professor in the Department of Psychology and Counseling at Governors State University. She has worked with children, adolescents, and adults in settings which include community agencies and a university counseling center. Her research interests are in the internationalization of counseling, homelessness, and spirituality in counseling.

Jill A. Lumsden, EdS, is associate director of Career Counseling, Education to Careers, at University of Phoenix. She has worked in a variety of career services roles, including career counseling, instruction, training, and administration. Her particular areas of interest include electronic portfolios, distance career counseling, and career assessment.

Wei-Cheng J. Mau, PhD, NCC, is a professor in the Department of Counseling, Leadership, Educational and School Psychology at Wichita State University. He has worked at college counseling centers and researched at the American College Testing Program. His research interests include career assessment, education/vocation aspirations, and career decision-making of female and minority students.

Mary-Catherine McClain, EdS, MS, is an instructor and career advisor in the Career Center at the Florida State University as well as a current student in the Combined Doctoral Program of Counseling Psychology and School Psychology. Her research interests include the integration of mental health and career concerns, career readiness, motivational interviewing, student engagement, eating disorders, and coping with Attention Deficit Hyperactivity Disorder.

Julian R. McCullough, MAEd, is an adjunct professor in the Department of Counseling and School Psychology at Seattle University. He is also a professional school counselor, working with children, adolescents, and their families. He has served on committees at both the state and national level. His research interests include social justice issues in counseling and school counseling.

Dixie D. Meyer, PhD, PLPC, NCC, is an assistant professor in the Department of Counseling and Family Therapy at Saint Louis University. She has worked with individuals, couples, families, and groups in a variety of clinical settings including university counseling centers, schools, hospitals, and community agencies. Her research interests include assessment, neurobiological applications in counseling, drama therapy, and couples counseling.

Rebecca E. Michel, PhD, LCPC, NCC, is an assistant professor in the Department of Psychology and Counseling at Governors State University. She has provided counseling for clients/students across the lifespan, in K-12 educational settings, university counseling centers, and community agencies. Her research interests include career and life satisfaction, social justice and advocacy in counselor preparation, relationship violence intervention, and international partnership building.

Carrie A. Wachter Morris, PhD, NCC, ACS, is an associate professor of Educational Studies and co-chair of the school counseling program at Purdue University. She has worked with individuals, families, and groups in both school and clinical mental health settings. Her research interests include the scholarship of teaching and learning in counselor education and crisis prevention and intervention.

Deidre L. Muth is a graduate student in the Department of Counseling Education at California University of Pennsylvania. She is in the school counseling program and intends to work as a professional school counselor in the K-12 educational system.

Margaret M. Nauta, PhD, is a professor in the Department of Psychology at Illinois State University. She has provided career counseling to individuals and groups at several university counseling centers and at a VA medical center. Her research interests include career assessment, factors influencing women's career choices, and the role of self-efficacy in career decision-making.

Rebecca A. Newgent, PhD, LCPC, NCC, is professor and chairperson in the Department of Counselor Education at Western Illinois University–Quad Cities. She has counseled clients in a variety of settings, including an outpatient community mental health center for adults with severe emotional disabilities, university counseling and development centers, parochial family-service agencies, private practice, and a county psychiatric emergency center. Her research interests include measurement and evaluation in counseling, counseling/clinical/supervision, and at-risk children concerns (peer victimization/bullying, academic, behavior, and social problems).

About the Authors

Spencer G. Niles is a Distinguished Professor and department head for Educational Psychology, Counseling, and Special Education at the Pennsylvania State University. He is the recipient of the National Career Development Association's (NCDA) Eminent Career Award and is also a Fellow in NCDA and American Counseling Association. He served as President for NCDA and Editor for *Career Development Quarterly,* and is currently the Editor of the *Journal of Counseling & Development* and a member of the Executive Committee for the International Centre for Career Development and Public Policy.

Debra S. Osborn, PhD, NCC, is an assistant professor in the Educational Psychology and Learning Systems Department at Florida State University and has worked more than 15 years as a counselor educator. She has worked with individuals in school and university settings on career development concerns. Her research interests include the design and use of technology in counseling, innovation and effectiveness in counselor education, and the design and use of assessments in career services.

Lauren K. Osborne, MS, is a doctoral student in Counseling Psychology at the University of Southern Mississippi. She has worked with individuals and groups at her university's clinic on a variety of issues, including career development. Her research interests include career decision making and career identity, especially as they relate to veteran populations as they make their transitions from military service to the civilian workforce.

Christen Opsal is a coordinator at the Institute on Community Integration. Since 2001, she has served in a variety of capacities as an editor and researcher. She is currently working on research and dissemination projects related to community college retention, youth with intellectual disabilities attending college, and the transition to adulthood for youth with disabilities. She is completing her PhD and is a teaching specialist in the Department of Organizational Leadership, Policy, and Development at the University of Minnesota's College of Education and Human Development.

John Patrick, PhD, is a professor in the Counselor Education Department at California University of Pennsylvania. His research areas of interest are career counseling and use of the creative arts in counseling.

Paul R. Peluso, PhD, LMHC, LMFT, is an associate professor and doctoral program coordinator at Florida Atlantic University. He is the co-author of four books, including *Changing Aging, Changing Family Therapy: Practicing with 21st Century Realities, Couples Therapy: Integrating Theory, Research, & Practice* (Love Publishing), and *Principles of Counseling and Psychotherapy: Learning the Essential Domains and Nonlinear Thinking of Master Practitioners* (Routledge Publishing), as well as the editor of the book *Infidelity: A Practitioner's Guide to Working with Couples in Crisis* (Routledge Publishing). Dr. Peluso is the author of more than 25 articles and 12 chapters related to the therapeutic relationship, family therapy, couples counseling, and Adlerian Theory.

Michelle Perepiczka, PhD, LMHC, RPTS, CSC (Provisional), NCC, is an assistant professor in the school counseling department at New York Institute of Technology. She has worked with children, adults, and groups in a variety of settings including psychiatric hospitals, domestic violence agencies, preventative agencies, schools, and private practice. Her research interests include wellness in counselor preparation and community mental health as well as integration of technology into counselor education.

Bethany L. Perkins, MEd, is a doctoral student in the Counseling Psychology program at Lehigh University. She has worked with individuals, groups, and families in a number of settings, including college counseling centers, partial hospital programs, transitional outpatient programs, and school-based community clinics. Her primary research interests include sexual minority identities, aging, trauma, social support, and their relations to mental health.

QuaVaundra Perry, MS, is a doctoral candidate in Counseling Psychology at the University of North Texas. Her clinical experience includes working with individuals, couples, and families in a variety of settings including university counseling centers, outpatient community clinics, and a VA hospital. Her clinical and research interests include multicultural and familial influences on career development, assessment, and supervision.

Dale Pietrzak, EdD, LPC-MH, CCMHC, is the Director of Academic Evaluation and Assessment at University of South Dakota. He has worked with individuals, families, and groups in a variety of clinical settings, including schools, psychiatric hospitals, university counseling centers, corrections, and outpatient mental health. His research interests include assessment and diagnosis, and outcome research.

Mary Podmostko, EdD, the assistant director of Project 10: Transition Education Network at the University of South Florida St. Petersburg. Project 10 assists Florida school districts in building capacity to provide secondary transition services to students with disabilities in order to improve their academic success and post-school outcomes. She has a masters' degree in Collaborative Vocational Evaluation and has taught career development at the high school level. She has also managed a number of workforce development programs, including dropout prevention, school-to-work, welfare-to-work, Job Training Partnership Act, leadership development, registered apprenticeship, and an independent postsecondary school.

Julia Y. Porter, PhD, LPC, NCC, NCSC, is a professor of Counselor Education and associate dean of the Division of Education at Mississippi State University–Meridian. She has worked with individuals and groups in a variety of educational settings, including career centers, university counseling centers, and schools. Her research interests focus on student development issues related to wellness and on the effectiveness of counseling practices used to address developmental wellness issues.

Shawn Powell, PhD, ABPP, is the dean of Social and Behavioral Sciences at Casper College. He is an adjunct faculty member for the Department of Psychology at the University of Wyoming. He is a licensed psychologist and board certified as a school psychologist. He is a past-president of the American Academy of School Psychology, the Wyoming Psychological Association, and the Wyoming School Psychology Association.

Sally J. Power, PhD, is professor emerita of the Management Department at the University of St. Thomas in Minneapolis–St. Paul, Minnesota, and now works primarily in the area of career management in mid-career. She has also taught and consulted with for-profit and not-for-profit organization managers and other workers on a range of issues related to organizational behavior. Her research interests include comparing the Myers-Briggs Type Indicator to the Herrmann Brain Dominance Instrument, business ethics, and the challenges of career management in midcareer. She is the author of *The Mid-Career Success Guide* (2006, Praeger Publishing).

Elizabeth A. Prosek, PhD, NCC, is an assistant professor in the Department of Counseling and Higher Education at the University of North Texas. Her clinical experience includes community in-home counseling, community outpatient counseling, university supervision, and director of a grant funded in-school program. Her research interests include diagnosis and assessment, counseling underserved populations, and issues in counselor education.

Matthew Putts, MS, LPCA, CRC, is a PhD student and research assistant in the Department of Addictions and Rehabilitation Studies at East Carolina University. He is an experienced community rehabilitation agency manager of employment programs, has worked with individuals with varying disabilities, and currently provides counseling and vocational assessments in a clinic. His research interests include posttraumatic stress disorder (PTSD), the intersection of PTSD and psychosis, motivational interviewing, and rehabilitation counseling and assessment for veterans.

Manivong J. Ratts, PhD, NCC, is an associate professor in the Department of Counseling and School Psychology at Seattle University. Dr. Ratts has extensive experience in career counseling as a community college counselor at William Rainey Harper College, College of DuPage, and Portland Community College. His research interests are in the area of social justice and advocacy in the counseling profession.

Mark C. Rehfuss, PhD, LPC, ACS, is an assistant professor and director of the distance learning Human Services program in the Department of Counseling and Human Services at Old Dominion University. He has worked as a counselor with children, adolescents, adults, and families as well as provided individual career

About the Authors

counseling and career workshops for university students and adults in career transition. His research interests include career counseling and guidance, narrative career interventions, counselor education and supervision, qualitative research methods, and clinical mental health.

Ciemone S. Rose, MA, NCC, is a doctoral student in the Counseling Psychology program at Indiana University. Her research interests include career counseling interventions for racial/ethnic minorities, the risk and protective factors of LGB persons of color, and individuals with intersecting marginalized identities. She currently works as a counselor with middle and older adult populations in nursing and rehabilitation settings. Her clinical training experiences include work in Chicago, with substance abusers and persons living with HIV, and juveniles and their families involved in the Monroe County probation system in Bloomington, IN.

David Rothman is a senior psychology major at The College of New Jersey. David has worked as a research assistant in various labs at the college and worked as a research assistant for the War Related Illness and Injury Study Center at the East Orange Department of Veterans Affairs. He holds NIH and Department of Veterans Affairs certificates for research with Human Subjects and is currently working as a civilian contractor for the VA.

Jeff Samide is an associate professor in the Counselor Education Department at California University of Pennsylvania. His research areas of interest are career counseling, existentialism and spiritualism, and the use of technology in counseling.

James P. Sampson, Jr., PhD, is the Mode L. Stone Distinguished Professor of Counseling and Career Development in the Department of Educational Psychology and Learning Systems, Co-Director of the Center for the Study of Technology in Counseling and Career Development, and Associate Dean in the College of Education, all at the Florida State University. His research interests include information and communication technology in counseling and the design of career counseling and guidance services.

Eleanor E. Sanford-Moore, PhD, is senior vice-president for research and development at Meta-Metrics, Inc. Her research interests include mathematics instruction, mathematics and reading assessment development, large-scale testing and measurement, and the examination of reading and mathematics demands of postsecondary and career endeavors as they relate to student abilities.

William I. Sauser, Jr., PhD, is a professor of Management and Higher Education at Auburn University. Dr. Sauser earned his BS in Management and his MS and PhD in Industrial/Organizational Psychology at the Georgia Institute of Technology, and an MA in Business Ethics from the University of Wales. He is licensed to practice psychology in Alabama and holds specialty diplomas in Industrial/Organizational Psychology and Organizational and Business Consulting Psychology from the American Board of Professional Psychology. Dr. Sauser's interests include organizational development, strategic planning, human relations in the workplace, business ethics, and continuing professional education. He is a Fellow of the American Council on Education and the Society for Advancement of Management. Dr. Sauser is also a Commissioned Lay Pastor in the Presbyterian Church (USA) and serves as pastor of the Union Springs (Alabama) Presbyterian Church.

Lisa Severy, PhD, LPC, is assistant vice chancellor of Student Affairs and Director of Career Services at the University of Colorado Boulder. She has published numerous books and articles in career development, mostly related to narrative counseling and empowering clients by helping them author their own stories. In addition, she is a proud and passionate member of the National Career Development Association.

Eugene P. Sheehan, PhD, has been the dean of the College of Education and Behavioral Sciences at the University of Northern Colorado for the past 12 years. He worked as a personnel psychologist and vocational evaluator prior to entering the academy. He currently is interested in teacher quality and assessment.

Donna S. Sheperis, PhD, LPC, NCC, ACS, is a core faculty member in the Mental Health Counseling Program of Walden University and has more than 20 years of experience in community counseling settings. She has served as co-chair of the American Counseling Association Ethics Committee and has authored nine articles in peer reviewed journals, nine book chapters, an instructor's manual to a research text, and has a foundational textbook in clinical mental health counseling in press. Dr. Sheperis presents regularly on a variety of topics and has received numerous awards for her teaching, scholarship, and research. Her primary areas of interest include counselor development, assessment of mental health and coping, counseling ethics, and supervision.

Marie F. Shoffner, PhD, is an associate professor in the Department of Counselor Education at Virginia Commonwealth University. Her research interests include the career development of underrepresented populations in STEM (Science, Technology, Engineering, and Mathematics), and the professional development of doctoral students in counselor education.

W. Matthew Shurts, PhD, is an associate professor in the Department of Counseling and Educational Leadership at Montclair State University. He has a background in community/mental health counseling and has worked with numerous clinical settings including inpatient behavioral health centers, youth group homes, and outpatient community counseling agencies. His research interests include premarital and pre-union counseling, romantic relationship development, and counselor education pedagogy.

Jacqueline J. Peila-Shuster, PhD, NCC, is an assistant professor of Counseling and Career Development at Colorado State University. She has worked as a career counselor in the university setting and continues to participate in pro bono career counseling with a variety of clientele. Her counseling and research interests include career counseling, retirement, and strengths-based interventions and approaches to career and life planning.

Steven R. Sligar, EdD, CVE, PVE, is an associate professor and director of the graduate program in vocational evaluation in the Department of Addictions and Rehabilitation Counseling at East Carolina University. He has conducted vocational evaluations with individuals who have disabilities specializing with those who are deaf and/or blind in private community rehabilitation programs or state vocational rehabilitation agencies. His research interests include accessibility, program administration, and vocational evaluation.

Michael J. Stebleton, PhD, is an assistant professor in the Department of Postsecondary Teaching and Learning at the University of Minnesota–Twin Cities. His teaching and research interests focus on career development, multicultural student development, college student success, and retention issues. Most recently, he helped to implement the StrengthsQuest program into a first-year experience course for new students in the College of Education and Human Development. Dr. Stebleton's published research on career-related issues appears in *The Career Development Quarterly, Journal of College and Character, Journal of Career Development,* and other journals.

Jacqueline M. Swank, PhD, LMHC, LCSW, RPT-S, is an assistant professor of Counselor Education in the School of Human Development and Organizational Studies in Education at the University of Florida. She has clinical experience working with children and adolescents and their families in residential, inpatient, day treatment, and outpatient settings. Her research interests include counselor development, assessment, and play, adventure, and nature-based interventions with at-risk children and adolescents.

Mei Tang, PhD, LPC, is a professor of Counseling in the School of Human Services at the University of Cincinnati. She has actively published and presented in the areas of career development and assessment, counseling ethnic minorities, counseling school-age population, and cross-cultural issues in counselor education. She has served on editorial boards of *Career Development Quarterly* and *Journal of Counseling and Development.* She has also been active in community service, providing consultation with a local school district to help at-risk youth through guidance curriculum revision and grant-funded prevention projects.

About the Authors

Joe Timmons has worked with adolescents and adults with disabilities in rehabilitation and educational settings for more than 28 years. Since 2003, he has been a coordinator and Research Fellow at the Institute on Community Integration (ICI) at the University of Minnesota. His work at ICI has focused on the transition of youth with disabilities to adulthood, and he has authored or co-authored more than 20 publications to support individuals and their families. Joe is working on completing a master's degree in Social Work.

Tammi Vacha-Haase, PhD, is a professor in the Department of Psychology at Colorado State University. A licensed psychologist, she specializes in geropsychology and currently serves as the director for the Aging Clinic of the Rockies. She focuses on increasing the well-being of older adults and their families through clinical practice and research.

Janet E. Wall, EdD, CDFI, MCDP, is founder and president of Sage Solutions and http://www.CEU-onestop.com. She is an award-winning author, teacher, trainer, and career practitioner with interests in career and workforce development, assessment, vocational interests and abilities, technology, and the development of online courses for persons in the career development field. Contact her at careerfacilitator@janetwall.net.

Joshua C. Watson, PhD, LPC, NCC, is an associate professor in the Department of Counseling and Educational Psychology at Mississippi State University–Meridian. He has worked in a variety of clinical settings, including community mental health agencies, psychiatric hospitals, university counseling centers, and vocational rehabilitation centers, as well as maintaining a private practice. His research interests include adolescent wellness, assessment training, technology integration in counselor education, and counseling athletes.

Susan Whiston, PhD, is a professor in the Department of Counseling and Educational Psychology at Indiana University. She teaches career counseling, assessment, and other courses in the counseling program. Her research has primarily focused on identifying effective methods for delivering career and school counseling interventions, and she has written books, numerous book chapters, and more than 50 journal articles. Her clinical work has mostly centered on career counseling and she has worked with adolescents, college students, and adults.

Cornelia R. Wilson, EdD, PMHCNS, LPCC, is an emeritus professor of Nursing, having retired after 37 years of teaching and supervising nursing students at the University of Cincinnati. She is a Fellow of the American Academy of Nursing, and is the founding president and CEO of a nurse-managed clinic which serves indigent and homeless adults with serious and chronic mental, emotional, behavioral, and substance abuse disorders. Her research interests include homelessness; assessment, diagnosis, and treatment of mental, emotional, behavioral, and substance abuse disorders; and integrated service delivery.

F. Robert Wilson, PhD, LPCC, is an emeritus professor of Counseling, having retired after 35 years teaching and supervising counseling students at the University of Cincinnati. He is a past-president of the Association for Assessment and Research in Counseling. He served on the governing board for and is a Fellow of the American Counseling Association. In his clinical practice, he treats indigent and homeless adults with serious and chronic mental, emotional, behavioral, and substance use disorders at an inner-city mental health clinic. He has served on the editorial boards of several professional journals including *Measurement and Evaluation in Counseling and Development* and *Educational and Psychological Measurement.* He has actively published and presented in the areas of assessment, diagnosis, and treatment of mental, emotional, behavioral, and substance abuse disorders; counselor education and supervision; and research methodology.

Emily Bullock-Yowell, PhD, is an associate professor of Psychology at the University of Southern Mississippi and program coordinator of the department's Counseling Psychology master's program. Her research and student training focus in the area of career development, including career assessment, Holland's Theory, and the Cognitive Information Processing (CIP) Approach. She has worked with clients in a variety of settings regarding diverse issues, including personal career development. Currently, she trains doctoral and master's students in a manualized, CIP career counseling group treatment through her program's training clinic.

Peter Zachar, PhD, is a professor of Psychology at Auburn University Montgomery. His research interests lie at the intersection of the philosophy of psychiatry and the philosophy of science. He also writes about the classification of emotions.

APPENDIX A

A COUNSELOR'S GUIDE
USER'S MATRIX

Appendix A: Counselors Guide User's Matrix

INSTRUMENT NAME	Achievement	Aptitude	Interest	Values/Satisfaction/Environments	Career Development/Maturity	Personality	Elementary School	Junior High/Middle School	Senior High School	2-Year or 4-Year College	Adult Education/Training	Business & Industry/Employment	Special Populations
Ability Explorer		*						*	*	*			
ACCU Vision - Workplace Success Skills System	*								*		*	*	
Activity Vector Analysis (AVA)	*				*	*						*	
Adaptability Test		*											*
Adult Basic Learning Exam (ABLE)	*									*	*		*
Adult Career Concerns Inventory (ACCI)					*					*	*	*	
Adult Measure of Essential Skills (AMES)	*									*	*	*	
Adult Personality Inventory (API)						*				*	*	*	
Applicant Review						*						*	
ARC Self-Determination Scale (ARC-SDS)					*	*			*			*	*
Armed Services Vocational Aptitude Battery (ASVAB - CEP)		*	*	*					*	*			
Armed Services-Civilian Vocational Interest Survey		*						*	*		*		
Assessment of Career Decision Making (ACDM)					*				*	*			
Ball Aptitude Battery (BAB)		*							*	*	*		
Barriers to Employment Success Inventory (BESI)					*				*		*		*
Barsch Learning Styles Inventory - Revised						*			*		*		*
Basic Skills Locator Test	*								*		*		*
Becker Work Adjustment Profile (BWAP)					*				*		*		*
Bennett Hand Tool Dexterity Test (BHTDT)		*							*		*	*	*
Bennett Mechanical Comprehension Test (BMCT)		*							*	*	*	*	
Brigance Transition Skills Inventory (TSI)	*				*								*
Business Careers Interest Inventory (BCII)			*							*		*	
California Life Goals Evaluation Schedules				*					*	*	*	*	
California Psychological Inventory (CPI)						*			*	*	*	*	
Campbell Interest & Skills Survey (CISS)			*						*	*		*	
Campbell Organizational Survey				*								*	
Career Ability Placement Survey (CAPS)		*						*	*	*	*		
Career Action Inventory					*					*	*	*	
Career Anchors: Discovering Your Real Values				*							*	*	
Career and Vocational Form of the SOI-LA Basic Test	*								*	*	*	*	
Career Assessment Battery (CAB)			*						*	*	*		*
Career Assessment Inventory (CAI)			*						*	*	*	*	
Career Attitudes and Strategies Inventory (CASI)					*					*	*	*	
Career Awareness Inventory (CAI)					*		*	*	*				
Career Beliefs Inventory (CBI)					*				*	*	*	*	
Career Commitment Measure				*	*				*	*	*		
Career Compass			*					*	*				
Career Decision Profile					*				*	*	*		
Career Decision Scale (CDS)					*				*	*			
Career Decision Self-Efficacy (CDSE) Scale					*				*	*	*		
Career Development Inventory (CDI)					*				*	*	*		
Career Development Profile					*							*	
Career Directions Inventory (CDI)			*						*	*	*		
Career Exploration Inventory (CEI)			*						*		*		
Career Exploration Series (CES)			*					*	*	*	*		
Career Factors Inventory					*				*	*	*		
Career Finder			*				*	*	*	*	*		
Career Genogram					*			*	*	*	*		

546

A COUNSELOR'S GUIDE TO CAREER ASSESSMENTS INSTRUMENTS

INSTRUMENT NAME	CHARACTERISTICS						USE						
	Achievement	Aptitude	Interest	Values/Satisfaction/Environments	Career Development/Maturity	Personality	Elementary School	Junior High/Middle School	Senior High School	2-Year or 4-Year College	Adult Education/Training	Business & Industry/Employment	Special Populations
Career Guidance Inventory			*					*	*	*			
Career Interest Inventory (CII)			*					*	*	*	*		
Career Inventories for the Learning Disabled (CILD)		*	*			*							
Career IQ and Interest Test (CIQIT)		*	*						*	*		*	
CareerKey			*						*	*	*		
Career Leverage Inventory					*						*		
Career Maturity Inventory (CMI)					*				*	*	*		
Career Occupational Preference System Interest Inventory (COPS)			*						*	*	*	*	
Career Orientation Placement and Evaluation Survey (COPES)				*					*	*	*	*	
Career Planning Survey		*	*						*	*	*	*	
Career Profile Assessment		*	*						*	*			
Career Programs Assessment Test (CPAT)	*									*	*	*	
Career Search Efficacy Scale					*					*	*	*	
CareerScope		*	*						*	*	*	*	
Career Style Interview			*	*	*				*	*	*	*	
Career SnapShot 2001		*							*	*		*	
Career Technical Assistance Program (C-Tap)	*								*	*		*	
Career Thoughts Inventory (CTI)					*				*	*	*		
Career Values Scale				*						*	*	*	
Childhood Career Development Scale (CCDS)					*		*	*					
CITE Learning Styles Inventory					*		*	*	*	*		*	*
Clerical Abilities Battery (CAB)	*	*							*	*	*	*	
Clerical Skills Test Series	*	*							*	*	*	*	
Clifton StrengthsFinder/StrengthsFinder 2.0						*			*	*	*	*	
COIN Basic Skills and Career Interest Survey		*	*						*		*		
COIN Career Targets			*					*	*				
COIN Clue					*			*					
COIN Educational Inventory			*						*				
College Major Interest Inventory (CMII)			*						*	*			
Comprehensive Ability Battery (CAB)		*							*	*	*	*	
Comprehensive Personality Profile						*				*	*	*	
Computer Operator Aptitude Battery (COAB)		*								*	*	*	
Computer Programmer Aptitude Battery (CPAB)		*								*	*	*	
Crawford Small Parts Dexterity Test (CSPDT)		*								*		*	*
Curtis Interest Scale			*							*	*	*	
Customer Service Skills Assessment Program	*									*		*	
Deal-Me-In/It's In the Cards			*							*	*	*	
Differential Aptitudes Test (DAT)		*						*	*	*	*		
Dole Vocational Sentence Completion Blank			*					*	*	*			
Dvorine Color Vision Test		*							*	*	*	*	
Educational Interest Inventory, Revised Edition (EII)			*						*	*	*		
Edwards Personal Preference Schedule (EPPS)						*				*	*	*	
Employability Competency System Appraisal Test (ECS Appraisal)	*								*	*	*	*	
Employability Inventory					*				*	*	*	*	
Employability Maturity Interview					*				*		*		*
Employee Aptitude Survey (EAS)		*									*	*	
Employee Effectiveness Profile						*						*	
Employee Reliability Inventory						*					*	*	*

Appendix A: Counselors Guide User's Matrix

INSTRUMENT NAME	Achievement	Aptitude	Interest	Values/Satisfaction/Environments	Career Development/Maturity	Personality	Elementary School	Junior High/Middle School	Senior High School	2-Year or 4-Year College	Adult Education/Training	Business & Industry/Employment	Special Populations
Endorale Seversen Transition Rating Scale	*				*								*
ETSA Tests (Employers' Tests and Services Association)	*	*							*	*	*	*	*
Evaluating the Participant's Employability Skills					*				*	*	*		
Expanded Skills Confidence Inventory		*							*	*	*	*	
Explore	*	*						*					
Explore the World of Work (E-WOW)			*								*		*
Flanagan Aptitude Classification Test (FACT)		*							*	*	*	*	*
Flanagan Industrial Tests (FIT)		*									*	*	*
Fleishman Job Analysis Survey (F-JAS)				*								*	
Forer Vocational Survey						*			*	*	*		
Functional Assessment Inventory	*				*								*
Fundamental Interpersonal Relations Orientation-Behavior (FIRO-B)						*			*	*	*	*	
Future Career Autobiography			*	*				*	*				
Geist Picture Interest Inventory			*										*
General Clerical Test (GCT)		*							*	*	*		
Gordon Occupational Checklist II			*					*	*		*		
Gordon Personal Profile-Inventory (GPP-I)						*			*	*	*	*	
Group Test of Musical Ability		*					*	*					
Guide for Occupational Exploration (GOE) Inventory			*					*	*		*		
Guilford-Zimmerman Interest Inventory			*	*						*	*	*	
Guilford-Zimmerman Temperament Survey (GZTS)						*			*	*	*	*	
Hall Occupational Orientation Inventory (HOOI)			*					*	*	*	*		
Harrington-O'Shea Career Decision-Making System (CDM)			*					*	*	*	*		
Hay Aptitude Test Battery		*									*	*	
Highlands Ability Battery (tHAB)		*						*	*	*	*		
High School Career-Course Planner			*					*	*				
Individual Style Survey (ISS)				*					*	*	*	*	
Industrial Reading Test (IRT)	*	*							*	*	*	*	
Insight Inventory						*			*	*	*	*	
Intelligent Career Card Sorts			*						*	*	*		
Interest Explorer with ITED	*		*							*			
Interest, Determination, Exploration & Assessment System (IDEAS)			*					*	*		*		*
Intuitive Mechanics		*							*	*	*	*	
IPI Aptitude-Intelligence Test Series		*			*							*	
Jackson Personality Inventory (JPI)						*			*	*	*	*	
Jackson Vocational Interest Inventory (JVIS)			*						*	*	*		
Job Choice Decision-Making Exercise						*			*	*	*	*	
Job Descriptive Index, Revised (JDI Rev)	*	*		*							*	*	
Job Effectiveness Prediction System (JEPS)	*											*	
Job Search Attitude Inventory					*			*	*	*	*		
Job Seeking Skills Assessment					*					*		*	*
Job Skills	*								*	*	*		
Job Skills Tests	*	*								*	*		*
Job Style Indicator (JSI)				*							*	*	
Job Survival and Success Scale (JSSS)					*	*			*	*	*		
Judgement of Occupational Behavior-Orientation 2000+ (JOB-O 2000)			*				*	*	*		*		*
Keirsey Character Sorter						*				*	*	*	
Keirsey Temperament Sorter II						*				*	*	*	

A Counselor's Guide To Career Assessments Instruments

INSTRUMENT NAME	Achievement	Aptitude	Interest	Values/Satisfaction/Environments	Career Development/Maturity	Personality	Elementary School	Junior High/Middle School	Senior High School	2-Year or 4-Year College	Adult Education/Training	Business & Industry/Employment	Special Populations
Knowdell Career Values Card Sort				*						*	*	*	
Knowdell Motivated Skills Card Sort		*		*				*	*	*	*	*	
Knowdell Occupational Interests Card Sort			*					*	*	*	*	*	
Kuder Career Interest Assessment			*					*	*	*	*	*	
Kuder Skills Confidence Assessment		*		*				*	*	*	*	*	
Kuder Work Values Assessment				*				*	*	*	*	*	
LCCE Competency Assessments: Knowledge and Performance	*	*											*
Learning Skills Profile	*	*						*	*	*	*	*	
Learning Style Profile						*		*	*		*		*
Learning Styles Inventory						*	*	*	*		*		*
Learning/Working Styles Inventory						*			*		*		*
Leisure to Occupations Connection Search (LOC)			*					*	*		*		
Leisure/Work Search Inventory			*						*		*		
Life Role Analysis				*						*	*		
Mapping Possible Selves					*				*	*	*		
McCarron-Dial System (MDS)		*				*							*
Mechanical Aptitudes													
Mechanical Movements		*							*		*	*	*
Meyer-Kendall Assessment Survey (MKAS)						*						*	
Microcomputer Evaluation of Career Areas (MECA)		*	*										*
Minnesota Clerical Test (MCT)		*							*	*	*	*	*
Minnesota Importance Questionnaire (MIQ)				*						*	*		
Minnesota Job Description Questionnaire (MJDQ)				*								*	
Minnesota Paper Form Board-Revised		*							*	*	*	*	
Minnesota Rate of Manipulation Test, 1969 Edition (MRMT)		*						*	*	*	*	*	*
Minnesota Satisfaction Questionnaire (MSQ)				*							*	*	
Minnesota Satisfactoriness Scales (MSS)					*							*	
Minnesota Spatial Relations Test, Revised Edition (MSRT)		*							*	*	*	*	*
Missouri Occupational Card Sort (MOCS)			*						*	*	*	
Motivational Appraisal of Personal Potential		*	*			*		*	*		*		
Multidimensional Aptitude Battery (MAB)		*							*	*	*		*
Musical Aptitude Profile		*					*	*	*				
My Career Chapter			*	*	*			*	*	*	*		
My System of Career Influences			*	*	*			*	*	*	*		
My Vocational Situation (MVS)					*			*	*	*	*		
Myers-Briggs Type Indicator (MBTI)						*			*	*	*	*	
Neo Personality Inventory (NEO-PI-3)						*				*	*	*	
NOCTI Occupational Competency Tests	*								*	*	*	*	
Occupational Aptitude Survey & Interest Schedule-3 (OASIS-3)		*	*					*	*				*
Occupational Clues			*	*				*	*	*	*	
Occupational Personality Assessment			*			*					*	*	
Occupational Personality Questionnaire						*					*	*	
Occupational Preference Inventory		*	*			*			*	*	*	
Occupational Stress Inventory-Revised (OSI-R)						*					*	*	
O'Conner Finger Dexterity Test		*						*	*		*	*	*
O'Conner Tweezer Dexterity Test		*						*	*		*	*	*
Office Skills Test		*							*	*	*	*	
O*NET Ability Profiler			*						*	*	*	

549

Appendix A: Counselors Guide User's Matrix

INSTRUMENT NAME	CHARACTERISTICS						USE						
	Achievement	Aptitude	Interest	Values/Satisfaction/Environments	Career Development/Maturity	Personality	Elementary School	Junior High/Middle School	Senior High School	2-Year or 4-Year College	Adult Education/Training	Business & Industry/Employment	Special Populations
O*NET Interest Inventory/Computerized Interest Profiler				*					*	*	*		
O*NET Work Importance Locator/Computerized Work Importance Profiler					*				*	*	*		
Pennsylvania Bi-Manual Worksample		*							*		*	*	*
Perceptual Speed		*							*	*	*	*	*
Personal Audit						*			*	*	*	*	
Personal Skills Map (PSM)						*	*	*	*	*	*	*	
Personal Style Indicator (PSI)				*		*					*	*	
Personality Research Form (PRF)						*		*	*	*	*	*	
Personnel Tests for Industry (PTI)		*											*
Pictorial Inventory of Careers (PIC)			*					*	*		*		*
Picture Interest Career Survey (PICS -2)				*				*	*	*	*		*
Pictorial Reasoning Test			*					*	*	*			
Plan	*	*	*						*				
Position Analysis Questionnaire (PAQ)				*								*	
Position Classification Inventory (PCI)				*								*	
Practical Assessment Exploration System (PAES)	*		*		*								*
Preliminary Diagnostic Questionnaire	*	*			*	*							*
Prevocational Assessment Screen (PAS)		*											*
Professional Employment Test		*										*	
PSI Basic Skills Test	*	*										*	*
Purdue Pegboard		*								*	*	*	*
Quality of Life Inventory				*	*					*	*	*	
Reading-Free Vocational Interest Inventory (RFVII)			*										*
Responsibility and Independence Scale for Adolescents	*				*								*
Retirement Activities Card Sort			*								*	*	
Revised Beta Examination-Third Edition (BETA-III)		*									*	*	*
Rokeach Value Survey				*				*	*	*	*	*	
Sales Attitude Checklist						*						*	
Salience Inventory (SI)				*				*	*	*	*	*	
Scholastic Level Exam (SLE)		*							*	*	*	*	*
School to Work Career Survey			*					*	*	*			
Schubert General Ability Battery (GAB)		*							*	*	*	*	
Self Directed Search (SDS)			*						*	*	*	*	*
Self-Motivated Career Planning						*			*	*	*		
Sixteen Personality Factors (16PF)						*			*	*	*	*	
Skills Assessment Module (SAM)		*											*
Skills Confidence Inventory		*							*	*	*	*	
Social & Prevocational Information Battery (SPIB)	*				*								*
Space Relations (Paper Puzzles)		*								*	*	*	*
SRA Test of Mechanical Concepts		*						*	*	*	*	*	*
Strategic Assessment of Readiness for Training (START)						*					*	*	
Street Survival Skills Questionnaire (SSSQ)	*				*								*
Strength Deployment Inventory						*					*	*	
Stromberg Dexterity Test (SDT)		*							*	*	*	*	*
Strong Interest Inventory (SII)			*						*	*	*	*	
Student Styles Questionnaire (SSQ)						*	*	*					
Study of Values				*					*	*	*	*	
Styles of Teamwork Inventory						*						*	

A Counselor's Guide To Career Assessments Instruments

INSTRUMENT NAME	Achievement	Aptitude	Interest	Values/Satisfaction/Environments	Career Development/Maturity	Personality	Elementary School	Junior High/Middle School	Senior High School	2-Year or 4-Year College	Adult Education/Training	Business & Industry/Employment	Special Populations
Success Skills 2000	*	*				*			*	*	*	*	
SureHire						*					*	*	
Survey of Interpersonal Values (SIV)				*					*	*	*	*	
Survey of Personal Values (SPV)				*					*	*	*	*	
Survey of Work Styles (SWS)						*					*	*	
Survey of Work Values				*					*	*	*	*	
Talent Assessment Program (TAP)		*											*
Technical Test Battery		*								*	*	*	
Technology and Internet Assessment	*	*						*	*	*	*	*	
Temperament Comparator (TC)						*						*	
Test of Adult Basic Education (TABE)	*								*	*	*	*	*
Tests for Everyday Living (TEL)	*				*								*
Thurstone Temperament Schedule						*			*	*	*		
Training House Assessment Kit	*	*				*						*	
Transition Behavior Scale					*	*							*
Transition Planning Inventory (TPI)					*								*
Transition-to-Work Inventory					*			*	*		*		*
UNIACT IV			*						*	*			
USES Basic Occupational Literacy Test (BOLT)	*												*
USES General Aptitude Test Battery (GATB)		*						*	*	*	*	*	
USES Interest Inventory (USESII)			*						*		*		*
Valpar 300 Series Dexterity Modules		*							*	*	*		*
Valpar Aviator	*	*	*						*		*		*
Valpar Component Work Sample Series		*							*				*
Valpar Pro 3000	*	*			*				*	*	*		*
Valpar Test of Essential Skills (VTES)	*								*	*	*		*
Values Preference Indicator				*							*	*	
Values Scale (VS)				*				*	*	*	*		
Viewpoint						*						*	
Vocational Adaptation Rating Scales (VARS)	*				*								*
Vocational Assessment & Curriculum Guide	*				*								*
Vocational Behavior Checklist (VBC)					*						*		*
Vocational Decision-Making Interview					*								*
Vocational Evaluation Systems (Singer)		*	*					*	*				*
Vocational Implications of Personality (VIP)						*		*	*	*	*	*	*
Vocational Interest Assessment System (VIAS)			*					*	*		*		*
Vocational Interest Exploration (VIE) System			*					*	*		*		*
Vocational Interest Inventory & Exploration Survey (VOC-TIES)			*					*	*		*		*
Vocational Interest Temperament and Aptitude System (VITAS)		*	*								*		*
Vocational Preference Inventory			*			*				*	*	*	*
Vocational Training Inventory and Exploration Survey (VOC-TIES)		*											*
Vocational Transit		*											
VOC-TECH Quick Screener (VTQS)		*	*							*			*
V-TECS Assessments	*									*	*	*	*
Watson-Glaser Critical Thinking Appraisal		*										*	
Wesman Personnel Classification Test (PCT)		*										*	
Wide Range Achievement Test (WRAT)	*												*
Wide Range Interest Opinion Test (WRIOT)			*										*

551

Appendix A: Counselors Guide User's Matrix

INSTRUMENT NAME	Achievement	Aptitude	Interest	Values/Satisfaction/Environments	Career Development/Maturity	Personality	Elementary School	Junior High/Middle School	Senior High School	2-Year or 4-Year College	Adult Education/Training	Business & Industry/Employment	Special Populations
Wiesen Test of Mechanical Aptitude		*							*	*	*	*	
Wonderlic Basic Skills Test		*									*	*	*
Wonderlic Personnel Test		*										*	
Work Adjustment Inventory					*	*							*
Work Environment Scale				*								*	
Work Exploration Checklist			*					*	*		*		
WorkKeys Assessments	*								*	*	*	*	
Work Motivation Inventory (WMI)				*								*	
Work Performance Assessment					*	*							*
Work Personality Profile					*	*							*
Work Preference Questionnaire			*									*	
Work Readiness Cognitive Screen (WCS)		*									*		*
Work Skills Development Package (WSD)	*	*											*
Work Temperament Inventory					*	*							*
Workmate				*				*	*		*		
Workplace Skills Survey		*							*	*	*		
World of Work Inventory (WOWI)	*	*	*	*					*	*	*		*

Note. Instruments in boldface were reviewed in Chapters 10-16.

APPENDIX B

SUPPLEMENTAL
ONLINE RESOURCES

Because weblinks change frequently, be sure to search for
periodical names on the Internet.

Appendix B: Supplemental Online Resources

Available on the NCDA Webpage (http://www.ncda.org)

Publisher Contact Information

Instructor Materials (Password protected; PowerPoint templates and test bank items)

Test Standards and Codes

Responsibilities of Users of Standardized Tests, Third Edition

Code of Fair Testing Practices in Education: http://www.apa.org/science/programs/testing/fair-testing.pdf

Rights and Responsibilities of Test Takers: Guidelines and Expectations: http://www.apa.org/science/programs/testing/rights.aspx

Standards for Multicultural Assessment, Fourth Edition

Periodicals that Publish Test Research and Reviews

Assessment

The Career Development Quarterly

The Counseling Psychologist

Counseling Outcome Research and Evaluation

Counselor Education and Supervision

Educational and Psychological Measurement

Journal of Applied Psychology

Journal of Career Assessment

Journal of Career Development

Journal of Counseling and Development

Journal of Counseling Psychology

Journal of Educational Measurement

Journal of Personality Assessment

Journal of Psychoeducational Assessment

Journal of Vocational Behavior

NewsNotes

Measurement and Evaluation in Counseling and Development

Professional School Counseling

Psychology in the Schools

School Psychology Review

Additional Career Assessment Websites

Association of Assessment and Research in Counseling test reviews: http://www.aarc.net

Achieve: http://www.achieve.org

America's Career Resource Network: http://www.acrnnetwork.org

American Counseling Association: http://www.counseling.org

American Psychological Association: http://www.apa.org

Association of Computer-Based Systems for Career Information: http://www.acsci.org

ATP Test Publishers: http://www.testpublishers.org

Buros Test Reviews Online: http://www.buros.unl.edu

National Alliance for Secondary Education and Transition: http://www.nasetalliance.org

National Collaborative on Workforce and Disability: http://www.ncwd-youth.info

O*NET Resource Center: http://www.onetcenter.org

U.S. Department of Education: http://www.ed.gov

VRI Career Planning Solutions: http://www.vri.org

Index

556

AUTHOR INDEX

Authors

B
Bremer, Christine, 63

C
Carr, Darrin L., 33
Cato, Sibyl, 75

D
Dozier, Casey, 33

E
Evans, Kathy M., 49

G
Gysbers, Norman C., 75

H
Hays, Danica G., vii, 3, 509
Herr, Edwin L., 11

L
Lapan, Richard T., 75
Lumsden, Jill A., 33

M
McClain, Mary-Catherine, 33

N
Niles, Spencer G., 11

O
Opsal, Chris, 63
Osborn, Debra S., vii, 33

P
Podmostko, Mary, 63

R
Rose, Ciemone S., 101

S
Sampson, Jr., James P., 33

T
Tang, Mei, 85
Timmons, Joe, 63

W
Wall, Janet E., 23
Whiston, Susan C., 101
Whitfield, Edwin A., v
Wilson, Cornelia R., 85
Wilson, F. Robert, 85
Wood, Chris, 3

Developers

A
ACT, Inc., 157, 195, 197
Allport, Robert B., 285
Amundson, Norman, 475
Anderson, Mary Z., 451
Anderson, Terry, 397
Artese, Victor S., 153
Arthur, Michael, 475

B
Becker, Ralph L., 421, 447
Bedeian, Arthur, 311
Bennett, George K., 183
Betz, Nancy E., 243, 279, 315
Borgen, Fred H., 243, 279
Brady, Robert, 443
Brigance, Albert H., 427
Briggs, Katharine C., 385
Brolin, Donn E., 437

C
Campbell, David, 226
Carson, Kerry, 311
Cattell, A. Karen, 401
Cattell, Heather E.P., 401
Cattell, Raymond B., 401
Center for Creative Leadership in conjunction with
Ellen Ernst Kossek, 363
Chartrand, Judy M., 325
Chung, Y. Barry, 451
Clark, Gary, 168
Clonts, Winifred L., 153
Costa, Paul T., 391
Croteau, James, 451
CTB/McGraw Hill, 147

Author Index

D
DiStefano, Teresa, 451

E
Emanuel, Lazar, 141

F
Farr, Michael, 239
Feller, Rich, 251
Frisch, Michael B., 359

G
Gardner, Eric F., 121
Geist, Harold, 433
Glavin, Kevin, 465
Glutting, Joseph J., 295, 409
Good, Glenn, 329
Gough, Harrison, 368
Gysbers, Norman C., 487

H
Hall, Lacy G., 247
Harmon, Lenore W., 243, 279
Harrington, Joan C., 116
Harrington, Thomas F., 116
Harris-Bowlsbey, JoAnn, 203
Heffernan, Mary, 329
Heppner, Mary J., 339
Hohner, Robin, 329
Holland, John L., 275
Holm, Cheryl, 329
Horton, Connie, 409

I
Industrial Psychology International Ltd., 163

J
Jackson, Douglas N., 233, 255, 380, 416
Jones, Lawrence K., 373
Jordaan, Jean Pierre, 319

K
Karlsen, Bjorn, 121
Keis, Ken, 291, 397
Knapp-Lee, Lisa, 177
Knapp, Lila F., 177
Knapp, Robert R., 177
Knowdell, Richard L., 481
Kopelman, Richard E., 285
Kossek, Ellen E., 363

L
Lenz, Janet G., 333
Lindeman, Richard, 302, 319

Liptak, John J., 307, 347, 351, 355
Long, Eliot R., 153

M
Malen, Ann, 329
Marshall, Anne, 503
Marshall, Connie W., 416
McCrae, Robert R., 391
McDonald, Robert, 135
McIlveen, Peter, 493
McMahon, Mary, 499
Morrill, Weston H., 325
Myers, Isabel B., 385
Myers, Roger, 319

N
Neidert, Gregory P. M., 219
Niles, Spencer G., 203
Nord, Dennis, 329

O
O'Shea, Arthur J., 251
Oakland, Thomas, 409
Okiishi, Rae W., 459
Ortman Nancy L., 219

P
Parker, Polly, 475
Parker, Randall M., 211
Patton, James, 168
Patton, Wendy, 499
Peterson, Gary W., 333

R
Rath, Tom, 377
Rayman, Jack, 203
Reardon, Robert C., 333
Rehfuss, Mark, 471
Ripley, Robert E., 219
Robbins, Steven B., 325
Robinson, Everett, 291, 397
Rovenpor, Janet L., 285

S
Sampson, Jr., James P., 333
Saunders, Denise E., 333
Savickas, Mark, 465
Schultheiss, Donna E., 343
Seashore, Harold G., 183
Shepard, Blythe, 503
Solberg, V. Scott, 329
Stead, Graham B., 343
Steel, Lawrence, 168

Strong, E.K., 279
Super, Donald, 302, 319
Synatschk, Katherine, 168

T

Taylor, Karen M., 315
Thompson, Albert, 302, 319
Trusty, Jerry, 203

U

U.S. Department of Defense Personnel
    Testing Division, 125
U.S. Department of Labor, Employment and
    Training Administration, 141, 261, 269

V

Vocational Research Institute, 171

W

Wall, Janet E., 116
Watson, Mark, 499
Wesman, Alexander G., 183
Wilkinson, Gary S., 295

Z

Zima, Nicole, 329
Zytowski, Donald, 203

Reviewers

A

Austin, James T., 422

B

Baker, Caroline A., 276
Baker, Spencer R., 303
Balkin, Richard S., 329
Bayne, Hannah B., 493
Berríos-Allison, Ana C., 476
Bobzien, Jonna L., 428
Bruno, Michelle L., 410
Bugaj, Albert M., 296
Bullock-Yowell, Emily E., 179
Burck, Andrew M., 149

C

Cameron, Erika R. N., 164
Campbell, Vicki L., 252
Carlson, Laurie A., 360
Carlstrom, Aaron H., 234
Chope, Robert C., 369
Comito, Nikki S., 127
Crockett, Stephanie A., 262

D

D'Costa, Ayres, 326
DeBlaere, Cirleen, 451
Del Corso, Jennifer J., 271
Dik, Bryan J., 248
Doubrava-Smith, Pamela, 329
Dykeman, Cass, 344

E

Ellison, Lori, 417
Enke, Serena, 434

F

Feller, Rich, 334
Fields, Justin R., 482
Fleenor, John W., 348
Foster, Linda H., 198

G

Geisinger, Kurt F., 122
Gibbons, Melinda M., 208
Gorin, Joanna, 143
Gratz, Zandra S., 448
Green, Kathy E., 308
Gross, Christi L., 127

H

Hauser, Mike, 378
Henfield, Malik S., 499
Hill, Tara, 240
Hillis, Katie, 378
Hughey, Kenneth F., 234

J

Jenkins, Jeffrey A., 280
Johnson, Kaprea F., 471

K

Kelley, Karl N., 184
Kinnier, Richard T., 143
Kirnan, Jean P., 340
Kuznetsova, Maria I., 169

L

La Guardia, Amanda C., 386
Lenz, A. Stephen, 212
Lomas, Gabriel I., 172
Lorelle, Sonya, 487

M

Mau, Wei-Cheng J., 117
McCullough, Julian R., 137
Meyer, Dixie, 352

Author Index

Michel, Rebecca E., 504
Morris, Carrie W., 311
Muth, Deidre L., 127

N
Nauta, Margaret M., 374
Newgent, Rebecca A., 363

O
Osborn, Debra S., 158
Osborne, Lauren K., 179

P
Patrick, John, 127
Peila-Shuster, Jacqueline J., 334
Peluso, Paul R., 398
Perepiczka, Michelle, 402
Perkins, Bethany L., 451
Perry, QuaVaundra A., 252
Pietrzak, Dale, 320
Porter, Julia Y., 443
Powell, Shawn, 169
Power, Sally J., 154
Prosek, Elizabeth A., 460
Putts, Matthew, 438

R
Ratts, Manivong J., 137
Rehfuss, Mark C. , 466
Rothman, David J., 340

S
Samide, Jeff, 127
Sanford-Moore, Eleanor E., 257
Sauser, Jr., William I., 356
Severy, Lisa E., 227
Sheehan, Eugene P., 220
Sheperis, Donna S., 291
Shoffner, Marie F., 191
Shurts, W. Matthew, 286
Sligar, Steven R., 438
Stebleton, Michael J., 392
Swank, Jacqueline M., 243

V
Vacha-Haase, Tammi, 434
Watson, Joshua C., 316

Z
Zachar, Peter, 382

SUBJECT INDEX

411 on Disability Disclosure, 66

A

A priori criteria, 93
Ability Explorer, 116-120, 546
Accommodations, 69-70
Achievement Gap, 51, 52
Activities of Daily Living (ADLs), 68
Adaption of career assessments, 15-16
Adult Basic Learning Examination, Second Edition
    (ABLE), 121-124, 546
Adult Career Concerns Inventory (ACCI), 13, 302-305,
    546
Advocacy
    American Counseling Association Advocacy
    Competencies, 50, 53, 75-79
    advocacy competence, defined, 75-76
    client/student advocacy level, 76-77
    community collaboration, 78, 81
    community/school level, 78
    personal advocacy, 75-77, 80-82
    policy advocacy, 75, 79-82
    program advocacy, 75, 77, 78, 80, 81, 82
    public arena level, 79-80
    self-advocacy, 67, 76
    systems advocacy, 78, 81
African American, Latino/Latina American, and Native
    American (ALANA), 51, 52
Alliance of Career Resource Professionals (ACRP),
    36, 39
America Creating Opportunities to Meaningfully
    Promote Excellence in Technology, Education, and
    Science (America COMPETES), 8
American Counseling Association (ACA), 7, 24, 25,
    27, 28, 49-50, 75, 79
American Counseling Association Advocacy
    competencies, 50, 53, 75-79
American Counseling Association Code of Ethics,
    24-25, 49, 89, 92
American Counseling Association Office of Public
    Policy and Legislation, 79
American Counseling Association Position Statement
    on High Stakes Testing, 28
American Counseling Association Public Policy and
    Legislative Agenda, 79
American Psychological Association (APA), 27

American School Counseling Association Ethical
    Standards for School Counselors, 26-27
American School Counseling Association Office of
    Research, 79
American School Counseling Association (ASCA), 26,
    27, 78, 411
Americans with Disabilities Act (ADA), 28, 66
Apps (mobile applications), 40, 42
Armed Services Vocational Aptitude Battery
    (ASVAB), 6, 51-52, 125-132, 546
Army Alpha, 6
Army Beta, 6
Artificial intelligence, 40-41
Ashland Interest Assessment, 416-419
Assessment
    assessment defined, 3
    considerations, 68-69
    four domains of, 64-65
    interpretation, *see also interpretation*, 8, 36,
    55-57, 97, 101, 103-105, 108
    preparing, 96
    process, defined, 12
    purpose of, 4-5, 86, 89
    sources of information, 9, 88-89
Assessments of Ability, 51-53
Association for Assessment and Research in
    Counseling Career Counseling Assessment and
    Evaluation Competencies, 25-26
Association for Assessment and Research in
    Counseling (AARC), 25, 27, 28, 101
Association of Computer-Based Systems for Career
    Information (ACSCI), 36
Association of Test Publishers, 24
Asynchronous communication, 40

B

Barriers to Employment Success Inventory, Fourth
    Edition (BESI, 4th ed.), 307-310, 546
Becker Work Adjustment Profile, Second Edition
    421-425, 546
Bibliographic Retrieval Service, 9
Boston Vocational Bureau, 5
Boundaryless careers, 15, 476
BRIGANCE Transition Skills Inventory, 427-431, 546
Buros Center for Testing Publications, 8

Subject Index

C

C-DAC Model, 13
California Psychological Inventory, Third Edition, 368-371, 546
Campbell Interest and Skill Survey (CISS), 226-231, 546
Career Ability Placement Survey (CAPS), 179, 546
Career and Life Explorer, Third Edition (CLE) 239-242, 546
Career assessment,
  domains, 88
  instrument selection, 23, 43, 85-97
  client factors, 86-87
  counselor factors, 87
  issues, 94-95
  strategies, 96-97
Career Beliefs Inventory, 13, 523,
Career Commitment Measure (CCM), 311-314, 546
Career construction counselors, 13
Career construction theory, 13, 466, 468
Career Decision Self-Efficacy Scale and Career Decision Self-Efficacy Scale-Short Form (CDSE-SF) 315-318, 546
Career Development Inventory, 319-323, 546
Career development process, 4
Career Directions Inventory, Second Edition (CDI) 233-237
Career education movement, 7
Career Explorer (CE), 275-278
Career Factors Inventory (CFI), 325-328, 546
Career foreclosure, 53
Career Genogram, 459-463, 546
Career Information Delivery Systems (CIDS), 16, 35-36
Career Interest Inventory, 183-188, 547
Career Interests, Preferences, and Strengths Inventory 168-170
Career interventions, 11, 12, 15-19, 476
Career Key, 373-376, 546
Career Occupational Preference System Interest Inventory (COPS), 179, 547
Career Orientation Placement and Evaluation Survey (COPES) 179, 547
Career Search Efficacy Scale (CSES) 329-331, 547
Career Style Interview (CSI), 13, 465-469, 547
Career Thoughts Inventory (CTI), 13, 333-337, 547
Career Transitions Inventory (CTI), 339-342
CareerScope: Career Assessment and Reporting System, Version 10, 171-175, 547
Carl D. Perkins Vocational and Applied Technology Education Act, 6

Carl D. Perkins Vocational and Technical Education Act of 2006, 6
Carl D. Perkins Vocational Education Act, 6
Carnegie Interest Inventory, 6
Childhood Career Development Scale (CCDS), 343-346, 547
Client/student advocacy level, 76-77
Clifton StrengthsFinder or StrengthsFinder 2.0, 377-380, 547
Clinical significance, 93
Code of Ethics,
  American Counseling Association, 24-25, 49, 89, 92
  Global Career Development Facilitator, 25-26
  National Board for Certified Counselors, 25
  National Career Development Association, 24, 25
Code of Fair Testing Practices in Education, 7, 27, 94
Coefficient alpha, 90, 123, 130, 156, 210, 265, 282, 287, 297, 298, 321, 330, 335, 341, 349, 361, 365, 383, 411, 418,
Cognitive information processing theory, 13, 334, 335
Community asset mapping, 71-72
Community collaboration, 78, 81
Community/school level, 78
Competencies,
  American Counseling Association Advocacy Competencies, 50, 53, 75-79
  Career Counseling Assessment and Evaluation Competencies, 25, 101
  Competencies in Assessment and Evaluation for School Counselors, 26
  Multicultural competencies, 50, 107-108
  National Career Development Association and Association for Assessment and Research in Counseling, Career Counselor Assessment and Evaluation Competencies, 25-26, 101
  National Career Development Association Career Counseling Competencies, 25-26
Comprehensive Employment Training Act of 1973, 7
Computer scoring, 103
Computer-assisted career assessment, 33-42
Computer-assisted career guidance systems, 12-13, 16-17
Computer-based test interpretation (CBTI), 36, 38-39
Computer-mediated career guidance systems, 12-13, 16-17
Concurrent measurements, 91
Concurrent validity, 91
Conducting assessments, 101-109
Construct validity, 91
Content validity, 55, 91
Content variables, 4

A COUNSELOR'S GUIDE TO CAREER ASSESSMENTS INSTRUMENTS

Convergent validity, 91
COPSystem Career Guidance Program, 177-182, 547
Correlation coefficient, 90-91
Cost recovery, 35
Cost-benefit ratios and analyses, 17-19
Council for the Accreditation of Counseling and Related Educational Programs (CACREP), 24-25, 49-50
Council for the Accreditation of Counseling and Related Education Programs Standards, 25
Council on Rehabilitation Education (CORE), 49
Counseling and Testing Centers, 6
Criterion-referenced, 103-104, 109,
Criterion-related validity, 91
Cronbach's Alpha, 90, 123, 130, 156, 210, 265, 282, 287, 297, 298, 321, 330, 335, 341, 349, 361, 365, 383, 411, 418,
Cultural bias, 50-51, 53, 58, 91, 108, 144, 265
Cultural replicability, 16
Cultural validity, 16
Culturally appropriate,
    administration, 108
    interpretation of assessment, 108
    selection of instruments, 108
Culturally competent, *see also multicultural competencies*, 49-50
Culturally encompassing information gathering, 107-108
Culturally Appropriate Career Assessment Model (CACAM), 55-57

D

Department of Health, Education, and Welfare's Office of Civil Rights, 7
Dictionary of Holland Codes, 13
Dictionary of Occupational Titles, 155
Differential Aptitude Tests for Personal and Career Assessment, DAT, 183-188, 547
Disability
    disclosure, 65-66
    undiagnosed, 65-66
Divergent validity, 91

E

Ecological assessments, environmental assessments, 70-71
Education of All Handicapped Children Act of 1975, 7
Elementary and Secondary Education Act of 1965, 67, 76
Employability Competency System Appraisal Test 189-193, 547

Equivalence, 89-90
Ethical standards and statements, 23-30
Evidence-based practice, 14, 17-19
Evidence-based stealth assessment, 41-42
Expanded Skills Confidence Inventory (ESCI), 243-246, 548
EXPLORE, 195-201, 548

F

Face validity, 91
Factorial validity, 91
Fairness model, 52
Faking, 92, 326, 370, 404, 524
Family Educational Rights and Privacy Act, 7, 131
Federal Vocational Education Programs Guidelines for Eliminating Discrimination and Denial of Services on the Basis of Race, Color, National Origin, Sex, and Education Amendments of 1972, 7
Flores et al. (2003) model, 107-108
Focus clients, 63-73
    defined, 63
Formal assessment technique, 12
Formal career assessment tools, 86, 88-89
Functional limitations, 71
Functional skills and abilities, 68-69, 71
Functional Vocational Evaluations (FVEs), 68
Future Career Autobiography, 471-473, 548

G

Geist Picture Interest Inventory, Revised Eighth Printing, 433-436, 548
Global Career Development Facilitator Code of Ethics, 25-26
Global economy, 11, 15, 75
Group testing, developments in, 6
Guidelines for Assessment of Sex Bias and Sex Fairness in Career Interest Inventories, 7
Guidelines for computer-based testing, 24

H

Hall Occupational Orientation Inventory, Fourth Edition (HALL), 247-250, 548
Harrington-O'Shea Career Decision Making System-Revised (CDM-R), 53, 119, 251-254, 548
High stakes testing, 27-28, 52-53, 91-92
Highlands Ability Battery, 135-140, 548
Holland Code, *see also Self Directed Search and Career Explorer*, 12-13, 42, 54, 209, 228, 240-241, 374
    RIASEC, 2, 129, 130, 229, 263-266, 374, 443-445, 467

Subject Index

Holland-type, clusters and scales, 295, 296, 298
Holland, John, 12-13, 126, 129, 130, 228, 252, 275-278, 443, 467, 483
Homogeneity, *see also internal consistency*, 89-90

I

Individualized Education Plans (IEP), 7, 65, 430, 440,
Individualized Plan for Employment, 65
Individuals with Disabilities Education Act (IDEA), 7, 169
Individuals with Disabilities Improvement Act of 2004, 7
Informal assessment technique, 12
Informal career assessment tools, 86, 88
Integration of career services, 80
Intelligent Career Card Sort, 475-479, 548
Interest assessments, 53-54
Interest inventory, 5-6, 53-54, 104-105, 107
Internal consistency, 53, 90
Internalized oppression, 50, 55
International Test Commission, 16
Internet-based assessment, limitations and issues, 37-40
Internet-based career assessment, 33, 35-36, 38-39, 95-96, 102
Interpretation, 8, 36, 55-57, 97, 101, 103-108
    Americans with Disabilities Act, 28
    ethical standards, 24-28
    interpreting reliability coefficients, 90-91
    interpreting validity coefficients, 92-93
    multicultural considerations, 49, 55-57, 106-108
    norm-referenced, 104-105
Interpretative reports, problems in the design of, 38
Interviews, 12, 68-69
Inventory of Work-Relevant Abilities, 53
Item response theory, 156

J

Jackson Personality Inventory-Revised, 380-384, 548
Jackson Vocational Interest Survey, Second Edition, 255-259, 548
Job Accommodation Network (JAN), 70
Job placement, 5
Job placement, individuals with disabilities, 70
Job Search Attitude Inventory, Fourth Edition (JSAI), 347-350, 548
Job Search Knowledge Scale (JSKS), 351-354
Job Survival and Success Scale, Second Edition (JSSS), 355-358, 548
Job Training Partnership Act of 1982, 7
Joint Committee on Testing Practices, 38, 39, 96

K

Knowdell Card Sorts, 481-486, 549
Knowledge workers, 14-15
Krumboltz, John, 13
Kuder Career Interest Assessment, 203-210, 549
Kuder Career Planning System, 203-210
Kuder Preference Record, 6
Kuder Skills Confidence Assessment, 203-210, 549
Kuder Work Values Assessment, 203-210, 549

L

Learning organizations, 14
Legislation, 3, 6-7, 52, 71, 79-80
Life Centered Career Education Competency Assessment: Knowledge and Performance Batteries, 437-441
Life Role Analysis, 487-491, 549
Life-long learning, 15
Limitations,
    computer-assisted career assessment, 37-40
    testing context and environment, 88
Long-term unemployment, 11

M

Macrolevel approaches, 76
Manpower Development Training Act of 1962, 7
Meaning making process, 13, 87, 88, 97, 106, 476
Mental Measurements Yearbook (MMY), 9, 89, 95
Meta-analyses, 18-19
Microlevel approaches, 76
Modal profile, 383
Model Guidelines for Preemployment Integrity Testing, 24
Multicultural assessment models, 55-57, 107-108
    Culturally-Appropriate Career Assessment Model (CACAM), 55-57
    Flores et al. (2003) model, 107-108
    Multicultural Assessment Process (MAP), 57
Multicultural career assessment, 49-59
Multicultural competencies, 50, 107-108
Multicultural considerations, 49-59, 106-108
Multimedia technology, 36, 38-41
Multimedia-based generalized test interpretation, 36, 38
My Career Chapter, 493-497, 549
My System of Career Influences, 499-502, 549
My Vocational Situation (MVS), 12, 336, 341, 549
Myers-Briggs Type Indicator (MBTI), 54, 385-389, 393, 410, 411, 549

A Counselor's Guide To Career Assessments Instruments

N

Narrative interpretative reports, 38
National Board for Certified Counselors (NBCC), 7, 17, 24, 25
National Board for Certified Counselors Code of Ethics, 25
National Career Development Association and Association for Assessment and Research in Counseling, Career Counseling Assessment and Evaluation Competencies, 25-26, 101
National Career Development Association Career Counseling Competencies, 25-26
National Career Development Association Code of Ethics, 24, 25
National Collaborative on Workforce and Disability for Youth (NCWD/Youth), 63, 66
National Council on Measurement in Education (NCME), 24, 27
National Defense Education Act (NDEA), 6, 8
National Fair Access Coalition on Testing (FACT), 95
National Institute of Education (NIE), 7
NEO Personality Inventory, 3, 391-395, 549
No Child Left Behind Act (NCLB), 27, 52
Non-timed standardized inventories, 12
Norm-referenced, 69, 103-104
Normative populations, 50
Normative sample, 93
Norms, 93-94

O

O*NET Ability Profiler, 51, 52, 57, 141-145, 549
O*NET Interest Profiler and Computerized O*NET Interest Profiler (IP, CIP), 261-267, 550
O*NET Work Importance Profiler and Work Importance Locator (WIP) (WIL), 269-274, 550
Occupational Aptitude Survey and Interest Schedule, Third Edition, OASIS, 3, 211-217, 549
Occupational information, 13, 17, 35
Operational Best Practices for Statewide Large-Scale Assessment Programs, 24

P

Parsons, Frank, 5, 8, 85
Patter, 87
Percentile rank and percentile scores, 104
Person-centered planning, 67-69
Personal advocacy, 75-77, 80-82
Personal development, 4
Personal Style Indicator, 397-400, 550
Personality assessment, 54-55
Personality inventories, 16, 54-55

Picture Interest Career Survey, Second Edition, 443-445, 550
PLAN, 197-201, 550
Policy advocacy, 75, 79-82
Possible Selves Mapping, 503-507, 549
Postmodern approach, 106, 273
Practical significance, 93
Practitioner-assisted assessment, 34
Pre-employment testing, 27-28
Predictive validity, 91
Process variables, 4
Program advocacy, 75, 77, 78, 80, 81, 82
Program evaluation, 77-78, 345, 346, 425
Program Results-Based Evaluation (PRBE), 78
Proportion of variance, 90
Psychometrics, 87-88, 95
Public arena level, 79-80

Q

Qualitative assessment, 55, 85, 94
Quality of Life Inventory (QOLI), 359-362, 550

R

Reading–Free Vocational Interest Inventory, Second Edition 447-450, 550
Reliability, 89-91
 test-retest reliability, 53, 77, 89-90
Reliability coefficient, 90-91
Resource mapping, 71-72
Responsibilities of Users of Standardized Tests (RUST Statement), 7, 26, 27
Results, communication of, 105-106
RIASEC, *see Holland Code*
Rights and Responsibilities of Test Takers: Guidelines and Expectations, 29
Rights and Responsibilities of Test Takers: Guidelines and Responsibilities, 7
Risk factors, 66, 72
RUST Statement, 7, 26, 27

S

Salience Inventory, 13, 522
SCANS report, 7
Scholastic Assessment Test (SAT), 51
School counseling programs, 78
School to Work Opportunities Act of 1994, 7
Science, technology, engineering, and mathematics (STEM), 8, 118
Score stability, *see test-retest reliability*
Screening, 37, 38, 42
Searchable On-line Accommodation Resource (SOAR), 70

Subject Index

Section 504 of the Rehabilitation Act of 1973, 7
Selecting a career assessment instrument, 23, 43, 85-97, 94-95
Self-advocacy, 67, 76
Self-assessment, 34
Self-Directed Search, Fourth Edition (SDS), 41-42, 53 275-278, 550
Self-estimate of ability, 53
Sequential life stages, 14
Significance, 92-93
    clinical significance, 93
    personal significance, 93
    statistical significance, 91, 92-93
Siri, artificial intelligence, 40-41
Situational work assessments, 70-71
Sixteen Personality Factor Questionnaire (16PF), 54-55, 401-407, 550
Skills Confidence Inventory, 107, 279-284, 550
Social desirability response bias, 299-300, 404, 524
Social justice, 17-18, 49-50
Social media, 40
Soft skills, 14, 70, 159-161, 356
Stability, 89-90, 253, 322, 357, 370, 383
Standard error of measurement, 19, 104-105, 150, 161, 186, 200, 345, 406, 423
Standard Occupation Classification (SOC), 173
Standards for Educational and Psychological Testing, 3, 7, 24, 37, 39-40, 102
Standards for Multicultural Assessment, 28
Standards for Qualifications of Test Users, 27
Standards relevant to career counselors and practitioners, 25-26
Standards relevant to Professional Counselors, 24-25
Standards relevant to the test taker, 29
Statistical significance, 91, 92-93
Stereotype threat, 52, 53, 56
Strong Interest Inventory (SII), 279-284, 550
Strong Vocational Interest Blank, 6, 249, 258, 280
Student Styles Questionnaire, 409-413, 550
Study of Values, Fourth Edition (SOV), 285-289
Subjective career experience, 13
Summary of Performance (SOP), 66-67
Super, Donald, 13, 302-304, 319, 320, 344, 489
Synchronous communication, 40-41
Systemic challenges, 71-72
Systems advocacy, 78, 81

T

t-scores, 104, 164, 165, 334, 360, 361, 391, 409, 410, 422, 423, 433, 435
Technical quality of tests, 87
Test accommodations, 28, 64, 69-70, 102

Test adaption, 15-16
Test administration, 101-102
Test bias, 52
Test expense, 95
Test interpretation, 103
Test of Adult Basic Education, 147-152, 551
Test purpose, 95
Test review structure, 94
Test scoring, 103
Test selection, 23, 43, 85-97
Test-retest reliability, 53, 77, 89-90
Testing and Assessment: A Guide to Good Practices for Workforce Investment Professionals, 28-29
Tests in Print, 9, 89, 95
Tests of cognitive ability, 51-52
Therapeutic assessment, 106
Time horizons, 14
Timed standardized tests, 12
Trait-and-Factor Approach, 5
Transition services, 7, 66-67, 438

U

Ubiquitous assessment, 41-42
Universal Design for Learning (UDL), 64, 72

V

Validation evidence, 103, 105-109
Validity, 91-93
    content validity, 55, 91
    criterion-related validity, 91
    construct validity, 91
    concurrent validity, 91
    predictive validity, 91
    convergent validity, 91
    divergent validity, 91
    factorial validity, 91
    face validity, 91
    validity coefficient, 92-93
Validity coefficients, 92-93
Values Inventory, the, 13
Values Preference Indicator (VPI), 291-294, 551
Vocational assessments, 5-6, 64
Vocational choice, 5
Vocational Education Act of 1963, 6
Vocational Education Program, 6-7
Vocational Evaluation and Career Assessment Professionals (VECAP), 64
Vocational Preference Inventory, 12-13, 375, 551

W

Watson, artificial intelligence, 40-41
Web-based systems, 16-17, 35

Wide Range Interest and Occupation Test, Second
  Edition (WRIOT-2), 295-299 , 551
Wonderlic Basic Skills Test, 153-156, 552
Work Values Inventory, 13, 207, 209
Workforce Investment Act of 1998, 7
WorkKeys Assessment, 157-162, 552
WorkLife Indicator (WLI), 363-366
Workplace Sexual Identity Management Measure,
  451-455
Workplace Skills Survey, 163-166, 552
World Bank, The, 15
World of Work Inventory (WOWI) 219-223, 552
World-of-Work Map, 195, 198, 200

Y

Yerkes, Robert, 6

Z

z-scores, 104, 404

568